The Art of the Critic

The Art of the Critic

Literary Theory and Criticism from the Greeks to the Present

Volume 4
The Enlightenment

EDITED WITH AN INTRODUCTION BY

HAROLD BLOOM

Sterling Professor of the Humanities, Yale University

1987
CHELSEA HOUSE PUBLISHERS
NEW YORK   NEW HAVEN   PHILADELPHIA

Project Editor: James Uebbing
Editorial Coordinator: Karyn Gullen Browne
Editorial Staff: Neal Dolan, Richard Fumosa, Stephen Mudd
Design: Susan Lusk

Printed and bound in the United States of America

Library of Congress Cataloging in Publication Data
Main entry under title:

The Art of the Critic

    Includes bibliographies.
    Contents: v. 1. Classical and medieval—   —v. 4.
The enlightenment.
    1. Criticism—Collected works. 2. Literature—
Philosophy—Collected works. I. Bloom, Harold.
PN86.A77   1985   809   84–15547
ISBN 0–87754–493–X (set)
    0–87754–497–2 (vol. 4)

Contents

Index and Glossary are contained in Volume 11

Dr. Johnson
And Neo-Classical Wisdom

Harold Bloom

1

There lurks, perhaps, in every known heart a desire of distinction which inclines every man first to hope, and then to believe, that Nature has given him something peculiar to himself. This vanity makes one mind nurse aversions and another actuate desires, till they rise by art much above their original state of power and as affectation, in time, improves to habit, they at last tyrannize over him who at first encouraged them only for show.

—JOHNSON, in a letter to Boswell, 8 December 1763

DR. SAMUEL JOHNSON, in the judgment of many (myself included), is the strongest critic in the varied history of Western literary culture. In the Anglo-American tradition, his only near rival would seem to be William Hazlitt, who has something like Johnson's energy, intellect, and knowledge, but lacks the full compass of Johnson's human sympathies, and is simply not as wise. Johnson shows us that criticism, as a literary art, joins itself to the ancient genre of wisdom writing, and so is descended from Koheleth (Ecclesiastes) and Jesus Ben Sirach (Ecclesiasticus). If you search for Johnson's precursor, turn from Aristotle or even from Ben Jonson, father of English neoclassicism, and find the forerunner of *Rasselas* and *The Rambler* in Koheleth:

> Whatsoever thy hand findeth to do, do it with thy might; for there is no work, nor device, nor knowledge, nor wisdom, in the grave, whither thou goest.

The mind of Johnson, confronting the Biblical Preacher's words, was altered permanently. Indeed, Johnson is so strong a writer, that he nearly achieves the metaleptic reversal of making us believe that the author of Ecclesiastes has read deeply in Samuel Johnson. Sometimes I find myself reading Ecclesiastes aloud, and become confused, believing that I am reading *Rasselas:*

> It is better to hear the rebuke of the wise, than for a man to hear the song of fools.

For as the crackling of thorns under a pot, so is the laughter of the fool: this also is vanity.

Johnson teaches us that the authority of criticism as a literary genre depends upon the human wisdom of the critic, and not upon the rightness or wrongness of either theory or *praxis*. Hazlitt observed that the arts, including literature, are not progressive, and this includes criticism as a branch of the literary art. There always will be those setting rules for criticism, down to current Gallic versions of formalism, linguistic skepticism, and even psycholinguistics, but they have not given and will not give us literary criticism, which will go on being the wisdom of interpretation and the interpretation of wisdom. Johnson and Hazlitt, Ruskin and Pater, Oscar Wilde and Kenneth Burke, all in different but related ways show us that memorable criticism is experiential criticism, that there is no method except oneself, and most profoundly that it is "objectivity" which turns out to be easy, vulgar, and therefore disgusting. True critical subjectivity or personality is hardly an abandonment to self, but is a difficult achievement, dependent upon learning, intellect, and the mystery of individual vitality. "Objectivity" turns out to be a digest of the opinions of others, whether those opinions mask as philosophy, science, or the social conventions of the academies:

> Minim professes great admiration of the wisdom and munificence by which the academies of the Continent were raised, and often wishes for some standard of taste, for some tribunal, to which merit may appeal from caprice, prejudice, and malignity.
>
> *(Idler)* No. 61

Mr. Dick Minim we have in abundance these bad days; he pours forth tomes denouncing interpretation, and calling for rules, principles, methods that will turn Anglo-American criticism into a Germano-Gallic "human science." "Rigor, Rigor!" cries our contemporary Minim, while he keeps reminding us that poems and stories are written in and by language. Dr. Samuel Johnson, who had not the benefits of the Hegelian philosophy and its Franco-Heideggerian revisionists, did what he could with what he had, as here on Shakespeare's *Henry IV* plays:

> But *Falstaff* unimitated, unimitable *Falstaff*, how shall I describe thee? Thou compound of sense and vice; of sense which may be admired but not esteemed, of vice which may be despised, but hardly detested. . . . Yet the man thus corrupt, thus despicable, makes himself necessary to the prince that despises him, by the most pleasing of all qualities, perpetual gaiety, by an unfailing power of exciting laughter, which is the more freely indulged, as his wit is not of the splendid or ambitious kind, but consists in easy escapes and sallies of levity, which make sport but raise no envy.

That the balance of this judgment is admirable, and unmatched, is palpable. But the critical magnificence surpasses mere balance, and is a crucial insight into Shakespearean representation. Falstaff is "unimitated"; he is not a mimesis, but a supermimesis of essential nature. He is also "unimitable," because he is a form more real than living man; he contains us, not we him. His "perpetual gaiety," his wit of "easy escapes and sallies of levity," a wit that exempts him from envy, testify to his unique nature as a person without a superego. Without a superego to admonish the ego to forsake its aggressivities (while punishing the ego all the more each time it abandons an aggressive drive), we would be as Falstaff, in a condition of perpetual gaiety, because our death drive, like Falstaff's, would have been subsumed by play, by easy escapes and sallies of levity. What Nietzsche failed to represent by his frequently bathetic Zarathustra, and what Freud assumed was beyond representation, Johnson shows us that Shakespeare triumphantly had accomplished in Sir John Falstaff. Johnson, greatest of critics, can teach the rest of us that the essence of poetry is *invention*. Invention is how meaning gets started, and Johnson implicitly demonstrates that Shakespeare, more even than Homer or the Bible, was the work most abundant in original invention.

Yet that is only part of how superbly suggestive Johnson upon Shakespeare is. Falstaff's admirable if not estimable sense makes itself necessary to us as well as to Hal, Bolingbroke's son, because we too lack perpetual gaiety, because we all of us, like Samuel Johnson, are too much punished by our superegos. Falstaff's sense, his unfailing power, is the sense and power of how meaning gets started, of how invention is accomplished. In the terms of Freudian reductiveness, meaning gets started rather than repeated when the superego is overcome, but in the Freudian reduction the superego cannot be overcome. Shakespeare, the most inventive and original of all writers, ever, is able to generate an almost totally fresh meaning through the exuberance of Falstaff's triumphant will to power over language. Such a will, whether in writing or speaking, can work its way only through diction, through a choice of words that pragmatically amounts to a series of choices in language. Johnson was both a critic of power (invention) and of the will to diction, and he understood the reflection of power by choice of language better than any critic has been able to convey since.

2

Johnson's greatest work as a critic is *The Lives of the Poets*, written between 1777 and 1781. Yet everything about this work is peculiar, since the *Lives* are introductions to a very odd collection of the British poets, chosen for the most part not by Johnson, but by the booksellers. Fifty poets are represented, with Oliver Goldsmith, Johnson's close friend, excluded and such bards as Roscommon, Pomfret, Dorset, Stepney, Sprat, Fenton, Yalden, and Lyttelton included, as though they were canonical. Johnson mostly shrugs them off, even when he had suggested them, remarking amiably enough in his *Life of Yalden*:

Of his poems, many are of that irregular kind, which, when he formed his poetical character, was supposed to be Pindarick. Having fixed his attention on Cowley as a model, he has attempted in some sort to rival him, and has written a *Hymn to Darkness,* evidently as a counter-part to Cowley's *Hymn to Light.*

Alas, poor Yalden! He is remembered now, if at all, only for that remark, and for the rather grand Johnsonian sentence that concludes his *Life:*

> Of his other poems it is sufficient to say that they deserve perusal, though they are not always exactly polished, though the rhymes are sometimes very ill sorted, and though his faults seem rather the omissions of idleness than the negligence of enthusiasm.

A bit earlier, Johnson had quoted Yalden's unfortunate line in which Jehovah contemplates the new created Light:

> A while th'Almighty wondering stood.

Alas, poor Yalden! We can never forget the Johnsonian observation upon this:

> He ought to have remembered that Infinite Knowledge can never wonder. All wonder is the effect of novelty upon Ignorance.

That last sentence is an epitome of the neoclassic critical stance, and could be Ben Jonson deprecating the followers of Spenser, or Samuel Johnson himself dismissing the poetry of Sensibility, the swerve away from Pope and back to Milton, in Gray, Collins, and the Wartons. In his *Life of Gray,* Johnson is superbly honest and direct in admitting his lack of pleasure in the poetry, and particularly in the two great Pindarics, *The Bard* and *The Progress of Poesy.* Boswell, in the *Life of Johnson,* reports the critic as dismissing Gray's Odes: "they are but cucumbers after all." The dismissal is especially hurtful if an American remembers that Johnson means the British cucumber, an ungainly and rough vegetable whose baroque outlines do suggest the shape of a Gray Pindaric upon the page.

The masterpiece of the *Lives* is the long and beautiful meditation upon Pope. Pope and Dryden, Johnson had by heart; he seems to have had total recall of their work. Swift was a profound problem for Johnson. Despite their intellectual affinities, or perhaps because of them, Johnson was unnerved by Swift. *A Tale of a Tub,* much as I myself am frightened by it, is certainly the most powerful discursive prose work in the English language. Johnson seems to have been even more frightened by it. He called it "this wild work" and wrote of it with a kind of traumatic response:

> of this book charity may be persuaded to think that it might be written by a man of a peculiar character, without ill intention; but it is certainly of dangerous example.

Scholars have surmised that Johnson feared joining Swift in madness. That seems to me a little too simple. Certainly Johnson, like many men and many women, feared dying badly:

> But few there are whom hours like these await,
> Who set unclouded in the gulfs of fate.
> From Lydia's monarch should the search descend,
> By Solon cautioned to regard his end,
> In life's last scene what prodigies surprise,
> Fears of the brave, and follies of the wise?
> From Marlborough's eyes the streams of dotage flow,
> And Swift expires a driveller and a show.

Swift's terrible irony, savage beyond measure, is antithetical to Johnson's empirical and humane stance. Neoclassical literary theory, which culminated in Johnson, emphasizes the virtues of moral instruction, imitation, and refinement, in the sense of improving the tradition without necessarily revising it. But Swift, though he agreed with this in the abstract, hardly possessed an Horatian temperament. His ferocity, perhaps unparalleled among the great writers, emerges fully only in *A Tale of a Tub*, as Johnson carefully notes:

> It exhibits a vehemence and rapidity of mind, a copiousness of images, and vivacity of diction, such as he afterwards never possessed or never exerted. It is of a mode so distinct and peculiar that it must be considered by itself. . . .

That is to say, in Johnson's own terms, Swift's extraordinary nightmare of a book exhibits supreme invention, and the essence of poetry is invention, according to Johnson himself. We all of us have a favorite writer; as I grow older, Johnson is mine, as Pope was Johnson's. We tend to confederate Swift and Pope in our minds; they were close friends, political and literary allies, and they divide the glory of the British Augustans between them, in an age of satire. But Johnson was at ease with Pope, and uncomfortable with Swift. As a wisdom writer, he knew the difference between them. Pope, like Addison, has a link to Francis Bacon, as does Johnson. Swift is not a wisdom writer, but something darker and stronger.

3

Johnson, in my judgment, remains Shakespeare's best critic, precisely because Shakespeare compels Johnson to retreat from neoclassicism and to stand upon the common sense of British naturalism in order to accept and admire Shakespeare's mimetic triumphs. In his *Preface to Shakespeare*, Johnson gives us the inevitable starting point for thinking about Shakespearean representation:

> There is a vigilance of observation and accuracy of distinction which books and precepts cannot confer; from this almost all original and native excellence proceeds. *Shakespeare* must have looked upon

mankind with perspicacity, in the highest degree curious and attentive. Other writers borrow their characters from preceding writers, and
diversify them only by the accidental appendages of present manners;
the dress is a little varied, but the body is the same. Our authour had
both matter and form to provide; for except the characters of *Chaucer,*
to whom I think he is not much indebted, there were no writers in
English, and perhaps not many in other modern languages, which
shewed life in its native colours.

Probably Johnson underestimated Shakespeare's indebtedness to
Chaucer. *A Midsummer Night's Dream* and *Troilus and Cressida* owe much to
Chaucer, and possibly *Romeo and Juliet* does also. More crucially, there is a
complex link between Chaucer's strongest figures, the Pardoner and the Wife
of Bath, and the magnificent Falstaff. Chaucer may well have given
Shakespeare something of that greatest gift they share: they are the first
writers whose personages change *by listening to themselves speak.* But I add
little to Johnson here, since he so massively indicates that only Chaucer and
Shakespeare represent reality in reality's own colors, and one of the most
essential of those colors or tropes is the effect of our words upon ourselves. It
is on the central issue of Shakespeare's greatest strength, which is his mode of
so representing reality as to compel aspects of reality, that otherwise we could
not know, to appear, that Johnson achieves his most useful insight:

> Though he had so many difficulties to encounter, and so little
> assistance to surmount them, he has been able to obtain an exact
> knowledge of many modes of life, and many casts of native disposi-
> tions; to vary them with great multiplicity; to mark them by nice
> distinctions; and to shew them in full view by proper combinations. In
> this part of his performances he had none to imitate, but has himself
> been imitated by all succeeding writers; and it may be doubted,
> whether from all his successors more maxims of theoretical knowl-
> edge, or more rules of practical prudence, can be collected, than he
> alone has given to his country.

Johnson splendidly recognizes that Shakespeare's legacy is both in
cognitive awareness or theoretical knowledge, and in wisdom or practical
prudence. Shakespeare attained "exact knowledge," and represented it in full
view; he therefore surpassed the metaphysicians in epistemological certainty,
and the moralists in pragmatic measurement. An original who established a
contingency that governs all writers since, Shakespeare clearly sets the
standard for representation itself. This is Johnson's most complex realization
about Shakespeare, and therefore about imaginative literature. To know many
modes of life, and so many casts of native dispositions, is here very much a
knowing indistinguishable from representation, from the allied acts of varying
with multiplicity, marking by nice distinctions, and showing in full view. To
vary, mark, and show is not apart from the knowing, but *is* the knowing.
Shakespeare, Johnson implies, creates representations so original that concep-

tually *they contain us,* and continue to shape our psychology of motivation. To have created the modern representation of the mind was the achievement neither of Montaigne nor (belatedly) of Freud, but of Shakespeare alone. What Johnson teaches us is that Shakespeare invented our psychology, to an astonishing degree.

4

Boswell's "Johnson" is of course, a fiction, but so is Boswell's "Boswell" in the *London Journal,* and so, in a related sense, is Johnson's "Johnson," the Ecclesiastes-like wisdom writer of *The Rambler, Rasselas, The Vanity of Human Wishes,* the *Preface to Shakespeare,* and the *Lives of the Poets.* When we read the *Life of Johnson,* we begin with the assumption that Dr. Samuel Johnson is not of the company of Sir John Falstaff, even though we delight to imagine them both as monarchs of conversation enthroned in their proper context, the tavern. Yet there is a sense in which Johnson is not only a conversational genius in himself, but the cause of grand conversation in other men and women just as Falstaff is the cause of wit in others. Witness Boswell's delicious account of the meeting between Johnson and an old college acquaintance, Edwards, after a separation of some forty-nine years. Nothing could be more memorable than a famous observation by the amiable Edwards: "You are a philosopher, Dr. Johnson. I have tried too in my time to be a philosopher; but, I don't know how, cheerfulness was always breaking in!"

Whether this truly was Edwards's, or is Boswell's own superb invention, we cannot know. What we do know is that Johnson was his own invention, and not Boswell's. Johnson without Boswell has rather a smaller audience now than Boswell without Johnson, but it is fit audience though few. "Boswell with Johnson" might be a proper description for the authorship of the *Life of Johnson.* It may even be divided thus; if *ethos* is the *daimon,* or character is fate, then Johnson is the author of the deepest portion of the *Life,* because Johnson's character is anything but Boswell's creation. The *ethos* of the greatest English writer of wisdom literature is as clearly recognizable in the *Life of Johnson* as it is in the *Life of Savage* or the *Life of Pope.* But if *pathos* is the swerve away from overdetermination, or personality is freedom, then the personality of Johnson, in the *Life of Johnson,* truly is Boswell's creation. So endearing is that personality, so vital is it to us as readers, that Boswell's Johnson, like Shakespeare's Falstaff, has become a permanent image of human freedom. Freedom from what, in Johnson's case? Falstaff is free of the superego, while Johnson is tormented by that psychic agency. Johnson, I think, has so strong an ego that paradoxically he is free of the ego, free of the ego's narcissistic investment in a self, which becomes its own self. Johnson, particularly in Boswell, though uncannily dark, and shadowed by presentiments, does not manifest either of Kierkegaard's two inevitable despairs: the despair of having failed to become oneself, or the still greater despair of having become oneself. It may be Boswell's greatest triumph that he gives us Dr. Johnson as a hero of consciousness, a man strong enough to live without illusions and without deceit.

Boswell's Johnson is eminently a humorist, and though a moralist, he is generally too wise to present his wisdom without humor. There are hundreds of instances in the *Life,* but I have a special fondness for a breakfast conversation between Johnson and Boswell on June 5, 1781, when the doctor was already seventy-two years in age:

> On Tuesday, June 5, Johnson was to return to London. He was very pleasant at breakfast; I mentioned a friend of mine having resolved never to marry a pretty woman. JOHNSON. 'Sir, it is a very foolish resolution to resolve never to marry a pretty woman. Beauty is of itself very estimable. No, Sir, I would prefer a pretty woman, unless there are objections to her. A pretty woman may be foolish; a pretty woman may be wicked; a pretty woman may not like me. But there is no such danger in marrying a pretty woman as is apprehended; she will not be persecuted if she does not invite persecution. A pretty woman, if she has a mind to be wicked, can find a readier way than another; and that is all.'

"And that is all," but as always with Boswell's Johnson, that is a great deal.

5

Boswell's greatest achievement, in the *Life,* is that he persuades us that his Johnson is *the* Johnson, which many incessant readers of Johnson (myself included) do not like to admit. Yet so strong is Boswell's imagination of Johnson that we tend to read it into Johnson whenever we read the sage, so that we never can be free of Boswell, once we have read the *Life of Johnson.* Even the greatest of modern scholar-critics of Johnson, my teacher W. K. Wimsatt, Jr., who was certainly the most Johnsonian personality I will ever know, is pervaded by Boswell, consciously and unconsciously, throughout his magnificent *The Prose Style of Johnson.* Wimsatt powerfully conveys Johnson's dislike of mere history and related love of biography, which is based upon a dislike of the plainness of fact, not as opposed to fiction, but as opposed to elaboration and its possibilities. On this account, Boswell in the *Life of Johnson* is more Johnsonian than even Johnson could have been. The true test for Boswell's masterpiece would thus be set by Johnson himself, in *Rambler* No. 3:

> The task of an author is, either to teach what is not known, or to recommend known truths by his manner of adorning them; either to let new light in upon the mind, and open new scenes to the prospect, or to vary the dress and situation of common objects, so as to give them fresh grace and more powerful attractions, to spread such flowers over

the regions through which the intellect has already made its progress, as may tempt it to return, and take a second view of things hastily passed over or negligently regarded.

This task of elaboration by adornment, variation, refinement is the project of both Pope in his poetry and Boswell in the *Life of Johnson*. What Johnson praised in Pope, we must praise in Boswell: if Boswell be not a biographer, where is biography to be found? Boswell is both neoclassical, as suits a follower of Johnson, and an apostle of sentiment, of sensibility and the Sublime, as was inevitable for a literary consciousness in Boswell's own generation. Johnson, though far shrewder and more humane in *praxis* than in critical theory, was something of a cultural reactionary. This hardly matters, since Shakespeare and even Milton (despite Johnson's strong prejudice against Milton) caused Johnson to overthrow his own critical speculations.

The Art of the Critic

Anthony Ashley Cooper Third Earl of Shaftesbury

1671–1713

Born of a noble family of intellectual distinction, Anthony Ashley Cooper played a unique role in the history of English moral and aesthetic philosophy and criticism. His grandfather, the first earl, was friendly with John Locke, so it is not surprising that as a result of the observance of family tradition, the young Cooper was brought up according to the educational precepts of the great English philosopher. After a period of continental travel, Shaftesbury returned to England in 1689 and spent several years absorbed in study. After a brief episode in which he flirted with politics his health (which was always delicate) forced him to retire to a life of learned endeavor. In 1698, Shaftesbury returned to Europe for a year that proved to be one of the most important of his life. In Holland he cultivated the friendship of Le Clerc, Bayle, and other prominent thinkers. Upon returning to England to assume his father's title, he had already formed the basis of his prodigious culture. It was probably then—at the age of twenty—that Shaftesbury surreptitiously published his fledgling work, *An Inquiry Concerning Virtue*.

With the accession of Queen Anne, Shaftesbury was deprived of the vice-admiralty of Dorset, and could then turn to writing with less distraction. His letter to Lord Somers, which bears the title *Concerning Enthusiasm* (1707), is one of his best known writings. During the last decade of his life he turned his attention to aesthetic and philosophical questions, with emphasis on the theory of wit and humor, and on the historical problem of the different kinds of taste. The publication of his *Characteristicks of Men, Manner, Opinions and Times* in 1711 revealed these interests in their most systematic expression. In July of that year he moved to Naples for reasons of health. He died on February 4, 1713, in Dorstshire.

The influence of Shaftesbury on Continental, and particularly German, thought is considerable. Herder, Lessing, and Goethe admired him greatly; Leibniz and the *philosophes* did not hesitate to acknowledge their debt to him. Until Byron no Englishman would make such an impression on his European successors and contemporaries. In the sphere of ethical speculation Shaftesbury was a key figure in the development of subsequent English philosophy as well. Hume and Adam Smith may be counted among his descendants, and Pope would not have been able to elaborate his view of philosophy in his *Essay on Man* without the example of Anthony Ashley Cooper to guide him.

A LETTER CONCERNING ENTHUSIASM

Section I

My Lord,

Now, you are return'd to . . . , and before the Season comes that must engage you in the weightier Matters of State; if you care to be entertain'd a while with a sort of idle Thoughts, ⟨such as⟩ pretend only to Amusement, and have no relation to Business or Affairs, you may cast your Eye slightly on what you have before you; and if there be any thing inviting, you may read it over at your leisure.

It has been an establish'd Custom for Poets, at the entrance of their Work, to address themselves to some Muse: and this Practice of the Antients has gain'd so much Repute, that ⟨even⟩ in our days we find it almost constantly imitated. I cannot but fancy however, that this Imitation, which passes so currently with other Judgments, must at some time or other have stuck a little with your Lordship; who is us'd to examine Things by a better Standard than that of Fashion or the common Taste. You must certainly have observ'd our Poets under a remarkable Constraint, when oblig'd to assume this Character: and you have wonder'd, perhaps, why that Air of Enthusiasm which sits so gracefully with an Antient, shou'd be so spiritless and aukard in a Modern. But as to this Doubt, your Lordship wou'd have soon resolv'd your self: and it cou'd only serve to bring a-cross you a Reflection which you have often made, on many occasions besides; *That Truth is the most powerful thing in the World,* since even Fiction it self must be govern'd by it, and can only please by its resemblance. The Appearance of Reality is necessary to make any Passion aggreeably represented: and to be able to move others, we must first be mov'd our-selves, or at least seem to be so, upon some probable Grounds. Now what possibility is there that a Modern, who is known never to have worship'd Apollo, or own'd any such Diety as the Muses, shou'd persuade us to enter into his pretended Devotion, and move us by his feign'd Zeal in a Religion out of date? But as for the Antients, 'tis known they deriv'd both their Religion and Polity from the Muses Art. How natural therefore must it have appear'd in any, but especially a Poet of those times, to address himself in Raptures of Devotion to those acknowledg'd Patronesses of Wit and Science? Here the Poet might with probability feign an Extasy, tho he really felt none: and supposing it to have been mere Affectation, it wou'd look however like something natural, and cou'd not fail of pleasing.

But perhaps, my Lord, there was a further Mystery in the case. Men, your

Lordship knows, are wonderfully happy in a Faculty of deceiving themselves, whenever they set heartily about it: and a very small Foundation of any Passion will serve us, not only to act it well, but even to work our-selves into it beyond our own reach. Thus by a little Affectation in Love-Matters, and with the help of a Romance or Novel, a Boy of Fifteen, or a grave Man of Fifty, may be sure to grow a very natural Coxcomb, and feel the *Belle Passion* in good earnest. A Man of tolerable Good-Nature, who happens to be a little piqu'd, may, by improving his Resentment, become a very Fury for Revenge. Even a good Christian, who wou'd needs be over-good, and thinks he can never believe enough, may, by a small Inclination well improv'd, extend his Faith so largely, as to comprehend in it not only all Scriptural and Traditional Miracles, but a solid System of Old-Wives Storys. Were it needful, I cou'd put your Lordship in mind of an Eminent, Learned, and truly Christian Prelate you once knew, who cou'd have given you a full account of his Belief in Fairys. And this, methinks, may serve to make appear, how far an antient Poet's Faith might possibly have been rais'd, together with his Imagination.

But we Christians, who have such ample Faith ourselves, will allow nothing to poor Heathens. They must be Infidels in every sense. We will not allow 'em to believe so much as their own Religion; which we cry is too absurd to have been credited by any besides the mere Vulgar. But if a Reverend Christian Prelate may be so great a Volunteer in Faith, as beyond the ordinary Prescription of the Catholick Church, to believe in Fairys; why may not a Heathen Poet in the ordinary way of his Religion be allow'd to believe in Muses? For these, your Lordship knows, were so many Divine Persons in the Heathen Creed, and were essential in their System of Theology. The God-desses had their Temples and Worship, the same as the other Deitys: And to disbelieve the Holy Nine, or their Apollo, was the same as to deny Jove himself, and must have been esteem'd equally Profane and Atheistical by the generality of sober Men. Now what a mighty advantage must it have been to an antient Poet to be thus Orthodox, and by the help of his Education, and a Good-Will into the bargain, to work himself up to ⟨the⟩ Belief of a Divine Presence and Heavenly Inspiration? It was never surely the Business of Poets in those days to call Revelation in question, when it evidently made so well for their Art. On the contrary, they cou'd not fail to animate their Faith as much as possible; when by a single Act of it, well inforc'd, they cou'd raise themselves into such Angelical Company.

How much the Imagination of such a Presence must exalt a Genius, we may observe merely from the Influence which an ordinary Presence has over Men. Our modern Wits are more or less rais'd by the Opinion they have of their Company, and the Idea they form to themselves of the Persons to whom they make their Addresses. A common Actor of the Stage will inform us how much a full Audience of the Better Sort exalts him above the common pitch. And you, my Lord, who are the noblest Actor, and of the noblest Part assign'd to any Mortal on this earthly Stage, when you are acting for Liberty and Mankind; does not the publick Presence, that of your Friends, and the Well-wishers to your Cause, add something to your Thought and Genius? Or is that Sublime of

Reason, and that Power of Eloquence, which you discover in publick, no more than what you are equally Master of in private, and can command at any time, alone, or with indifferent Company, or in any easy or cool hour? This indeed were more Godlike; but ordinary Humanity, I think, reaches not so high.

For my own part, My Lord, I have really so much need of some considerable Presence or Company to raise my Thoughts on any occasion, that when alone, I must endeavour by Strength of Fancy to supply this want; and in default of a Muse, must inquire out some Great Man of a more than ordinary Genius, whose imagin'd Presence may inspire me with more than what I feel at ordinary hours. And thus, my Lord, have I chosen to address my self to your Lordship; tho without subscribing my Name: allowing you, as a Stranger, the full Liberty of reading no more than what you may have a fancy for; but reserving to my self the privilege of imagining you read all, with particular notice, as a Friend, and one whom I may justifiably treat with the Intimacy and Freedom which follows.

Section II

If the knowing well how to expose any Infirmity or Vice were but a sufficient Security for the Vertue which is contrary, how excellent an Age might we be presum'd to live in! Never was there in our Nation a time known, when Folly and Extravagance of every kind ⟨were⟩ more sharply inspected, or more wittily ridicul'd. And one might hope at least from this good Symptom, that our Age was in no declining State; since whatever our Distempers are, we stand so well affected to our Remedys. To bear the being told of Faults, is in private Persons the best token of Amendment. 'Tis seldom that a Publick is thus dispos'd. For where Jealousy of State, or the Ill Lives of the Great People, or any other Cause is powerul enough to restrain the Freedom of Censure in any part, it in effect destroys the Benefit of it in the whole. There can be no impartial and free Censure of Manners where any peculiar Custom or National Opinion is set apart, and not only exempted from Criticism, but even flatter'd with the highest Art. 'Tis only in a free Nation, such as ours, that Imposture has no Privilege; and that neither the Credit of a Court, the Power of a Nobility, nor the Awfulness of a Church can give her protection, or hinder her from being arraign'd in every Shape and Appearance. 'Tis true, this Liberty may seem to run too far. We may perhaps be said to make ill use of it.———So every one will say, when he himself is touch'd, and his Opinion freely examin'd. But who shall be Judg of what may be freely examin'd, and what may not? Where Liberty may be us'd; and where it may not? What Remedy shall we prescribe to this in general? Can there be a better than from that Liberty it self which is complain'd of? If Men are vicious, petulant or abusive; the Magistrate may correct them—But if they reason ill, 'tis Reason still must teach 'em to do better. Justness of Thought and Stile, Refinement in Manners, good Breeding, and Politeness of every kind, can come only from the Trial and Experience of what is best. Let but the Search go freely on, and the right Measure of every thing will soon be found. Whatever Humour has got the start, if it be unnatural, it cannot hold: and the Ridicule, if ill plac'd at first, will certainly fall at last where it deserves.

I have often wonder'd to see Men of Sense so mightily alarm'd at the approach of any thing like Ridicule on certain Subjects; as if they mistrusted their own Judgment. For what Ridicule can lie against Reason? Or how can any one of the least Justness of Thought endure a Ridicule wrong plac'd? Nothing is more ridiculous than this it self. The Vulgar, indeed, may swallow any sordid Jest, any mere Drollery or Buffoonery; but it must be a finer and truer Wit that takes with the Men of Sense and Breeding. How comes it to pass then, that we appear such Cowards in reasoning, and are so afraid to stand the Test of Ridicule?——— O! say we, the Subjects are too grave———Perhaps so: but let us see first whether they are really grave or no: for in the manner we may conceive 'em, they may peradventure be very grave and weighty in our Imagination; but very ridiculous and impertinent in their own nature. Gravity is of the very Essence of Imposture. It does not only ⟨make us mistake⟩ other Things, but is apt perpetually almost to mistake it self. For ⟨even⟩ in common Behaviour, how hard a thing is it for the grave Character to keep long out of the limits of the formal one? We can never be too grave, if we can but be assur'd we are really ⟨what we suppose⟩: and we can never too much honour or revere any thing for grave; if we are assur'd the Thing is grave, as we apprehend it. The main Point is to know always true Gravity from the false: and this can only be, by carrying the Rule constantly with us, and freely applying it not only to the Things about us, but to our-selves. For if unhappily we lose the Measure in our-selves, we shall soon lose it in every thing besides. Now what Rule or Measure is there in the World, ⟨except in the considering of⟩ the real Temper of Things, to find which are truly serious, and which ridiculous? And how can this be done, ⟨unless⟩ by applying the Ridicule, to see whether it will bear? But if we fear to apply this Rule in any thing, what Security can we have against the Imposture of Formality in all things? We have allow'd our-selves to be Formalists in one Point; and the same Formality may rule us as it pleases in all other.

'Tis not in every Disposition that we are capacitated to judg of things. We must beforehand judg of our own Temper, and accordingly of other things that fall under our Judgment. But we must never more pretend to judg of things, or of our own Temper in judging them, when we have given up our preliminary Right of Judgment, and under a Presumption of Gravity, have allow'd our selves to be most ridiculous, and to admire profoundly the most ridiculous Things in nature, at least for ought we know. For having resolv'd never to try, we can never be sure.

Ridiculum acri
Fortius & melius magnas plerumque secat res.
Hor. Sat. 10.

This, my Lord, I may safely aver, is so true a thing in itself, and so well known for Truth by the cunning Formalists of the Age, that they can better bear to have their Impostures rail'd at, with all the Bitterness and Vehemence imaginable, than to have them touch'd ever so gently in this other way. They know very well, that as Modes and Fashions, so Opinions, tho ever so ridiculous, are kept up by Solemnity: and that those formal Notions which grew up probably in an ill Mood, and have been conceiv'd in sober Sadness, are never to be remov'd but in a sober kind of Chearfulness, and by a more easy and pleasant way of Thought. There is a Melancholy which accompanys all Enthusiasm. Be it Love or Religion (for there are Enthusiasms in both) nothing can put a stop to the growing mischief of either, till the Melancholy be remov'd, and the Mind at liberty to hear what can be said against the Ridiculousness of an Extreme in either way.

It was heretofore the Wisdom of some wise Nations, to let People be Fools as much as they pleas'd, and never to punish seriously what deserv'd only to be laugh'd at, and was after all best cur'd by that innocent Remedy. There are certain Humours in Mankind, which of necessity must have vent. The Human Mind and Body are both of 'em naturally subject to Commotions: and as there are strange Ferments in the Blood, which in many Bodys occasion an extraordinary discharge; so in Reason too, there are heterogeneous Particles which must be thrown off by Fermentation. Shou'd Physicians endeavour absolutely to allay those Ferments of the Body, and strike in the Humours which discover themselves in such Eruptions, they might, instead of making a Cure, bid fair perhaps to raise a Plague, and turn a Spring-Ague or an Autumn-Surfeit into an epidemical malignant Fever. They are certainly as ill Physicians in the Body-Politick, who wou'd needs be tampering with these mental Eruptions; and under the specious pretence of healing this Itch of Superstition, and saving Souls from the Contagion of Enthusiasm, shou'd set all Nature in an uproar, and turn a few innocent Carbuncles into an Inflammation and mortal Gangrene.

We read in History that Pan, when he accompany'd Bacchus in an Expedition to the Indies, found means to strike a Terror thro a Host of Enemys, by the help of a small Company, whose Clamors he manag'd to good advantage among the ecchoing Rocks and Caverns of a woody Vale. The hoarse bellowing of the Caves, join'd to the hideous aspect of such dark and desart Places, rais'd such a Horror in the Enemy, that in this state their Imagination help'd 'em to hear Voices, and doubtless to see Forms too, that were more than Human: whilst the Uncertainty of what they fear'd made their Fear yet greater, and spread it faster by implicit Looks than any Narration cou'd convey it. And this was what in after-times Men call'd a Pannick. The Story indeed gives a good Hint of the nature of this Passion, which can hardly be without some mixture of Enthusiasm, and Horrors of a superstitious kind.

We may with good reason call every Passion Pannick which is rais'd in a Multitude, and convey'd by Aspect, or as it were by Contact or Sympathy. Thus popular Fury may be call'd Pannick, when the Rage of the People, as we have sometimes known, has put them beyond themselves; especially where

Religion has had to do. And in this state their very Looks are infectious. The Fury flies from Face to Face: and the Disease is no sooner seen than caught. Those who in a better Situation of Mind have ⟨beheld⟩ a Multitude under the power of this Passion, have own'd that they saw in the Countenances of Men something more ghastly and terrible than at other times is express'd on the most passionate occasions. Such force has Society in ill, as well as in good Passions: and so much stronger any Affection is for being social and communicative.

Thus, my Lord, there are many Pannicks in Mankind, besides merely that of Fear. And thus is Religion also Pannick; when Enthusiasm of any kind gets up; as oft, on melancholy occasions, it will do. For Vapors naturally rise; and in bad times especially, when the Spirits of Men are low, as either in publick Calamitys, or during the Unwholesomness of Air or Diet, or when Convulsions happen in Nature, Storms, Earthquakes, or other amazing Prodigys: at this season the Pannick must needs run high, and the Magistrate of necessity give way to it. For to apply a serious Remedy, and to bring the Sword, or Fasces, as a Cure, must make the Case more melancholy, and increase the very Cause of the Distemper. To forbid Mens natural Fears, and to endeavour the overpowering them by other Fears, must needs be a most unnatural Method. The Magistrate, if he be any Artist, shou'd have a gentler hand; and instead of Causticks, Incisions, and Amputations, shou'd be using the softest Balms; and with a kind Sympathy entering into the Concern of the People, and taking, as it were, their Passion upon him, shou'd, when he has sooth'd and satisfy'd it, endeavour, by chearful ways, to divert and heal it.

This was antient Policy: and hence (as a notable Author of our Nation expresses it) ⟨'tis⟩ necessary a People shou'd have a Publick Leading in Religion. For to deny the Magistrate a Worship, or take away a National Church, is as mere Enthusiasm as the Notion which sets up Persecution. For why shou'd there not be publick Walks, as well as private Gardens? Why not publick Librarys, as well as private Education and Home-Tutors? But to prescribe bounds to Fancy and Speculation, to regulate Mens Apprehensions and religious Beliefs or Fears, to suppress by Violence the natural Passion of Enthusiasm, or to endeavour to ascertain it, or reduce it to one Species, or bring it under any one Modification, is in truth no better Sense, nor deserves a better Character, than what the Comedian declares of the like Project in the Affair of Love—

> *Nihilo plus agas*
> *Quàm si des operam ut cum ratione insanias.*

Not only the Visionarys and Enthusiasts of all kinds were tolerated, your Lordship knows, by the Antients: but on the other side, Philosophy had as free a course, and was permitted as a Ballance against Superstition. And whilst some Sects, such as the Pythagorean and latter Platonick, join'd in with the Superstition and Enthusiasm of the Times; the Epicurean, the Academick, and others, were allow'd to use all the Force of Wit and Raillery against it. And thus matters were ⟨happily⟩ ballanc'd; Reason had fair Play; Learning and

Science flourish'd. Wonderful was the Harmony and Temper that arose from all these Contrarietys. Thus Superstition and Enthusiasm were mildly treated; and being let alone, they never rag'd to that degree as to occasion Bloodshed, Wars, Persecutions and Devastations in the World. But a new sort of Policy, which extends it self to another World, and considers the future Lives and Happiness of Men rather than the present, has made us leap the Bounds of natural Humanity; and out of a supernatural Charity, has taught us the way of plaguing one another most devoutly. It has rais'd an Antipathy which no temporal Interest cou'd ever do; and entail'd upon us a mutual Hatred to all Eternity. And now Uniformity in Opinion (a hopeful Project!) is look'd on as the only Expedient against this Evil. The saving of Souls is now the Heroick Passion of exalted Spirits; and is become in a manner the chief care of the Magistrate, and the very end of Government it-self.

If Magistracy shou'd vouchsafe to interpose thus much in other Sciences, I am afraid we shou'd have as bad Logick, as bad Mathematicks, and in every kind as bad Philosophy, as we often have Divinity, in Countrys where a precise Orthodoxy is settled by Law. 'Tis a hard matter for a Government to settle Wit. If it does but keep us sober and honest, 'tis likely we shall have as much Ability in our spiritual as in our temporal Affairs: and if we can but be trusted, we shall have Wit enough to save our-selves, when no prejudice lies in the way. But if Honesty and Wit be insufficient for this saving Work, 'tis in vain for the Magistrate to meddle with it: since if he be ever so vertuous or wise, he may be as soon mistaken as another Man. I am sure the only way to save Mens Sense, or preserve Wit at all in the World, is to give Liberty to Wit. Now Wit can never have its Liberty, where the Freedom of Raillery is taken away: For against serious Extravagances and spleenitick Humours there is no Remedy but this.

We have indeed full Power over all other Modifications of Spleen. We may treat other Enthusiasms as we please. We may ridicule Love, or Gallantry, or Knight-Errantry to the utmost; and we find, that in these latter days of Wit, the Humour of this kind, which was once so prevalent, is pretty well declin'd. The Crusades, the rescuing of Holy Lands, and such devout Gallantrys are in less request than formerly: But if something of this militant Religion, something of this Soul-rescuing Spirit, and Saint-Errantry prevails still, we need not wonder, when we consider in how solemn a manner we treat this Distemper, and how preposterously we go about to cure Enthusiasm.

I can hardly forbear fancying, that if we had but an Inquisition, or some formal Court of Judicature, with grave Officers and Judges, erected to restrain Poetical Licence, and in general to suppress that Fancy and Humour of Versification; but in particular that most extravagant Passion of Love, as it is set out by Poets, in its Heathenish Dress of Venus's and Cupid's: if the Poets, as Ringleaders and Teachers of this Heresy, were under grievous Penaltys forbid to enchant the People by their vein of Rhyming; and if the People, on the other side, were under proportionable Penaltys forbid to hearken to any such Charm, or lend their Attention to any Love-Tale, so much as in a Play, a Novel, or a Ballad; we might perhaps see a new Arcadia arising out of this heavy

Persecution: Old People and Young wou'd be seiz'd with a versifying Spirit: We shou'd have Field-Conventicles of Lovers and Poets: Forests wou'd be fill'd with romantick Shepherds and Shepherdesses; and Rocks resound with Ecchoes of Hymns and Praises offer'd to the Powers of Love. We might indeed have a fair Chance, by this Management, to bring back the whole Train of Heathen Gods, and set our cold Northern Island burning with as many Altars to Venus and Apollo, as ⟨were⟩ formerly ⟨in⟩ Cyprus, Delos, or any of those warmer Grecian Climates.

Section III

But, my Lord, you may perhaps wonder, that having been drawn into such a serious Subject as Religion, I shou'd forget my self so far as to give way to Raillery and Humour. I must own to you, my Lord, 'tis not merely thro Chance that this has happen'd. To say truth, I hardly care so much as to think on this Subject, much less to write on it, without endeavouring to put my self in as good Humour as is possible. People indeed, who can endure no middle Temper, but are all Air and Humour, know little of the Doubts and Scruples of Religion, and are safe from any immediate Influence of devout Melancholy or Enthusiasm; which requires more Deliberation and thoughtful Practice to fix it self in a Temper, and grow habitual. But be the Habit what it will; to be deliver'd of it at so sad a Cost as Inconsiderateness, or Madness, is what I wou'd never wish to be my Lot. I had rather stand all Adventures with Religion, than endeavour to get rid of the Thoughts of it by Diversion. All I contend for, is to think of it in a right Humour: and that this goes more than half way towards thinking rightly of it, is what I shall endeavour to demonstrate.

Good Humour is not only the best Security against Enthusiasm, but the best Foundation of Piety and true Religion: For if right Thoughts and worthy Apprehensions of the Supreme Being, are fundamental to all true Worship and Adoration; 'tis more than probable, that we shall never miscarry in this respect, ⟨except⟩ thro ill Humour only. Nothing ⟨beside⟩ ill Humour, either natural or forc'd, can bring a Man to think seriously that the World is govern'd by any devilish or malicious Power. I very much question whether any thing, besides ill Humour, can be the Cause of Atheism. For there are so many Arguments to persuade a Man in Humour, that, in the main, all things are kindly and well dispos'd, that one wou'd think it impossible for him to be so far out of conceit with Affairs, as to imagine they all ran at Adventures; and that the World, as venerable and wise a Face as it carry'd, had neither Sense nor Meaning in it. This however I am persuaded of, that nothing ⟨beside⟩ ill Humour can give us dreadful or ill Thoughts of a Supreme Manager. Nothing can persuade us of Sullenness or Sourness in such a Being, ⟨beside the actual⟩ sore-feeling of somewhat of this kind within our-selves: and if we are afraid of bringing good Humour into Religion, or thinking with Freedom and Pleasantness on such a

Subject as God; 'tis because we conceive the Subject so like our-selves, and can hardly have a Notion of Majesty and Greatness without Stateliness and Moroseness accompanying it.

This, however, is the just Reverse of that Character, which we own to be most divinely Good, when we see it, as we sometimes do, in Men of highest Power among us. If they pass for truly Good, we dare treat them freely, and are sure they will not be displeas'd with this Liberty. They are doubly Gainers by this Goodness of theirs. For the more they are search'd into and familiarly examin'd, the more their Worth appears; and the Discoverer, charm'd with his Success, esteems and loves more than ever, when he has prov'd this additional Bounty in his Superior, and reflects on that Candor and Generosity he has experienc'd. Your Lordship knows more perhaps of this Mystery than any one. How else shou'd you have been so belov'd in Power, and out of Power so adher'd to, and still more belov'd?

Thank Heaven! there are even in our own Age some such Examples. In former Ages there have been many such. We have known mighty Princes, and even Emperors of the World, who cou'd bear unconcernedly not only the free Censure of their Actions, but the most spiteful Reproaches and Calumnys, even to their faces. Some perhaps may wish there had never been such Examples found in Heathens: but more especially, that the occasion had never been given by Christians. 'Twas more the Misfortune indeed of Mankind in general, than of Christians in particular, that some of the earlier Roman Emperors were such Monsters of Tyranny, and began a Persecution, not on religious Men merely, but on all that were suspected of Worth or Vertue. What cou'd have been a higher Honour or Advantage to Christianity, than to be persecuted by a Nero? But better Princes, who came after, were persuaded to remit these severe Courses. 'Tis true, the Magistrate might possibly have been surpriz'd with the newness of a Notion, which he might pretend, perhaps, did not only destroy the Sacredness of his Power, but treated him and all Men as profane, impious, and damn'd, who enter'd not into certain particular Modes of Worship, of which there had been formerly so many thousand kinds instituted, all of 'em compatible and sociable till that time. However, such was the Wisdom of some succeeding Ministrys, that the edge of Persecution was much abated; and even that Prince, who was esteem'd the greatest Enemy of the Christian Sect, and who himself had been educated in it, was a great Restrainer of Persecution, and wou'd allow of nothing further than a Resumption of Church-Lands and publick Schools, without any attempt on the Goods or Persons even of those who branded the State-Religion, and made a Merit of affronting the publick Worship.

'Tis well we have the Authority of a sacred Author in our Religion, to assure us, that the Spirit of Love and Humanity is above that of Martyrs. Otherwise, one might be a little scandaliz'd, perhaps, at the History of many of our primitive Confessors and Martyrs, even according to our own accounts. There is hardly now in the World so good a Christian (if this be indeed the Mark of a good one) who, supposing he liv'd at Constantinople, or elsewhere under the Protection of the Turks, wou'd think it fitting or decent to give any

Disturbance to their Mosque-Worship. And as good Protestants, my Lord, as you and I are, we shou'd scarce think him better than a rank Enthusiast, who, out of Hatred to the Romish Idolatry, shou'd, in time of high Mass (where Mass perhaps was by Law establish'd) interrupt the Priest with Clamors, or fall foul on his Images and Relicks.

There are some, it seems, of our good Brethren, the French Protestants, lately come among us, who are mightily taken with this Primitive way. They have set a-foot the Spirit of Martyrdom to a wonder in their own Country; and they long to be trying it here, if we will give 'em leave, and afford 'em the Occasion: that is to say, if we will only do 'em the Favour to hang or imprison 'em; if we will only be so obliging as to break their Bones for 'em, after their Country fashion, blow up their Zeal, and stir a-fresh the Coals of Persecution. But no such Grace can they hitherto obtain of us. So hard-hearted we are, that notwithstanding their own Mob are willing to bestow kind Blows upon 'em, and fairly stone 'em now and then in the open Street; tho the Priests of their own Nation wou'd gladly give 'em their desir'd Discipline, and are earnest to light their probationary Fires for 'em; we English Men, who are Masters in our own Country, will not suffer the Enthusiasts to be thus us'd. Nor can we be suppos'd to act thus in envy to their Phenix-Sect, which it seems has risen out of the Flames, and wou'd willingly grow to be a new Church by the same manner of Propagation as the old one, whose Seed was truly said to be from the Blood of the Martyrs.

But how barbarous still, and more than heathenishly cruel, are we tolerating English Men! For, not contented to deny these Prophesying Enthusiasts the Honour of a Persecution, we have deliver'd 'em over to the cruellest Contempt in the World. I am told, for certain, that they are at this very time the Subject of a choice Droll or Puppet-Shew at Bart'lemy-Fair. There, doubtless, their strange Voices and involuntary Agitations are admirably well acted, by the Motion of Wires, and Inspiration of Pipes. For the Bodys of the Prophets, in their State of Prophecy, being not in their own power, but (as they say themselves) mere passive Organs, actuated by an exterior Force, having nothing natural, or resembling real Life, in any of their Sounds or Motions: so that how aukardly soever a Puppet-Shew may imitate other Actions, it must needs represent this Passion to the Life. And whilst Bart'lemy-Fair is in possession of this Privilege, I dare stand Security to our National Church, that no Sect of Enthusiasts, no new Venders of Prophecy or Miracles, shall ever get the Start, or put her to the trouble of trying her Strength with 'em, in any Case.

Happy it was for us, that when Popery had got possession, Smithfield was us'd in a more tragical way. Many of our first Reformers, 'tis fear'd, were little better than Enthusiasts: and God knows whether a Warmth of this kind did not considerably help us in throwing off that spiritual Tyranny. So that had not the Priests, as is usual, prefer'd the love of Blood to all other Passions, they might in a merrier way, perhaps, have evaded the greatest Force of our reforming Spirit. I never heard that the antient Heathens were so well advis'd in their ill Purpose of suppressing the Christian Religion in its first Rise, as to make use, at any time, of this Bart'lemy-Fair Method. But this I am persuaded of, that had the Truth of the Gospel been any way surmountable, they wou'd have bid much fairer for the silencing it, if they had chose to bring our primitive Founders upon the Stage in a pleasanter way than that of Bear-Skins and Pitch-Barrels.

The Jews were naturally a very cloudy People, and wou'd endure little Raillery in any thing; much less in what belong'd to any Religious Doctrines or Opinions. Religion was look'd upon with a sullen Eye; and Hanging was the only Remedy they cou'd prescribe for any thing that look'd like setting up a new Revelation. The sovereign Argument was, Crucify, Crucify. But with all their Malice and Inveteracy to our Saviour, and his Apostles after him, had they but taken the Fancy to act such Puppet-Shews in his Contempt, as at this hour the Papists are acting in his Honour; I am apt to think they might possibly have done our Religion more Harm, than by all their other ways of Severity.

I believe our great and learned Apostle found less Advantage from the easy Treatment of his Athenian Antagonists, than from the surly and curst Spirit of the most persecuting Jewish Citys. He made less Improvement of the Candour and Civility of his Roman Judges, than of the Zeal of the Synagogue, and Vehemence of his National Priests. Tho when I consider this Apostle as appearing either before the witty Athenians, or before a Roman Court of Judicature, in the Presence of their great Men and Ladys, and see how handsomly he accommodates himself to the Apprehensions and Temper of those politer People, I do not find that he declines the way of Wit or good Humour; but, without Suspicion of his Cause, is willing generously to commit it to this Proof, and try it against the Sharpness of any Ridicule that might be offer'd.

But tho the Jews were never pleas'd to try their Wit or Malice this way against our Saviour or his Apostles; the irreligious part of the Heathens had try'd it long before against the best Doctrines and best Characters of Men that had ever arisen amongst 'em. Nor did this prove in the end any Injury, but on the contrary the highest Advantage to those very Characters and Doctrines, which, having stood the Proof, were found so solid and just. The divinest Man that had appear'd ever in the Heathen World, was in the height of witty Times, and by the wittiest of all Poets, most abominably ridicul'd, in a whole Comedy writ and acted on purpose. But so far was this from sinking his Reputation, or suppressing his Philosophy, that they both increas'd the more for it; and he apparently grew to be more the Envy of other Teachers. He was not only contented to be ridicul'd; but, that he might help the Poet as much as possible, he presented himself openly in the Theater; that his real Figure (which was no advantageous one) might be compar'd with that which the witty Poet had brought as his Representative on the Stage. Such was his good Humour. Nor cou'd there be in the World a greater Testimony of the invincible Goodness of the Man, or a greater Demonstration, that there was no Imposture either in his Character or Opinions. For that Imposture shou'd dare sustain the encounter of a grave Enemy, is no wonder. A solemn Attack, she knows, is not of such danger to her. There is nothing she abhors or dreads like Pleasantness and good Humour.

Section IV

In short, my Lord, the melancholy way of treating Religion is that which, according to my Apprehension, renders it so tragical, and is the occasion of its acting in reality such dismal Tragedys in the World. And my Notion is, that provided we treat Religion with good Manners, we can never use too much good Humour, or examine it with too much Freedom and Familiarity. For, if it be genuine and sincere, it will not only stand the Proof, but thrive and gain Advantage from hence; if it be spurious, or mixt with any Imposture, it will be detected and expos'd.

The melancholy way in which we have been taught Religion, makes us unapt to think of it in good Humour. 'Tis in Adversity chiefly, or in ill Health, under Affliction, or Disturbance of Mind, or Discomposure of Temper, that we have recourse to it. Tho in reality we are never so unfit to think of it as at such a heavy and dark Hour. We can never be fit to contemplate any thing above us, when we are in no Condition to look into our-selves, and calmly examine the Temper of our own Mind and Passions. For then it is we see Wrath, and Fury, and Revenge, and Terrors in the Deity; when we are full of Disturbances and Fears within, and have, by Sufferance and Anxiety, lost so much of the natural Calm and Easiness of our Temper.

We must not only be in ordinary good Humour, but in the best of Humours, and in the sweetest, kindest Disposition of our Lives, to understand well what true Goodness is, and what those Attributes imply, which we ascribe with such Applause and Honour to the Deity. We shall then be able to see best, whether those Forms of Justice, those Degrees of Punishment, that Temper of Resentment, and those Measures of Offence and Indignation, which we vulgarly suppose in God, are sutable to those original Ideas of Goodness, which the same Divine Being, or Nature under him, has implanted in us, and which we must necessarily presuppose, in order to give him Praise or Honour in any kind. This, my Lord, is the Security against all Superstition: To remember, that there is nothing in God but what is Godlike; and that He is either *not at all*, or *truly and perfectly Good*. But when we are afraid to use our Reason freely, even on that very Question, Whether He really be, or not; we then actually presume him bad, and flatly contradict that pretended Character of Goodness and Greatness; whilst we discover this mistrust of his Temper, and fear his Anger and Resentment, in the case of this Freedom of Inquiry.

We have a notable Instance of this Freedom in one of our sacred Authors. As patient as Job is said to be, it cannot be deny'd ⟨that⟩ he makes bold enough with God, and takes his Providence roundly to task. His Friends, indeed, plead hard with him, and use all Arguments, right or wrong, to patch up Objections, and set the Affairs of Providence upon an equal foot. They make a Merit of saying all the Good they can of God, at the very stretch of their Reason, and sometimes quite beyond it. But this, in Job's opinion, is flattering God, accepting of God's Person, and even mocking him. And no wonder. For, what Merit can there be in believing God, or his Providence, upon frivolous and weak grounds? What Vertue in assuming an Opinion contrary to the appearance of Things, and resolving to hear nothing that may be said against it? Excellent Character of the God of Truth! that he shou'd be offended at us, for having refus'd to put the lye upon our Understandings, as much as in us lay; and be satisfy'd with us for having believ'd, at a venture, and against our Reason, what might have been the greatest Falsehood in the world, for any thing we cou'd bring as a Proof or Evidence to the contrary!

It is impossible that any ⟨besides⟩ an ill-natur'd Man can wish against the Being of a God: for this is wishing against the Publick and even against one's private Good too, if rightly understood. But if a Man has not any such Ill-will to stifle his Belief, he must have surely an unhappy Opinion of God, and believe him not so good by far as he knows Himself to be, if he imagines that an impartial use of his Reason, in any matter of Speculation whatsoever, can make him run any Risk Hereafter; and that a mean Denial of his Reason, and an Affectation of Belief in any Point too hard for his Understanding, can intitle him to any Favour in another World. This is being Sycophants in Religion, mere Parasites of Devotion. 'Tis using God as the crafty Beggars use those they address to, when they are ignorant of their Quality. The Novices amongst 'em may innocently come out, perhaps, with a *Good Sir!* or a *Good Forsooth!* But with the old Stagers, no matter who they meet in a Coach, 'tis always *Good your Honour!* or *Good your Lordship!* or *Your Ladyship!* For if there shou'd be really a Lord in the case, we shou'd be undone (say they) for want of giving the Title: But if the Party shou'd be no Lord, there wou'd be no Offence; it wou'd not be ill taken.

And thus it is in Religion. We are highly concern'd how to beg right; and think all depends upon hitting the Title, and making a good Guess. 'Tis the most beggarly Refuge imaginable, which is so mightily cry'd up, and stands as a great Maxim with many able Men; "That they shou'd strive to have Faith, and believe to the utmost: because if, after all, there be nothing in the matter, there will be no harm in being thus deceiv'd; but if there be any thing, it will be fatal for them not to have believ'd to the full." But they are so far mistaken, that whilst they have this Thought, 'tis certain they can never believe either to their Satisfaction and Happiness in this World, or with any advantage of Recommendation to another. For besides that our Reason, which knows the Cheat, will never rest thorowly satisfy'd on such a Bottom, but turn us often a-drift, and toss us in a Sea of Doubt and Perplexity; we cannot but actually grow worse in our Religion, and entertain a worse Opinion still of a Supreme Deity, whilst our Belief is founded on so injurious a Thought of him.

To love the Publick, to study universal Good, and to promote the Interest of the whole World, as far as lies within our power, is surely the Height of Goodness, and makes that Temper which we call Divine. In this Temper, my Lord, (for surely you shou'd know it well) 'tis natural for us to wish that others shou'd partake with us, by being convinc'd of the Sincerity of our Example. 'Tis natural for us to wish our Merit shou'd be known; particularly, if it be our Fortune to have serv'd a Nation as a good Minister; or as some Prince, or Father of a Country, to have render'd happy a considerable Part of Mankind under our Care. But if it happen'd, that of this Number there shou'd be some so ignorantly bred, and of so remote a Province, as to have lain out of the hearing of our Name and Actions; or hearing of 'em, shou'd be so puzzl'd with odd and contrary Storys told up and down concerning us, that they knew not what to think, whether there were really in the World any such Person as our-self: Shou'd we not, in good truth, be ridiculous to take offence at this? And shou'd we not pass for extravagantly morose and ill-humour'd, if instead of treating the matter in Raillery, we shou'd think in earnest of revenging our selves on the offending Partys, who, out of their rustick Ignorance, ill Judgment, or Incredulity, had detracted from our Renown?

How shall we say then? Does it really deserve Praise, to be thus concern'd about it? Is the doing Good for Glory's sake, so divine a thing? or, Is it not diviner, to do Good even where it may be thought inglorious, even to the Ingrateful, and to those who are wholly insensible of the Good they receive? How comes it then that what is so divine in us, shou'd lose its Character in the Divine Being? And that according as the Deity is represented to us, he shou'd more resemble the weak, womanish, and impotent part of our Nature, than the generous, manly, and divine?

Section V

One wou'd think, my Lord, it were in reality no hard thing to know our own Weaknesses at first Sight, and distinguish the Features of human Frailty, with which we are so well acquainted. One wou'd think it were easy to understand, that Provocation and Offence, Anger, Revenge, Jealousy in point of Honour or Power, Love of Fame, Glory, and the like, belong only to limited Beings, and are necessarily excluded a Being which is perfect and universal. But if we have never settl'd with our selves any Notion of what is morally excellent; or if we cannot trust to that Reason which tells us, that nothing ⟨beside⟩ what is so, can have place in the Deity; we can neither trust to any thing that others relate of him, or that himself reveals to us. We must be satisfy'd before-hand, that he is good, and cannot deceive us. Without this, there can be no real religious Faith, or Confidence. Now, if there be really something previous to Revelation, some antecedent Demonstration of Reason, to assure us, that God is, and withal, that he is so good as not to deceive us; the same Reason, if we will trust to it, will demonstrate to us, that God is so good, as to exceed the very best of us in Goodness. And after this manner we can have no Dread or Suspicion to render us uneasy: for it is Malice only, and not Goodness, that can make us afraid.

There is an odd way of reasoning, but in certain Distempers of Mind very sovereign to those who can apply it; and it is this: "There can be no Malice but where Interests are oppos'd. A universal Being can have no Interest opposite; and therefore can have no Malice." If there be a general Mind, it can have no particular Interest: But the general Good, or Good of the Whole, and its own private Good, must of necessity be one and the same. It can intend nothing besides, nor aim at any thing beyond, nor be provok'd to any thing contrary. So that we have only to consider, whether there be really such a thing as a Mind that has relation to the Whole, or not. For if unhappily there be no Mind, we may comfort our selves, however, that Nature has no Malice: If there be really a Mind, we may rest satisfy'd, that it is the best natur'd one in the World. The last Case, one wou'd imagine, shou'd be the most comfortable; and the Notion of a common Parent less frightful than that of forlorn Nature, and a fatherless World. Tho, as Religion stands amongst us, there are many good People who wou'd have less Fear in being thus expos'd; and wou'd be easier, perhaps, in their ⟨Minds⟩, if they were assur'd they had only mere Chance to trust to. For no body trembles to think there shou'd be no God; but rather, that there shou'd be one. This however wou'd be otherwise, if Deity were thought as kindly of as Humanity; and we cou'd be persuaded to believe, that if there really was a God, the highest Goodness must of necessity belong to him, without any of those Defects of Passion, those Meannesses and Imperfections which we acknowl-edg such in ourselves, which as good Men we endeavour all we can to be superior to, and which we find we every day conquer as we grow better.

Methinks, my Lord, it wou'd be well for us, if before we ascended into the higher Regions of Divinity, we wou'd vouchsafe to descend a little into our-selves, and bestow some poor Thoughts upon plain honest Morals. When we had once look'd into our selves, and distinguish'd well the nature of our own Affections, we shou'd probably be fitter Judges of the Divineness of a Character, and discern better what Affections were sutable or unsutable to a perfect Being. We might then understand how to love, and praise, when we had acquir'd some consistent Notion of what was laudable or lovely. Otherwise we might chance to do God little Honour, when we intended him the most. For 'tis hard to imagine, what Honour can arise to the Deity from the Praises of Creatures, who are unable to discern what is Praise-worthy or Excellent in their own Kind.

If a Musician were cry'd up to the Skys by a certain Set of People who had no Ear in Musick, he wou'd surely be put to the Blush, and cou'd hardly, with a good Countenance, accept the Benevolence of his Auditors, till they had acquir'd a more competent Apprehension of him, and cou'd by their own Senses find out something that was really good in his Performance. Till this were brought about, there wou'd be little Glory in the case; and the Musician, tho ever so vain, wou'd have little reason to be contented.

They who affect Praise the most, had rather not be taken notice of, than be impertinently applauded. I know not how it comes about, that He who is ever said to do Good the most disinterestedly, shou'd be thought desirous of being prais'd so lavishly, and be supposed to set so high a Rate upon so cheap and low a Thing, as ignorant Commendation, and forc'd Applause.

⟨'Tis⟩ not the same with Goodness as with other Qualitys, which we may understand very well, and yet not possess. We may have an excellent Ear in Musick, without being able to perform in any kind. We may judg well of Poetry, without being Poets, or possessing the least of a Poetick Vein: But we can have no tolerable Notion of Goodness, without being tolerably good. So that if the Praise of a Divine Being be so great a part of his Worship, we shou'd, methinks, learn Goodness, were it for nothing else but that we might learn, in some tolerable manner, how to praise. For the praise of Goodness from an unsound hollow Heart, must certainly make the greatest Dissonance in the World.

Section VI

Other Reasons, my Lord, there are, why this plain home-spun Philosophy, of looking into our-selves, may do us wond'rous Service, in rectifying our Errors in Religion. For there is a sort of Enthusiasm of second hand. And when Men find no original Commotions in themselves, no prepossessing Pannick that bewitches 'em, they are apt still, by the Testimony of others, to be impos'd on, and led credulously into the Belief of many false Miracles. And this Habit may make 'em variable, and of a very inconstant Faith, easy to be carry'd away with every Wind of Doctrine, and addicted to every upstart Sect or Superstition. But the knowledg of our Passions in their very Seeds, the measuring well the Growth and Progress of Enthusiasm, and the judging rightly of its natural Force, and what command it has over our very Senses, may teach us to oppose more successfully those Delusions which come arm'd with the specious Pretext of moral Certainty, and Matter of Fact.

The new prophesying Sect, I made mention of above, pretend, it seems, among many other Miracles, to have had a most signal one, acted premeditately, and with warning, before many hundreds of People, who actually give Testimony to the Truth of it. But I wou'd only ask, Whether there were present, among those hundreds, any one Person, who having never been of their Sect, or addicted to their Way, will give the same Testimony with them? I must not be contented to ask, Whether such a one had been wholly free of that particular Enthusiasm? but, Whether, before that time, he was esteem'd of so sound a Judgment, and clear a Head, as to be wholly free of Melancholy, and in all likelihood incapable of all Enthusiasm besides? For otherwise, the Pannick may have been caught; the Evidence of the Senses lost, as in a Dream; and the Imagination so inflam'd, as in a moment to have burnt up every Particle of Judgment and Reason. The combustible Matters lie prepar'd within, and ready to take fire at a Spark; but chiefly in a Multitude seiz'd with ⟨the same⟩ Spirit. No wonder if the Blaze arises so of a sudden; when innumerable Eyes glow with the Passion, and heaving Breasts are labouring with Inspiration: When not the Aspect only, but the very Breath and Exhalations of Men are infectious, and the inspiring Disease imparts it-self by insensible Transpiration. I am not a Divine good enough to resolve what Spirit that was which prov'd so catching among the antient Prophets, that even the profane Saul was taken by it. But I learn from holy Scripture, that there was the evil, as well as the good Spirit of Prophecy. And I find by present Experience, as well as by all Historys, Sacred and Profane, that the Operation of this Spirit is every where the same, as to the bodily Organs.

A Gentleman who has writ lately in defence of reviv'd Prophecy, and has since fallen himself into the prophetick Extasys, tells us, "That the antient Prophets had the Spirit of God upon them under Extasy, with divers strange Gestures of Body denominating them Madmen, (or Enthusiasts) as appears evidently, says he, in the Instances of Balaam, Saul, David, Ezekiel, Daniel, &c." And he proceeds to justify this by the Practice of the Apostolick Times, and by the Regulation which the Apostle himself applys to these seemingly irregular Gifts, so frequent and ordinary (as our Author pretends) in the primitive Church, on the first rise and spreading of Christianity. But I leave it to him to make the Resemblance as well as he can between his own and the Apostolick way. I only know, that the Symptoms he describes, and which himself (poor Gentleman!) labours under, are as Heathenish as he can possibly pretend them to be Christian. And when I saw him lately under an Agitation (as they call it) uttering Prophecy in a pompous Latin Stile, of which, out of his Extasy, it seems, he is wholly incapable; it brought into my Mind the Latin Poet's Description of the Sybil, whose Agonys were so perfectly like these.

> Subitò non vultus, non color unus,
> Non comptae mansere comae; sed pectus anhelum,
> Et rabie fera corda tument; majorque videri
> Nec mortale sonans: afflata est Numine quando
> Jam propiore Dei.
>
> Virg. Æn. Lib. 6

And again, presently after:

> Immanis in antro
> Bacchatur Vates, magnum si pectore possit
> Excussisse Deum: tanto magis Ille fatigat
> Os rabidum, fera corda domans, FINGITQUE PREMENDO.

Which is the very Stile of our experienc'd Author. "For the Inspir'd (says he) undergo a Probation, wherein the Spirit, by frequent Agitations, forms the Organs, ordinarily for a Month or two before Utterance."

The Roman Historian, speaking of a most horrible Enthusiasm that broke out in Rome long before his days, describes this Spirit of Prophecy; *Viros, velut mente captâ, cum jactatione fanaticâ corporis vaticinari.* Liv. 39. The detestable Things ⟨which are further related of these Enthusiasts,⟩ I wou'd not willingly transcribe: but the Senate's mild Decree in so execrable a Case, I can't omit copying; being satisfy'd, that tho your Lordship has read it before now, you can read it again and again with admiration: *In reliquum deinde* (says Livy) *S.C. cautum est, &c. Si quis tale sacrum solenne & necessarium duceret, nec sine Religione & Piaculo se id omittere posse; apud Praetorem Urbanum profiteretur: Praetor Senatum consuleret. Si ei permissum esset, cùm in Senatu centum non minus essent, ita id sacrum faceret; dum ne plus quinque sacrificio interessent, neu qua pecunia communis, neu quis Magister sacrorum, aut Sacerdos esset.*

So necessary it is to give way to this Distemper of Enthusiasm, that even the Philosopher who bent the whole Force of his Philosophy against Superstition, appears to have left room for visionary Fancy, and to have indirectly tolerated Enthusiasm. For it is hard to imagine, that one who had so little religious Faith as Epicurus, shou'd have so vulgar a Credulity, as to believe those accounts of Armys and Castles in the Air, and such visionary Phaenomena. Yet he allows them; and then thinks to solve 'em by his Effluvia, and Aerial Looking-glasses, and I know not what other Stuff: which his Latin Poet, however, sets off beautifully, as he does all.

> *Rerum Simulacra vagari*
> *Multa, modis multis, in cunctas undique parteis*
> *Tenuia, quae facilè inter se junguntur in auris,*
> *Obvia cùm veniunt, ut aranea bracteaque auri*
> * * *
> *Centauros itaque, & Scyllarum Membra videmus,*
> *Cerbereasque canum facies, simulacraque eorum*
> *Quorum morte obita tellus amplectitur ossa:*
> *Omne genus quoniam passim simulacra feruntur,*
> *Partim sponte suâ quae fiunt aere in ipso;*
> *Partim quae variis ab rebus cumque recedunt.*
>   Lucret.l.4

'Twas a sign that this Philosopher believ'd there was a good Stock of Visionary Spirit originally in Human Nature. He was so satisfy'd that Men were inclin'd to see Visions, that rather than they shou'd go without, he chose to make 'em to their hand. Notwithstanding he ⟨deny'd⟩ the Principles of Religion to be natural, he was forc'd tacitly to allow there was a wondrous Disposition in Mankind towards supernatural Objects; and that if these Ideas were vain, they were yet in a manner innate, or such as Men were really born to, and cou'd hardly by any means avoid. From which Concession a Divine, methinks, might raise a good Argument against him, for the Truth as well as the Usefulness of Religion. But so it is: whether the matter of Apparition be true or false, the Symptoms are the same, and the Passion of equal force in the Person who is Vision-struck. The *Lymphatici* of the Latins were the *Nympholepti* of the Greeks. They were Persons said to have seen some Species of Divinity, as either some Rural Deity, or Nymph, which threw them into such Transports as overcame their Reason. The Extasys express'd themselves outwardly in Quakings, Tremblings, Tossings of the Head and Limbs, Agitations, and (as Livy calls them) Fanatical Throws or Convulsions, extempory Prayer, Prophecy, Singing, and the like. All Nations have their Lymphaticks of some kind or another; and all Churches (Heathen as well as Christian) have had their Complaints against Fanaticism.

One wou'd think the Antients imagin'd this Disease had some relation to that which they call'd *Hydrophoby*. Whether the Antient Lymphaticks had any way like that of biting, to communicate the Rage of their Distemper, I can't so positively determine. But certain Fanaticks there have been since the time of the Antients, who have had a most prosperous Faculty of communicating the Appetite of the Teeth. For since first the snappish Spirit got up in Religion, all Sects have been at it, as the saying is, *Tooth and Nail;* and are never better pleas'd, than in worrying one another without mercy.

So far indeed the innocent kind of Fanaticism extends it self, that when the Party is struck by the Apparition, there follows always an Itch of imparting it, and kindling the same fire in other Breasts. For thus Poets are Fanaticks too. And thus Horace either is, or feigns himself Lymphatick, and shews what an Effect the Vision of the Nymphs and Bacchus had on him.

> *Bacchum in remotis carmina rupibus*
> *Vidi docentem, credite posteri,*
> *NYMPHASque discentes,——*
> *Evoe! recenti mens trepidat metu,*
> *Plenoque Bacchi pectore turbidum*
> *LYMPHATVR——*
>
> Od. 19. L. 2.

No Poet (as I ventur'd to say at first to your Lordship) can do any thing great in his own way, without the Imagination or Supposition of a Divine Presence, which may raise him to some degree of this Passion we are speaking of. Even the cold Lucretius makes use of Inspiration, when he writes against it; and is forc'd to raise an Apparition of Nature, in a Divine Form, to animate and conduct him in his very Work of degrading Nature, and despoiling her of all her seeming Wisdom and Divinity.

> *Alma* VENUS, *coeli subter labentia signa*
> *Quae mare navigerum, quae terras frugiferenteis*
> *Concelebras——*
> *Quae quoniam rerum naturam sola gubernas,*
> *Nec sine te quidquam dias in luminis oras*
> *Exoritur, neque fit laetum neque amabile quidquam:*
> *Te sociam studeo scribundis versibus esse,*
> *Quos Ego de rerum naturâ pangere conor*
> MEMMIADÆ *nostro.*
>
> Lucret. 1. I.

Section VII

The only thing, my Lord, I wou'd infer from all this, is, that Enthusiasm is wonderfully powerful and extensive; that it is a matter of nice Judgment, and the hardest thing in the world to know fully and distinctly; since even Atheism is not exempt from it. For, as some have well remark'd, there have been Enthusiastical Atheists. Nor can Divine Inspiration, by its outward Marks, be easily distinguish'd from it. For Inspiration is a real feeling of the Divine Presence, and Enthusiasm a false one. But the Passion they raise is much alike. For when the Mind is taken up in Vision, and fixes its view either on any real Object, or mere Specter of Divinity; when it sees, or thinks it sees any thing prodigious, and more than human; its Horrour, Delight, Confusion, Fear, Admiration, or whatever Passion belongs to it, or is uppermost on this occasion, will have something vast, immane, and (as Painters say) beyond Life. And this is what gave occasion to the name of Fanaticism, as it was us'd by the Antients in its original Sense, for an Apparition transporting the Mind.

Something there will be of Extravagance and Fury, when the Ideas or Images receiv'd are too big for the narrow human Vessel to contain. So that Inspiration may be justly call'd Divine Enthusiasm: For the Word it self signifies Divine Presence, and was made use of by the Philosopher whom the earliest Christian Fathers call'd Divine, to express whatever was sublime in human Passions. This was the Spirit he allotted to Heroes, Statesmen, Poets, Orators, Musicians, and even Philosophers themselves. Nor can we, of our own accord, forbear ascribing to a noble Enthusiasm, whatever is greatly perform'd by any of These. So that almost all of us know something of this Principle. But to know it as we shou'd do, and discern it in its several kinds, both in our-selves, and others; this is the great Work, and by this means alone we can hope to avoid Delusion. For to judg the Spirits whether they are of God, we must antecedently judg our own Spirit; whether it be of Reason, and sound Sense; whether it be fit to judg at all, by being sedate, cool, and impartial; free of every byassing Passion, every giddy Vapour, or melancholy Fume. This is the first Knowledg and previous Judgment: to understand ourselves, and know what Spirit we are of. Afterwards we may judg the Spirit in others, consider what their personal Merit is, and prove the Validity of their Testimony by the Solidity of their Brain. By this means we may prepare our-selves with some Antidote against Enthusiasm. And this is what I have dar'd affirm is best perform'd by keeping to Good Humour. For otherwise the Remedy itself may turn to the Disease.

And now, my Lord, having after all, in some measure, justify'd Enthusiasm, and own'd the Word; if I appear extravagant, in addressing to you after the manner I have done, you must allow me to plead an Impulse. You must suppose me (as with truth you may) most passionately yours; and with that Kindness which is natural to you on other occasions, you must tolerate your Enthusiastick Friend, who, excepting only in the case of this over-forward Zeal, can never but appear, with the highest Respect.

Joseph Addison
1672–1719

Sir Richard Steele
1672–1729

Joseph Addison, the eighteenth century's preeminent prose stylist, was born in Milston, Wiltshire, on May 1, 1672. He attended several different grammar schools, the last being the Charterhouse, where he made the acquaintance of his future literary associate Richard Steele. By the time he entered Queen's College, Oxford, he had begun to show his literary mettle. His performance in Latin verse composition earned him a fellowship in Magdalen College which lasted until 1711. These early efforts are included in the *Musae Anglicanae* of 1691–99, and are said to have elicited the approbation of Boileau. His first Latin translations and English verse followed shortly thereafter, with the publication of a poem dedicated to Dryden and a partial translation of Virgil's fourth georgic in Dryden's series of *Miscellanies*. Conspicuous among his early compositions are the *Account of the Greatest English Poets* (1694) and the *Pax Guglielmi,* occasioned by the Peace of Ryswick (1697), both typical seventeenth-century bids for patronage. These early productions pertain to the same pre-Augustan literary milieu as such works as Gerard Langbaine's *Account of the English Dramatic Poets* (1692), and may be said to partake of the same antiquarian and commemorative air of the dying Baroque. Yet something new is stirring; the studied Latinate diction is in the process of breaking up; and what emerges is a style unprecedented in the development of English prose, a style characterized by an evenhanded variation of conversational form with eloquent moral insight.

This change in style marks the rise of the essayist as *arbiter elegantiarum* to the middle classes. The literary compositions of the period of Addison's journey to the Continent, while interesting in their own right, are, as Dr. Johnson indicates, substantively negligible; what is of importance to students of Addison in particular, and eighteenth century prose style in general, is the initiation of those two literary ventures whose epoch-making quality is entirely out of proportion to the relative brevity of their existence: the *Tatler* and the *Spectator*. Between April, 1709 and January, 1711, the former, which was founded by Steele, came to rely more and more on Addison's contributions. If the *Tatler*'s orientation was political and controversial, the *Spectator* from its inception was characterized by a detached and pleasant narration, guided by the fictional persona (one among many) of Mr. Spectator himself. In contrast to the rancorous factionalism that made Addison's own tragedy, *Cato* (1713), such a wild success on the stage, the calm and easy numbers of the *Spectator* consistently offered a gentle and purposive moral satire, interspersed with critical commentaries on literature, manners, imagination, the feminine, and other eighteenth-century *topoi* of polite society. It is not by accident that Johnson finds the predecessors of the *Spectator* in the courtly manuals of Castiglione and Della Casa, and the elegant and didactic works of La Bruyère; even more to the point is his comparison of such apparently disparate institutions as the Royal Society and the apolitical periodical paper (viz., the *Tatler*) which had as their common purpose "to divert the attention of the people from publick discontent."

After 1713, Addison contributed to the *Guardian,* a new venture of Steele's. This periodical lacks the moral criteria of the *Spectator,* and has been faulted by many (mainly eighteenth-century detractors) for its excessive facetiousness as well as narrow political concerns. Addison in the meanwhile enjoyed the good graces of the recently installed Hanoverian dynasty, being appointed Secretary of State for a brief tenure up to March 1718. He seems not to have found this job to his liking; a shy and retiring man, he was not given to playing the orator, but rather represented the coffee-table conversationalist *par excellence*. At the time of his death, Addison was engaged in a political controversy with his old friend Steele, though there is evidence to the effect that Steele's love for his old school companion was not severely impaired by this last of their political disagreements.

Steele was born in the same year as his friend on March 12, in Dublin. Because his father died when Steele was six years old, the boy was placed under the tutelage of his maternal uncle, Henry Gascoigne, secretary and confidant to the Dukes of Ormonde. Through the influence of the Duke, Steele was guaranteed a position in the Charterhouse School, where he first made Addison's acquaintance. Their friendship continued at Oxford, where Steele served as a postmaster in Merton College. Before taking a degree he ran off to enlist in the army. For reasons that remain unclear, Steele seems to have lost his uncle's favor, and in so doing "the succession to a very good estate in the county of Wexford in Ireland" as well. Within a few years, however, Steele found a generous patron in the person of Lord Cutts; moreover, a well-timed reference to William III in the *Christian Hero* (a composition that subsequently earned its author an undeserved reputation for priggishness) gained him the patronage of the monarch himself. The period 1701–1705 saw the composition and production of three comedies, written to vindicate himself from the charges of prudery. Steele had to wait until 1722, however, to have a true comic success with *The Conscious Lovers*.

Before starting in on the *Tatler* under the pseudonym of Sir Isaac Bickerstaff in 1709, Steele wrote for the official government *Gazette* with the unfortunate task of "keeping the paper very innocent and very insipid." It is said that Addison, who was not initially aware of the real identity of Isaac Bickerstaff, recognized it to be Steele as a result of reading a remark he had repeated to his friend many years earlier concerning Dido's meeting with Aeneas in the cave. All in all, Steele wrote almost two-hundred and thirty of the two-hundred and seventy-one numbers of the *Tatler,* while Addison and others (notably Swift) were more responsible for the composition of the *Spectator*.

A year after the cessation of the last number of that paper, Defoe and an almost unanimous Tory contingent succeeded in expelling Steele from Parliament, where he sat as a Whig member from Stockbridge. The pamphlet he wrote in his defense, published in 1714 with an address to his ally Walpole, is of considerable biographical interest. With the accession of the Hanoverians in 1714, however, self-defense was rendered needless: Steele found himself showered with favors, culminating in knighthood in 1715. The accession of his long-time ally Walpole to the Chancellorship of the Exchequer further strengthened Steele's position. Nevertheless, his profligacy managed to get the better of him; when he retired to the country to escape his debts, he suffered a seizure and died on September 1, 1729.

THE TATLER

FROM

Number 29

June 16, 1709

I am just come hither at ten at night, and have, ever since six, been in the most celebrated, though most nauseous company in town; the two leaders of the society were a Critic and a Wit. These two gentlemen are great opponents on all occasions, not discerning that they are the nearest each other, in temper and talents, of any two classes of men in the world; for to profess judgment, and to profess wit, both arise from the same failure; which is want of judgment. The poverty of the Critic this way proceeds from the abuse of his faculty; that of the Wit, from the neglect of it. It is a particular observation I have always made, that of all mortals a critic is the silliest; for by inuring himself to examine all things, whether they are of consequence or not, he never looks upon any thing but with a design of passing sentence upon it; by which means he is never a companion but always a censor. This makes him earnest upon trifles, and dispute on the most indifferent occasions with vehemence. If he offers to speak or write, that talent which should approve the work of the other faculties, prevents their operation. He comes upon action in armour, but without weapons; he stands in safety, but can gain no glory. The wit, on the other hand, has been hurried so long away by imagination only, that judgment seems not to have ever been one of his natural faculties. This gentleman takes himself to be as much obliged to be merry, as the other to be grave. A thorough Critic is a sort of Puritan in the polite world. As an enthusiast in religion stumbles at the ordinary occurrences of life, if he cannot quote scripture examples on the occasion; so the Critic is never safe in his speech or writing, without he has, among the celebrated writers, an authority for the truth of his sentence. You will believe we had a very good time with these brethren, who were so far out of the dress of their native country, and so lost in its dialect, that they were as much strangers to themselves, as to their relation to each other. They took up the whole discourse; sometimes the Critic grew passionate, and when reprimanded by the Wit for any trip or hesitation in his voice, he would answer, "Mr. Dryden makes such a character, on such an occasion, break off in the same manner: so that the stop was according to nature, and as a man in a passion should do." The Wit, who is as far gone in letters as himself, seems to be at a loss to answer such an apology; and concludes only that though his anger is justly vented, it wants fire in the utterance. If wit is to be measured by the circumstances of time and place, there is no man has generally so little of that talent as he who is a Wit by profession. What he says, instead of arising from the occasion, has an occasion invented to bring it in. Thus he is new for no other reason, but that he talks like nobody else; but has taken up a method of his own, without commerce of dialogue with other people. The lively Jasper Dactyle is one of this character. He seems to have made a vow to be witty to his life's end. When you meet him, "What do you think," says he, "I have been entertaining myself with?" Then out comes a premeditated turn; to which it is to no purpose to answer, for he goes on in the same strain of thought he designed without your speaking. Therefore I have a general answer to all he can say; as, "Sure there never was any creature had so much fire!" Spondee, who is a critic, is seldom out of this fine man's company. They have no manner of affection for each other, but keep together like Novel and Oldfox in the Plain Dealer, because they shew each other. I know several men of sense who can be diverted with this couple; but I see no curiosity in the thing, except it be, that Spondee is dull, and seems dull; but Dactyle is heavy with a brisk face. It must be owned also that Dactyle has almost vigour enough to be a coxcomb; but Spondee, by the lowness of his constitution, is only a blockhead. . . .

Number 158

Thursday, April 13, 1710

Facient næ intelligendo, ut nihil intelligant.
TER.

While they pretend to know more than others, they know nothing in reality.

Tom Folio is a broker in learning, employed to get together good editions, and stock the libraries of great men. There is not a sale of books begins until Tom Folio is seen at the door. There is not an auction where his name is not heard, and that too in the very nick of time, in the critical moment, before the last decisive stroke of the hammer. There is not a subscription goes forward in which Tom is not privy to the first rough draught of the proposals; nor a catalogue printed that doth not come to him wet from the press. He is an universal scholar, so far as the title-page of all authors; knows the manuscripts in which they were discovered, the editions through which they have passed, with the praises or censures which they have received from the several members of the learned world. He has a greater esteem for Aldus and Elzevir, than for Virgil and Horace. If you talk of Herodotus, he breaks out into a panegyric upon Harry Stephens. He thinks he gives you an account of an author when he tells you the subject he treats of, the name of the editor, and the year in which it was printed. Or if you draw him into further particulars, he cries up the goodness of the paper, extols the diligence of the corrector, and is transported with the beauty of the letter. This he looks upon to be sound learning, and substantial criticism. As for those who talk of the fineness of style, and the justness of thought, or describe the brightness of any particular passages; nay, though they themselves write in the genius and spirit of the author they admire; Tom looks upon them as men of superficial learning, and flashy parts.

I had yesterday morning a visit from this learned *ideot,* for *that* is the light in which I consider every pedant, when I discover in him some little touches of the coxcomb, which I had not before observed. Being very full of the figure which he makes in the republic of letters, and wonderfully satisfied with his great stock of knowledge, he gave me broad intimations that he did not believe in all points as his forefathers had done. He then communicated to me a thought of a certain author upon a passage of Virgil's account of the dead, which I made the subject of a late paper. This thought hath taken very much among men of Tom's pitch and understanding, though universally exploded by all that know how to construe Virgil, or have any relish of antiquity. Not to trouble my reader with it, I found upon the whole that Tom did not believe a future state of rewards and punishments, because Æneas, at his leaving the empire of the dead, passed through the gate of ivory, and not through that of horn. Knowing that Tom had not sense enough to give up an opinion which he had once received, that I might avoid wrangling, I told him, "that Virgil possibly had his oversights as well as another author." "Ah! Mr. Bickerstaff," says he, you would have another opinion of him, if you would read him in Daniel Heinsius's edition. I have perused him myself several times in that edition," continued he: "and after the strictest and most malicious examination, could find but two faults in him; one of them is in the Æneids, where there are two commas instead of a parenthesis; and another in the third Georgic, where you may find a semicolon turned upside down." "Perhaps," said I, "these were not Virgil's faults, but those of the transcriber." "I do not design it," says Tom, "as a reflection on Virgil; on the contrary, I know that all the manuscripts declaim against such a punctuation. Oh! Mr. Bickerstaff," says he, "what would a man give to see one simile of Virgil writ in his own hand!" I asked him which was the simile he meant; but was answered, any simile in Virgil. He then told me all the secret history in the commonwealth of learning; of modern pieces that had the names of ancient authors annexed to them; of all the books that were now writing or printing in the several parts of Europe; of many amendments which are made and not yet published, and a thousand other particulars, which I would not have my memory burdened with for a Vatican.

At length, being fully persuaded that I thoroughly admired him, and looked upon him as a prodigy of learning, he took his leave. I know several of Tom's class, who are professed admirers of Tasso, without understanding a word of Italian: and one in particular, that carries a *Pastor Fido* in his pocket, in which, I am sure, he is acquainted with no other beauty but the clearness of the character.

There is another kind of Pedant, who, with all Tom Folio's impertinencies, hath greater superstructures and embellishments of Greek and Latin; and is still more insupportable than the other, in the same degree as he is more learned. Of this kind very often are editors, commentators, interpreters, scholiasts, and critics; and, in short, all men of deep learning without common sense. These persons set a greater value on themselves for having found out the meaning of a passage in Greek, than upon the author for having written it; nay, will allow the passage itself not to have any beauty in it, at the same time that they would be considered as the greatest men of the age, for having interpreted it. They will look with contempt on the most beautiful poems that have been composed by any of their contemporaries; but will lock themselves up in their studies for a twelvemonth together, to correct, publish, and expound such trifles of antiquity, as a modern author would be contemned for. Men of the strictest morals, severest lives, and the gravest professions, will write volumes upon an idle sonnet, that is originally in Greek or Latin; give editions of the most immoral authors; and spin out whole pages upon the various readings of a lewd expression. All that can be said in excuse for them is, that their works sufficiently shew they have no taste of their authors; and that what they do in this kind, is out of their great learning, and not out of any levity or lasciviousness of temper.

A pedant of this nature is wonderfully well described in six lines of Boileau, with which I shall conclude his character.

> *Un Pedant enyvré de sa vaine science,*
> *Tout herissé de Grec, tout bouffi d'arrogance;*
> *Et qui de mille auteurs retenus mot pour mot,*
> *Dans sa tête entassez n'a souvent fait qù'un sot,*
> *Croit qu'un livre fait tout, & que sans Aristote*
> *La raison ne voit goute, & le bon sens radote.*

> Brim-full of learning see that pedant stride,
> Bristling with horrid Greek, and puff'd with pride!
> A thousand authors he in vain has read,
> And with their maxims stuff'd his empty head;
> And thinks that, without Aristotle's rule,
> Reason is blind, and common sense a fool.
>
> Wynne.

Number 163

Tuesday, April 25, 1710

Idem inficeto est inficetior rure,
Simul poemata attigit; neque idem unquam
Æquè est beatus, ac poema cum scribit:
Tam gaudet in se, tamque se ipse miratur.
Nimirum idem omnes fallimur; neque est quisquam
Quem non in aliquâ re videre Suffenum
Possis

Catul. *de Suffeno*, xx. 14.

Suffenus has no more wit than a mere clown, when he attempts to write verses; and yet he is never happier than when he is scribbling; so much does he admire himself and his compositions. And, indeed, this is the foible of every one of us; for there is no man living who is not a Suffenus in one thing or other.

I yesterday came hither about two hours before the company generally make their appearance, with a design to read over all the newspapers; but, upon my sitting down, I was accosted by Ned Softly, who saw me from a corner in the other end of the room, where I found he had been writing something. "Mr. Bickerstaff," says he, "I observe by a late paper of yours, that you and I are just of a humour, for you must know, of all impertinences, there is nothing which I so much hate as news. I never read a Gazette in my life; and never trouble my head about our armies, whether they win or lose, or in what part of the world they lie encamped." Without giving me time to reply, he drew a paper of verses out of his pocket, telling me, "that he had something which would entertain me more agreeably; and that he would desire my judgment upon every line, for that we had time enough before us until the company came in."

Ned Softly is a very pretty poet, and a great admirer of easy lines. Waller is his favourite: and as that admirable writer has the best and worst verses of any among our great English poets, Ned Softly has got all the bad ones without book; which he repeats upon occasion, to shew his reading, and garnish his conversation. Ned is indeed a true English reader, incapable of relishing the great and masterly strokes of this art; but wonderfully pleased with the little Gothic ornaments of epigrammatical conceits, turns, points, and quibbles; which are so frequent in the most admired of our English poets, and practised by those who want genius and strength to represent, after the manner of the ancients, simplicity in its natural beauty and perfection.

Finding myself unavoidably engaged in such a conversation, I was resolved to turn my pain into a pleasure, and to divert myself as well as I could with *so very odd* a fellow. "You must understand," says Ned, "that the sonnet I am going to read to you was written upon a lady, who shewed me some verses of her own making, and is perhaps the best *poet* of our age. But you shall hear it."

Upon which he began to read as follows:

To Mira, on Her Incomparable Poems

I

When dress'd in laurel wreaths you shine,
   And tune your soft melodious notes,
You seem a sister of the Nine,
   Or Phœbus' self in petticoats.

II

I fancy, when your song you sing,
   (Your song you sing with so much art)

> Your pen was pluck'd from Cupid's wing;
> For, ah! it wounds me like his dart.

"Why," says I, "this is a little nosegay of conceits, a very lump of salt; every verse has something in it that piques; and then the *dart* in the last line is certainly as pretty a sting in the tail of an epigram, for so I think you critics call it, as ever entered into the thought of a poet." "Dear Mr. Bickerstaff," says he, shaking me by the hand, "every body knows you to be a judge of these things; and to tell you truly, I read over Roscommon's translation of 'Horace's Art of Poetry' three several times, before I sat down to write the sonnet which I have shewn you. But you shall hear it again, and pray observe every line of it; for not one of them shall pass without your approbation.

> When dress'd in laurel wreaths you shine,

"That is," says he, "when you have your garland on; when you are writing verses." To which I replied, "I know your meaning: a metaphor!" "The same," said he, and went on.

> And tune your soft melodious notes,

"Pray observe the gliding of that verse, there is scarce a consonant in it: I took care to make it run upon liquids. Give me your opinion of it." "Truly," said I, "I think it is as good as the former." "I am very glad to hear you say so," says he; "but mind the next.

> You seem a sister of the Nine,

"That is," says he, "you seem a sister of the Muses; for, if you look into ancient authors, you will find it was their opinion, that there were nine of them." "I remember it very well," said I, "but pray proceed."

> Or Phœbus' self in petticoats.

"Phœbus," says he, "was the god of Poetry. These little instances, Mr. Bickerstaff, shew a gentleman's reading. Then to take off from the air of learning, which Phœbus and the Muses had given to this first stanza, you may observe, how it falls all of a sudden into the familiar; "in Petticoats!"

> Or Phœbus' self in petticoats.

"Let us now," says I, "enter upon the second stanza; I find the first line is still a continuation of the metaphor."

> I fancy, when your song you sing,

"It is very right," says he, "but pray observe the turn of words in those two lines. I was a whole hour in adjusting *of* them, and have still a doubt upon me, whether in the second line it should be, "Your song you sing; or, You sing your song!" You shall hear them both:

> I fancy, when your song you sing,
> (Your song you sing with so much art)

Or,

> I fancy, when your song you sing,
>   (You sing your song with so much art)

"Truly," said I, "the turn is so natural either way, that you have made me almost giddy with it." "Dear Sir," said he, grasping me by the hand, "you have a great deal of patience; but pray what do you think of the next verse?"

> Your pen was pluck'd from Cupid's wing;

"Think!" says I; "I think you have made Cupid look like a little goose." "That was my meaning," says he: "I think the ridicule is well enough hit off. But we come now to the last, which sums up the whole matter."

> For, ah! it wounds me like his dart.

"Pray how do you like that *Ah!* doth it not make a pretty figure in that place? *Ah!*—it looks as if I felt the dart, and cried out as being pricked with it.

> For, ah! it wounds me like his dart.

"My friend Dick Easy," continued he, "assured me, he would rather have written that *Ah!* than *to* have been the author of the Æneid. He indeed objected, that I made Mira's pen like a quill in one of the lines, and like a dart in the other. But as to that—" "Oh! as to that," says I, "it is but supposing Cupid to be like a porcupine, and his quills and darts will be the same thing." He was going to embrace me for the hint; but half a dozen critics coming into the room, whose faces he did not like, he conveyed the sonnet into his pocket, and whispered me in the ear, "he would show me it again as soon as his man had written it over fair."

Number 165

Saturday, April 29, 1710

It has always been my endeavour to distinguish between realities and appearances, and to separate true merit from the pretence to it. As it shall ever be my study to make discoveries of this nature in human life, and to settle the proper distinctions between the virtues and perfections of mankind, and those false colours and resemblances of them that shine alike in the eyes of the vulgar; so I shall be more particularly careful to search into the various merits and pretences of the learned world. This is the more necessary, because there seems to be a general combination among the pedants to extol one another's labours, and cry up one another's parts; while men of sense, either through that modesty which is natural to them, or the scorn they have for such trifling commendations, enjoy their stock of knowledge, like a hidden treasure, with satisfaction and silence. Pedantry indeed in learning is like hypocrisy in religion, a form of knowledge without the power of it; that attracts the eyes of the common people; breaks out in noise and show; and finds its reward not from any inward pleasure that attends it, but from the praises and approbations which it receives from men.

Of this shallow species there is not a more importunate, empty, and conceited animal, than that which is generally known by the name of a Critic. This, in the common acceptation of the word, is one that, without entering into the sense and soul of an author, has a few general rules, which, like mechanical instruments, he applies to the works of every writer; and as they quadrate with them, pronounces the author perfect or defective. He is master of a certain set of words, as *Unity, Style, Fire, Phlegm, Easy, Natural, Turn, Sentiment,* and the like; which he varies, compounds, divides, and throws together, in every part of his discourse, without any thought or meaning. The marks you may know him by are, an elevated eye, and dogmatical brow, a positive voice, and a contempt for every thing that comes out, whether he has read it or not. He dwells altogether in generals. He praises or dispraises in the lump. He shakes his head very frequently at the pedantry of universities, and bursts into laughter when you mention an author that is *not known* at Will's. He hath formed his judgment upon Homer, Horace, and Virgil, not from their own works, but from those of Rapin and Bossu. He knows his own strength so well, that he never dares praise any thing in which he has not a French author for his voucher.

With these extraordinary talents and accomplishments, Sir Timothy Tittle *puts men in vogue,* or condemns them to obscurity; and sits as judge of life and death upon every author that appears in public. It is impossible to represent the pangs, agonies, and convulsions, which Sir Timothy expresses in every feature of his face, and muscle of his body, upon the reading of a bad poet.

About a week ago, I was engaged, at a friend's house of mine, in an agreeable conversation with his wife and daughters, when in the height of our mirth, Sir Timothy, who makes love to my friend's eldest daughter, came in amongst us, puffing and blowing as if he had been very much out of breath. He immediately called for a chair, and desired leave to sit down without any further ceremony. I asked him where he had been? whether he was out of order? He only replied, that he was quite spent, and fell a cursing in soliliquy. I could hear him cry, "A wicked rogue—An execrable wretch—Was there ever such a monster!"—The young ladies upon this began to be affrighted, and asked, whether any one had hurt him? He answered nothing, but still talked to himself. "To lay the first scene," says he, "in St. James's-park, and the last in Northamptonshire!" "Is that all?" said I. "Then I suppose you have been at the rehearsal of a play this morning." "Been!" says he, "I have been at Northampton, in the Park, in a lady's bed-chamber, in a dining-room, every where; the rogue has led me such a dance—" Though I could scarce forbear laughing at his discourse, I told him I was glad it was no worse, and that he was only metaphorically weary. "In short, Sir," says he, "the author has not observed a single Unity in his whole play; the scene shifts in every dialogue;

the villain has hurried me up and down at such a rate, that I am tired off my legs." I could not but observe with some pleasure, that the young lady whom he made love to, conceived a very just aversion towards him, upon seeing him so very passionate in trifles. And as she had that natural sense which makes her a better judge than a thousand critics, she began to rally him upon this foolish humour. "For my part," says she, "I never knew a play take that was written up to your rules, as you call them." "How, Madam!" says he, "is that your opinion? I am sure you have a better taste." "It is a pretty kind of magic," says she, "the poets have, to transport an audience from place to place without the help of a coach and horses; I could travel round the world at such a rate. It is such an entertainment as an enchantress finds when she fancies herself in a wood, or upon a mountain, at a feast, or a solemnity; though at the same time she has never stirred out of her cottage." "Your simile, Madam," says Sir Timothy, "is by no means just." "Pray," says she, "let my similes pass without a criticism. I must confess," continued she (for I found she was resolved to exasperate him,) "I laughed very heartily at the last new comedy which you found so much fault with." "But, Madam," says he, "you ought not to have laughed; and I defy any one to shew me a single rule that you could laugh by." "Ought not to laugh!" says she; "pray who should hinder me?" "Madam," says he, "there are such people in the world as Rapin, Dacier, and several others, that ought to have spoiled your mirth." "I have heard," says the young lady, "that your great critics are always very bad poets: I fancy there is as much difference between the works of the one and the other, as there is between the carriage of a dancing-master and a gentleman. I must confess," continued she, "I would not be troubled with so fine a judgment as yours is; for I find you feel more vexation in a bad comedy, than I do in a deep tragedy." "Madam," says Sir Timothy, "that is not my fault; they should learn the art of writing." "For my part," says the young lady, "I should think the greatest art in your writers of comedies is to please." "To please!" says Sir Timothy; and immediately fell a laughing. "Truly," says she, "that is my opinion." Upon this, he composed his countenance, looked upon his watch, and took his leave.

I hear that Sir Timothy has not been at my friend's house since this notable conference, to the great satisfaction of the young lady, who by this means has got rid of a very impertinent fop.

I must confess, I could not but observe, with a great deal of surprise, how this gentleman, by his ill-nature, folly, and affectation, had made himself capable of suffering so many imaginary pains, and looking with such a senseless severity upon the common diversions of life.

THE GUARDIAN

Number 12

Wednesday, March 25

Vel quia nil rectum, nisi quod placuit sibi, ducunt:
Vel quia turpe putant parere minoribus—
Hor. Ep. i. l. 2. v. 84

IMITATED

You'd think no fools disgrac'd the former reign,
Did not some grave examples yet remain,
Who scorn a lad shou'd match his father's skill,
And having once been wrong, will be so still.

POPE

When a poem makes its first appearance in the world, I have always observed, that it gives employment to a greater number of criticks, than any other kind of writing. Whether it be that most men, at some time of their lives, have tried their talent that way, and thereby think they have a right to judge; or whether they imagine, that their making shrewd observations upon the polite arts, gives them a pretty figure; or whether there may not be some jealousy and caution in bestowing applause upon those who write chiefly for fame. Whatever the reasons be, we find few discouraged by the delicacy and danger of such an undertaking.

I think it certain that most men are naturally not only capable of being pleased with that which raises agreeable pictures in the fancy, but willing also to own it. But then there are many, who, by false applications of some rules ill-understood, or out of deference to men whose opinions they value, have formed to themselves certain schemes and systems of satisfaction, and will not be pleased out of their own way. These are not criticks themselves, but readers of criticks, who, without the labour of perusing authors, are able to give their characters in general; and know just as much of the several species of poetry, as those who read books of geography do of the genius of this or that people or nation. These gentlemen deliver their opinions sententiously, and in general terms; to which it being impossible readily to frame complete answers, they have often the satisfaction of leaving the board in triumph. As young persons, and particularly the ladies, are liable to be led aside by these tyrants in wit, I shall examine two or three of the many stratagems they use, and subjoin such precautions as may hinder candid readers from being deceived thereby.

The first I shall take notice of is an objection commonly offered, viz. "That such a poem hath indeed 'some good lines in it, but it is not a regular piece.'" This for the most part is urged by those whose knowledge is drawn from some famous French criticks, who have written upon the epic poem, the drama, and the great kinds of poetry, which cannot subsist without great regularity; but ought by no means to be required in odes, epistles, panegyricks, and the like, which naturally admit of greater liberties. The enthusiasm in odes, and the freedom of epistles, is rarely disputed: But I have often heard the poems upon publick occasions written in heroick verse, which I choose to call panegyricks, severely censured upon this account; the reason whereof I cannot guess, unless it be, that because they are written in the same kind of numbers and spirit as an epic poem, they ought therefore to have the same regularity. Now an epic poem consisting chiefly in narration, it is necessary that the incidents should be related in the same order that they are supposed to have been transacted. But in works of the abovementioned kind, there is no more reason that such order should be observed, than that an oration should be as methodical as a history. I think it sufficient that the great hints, suggested from the subject, be so disposed, that the first may naturally prepare the reader for what follows, and so on: and that their places cannot be changed without disadvantage to the whole. I will add further, that sometimes gentle deviations, sometimes bold and even abrupt digressions, where the dignity of the subject seems to give the impulse, are proofs of a noble genius; as winding about and returning artfully to the main design, are marks of address and dexterity.

Another artifice made use of by pretenders to criticism, is an insinuation, "That all that is good is borrowed from the ancients." This is very common in the mouths of pedants, and perhaps in their hearts too; but is often urged by men of no great learning, for reasons very obvious. Now nature being still the same, it is impossible for any modern writer to paint her otherwise than the ancients have done. If, for example, I was to describe the general's horse at the battle of Blenheim as my fancy represented such a noble beast, and that description should resemble what Virgil hath drawn for the horse of his hero, it would be almost as ill-natured to urge that I had stolen my description from Virgil, as to reproach the Duke of Marlborough for fighting only like Æneas. All that the most exquisite judgment can perform is, out of that great variety of circumstances, wherein natural objects may be considered, to select the most beautiful; and to place images in such views and lights, as will affect the fancy after the most delightful manner. But over and above a just painting of nature, a learned reader will find a new beauty supperadded in a happy imitation of some famous ancient, as it revives in his mind the pleasure he took in his first reading such an author. Such copyings as these give that kind of double delight which we perceive when we look upon the children of a beautiful couple; where the eye is not more charmed with the symmetry of the parts, than the mind by observing the resemblance transmitted from parents to their offspring, and the mingled features of the father and mother. The phrases of Holy Writ, and allusions to several passages in the inspired writings, (though not produced as proofs of doctrine) add majesty and authority to the noblest discourses of the pulpit: in like manner an imitation of the air of Homer and Virgil raises the dignity of modern poetry, and makes it appear stately and venerable.

The last observation I shall make at present is upon the disgust taken by those criticks, who put on their clothes prettily, and dislike every thing that is not written WITH EASE. I hereby therefore give the genteel part of the learned world to understand, that every thought which is agreeable to nature, and exprest in language suitable to it, is written with Ease. There are some things which must be written with strength, which nevertheless are easy. The statue of the gladiator, though represented in such a posture as strains every muscle, is as easy as that of Venus; because the one expresses strength and fury as naturally as the other doth beauty and softness. The passions are sometimes to be roused, as well as the fancy to be entertained; and the soul to be exalted and enlarged, as well as soothed. This often requires a raised figurative stile; which readers of low apprehensions or soft and languid dispositions (having heard of the words, fustian and bombast) are apt to reject as stiff and affected language. But nature and reason appoint different garbs for different things; and since I write this to the men of dress, I will ask them if a soldier who is to mount a breach should be adorned like a beau, who is spruced up for a ball?

THE SPECTATOR

Number 39

Saturday, April 14, 1711

Multa fero, ut placem genus irritabile vatum,
Cum scribo———

HOR., 2 Ep., ii, 102.

IMITATED

Much do I suffer, much, to keep in peace
This jealous, waspish, wrong-headed rhyming race.

POPE

As a perfect tragedy is the noblest production of human nature, so it is capable of giving the mind one of the most delightful and most improving entertainments. A virtuous man (says Seneca) struggling with misfortunes, is such a spectacle as gods might look upon with pleasure; and such a pleasure it is which one meets with in the representation of a well-written tragedy. Diversions of this kind wear out of our thoughts everything that is mean and little. They cherish and cultivate that humanity which is the ornament of our nature. They soften insolence, soothe affliction, and subdue the mind to the dispensations of Providence.

It is no wonder, therefore, that in all the polite nations of the world, this part of the drama has met with public encouragement.

The modern tragedy excels that of Greece and Rome in the intricacy and disposition of the fable; but, what a Christian writer would be ashamed to own, falls infinitely short of it in the moral part of the performance.

This I may show more at large hereafter: and in the meantime, that I may contribute something toward the improvement of the English tragedy, I shall take notice, in this and in other following papers, of some particular parts in it that seem liable to exception.

Aristotle observes, that the Iambic verse in the Greek tongue was the most proper for tragedy; because at the same time that it lifted up the discourse from prose, it was that which approached nearer to it than any other kind of verse. "For," says he, "we may observe that men in ordinary discourse very often speak iambics without taking notice of it." We may make the same observation of our English blank verse, which often enters into our common discourse, though we do not attend to it, and is such a due medium between rhyme and prose, that it seems wonderfully adapted to tragedy. I am therefore very much offended when I see a play in rhyme; which is as absurd in English, as a tragedy of hexameters would have been in Greek or Latin. The solecism is, I think, still greater in those plays that have some scenes in rhyme and some in blank verse, which are to be looked upon as two several languages; or where we see some particular similes dignified with rhyme at the same time that everything about them lies in blank verse. I would not however debar the poet from concluding his tragedy, or, if he pleases, every act of it, with two or three couplets, which may have the same effect as an air in the Italian opera after a long recitativo, and give the actor a graceful exit. Beside that, we see a diversity of numbers in some parts of the old tragedy in order to hinder the ear from being tired with the same continued modulation of voice. For the same reason I do not dislike the speeches in our English tragedy that close with a hemistich, or half verse, notwithstanding the person who speaks after it begins a new verse, without filling up the preceding one; nor with abrupt pauses and breakings off in the middle of a verse, when they humor any passion that is expressed by it.

Since I am upon this subject, I must observe that our English poets have succeeded much better in the style than in the sentiment of their tragedies. Their language is very often noble and sonorous, but the sense either very trifling or very common. On the contrary, in the ancient tragedies, and indeed in those of Corneille and Racine, though the expressions are very great, it is the thought that bears them up and swells them. For my own part, I prefer a noble sentiment that is depressed with homely language, infinitely before a vulgar one that is blown up with all the sound and energy of expression. Whether this defect in our tragedies may arise from want of genius, knowledge, or experience in the writers, or from their compliance with the vicious taste of their readers, who are better judges of the language than of the sentiments, and consequently relish the one more than the other, I cannot determine. But I believe it might rectify the conduct both of the one and of the other, if the writer laid down the whole contexture of his dialogue in plain English, before he turned it into blank verse: and if the reader, after the perusal of a scene, would consider the naked thought of every speech in it, when divested of all its tragic ornaments. By this means, without being imposed upon by words, we may judge impartially of the thought, and consider whether it be natural or great enough for the person that utters it, whether it deserves to shine in such a blaze of eloquence, or show itself in such a variety of lights as are generally made use of by the writers of our English tragedy.

I must in the next place observe, that when our thoughts are great and just, they are often obscured by the sounding phrases, hard metaphors, and forced expressions in which they are clothed. Shakspeare is often very faulty in this particular. There is a fine observation in Aristotle to this purpose, which I have never seen quoted. The expression, says he, ought to be very much labored in the inactive parts of the fable, as in descriptions, similitudes, narrations, and the like; in which the opinions, manners, and passions of men are not represented; for these (namely, the opinions, manners, and passions) are apt to be obscured by pompous phrases and elaborate expressions. Horace, who copied most of his criticisms after Aristotle, seems to have had his eye on the foregoing rule, in the following verses:

Et tragicus plerumque dolet sermone pedestri;
Telephus et Peleus, cum pauper et exul uterque.
Projicit ampullas et sesquipedalia verba,
Si curat cor spectantis tetigisse querela.

HOR., *Ars Poet.*, ver. 95.

Tragedians, too, lay by their state to grieve:
Peleus and Telephus, exil'd and poor,
Forget their swelling and gigantic words.

ROSCOMMON.

Among our modern English poets, there is none who has a better turn for tragedy than Lee; if, instead of favoring the impetuosity of his genius, he had restrained it, and kept it within its proper bounds. His thoughts are wonderfully suited to tragedy, but frequently lost in such a cloud of words that it is hard to see the beauty of them. There is an infinite fire in his works, but so involved in smoke that it does not appear in half its luster. He frequently succeeds in the passionate parts of the tragedy, but more particularly where he slackens his efforts, and eases his style of those epithets and metaphors in which he so much abounds. What can be more natural, more soft, or more passionate, than that line in Statira's speech where she describes the charms of Alexander's conversation?

Then he would talk—Good gods! how he would talk!

That unexpected break in the line, and turning the description of his manner of talking into an admiration of it, is inexpressibly beautiful, and wonderfully suited to the fond character of the person that speaks it. There is a simplicity in the words that outshines the utmost pride of expression.

Otway has followed nature in the language of his tragedy, and therefore shines in the passionate parts more than any of our English poets. As there is something familiar and domestic in the fable of his tragedy, more than in those of any other poet, he has little pomp, but great force in his expressions. For which reason, though he has admirably succeeded in the tender and melting part of his tragedies, he sometimes falls into too great familiarity of phrase in those parts, which, by Aristotle's rule, ought to have been raised and supported by the dignity of expression.

It has been observed by others, that this poet has founded his tragedy of *Venice Preserved* on so wrong a plot, that the greatest characters in it are those of rebels and traitors. Had the hero of this play discovered the same good qualities in the defense of his country that he showed for its ruin and subversion, the audience could not enough pity and admire him; but as he is now represented, we can only say of him what the Roman historian says of Catiline, that his fall would have been glorious (*si pro patriâ sic concidisset*), had he so fallen in the service of his country.—C.

Number 40

Monday, April 16, 1711

Ac ne forte putes me quæ facere ipse recusem,
Cum recte tractant alii, laudare maligne;
Ille per extentum funem mihi posse videtur
Ire poeta, meum qui pectus inaniter angit,
Irritat, mulcet, falsis terroribus implet,
Ut magus; et modo me Thebis, modo ponit Athenis.

HOR., 2 Ep., i, 208

IMITATED

Yet lest you think I rally more than teach,
Or praise, malignant, arts I cannot reach,
Let me for once presume t'instruct the times,
To know the poet from the man of rhymes;
'Tis he, who gives my breast a thousand pains,
Can make me feel each passion that he feigns;
Enrage, compose, with more than magic art,
With pity, and with terror, tear my heart;
And snatch me o'er the earth, or through the air,
To Thebes, to Athens, when he will, and where.

POPE

The English writers of tragedy are possessed with a notion, that when they represent a virtuous or innocent person in distress, they ought not to leave him till they have delivered him out of his troubles, or made him triumph over his enemies. This error they have been led into by a ridiculous doctrine in modern criticism, that they are obliged to an equal distribution of rewards and punishments, and an impartial execution of poetical justice. Who were the first that established this rule I know not; but I am sure it has no foundation in nature, in reason, or in the practice of the ancients. We find that good and evil happen alike to all men on this side the grave; and as the principal design of tragedy is to raise commiseration and terror in the minds of the audience, we shall defeat this great end, if we always make virtue and innocence happy and successful. Whatever crosses and disappointments a good man suffers in the body of the tragedy, they will make but a small impression on our minds, when we know that in the last act he is to arrive at the end of his wishes and desires. When we see him engaged in the depth of his afflictions, we are apt to comfort ourselves, because we are sure he will find his way out of them; and that his grief, how great soever it may be at present, will soon terminate in gladness. For this reason, the ancient writers of tragedy treated men in their plays, as they are dealt with in the world, by making virtue sometimes happy and sometimes miserable, as they found it in the fable which they made choice of, or as it might affect the audience in the most agreeable manner. Aristotle considers the tragedies that were written in either of these kinds, and observes, that those which ended unhappily had always pleased the people, and carried away the prize in the public disputes of the stage, from those that ended happily. Terror and commiseration leave a pleasing anguish on the mind, and fix the audience in such a serious composure of thought, as is much more lasting and delightful than any little transient starts of joy and satisfaction. Accordingly we find, that more of our English tragedies have succeeded, in which the favorites of the audience sink under their calamities, than those in which they recover themselves out of them. The best plays of this kind are, *The Orphan, Venice Preserved, Alexander the Great, Theodosius, All for Love, Œdipus, Oroonoko, Othello,* etc. *King Lear* is an admirable tragedy of the same kind, as Shakspeare wrote it; but as it is reformed according to the chimerical notion of poetical justice, in my humble opinion it has lost half its beauty. At the same time I must allow, that there are very noble tragedies which have been framed upon the other plan, and have ended happily; as indeed most of the good tragedies, which have been written since the starting of the above-mentioned criticism, have taken this turn: as *The Mourning Bride, Tamerlane, Ulysses, Phædra and Hippolytus,* with most of Mr. Dryden's. I must also allow, that many of Shakspeare's, and several of the celebrated tragedies of antiquity, are in the same form. I do not therefore dispute against this way of writing tragedies, but against the criticism that would establish this as the only method; and by that means would very much cramp the English tragedy, and perhaps give a wrong bent to the genius of our writers.

The tragi-comedy, which is the product of the English theater, is one of the most monstrous inventions that ever entered in a poet's thoughts. An author might as well think of weaving the adventures of Æneas and Hudibras into one poem, as of writing such a piece of motley sorrow. But the absurdity of these performances is so very visible, that I shall not insist upon it.

The same objections which are made to tragi-comedy, may in some measure be applied to all tragedies that have a double plot in them; which are likewise more frequent upon the English stage, than upon any other; for though the grief of the audience, in such performances, be not changed into another passion, as in tragi-comedies; it is diverted upon another object, which weakens their concern for the principal action, and breaks the tide of sorrow, by throwing it into different channels. This inconvenience, however, may in a great measure be cured, if not wholly removed, by the skillful choice of an under plot, which may bear such a near relation to the principal design, as to contribute toward the completion of it, and be concluded by the same catastrophe.

There is also another particular, which may be reckoned among the blemishes, or rather the false beauties of our English tragedy: I mean those particular speeches which are commonly known by the name of Rants. The warm and passionate parts of a tragedy are always the most taking with the audience; for which reason we often see the players pronouncing, in all the violence of action, several parts of the tragedy which the author wrote with great temper, and designed that they should have been so acted. I have seen

Powell very often raise himself a loud clap by this artifice. The poets that were acquainted with this secret, have given frequent occasion for such emotions in the actor, by adding vehemence to words where there was no passion, or inflaming a real passion into fustian. This hath filled the mouths of our heroes with bombast; and given them such sentiments as proceed rather from a swelling than a greatness of mind. Unnatural exclamations, curses, vows, blasphemies, a defiance of mankind, and an outraging of the gods, frequently pass upon the audience for towering thoughts, and have accordingly met with infinite applause.

I shall here add a remark, which I am afraid our tragic writers may make an ill use of. As our heroes are generally lovers, their swelling and blustering upon the stage very much recommends them to the fair part of the audience. The ladies are wonderfully pleased to see a man insulting kings, or affronting the gods, in one scene, and throwing himself at the feet of his mistress in another. Let him behave himself insolently toward the men, and abjectly before the fair one, and it is ten to one but he proves a favorite with the boxes. Dryden and Lee, in several of their tragedies, have practiced this secret with good success.

But to show how a rant pleases beyond the most just and natural thought that is not pronounced with vehemence, I would desire the reader, when he sees the tragedy of Œdipus, to observe how quietly the hero is dismissed at the end of the third act, after having pronounced the following lines, in which the thought is very natural, and apt to move compassion:

> To you, good gods, I make my last appeal;
> Or clear my virtues, or my crimes reveal.
> If in the maze of fate I blindly run,
> And backward tread those paths I sought to shun;
> Impute my errors to your own decree!
> My hands are guilty, but my heart is free.

Let us then observe with what thunder-claps of applause he leaves the stage, after the impieties and execrations at the end of the fourth act; and you will wonder to see an audience so cursed and so pleased at the same time.

> O that, as oft I have at Athens seen

[*Where, by the way, there was no stage till many years after* Œdipus.]

> The stage arise, and the big clouds descend;
> So now, in every deed, I might behold
> This pon'drous globe, and all yon marble roof,
> Meet, like the hands of Jove, and crush mankind;
> For all the elements, etc.

Number 61

Thursday, May 10, 1711

Non equidem studeo bullatis ut mihi nugis
Pagina turgescat, dare pondus idonea fumo.
PERS., Sat. v, 19.

'Tis not indeed my talent to engage
In lofty trifles, or to swell my page
With wind and noise.

DRYDEN

There is no kind of false wit which has been so recommended by the practice of all ages, as that which consists in a jingle of words, and is comprehended under the general name of punning. It is indeed impossible to kill a weed which the soil has a natural disposition to produce. The seeds of punning are in the minds of all men; and though they may be subdued by reason, reflection, and good sense, they will be very apt to shoot up in the greatest genius that is not broken and cultivated by the rules of art. Imitation is natural to us, and when it does not raise the mind to poetry, painting, music, or other more noble arts, it often breaks out in puns and quibbles.

Aristotle, in the eleventh chapter of his book of rhetoric, describes two or three kinds of puns, which he calls paragrams, among the beauties of good writing, and produces instances of them out of some of the greatest authors in the Greek tongue. Cicero has sprinkled several of his works with puns, and in his book where he lays down the rules of oratory, quotes abundance of sayings as pieces of wit, which also upon examination prove arrant puns. But the age in which the pun chiefly flourished was in the reign of King James the First. That learned monarch was himself a tolerable punster, and made very few bishops or privy-counselors that had not some time or other signalized themselves by a clinch or a conundrum. It was therefore in this age that the pun appeared with pomp and dignity. It had been before admitted into merry speeches and ludicrous compositions but was now delivered with great gravity from the pulpit, or pronounced in the most solemn manner at the council table. The greatest authors, in their most serious works, made frequent use of puns. The sermons of Bishop Andrews, and the tragedies of Shakspeare are full of them. The sinner was punned into repentance by the former, as in the latter nothing is more usual than to see a hero weeping and quibbling for a dozen lines together.

I must add to these great authorities, which seem to have given a kind of sanction to this piece of false wit, that all the writers of rhetoric have treated of punning with very great respect, and divided the several kinds of it into hard names, that are reckoned among the figures of speech, and recommended as ornaments in discourse. I remember a country schoolmaster of my acquaintance told me once, that he had been in company with a gentleman whom he looked upon to be the greatest paragrammatist among the moderns. Upon inquiry, I found my learned friend had dined that day with Mr. Swan, the famous punster; and desiring him to give me some account of Mr. Swan's conversation, he told me that he generally talked in the *Paranomasia*, that he sometimes gave into the *Place*, but that in his humble opinion he shone most in the *Antanaclasis*.

I must not here omit, that a famous university of this land was formerly very much infested with puns; but whether or no this might not arise from the fens and marshes in which it was situated, and which are now drained, I must leave to the determination of more skillful naturalists.

After this short history of punning, one would wonder how it should be so entirely banished out of the learned world as it is at present, especially since it had found a place in the writings of the most ancient polite authors. To account for this, we must consider that the first race of authors, who were the great heroes in writing, were destitute of all rules and arts of criticism; and for that reason, though they excel later writers in greatness of genius, they fell short of them in accuracy and correctness. The moderns cannot reach their beauties, but can avoid their imperfections. When the world was furnished with these authors of the first eminence, there grew up another set of writers, who gained themselves a reputation by the remarks which they made on the works of those who preceded them. It was one of the employments of these secondary authors to distinguish the several kinds of wit by terms of art, and to consider them as more or less perfect according as they were founded in truth. It is no wonder, therefore, that even such authors as Isocrates, Plato, and Cicero, should have such little blemishes as are not to be met with in authors of a much inferior character, who have written since those several blemishes were discovered. I do not find that there was a proper separation made between puns and true wit by any of the ancient authors, except Quinctilian and Longinus. But when this distinction was once settled, it was very natural for all men of sense to agree in it. As for the revival of this false wit, it happened about the time of the revival of letters; but as soon as it was once detected, it immediately vanished and disappeared. At the same time there is no question, but as it has sunk in one age and risen in another, it will again recover itself in some distant period of time, as pedantry and ignorance shall prevail upon wit and sense. And, to speak the truth, I do very much apprehend, by some of the last winter's productions, which had their sets of admirers, that our posterity will in a few years degenerate into a race of punsters: at least, a man may be very excusable for any apprehensions of this kind, that has seen acrostics handed about the town with great secrecy and applause; to which I must also add a little epigram called the Witches' Prayer, that fell into verse when it was read either backward or forward, excepting only that it cursed one way and blessed the other. When one sees there are actually such painstakers among our British wits, who can tell what it may end in? If we must lash one another, let it be with the manly strokes of wit and satire; for I am of the old philosopher's opinion, that if I must suffer from one or the other, I would rather it should be from the paw of a lion than from the hoof of an ass. I do not speak this out of any spirit of party. There is a most crying dullness on both sides. I have seen tory acrostics and whig anagrams, and do not quarrel with either of them because they are whigs or tories, but because they are anagrams and acrostics.

But to return to punning. Having pursued the history of a pun, from its original to its downfall, I shall here define it to be a conceit arising from the use of two words that agree in the sound, but differ in the sense. The only way, therefore, to try a piece of wit, is to translate it into a different language. If it bears the test, you may pronounce it true; but if it vanishes in the experiment, you may conclude it to have been a pun. In short, one may say of a pun as the countryman described his nightingale, that it is *"vox et præterea nihil,"* "a sound, and nothing but a sound." On the contrary, one may represent true wit by the description which Aristenetus makes of a fine woman; when she is dressed she is beautiful, when she is undressed she is beautiful; or, as Mercerus has translated it more emphatically, *"Induitur, formosa est: exuitur, ipsa forma est."*—C.

Number 62

Friday, May 11, 1711

Scribendi recte sapere est et principium, et fons.
Hor., *Ars. Poet.*, ver. 309
Sound judgment is the ground of writing well.
Roscommon

Mr. Locke has an admirable reflection upon the difference of wit and judgment, whereby he endeavors to show the reason why they are not always the talents of the same person. His words are as follow: "And hence, perhaps, may be given some reason of that common observation, 'That men who have a great deal of wit, and prompt memories, have not always the clearest judgment or deepest reason.' For wit lying most in the assemblage of ideas, and putting those together with quickness and variety wherein can be found any resemblance or congruity, thereby to make up pleasant pictures, and agreeable visions in the fancy; judgment, on the contrary, lies quite on the other side, in separating carefully one from another ideas wherein can be found the least difference, thereby to avoid being misled by similitude, and by affinity to take one thing for another. This is a way of proceeding quite contrary to metaphor and allusion; wherein, for the most part, lies that entertainment and pleasantry of wit, which strikes so lively on the fancy, and is therefore so acceptable to all people."

This is, I think, the best and most philosophical account that I have ever met with of wit, which generally, though not always, consists in such a resemblance and congruity of ideas as this author mentions. I shall only add to it, by way of explanation, that every resemblance of ideas is not that which we

call wit, unless it be such a one that gives delight and surprise to the reader.
These two properties seem essential to wit, more particularly the last of them.
In order, therefore, that the resemblance in the ideas be wit, it is necessary that
the ideas should not lie too near one another in the nature of things; for where
the likeness is obvious, it gives no surprise. To compare one man's singing to
that of another, or to represent the whiteness of any object by that of milk and
snow, or the variety of its colors by those of the rainbow, cannot be called wit,
unless, beside this obvious resemblance, there be some farther congruity
discovered in the two ideas, that is capable of giving the reader some surprise.
Thus when a poet tells us the bosom of his mistress is as white as snow, there
is no wit in the comparison; but when he adds, with a sigh, it is as cold too, it
then grows into wit. Every reader's memory may supply him with innumerable
instances of the same nature. For this reason, the similitudes in heroic poets,
who endeavor rather to fill the mind with great conceptions than to divert it
with such as are new and surprising, have seldom anything in them that can
be called wit. Mr. Locke's account of wit, with this short explanation,
comprehends most of the species of wit, as metaphors, similitudes, allegories,
enigmas, mottoes, parables, fables, dreams, visions, dramatic writings, burlesque, and all the methods of allusion. There are many other species of wit
(how remote soever they may appear at first sight from the foregoing
description) which upon examination will be found to agree with it.

As true wit generally consists in this resemblance and congruity of ideas,
false wit chiefly consists in the resemblance and congruity sometimes of single
letters, as in anagrams, chronograms, lipograms, and acrostics; sometimes of
syllables, as in echoes and doggerel rhymes: sometimes of words, as in puns
and quibbles; and sometimes of whole sentences or poems, cast into the
figures of eggs, axes, or altars: nay, some carry the notion of wit so far, as to
ascribe it even to external mimicry; and to look upon a man as an ingenious
person that can resemble the tone, posture, or face of another.

As true wit consists in the resemblance of ideas, and false wit in the
resemblance of words, according to the foregoing instances; there is another
kind of wit which consists partly in the resemblance of ideas, and partly in the
resemblance of words, which for distinction-sake I shall call mixed wit. This
kind of wit is that which abounds in Cowley, more than in any other author
that ever wrote. Mr. Waller has likewise a great deal of it. Mr. Dryden is very
sparing in it. Milton had a genius much above it. Spenser is in the same class
with Milton. The Italians, even in their epic poetry, are full of it. Monsieur
Boileau, who formed himself upon the ancient poets, has everywhere rejected
it with scorn. If we look after mixed wit among the Greek writers, we shall find
it nowhere but in the epigrammatists. There are indeed some strokes of it in
the little poem ascribed to Musæus, which by that, as well as many other
marks, betrays itself to be a modern composition. If we look into the Latin
writers, we find none of this mixed wit in Virgil, Lucretius, or Catullus; very
little in Horace, but a great deal of it in Ovid, and scarce anything else in
Martial.

Out of the innumerable branches of mixed wit, I shall choose one instance which may be met with in all the writers of this class. The passion of love, in its nature, has been thought to resemble fire; for which reason the words fire and flame are made use of to signify love. The witty poets therefore have taken an advantage from the double meaning of the word fire, to make an infinite number of witticisms. Cowley, observing the cold regard of his mistress's eyes, and at the same time their power of producing love in him, considers them as burning-glasses made of ice; and finding himself able to live in the greatest extremeties of love, concludes the torrid zone to be habitable. When his mistress has read his letter written in juice of lemon, by holding it to the fire, he desires her to read it over a second time by love's flame. When she weeps, he wishes it were inward heat that distilled those drops from the limbeck. When she is absent, he is beyond eighty, that is thirty degrees nearer the pole than when she is with him. His ambitious love is a fire that naturally mounts upward; his happy love is the beams of heaven, and his unhappy love flames of hell. When it does not let him sleep, it is a flame that sends up no smoke; when it is opposed by counsel and advice, it is a fire that rages the more by the winds blowing upon it. Upon the dying of a tree, in which he had cut his loves, he observed that his written flames had burnt up and withered the tree. When he resolves to give over his passion, he tells us that one burnt like him forever dreads the fire. His heart is an Ætna, that instead of Vulcan's shop, incloses Cupid's forge in it. His endeavoring to drown his love in wine, is throwing oil upon the fire. He would insinuate to his mistress that the fire of love, like that of the sun (which produces so many living creatures), should not only warm, but beget. Love in another place cooks pleasure at his fire. Sometimes the poet's heart is frozen in every breast, and sometimes scorched in every eye. Sometimes he is drowned in tears and burnt in love, like a ship set on fire in the middle of the sea.

The reader may observe in every one of these instances, that the poet mixes the qualities of fire with those of love; and in the same sentence, speaking of it both as a passion and as real fire, surprises the reader with those seeming resemblances or contradictions, that make up all the wit in this kind of writing. Mixed wit therefore is a composition of pun and true wit, and is more or less perfect as the resemblance lies in the ideas or in the words. Its foundations are laid partly in falsehood and partly in truth; reason puts in her claim for one half of it, and extravagance for the other. The only province therefore for this kind of wit is epigram, or those little occasional poems that in their own nature are nothing else but a tissue of epigrams. I cannot conclude this head of mixed wit, without owning that the admirable poet, out of whom I have taken the examples of it, had as much true wit as any author that ever wrote; and indeed, all other talents of an extraordinary genius.

It may be expected since I am upon this subject, that I should take notice of Mr. Dryden's definition of wit; which, with all the deference that is due to the judgment of so great a man, is not so properly a definition of wit as of good writing in general. Wit, as he defines it, is "a propriety of words and thoughts adapted to the subject." If this be a true definition of wit, I am apt to think that Euclid was the greatest wit that ever set pen to paper. It is certain there never was a greater propriety of words and thoughts adapted to the subject, than what that author has made use of in his Elements. I shall only appeal to my reader if this definition agrees with any notion he has of wit. If it be a true one, I am sure Mr. Dryden was not only a better poet, but a greater wit, than Mr. Cowley; and Virgil a much more facetious man than either Ovid or Martial.

Bouhours, whom I look upon to be the most penetrating of all French critics has taken pains to show, that it is impossible for any thought to be beautiful which is not just, and has not its foundation in the nature of things; that the basis of all wit is truth; and that no thought can be valuable, of which good sense is not the groundwork. Boileau has endeavored to inculcate the same notion in several parts of his writings, both in prose and verse. This is that natural way of writing, that beautiful simplicity, which we so much admire in the compositions of the ancients; and which nobody deviates from, but those who want strength of genius to make a thought shine in its own natural beauties. Poets who want this strength of genius to give that majestic simplicity to nature, which we so much admire in the works of the ancients, are forced to hunt after foreign ornaments, and not to let any piece of wit of what kind soever escape them. I look upon these writers as Goths in poetry, who, like those in architecture, not being able to come up to the beautiful simplicity of the old Greeks and Romans, have endeavored to supply its place with all the extravagances of an irregular fancy. Mr. Dryden makes a very handsome observation on Ovid's writing a letter from Dido to Æneas, in the following words: "Ovid," says he, speaking of Virgil's fiction of Dido and Æneas, "takes it up after him, even in the same age, and makes an ancient heroine of Virgil's new-created Dido, dictates a letter for her just before her death to the ungrateful fugitive, and very unluckily for himself, is for measuring a sword with a man so much superior in force to him on the same subject. I think I may be judge of this, because I have translated both. The famous author of the Art of Love has nothing of his own; he borrows all from a greater master in his own profession, and, which is worse, improves nothing which he finds. Nature fails him, and, being forced to his old shift, he has recourse to witticism. This passes indeed with his soft admirers, and gives him the preference to Virgil in their esteem."

Were I not supported by so great an authority as that of Mr. Dryden, I should not venture to observe, that the taste of most of our English poets, as well as readers, is extremely Gothic. He quotes Monsieur Segrais, for a threefold distinction of the readers of poetry; in the first of which he comprehends the rabble of readers, whom he does not treat as such with regard to their quality, but to their numbers and the coarseness of their taste. His words are as follow: "Segrais has distinguished the readers of poetry, according to their capacity of judging, into three classes." [He might have said the same of writers too, if he had pleased.] "In the lowest form he places those whom he calls Les Petits Esprits, such things as our upper-gallery audience in a playhouse; who like nothing but the husk and rind of wit, and prefer a quibble, a conceit, an epigram, before solid sense and elegant expression. These are mob readers. If Virgil and Martial stood for parliament-men, we know already who would carry it. But though they made the greatest appearance in the field, and cried the loudest, the best of it is, they are but a sort of French Huguenots, or Dutch boors, brought over in herds, but not naturalized; who have not lands of two pounds per annum in Parnassus, and therefore are not priveliged to poll. The authors are of the same level, fit to represent them on a mountebank's stage, or to be masters of the ceremonies in a bear-garden; yet these are they who have the most admirers. But it often happens, to their mortification, that as their readers improve their stock of sense (as they may by reading better books, and by conversation with men of judgment), they soon forsake them."

I must not dismiss this subject without observing, that as Mr. Locke in the passage above-mentioned has discovered the most fruitful source of wit, so there is another of a quite contrary nature to it, which does likewise branch itself out into several kinds. For not only the resemblance, but the opposition of ideas, does very often produce wit; as I could show in several little points, turns, and antitheses, that I may possibly enlarge upon in some future speculation.—C.

Number 267

Saturday, January 5, 1711–12

Cedite Romani scriptores, cedite Graii.
PROPERT. *El.* 34, lib. 2, ver. 95.
Give place, ye Roman and ye Grecian wits.

There is nothing in nature so irksome as general discourses, especially when they turn chiefly upon words. For this reason I shall wave the discussion of that point which was started some years since, whether Milton's Paradise Lost may be called an heroic poem? Those who will not give it that title, may call it (if they please) a divine poem. It will be sufficient to its perfection, if it has in it all the beauties of the highest kind of poetry: and as for those who allege it is not an heroic poem, they advance no more to the diminution of it, than if they should say Adam is not Æneas, nor Eve Helen.

I shall therefore examine it by the rule of epic poetry, and see whether it falls short of the Iliad or Æneid, in the beauties which are essential to that kind of writing. The first thing to be considered in an epic poem is the fable, which is perfect or imperfect, according as the action which it relates is more or less so. This actor should have three qualifications in it. First, it should be but one action. Secondly, it should be an entire action; and Thirdly, it should be a great action. To consider the action of the Iliad, Æneid, and Paradise Lost, in these three several lights. Homer, to preserve the unity of his action, hastens into the midst of things, as Horace has observed. Had he gone up to Leda's egg, or begun much later, even at the rape of Helen, or the investing of Troy, it is manifest that the story of the poem would have been a series of several actions. He therefore opens his poem with the discord of his princes, and artfully interweaves, in the several succeeding parts of it, an account of everything material which relates to them, and had passed before that fatal dissension. After the same manner Æneas makes his first appearance in the Tyrrhene seas, and within sight of Italy, because the action proposed to be celebrated was that of his settling himself in Latium. But because it was necessary for the reader to know what had happened to him in the taking of Troy, and in the preceding parts of his voyage, Virgil makes his hero relate it by way of episode in the second and third books of the Æneid. The contents of both which books come before those of the first book in the thread of the story, though for preserving this unity of action they follow them in the disposition of the poem. Milton, in imitation of these two great poets, opens his Paradise Lost with an infernal council plotting the fall of man, which is the action he proposed to celebrate; and as for those great actions, which preceded in point of time, the battle of the angels, and the creation of the world (which would have entirely destroyed the unity of the principal action, had he related them in the same order that they happened), he cast them in the fifth, sixth, and seventh books, by way of episode to this noble poem.

Aristotle himself allows, that Homer has nothing to boast of as to the unity of his fable, though at the same time that great critic and philosopher endeavored to palliate this imperfection in the Greek poet, by imputing it in some measure to the very nature of an epic poem. Some have been of opinion, that the Æneid also labors in this particular, and has *Episodes* which may be looked upon as excrescences rather than as parts of the action. On the contrary, the poem which we have now under our consideration, hath no other episodes than such as naturally arise from the subject, and yet is filled with such a multitude of astonishing incidents, that it gives us at the same time a pleasure of the greatest variety and of the greatest simplicity; uniform in its nature, though diversified in the execution.

I must observe also, that as Virgil, in the poem which was designed to celebrate the origin of the Roman empire, has described the birth of its great rival, the Carthaginian commonwealth; Milton, with the like art in his poem on the fall of man, has related the fall of those angels who are his professed enemies. Beside the many other beauties in such an episode, its running parallel with the great action of the poem, hinders it from breaking the unity so much as another episode would have done, that had not so great affinity with the principal subject. In short this is the same kind of beauty which the critics admire in the Spanish Friar, or the Double Discovery, where the two different plots look like counterparts and copies of one another.

The second qualification required in the action of an epic poem is, that it should be an entire action. An action is entire when it is complete in all its parts; or as Aristotle describes it, when it consists of a beginning, a middle, and an end. Nothing should go before it, be intermixed with it, or follow after it, that is not related to it. As, on the contrary, no single step should be omitted in that just and regular process which it must be supposed to take from its origin to its consummation. Thus we see the anger of Achilles in its birth, its continuance, and effects; and Æneas's settlement in Italy carried on through all the oppositions in his way to it both by sea and land. The action in Milton excels (I think) both the former in this particular; we see it contrived in hell, executed upon earth, and punished by Heaven. The parts of it are told in the most distinct manner, and grow out of one another in the most natural order.

The third qualification of an epic poem is its greatness. The anger of Achilles was of such consequence that it embroiled the kings of Greece, destroyed the heroes of Troy, and engaged all the gods in factions. Æneas's settlement in Italy produced the Cæsars and gave birth to the Roman empire. Milton's subject was still greater than either of the former; it does not determine the fate of single persons or nations; but of a whole species. The united powers of hell are joined together for the destruction of mankind, which they effected in part, and would have completed, had not Omnipotence itself interposed. The principal actors are man in his greatest perfection, and woman in her highest beauty. Their enemies are the fallen angels; the Messiah their friend, and the Almighty their protector. In short everything that is great in the whole circle of being, whether within the verge of nature, or out of it, has a proper part assigned it in this admirable poem.

In poetry, as in architecture, not only the whole, but the principal members, and every part of them, should be great. I will not presume to say, that the book of games in the Æneid, or that in the Iliad, are not of this nature: nor to reprehend Virgil's simile of the top, and many others of the same kind in the Iliad, as liable to any censure in this particular; but I think we may say, without derogating from those wonderful performances, that there is an unquestionable magnificence in every part of Paradise Lost, and indeed a much greater than could have been formed upon any pagan system.

But Aristotle, by the greatness of the action, does not only mean that it should be great in its nature, but also in its duration, or in other words, that it should have a due length in it, as well as what we properly call greatness. The just measure of this kind of magnitude, he explains by the following similitude: An animal no bigger than a mite, cannot appear perfect to the eye, because the sight takes it in at once, and has only a confused idea of the whole, and not a distinct idea of all its parts; if, on the contrary, you should suppose an animal of ten thousand furlongs in length, the eye would be so filled with a single part of it, that it could not give the mind an idea of the whole. What these animals are to the eye, a very short or a very long action would be to the memory. The first would be, as it were, lost and swallowed up by it, and the other difficult to be contained in it. Homer and Virgil have shown their principal art in this particular; the action of the Iliad, and that of the Æneid, were in themselves exceedingly short, but are so beautifully extended and diversified by the invention of episodes, and the machinery of gods, with the like poetical ornament, that they make up an agreeable story, sufficient to employ the memory without overcharging it. Milton's action is enriched with such a variety of circumstances, that I have taken as much pleasure in reading the contents of his books, as in the best invented story I ever met with. It is possible, that the traditions on which the Iliad and Æneid were built, had more circumstances in them than the history of the fall of man, as it is related in Scripture. Beside, it was easier for Homer and Virgil to dash the truth with fiction, as they were in no danger of offending the religion of their country by it. But as for Milton, he had not only a very few circumstances upon which to raise his poem, but was also obliged to proceed with the greatest caution in everything that he added out of his own invention. And indeed, notwithstanding all the restraint he was under, he has filled his story with so many surprising incidents, which bear so close an analogy with what is delivered in holy writ, that it is capable of pleasing the most delicate reader, without giving offense to the most scrupulous.

The modern critics have collected from several hints in the Iliad and Æneid the space of time, which is taken up by the action of each of those poems; but as a great part of Milton's story was transacted in regions that lie out of the reach of the sun and the sphere of the day, it is impossible to gratify the reader with such a calculation, which indeed would be more curious than instructive; none of the critics, either ancient or modern, having laid down rules to circumscribe the action of an epic poem with any determined number of years, days, or hours.

This piece of criticism on Milton's Paradise Lost shall be carried on in the following Saturday's paper.—L.

Number 273

Saturday, January 12, 1711–12

—Notandi sunt tibi mores.
Hor., Ars. Poet., ver. 156
Note well the manners.

Having examined the action of Paradise Lost, let us in the next place consider the actors. This is Aristotle's method of considering, first the fable, and secondly the manners; or, as we generally call them, in English, the fable and the characters.

Homer has excelled all the heroic poets that ever wrote in the multitude and variety of his characters. Every God that is admitted into his poem, acts a part which would have been suitable to no other deity. His princes are as much distinguished by their manners, as by their dominions; and even those among them, whose characters seem wholly made up of courage, differ from one another as to the particular kinds of courage in which they excel. In short, there is scarce a speech or action in the Iliad, which the reader may not ascribe to the person who speaks or acts, without seeing his name at the head of it.

Homer does not only outshine all other poets in the variety, but also in the novelty of his characters. He has introduced among his Grecian princes a person who had lived thrice the age of man, and conversed with Theseus, Hercules, Polyphemus, and the first race of heroes. His principal actor is the son of a goddess, not to mention the offspring of other deities, who have likewise a place in his poem, and the venerable Trojan prince, who was the father of so many kings and heroes. There is in these several characters of Homer, a certain dignity as well as novelty, which adapts them in a more peculiar manner to the nature of a heroic poem. Though, at the same time, to give them the greater variety, he has described a Vulcan, that is a buffoon, among his gods, and a Thersites among his mortals.

Virgil falls infinitely short of Homer in the characters of his poem, both as to their variety and novelty. Æneas is indeed a perfect character; but as for Achates, though he is styled the hero's friend, he does nothing in the whole poem which may deserve that title. Gyas, Mnestheus, Sergestus, and Cloanthes, are all of them men of the same stamp and character.

—*Fortemque Gyan, fortemque Cloanthem.*

There are, indeed, several natural incidents in the part of Ascanius; and that of Dido cannot be sufficiently admired. I do not see anything new or particular in Turnus. Pallas and Evander are remote copies of Hector and Priam, as Lausus and Mezentius are almost parallels to Pallas and Evander. The characters of Nisus and Euryalus are beautiful, but common. We must not forget the parts of Sinon, Camilla, and some few others, which are fine improvements on the Greek poet. In short, there is neither that variety nor novelty in the persons of Æneid, which we meet with in those of the Iliad.

If we look into the characters of Milton, we shall find that he has introduced all the variety his fable was capable of receiving. The whole species of mankind was in two persons at the time to which the subject of his poem is confined. We have, however, four distinct characters in these two persons. We see man and woman in the highest innocence and perfection, and in the most abject state of guilt and infirmity. The two last characters are, indeed, very common and obvious, but the two first are not only more magnificent, but more new than any characters either in Virgil or Homer, or indeed in the whole circle of nature.

Milton was so sensible of this defect in the subject of his poem, and of the few characters it would afford him, that he has brought into it two actors of a shadowy and fictitious nature, in the persons of Sin and Death, by which means he has wrought into the body of his fable a very beautiful and well-invented allegory. But notwithstanding the fineness of this allegory may atone for it in some measure, I cannot think that persons of such a chimerical existence are proper actors in an epic poem; because there is not that measure of probability annexed to them, which is requisite in writings of this kind, as I shall show more at large hereafter.

Virgil has indeed admitted Fame as an actress in the Æneid, but the part she acts is very short, and none of the most admired circumstances in that divine work. We find in mock-heroic poems, particularly in the Dispensary and the Lutrin, several allegorical persons of this nature, which are very beautiful in these compositions, and may perhaps be used as an argument, that the authors of them were of opinion such characters might have a place in an epic work. For my own part, I should be glad the reader would think so, for the sake of the poem I am now examining: and must further add, that if such empty, unsubstantial beings may be ever made use of on this occasion, never were any more nicely imagined, and employed in more proper actions, than those of which I am now speaking.

Another principal actor in this poem is the great enemy of mankind. The part of Ulysses in Homer's Odyssey is very much admired by Aristotle, as perplexing that fable with very agreeable plots and intricacies, not only by the many adventures in his voyage, and the subtilty of his behavior, but by the various concealments and discoveries of his person in several parts of that poem. But the crafty being I have now mentioned makes a much longer voyage than Ulysses, puts in practice many more wiles and stratagems, and hides himself under a greater variety of shapes and appearances, all of which are severally detected, to the great delight and surprise of the reader.

We may likewise observe with how much art the poet has varied several characters of the persons that speak in his infernal assembly. On the contrary, how has he represented the whole Godhead exerting itself toward man in its full benevolence under the threefold distinction of a Creator, a Redeemer, and a Comforter!

Nor must we omit the person of Raphael, who, amidst his tenderness and friendship for man, shows such a dignity and condescension in all his speech and behavior, as are suitable to a superior nature. The angels are, indeed, as much diversified in Milton, and distinguished by their proper parts, as the gods are in Homer and Virgil. The reader will find nothing ascribed to Uriel, Gabriel, Michael, or Raphael; which is not in a particular manner suitable to their respective characters.

There is another circumstance in the principal actors of the Iliad and Æneid, which gives a peculiar beauty to those two poems, and was therefore contrived with very great judgment. I mean the authors having chosen for their heroes, persons who were so nearly related to the people for whom they wrote. Achilles was a Greek, and Æneas the remote founder of Rome. By this means their countrymen (whom they principally propose to themselves for their readers) were particularly attentive to all the parts of their story, and sympathized with their heroes in all their adventures. A Roman could not but rejoice in the escapes, successes, and victories, of Æneas, and be grieved at any defeats, misfortunes, or disappointments that befel him; as a Greek must have had the same regard for Achilles. And it is plain, that each of those poems have lost this great advantage, among those readers to whom their heroes are as strangers, or indifferent persons.

Milton's poem is admirable in this respect, since it is impossible for any of its readers, whatever nation, country, or people, he may belong to, not to be related to the persons who are the principal actors in it; but what is still infinitely more to its advantage, the principal actors in this poem are not only our progenitors, but our representatives. We have an actual interest in everything they do, and no less than our utmost happiness is concerned, and lies at stake in all their behavior.

I shall subjoin, as a corollary to the foregoing remark, an admirable observation out of Aristotle, which has been very much misrepresented in the quotations of some modern critics: "If a man of perfect and consummate virtue falls into a misfortune, it raises our pity, but not our terror, because we do not fear that it may be our own case, who do not resemble the suffering person." But, as that great philosopher adds "if we see a man of virtue mixed with infirmities fall into any misfortune, it does not only raise our pity but our terror; because we are afraid that the like misfortunes may happen to ourselves, who resemble the character of the suffering person."

I shall take another opportunity to observe, that a person of an absolute and consummate virtue should never be introduced into tragedy, and shall only remark in this place, that the foregoing observation of Aristotle, though it may be true in other occasions, does not hold in this; because in the present case, though the persons who fall into misfortune are of the most perfect and consummate virtue, it is not to be considered as what may possibly be, but what actually is our own case; since we are embarked with them on the same bottom, and must be partakers of their happiness or misery.

In this, and some other very few instances, Aristotle's rules for epic poetry (which he had drawn from his reflections upon Homer) cannot be supposed to quadrate exactly with the heroic poems which have been made since his time; since it is plain his rules would still have been more perfect, could he have perused the Æneid, which was made some hundred years after his death.

In my next; I shall go through other parts of Milton's poem; and hope that what I shall there advance, as well as what I have already written, will not only serve as a comment upon Milton, but upon Aristotle.—L.

Number 279

Saturday, January 19, 1711–12

Reddere personæ scit convenientia cuique
HOR. *Ars Poet.*, v, 316.
He knows what best befits each character.

We have already taken a general survey of the fable and characters in Milton's Paradise Lost. The parts which remain to be considered, according to Aristotle's method, are the sentiments and the language. Before I enter upon the first of these, I must advertise my reader, that it is my design, as soon as I have finished my general reflections on these four several heads, to give particular instances out of the poem which is now before us of beauties and imperfections which may be observed under each of them, as also of such other particulars as may not properly fall under any of them. This I thought fit to premise, that the reader may not judge too hastily of this piece of criticism, or look upon it as imperfect, before he has seen the whole extent of it.

The sentiments in an epic poem are the thoughts and behavior which the author ascribes to the persons whom he introduces, and are just when they are conformable to the characters of the several persons. The sentiments have likewise a relation to things as well as persons, and are then perfect when they are such as are adapted to the subject. If in either of these cases the poet endeavors to argue or explain, to magnify or diminish, to raise love or hatred, pity or terror, or any other passion, we ought to consider whether the sentiments he makes use of are proper for those ends. Homer is censured by the critics for his defect as to this particular in several parts of the Iliad and Odyssey, though at the same time those who have treated this great poet with candor, have attributed this defect to the times in which he lived. It was the fault of the age and not of Homer, if there wants that delicacy in some of his sentiments, which now appears in the works of men of a much inferior genius. Beside, if there are blemishes in any particular thoughts, there is an infinite beauty in the greatest part of them. In short, if there are many poets who would not have fallen into the meanness of some of his sentiments, there are none who could have risen up to the greatness of others. Virgil has excelled all others in the propriety of his sentiments. Milton shines likewise very much in this particular: nor must we omit one consideration which adds to his honor and reputation. Homer and Virgil introduced persons whose characters are commonly known among men, and such as are to be met with either in history or in ordinary conversation. Milton's characters, most of them, lie out of nature, and were to be formed purely by his own invention. It shows a greater genius in Shakspeare to have drawn his Caliban, than his Hotspur, or Julius Cæsar: the one was to be supplied out of his own imagination, whereas the other might have been formed upon tradition, history, and observation. It was much easier therefore for Homer to find proper sentiments for an assembly of Grecian generals, than for Milton to diversify his infernal council with proper characters, and inspires them with a variety of sentiments. The love of Dido and Æneas are only copies of what has passed between other persons. Adam and Eve, before the fall, are a different species from that of mankind, who are descended from them; and none but a poet of the most unbounded invention, and the most exquisite judgment, could have filled their conversation and behavior with so many apt circumstances during their state of innocence.

Nor is it sufficient for an epic poem to be filled with such thoughts as are natural, unless it abound also with such as are sublime. Virgil in this particular falls short of Homer. He has not indeed so many thoughts that are low and vulgar; but at the same time has not so many thoughts that are sublime and noble. The truth of it is, Virgil seldom rises into very astonishing sentiments, where he is not fired by the Iliad. He everywhere charms and pleases us by the force of his own genius; but seldom elevates and transports us where he does not fetch his hints from Homer.

Milton's chief talent, and indeed his distinguishing excellence, lies in the sublimity of his thoughts. There are others of the moderns who rival him in every other part of poetry; but in the greatness of his sentiments he triumphs over all the poets, both modern and ancient, Homer only excepted. It is impossible for the imagination of man to distend itself with greater ideas, than those which he has laid together in his first, second, and sixth books. The seventh, which describes the creation of the world, is likewise wonderfully sublime, though not so apt to stir up emotion in the mind of the reader, nor consequently so perfect in the epic way of writing, because it is filled with less action. Let the judicious reader compare what Longinus has observed on several passages in Homer, and he will find parallels for most of them in the Paradise Lost.

From what has been said we may infer, that as there are two kinds of sentiments, the natural and the sublime, which are always to be pursued in a heroic poem, there are also two kinds of thoughts which are carefully to be avoided. The first are such as are affected and unnatural; the second such as are mean and vulgar. As for the first kind of thoughts, we meet with little or nothing that is like them in Virgil. He has none of those trifling points and puerilities that are so often to be met with in Ovid, none of the epigrammatic turns of Lucan, none of those swelling sentiments which are so frequent in Statius and Claudian, none of those mixed embellishments of Tasso. Everything is just and natural. His sentiments show that he had a perfect insight into human nature, and that he knew everything which was the most proper to affect it.

Mr. Dryden has in some places, which I may hereafter take notice of, misrepresented Virgil's way of thinking as to this particular, in the translation he has given us of the Æneid. I do not remember that Homer any where falls into the faults above-mentioned, which were indeed the false refinements of latter ages. Milton, it must be confessed, has sometimes erred in this respect, as I shall show more at large in another paper; though considering how all the poets of the age in which he wrote were infected with this wrong way of thinking, he is rather to be admired that he did not give more into it, than that he did sometimes comply with the vicious taste which still prevails so much among modern writers.

But since several thoughts may be natural which are low and groveling, an epic poet should not only avoid such sentiments as are unnatural or affected, but also such as are mean and vulgar. Homer has opened a great field of raillery to men of more delicacy than greatness of genius by the homeliness of some of his sentiments. But as I have before said, these are rather to be imputed to the simplicity of the age in which he lived, to which I may also add, of that which he described, than to any imperfection in that divine poet. Zoilus among the ancients, and Monsieur Perrault among the moderns, pushed their ridicule very far upon him, on account of some such sentiments. There is no blemish to be observed in Virgil under this head, and but a very few in Milton.

I shall give but one instance of this impropriety of thought in Homer, and at the same time compare it with an instance of the same nature, both in Virgil and Milton. Sentiments which raise laughter can very seldom be admitted with any decency into a heroic poem, whose business it is to excite passions of a much nobler nature. Homer, however, in his characters of Vulcan and Thersites, in his story of Mars and Venus, in his behavior of Irus, and in other passages, has been observed to have lapsed into the burlesque character, and to have departed from that serious air which seems essential to the magnificence of an epic poem. I remember but one laugh in the whole Æneid, which rises in the fifth book, upon Monœtes, where he is represented as thrown overboard, and drying himself upon a rock. But this piece of mirth is so well-timed that the severest critic can have nothing to say against it; for it is the book of games and diversions, where the reader's mind may be supposed sufficiently relaxed for such an entertainment. The only piece of pleasantry in Paradise Lost, is where the evil spirits are described as rallying the angels upon the success of their newly-invented artillery. This passage I look upon to be the most exceptionable in the whole poem, as being nothing else but a string of puns, and those, too, very indifferent ones:

> ———Satan beheld their plight,
> And to his mates thus in derision call'd:
> "O friends, why come not on those victors proud?"
> Ere while they fierce were coming; and when we,
> To entertain them fair with open front
> And breast (what could we more?) propounded terms
> Of composition, straight they chang'd their minds,
> Flew off, and into strange vagaries fell
> As they would dance; yet for a dance they seem'd
> Somewhat extravagant, and wild: perhaps
> For joy of offer'd peace; but I suppose
> If our proposals once again were heard,
> We should compel them to a quick result."
> To whom thus Belial in like gamesome mood:
> "Leader, the terms we sent were terms of weight,
> Of hard contents, and full of force urged home:
> Such as we might perceive amus'd them all,
> And stumbled many; who receives them right,
> Had need from head to foot well understand;
> Not understood, this gift they have beside,
> They show us when our foes walk not upright."
> Thus they among themselves in pleasant vein
> Stood scoffing———
>
> MILTON's *Par. Lost,* b. vi, 1. 609, etc.

Number 285

Saturday, January 26, 1711–12

Ne, quieunque Deus, quicunque adhibebitur heros,
Regali conspectus in auro nuper et ostro,
Migret in obscuras humili sermone tabernas;
Aut, dum vitat humum, nubes et inania captet.
                                  HOR., *Ars. Poet.*, ver. 227.
But then they did not wrong themselves so much,
To make a god, a hero, or a king,
(Stript of his golden crown, and purple robe)
Descend to a mechanic dialect;
Nor (to avoid such meanness) soaring high,
With empty sound, and airy notions fly.
                                            ROSCOMMON

Having already treated of the fable, the characters, and sentiments in Paradise Lost, we are in the last place, to consider the language; and as the learned world is very much divided upon Milton as to this point, I hope they will excuse me if I appear particular in any of my opinions, and incline to those who judge most advantageously of the author.

It is requisite that the language of a heroic poem should be both perspicuous and sublime. In proportion as either of these two qualities are wanting, the language is imperfect. Perspicuity is the first and most necessary qualification; insomuch that a good-natured reader sometimes overlooks a little slip even in the grammar or syntax, where it is impossible for him to mistake the poet's sense. Of this kind is that passage in Milton, wherein he speaks of Satan:

————God and his Son except,
Created thing naught valu'd he nor shunn'd:

and that in which he describes Adam and Eve:

Adam the goodliest man of men since born
His sons, the fairest of her daughters Eve.

It is plain, that in the former of these passages, according to the natural syntax, the Divine Persons mentioned in the first line are represented as created beings; and that, in the other, Adam and Eve are confounded with their sons and daughters. Such little blemishes as these, when the thought is great and natural, we should, with Horace, impute to a pardonable inadvertency, or to the weakness of human nature, which cannot attend to each minute particular, and give the last finishing to every circumstance in so long a work. The ancient critics, therefore, who were actuated by a spirit of candor, rather than that of caviling, invented certain figures of speech, on purpose to palliate little errors of this nature in the writings of those authors who had so many greater beauties to atone for them.

If clearness and perspicuity were only to be consulted, the poet would have nothing else to do but to clothe his thoughts in the most plain and natural expressions. But since it often happens that the most obvious phrases, and those which are used in ordinary conversation, become too familiar to the ear, and contract a kind of meanness by passing through the mouths of the vulgar; a poet should take particular care to guard himself against idiomatic ways of speaking. Ovid and Lucan have many poornesses of expression upon this account, as taking up with the first phrases that offered, without putting themselves to the trouble of looking after such as would not only have been natural, but also elevated and sublime. Milton has but few failings in this kind, of which, however, you may meet with some instances, as in the following passages:

> Embryos and idiots, eremites and friars,
> White, black, and gray, with all their trumpery
> Here pilgrims roam——
> ——A while discoursed they hold,
> No fear lest dinner cool; when thus began
> Our author——
> Who of all ages to succeed, but feeling
> The evil on him brought by me, will curse
> My head,—ill fare our ancestor impure,
> For this we may thank Adam.——

The great masters in composition know very well that many an elegant phrase becomes improper for a poet or an orator, when it has been debased by common use. For this reason the works of ancient authors, which are written in dead languages, have a great advantage over those which are written in languages that are now spoken. Were there any mean phrases or idioms in Virgil or Homer, they would not shock the ear of the most delicate modern reader, so much as they would have done that of an old Greek or Roman, because we never hear them pronounced in our streets, or in ordinary conversation.

It is not therefore sufficient, that the language of an epic poem be perspicuous, unless it be also sublime. To this end it ought to deviate from the common forms and ordinary phrases of speech. The judgment of a poet very much discovers itself in shunning the common roads of expression, without falling into such ways of speech as may seem stiff and unnatural: he must not swell into a false sublime, by endeavoring to avoid the other extreme. Among the Greeks, Æschylus, and sometimes Sophocles, were guilty of this fault; among the Latins, Claudian and Statius; and among our own countrymen, Shakspeare and Lee. In these authors the affectation of greatness often hurts the perspicuity of the style, as in many others the endeavor after perspicuity prejudices its greatness.

Aristotle has observed, that the idiomatic style may be avoided, and the sublime formed, by the following methods. First, by the use of metaphors: such are those of Milton:

> Imparadis'd in one another's arms.
> ———And in his hand a reed
> Stood waving tipp'd with fire.———
> The grassy clods now calv'd———
> Spangled with eyes———.

In these and innumerable other instances, the metaphors are very bold but just; I must however observe, that if the metaphors are not so thick sown in Milton, which always savors too much of wit, that they never clash with one another, which, as Aristotle observes, turns a sentence into a kind of enigma or riddle; and that he seldom has recourse to them where the proper and natural words will do as well.

Another way of raising the language, and giving it a poetical turn, is to make use of the idioms of other tongues. Virgil is full of the Greek forms of speech, which the critics call Hellenisms, as Horace in his odes abounds with them much more than Virgil. I need not mention the several dialects which Homer has made use of for this end. Milton, in conformity with the practice of the ancient poets, and with Aristotle's rule, has infused a great many Latinisms, as well as Græcisms, and sometimes Hebraisms, into the language of his poem; as toward the beginning of it:

> Nor did they not perceive the evil plight
> In which they were, or the fierce pains not feel.
> Yet to their general's voice they soon obey'd—
> ———Who shall tempt with wandering feet
> The dark unbottom'd infinite abyss,
> And through the palpable obscure find out
> His uncouth way, or spread his airy flight
> Upborne with indefatigable wings
> Over the vast abrupt?
> ———So both ascend
> In the visions of God.
>
> Book II

Under this head may be reckoned the placing the adjective after the substantive, the transposition of words, the turning the adjective into a substantive, with several other foreign modes of speech which this poet has naturalized to give his verse the greater sound, and throw it out of prose.

The third method mentioned by Aristotle, is what agrees with the genius of the Greek language more than with that of any other tongue, and is therefore more used by Homer than by any other poet. I mean the lengthening of a phrase by the addition of words, which may either be inserted or omitted, as also by extending or contracting of particular words by the insertion or omission of certain syllables. Milton has put in practice this method of raising his language, as far as the nature of our tongue will permit, as in the passage above-mentioned, eremite, for what is hermit in common discourse. If you observe the measure of his verse, he has with great judgment suppressed a syllable in several words, and shortened those of two syllables into one; by which method, beside the above-mentioned advantage, he has given a greater variety to his numbers. But this practice is more particularly remarkable in the names of persons and of countries, as Beelzebub, Hessebon, and in many other particulars, wherein he has either changed the name, or made use of that which is not the most commonly known, that he might the better deviate from the language of the vulgar.

The same reason recommended to him several old words; which also makes his poem appear the more venerable, and gives it a greater air of antiquity.

I must likewise take notice, that there are in Milton several words of his own coining, as "cerberean, miscreated, hell-doomed, embryon atoms," and many others. If the reader is offended at this liberty in our English poet, I would recommend to him a discourse in Plutarch, which shows us how frequently Homer has made use of the same liberty.

Milton, by the above-mentioned helps, and by the choice of the noblest words and phrases which our tongue would afford him, has carried our language to a greater height than any of the English poets have ever done before or after him, and made the sublimity of his style equal to that of his sentiments.

I have been the more particular in these observations on Milton's style, because it is in that part of him in which he appears the most singular. The remarks I have here made upon the practice of other poets, with my observations out of Aristotle, will perhaps alleviate the prejudice which some have taken to his poem upon this account; though after all I must confess that I think his style, though admirable in general, is in some places too much stiffened and obscured by the frequent use of those methods which Aristotle has prescribed for the raising of it.

This redundancy of those several ways of speech which Aristotle calls "foreign language," and with which Milton has so very much enriched, and in some places darkened, the language of his poem, was the more proper for his use, because his poem is written in blank verse. Rhyme, without any other assistance, throws the language off from prose, and very often makes an indifferent phrase pass unregarded; but where the verse is not built upon rhymes, there pomp of sound and energy of expression are indispensably necessary to support the style, and keep it from falling into the flatness of prose.

Those who have not a taste for this elevation of style, and are apt to ridicule a poet when he departs from the common forms of expression, would do well to see how Aristotle has treated an ancient author called Euclid, for his insipid mirth upon this occasion. Mr. Dryden used to call these sort of men his prose-critics.

I should, under this head of the language, consider Milton's numbers, in which he has made use of several elisions, which are not customary among other English poets, as may be particularly observed in his cutting off the letter Y, when it precedes a vowel. This, and some other innovations in the measure of his verse, has varied his numbers in such a manner, as makes them incapable of satiating the ear, and cloying the reader, which the same uniform measure would certainly have done, and which the perpetual returns of rhyme never fail to do in long narrative poems. I shall close these reflections upon the language of Paradise Lost with observing, that Milton has copied after Homer rather than Virgil in the length of his periods, the copiousness of his phrases, and the running of his verses into one another.

Number 315

Saturday, March 1, 1711–12

Nec Deus intersit, nisi dignus vindice nodus
Inciderit———

> Hor., *Ars. Poet.*, ver. 191
> Never presume to make a god appear,
> But for a business worthy of a god.
>
> Roscommon

Horace advises a poet to consider thoroughly the nature and force of his genius. Milton seems to have known perfectly well wherein his strength lay, and has therefore chosen a subject entirely conformable to those talents of which he was master. As his genius was wonderfully turned to the sublime, his subject was the noblest that could have entered into the thoughts of man. Everything that is truly great and astonishing has a place in it. The whole system of the intellectual world; the chaos, and the creation; heaven, earth, and hell; enter into the constitution of his poem.

Having in the first and second books represented the infernal world with all its horrors, the thread of his fable naturally leads him into the opposite regions of bliss and glory.

If Milton's majesty forsakes him anywhere, it is in those parts of his poem where the divine persons are introduced as speakers. One may, I think, observe, that the author proceeds with a kind of fear and trembling, while he describes the sentiments of the Almighty. He dares not give his imagination its full play, but chooses to confine himself to such thoughts as are drawn from the books of the most orthodox divines, and to such expressions as may be met with in Scripture, the beauties, therefore, which we are to look for in these speeches, are not of a poetical nature, nor so proper to fill the mind with sentiments of grandeur, as with thoughts of devotion. The passions which they are designed to raise, are a divine love and religious fear. The particular beauty of the speeches in the third book, consists in that shortness and perspicuity of style, in which the poet has couched the greatest mysteries of Christianity, and drawn together in a regular scheme, the whole dispensation of Providence with respect to man. He has represented all the abstruse doctrines of predestination, free-will and grace, as also the great points of the incarnation and redemption (which naturally grow up in a poem that treats of the fall of man), with great energy of expression, and in a clearer and stronger light than I ever met with in any other writer. As these points are dry in themselves to the generality of readers, the concise and clear manner in which he has treated them is very much to be admired, as is likewise that particular art which he has made use of in the interspersing of all those graces of poetry which the subject was capable of receiving.

The survey of the whole creation, and of everything that is transacted in it, is a prospect worthy of Omniscience, and as much above that in which Virgil has drawn his Jupiter, as the Christian idea of the Supreme being is more rational and sublime than that of the Heathens. The particular objects on which he is described to have cast his eye, are represented in the most beautiful and lively manner:

> "Now had th' Almighty Father from above
> (From the pure empyrean where he sits
> High thron'd above all height) bent down his eye,
> His own works and their works at once to view.
> About him all the sanctities of heaven
> Stood thick as stars, and from his sight receiv'd
> Beatitude past utt'rance. On his right
> The radiant image of his glory sat,
> His only Son. On earth he first beheld
> Our two first parents, yet the only two
> Of mankind, in the happy garden plac'd,
> Reaping immortal fruits of joy and love;
> Uninterrupted joy, unrival'd love,
> In blissful solitude. He then survey'd
> Hell and the gulf between, and Satan there
> Coasting the wall of heav'n on this side night,
> In the dull air sublime; and ready now
> To stoop with varied wings and willing feet
> On the bare outside of this world, that seem'd
> Firm land imbosom'd without firmament;
> Uncertain which, in ocean, or in air,
> Him God beholding from his prospect high,
> Wherein past, present, future, he beholds,
> Thus to his only Son foreseeing spake."

Satan's approach to the confines of the creation is finely imaged in the beginning of the speech which immediately follows. The effects of this speech in the blessed spirits, and in the divine person to whom it was addressed, cannot but fill the mind of the reader with a secret pleasure and complacency:

> "Thus while God spake, ambrosial fragrance fill'd
> All heav'n, and in the blessed spirits elect
> Sense of new joy ineffable diffus'd.
> Beyond compare the Son of God was seen
> Most glorious; in him all his Father shone
> Substantially expressed; and in his face
> Divine compassion visibly appear'd,
> Love without end, and without measure grace."

I need not point out the beauty of that circumstance wherein the whole host of angels are represented as standing mute; nor show how proper the occasion was to produce such a silence in heaven. The close of this divine colloquy, with the hymn of angels that follows upon it, are so wonderfully beautiful and poetical, that I should not forbear inserting the whole passage, if the bounds of my paper would give me leave:

> "No sooner had the Almighty ceas'd but all
> The multitude of angels with a shout!
> (Loud as from numbers without number, sweet
> As from blest voices) utt'ring joy, heav'n rung
> With jubilee, and loud hosannas fill'd
> Th' eternal regions," etc., etc.

Satan's walk upon the outside of the universe, which at a distance appeared to him of a globular form, but upon his nearer approach looked like an unbounded plain, is natural and noble; as his roaming upon the frontiers of the creation, between that mass of matter which was wrought into a world, and that shapeless, unformed heap of materials which still lay in chaos and confusion, strikes the imagination with something astonishingly great and wild. I have before spoken of the Limbo of Vanity, which the poet places upon this outermost surface of the universe, and shall here explain myself more at large on that and other parts of the poem, which are of the same shadowy nature.

Aristotle observes that the fable of an epic poem should abound in circumstances that are both credible and astonishing; or, as the French critics choose to phrase it, the fable should be filled with the probable and the marvelous. This rule is as fine and just as any in Aristotle's whole Art of Poetry.

If the fable is only probable, it differs nothing from a true history; if it is only marvelous, it is no better than a romance. The great secret, therefore, of heroic poetry, is to relate such circumstances as may produce in the reader at the same time both belief and astonishment. This is brought to pass in a well-chosen fable, by the account of such things as have really happened, or at least of such things as have happened according to the received opinions of mankind. Milton's fable is a masterpiece of this nature: as the war in heaven, the condition of the fallen angels, the state of innocence, the temptation of the serpent and the fall of man; though they are very astonishing in themselves, and are not only credible, but actual points of faith.

The next method of reconciling miracles with credibility, is by a happy invention of the poet; as in particular, when he introduces agents of a superior nature, who are capable of effecting what is wonderful, and what is not to be met with in the ordinary course of things. Ulysses' ship being turned into a rock, and Æneas's fleet into a shoal of water-nymphs, though they are very surprising accidents, are nevertheless probable when we are told, that they were the gods who thus transformed them. It is this kind of machinery which fills the poems both of Homer and Virgil with such circumstances as are wonderful but not impossible, and so frequently produce in the reader the most pleasing passion that can rise in the mind of man, which is admiration. If there be any instance in the Æneid liable to exception upon this account, it is in the beginning of the third book, where Æneas is represented as tearing up the myrtle that dropped blood. To qualify this wonderful circumstance, Polydorus tells a story from the root of the myrtle, that the barbarous inhabitants of the country having pierced him with spears and arrows, the wood which was left in his body took root in his wounds, and gave birth to that bleeding tree. This circumstance seems to have the marvelous without the probable, because it is represented as proceeding from natural causes, without the interposition of any god, or other supernatural power capable of producing it. The spears and arrows grow of themselves without so much as the modern help of enchantment. If we look into the fiction of Milton's fable, though we find it full of surprising incidents, they are generally suited to our notions of the things and persons described, and tempered with a due measure of probability. I must only make an exception to the Limbo of Vanity, with his Episode of Sin and Death, and some of the imaginary persons in his chaos. These passages are astonishing, but not credible; the reader cannot so far impose upon himself as to see a possibility in them; they are the description of dreams and shadows, not of things or persons. I know that many critics look upon the stories of Circe, Polypheme, the Sirens, nay the whole Odyssey and Iliad, to be allegories: but allowing this to be true, they are fables, which, considering the opinions of mankind that prevailed in the age of the poet, might possibly have been according to the letter. The persons are such as might have acted what is ascribed to them, as the circumstances in which they are represented might possibly have been truths and realities. This appearance of probability is so absolutely requisite in the greater kinds of poetry, that Aristotle observes the ancient tragic writers made use of the names of such great men as had actually lived in the world, though the tragedy proceeded upon adventures they were never engaged in, on purpose to make the subject more credible. In a word, beside the hidden meaning of an epic allegory, the plain, literal sense ought to appear probable. The story should be such as an ordinary reader may acquiesce in, whatever natural, moral, or political truth may be discovered in it by men of greater penetration.

Satan, after having long wandered upon the surface or outmost wall of the universe, discovers at last a wide gap in it, which led into the creation, and is described as the opening through which the angels pass to and fro into the lower world, upon their errands to mankind. His sitting upon the brink of this passage, and taking a survey of the whole face of nature that appeared to him new and fresh in all its beauties, with the simile illustrating the circumstances, fills the mind of the reader with as surprising and glorious an idea as any that arises in the whole poem. He looks down into that vast hollow of the universe with the eye, or (as Milton calls it in his first book) with the ken of an angel. He surveys all the wonders in the immense amphitheater that lies between both the poles of heaven, and takes in at one view the whole round of the creation.

His flight between the several worlds that shone on every side of him, with the particular description of the sun, are set forth in all the wantonness of a luxuriant imagination. His shape, speech, and behavior upon his transforming himself into an angel of light, are touched with exquisite beauty. The poet's thoughts of directing Satan to the sun, which, in the vulgar opinion of mankind, is the most conspicuous part of the creation, and the placing in it an angel, is a circumstance very finely contrived, and the more adjusted to a poetical probability, as it was a received doctrine among the most famous philosophers, that every orb had its intelligence; and as an apostle in sacred writ is said to have seen such an angel in the sun. In the answer which this angel returns to the disguised evil spirit, there is such a becoming majesty as is altogether suitable to a superior being. The part of it in which he represents himself as present at the creation, is very noble in itself, and not only proper where it is introduced, but requisite to prepare the reader for what follows in the seventh book:

> "I saw when at his word the formless mass,
> This world's material mould, came to a heap:
> Confusion heard his voice, and wild Uproar
> Stood rul'd, stood vast infinitude confin'd,
> Till at his second bidding Darkness fled,
> Light shone," etc.

In the following part of the speech he points out the earth with such circumstances, that the reader can scarce forbear fancying himself employed on the same distant view of it:

> "Look downward on that globe, whose hither side
> With light from hence, though but reflected shines:
> That place is earth, the seat of man, that light
> His day," etc.

I must not conclude my reflections upon this third book of Paradise Lost, without taking notice of that celebrated complaint of Milton with which it opens, and which certainly deserves all the praises that have been given it; though, as I have before hinted, it may rather be looked upon as an excrescence, than as an essential part of the poem. The same observation might be applied to that beautiful digression upon hypocrisy in the same book.

Number 321

Saturday, March 8, 1711–12

Nec satis est pulchra esse poemata, dulcia sunto.
                              Hor., *Ars. Poet.*, ver. 99
'Tis not enough a poem's finely writ:
It must affect and captivate the soul.

Those who know how many volumes have been written on the poems of
Homer and Virgil will easily pardon the length of my discourse upon Milton.
The Paradise Lost, is looked upon, by the best judges, as the greatest
production, or at least the noblest work of genius, in our language, and
therefore deserves to be set before an English reader in its full beauty. For
this reason, though I have endeavored to give a general idea of its graces and
imperfections in my first six papers, I thought myself obliged to bestow one
upon every book in particular. The first three books I have already dispatched,
and am now entering upon the fourth. I need not acquaint my reader that there
are multitudes of beauties in this great author, especially in the descriptive
parts of this poem, which I have not touched upon; it being my intention to
point out those only which appear to be the most exquisite, or those which are
not so obvious to ordinary readers. Every one that has read the critics who have
written upon the Odyssey, the Iliad, and the Æneid, knows very well, that
though they agree in their opinions of the great beauties in those poems, they
have, nevertheless, each of them discovered several master-strokes, which
have escaped the observation of the rest. In the same manner, I question not
but any writer who shall treat of this subject after me, may find several
beauties in Milton, which I have not taken notice of. I must likewise observe,
that as the greatest masters of critical learning differ among one another, as to
some particular points in an epic poem, I have not bound myself scrupulously
to the rules which any of them have laid down upon that art, but have taken
the liberty sometimes to join with one, and sometimes with another, and
sometimes to differ from all of them, when I have thought that the reason of
the thing was on my side.

We may conclude the beauties of the fourth book under three heads. In
the first are those pictures of still-life, which we meet with in the description
of Eden, Paradise, Adam's Bower, etc. In the next are the machines, which
comprehend the speeches and behavior of the good and bad angels. In the last
is the conduct of Adam and Eve, who are the principal actors in the poem.

In the description of Paradise, the poet has observed Aristotle's rule of
lavishing all the ornaments of diction on the weak inactive parts of the fable
which are not supported by the beauty of sentiments and characters. Accordingly the reader may observe, that the expressions are more florid and
elaborate in these descriptions, than in most other parts of the poem. I must
further add, that though the drawings of gardens, rivers, rainbows, and the like
dead pieces of nature, are justly censured in an heroic poem, when they run

out into an unnecessary length—the description of Paradise would have been faulty, had not the poet been very particular in it, not only as it is the scene of the principal action, but as it is requisite to give us an idea of that happiness from which our first parents fell. The plan of it is wonderfully beautiful, and formed upon the short sketch which we have of it in holy writ. Milton's exuberance of imagination has poured forth such a redundancy of ornaments on this seat of happiness and innocence, that it would be endless to point out each particular.

I must not quit this head without further observing, that there is scarce a speech of Adam or Eve in the whole poem, wherein the sentiments and allusions are not taken from this their delightful habitation. The reader, during their whole course of action, always finds himself in the walks of Paradise. In short, as the critics have remarked, that in those poems wherein shepherds are the actors, the thoughts ought always to take a tincture from the woods, fields, and rivers; so we may observe, that our first parents seldom lose sight of their happy station in anything they speak or do: and if the reader will give me leave to use the expression, that their thoughts are always "paradisaical."

We are in the next place to consider the machines of the fourth book. Satan being now within prospect of Eden, and looking round upon the glories of the creation, is filled with sentiments different from those which he discovered while he was in hell. The place inspires him with thoughts more adapted to it. He reflects upon the happy condition from whence he fell, and breaks forth into a speech that is softened with several transient touches of remorse and self-accusation: but at length he confirms himself in impenitence; and in his design of drawing man into his own state of guilt and misery. This conflict of passions is raised with a great deal of art, as the opening of his speech to the sun is very bold and noble:

> "O thou that, with surprising glory crown'd,
> Look'st from thy sole dominion like the god
> Of this new world; at whose sight all the stars
> Hide their diminished heads; to thee I call,
> But with no friendly voice; and add thy name,
> O Sun! to tell thee how I hate thy beams,
> That bring to my remembrance from what state
> I fell, how glorious once above thy sphere."

This speech is, I think, the finest that is ascribed to Satan, in the whole poem. The evil spirit afterward proceeds to make his discoveries concerning our first parents, and to learn after what manner they may be best attacked. His bounding over the walls of Paradise; his sitting in the shape of a cormorant upon the tree of life, which stood in the center of it, and overtopped all the other trees of the garden; his alighting among the herd of animals, which are so beautifully represented as playing about Adam and Eve, together with his transforming himself into different shapes, in order to hear their conversation; are circumstances that give an agreeable surprise to the reader, and are

devised with great art, to connect that series of adventures in which the poet
has engaged this artificer of fraud.

The thought of Satan's transformation into a cormorant, and placing
himself on the tree of life, seems raised upon that passage in the Iliad, where
two deities are described as perching on the top of an oak in the shape of
vultures.

His planting himself at the ear of Eve under the form of a toad, in order to
produce vain dreams and imaginations, is a circumstance of the same nature:
as his starting up in his own form is wonderfully fine, both in the literal
description, and in the moral which is concealed under it. His answer upon
being discovered, and demanded to give an account of himself, is conformable
to the pride and intrepidity of his character:

> "Know ye not, then," said Satan, fill'd with scorn,
> "Know ye not me! Ye knew me once no mate
> For you, there sitting where you durst not soar;
> Not to know me argues yourself unknown,
> The lowest of your throng"

Zephon's rebuke, with the influence it had on Satan, is exquisitely
graceful and moral. Satan is afterward led away to Gabriel, the chief of the
guardian angels, who kept watch in Paradise. His disdainful behavior on this
occasion is so remarkable a beauty, that the most ordinary reader cannot but
take notice of it. Gabriel's discovering his approach at a distance, is drawn with
great strength and liveliness of imagination:

> "O friends, I hear the tread of nimble feet
> Hasting this way, and now by glimpse discern
> Ithuriel and Zephon through the shade,
> And with them comes a third of regal port
> But faded splendor wan; who by his gait
> And fierce demeanor seems the prince of hell;
> Not likely to part hence without contest;
> Stand firm, for in his look defiance low'rs."

The conference between Gabriel and Satan abounds with sentiments
proper for the occasion, and suitable to the persons of the two speakers. Satan
clothing himself with terror when he prepares for the combat is truly sublime,
and at least equal to Homer's description of Discord, celebrated by Longinus,
or to that of Fame in Virgil, who are both represented with their feet standing
upon the earth, and their heads reaching above the clouds:

> While thus he spake, th' angelic squadron bright
> Turn'd fiery red, sharp'ning in mooned horns
> Their phalanx, and began to hem him around
> With ported spears, etc.
> ———On the other side Satan alarm'd,
> Collecting all his might, dilated stood

> Like Teneriffe or Atlas unremoved.
> His stature reach'd the sky, and on his crest
> Sat Horror plum'd.

I must here take notice, that Milton is everywhere full of hints, and sometimes literal translations, taken from the greatest of the Greek and Latin poets. But this I may reserve for a discourse by itself, because I would not break the thread of these speculations, that are designed for English readers, with such reflections as would be of no use but to the learned.

I must, however, observe in this place, that the breaking off of the combat between Gabriel and Satan, by the hanging out of the golden scales in heaven, is a refinement upon Homer's thought, who tells us, that before the battle between Hector and Achilles, Jupiter weighed the event of it in a pair of scales. The reader may see the whole passage in the 22d Iliad.

Virgil, before the last decisive combat, describes Jupiter in the same manner, as weighing the fates of Turnus and Æneas. Milton, though he fetched this beautiful circumstance from the Iliad and Æneid, does not only insert it as a poetical embellishment, like the authors above-mentioned, but makes an artful use of it for the proper carrying on of his fable, and for the breaking off the combat between the two warriors, who were upon the point of engaging. To this we may further add, that Milton is the more justified in this passage, as we find the same noble allegory in holy writ, where a wicked prince, some few hours before he was assaulted and slain, is said to have been "weighed in the scales, and to have been found wanting."

I must here take notice, under the head of the machines, that Uriel's gliding down to the earth upon a sunbeam, with the poet's device to make him descend, as well in his return to the sun as in his coming from it, is a prettiness that might have been admired in a little fanciful poet, but seems below the genius of Milton. The description of the host of armed angels walking their nightly round in Paradise is of another spirit:

> So saying, on he led his radiant files,
> Dazzling the moon;

as that account of the hymns which our first parents used to hear them sing in these their midnight walks is altogether divine, and inexpressibly amusing to the imagination.

We are, in the last place, to consider the part which Adam and Eve act in the fourth book. The description of them as they first appeared to Satan, is exquisitely drawn, and sufficient to make the fallen angel gaze upon them with all that astonishment, and those emotions of envy, in which he is represented:

> Two of far nobler shape, erect and tall,
> Godlike erect, with native honor clad
> In naked majesty, seem'd lords of all;
> And worthy seem'd; for in their looks divine
> The image of their glorious Maker shone,
> Truth, wisdom, sanctitude severe and pure;

> Severe, but in true filial freedom plac'd;
> For contemplation he and valor form'd,
> For softness she and sweet attractive grace,
> He for God only, she for God in him.
> His fair large front, and eye sublime, declared
> Absolute rule: and hyacinthian locks
> Round from his parted forelock manly hung
> Clust'ring, but not beneath his shoulders broad.
> She, as a vail, down to her slender waist
> Her unadorned golden tresses wore.
> Dishevel'd, but in wanton ringlets wav'd.
> So pass'd they naked on, nor shunn'd the sight
> Of God or angel, for they thought no ill:
> So hand in hand they pass'd, the loveliest pair
> That ever since in love's embraces met.

There is a fine spirit of poetry in the lines which follow, wherein they are described as sitting on a bed of flowers by the side of a fountain, amidst a mixed assembly of animals.

The speeches of these two first lovers flow equally from passion and sincerity. The professions they make to one another are full of warmth; but at the same time founded on truth. In a word, they are the gallantries of Paradise:

> ——When Adam, first of men
> "Sole partner and sole part of all these joys,
> Dearer thyself than all;
> But let us ever praise Him, and extol
> His bounty, following our delightful task,
> To prune these growing plants, and tend these flow'rs,
> Which were it toilsome, yet with thee were sweet."
> To whom thus Eve replied: "O thou for whom,
> And from whom, I was form'd, flesh of thy flesh,
> And without whom am to no end, my guide
> And head, what thou hast said is just and right.
> For we to Him indeed all praises owe,
> And daily thanks: I chiefly, who enjoy
> So far the happier lot, enjoying thee
> Pre-eminent by so much odds, while thou
> Like consort to thyself canst nowhere find," etc.

The remaining part of Eve's speech, in which she gives an account of herself upon her first creation, and the manner in which she was brought to Adam, is, I think, as beautiful a passage as any in Milton, or perhaps in any other poet whatsoever. These passages are all worked off with so much art, that they are capable of pleasing the most delicate reader without offending the most severe.

"That day I oft remember, when from sleep," etc.

A poet of less judgment and invention than this great author, would have found it very difficult to have filled these tender parts of the poem with sentiments proper for a state of innocence; to have described the warmth of love, and the professions of it, without artifice or hyperbole; to have made the man speak the most endearing things without descending from his natural dignity, and the woman receiving them without departing from the modesty of her character: in a word, to adjust the prerogatives of wisdom and beauty, and make each appear to the other in its proper force and loveliness. This mutual subordination of the two sexes is wonderfully kept up in the whole poem, as particularly in the speech of Eve I have before mentioned, and upon the conclusion of it in the following lines:

> So spake our general mother, and with eyes
> Of conjugal attraction unreprov'd,
> And meek surrender, half-embracing lean'd
> On our first father; half her swelling breast
> Naked met his under the flowing gold
> Of her loose tresses hid; he in delight
> Both of her beauty and submissive charms
> Smil'd with superior love.

The poet adds, that the devil turned away with envy at the sight of so much happiness.

We have another view of our first parents in their evening discourses, which is full of pleasing images and sentiments suitable to their condition and characters. The speech of Eve in particular, is dressed up in such a soft and natural turn of words and sentiments, as cannot be sufficiently admired.

I shall close my reflections upon this book with observing the masterly transition which the poet makes to their evening worship in the following lines:

> Thus at their shady lodge arriv'd, both stood,
> Both turned, and under open sky ador'd
> The God that made both sky, air, earth, and heav'n,
> Which they beheld, the moon's resplendent globe,
> And starry pole: "Thou also mad'st the night,
> Maker omnipotent, and thou the day," etc.

Most of the modern heroic poets have imitated the ancients, in beginning a speech without premising that the person said thus or thus; but as it is easy to imitate the ancients in the omission of two or three words, it requires judgment to do it in such a manner as they shall not be missed, and that the speech may begin naturally without them. There is a fine instance of this kind out of Homer, in the twenty-third chapter of Longinus.

Number 339

Saturday, March 29, 1712

————*Ut his exordia primis*
Omnia, et ipse tener mundi concreverit orbis.
Tum durare solum et discludere Nerea ponto
Cœperit, et rerum paullatim sumere formas.

VIRG., *Ecl.* vi, 33

He sung the secret seeds of nature's frame,
How seas, and earth, and air, and active flame,
Fell through the mighty void, and in their fall,
Were blindly gather'd in this goodly ball.
The tender soil then stiff'ning by degrees,
Shut from the bounded earth the bounding seas;
The earth and ocean various forms disclose,
And a new sun to the new world arose.

DRYDEN

Longinus has observed, that there may be a loftiness in sentiments where there is no passion, and brings instances out of ancient authors to support this his opinion. The pathetic, as that great critic observes, may animate and inflame the sublime, but is not essential to it. Accordingly, as he further remarks, we very often find that those who excel most in stirring up the passions very often want the talent of writing in the great and sublime manner, and so on the contrary. Milton has shown himself a master in both these ways of writing. The seventh book, which we are now entering upon, is an instance of that sublime which is not mixed and worked up with passion. The author appears in a kind of composed and sedate majesty; and though the sentiments do not give so great an emotion as those in the former book, they abound with as magnificent ideas. The sixth book, like a troubled ocean, represents greatness in confusion; the seventh affects the imagination like the ocean in a calm, and fills the mind of the reader, without producing in it anything like tumult or agitation.

The critic above-mentioned, among the rules which he lays down for succeeding in the sublime way of writing, proposes to his reader, that he should imitate the most celebrated authors who have gone before him, and have been engaged in works of the same nature; as in particular that, if he writes on a poetical subject, he should consider how Homer would have spoken on such an occasion. By this means one great genius often catches the flame from another, and writes in his spirit, without copying servilely after him. There are a thousand shining passages in Virgil, which have been lighted up by Homer.

Milton, though his own natural strength of genius was capable of furnishing out a perfect work, has doubtless very much raised and ennobled his conceptions by such an imitation as that which Longinus has recommended.

In this book, which gives us an account of the six days' works, the poet received but very few assistances from heathen writers, who are strangers to the wonders of creation. But as there are many glorious strokes of poetry upon this subject in holy writ, the author has numberless allusions to them through the whole course of this book. The great critic I have before mentioned, though a heathen, has taken notice of the sublime manner in which the lawgiver of the Jews has described the creation in the first chapter of Genesis; and there are many other passages in Scripture which rise up to the same majesty, where the subject is touched upon. Milton has shown his judgment very remarkably, in making use of such of these as were proper for his poem, and in duly qualifying those strains of eastern poetry which were suited to readers whose imaginations were set to a higher pitch than those of colder climates.

Adam's speech to the angel, wherein he desires an account of what had passed within the regions of nature before the creation, is very great and solemn. The following lines, in which he tells him, that the day is not too far spent for him to enter upon such a subject, are exquisite in their kind:

> And the great light of day yet wants to run
> Much of his race, though steep; suspense in heav'n
> Held by thy voice, thy potent voice he hears,
> And longer will delay to hear thee tell
> His generation, etc.

The angel's encouraging our first parents in a modest pursuit after knowledge, with the causes which he assigns for the creation of the world, are very just and beautiful. The Messiah, by whom, as we are told in Scripture, the heavens were made, goes forth in the power of his Father, surrounded with a host of angels, and clothed with such a majesty as becomes his entering upon a work which, according to our conceptions, appears the utmost exertion of Omnipotence. What a beautiful description has our author raised upon that hint in one of the prophets! "And behold there came four chariots out from between two mountains, and the mountains were mountains of brass:"

> About his chariot numberless were pour'd
> Cherub and seraph, potentates and thrones,
> And virtues, winged spirits, and chariots wing'd
> From the armory of God, where stand of old
> Myriads between two brazen mountains lodg'd
> Against a solemn day, harness'd at hand,
> Celestial equipage! and now came forth
> Spontaneous, for within them spirit liv'd,
> Attendant on the Lord: Heav'n open'd wide
> Her ever-during gates, harmonious sound!
> On golden hinges moving

I have before taken notice of these chariots of God, and of these gates of heaven; and shall here only add, that Homer gives us the same idea of the latter, as opening of themselves; though he afterward takes off from it, by telling us that the hours first of all removed those prodigious heaps of clouds which lay as a barrier before them.

I do not know anything in the whole poem more sublime than the description which follows, where the Messiah is represented at the head of his angels, as looking down into the chaos, calming its confusion, riding into the midst of it, and drawing the first outline of the creation:

> On heav'nly ground they stood, and from the shore
> They view'd the vast immeasureable abyss
> Outrageous as a sea, dark, wasteful, wild,
> Up from the bottom turn'd by furious winds
> And surging waves, as mountains to assault
> Heav'n's height, and with the center mix the pole.
> "Silence, ye troubled waves; and thou, deep, peace!"
> Said then th' omnific Word, "Your discord end!"
> Nor staid, but on the wings of cherubim
> Up-lifted, in paternal glory rode
> Far into Chaos,and the world unborn;
> For Chaos heard his voice. Him all his train
> Follow'd in bright procession, to behold
> Creation, and the wonders of his might.
> Then stay'd the fervid wheels; and in his hand
> He took the golden compasses, prepar'd,
> In God's eternal store to circumscribe
> This universe and all created things:
> One foot he centered, and the other turn'd
> Round through the vast profundity obscure,
> And said, "Thus far extend, thus far thy bounds,
> This be thy just circumference, O world!"

The thought of the golden compasses is conceived altogether in Homer's spirit, and is a very noble incident in this wonderful description. Homer, when he speaks of the gods, ascribes to them several arms and instruments with the same greatness of imagination. Let the reader only peruse the description of Minerva's ægis or buckler, in the fifth book of the Iliad, with her spear, which would overturn whole squadrons, and her helmet that was sufficient to cover an army drawn out of a hundred cities. The golden compasses, in the above-mentioned passage, appear a very natural instrument in the hand of him whom Plato somewhere calls the Divine Geometrician. As poetry delights in clothing abstracted ideas in allegories and sensible images, we find a magnificent description of the creation formed after the same manner in one of the prophets, wherein he describes the Almighty Architect as measuring the waters in the hollow of his hand, meting out the heavens with his span, comprehending the dust of the earth in a measure, weighing the mountains in scales, and the hills in a balance. Another of them describing the Supreme

Being in this great work of creation, represents him as laying the foundations of the earth, and stretching a line upon it; and, in another place, as garnishing the heavens, stretching out the north over the empty place, and hanging the earth upon nothing. This last noble thought Milton has expressed in the following verse:

> And earth self-balanc'd on her center hung.

The beauties of description in this book lie so very thick, that it is impossible to enumerate them in this paper. The poet has employed on them the whole energy of our tongue. The several great scenes of the creation rise up to view one after another, in such a manner, that the reader seems present at this wonderful work, and to assist among the choirs of angels who are the spectators of it. How glorious is the conclusion of the first day!

> ——Thus was the first day ev'n and morn:
> Nor past uncelebrated, nor unsung,
> By the celestial choirs, when orient light
> Exhaling first from darkness they beheld;
> Birth-day of heav'n and earth! with joy and shout
> The hollow universal orb they fill'd.

We have the same elevation of thought in the third day, when the mountains were brought forth and the deep was made:

> Immediately the mountains huge appear
> Emergent, and their broad bare backs upheave
> Into the clouds, their tops ascend the sky:
> So high as heav'n the tumid hills, so low
> Down sunk a hollow bottom broad and deep,
> Capacious bed of waters

We have also the rising of the whole vegetable world described in this day's work, which is filled with all the graces that other poets have lavished on their description of the spring, and leads the reader's imagination into a theater equally surprising and beautiful.

The several glories of the heavens make their appearance on the fourth day:

> First in his east the glorious lamp was seen,
> Regent of day, and all the horizon round
> Invested with bright rays, jocund to run
> His longitude through heaven's high road; the gray
> Dawn, and the Pleiades before him danc'd,
> Shedding sweet infuence. Less bright the moon,
> But opposite in level'd west was set
> His mirror, with full face borrowing her light
> From him, for other lights she needed none

> In that aspect, and still that distance keeps
> Till night; then in the east her turn she shines,
> Revolv'd on heaven's great axle, and her reign
> With thousand lesser lights dividual holds,
> With thousand thousand stars, that then appear'd
> Spangling the hemisphere

One would wonder how the poet could be so concise in his description of the six days' works, as to comprehend them within the bounds of an episode, and at the same time, so particular, as to give us a lively idea of them. This is still more remarkable in his account of the fifth and sixth days, in which he has drawn out to our view the whole animal creation, from the reptile to the behemoth. As the lion and the leviathan are two of the noblest productions in the world of living creatures, the reader will find a most exquisite spirit of poetry in the account which our author gives us of them. The sixth day concludes with the formation of man, upon which the angel takes occasion, as he did after the battle in heaven, to remind Adam of his obedience, which was the principal design of this his visit.

The poet afterward represents the Messiah returning into heaven, and taking a survey of his great work. There is something inexpressibly sublime in this part of the poem, where the author describes that great period of time, filled with so many glorious circumstances; when the heavens and earth were finished; when the Messiah ascended up in triumph through the everlasting gates; when he looked down with pleasure upon his new creation; when every part of nature seemed to rejoice in its existence, when the morning-stars sang together, and all the sons of God shouted for joy.

> So ev'n and morn accomplish'd the sixth day:
> Yet not till the Creator from his work
> Desisting, though unwearied, up return'd.
> Up to the heaven of heavens, his high abode;
> Thence to behold his new created world
> Th' addition of his empire, how it show'd
> In prospect from his throne, how good, how fair,
> Answering his great idea. Up he rode,
> Follow'd with acclamation and the sound
> Symphonious of ten thousand harps, that tun'd
> Angelic harmonies: the earth, the air
> Resounded (thou rememberest, for thou heard'st)
> The heavens and all the constellations rung,
> The planets in their station list'ning stood,
> While the bright pomp ascended jubilant.
> "Open, ye everlasting gates!" they sung,
> "Open, ye heavens, your living doors! let in
> The great Creator from his work return'd
> Magnificent, his six days' work—a world."

I cannot conclude this book upon the creation, without mentioning a poem which has lately appeared under that title. [Creation, a philosophical poem; demonstrating the existence and providence of God. In seven books. By Sir Richard Blackmore, Knt. M.D., and fellow of the college of physicians in London.] The work was undertaken with so good an intention, and is executed with so great a mastery, that it deserves to be looked upon as one of the most useful and noble productions in our English verse. The reader cannot but be pleased to find the depths of philosophy enlivened with all the charms of poetry, and to see so great a strength of reason amid so beautiful a redundancy of the imagination. The author has shown us that design in all the works of nature which necessarily leads us to the knowledge of the first cause. In short, he has illustrated, by numberless and incontestable instances, that divine wisdom which the son of Sirach has so nobly ascribed to the Supreme Being in his formation of the world, when he tells us, that "He created her, he saw her, and numbered her, and poured her out upon all his works."—L.

Number 409

Thursday, June 19, 1712

Musæo contingere cuncta lepore.

LUCR. i, 933

To grace each subject with enliv'ning wit.

Gratian very often recommends fine taste as the utmost perfection of an accomplished man.

As this word arises very often in conversation, I shall endeavor to give some account of it, and to lay down rules how we may know whether we are possessed of it, and how we may acquire that fine taste of writing which is so much talked of among the polite world.

Most languages make use of this metaphor to express that faculty of the mind which distinguishes all the most concealed faults and nicest perfections in writing. We may be sure this metaphor would not have been so general in all tongues, had there not been a very great conformity between that mental taste, which is the subject of this paper, and that sensitive taste, which gives us a relish of every different flavor that affects the palate. Accordingly we find there are as many degrees of refinement in the intellectual faculty as in the sense which is marked out by this common denomination.

I knew a person who possessed the one in so great a perfection, that, after having tasted ten different kinds of tea, he would distinguish, without seeing the color of it, the particular sort which was offered him; and not only so, but any two sorts of them that were mixed together in an equal proportion; nay, he has carried the experiment so far, as, upon tasting the composition of three different sorts, to name the parcels from whence the three several ingredients were taken. A man of a fine taste in writing will discern, after the same manner, not only the general beauties and imperfections of an author, but discover the several ways of thinking and expressing himself, which diversify him from all other authors, with the several foreign infusions of thought and language, and the particular authors from whom they were borrowed.

After having thus far explained what is generally meant by a fine taste in writing, and shown the propriety of the metaphor which is used on this occasion, I think I may define it to be "that faculty of the soul, which discerns the beauties of an author with pleasure, and the imperfections with dislike." If a man would know whether he is possessed of this faculty, I would have him read over the celebrated works of antiquity, which have stood the test of so many different ages and countries, or those works among the moderns which have the sanction of the politer part of our cotemporaries. If, upon the perusal of such writings, he does not find himself delighted in an extraordinary manner, or if, upon reading the admired passages in such authors, he finds a coldness and indifference in his thoughts, he ought to conclude, not (as is too usual among tasteless readers) that the author wants those perfections which have been admired in him, but that he himself wants the faculty of discovering them.

He should, in the second place, be very careful to observe, whether he tastes the distinguishing perfections, or, if I may be allowed to call them so, the specific qualities of the author whom he peruses; whether he is particularly pleased with Livy for his manner of telling a story, with Sallust for his entering into those internal principles of action which arise from the characters and manners of the persons he describes, or with Tacitus for displaying those outward motives of safety and interest which gave birth to the whole series of transactions which he relates.

He may likewise consider how differently he is affected by the same thought which presents itself in a great writer, from what he is when he finds it delivered by a person of an ordinary genius; for there is as much difference in apprehending a thought clothed in Cicero's language, and that of a common author, as in seeing an object by the light of a taper, or by the light of the sun.

It is very difficult to lay down rules for the acquirement of such a taste as that I am here speaking of. The faculty must, in some degree, be born with us; and it very often happens, that those who have other qualities in perfection, are wholly void of this. One of the most eminent mathematicians of the age has assured me, that the greatest pleasure he took in reading Virgil was in examining Æneas's voyage by the map; as I question not but many a modern compiler of history would be delighted with little more in that divine author than the bare matter of fact.

But, notwithstanding this faculty must in some measure be born with us, there are several methods for cultivating and improving it, and without which it will be very uncertain, and of little use to the person that possesses it. The most natural method for this purpose is to be conversant among the writings of the most polite authors. A man who has any relish for fine writing, either discovers new beauties, or receives stronger impressions, from the masterly strokes of a great author, every time he peruses him; beside that he naturally wears himself into the same manner of speaking and thinking.

Conversation with men of a polite genius is another method for improving our natural taste. It is impossible for a man of the greatest parts to consider anything in its whole extent, and in all its variety of lights. Every man, beside those general observations which are to be made upon an author, forms several reflections that are peculiar to his own manner of thinking; so that conversation will naturally furnish us with hints which we did not attend to, and make us enjoy other men's parts and reflections as well as our own. This is the best reason I can give for the observation which several have made, that men of great genius in the same way of writing seldom rise up singly, but at certain periods of time appear together, and in a body; as they did at Rome in the reign of Augustus, and in Greece about the age of Socrates. I cannot think that Corneille, Racine, Moliere, Boileau, La Fontaine, Bruyere, Bossu, or the Daciers, would have written so well as they have done, had they not been friends and cotemporaries.

It is likewise necessary for a man who would form to himself a finished taste of good writing, to be well versed in the works of the best critics, both ancient and modern. I must confess that I could wish there were authors of this kind, who, beside the mechanical rules, which a man of very little taste may discourse upon, would enter into the very spirit and soul of fine writing, and show us the several sources of that pleasure which rises in the mind upon the perusal of a noble work. Thus, although in poetry it be absolutely necessary that the unities of time, place, and action, with other points of the same nature, should be thoroughly explained and understood, there is still something more essential to the art, something that elevates and astonishes the fancy, and gives a greatness of mind to the reader, which few of the critics beside Longinus have considered.

Our general taste in England is for epigram, turns of wit, and forced conceits, which have no manner of influence either for the bettering or enlarging the mind of him who reads them, and have been carefully avoided by the greatest writers both among the ancients and moderns. I have endeavored, in several of my speculations, to banish this Gothic taste which has taken possession among us. I entertained the town for a week together with an essay upon wit, in which I endeavored to detect several of those false kinds which have been admired in the different ages of the world, and at the same time to show wherein the nature of true wit consists. I afterward gave an instance of the great force which lies in a natural simplicity of thought to affect the mind of the reader from such vulgar pieces as have little else beside this single qualification to recommend them. I have likewise examined the works of the greatest poet which our nation, or perhaps any other, has produced, and particularized most of those rational and manly beauties which give a value to that divine work. I shall next Saturday enter upon an essay on "The Pleasures of the Imagination," which, though it shall consider that subject at large, will perhaps suggest to the reader what it is that gives a beauty to many passages of the finest writers both in prose and verse. As an undertaking of this nature is entirely new, I question not but it will be received with candor.

Number 592

Friday, September 10, 1714

Studium sine divite vena.
Hor., *Ars Poet.* ver. 409
Art without a vein.
                                    Roscommon.

I look upon the playhouse as a world within itself. They have lately furnished the middle region of it with a new set of meteors, in order to give the sublime to many modern tragedies. I was there last winter at the first rehearsal of the new thunder, which is much more deep and sonorous than any hitherto made use of. They have a Salmoneus behind the scenes who plays it off with great success. Their lightnings are made to flash more briskly than heretofore; their clouds are also better furbelowed, and more voluminous; not to mention a violent storm locked up in a great chest, that is designed for the Tempest. They are also provided with above a dozen showers of snow, which, as I am informed, are the plays of many unsuccessful poets artificially cut and shredded for that use. Mr. Rymer's Edgar is to fall in snow at the next acting of *King Lear,* in order to heighten, or rather to alleviate, the distress of that unfortunate prince; and to serve by way of decoration to a piece which that great critic has written against.

I do not indeed wonder that the actors should be such professed enemies to those among our nation who are commonly known by the name of critics, since it is a rule among these gentlemen to fall upon a play, not because it is ill written, but because it takes. Several of them lay it down as a maxim, that whatever dramatic performance has a long run, must of necessity be good for nothing; as though the first precept in poetry were "not to please." Whether this rule holds good or not, I shall leave to the determination of those who are better judges than myself; if it does, I am sure it tends very much to the honor of those gentlemen who have established it; few of their pieces having been disgraced by a run of three days, and most of them being so exquisitely written, that the town would never give them more than one night's hearing.

I have a great esteem for a true critic, such as Aristotle and Longinus among the Greeks; Horace and Quintilian among the Romans; Boileau and Dacier among the French. But it is our misfortune that some, who set up for professed critics among us, are so stupid, that they do not know how to put ten words together with elegance or common propriety; and withal so illiterate, that they have no taste of the learned languages, and therefore criticise upon old authors only at second-hand. They judge of them by what others have written, and not by any notions they have of the authors themselves. The words unity, action, sentiment, and diction pronounced with an air of authority, give them a figure among unlearned readers, who are apt to believe they are very deep because they are unintelligible. The ancient critics are full of the praises of their cotemporaries; they discover beauties which escaped the observation of the vulgar, and very often find out reasons for palliating and excusing such little slips and oversights as were committed in the writings of eminent authors. On the contrary, most of the smatterers in criticism, who appear among us, make it their business to vilify and depreciate every new production that gains applause, to decry imaginary blemishes, and to prove, by far-fetched arguments, that what pass for beauties in any celebrated piece are faults and errors. In short, the writings of these critics, compared with those of the ancients, are like the works of the sophists compared with those of the old philosophers.

Envy and cavil are the natural fruits of laziness and ignorance; which was probably the reason, that in the heathen mythology, Momus is said to be the son of Nox and Somnus, of darkness and sleep. Idle men, who have not been at the pains to accomplish or distinguish themselves, are very apt to detract from others; as ignorant men are very subject to decry those beauties in a celebrated work which they have not eyes to discover. Many of our sons of Momus, who dignify themselves by the name of critics, are the genuine descendants of these two illustrious ancestors. They are often led into those numerous absurdities in which they daily instruct the people, by not considering that, first, there is sometimes a greater judgment shown in deviating from the rules of art than in adhering to them; and, secondly, that there is more beauty in the works of a great genius, who is ignorant of all the rules of art, than in the works of a little genius, who not only knows but scrupulously observes them.

First, We may often take notice of men who are perfectly acquainted with all the rules of good writing, and notwithstanding choose to depart from them on extraordinary occasions. I could give instances out of all the tragic writers of antiquity who have shown their judgment in this particular; and purposedly receded from an established rule of the drama, when it has made way for a much higher beauty than the observation of such a rule would have been. Those who have surveyed the noblest pieces of architecture and statuary, both ancient and modern, know very well that there are frequent deviations from art in the works of the greatest masters, which have produced a much nobler effect than a more accurate and exact way of proceeding could have done. This often arises from what the Italians call the *gusta grande* in these arts, which is what we call the sublime in writing.

In the next place, our critics do not seem sensible that there is more beauty in the works of a great genius, who is ignorant of the rules of art, than in those of a little genius, who knows and observes them. It is of these men of genius that Terence speaks, in opposition to the little artificial cavilers of his time:

> *Quorum æmulari exoptat negligentiam*
> *Potius, quam istorum obscuram diligentiam.*

> Whose negligence he would rather imitate than these men's obscure diligence.

A critic may have the same consolation in the ill success of his play as Dr. South tells us a physician has at the death of a patient, that he was killed *secundum artem*. Our inimitable Shakspeare is a stumbling-block to the whole tribe of these rigid critics. Who would not rather read one of his plays, where there is not a single rule of the stage observed, than any production of a modern critic, where there is not one of them violated. Shakspeare was indeed born with all the seeds of poetry, and may be compared to the stone in Pyrrhus' ring, which as Pliny tells us, had the figure of Apollo and the nine Muses in the veins of it, produced by the spontaneous hand of nature, without any help from art.

John Gay
1685–1732

John Gay is remembered as one of the liveliest playwrights of the Restoration. Born at Barnstaple on September 16, 1685, he spent his youth in part with his uncle, a Nonconformist minister, and in part apprenticed to a silk mercer in London. A man of undistinguished background and education, Gay, like Samuel Johnson after him, eked out a livelihood in literary drudgery. But unlike Johnson, no ornate Latinisms flowed from his pen. His first works of note include some details of biography (*Rural Sports*, 1713) and some examples of laudatory verse, not surprisingly in honor of Pope (viz., *Lintot's Miscellany*, 1712, in which he contributed an "Epistle to Bernard Lintot.") Swift obtained for him the post of secretary to the ambassador to the court of Hanover, but Queen Anne's death prevented him from assuming the position.

Gay was nonetheless fortunate in his dealings with patrons. At one point or another, Pope, Swift, the Earl of Bath, and the Earl of Burlington, all assisted him in one way or another. His dry wit was much in fashion: it could be said that his taste fit the times admirably. No mean satirist, he ridiculed the pastoral conventions (to great effect) in his *Shepherd's Week* (1714). *Poems on Several Occasions* apparently made him financially secure. From 1722 to 1729, he obtained lodgings in the palace at Whitehall; the yearly salary he received as commissioner of the lotteries and other monies combined to make him one of the richest literati in England.

Soon he was to become one of the country's most notorious writers as well. With the production of the *Beggar's Opera*, in 1729, he came to know his greatest success. This, his most characteristic play, has won him a secure place in the English literary pantheon. It was this piece that was reputed to have made "the Rich gay and Gay rich", satirizing the high and mighty of its day by skillfully encasing its caricatures and characterizations under the dramatic guises of highwaymen, thieves, drabs, and robbers. The play is famous not only for its comic genius, its satiric efficacy and the pointed and piquant nature of its wit; its melodies were on the lips of all of London and it finally succeeded in accomplishing what was perhaps the most important feat of all: that of driving the Italian Opera from the English Stage, which it had occupied since the middle of the seventeenth century. A sequel, *Polly*, was proscribed by the censor; no less a personage than the Duchess of Queensberry was dismissed from court for soliciting on the behalf of the play within the confines of the palace. Provided with the favor of this noblewoman and the funds he had acquired as a result of his other literary and operatic ventures, Gay found it expedient to retire to a life of luxury and write his *Fables* (1738). These small masterpieces proved to be of astonishing popularity. John

Gay died in 1732 (the *Fables,* published posthumously, were part of his patrimony to his two sisters) and is interred in Westminster Abbey under a stone which bears the delightful lines

> Life is a jest, and all things show it,
> I thought so once, and now I know it.

THE PRESENT STATE OF WIT

Sir,

You Acquaint me in your last, that you are still so busie Building at ——, that your Friends must not hope to see you in Town this Year: At the same time you desire me that you may not be quite at a loss in Conversation among the *Beau Monde* next Winter, to send you an account of the present State of Wit in Town; which, without further Preface, I shall therefore endeavour to perform, and give you the Histories and Characters of all our Periodical Papers, whether Monthly, Weekly, or Diurnal, with the same freedom I used to send you our other Town News.

I shall only premise, that as you know I never cared one Farthing either for Whig or Tory, So I shall consider our Writers purely as they are such, without any respect to which Party they may belong.

Dr. King has for some time lain down his *Monthly Philosophical Transactions,* which the Title Page informed us at first, were only to be continued as they Sold; and tho' that Gentleman has a World of Wit, yet as it lies in one particular way of Raillery, the Town soon grew weary of his Writings; tho' I cannot but think, that their Author deserves a much better Fate, than to Languish out the small remainder of his Life in the Fleet Prison.

About the same time that the Doctor left off Writing, one Mr. Ozell put out his *Monthly Amusement,* (which is still continued) and as it is generally some French Novel or Play indifferently Translated, is more or less taken Notice of, as the Original Piece is more or less Agreeable.

As to our Weekly Papers, the Poor *Review* is quite exhausted, and grown so very Contemptible, that tho' he has provoked all his Brothers of the Quill round, none of them will enter into a Controversy with him. This Fellow, who had excellent Natural Parts, but wanted a small Foundation of Learning, is a lively instance of those Wits, who, as an Ingenious Author says, will endure but one Skimming.

The Observator was almost in the same Condition, but since our Party-Struggles have run so high, he is much mended for the better; which is imputed to the Charitable Assistance of some out-lying Friends.

These Two Authors might, however, have flourish'd some time longer, had not the Controversie been taken up by much abler Hands.

The Examiner is a Paper, which all Men, who speak without Prejudice, allow to be well Writ. Tho' his Subject will admit of no great Variety, he is continually placing it in so many different Lights, and endeavouring to inculcate the same thing by so many Beautiful Changes of Expressions, that Men, who are concern'd in no Party, may Read him with Pleasure. His way of assuming the Question in Debate, is extremely Artful; and his Letter to Crassus, is, I think, a Master-piece. As these Papers are suppos'd to have been

Writ by several Hands, the Criticks will tell you, That they can discern a difference in their Stiles and Beauties, and pretend to observe, that the first *Examiners* abound chiefly in Wit, the last in Humour.

Soon after their first appearance, came out a Paper from the other Side, called the *Whig Examiner,* writ with so much Fire, and in so excellent a Stile, as put the Tories in no small pain for their favourite Hero, every one cry'd Bickerstaff must be the Author, and People were the more confirm'd in this opinion, upon its being so soon lay'd down; which seem'd to shew, that it was only writ to bind the *Examiners* to their good Behavior, and was never design'd to be a Weekly Paper. The *Examiners* therefore have no one to Combat with at present, but their Friend the *Medley;* The Author of which Paper, tho' he seems to be a Man of good Sense, and expresses it luckily enough now and then, is, I think, for the most part, perfectly a Stranger to fine Writing.

I presume I need not tell you that the *Examiner* carries much the more Sail, as 'tis supposed to be writ by the Direction, and under the Eye of some Great Persons who sit at the helm of Affairs, and is consequently look'd on as a sort of publick Notice which way they are steering us.

The reputed Author is Dr. S—t, with the assistance, sometimes, of Dr. Att—y, and Mr. P—r.

The Medley, is said to be Writ by Mr. Old—n, and supervised by Mr. Mayn—g, who perhaps might intirely write those few Papers which are so much better than the rest.

Before I proceed further in the account of our Weekly Papers, it will be necessary to inform you, that at the beginning of the Winter, to the infinite suprize of all Men, Mr. Steele flung up his *Tatler,* and instead of *Isaac Bickerstaff* Esq; Subscrib'd himself *Richard Steele* to the last of those Papers, after an handsome Compliment to the Town for their kind acceptance of his Endeavours to divert them. The Chief Reason he thought fit to give for his leaving off writing, was, that having been so long look'd on in all publick Places and Companies as the Author of those Papers, he found that his most intimate Friends and Acquaintance were in Pain to Act or Speak before him. The Town was very far from being satisfied with this Reason; and most People judg'd the true cause to be, either that he was quite spent, and wanted matter to continue his undertaking any longer, or that he lay'd it down as a sort of Submission to, and Composition with the Government for some past Offences; Or lastly, that he had a Mind to vary his Shape, and appear again in some new light.

However that were, his disappearing seem'd to be bewailed as some general Calamity, every one wanted so agreeable an Amusement, and the Coffee-houses began to be sensible that the Esquires Lucubrations alone, had brought them more Customers than all their other News Papers put together.

It must indeed be confess'd, that never Man threw up his Pen under Stronger Temptations to have imployed it longer: His Reputation was at a greater height than, I believe, ever any living Author's was before him. 'Tis reasonable to suppose that his Gains were proportionably considerable; Every one Read him with Pleasure and Good Will, and the Tories, in respect to his other Good Qualities, had almost forgiven his unaccountable Imprudence in declaring against them.

Lastly, It was highly improbable that if he threw off a Character, the Ideas of which were so strongly impress'd in every one's mind, however finely he might write in any new form, that he should meet with the same reception.

To give you my own thoughts of this Gentleman's Writings, I shall in the first place observe, that there is this noble difference between him and all the rest of our Polite and Gallant Authors: The latter have endeavour'd to please the Age by falling in with them, and incouraging them in their fashionable Vices, and false notions of things. It would have been a jest, sometime since, for a Man to have asserted, that any thing Witty could be said in praise of a Marry'd State, or that Devotion and Virtue were any way necessary to the Character of a fine Gentleman. Bickerstaff ventur'd to tell the Town, that they were a parcel of Fops, Fools, and vain Cocquets; but in such a manner, as even pleased them, and made them more than half enclin'd to believe that he spoke Truth.

Instead of complying with the false Sentiments or Vicious tasts of the Age, either in Morality, Criticism, or Good Breeding, he has boldly assur'd them, that they were altogether in the wrong, and commanded them with an Authority, which perfectly well became him, to surrender themselves to his Arguments, for Vertue and Good Sense.

'Tis incredible to conceive the effect his Writings have had on the Town; How many Thousand follies they have either quite banish'd, or given a very great check to; how much Countenance they have added to Vertue and Religion; how many People they have render'd happy, by shewing them it was their own fault if they were not so; and lastly, how intirely they have convinc'd our Fops, and Young Fellows, of the value and advantages of Learning.

He has indeed rescued it out of the hands of Pedants and Fools, and discover'd the true method of making it amiable and lovely to all mankind: In the dress he gives it, 'tis a most welcome guest at Tea-tables and Assemblies, and is relish'd and caressed by the Merchants on the Change; accordingly, there is not a Lady at Court, nor a Banker in Lumbard-Street, who is not verily perswaded, that Captain Steele is the greatest Scholar, and best Casuist, of any Man in England.

Lastly, His Writings have set all our Wits and Men of Letters upon a new way of thinking, of which they had little or no Notion before; and tho' we cannot yet say that any of them have come up to the Beauties of the Original, I think we may venture to affirm, that every one of them Writes and Thinks much more justly than they did some time since.

The vast variety of Subjects which he has treated of in so different manners, and yet All so perfectly well, made the World believe that 'twas impossible they should all come from the same hand. This set every one upon guessing who was the Esquires Friend, and most people at first fancied it must be Dr. Swift; but it is now no longer a Secret, that his only great and constant assistant was Mr. Addison.

This is that excellent Friend to whom Mr. Steele ow's so much, and who refuses to have his Name set before those Pieces, which the greatest pens in

England would be Proud to own. Indeed, they could hardly add to this Gentleman's Reputation, whose Works in Latin and English Poetry, long since convinc'd the World, that he was the greatest Master in Europe of those Two Languages.

I am assur'd from good hands, That all the Visions, and other Tracts in that way of Writing, with a very great number of the most exquisite Pieces of Wit and Raillery throughout the Lucubrations, are intirely of this Gentleman's Composing; which may in some Measure account for that different Genius, which appears in the Winter Papers from those of the Summer; at which time, as the *Examiner* often hinted, this Friend of Mr. Steele's was in Ireland.

Mr. Steele confesses in his last Volume of the *Tatlers,* that he is oblig'd to Dr. Swift for his *Town Shower,* and the *Description of the Morn,* with some other hints received from him in Private Conversation.

I have also heard, that several of those Letters, which came as from Unknown Hands, were writ by Mr. Henly; which is an Answer to your Query, Who those Friends are, whom Mr. Steele speaks of in his last *Tatler?*

But to proceed with my account of our other Papers: The Expiration of Bickerstaff's Lucubrations, was attended with much the same Consequences as the Death of Melibæus's Ox in Virgil; as the latter engendred Swarms of Bees, the former immediately produc'd whole Swarms of little Satyrical Scriblers.

One of these Authors, call'd himself *The Growler,* and assur'd us, that to make amends for Mr. Steele's Silence, he was resolv'd to Growl at us Weekly, as long as we should think fit to give him any Encouragement. Another Gentleman, with more Modesty, call'd his Paper *The Whisperer;* and a Third, to Please the Ladies, Christen'd his, *The Tell-Tale.*

At the same time came out several *Tatlers;* each of which, with equal Truth and Wit, assur'd us, That he was the Genuine Isaac Bickerstaff.

It may be observ'd, That when the Esquire laid down his Pen, tho' he could not but foresee that several Scriblers would soon snatch it up, which he might, one would think, easily have prevented, he Scorn'd to take any further Care about it, but left the Field fairly open to any Worthy Successor. Immediately some of our Wits were for forming themselves into a Club, headed by one Mr. Harrison, and trying how they could shoot in this Bow of Ulysses; but soon found that this sort of Writing, requires so fine and particular a manner of Thinking, with so exact a Knowledge of the World, as must make them utterly Despair of Success.

They seem'd indeed at first to think, that what was only the Garnish of the former *Tatlers,* was that which recommended them, and not those Substantial Entertainments which they every where abound in.

Accordingly, they were continually talking of their *Maid, Night-Cap, Spectacles,* and *Charles Lillie.* However there were now and then some faint endeavours at Humour and Sparks of Wit, which the Town, for want of better Entertainment, was content to hunt after, through an heap of Impertinencies; but even those are at present, become wholly invisible, and quite swallow'd up in the Blaze of the Spectator.

You may remember I told you before, that one Cause assign'd for the laying down of the *Tatler* was, want of Matter; and indeed this was the prevailing Opinion in Town, when we were Supriz'd all at once by a Paper called *The Spectator*, which was promised to be continued every day, and was writ in so excellent a Stile, with so nice a Judgment, and such a noble profusion of Wit and Humour, that it was not difficult to determine it could come from no other hands but those which had penn'd the Lucubrations.

This immediately alarm'd these Gentlemen, who (as 'tis said Mr. Steele phrases it) had The Censorship in Commission. They found the new *Spectator* come on like a Torrent and swept away all before him; they despaired ever to equal him in Wit, Humour, or Learning; (which had been their true and certain way of opposing him) and therefore, rather chose to fall on the Author, and to call out for help to all Good Christians, by assuring them again and again, that they were the First, Original, True, and Undisputed Isaac Bickerstaff.

Mean while *The Spectator*, whom we regard as our shelter from that Flood of False Wit and Impertinence which was breaking in upon us, is in every ones Hand, and a constant Topick for our Morning Conversation at Tea-Tables, and Coffee-Houses. We had at first indeed no manner of Notion, how a Diurnal Paper could be continu'd in the Spirit and Stile of our present *Spectators;* but to our no small Surprize, we find them still rising upon us, and can only wonder from whence so Prodigious a Run of Wit and Learning can proceed; since some of our best Judges seem to think that they have hitherto, in general, out-shone even the Esquires first *Tatlers*.

Most People Fancy, from their frequency, that they must be compos'd by a Society; I, with all, Assign the first Places to Mr. Steele and His Friend.

I have often thought that the Conjunction of those two Great Genius's (who seem to stand in a Class by themselves, so high above all our other Wits) resembled that of two famous States-men in a late Reign, whose Characters are very well expressed in their two Mottoes (*viz.*) *Prodesse quam conspici*, and *Otium cum Dignitate*. Accordingly the first was continually at work behind the Curtain, drew up and prepared all those Schemes and Designs, which the latter Still drove on, and stood out exposed to the World to receive its Praises or Censures.

Mean time, all our unbyassed wellwishers to Learning, are in hopes, that the known Temper and Prudence of one of these Gentlemen, will hinder the other from ever lashing out into Party, and rend'ring that wit which is at present a Common Good, Odious and Ungrateful to the better part of the Nation.

If this piece of imprudence do's not spoil so excellent a Paper, I propose to my self, the highest Satisfaction, in Reading it with you over a Dish of Tea, every Morning next Winter.

As we have yet had nothing new since the *Spectator*, it only remains for me to assure you, that I am

Yours, &c.

Westminster,
May 3, 1711

J. G.

POSTSCRIPT

Upon a Review of my letter, I find I have quite forgot *The British Apollo;* which might possibly happen, from its having of late Retreated out of this end of the Town into the City; where I am inform'd however, That it still recommends its self by deciding Wagers at Cards, and giving good Advice to the Shop-keepers, and their Apprentices.

Jonathan Swift

1667–1745

If the greater portion of eighteenth century English prose were suddenly obliterated, with the exception of the works of Swift, the finest satire of the era would remain intact. Even Pope cannot measure up to Swift's brilliance and the sustained moral force of his imagination. It is no accident that he represents the standard by which all great English satire is measured. To deem a writer "Swiftian" is at once a high appraisal of comic genius as well as a term that denotes outlandish irony of content coupled with an apparently serious and matter-of-fact tone. A man of contradictions—not the least of which was the marked contrast between his perfect, detached appeal to logic and good sense while putting forth the most incredible, well-nigh unspeakable satiric proposals—Swift did have a consistent program. This was the redress of what he considered to be evil. Swift exposed hypocrisy and dissected the anatomy of oppression. Waging war with his pen, he was often more effective in his attack on civil and literary abuses than those whose voices were more strident, or those whose power had the support of arms or money.

Swift was born on November 7, 1667, in Dublin. On his father's side he was distantly related to Dryden. When he was six he entered the Kilkenny School, where he proved an indifferent student. Along with Congreve, he entered Trinity College. Upon the death of his uncle, who had supported him financially, Swift was obliged to leave for England. It was at Moor Park, near Farnham, that he became the secretary and amanuensis of Sir William Temple, a distinguished diplomat and man of letters. Under his influence Swift made his first forays into literary composition. The fruits of these early labors proved to be nothing more than a mediocre attempt to shape verses in the Pindaric style.

At Moor Park Swift encountered Esther Johnson, who became the "Stella" of his journals and the first love of his life. When Swift met "Stella," she was eight years old. Only later did their "curious friendship" become an all-absorbing, passionate romance. But at that time Swift was just beginning to teach Esther the rudiments of reading, while serving the Temple household and occasionally undertaking secret diplomatic missions at his master's behest.

Though Swift enjoyed the full confidence of Temple and was deeply attached to him personally, he soon grew annoyed when it became clear that Temple delayed in obtaining preferment for him. In 1694 Swift left England for Ireland, but he soon returned to Temple's service, where he stayed until the latter's death in 1699. In 1697 Swift produced his first "Swiftian" satire, a defense of Temple's stand in a literary debate that had started in France and which ranged the distinguished elder critic against the pompous classical philologist Bentley. This work, entitled *The Battle of the Books,* refuted what the satirist regarded as a good example of supercilious pedantry, while defending the position Temple had put forth in his *Essay upon Ancient and Modern Learning* (1692).

When Temple died Swift began to cast about for some new employment, but he was not immediately successful. Before long he was back in Ireland, where he eventually secured a number of minor ecclesiastical livings. It did not take long for this hotheaded young Irishman to become embroiled in political debate. By 1701 he had written an anti-Tory tract that was so good that it was attributed to other well-known hands; but it was in 1704, with the publication of the masterful *Tale of a Tub,* that Swift began to display the true range of his comic genius and his almost preternatural gift for invective.

Between 1701, when Swift had taken his Doctor of Divinity degree at Trinity, and 1704, he lived in England, where he made the acquaintance of Pope, Steele, and Addison. By 1710 Swift was regarded as the most brillian polemicist among the literati of Britain. Not only was this clever young clergyman friendly with the greatest wits of his day; he had also written the most outrageous ecclesiastical satire in the English language—his *Argument to prove that the abolishing of Christianity in England may, as things now stand, be attended with some inconveniencies* (1708).

In 1708 Swift perpetrated one of the most amusing hoaxes in the history of English literature. Claiming to be a curmudgeonly old astrologer, Isaac Bickerstaff, Swift predicted the death of John Partridge, a Protestant extremist for whom he had scant affection. When the testy Partridge objected by pointing out Bickerstaff's error, Swift responded by making a complete fool of him in print. When Swift began to write for Steele's *Tatler* in 1709, it seemed natural to him to adopt the persona of Bickerstaff.

Swift's conversion to the Tory party was the result of many factors, not the least among which was the cool reception he was accorded by the powerful Whig Godolphin. Before long he became the ally of the leaders of the Tory party, Oxford and Bolingbroke. In 1713 Swift—backed by his powerful friends—wrested from Queen Anne a considerable token of her favor, the deanery of St. Patrick's, Dublin. With the fall of Oxford and the death of the Queen, Swift felt it best to move to Ireland for good, where he overcame the initally cool reception of his countrymen and soon became the most popular (and effective) champion of their rights.

The transfer of Swift from London to Dublin meant a fall from the pinnacle of literary and political power to the depths of obscurity. In London he had conceived of Martinus Scriblerus with Arbuthnot; had hobnobbed with Pope, written essays for Addison and Steele, and penned such satires as the *Meditation on a Broomstick* and written such history as he was capable of in his *History of the Four Last Years of the Reign of Queen Anne.* In Dublin he soon became embroiled in the Drapier affair, which caused him to rise out of his seclusion and become the leading light of Irish patriotism. William Wood, a royal sycophant who had obtained the right to mint the halfpence for Ireland in such a way that he could pocket the difference between the nominal and real value of the new coins, had completely enraged the Irish people. Swift took up the cudgel (i.e., his pen) and wrote a series of devastating attacks on Wood and M. B. Drapier, the official who had issued the patent to Wood. The authorities made numerous attempts to discover the authorship of these *Drapier Letters* (1724), but Ireland hid her champion well. Swift's notoriety had never been so widespread as when his name was, at least in official circles, hidden from view.

Soon after the successful outcome of the Drapier affair—which ended with the revocation of Wood's patent—a certain strange new book was presented anonymously to the world. This was *Travels Into Several Remote Nations of the World* in four parts, by one Lemuel Gulliver (1726), a work that firmly established Swift's reputation in the world of great satire. Though Swift was wary of the effect such a book would produce, his precautions were unnecessary: its success was immense. *Gulliver's Travels,* as it came to be known, and that outrageous masterpiece of perfect wit, *A Modest Proposal for Preventing the Children of Poor People from Being a Burden to Their Parents and Country* (1729) stand as the twin pinnacles of Swift's oeuvre, and of satire in general. In these two works the satiric genius of a Lucan or a Juvenal was equalled, if not surpassed; modern literature has nothing else of such invention, and such moral import, to offer in comparison with antique satire.

Swift died on October 19, 1745, a broken man. Having suffered the onset of madness in his latest years, he seems to have succumbed to it, and died insane. He was interred next to Stella at St. Patrick's, where he won such widespread fame during his lifetime.

A Tritical Essay[1]

Upon the Faculties of the Mind

Philosophers say, that a man is a microcosm, or little world, resembling in miniature every part of the great; and, in my opinion, the body natural may be compared to the body politic; and if this be so, how can the Epicurean's opinion be true, that the universe was formed by a fortuitous concourse of atoms, which I will no more believe, than that the accidental jumbling of the letters in the alphabet, could fall by chance into a most ingenious and learned treatise of philosophy. *Risum teneatis amici—Hor.* This false opinion must needs create many more; 'tis like an error in the first concoction, which cannot be corrected in the second; the foundation is weak, and whatever superstructure you raise upon it, must, of necessity, fall to the ground. Thus, men are led from one error to another, until, with Ixion, they embrace a cloud instead of Juno, or, like the dog in the fable, lose the substance in gaping at the shadow. For such opinions cannot cohere; but, like the iron and clay in the toes of Nebuchadnezzar's image, must separate and break in pieces. I have read in a certain author, that Alexander wept because he had no more worlds to conquer; which he need not have done, if the fortuitous concourse of atoms could create one; but this is an opinion, fitter for that many-headed beast, the vulgar, to entertain, than for so wise a man as Epicurus; the corrupt part of his sect only borrowed his name, as the monkey did the cat's claw to draw the chestnut out of the fire.

However, the first step to the cure, is to know the disease; and though truth may be difficult to find, because, as the philosopher observes, she lives in the bottom of a well, yet we need not, like blind men, grope in open daylight. I hope I may be allowed, among so many far more learned men, to offer my mite, since a stander-by may sometimes, perhaps, see more of the game, than he that plays it. But I do not think a philosopher obliged to account for every phenomenon in nature, or drown himself with Aristotle, for not being able to solve the ebbing and flowing of the tide, in that fatal sentence he passed upon himself, *Quia te non capio, tu capies me.*

Wherein he was at once the judge and the criminal, the accuser and executioner. Socrates, on the other hand, who said he knew nothing, was pronounced by the oracle to be the wisest man in the world.

But to return from this digression. I think it as clear as any demonstration in Euclid, that nature does nothing in vain: if we were able to dive into her secret recesses, we should find that the smallest blade of grass, or more contemptible weed, has its particular use; but she is chiefly admirable in her minutest compositions; the least and most contemptible insect most discovers the art of nature, if I may so call it; though nature, which delights in variety, will always triumph over art; and as the poet observes,

Naturam expellas furcâ licet, usque recurret.
                                                                        HOR.

But the various opinions of philosophers have scattered through the world as many plagues of the mind, as Pandora's box did those of the body; only with this difference, that they have not left hope at the bottom. And if Truth be not fled with Astrea, she is certainly as hidden as the source of Nile, and can be found only in Utopia. Not that I would reflect on those wise sages; which would be a sort of ingratitude; and he that calls a man ungrateful, sums up all the evil that a man can be guilty of.

Ingratum si dixeris, omnia dicis.

But, what I blame the philosophers for, (though some may think it a paradox,) is chiefly their pride; nothing less than an *ipse dixit,* and you must pin your faith on their sleeve. And though Diogenes lived in a tub, there might be, for aught I know, as much pride under his rags, as in the fine-spun garments of the divine Plato. It is reported of this Diogenes, that when Alexander came to see him, and promised to give him whatever he would ask, the cynic only answered; "Take not from me what thou canst not give me, but stand from between me and the light;" which was almost as extravagant as the philosopher, that flung his money into the sea, with this remarkable saying—
How different was this man from the usurer, who, being told his son would spend all he had got, replied, "He cannot take more pleasure in spending, than I did in getting it." These men could see the faults of each other, but not their own; those they flung into the bag behind; *non videmus id manticæ quod in tergo est.* I may perhaps be censured for my free opinions by those carping Momuses whom authors worship, as the Indians do the devil, for fear. They will endeavour to give my reputation as many wounds, as the man in the almanack; but I value it not; and perhaps like flies, they may buzz so often about the candle, till they burn their wings. They must pardon me, if I venture to give them this advice, not to rail at what they cannot understand; it does but discover that self-tormenting passion of envy, than which the greatest tyrant never invented a more cruel torment:

Invidiâ Siculi non invenere Tyranni
Tormentum majus—
                                                                        JUVEN.

I must be so bold to tell my critics and witlings, that they are no more judges of this, than a man that is born blind can have any true idea of colours. I have always observed, that your empty vessels sound loudest: I value their lashes as little as the sea did those of Xerxes, when he whipped it. The utmost favour a man can expect from them is, that which Polyphemus promised Ulysses, that he would devour him the last: they think to subdue a writer, as Cæsar did his enemy, with a *Veni, vidi, vici.* I confess I value the opinion of the judicious few, a R——r, a D——s, or a W——k; but for the rest, to give my judgment at once, I think the long dispute among the philosophers about a *vacuum,* may be determined in the affirmative, that it is to be found in a critic's head. They are at best but the drones of the learned world, who devour the honey, and will not work themselves: and a writer need no more regard them, than the moon does the barking of a little senseless cur. For, in spite of their terrible roaring, you may, with half an eye, discover the ass under the lion's skin.

But to return to our discourse: Demosthenes being asked what was the first part of an orator, replied, Action: what was the second, Action: what was the third, Action, and so on, *ad infinitum.* This may be true in oratory; but contemplation in other things, exceeds action. And, therefore, a wise man is never less alone, than when he is alone:

Nunquam minus solus, quam cum solus.

And Archimedes, the famous mathematician, was so intent upon his problems, that he never minded the soldiers who came to kill him. Therefore, not to detract from the just praise which belongs to orators, they ought to consider, that nature, which gave us two eyes to see, and two ears to hear, has given us but one tongue to speak; wherein, however, some do so abound, that the *virtuosi,* who have been so long in search for the perpetual motion, may infallibly find it there.

Some men admire republics, because orators flourish there most, and are the great enemies of tyranny; but my opinion is, that one tyrant is better than a hundred. Besides, these orators inflame the people, whose anger is really but a short fit of madness.

Ira furor brevis est—
Hor.

After which, laws are like cobwebs, which may catch small flies, but let wasps and hornets break through. But in oratory the greatest art is to hide art.

Artis est celare artem.

But this must be the work of time. We must lay hold on all opportunities, and let slip no occasion, else we shall be forced to weave Penelope's web, unravel in the night what we spun in the day. And therefore I have observed, that Time is painted with a lock before, and bald behind, signifying thereby, that we must take time (as we say) by the forelock, for when it is once past, there is no recalling it.

The mind of man is at first (if you will pardon the expression) like a *tabula rasa,* or like wax, which, while it is soft, is capable of any impression, till time has hardened it. And at length death, that grim tyrant, stops us in the midst of our career. The greatest conquerors have at last been conquered by death, which spares none, from the sceptre to the spade.

Mors omnibus communis.

All rivers go to the sea, but none return from it. Xerxes wept when he beheld his army, to consider that in less than a hundred years they would be all dead. Anacreon was choked with a grape-stone; and violent joy kills as well as violent grief. There is nothing in this world constant, but inconstancy; yet Plato thought, that if virtue would appear to the world in her own native dress, all men would be enamoured with her. But now, since interest governs the world, and men neglect the golden mean, Jupiter himself, if he came to the earth, would be despised, unless it were, as he did to Danae, in a golden shower. For men now-a-days worship the rising sun, and not the setting.

Donec eris felix multos numerabis amicos.

Thus have I, in obedience to your commands, ventured to expose myself to censure, in this critical age. Whether I have done right to my subject, must be left to the judgment of my learned reader: however, I cannot but hope, that my attempting of it may be encouragement for some able pen to perform it with more success.

NOTES

1. This essay is a parody on the pseudo-philosophical essays of the time, in which all sense was lost in the maze of inconsequential quotations. It was written in 1707–8, and the "Miscellanies" of 1711 places its publication in August, 1707.

THE TATLER

Number 230

September 26, 1710

The following Letter has laid before me many great and manifest Evils in the World of Letters which I had overlooked; but they open to me a very busie Scene, and it will require no small Care and Application to amend Errors which are become so universal. The Affectation of Politeness is exposed in this Epistle with a great deal of Wit and Discernment; so that whatever Discourses I may fall into hereafter upon the Subjects the Writer treats of, I shall at present lay the Matter before the World without the least Alteration from the Words of my Correspondent.

To Isaac Bickerstaff Esq;

SIR,

There are some Abuses among us of great Consequence, the Reformation of which is properly your Province, tho', as far as I have been conversant in your Papers, you have not yet considered them. These are, the deplorable Ignorance that for some Years hath reigned among our English Writers, the great Depravity of our Taste, and the continual Corruption of our Style. I say nothing here of those who handle particular Sciences, Divinity, Law, Physick, and the like; I mean, the Traders in History and Politicks, and the Belles Lettres; together with those by whom Books are not translated, but (as the common Expressions are) Done out of French, Latin, or other Language, and Made English. I cannot but observe to you, That till of late Years a Grub-street Book was always bound in Sheep-skin, with suitable Print and Paper, the Price never above a Shilling, and taken off wholly by common Tradesmen, or Country Pedlars. But now they appear in all Sizes and Shapes, and in all Places. They are handed about from Lapfulls in every Coffee-house to Persons of Quality, are shewn in Westminster-Hall and the Court of Requests. You may see them gilt, and in Royal Paper, of Five or Six hundred Pages, and rated accordingly. I would engage to furnish you with a Catalogue of English Books published within the Compass of Seven Years past, which at the first Hand would cost you a Hundred Pounds wherein you shall not be able to find Ten Lines together of common Grammar or common Sense.

These Two Evils, Ignorance and Want of Taste, have produced a Third; I mean, the continual Corruption of our English Tongue, which, without some timely Remedy, will suffer more by the false Refinements of Twenty Years past, than it hath been improved in the foregoing Hundred: And this is what

I design chiefly to enlarge upon, leaving the former Evils to your Animadversion.

But instead of giving you a List of the late Refinements crept into our Language, I here send you the Copy of a Letter I received some Time ago from a most accomplished Person in this Way of Writing, upon which I shall make some Remarks. It is in these Terms.

> *SIR,*
> 'I *Cou'dn't* get the Things you sent for all *about Town*. . . . I *thôt* to *ha'* come down my self, and then *I'd ha' brôut 'um;* but I *han't don't,* and I believe I *can't do't,* that's *Pozz.* . . . *Tom* begins to *gi'mself Airs* because *he's* going with the *Plenipo's.* . . . 'Tis said, the *French* King will *bamboozl' us agen,* which *causes many Speculations.* The *Jacks,* and others of that *Kidney,* are very *uppish,* and *alert upon't,* as you may see by their *Phizz's.* . . . *Will Hazzard* has got the *Hipps,* having lost *to the Tune of* Five hundr'd Pound, *thô* he understands Play very well, *no body better.* He has promis't me upon *Rep,* to leave off Play; but you know 'tis a Weakness *he's* too apt to *give into, thô* he has as much Wit as any Man, *no body more.* He has lain *incog* ever since. . . . The *Mobb's* very quiet with us now. . . . I believe you *thot* I *banter'd* you in my Last like a *Country Put.* . . . I *sha'n't* leave Town this Month, *&c.*

This Letter is in every Point an admirable Pattern of the present polite Way of Writing; nor is it of less Authority for being an Epistle. You may gather every Flower in it, with a Thousand more of equal Sweetness, from the Books, Pamphlets, and single Papers, offered us every Day in the Coffee-houses: And these are the Beauties introduced to supply the Want of Wit, Sense, Humour, and Learning, which formerly were looked upon as Qualifications for a Writer. If a Man of Wit, who died Forty Years ago, were to rise from the Grave on Purpose, How would he be able to read this Letter? And after he had got through that Difficulty, How would he be able to understand it? The first Thing that strikes your Eye is the Breaks at the End of almost every Sentence; of which I know not the Use, only that it is a Refinement, and very frequently practised. Then you will observe the Abbreviations and Elisions, by which Consonants of most obdurate Sound are joined together, without one softening Vowel to intervene; and all this only to make one Syllable of two, directly contrary to the Example of the Greeks and Romans; altogether of the Gothick Strain, and a natural Tendency towards relapsing into Barbarity, which delights in Monosyllables, and uniting of Mute Consonants; as it is observable in all the Northern Languages. And this is still more visible in the next Refinement, which consists in pronouncing the first Syllable in a Word that has many, and dismissing the rest; such as *Phizz, Hipps, Mobb, Poz. Rep.* and many more; when we are already overloaded with Monosyllables, which are the Disgrace of our Language. Thus we cram one Syllable, and cut off the rest; as the Owl fatten'd her Mice, after she had bit off their Legs to prevent their running away; and if ours be the same Reason for maiming our Words, it will certainly answer the End; for I am sure no other Nation will desire to borrow them. Some Words are hitherto but fairly split, and therefore only in their Way to Perfection, as *Incog* and *Plenipo:* But in a short Time 'tis to be hoped they will be further dock'd to *Inc* and *Plen.* This Reflexion has made me of late Years very impatient for a Peace, which I believe would save the Lives of many brave Words, as well as Men. The War has introduced Abundance of Polysyllables, which will never be able to live many more Campagnes; *Speculations, Operations, Preliminaries, Ambassadors, Pallisadoes, Communication, Circumvallation, Battalions,* as numerous as they are, if they attack us too frequently in our Coffee-houses, we shall certainly put them to Flight, and cut off the Rear.

The Third Refinement observable in the Letter I send you, consists in the Choice of certain Words invented by some Pretty Fellows; such as *Banter, Bamboozle, Country Put,* and *Kidney,* as it is there applied; some of which are now struggling for the Vogue, and others are in Possession of it. I have done my utmost for some Years past to stop the Progress of *Mobb* and *Banter,* but have been plainly borne down by Numbers, and betrayed by those who promised to assist me.

In the last Place, you are to take Notice of certain choice Phrases scattered through the Letter; some of them tolerable enough, till they were worn to Rags by servile Imitators. You might easily find them, though they were not in a different Print, and therefore I need not disturb them.

These are the false Refinements in our Style which you ought to correct: First, by Argument and fair Means; but if those fail, I think you are to make Use of your Authority as Censor, and by an Annual *Index Expurgatorius* expunge all Words and Phrases that are offensive to good Sense, and condemn those barbarous Mutilations of Vowels and Syllables. In this last Point the usual Pretence is, that they spell as they speak; A noble Standard for Language! to depend upon the Caprice of every Coxcomb, who, because Words are the Cloathing of our Thoughts, cuts them out, and shapes them as he pleases, and changes them oftner than his Dress. I believe, all reasonable People would be content that such Refiners were more sparing in their Words, and liberal in their Syllables: And upon this Head I should be glad you would bestow some Advice upon several young Readers in our Churches, who coming up from the University, full fraught with Admiration of our Town Politeness, will needs correct the Style of their Prayer Books. In reading the Absolution, they are very careful to say *pardons* and *absolves;* and in the Prayer for the Royal Family, it must be, *endue 'um, enrich 'um, prosper 'um,* and *bring 'um.* Then in their Sermons they use all the modern Terms of Art, *Sham, Banter, Mob, Bubble, Bully, Cutting, Shuffling,* and *Palming,* all which, and many more of the like Stamp, as I have heard them often in the Pulpit from such young Sophisters, so I have read them in some of those Sermons that have made most Noise of late. The Design, it seems, is to avoid the dreadful Imputation of Pedantry, to shew us, that they know the Town, understand Men and Manners, and have not been poring upon old unfashionable Books in the University.

I should be glad to see you the Instrument of introducing into our Style that Simplicity which is the best and truest Ornament of most Things in Life, which the politer Ages always aimed at in their Building and Dress, (*Simplex munditiis*) as well as their Productions of Wit. 'Tis manifest, that all new, affected Modes of Speech, whether borrowed from the Court, the Town, or the Theatre, are the first perishing Parts in any Language, and, as I could prove by many Hundred Instances, have been so in ours. The Writings of Hooker, who was a Country Clergyman, and of Parsons the Jesuit, both in the Reign of Queen Elizabeth, are in a Style that, with very few Allowances, would not offend any present Reader; much more clear and intelligible than those of Sir H. Wotton, Sir Robert Naunton, Osborn, Daniel the Historian, and several others who writ later; but being Men of the Court, and affecting Phrases then in Fashion, they are often either not to be understood, or appear perfectly ridiculous.

What Remedies are to be applied to these Evils I have not Room to consider, having, I fear, already taken up most of your Paper. Besides, I think it is our Office only to represent Abuses, and yours to redress them. I am, with great Respect,

      SIR,

                                     Your, &c.

A PROPOSAL

FOR CORRECTING, IMPROVING AND ASCERTAINING THE ENGLISH TONGUE

To the Most Honourable
Robert Earl of Oxford

My Lord,

What I had the Honour of mentioning to your Lordship some Time ago in Conversation, was not a new Thought, just then started by Accident or Occasion, but the Result of long Reflection; and I have been confirmed in my Sentiments by the Opinion of some very judicious Persons, with whom I consulted. They all agreed, That nothing would be of greater Use towards the Improvement of Knowledge and Politeness, than some effectual Method for Correcting, Enlarging, and Ascertaining our Language; and they think it a Work very possible to be compassed, under the Protection of a Prince, the Countenance and Encouragement of a Ministry, and the Care of proper Persons, chosen for such an Undertaking. I was glad to find your Lordship's Answer in so different a Style, from what hath been commonly made use of on such like Occasions, for some Years past; *That all such Thoughts must be deferred to a Time of Peace:* A Topick which some have carried so far, that they would not have us by any Means think of preserving our Civil or Religious Constitution, because we are engaged in a War abroad. It will be among the distinguishing Marks of your Ministry, My Lord, that you had a Genius above all such Regards; and that no reasonable Proposal for the Honour, the Advantage, or the Ornament of your Country, however foreign to your more immediate Office, was ever neglected by you. I confess, the Merit of this Candour and Condescension is very much lessened; because your Lordship hardly leaves us Room to offer our good Wishes; removing all our Difficulties, and supplying our Wants, faster than the most visionary Projector can adjust his Schemes. And therefore, my Lord, the Design of this Paper is not so much to offer you Ways and Means, as to complain of a Grievance, the Redressing of which is to be your own Work, as much as that of paying the Nation's Debts, or opening a Trade into the South-Sea; and although not of such immediate Benefit, as either of these, or any other of your glorious Actions, yet perhaps in future Ages not less to your Honor.

My Lord, I do here, in the Name of all the learned and polite Persons of the Nation, complain to your Lordship as First Minister, that our Language is extremely imperfect; that its daily Improvements are by no Means in Proportion to its daily Corruptions; that the Pretenders to polish and refine it, have chiefly multiplied Abuses and Absurdities; and, that in many Instances, it offends against every Part of Grammar. But lest your Lordship should think my Censure too severe, I shall take your leave to be more particular.

I believe your Lordship will agree with me in the Reason, why our Language is less refined than those of Italy, Spain, or France. It is plain, that the Latin Tongue in its Purity was never in this Island; towards the Conquest of which, few or no Attempts were made till the Time of Claudius: Neither was that Language ever so vulgar in Britain, as it is known to have been in Gaul and Spain. Further, we find that the Roman Legions here, were at length all recalled to help their Country against the Goths, and other barbarous Invaders. Mean time, the Britons left to shift for themselves, and daily harrassed by cruel Inroads from the Picts, were forced to call in the Saxons for their Defence; who consequently reduced the greatest Part of the Island to their own Power, drove the Britons into the most remote and mountainous Parts; and the Rest of the Country in Customs, Religion, and Language, became wholly Saxon. This I take to be the Reason why there are more Latin Words remaining in the British Tongue than in the old Saxon; which, excepting some few Variations in the Orthography, is the same in most original Words with our present English, as well as with the German and other Northern Dialects.

Edward the Confessor having lived long in France, appears to be the first, who introduced any Mixture of the French Tongue with the Saxon; the Court affecting what the Prince was fond of, and others taking it up for a Fashion, as it is now with us. William the Conqueror proceeded much further; bringing over with him vast Numbers of that Nation, scattering them in every Monastery, giving them great Quantities of Land, directing all Pleadings to be in that Language, and endeavouring to make it universal in the Kingdom. This, at least, is the Opinion generally received: But your Lordship hath fully convinced me, that the French Tongue made yet a greater Progress here under Harry the Second, who had large Territories on that Continent, both from his Father and his Wife; made frequent Journeys and Expeditions thither, and was always attended with a Number of his Countrymen, Retainers at his Court. For some Centuries after, there was a Constant Intercourse between France and England, by the Dominions we possessed there, and the Conquests we made: So that our Language, between two and three hundred Years ago, seems to have had a greater Mixture with the French than at present; many Words having been afterwards rejected, and some since the Time of Spencer; although we have still retained not a few, which have been long antiquated in France. I could produce several Instances of both Kinds, if it were of any Use or Entertainment.

To examine into the several Circumstances by which the Language of a Country may be altered, would force me to enter into a wide Field. I shall only observe, that the Latin, the French, and the English, seem to have undergone the same Fortune. The first, from the Days of Romulus to those of Julius Cæsar, suffered perpetual Changes; and by what we meet in those Authors who occasionally speak on that Subject, as well as from certain Fragments of old Laws; it is manifest that the Latin, three Hundred Years before Tully, was as unintelligible in his Time, as the English and French of the same Period are now: And these two have changed as much since William the Conqueror, (which is but little less than seven Hundred Years) as the Latin appears to have done in the like Term. Whether our Language, or the French, will decline as fast as the Roman did, is a Question that would perhaps admit more Debate than it is worth. There were many Reasons for the Corruptions of the last: As the Change of their Government into a Tyranny, which ruined the Study of Eloquence; there being no further Use or Encouragement for popular Orators: Their giving not only the Freedom of the City, but Capacity for Employments, to several Towns in Gaul, Spain, and Germany, and other distant Parts, as far as Asia; which brought a great Number of foreign Pretenders into Rome: The slavish Disposition of the Senate and People; by which the Wit and Eloquence of the Age were wholly turned into Panegyrick, the most barren of all Subjects: The great Corruption of Manners, and Introduction of foreign Luxury, with foreign Terms to express it: With several others that might be assigned: Not to mention those Invasions from the Goths and Vandals, which are too obvious to insist on.

The Roman Language arrived at great Perfection before it began to decay: The French, for these last Fifty Years, hath been polishing as much as it will bear; and appears to be declining by the natural Inconstancy of that People, as well as the Affectation of some late Authors, to introduce and multiply Cant Words, which is the most ruinous Corruption in any Language. La Bruyere, a late celebrated Writer among them, makes use of many new Terms which are not to be found in any of the common Dictionaries before his Time. But the English Tongue is not arrived to such a Degree of Perfection, as, upon that Account, to make us apprehend any Thoughts of its Decay: And if it were once refined to a certain Standard, perhaps there might be Ways to fix it for ever, or at least till we are invaded, and made a Conquest by some other State: And even then, our best Writings might probably be preserved with Care, and grow into Esteem, and the Authors have a chance for Immortality.

But without such great Revolutions as these, (to which we are, I think, less subject than Kingdoms upon the Continent,) I see no absolute Necessity why any Language should be perpetually changing; for we find many Examples to the contrary. From Homer to Plutarch, are above a Thousand Years; so long, at least, the Purity of the Greek Tongue may be allowed to last; and we know not how far before. The Grecians spread their Colonies round all the Coasts of Asia Minor, even to the Northern Parts, lying towards the Euxine; in every Island of the Ægean Sea, and several others in the Mediterranean; where the Language was preserved entire for many Ages, after they themselves became Colonies to Rome, and till they were overrun by the barbarous Nations, upon the Fall of that Empire. The Chinese have Books in their Language above two Thousand Years old; neither have the frequent Conquests of the Tartars been able to alter it. The German, Spanish, and Italian, have admitted few or no changes for some Ages past. The other Languages of Europe I know nothing of; neither is there any Occasion to consider them.

Having taken this Compass, I return to those Considerations upon our own Language, which I would humbly offer your Lordship. The Period wherein the English Tongue received most Improvement, I take to commence with the Beginning of Queen Elizabeth's Reign, and to conclude with the great Rebellion in Forty-two. It is true, there was a very ill Taste both of Style and Wit, which prevailed under King James the First; but that seems to have been corrected in the first Years of his Successor; who, among many other Qualifications of an excellent Prince, was a great Patron of Learning. From that great Rebellion to this present Time, I am apt to doubt whether the Corruptions in our Language have not, at least, equalled the Refinements of it; and these Corruptions very few of the best Authors in our Age have wholly escaped. During the Usurpation, such an Infusion of Enthusiastick Jargon prevailed in every Writing, as was not shaken off in many Years after. To this succeeded that Licentiousness which entered with the Restoration; and from infecting our Religion and Morals, fell to corrupt our Language: Which last, was not like to be much improved by those, who, at that Time, made up the Court of King Charles the Second; either such who had followed him in his Banishment, or who had been altogether conversant in the Dialect of those Fanatick Times; or young Men, who had been educated in the same Company; so that the Court, which used to be the Standard of Propriety, and Correctness of Speech, was then, and I think hath ever since continued the worst School in England, for that Accomplishment; and so will remain, till better Care be taken in the Education of our young Nobility; that they may set out into the World with some Foundation of Literature, in order to qualify them for Patterns of Politeness. The Consequence of this Defect upon our Language, may appear from the Plays, and other Compositions, written for Entertainment, within fifty Years past; filled with a Succession of affected Phrases, and new conceited Words, either borrowed from the current Style of the Court, or from those, who, under the Character of Men of Wit and Pleasure, pretended to give the Law. Many of these Refinements have already been long antiquated, and are now hardly intelligible; which is no Wonder, when they were the Product only of Ignorance and Caprice.

I have never known this great Town without one or more Dunces of Figure, who had Credit enough to give Rise to some new Word, and propagate it in most Conversations; although it had neither Humour nor Significancy. If it struck the present Taste, it was soon transferred into the Plays, and current Scribbles of the Week, and became an Addition to our Language; while the Men of Wit and Learning, instead of early obviating such Corruptions, were too often seduced to imitate and comply with them.

There is another Set of Men, who have contributed very much to the spoiling of the English Tongue; I mean the Poets, from the Time of the Restoration. These Gentlemen, although they could not be insensible how much our Language was already overstocked with Monosyllables, yet to save Time and Pains, introduced that barbarous Custom of abbreviating Words, to fit them to the Measure of their Verses; and this they have frequently done, so very injudiciously, as to form such harsh unharmonious Sounds, that none but a Northern Ear could endure. They have joined the most obdurate Consonants, without one intervening Vowel, only to shorten a Syllable: And their Taste in Time became so depraved, that what was at first a poetical Licence, not to be justified, they made their Choice; alledging, that the Words pronounced at length, sounded faint and languid. This was a Pretence to take up the same Custom in Prose; so that most of the Books we see now-a-days, are full of those Manglings and Abbreviations. Instances of this Abuse are innumerable: What does your Lordship think of the Words, *Drudg'd, Disturb'd, Rebuk'd, Fledg'd,* and a Thousand others, every where to be met in Prose, as well as Verse? Where, by leaving out a Vowel to save a Syllable, we form so jarring a Sound, and so difficult to utter, that I have often wondered how it could ever obtain.

Another Cause (and perhaps borrowed from the former) which hath contributed not a little to the maiming of our Language, is a foolish Opinion, advanced of late Years, that we ought to spell exactly as we speak; which beside the obvious Inconvenience of utterly destroying our Etymology, would be a Thing we should never see an End of. Not only the several Towns and Counties of England, have a different Way of pronouncing; but even here in London, they clip their Words after one Manner about the Court, another in the City, and a third in the Suburbs; and in a few Years, it is probable, will all differ from themselves, as Fancy or Fashion shall direct: All which reduced to Writing, would entirely confound Orthography. [It would be just as wise as to shape our Bodies to our Cloathes and not our Cloaths to our bodyes.] Yet many People are so fond of this Conceit, that it is sometimes a difficult Matter to read modern Books and Pamphlets; where the Words are so curtailed, and varied from their original Spelling, that whoever hath been used to plain English, will hardly know them by Sight.

Several young Men at the Universities, terribly possessed with the Fear of Pedantry, run into a worse Extream; and think all Politeness to consist in reading the daily Trash sent down to them from hence: This they call *knowing the World,* and *reading Men and Manners.* Thus furnished, they come up to Town; reckon all their Errors for Accomplishments, borrow the newest Set of Phrases; and if they take a Pen into their Hands, all the odd Words they have picked up in a Coffee-House, or a Gaming Ordinary, are produced as Flowers of Style; and the Orthography refined to the utmost. To this we owe those monstrous Productions, which under the Names of Trips, Spies, Amusements, and other conceited Appellations, have over-run us for some Years past. To this we owe that strange Race of Wits, who tell us they write to the Humour of the Age. And I wish I could say, these quaint Fopperies were wholly absent from graver Subjects. In short, I would undertake to shew your Lordship several Pieces, where the Beauties of this Kind are so predominant, that with all your Skill in Languages, you could never be able either to read or understand them.

But I am very much mistaken, if many of these false Refinements among us, do not arise from a Principle which would quite destroy their Credit, if it were well understood and considered. For I am afraid, my Lord, that with all the real good Qualities of our Country, we are naturally not very polite. This perpetual Disposition to shorten our Words, by retrenching the Vowels, is nothing else but a Tendency to lapse into the Barbarity of those Northern Nations from whom we are descended, and whose Languages labour all under the same Defect. For it is worthy our Observation, that the Spaniards, the French, and the Italians, although derived from the same Northern Ancestors with our selves, are, with the utmost Difficulty taught to pronounce our Words; which the Swedes and Danes, as well as the Germans and the Dutch, attain to with Ease, because our Syllables resemble theirs, in the Roughness and Frequency of Consonants. Now, as we struggle with an ill Climate to improve the nobler Kinds of Fruits; are at the Expence of Walls to receive and reverberate the faint Rays of the Sun, and fence against the Northern Blasts; we sometimes by the Help of a good Soil equal the Productions of warmer Countries, who have no need to be at so much Cost or Care: It is the same Thing with respect to the politer Arts among us; and the same Defect of Heat which gives a Fierceness to our Natures, may contribute to that Roughness of our Language, which bears some Analogy to the harsh Fruit of colder Countries. For I do not reckon, that we want a Genius more than the rest of our Neighbours: But your Lordship will be of my Opinion, that we ought to struggle with these natural Disadvantages as much as we can; and be careful whom we employ, whenever we design to correct them; which is a Work that hath hitherto been assumed by the least qualified Hands: So that if the Choice had been left to me, I would rather have trusted the Refinement of our Language, as far as it relates to Sound, to the Judgment of Women, than of illiterate Court-Fops, half-witted Poets, and University-Boys. For, it is plain, that Women in their Manner of corrupting Words, do naturally discard the Consonants, as we do the Vowels. What I am going to tell your Lordship, appears very trifling; that more than once, where some of both Sexes were in Company, I have persuaded two or three of each to take a Pen, and write down a Number of Letters joined together, just as it came into their Heads; and upon reading this Gibberish we have found that which the Men had writ, by the frequent encountering of rough Consonants, to sound like High-Dutch; and the other by the Women, like Italian, abounding in Vowels and Liquids. Now, although I would by no Means give Ladies the Trouble of advising us in the Reformation of our Language; yet I cannot help thinking, that since they have been left out of all Meetings, except Parties at Play, or where worse Designs are carried on, our Conversation hath very much degenerated.

In order to reform our Language; I conceive, my Lord, that a free judicious Choice should be made of such Persons, as are generally allowed to be best qualified for such a Work, without any regard to Quality, Party, or Profession. These to a certain Number, at least, should assemble at some appointed Time and Place, and fix on Rules by which they design to proceed. What Methods they will take, is not for me to prescribe. Your Lordship, and other Persons in great Employment, might please to be of the Number: And I am afraid, such a Society would want your Instruction and Example, as much as your Protection: For I have, not without a little Envy, observed of late the Style of some great Ministers very much to exceed that of any other Productions.

The Persons who are to undertake this work, will have the Example of the

French before them, to imitate where these have proceeded right, and to avoid their Mistakes. Besides the Grammar-part, wherein we are allowed to be very defective, they will observe many gross Improprieties, which however authorized by Practice, and grown familiar, ought to be discarded. They will find many Words that deserve to be utterly thrown out of our Language; many more to be corrected, and perhaps not a few, long since antiquated, which ought to be restored, on Account of their Energy and Sound.

But what I have most at Heart, is, that some Method should be thought on for Ascertaining and Fixing our Language for ever, after such Alterations are made in it as shall be thought requisite. For I am of Opinion, that it is better a Language should not be wholly perfect, than that it should be perpetually changing; and we must give over at one Time or other, or at length infallibly change for the worse: As the Romans did, when they began to quit their Simplicity of Style for affected Refinements; such as we meet in Tacitus and other Authors, which ended by Degrees in many Barbarities, even before the Goths had invaded Italy.

The Fame of our Writers is usually confined to these two Islands; and it is hard it should be limited in Time as much as Place, by the perpetual Variations of our Speech. It is your Lordship's Observation, that if it were not for the Bible and Common-Prayer-Book in the vulgar Tongue, we should hardly be able to understand any thing that was written among us an Hundred Years ago; which is certainly true: For those Books being perpetually read in Churches, have proved a Kind of Standard for Language, especially to the common People. And I doubt whether the Alterations since introduced, have added much to the Beauty or Strength of the English Tongue, although they have taken off a great deal from that Simplicity, which is one of the greatest Perfections in any Language. You, my Lord, who are so conversant in the sacred Writings, and so great a Judge of them in their Originals, will agree, that no Translation our Country ever yet produced, hath come up to that of the Old and New Testament: And by the many beautiful Passages which I have often had the Honour to hear your Lordship cite from thence, I am persuaded that the Translators of the Bible were Masters of an English Stile much fitter for that Work, than any we see in our present Writings; which I take to be owing to the Simplicity that runs through the Whole. Then, as to the greatest Part of our Liturgy, compiled long before the Translation of the Bible now in use, and little altered since; there seem to be in it as great Strains of true sublime Eloquence, as are any where to be found in our Language; which every Man of good Taste will observe in the Communion-Service, that of Burial, and other Parts.

But, where I say that I would have our Language, after it is duly correct, always to last; I do not mean that it should never be enlarged: Provided, that no Word, which a Society shall give a Sanction to, be afterwards antiquated and exploded, they may have Liberty to receive whatever new ones they shall find Occasion for: Because then the old Books will yet be always valuable according to their intrinsick Worth, and not thrown aside on Account of unintelligible Words and Phrases, which appear harsh and uncouth, only because they are out of Fashion. Had the Roman Tongue continued vulgar in that City till this Time; it would have been absolutely necessary, from the mighty Changes that have been made in Law and Religion; from the many Terms of Art required in Trade and in War; from the new Inventions that have happened in the World; from the vast spreading of Navigation and Commerce; with many other obvious Circumstances, to have made great Additions to that Language; yet the Antients would still have been read, and understood with Pleasure and Ease. The Greek Tongue received many Enlargements between the Time of Homer, and that of Plutarch; yet the former Author was probably as well understood in Trajan's Time, as the latter. What Horace says of *Words going off, and perishing like Leaves, and new ones coming in their Place,* is a Misfortune he laments, rather than a Thing he approves: But I cannot see why this should be absolutely necessary, or if it were, what would have become of his *Monumentum œre perennius.*

Writing by Memory only, as I do at present, I would gladly keep within my Depth; and therefore shall not enter into further Particulars. Neither do I pretend more than to shew the Usefulness of this Design, and to make some general Observations; leaving the rest to that Society, which I hope will owe its Institution and Patronage to your Lordship. Besides, I would willingly avoid Repetition; having about a Year ago, communicated to the Publick, much of what I had to offer upon this Subject, by the Hands of an ingenious Gentleman, who for a long Time did thrice a Week divert or instruct the Kingdom by his Papers; and is supposed to pursue the same Design at present, under the Title of *Spectator.* [In a Conversation some Time ago with the Person to whom these Productions are ascribed, I happened to mention the Proposall I have here made to Your Lordship; and in a few dayes after I observed that Author had taken the Hint and treated the same matter in one of his Papers, and with much Judgement, except where he is pleased to put so great a Compliment upon me, as I can never pretend to Deserve.] This Author, who hath tried the Force and Compass of our Language with so much Success, agrees entirely with me in most of my Sentiments relating to it: So do the greatest Part of the Men of Wit and Learning, whom I have had the Happiness to converse with: And therefore I imagine, that such a Society would be pretty unanimous in the main Points.

Your Lordship must allow, that such a Work as this, brought to Perfection, would very much contribute to the Glory of Her Majesty's Reign; which ought to be recorded in Words more durable than Brass, and such as our Posterity may read a thousand Years hence, with Pleasure as well as Admiration. I have always disapproved that false Compliment to Princes: That the most lasting Monument they can have, is the Hearts of their Subjects. It is indeed their greatest present Felicity to reign in their Subjects Hearts; but these are too perishable to preserve their Memories, which can only be done by the Pens of able and faithful Historians. And I take it to be your Lordship's Duty, as prime Minister, to give Order for inspecting our Language, and rendering it fit to record the History of so great and good a Princess. Besides, my Lord, as disinterested as you appear to the World, I am convinced, that no Man is more in the Power of a prevailing favourite Passion than your self; I mean, that Desire of true and lasting Honour, which you have born along with you through every Stage of your Life. To this you have often sacrificed your Interest, your Ease, and your Health: For preserving and encreasing this, you have exposed your Person to secret Treachery, and open Violence. There is not perhaps an Example in History of any Minister, who in so short a Time hath performed so many great Things, and overcome so many great Difficulties. Now, although I am fully convinced, that you fear God, honour your Queen, and love your Country, as much as any of your Fellow-Subjects; yet I must believe, that the Desire of Fame hath been no inconsiderable Motive to quicken you in the Pursuit of those Actions which will best deserve it. But, at the same Time, I must be so plain as to tell your Lordship, that if you will not take some Care to settle our Language, and put it into a State of Continuance, I cannot promise that your Memory shall be preserved above an Hundred Years, further than by imperfect Tradition.

As barbarous and ignorant as we were in former Centuries; there was more effectual Care taken by our Ancestors, to preserve the Memory of Times and Persons, than we find in this Age of Learning and Politeness, as we are pleased to call it. The rude Latin of the Monks is still very intelligible; whereas, had their Records been delivered down only in the vulgar Tongue, so barren and so barbarous, so subject to continual succeeding Changes; they could not now be understood, unless by Antiquaries, who made it their Study to expound them: And we must, at this Day, have been content with such poor Abstracts of our English Story, as laborious Men of low Genius would think fit to give us: And even these, in the next Age, would be likewise swallowed up in succeeding Collections. If Things go on at this Rate; all I can promise your Lordship, is, that about two Hundred Years hence, some painful Compiler, who will be at the Trouble of studying old Language, may inform the World, that in the Reign of Queen Anne, Robert Earl of Oxford, a very wise and excellent Man, was made High-Treasurer, and saved his Country, which in those Days was almost ruined by a foreign War, and a domestick Faction. Thus much he may be able to pick out, and willing to transfer into his new History; but the rest of your Character, which I, or any other Writer, may now value our selves by drawing; and the particular Account of the great Things done under your Ministry, for which you are already so celebrated in most Parts of Europe, will probably be dropt, on Account of the antiquated Style, and Manner they are delivered in.

How then shall any Man, who hath a Genius for History, equal to the best of the Antients, be able to undertake such a Work with Spirit and Chearfulness, when he considers, that he will be read with Pleasure but a very few Years, and in an Age or two shall hardly be understood without an Interpreter? This is like employing an excellent Statuary to work upon mouldring Stone. Those who apply their Studies to preserve the Memory of others, will always have some Concern for their own. And I believe it is for this Reason, that so few Writers among us, of any Distinction, have turned their Thoughts to such a discouraging Employment: For the best English Historian must lie under this Mortification, that when his Style grows antiquated, he will be only considered as a tedious Relater of Facts; and perhaps consulted in his Turn, among other neglected Authors, to furnish Materials for some future Collector.

I doubt your Lordship is but ill entertained with a few scattered Thoughts, upon a Subject that deserves to be treated with Ability and Care: However, I must beg Leave to add a few Words more, perhaps not altogether foreign to the same Matter. I know not whether that which I am going to say, may pass for Caution, Advice, or Reproach; any of which will be justly thought very improper from one in my Station, to one in yours. However, I must venture to affirm, that if Genius and Learning be not encouraged under your Lordship's Administration, you are the most inexcuseable Person alive. All your other Virtues, my Lord, will be defective without this: Your Affability, Candour, and good Nature; that perpetual Agreeableness of Conversation, so disengaged in the Midst of such a Weight of Business and Opposition; even your Justice, Prudence, and Magnanimity, will shine less bright without it. Your Lordship is universally allowed to possess a very large Portion in most Parts of Literature; and to this you owe the cultivating those many Virtues, which otherwise would have been less adorned, or in lower Perfection. Neither can you acquit your self of these Obligations, without letting the Arts, in their Turn, share your Influence and Protection. Besides, who knows but some true Genius may happen to arise under your Ministry, *exortus ut œtherius* Sol. Every Age might, perhaps, produce one or two of these to adorn it, if they were not sunk under the Censure and Obloquy of plodding, servile, imitating Pedants: I do not mean by a true Genius, any bold Writer, who breaks through the Rules of Decency to distinguish himself by the Singularity of Opinions; but one, who upon a deserving Subject, is able to open new Scenes, and discover a Vein of true and noble Thinking, which never entered into any Imagination before: Every stroke of whose Pen is worth all the Paper blotted by Hundreds of others in the Compass of their Lives. I know, my Lord, your Friends will offer in your Defence, that in your private Capacity, you never refused your Purse and Credit to the Service and Support of learned or ingenious Men: And that ever since you have been in publick Employment, you have constantly bestowed your Favours to the most deserving Persons. But I desire your Lordship not to be deceived: We never will admit to these Excuses; nor will allow your private Liberality, as great as it is, to attone for your excessive publick Thrift. But here again, I am afraid most good Subjects will interpose in your Defence, by alledging the desperate Condition you found the Nation in, and the Necessity there was for so able and faithful a Steward to retrieve it, if possible, by the utmost Frugality. We grant all this, my Lord; but then, it ought likewise to be considered, that you have already saved several Millions to the Publick; and that what we ask is too inconsiderable to break into any Rules of the strictest good Husbandry. The French King bestows about half a Dozen Pensions to learned Men in several Parts of Europe; and perhaps a Dozen in his own Kingdom; which, in the whole, do probably not amount to half the Income of many a private Commoner in England; yet have more contributed to the Glory of that Prince, than any Million he hath otherwise employed. For Learning, like all true Merit, is easily satisfied; whilst the False and Counterfeit is perpetually craving, and never thinks it hath enough. The smallest Favour given by a great Prince, as a Mark of Esteem, to reward the Endowments of the Mind, never fails to be returned with Praise and Gratitude, and loudly celebrated to the World. I have known, some Years ago, several Pensions given to particular Persons, (how deservedly I shall not enquire) any one of which, if divided into smaller Parcels, and distributed by the Crown to those who might, upon Occasion, distinguish themselves by some extraordinary Production of Wit or Learning; would be amply sufficient to answer the End. Or, if any such Persons were above Money, (as every great Genius certainly is, with very moderate Conveniences of Life) a Medal, or some Mark of Distinction, would do full as well.

But I forget my Province; and find my self turning Projector before I am aware; although it be one of the last Characters under which I should desire to appear before your Lordship; especially when I have the Ambition of aspiring to that of being, with the greatest Respect and Truth,

      My Lord,

        Your Lordship's

          most Obedient, most Obliged,

          and most Humble Servant,

                                      J. SWIFT

LONDON, Feb.
  22, 1711–12

A LETTER TO A YOUNG POET

Sir,

As I have always profess'd a Friendship for you, and have therefore been
more inquisitive into your Conduct and Studies than is usually agreeable to
young Men, so I must own I am not a little pleas'd to find, by your last Account,
that you have entirely bent your Thoughts to English Poetry, with Design to
make it your Profession and Business. Two Reasons incline me to encourage
you in this Study; one, the Narrowness of your present Circumstances; the
other, the great Use of Poetry to Mankind and Society, and in every Employment of Life. Upon these Views, I cannot but commend your wise Resolution
to withdraw so early from other unprofitable and severe Studies, and betake
yourself to that, which, if you have good Luck, will advance your Fortune, and
make you an Ornament to your Friends and your Country. It may be your
Justification, and farther Encouragement, to consider that History, Ancient or
Modern, cannot furnish you an Instance of one Person, eminent in any
Station, who was not in some Measure vers'd in Poetry, or at least a
Well-wisher to the Professors of it; neither would I despair to prove, if legally
call'd thereto, that it is impossible to be a good Soldier, Divine, or Lawyer, or
even so much as an eminent Bell-Man, or Ballad-Singer, without some Taste
of Poetry, and a competent Skill in Versification: But I say the less of this,
because the renowned Sir P. Sidney has exhausted the Subject before me, in
his Defence of Poesie, on which I shall make no other Remark but this, that he
argues there as if he really believed himself.

For my own part, having never made one Verse since I was at School,
where I suffered too much for my Blunders in Poetry, to have any Love to it
ever since, I am not able, from any Experience of my own, to give you those
Instructions you desire: neither will I declare (for I love to conceal my
Passions) how much I lament my Neglect of Poetry in those Periods of my Life,
which were properest for Improvements in that ornamental Part of Learning;
besides, my Age and Infirmities might well excuse me to you, as being
unqualify'd to be your Writing-Master, with Spectacles on, and a Shaking
Hand. However, that I may not be altogether wanting to you in an Affair of so
much importance to your credit and happiness, I shall here give you some
scatter'd thoughts upon the Subject, such as I have gather'd by Reading and
Observation.

There is a certain little Instrument, the first of those in Use with Scholars,
and the meanest, considering the Materials of it, whether it be a joint of
Wheaten-Straw (the old Arcadian Pipe), or just three inches of slender Wire,
or a stript Feather, or a Corking-Pin. Furthermore, this same diminutive Tool,
for the Posture of it, usually reclines its head on the Thumb of the Right Hand,
sustains the foremost Finger upon its Breast, and is it self supported by the

second. This is commonly known by the Name of a Fescue; I shall here therefore condescend to be this little Elementary Guide, and point out some Particulars which may be of Use to you in your Horn-Book of Poetry.

In the first Place, I am not yet convinc'd, that it is at all necessary for a modern poet to believe in God, or have any serious Sense of Religion; and in this Article you must give me Leave to suspect your Capacities; because Religion being what your Mother taught you, you will hardly find it possible, at least not easy, all at once to get over those early Prejudices, so far as to think it better to be a great Wit than a good Christian, tho' herein the General Practice is against you; so that if, upon Enquiry, you find in your self any such Softnesses, owing to the Nature of your Education, my Advice is, that you forthwith lay down your Pen, as having no farther Business with it in the Way of Poetry, unless you will be content to pass for an Insipid, or will submit to be hooted at by your Fraternity, or can disguise your Religion, as wellbred Men do their Learning, in Complaisance to Company.

For Poetry, as it has been manag'd for some Years past, by such as make a Business of it (and of such only I speak here, for I do not call him a Poet that writes for his Diversion, any more than that Gentleman a Fidler who amuses himself with a Violin) I say, our Poetry of late has been altogether disengag'd from the narrow Notions of Virtue and Piety, because it has been found by Experience of our Professors, that the smallest Quantity of Religion, like a single Drop of Malt-Liquor in Claret, will muddy and discompose the brightest Poetical Genius.

Religion supposes Heaven and Hell, the Word of God, and Sacraments, and twenty other Circumstances, which taken seriously, are a wonderful Check to Wit and Humour, and such as a true poet cannot possibly give into with a saving to his Poetical License; but yet it is necessary for him, that others should believe those Things seriously, that his Wit may be exercised on their Wisdom, for so doing: For tho' a Wit need not have Religion, religion is necessary to a Wit, as an Instrument is to the Hand that plays upon it: And for this the Moderns plead the Example of their great Idol Lucretius, who had not been by half so eminent a Poet (as he truly was), but that he stood tip-toe on Religion, *Religio pedibus subjecta,* and by that rising Ground had the advantage of all the poets of his own or following Times, who were not mounted on the same Pedestal.

Besides, it is farther to be observed, that Petronius, another of their Favourites, speaking of the Qualifications of a good Poet, insists chiefly on the *Liber Spiritus;* by which I have been ignorant enough heretofore to suppose he meant, a good Invention, or great Compass of Thought, or a sprightly Imagination: But I have learned a better Construction, from the Opinion and Practice of the Moderns; and taking it literally for a free Spirit, i.e. a Spirit, or Mind, free or disengag'd from all Prejudices concerning God, Religion, and another World, it is to me a plain Account why our present Sett of Poets are, and hold themselves oblig'd to be, Free-Thinkers.

But altho' I cannot recommend Religion upon the practice of some of our most eminent English Poets, yet I can justly advise you, from their Example, to be conversant in the Scriptures, and, if possible, to make yourself entirely Master of them: In which, however, I intend nothing less than imposing upon you a Task of Piety. Far be it from me to desire you to believe them, or lay any great Stress upon their Authority, (in that you may do as you think fit) but to read them as a Piece of necessary Furniture for a wit and a Poet; which is a very different View from that of a Christian. For I have made it my Observation, that the greatest Wits have been the best Textuaries: Our modern Poets are, all to a Man, almost as well read in the Scriptures as some of our Divines, and often abound more with the Phrase. They have read them Historically, Critically, Musically, Comically, Poetically, and every other Way except Religiously, and have found their Account in doing so. For the Scriptures are undoubtedly a Fund of Wit, and a subject for wit. You may, according to the modern Practice, be witty upon them or out of them: And to speak the Truth, but for them, I know not what our Play-wrights would do for Images, Allusions, Similitudes, Examples, or even Language itself. Shut up the Sacred Books, and I would be bound our Wit would run-down like an Alarm, or fall as the Stocks did, and ruin half the Poets in these Kingdoms. And if that were the Case, how would most of that Tribe, (all, I think, but the immortal Addison, who made a better Use of his Bible, and a few more) who dealt so freely in that Fund, rejoice that they had drawn out in Time, and left the present Generation of Poets to be the Bubbles?

But here I must enter one caution, and desire you to take notice, that in this advice of reading the Scriptures, I had not the least thought concerning your qualifications that way for Poetical Orders; which I mention, because I find a notion of that kind advanc'd by one of our English poets, and is, I suppose, maintain'd by the rest. He says to Spencer, in a pretended Vision,

> With Hands laid on, ordain me fit
> For the great Cure and Ministry of Wit.

Which Passage is, in my Opinion, a notable Allusion to the Scriptures, and making (but reasonable) Allowances for the small circumstance of Profaneness, bordering close upon Blasphemy, is inimitably fine; besides some useful Discoveries made in it, as, that there are Bishops in Poetry, that these Bishops must Ordain young poets, and with laying on Hands; and that Poetry is a Cure of Souls; and consequently speaking, those who have such Cures ought to be Poets, and too often are so: And indeed, as of old, Poets and Priests were one and the same Function, the Alliance of those ministerial Offices is to this Day happily maintain'd in the same Persons; and this I take to be the only justifiable Reason for that Appellation which they so much affect, I mean the modest Title of *Divine Poets*. However, having never been present at the Ceremony of ordaining to the Priesthood of Poetry, I own I have no Notion of the Thing, and shall say the less of it here.

The Scriptures then being generally both the Fountain and Subject of modern Wit, I could do no less than give them the Preference in your Reading. After a thorough Acquaintance with them, I would advise you to turn your

Thoughts to Human Literature, which yet I say more in Compliance with vulgar Opinions, than according to my own Sentiments.

For, indeed, nothing has supriz'd me more, than to see the Prejudices of Mankind as to this Matter of human Learning, who have generally thought it is necessary to be a good Scholar, in order to be a good Poet, than which nothing is falser in Fact, or more contrary to Practice and Experience. Neither will I dispute the Matter, if any Man will undertake to shew me one professed Poet now in Being, who is any thing of what may be justly called a Scholar; or is the worse Poet for that, but perhaps the better, for being so little encumber'd with the Pedantry of Learning: 'Tis true, the contrary was the Opinion of our Forefathers, which we of this Age have Devotion enough to receive from them on their own Terms, and unexamin'd, but not sense enough to preceive 'twas a gross Mistake in them. So Horace has told us.

Scribendi recte sapere est et principium et fons,
Rem tibi Socraticæ poterunt ostendere chartæ.

But to see the different Casts of Men's Heads, some not inferior to that Poet in Understanding (if you will take their own Word for it), do see no consequence in this rule, and are not ashamed to declare themselves of a contrary opinion. Do not many men write well in common account, who have nothing of that Principle? Many are too Wise to be Poets, and others too much Poets to be Wise. Must a man, forsooth, be no less than a philosopher to be a poet, when it is plain, that some of the greatest idiots of the age are our prettiest Performers that Way? And for this, I appeal to the Judgment and observation of Mankind. Sir Ph. Sidney's notable Remark upon this Nation, may not be improper to mention here. He says, "In our Neighbour-Country Ireland, where true learning goes very bare, yet are their poets held in devout Reverence;" which shews, that Learning is no way necessary either to the making a Poet, or judging of him. And farther to see the Fate of Things, notwithstanding our Learning here is as bare as ever, yet are our Poets not held, as formerly, in devout reverence, but are, perhaps, the most contemptible Race of Mortals now in this Kingdom, which is no less to be Wonder'd at than Lamented.

Some of the old Philosophers were Poets (as, according to the fore-mentioned Author, Socrates and Plato were; which, however, is what I did not know before) but that does not say that all Poets are, or that any need be Philosophers, otherwise than as those are so call'd who are a little out at the Elbows. In which sense the great Shakespear might have been a Philosopher; but was no Scholar, yet was an excellent Poet. Neither do I think a late most judicious Critick so much mistaken, as others do, in advancing this Opinion, that Shakespear had been a worse Poet had he been a better Scholar: And Sir W. Davenant is another instance in the same Kind. Nor must it be forgotten, that Plato was an avow'd enemy to Poets, which is, perhaps, the reason why Poets have been always at Enmity with his Profession; and have rejected all Learning and Philosophy for the Sake of that one Philosopher. As I take the Matter, neither Philosophy, nor any Part of Learning, is more necessary to poetry, (which, if you will believe the same Author, is the Sum of all Learning) than to know the Theory of Light, and the several Proportions and Diversifications of it in particular Colours, is to a good Painter.

Whereas therefore, a certain Author, call'd Petronius Arbiter, going upon the same Mistake, has confidently declar'd, the one Ingredient of a good Poet is *Mens ingenti literarum flumine inundata;* I do, on the contrary, declare, that this his Assertion (to speak of it in the softest Terms) is no better than an invidious and unhandsome Reflection on all the Gentlemen-Poets of these Times; for, with his good Leave, much less than a Flood, or Inundation, will serve the Turn, and to my certain Knowledge, some of our greatest Wits, in your poetical Way, have not as much real Learning as would cover a Six-Pence in the Bottom of a Bason; nor do I think the worse of them.

For, to speak my private Opinion, I am for every Man's working upon his own Materials, and producing only what he can find within himself, which is commonly a better Stock than the Owner knows it to be. I think Flowers of Wit ought to spring, as those in a Garden do, from their own Root and Stem, without Foreign Assistance. I would have a Man's Wit rather like a Fountain, that feeds itself invisibly, than a River, that is supply'd by several Streams from abroad.

Or if it be necessary, as the Case is with some barren Wits, to take in the Thoughts of others, in order to draw forth their own, as dry Pumps will not play till Water is thrown into them; in that Necessity, I would recommend some of the approv'd Standard-Authors of Antiquity for your Perusal, as a Poet and a Wit; because Maggots being what you look for, as Monkeys do for Vermin in their Keepers Heads, you will find they abound in good old Authors, as in rich old Cheese, not in the new; and for that Reason you must have the Classicks, especially the most Worm-eaten of them, often in your Hands.

But with this Caution, that you are not to use those Antients as unlucky Lads do their old Fathers, and make no Conscience of picking their Pockets and pillaging them. Your Business is not to steal from them, but to improve upon them, and make their Sentiments your own; which is an Effect of great Judgment; and tho' difficult, yet very possible, without the scurvy Imputation of Filching: For I humbly conceive, tho' I light my Candle at my Neighbour's Fire, that does not alter the Property, or make the Wyck, the Wax, or the Flame, or the whole Candle, less my own.

Possibly you may think it a very severe Task, to arrive at a competent Knowledge of so many of the Antients, as excel in their Way; and indeed it would be really so, but for the short and easy method lately found out of Abstracts, Abridgments, Summaries, &c. which are admirable Expedients for being very learned with little or no Reading; and have the same Use with Burning-Glasses, to collect the diffus'd Rays of Wit and Learning in Authors, and make them point with Warmth and Quickness upon the Reader's Imagination. And to this is nearly related that other modern Device of consulting Indexes, which is to read Books Hebraically, and begin where others usually end; and this is a compendious Way of coming to an Acquaintance with Authors: For authors are to be used like Lobsters, you must look for the best Meat in the Tails, and lay the Bodies back again in the Dish. Your cunningest Thieves (and what else are Readers who only read to borrow, i.e. to steal) use to cut off the Portmanteau from behind, without staying to dive into the Pockets of the owner. Lastly, you are taught thus much in the very Elements of Philosophy, for one of the first rules in Logick is, *Finis est primus in intentione.*

The learned World is therefore most highly indebted to a late painful and judicious Editor of the Classicks, who has labour'd in that new Way with exceeding Felicity. Every Author, by his Management, sweats under himself, being over-loaded with his own Index, and carries, like a North-Country Pedlar, all his Substance and Furniture upon his Back, and with as great Variety of Trifles. To him let all young Students make their Compliments for so much Time and Pains sav'd in the Pursuit of useful Knowledge; for whoever shortens a Road is a Benefactor to the Publick, and to every particular Person who has Occasion to travel that Way.

But to proceed. I have lamented nothing more in my Time, than the Disuse of some ingenious little Plays, in Fashion with young Folks, when I was a Boy, and to which the great Facility of that Age, above ours, in composing, was certainly owing; and if any Thing has brought a Damp upon the Versification of these Times, we have no farther than this to go for the Cause of it. Now could these Sports be happily reviv'd, I am of Opinion your wisest Course would be to apply your Thoughts to them, and never fail to make a Party when you can, in those profitable Diversions. For Example, Crambo is of extraordinary Use to good Rhiming, and Rhiming is what I have ever accounted the very Essential of a good Poet: And in that Notion I am not singular; for the aforesaid Sir P. Sidney has declar'd, That the chief Life of modern Versifying consisteth in the like sounding of Words, which we call rhime; which is an Authority, either without Exception or above any Reply. Wherefore, you are ever to try a good Poem as you would a sound Pipkin, and if it rings well upon the Knuckle, be sure there is no Flaw in it. Verse without Rhime is a Body without a Soul, (for the chief Life consisteth in the Rhime) or a Bell without a Clapper; which, in Strictness, is no Bell, as being neither of Use nor Delight. And the same ever-honoured Knight, with so musical an Ear, had that veneration for the Tuneableness and Chiming of verse, that he speaks of a Poet as one that has the Reverend Title of a Rhimer. Our celebrated Milton has done these Nations great Prejudice in this Particular, having spoil'd as many reverend rhimers, by his example, as he has made real Poets.

For which Reason, I am overjoy'd to hear, that a very ingenious Youth of this Town is now upon the useful Design (for which he is never enough to be commended) of bestowing Rhime upon Milton's *Paradise Lost,* which will make your Poem, in that only defective, more Heroick and Sonorous than it has hitherto been. I wish the Gentleman Success in the Performance; and, as it is a work in which a young Man could not be more happily employ'd, or appear in with greater Advantage to his Character, so I am concern'd that it did not fall out to be your Province.

With much the same View, I would recommend to you the witty Play of

Pictures and Motto's, which will furnish your Imagination with great Store of Images and suitable Devices. We of these Kingdoms have found our Account in this Diversion, as little as we consider or acknowledge it. For to this we owe our eminent Felicity in Posies of Rings, Motto's of Snuff-Boxes, the Humours of Sign-Posts, with their elegant inscriptions, &c. in which kind of Productions not any Nation in the World, no, not the Dutch themselves, will presume to rival us.

For much the same Reason it may be proper for you to have some Insight into the Play call'd *What is it like?* as of great Use in common Practice, to quicken slow Capacities, and improve the quickest: but the chief End of it is to supply the Fancy with Variety of Similies for all Subjects. It will teach you to bring Things to a Likeness which have not the least Conformity in Nature, which is properly Creation, and the very Business of a Poet, as his Name implies; and let me tell you, a good Poet can no more be without a Stock of Similies by him than a Shoe-Maker without his Lasts. He shou'd have them siz'd, and rang'd, and hung up in order in his Shop, ready for all Customers, and shap'd to the Feet of all sorts of Verse: And here I cou'd more fully (and I long to do it) insist upon the wonderful Harmony and Resemblance between a Poet and a Shoe-Maker, in many Circumstances common to both; such as the Binding of their Temples, the Stuff they work upon, and the Paring-Knife they use, &c. but that I would not digress, nor seem to trifle in so serious a Matter.

Now I say, if you apply yourself to these diminutive Sports (not to mention others of equal Ingenuity, such as Draw-Gloves, Cross-Purposes, Questions and Commands, and the rest) it is not to be conceived what Benefit (of Nature) you will find by them, and how they will open the Body of your Invention. To these devote your Spare Hours, or rather Spare all your Hours to them, and then you will act as becomes a wise Man, and make even Diversions an Improvement; like the inimitable Management of the Bee, which does the whole Business of Life at once, and at the same time both feeds, and works, and diverts itself.

Your own Prudence will, I doubt not, direct you to take a Place every Evening amongst the Ingenious, in the Corner of a certain Coffee-House in this Town, where you will receive a Turn equally right as to Wit, Religion, and Politicks: As likewise to be as frequent at the Play-House as you can afford, without selling your Books. For in our chast Theatre, even Cato himself might sit to the falling of the Curtain: Besides, you will sometimes meet with tolerable Conversation amongst the Players; they are such a kind of Men as may pass, upon the same sort of Capacities, for Wits off the Stage, as they do for fine Gentlemen upon it. Besides that, I have known a Factor deal in as good Ware, and sell as cheap, as the Merchant himself that employs him.

Add to this the Expediency of furnishing out your Shelves with a choice Collection of modern Miscellanies, in the gayest Edition; and of reading all sorts of Plays, especially the New, and above all, those of our own Growth, printed by Subscription, in which Article of Irish Manufacture I readily agree to the late Proposal, and am altogether for rejecting and renouncing every

Thing that comes from England; To what Purpose shou'd we go thither for Coals or Poetry when we have a Vein within ourselves equally Good and more Convenient? Lastly,

A common-place-Book is what a provident Poet cannot subsist without for this proverbial Reason, that great Wits have short Memories; and whereas on the other Hand, poets being Lyars by Profession, ought to have good Memories; to reconcile these, a Book of this sort is in the Nature of a Supplemental Memory, or a Record of what occurs remarkable in every Day's Reading or Conversation: There you enter not only your own Original Thoughts, (which, a hundred to one, are few and insignificant) but such of other Men as you think fit to make your own by entering them there. For take this for a Rule, when an Author is in your Books, you have the same Demand upon him for his Wit as a merchant has for your Money when you are in his.

By these few and easy Prescriptions (with the Help of a good Genius) 'tis possible you may in a short time arrive at the Accomplishments of a Poet, and shine in that Character. As for your manner of Composing, and choice of Subjects, I cannot take upon me to be your Director, but I will venture to give you some short Hints, which you may enlarge upon at your Leisure. Let me entreat you then by no Means to lay aside that Notion peculiar to our modern Refiners of Poetry, which is, That a Poet must never Write or Discourse as the ordinary Part of Mankind do, but in Number and Verse, as an Oracle; which I mention the rather, because upon this Principle I have known Heroes brought into the Pulpit, and a whole Sermon compos'd and deliver'd in Blank Verse, to the vast Credit of the Preacher, no less than the real Entertainment and great Edification of the Audience.

The secret of which I take to be this. When the Matter of such Discourses is but mere Clay, or, as we usually call it, sad Stuff, the Preacher, who can afford no better, wisely Moulds, and Polishes, and Drys, and Washes this piece of Earthen-Ware, and then Bakes it with Poetic Fire, after which it will ring like any Pan-crock, and is a good dish to set before common Guests, as every Congregation is that comes so often for Entertainment to one Place.

There was a good old Custom in Use, which our Ancestors had, of Invoking the Muses at the Entrance of their Poems, I suppose, by Way of craving a Blessing: This the graceless Moderns have in a great Measure laid aside, but are not to be followed in that Poetical Impiety; for altho' to nice Ears such Invocations may sound harsh and disagreeable (as tuning instruments is before a Concert) they are equally necessary. Again, you must not fail to dress your Muse in a Forehead-cloth of Greek or Latin, I mean, you are always to make use of a quaint Motto to all your Compositions; for, besides that this Artifice bespeaks the Reader's Opinion of the Writer's Learning, it is otherwise useful and commendable. A bright Passage in the Front of a Poem is a good Mark, like a Star in a Horse's Face, and the Piece will certainly go off the better for it. The *Os magna sonaturum*, which, if I remember right, Horace makes one qualification of a good Poet, may teach you not to gagg your Muse, or stint your Self in Words and Epithets (which cost you nothing) contrary to the Practice of some few out-of-the-way Writers, who use a natural and concise

Expression, and affect a Stile like unto a Shrewsbury-cake, Short and Sweet upon the Palate; they will not afford you a Word more than is necessary to make them intelligible, which is as poor and niggardly as it would be to set down no more Meat than your Company will be sure to eat up. Words are but Lacquies to Sense, and will dance attendance, without wages or Compulsion; *Verba non invita sequentur.*

Farthermore, when you set about Composing, it may be necessary, for your ease and better Distillation of Wit, to put on your worst Cloaths, and the worse the better; for an Author, like a Limbick, will yield the better for having a Rag about him: Besides that, I have observed a Gardener cut the outward Rind of a Tree (which is the Surtout of it), to make it bear well: And this is a natural Account of the usual Poverty of Poets, and is an Argument why Wits, of all Men living, ought to be ill Clad. I have always a secret Veneration for any one I observe to be a little out of Repair in his Person, as supposing him either a Poet or a Philosopher; because the richest Minerals are ever found under the most ragged and withered Surface of Earth.

As for your Choice of Subjects, I have only to give you this Caution, that as a handsome Way of Praising is certainly the most difficult Point in Writing or Speaking, I wou'd by no means advise any young Man to make his first Essay in Panegyrick, besides the Danger of it; for a particular Encomium is ever attended with more Ill-will than any general Invective, for which I need give no Reasons; wherefore, my Counsel is, that you use the Point of your Pen, not the Feather: Let your first Attempt be a *Coup d'Eclat* in the way of Libel, Lampoon or Satyr. Knock down half a score of Reputations, and you will infallibly raise your Own; and so it be with Wit, no matter how little Justice, for Fiction is your Trade.

Every great Genius seems to ride upon Mankind, like Pyrrhus on his Elephant; and the way to have the absolute Ascendant of your resty Nag, and to keep your Seat, is, at your first mounting, to afford him the Whip and Spurs plentifully, after which, you may travel the rest of the Day with great Alacrity. Once kick the world, and the world and you will live together at a reasonable good Understanding. You cannot but know, that these of your Profession have been called *Genus irritabile vatum,* and you will find it necessary to qualify yourself for that whaspish Society, by exerting your Talent of Satyr upon the first Occasion, and to abandon Good-nature, only to prove yourself a true Poet, which you will allow to be a valuable Consideration: In a Word, a young Robber is usually ent'red by a Murder: A young Hound is blooded when he comes first into the Field: A young Bully begins with killing his Man: And a young Poet must shew his Wit, as the other his Courage, by cutting and slashing, and laying about him, and banging Mankind.

Lastly, it will be your Wisdom to look out betimes for a good Service for your Muse, according to her Skill and Qualifications, whether in the Nature of a Dairy-Maid, a Cook, or Charwoman: I mean to hire out your Pen to a Party which will afford you both Pay and Protection; and when you have to do with the Press (as you will long to be there), take care to bespeak an importunate Friend to extort your Productions with an agreeable Violence; and which,

according to the Cue between you, you must surrender *digito male pertinaci:*
There is a Decency in this, for it no more becomes an Author in Modesty to
have a Hand in publishing his own Works, than a Woman in Labour to lay
herself.

I wou'd be very loth to give the least Umbrage of offence by what I have
here said, as I may do, if I should be thought to insinuate that these
Circumstances of good Writing have been unknown to, or not observed by, the
Poets of this Kingdom: I will do my Countrymen the Justice to say, they have
written by the foregoing Rules with great Exactness, and so far, as hardly to
come behind those of their Profession in England, in Perfection of low Writing.
The Sublime, indeed, is not so common with us; but ample Amends is made
for that want, in great Abundance of the Admirable and Amazing, which
appears in all our Compositions. Our very good Friend (the Knight aforesaid)
speaking of the Force of Poetry, mentions "rhiming to Death", which (adds he)
is said to be done in Ireland, and truly, to our Honour be it spoken, that Power,
in a great Measure, continues with us to this Day.

I would now offer some poor Thoughts of mine for the Encouragement of
Poetry in this Kingdom, if I could hope they would be agreeable. I have had
many an aking Heart for the ill Plight of that noble Profession here, and it has
been my late and early Study how to bring it into better Circumstances. And
surely, considering what Monstrous Wits in the Poetick Way do almost daily
start up and surprize us in this Town; what prodigious Genius's we have here
(of which I could give Instances without Number) and withal of what great
Benefit it may be to our Trade to encourage that Science here, (for it is plain
our Linen-Manufacture is advanced by the great Waste of Paper made by our
present Sett of Poets, not to mention other necessary Uses of the same to
Shop-keepers, especially Grocers, Apothecaries, and Pastry-Cooks; and I might
add, but for our Writers, the Nation wou'd in a little time be utterly destitute of
Bum-Fodder, and must of Necessity import the same from England and
Holland, where they have it in great abundance, by the indefatigable Labour
of their own Wits:) I say, these things consider'd, I am humbly of Opinion, it
would be worth the Care of our Governours to cherish Gentlemen of the Quill,
and give them all proper Encouragements here. And since I am upon the
Subject, I shall speak my mind very freely, and if I added, saucily, it is no more
than my Birth-right as a Briton.

Seriously then, I have many Years lamented the want of a Grub-Street in
this our large and polite City, unless the whole may be called one. And this I
have accounted an unpardonable Defect in our Constitution, ever since I had
any Opinions I could call my own. Everyone knows Grub-Street is a Market for
Small-Ware in Wit, and as necessary, considering the usual Purgings of the
human Brain, as the Nose is upon a Man's Face: And for the same Reasons we
have here a Court, a College, a Play-house, and beautiful Ladies, and fine
Gentlemen, and good Claret, and abundance of Pens, Ink, and Paper, (clear of
Taxes) and every other Circumstance to provoke Wit; and yet those whose
Province it is have not yet thought fit to appoint a Place for Evacuations of it,
which is a very hard Case, as may be judg'd by Comparisons.

And truly this Defect has been attended with unspeakable Inconveniences; for, not to mention the Prejudice done to the Commonwealth of Letters, I am of opinion we suffer in our Health by it: I believe our corrupted Air, and frequent thick Fogs, are in a great measure owing to the common exposal of our Wit, and that with good Management our poetical Vapours might be carry'd off in a common Drain, and fall into one Quarter of the Town, without infecting the whole, as the Case is at present, to the great Offence of our Nobility and Gentry, and others of nice Noses. When Writers of all Sizes, like Freemen of the City, are at liberty to throw out their Filth and excrementitious Productions in every Street as they please, what can the Consequence be, but that the Town must be poyson'd, and become such another Jakes, as by report of our great Travellers, Edinburgh is at Night, a thing well to be consider'd in these pestilential Times.

I am not of the Society for Reformation of Manners, but, without that pragmatical Title, I would be glad to see some Amendment in the matter before us: Wherefore I humbly bespeak the Favour of the Lord Mayor, the Court of Aldermen and Common Council, together with the whole Circle of Arts in this Town, and do recommend this Affair to their most political Consideration; and I persuade myself they will not be wanting in their best Endeavours, when they can serve two such good Ends at once, as both to keep the Town sweet, and encourage Poetry in it. Neither do I make any Exceptions as to Satyrical Poets and Lampoon Writers, in Consideration of their Office: For though indeed their Business is to rake into Kennels, and gather up the Filth of Streets and Families, (in which respect they may be, for aught I know, as necessary to the Town as Scavengers or Chimney sweeps) yet I have observed they too have themselves at the same Time very foul cloaths, and, like dirty Persons, leave more Filth and Nastiness than they sweep away.

In a Word, what I would be at (for I love to be plain in Matters of Importance to my Country) is, That some private Street, or blind Alley, of this Town may be fitted up at the Charge of the Publick, as an apartment for the Muses, (like those at Rome and Amsterdam, for their Female Relations) and be wholly consign'd to the Uses of our Wits, furnish'd compleatly with all Appurtenances, such as Authors, Supervisors, Presses, Printers, Hawkers, Shops, and Ware-Houses, abundance of Garrets, and every other Implement and Circumstance of Wit; the Benefit of which would obviously be this, viz. That we should then have a safe Repository for our best Productions, which at present are handed about in Single Sheets or Manuscripts, and may be altogether lost, (which were a Pity) or at the best are subject, in that loose Dress, like handsome Women, to great Abuses.

Another Point, that has cost me some melancholy Reflections, is the present State of the Play-House, the Encouragement of which hath an immediate influence upon the Poetry of the Kingdom; As a good Market improves the Tillage of the neighbouring Country, and enriches the Ploughman; neither do we of this Town seem enough to know or consider the vast Benefit of a Play-House to our City and Nation; that Single House is the Fountain of all our Love, Wit, Dress, and Gallantry. It is the school of Wisdom, for there we learn to know What's what; which, however, I cannot say is always in that Place sound Knowledge. There our young Folks drop their Childish Mistakes, and come first to perceive their Mothers Cheat of the Parsely-Bed; there too they get rid of Natural Prejudices, especially those of Religion and Modesty, which are great Restraints to a Free People. The same is a Remedy for the Spleen and Blushing, and several distempers occasion'd by the Stagnation of the Blood. It is likewise a School of Common Swearing; my young Master, who at first but minc'd an Oath, is taught there to mouth it gracefully, and to swear as he reads French, *ore rotundo*. Prophaneness was before to him in the Nature of his best Suit or holiday-cloathes; but upon frequenting the Play-house, Swearing, Cursing, and Lying, become like his Everyday coat, wastecoat, and Breeches. Now I say, common Swearing, a produce of this Country as plentiful as our Corn, thus cultivated by the Play-House, might, with Management, be of wonderful Advantage to the Nation, as a Projector of the Swearers Bank has prov'd at large. Lastly, the Stage in great Measure supports the Pulpit; for I know not what our Divines cou'd have to say there against the corruptions of the Age, but for the Play-house, which is the Seminary of them. From which it is plain, the Publick is a Gainer by the Play-House, and consequently ought to countenance it; and were I worthy to put in my Word, or prescribe to my Betters, I could say in what Manner.

I have heard that a certain Gentleman has great designs to serve the Publick in the Way of their Diversions, with due Encouragement; that is, if he can obtain some Concordatum-Money, or Yearly Salary, and handsome Contributions: And well he deserves the Favours of the Nation; for, to do him Justice, he has an uncommon Skill in Pastimes, having altogether apply'd his Studies that Way, and travell'd full many a League, by Sea and Land, for this his profound Knowledge. With that View alone he has visited all the Courts and Cities in Europe, and has been at more Pains than I shall speak of to take an exact Draught of the Play-House at the Hague, as a Model for a new one here. But what can a private Man do by himself in so publick an Undertaking? It is not to be doubted, but by his Care and Industry vast Improvements may be made, not only in our Play-House, (which is his immediate Province) but in our Gaming-Ordinaries Groom-Porter's, Lotteries, Bowling-Greens, Nine-pin Allies, Bear-Gardens, Cock-pits, Prizes, Puppet and Raree-shows, and whatever else concerns the elegant Divertisements of this Town. He is truly an Original Genius, and I felicitate this our Capital City on his Residence here, where I wish him long to live and flourish for the Good of the Commonwealth.

Once more: If any farther Applications shall be made on t'other Side, to obtain a Charter for a Bank here, I presume to make a Request, that Poetry may be a Sharer in that Privilege, being a Fund as real, and to the full as well grounded, as our Stocks; but I fear our Neighbours, who envy our Wit, as much as they do our Wealth or Trade, will give no Encouragement to either. I believe also, it might be proper to erect a Corporation of Poets in this City. I have been Idle enough in my Time, to make a Computation of Wits here, and do find we have three hundred performing Poets and upwards, in and about this Town, reckoning six Score to the Hundred, and allowing for Demi's like Pint Bottles; including also the several Denominations of Imitators, Translators, and Familiar-Letter-Writers, &c. One of these last has lately entertain'd the town with an original Piece, and such a one as, I dare say, the late British Spectator, in his Decline, would have call'd, An excellent Specimen of the true Sublime; or, A noble Poem; or, a fine Copy of Verses, on a Subject perfectly new, (the Author himself) and had given it a Place amongst his latest Lucubrations.

But, as I was saying, so many Poets, I am confident, are sufficient to furnish out a Corporation in point of Number. Then for the several Degrees of subordinate Members requisite to such a Body, there can be no Want; for altho' we have not one Masterly Poet, yet we abound with Wardens and Beadles, having a Multitude of Poetasters, Poetito's, Parcel-Poets, Poet-Apes, and Philo-Poets, and many of inferior Attainments in Wit, but strong Inclinations to it, which are by Odds more than all the rest. Nor shall I ever be at Ease, 'til this project of mine (for which I am heartily thankful to myself) shall be reduced to Practice. I long to see the Day, when our Poets will be a regular and distinct Body, and wait upon our Lord-mayor on publick Days, like other good Citizens, in Gowns turn'd up with Green instead of lawrels; and when I myself, who makes this Proposal, shall be free of their Company.

To conclude, what if our Government had a Poet-Laureat here, as in England? What if our University had a Professor of Poetry here as in England? What if our Lord-Mayor had a City Bard here, as in England? And, to refine upon England, What if every Corporation, Parish, and Ward in this Town, had a Poet in Fee, as they have not in England? Lastly, What if every one so qualify'd were obliged to add one more than usual to the Number of his Domesticks, and besides a fool and a Chaplain, (which are often united in one Person) would retain a Poet in his Family; for, perhaps, a Rhimer is as necessary amongst Servants of a House, as a Dobben with his Bells, at the Head of a Team: But these Things I leave to the Wisdom of my Superiors.

While I have been directing your Pen, I should not forget to govern my own, which has already exceeded the Bounds of a Letter: I must therefore take my Leave abruptly, and desire you, without farther Ceremony, to believe that I am, Sir,

                                                        Your most humble Servant.
Dec. 1. 1720.

Alexander Pope

1688–1744

Alexander Pope was born on May 31, 1688, the year William of Orange became King William III of England. Pope's family, being Roman Catholic, was obliged to leave London, and eventually settled on an estate at Benfield in Windsor Forest. They cultivated the company of other prominent Catholic families in the district, most notably Sir William Trumbull, under whose guidance Pope took his first steps in the study of literature. Soon the influential critic William Walsh took notice of the gifted youngster, and when the dramatist William Wycherley began to take an interest in the fledgling author's poetical works, a great future was predicted for him.

As a child, Pope's predilection for intense intellectual endeavour, combined with the effects of a severe tubercular infection, hastened the decay of his health. The young Pope offers a classic example of the zealous autodidact whose physical deterioration was exacerbated by long hours of study. Pope's deformity was to haunt him for the rest of his life, a fact which has inspired some of his less careful biographers to ascribe the acerbic and cruel aspect of his satiric genius to a constitutional bitterness associated with that deformity.

But the young Pope was no Shakespearean Richard, descanting on his own deformity, and such an interpretation of the facts of biography can shed little light on his literary works. Nevertheless, Pope's celebrated verbal rancor did have a direct connection with his illness. A hunchback, Pope was especially sensitive to insults when none were intended—as in the case of his relationship with Addison—but it is equally true that in at least one of his extended personal quarrels (with the pompous and difficult John Dennis) Pope did have to defend himself against brutal and explicit allusions to his deformity.

It is hardly surprising then, that in one of his first and most celebrated critical compositions, Pope held up the style of Dennis as an example of what was most deficient in the current literary scene. He did this in his *Essay on Criticism* (1711), which was to make his name in the literary circles of the capital. Addison reviewed it favorably in the two-hundred and thirty-fifth number of the *Spectator;* and though Pope's fame had been increasing for a number of years, it was the *Essay* which established his reputation. In 1712, Pope wrote the *Rape of the Lock,* a brightly irreverent mock-epic which set all London talking. In this work, Pope perfected that style, characterized by sharp sallies of wit and an evenness of tone, which Johnson was to admire so much when comparing him to Dryden:

> Dryden's performances were always hasty, either excited by some external occasion, or extorted by some domestick necessity; he composed without consideration, and published without correction. What

his mind simply could supply at call, or gather in one excursion, was all that he sought, or gave. The dilatory caution of Pope enabled him to condense his sentiments, to multiply his images, and to accumulate all that study might produce, or chance might supply. If the flights of Dryden therefore are higher, Pope continues longer on the wing. If of Dryden's fire the blaze is brighter, of Pope's the heat is more regular and constant. Dryden often surpasses expectation, and Pope never falls below it. Dryden is read with frequent astonishment, and Pope with perpetual delight.

Such a style may have provided perpetual delight for the reader, but it gave nothing by way of a livelihood for the author. Pope was famous, but poor; this was the main motive which drove him to translate Homer. The translation of the *Iliad*, done with the assistance of Broome and Thomas Parnell, proved to be an enormous success, and the profits which accrued to Pope by means of large numbers of subscriptions made him financially secure for life. And though the insufferable Richard Bentley is reputed to have said, "A fine poem, Mr. Pope, but you must not call it Homer," most readers thought highly of the translation. It even inspired Addison, at this point quite probably jealous of Pope, to encourage his associate Tickell to bring out a rival translation.

Around 1713—soon after writing the prologue for *Cato*—Pope broke with Addison and his Whig circle of friends and allied himself with such talented literary Tories as Swift, Arbuthnot, Gay, and others. This group formed the nucleus of what came to be known as the Scriblerus Club, dedicated to the vilification of dunces, especially of the Whig persuasion. Such works as Arbuthnot's *Memoirs of the Life, Works, and Discoveries of Martinus Scriblerus*, Swift's *Gulliver's Travels*, and Pope's own *Dunciad* (1738) were written in connection with the Scriblerus confraternity.

In the late 1730's Pope conceived of the idea of writing a series of philosophical poems on moral and domestic subjects; the first of these is the *Essay on Man* (1733). Though he did not complete this project, he did occupy himself with other projects, such as the edition of Shakespeare (1725), the first competent edition form of Shakespeare's works from a critical-textual stand-point. Presently Scriblerus had begun to disperse; but with Swift as his guest (1726–27) Pope collaborated on the miscellany which included the brilliant satire on literary mediocrity, *Peri Bathous, or the Art of Sinking in Poetry* (1727). During the latter part of his life Pope wrote several epistles, dialogues, and satires, in addition to his *Imitations of Horace*, which seemed to have been very highly regarded, so much so that Pope was deemed the English Horace.

In his last years Pope was beset by physical suffering. He died on May 31, 1744, at his estate at Twickenham.

AN ESSAY ON CRITICISM

'Tis hard to say, if greater Want of Skill
Appear in Writing or in Judging ill;
But, of the two, less dang'rous is th' Offence,
To tire our Patience, than mis-lead our Sense:
Some few in that, but Numbers err in this,
Ten Censure wrong for one who Writes amiss;
A Fool might once himself alone expose,
Now One in Verse makes many more in Prose.
   'Tis with our Judgments as our Watches, none
Go just alike, yet each believes his own.
In Poets as true Genius is but rare,
True Taste as seldom is the Critick's Share;
Both must alike from Heav'n derive their Light,
These born to Judge, as well as those to Write.
Let such teach others who themselves excell,
And censure freely who have written well.
Authors are partial to their Wit, 'tis true,
But are not Criticks to their Judgment too?
   Yet if we look more closely, we shall find
Most have the Seeds of Judgment in their Mind;
Nature affords at least a glimm'ring Light;
The Lines, tho' touch'd but faintly, are drawn right.
But as the slightest Sketch, if justly trac'd,   ⎫
Is by ill Colouring but the more disgrac'd,   ⎬
So by false Learning is good Sense defac'd;   ⎭
Some are bewilder'd in the Maze of Schools,
And some made Coxcombs Nature meant but Fools.
In search of Wit these lose their common Sense,
And then turn Criticks in their own Defence.
Each burns alike, who can, or cannot write,
Or with a Rival's, or an Eunuch's spite.
All Fools have still an Itching to deride,
And fain wou'd be upon the Laughing Side:
If Mævius Scribble in Apollo's spight,
There are, who judge still worse than he can write.
   Some have at first for Wits, then Poets past,
Turn'd Criticks next, and prov'd plain Fools at last;
Some neither can for Wits nor Criticks pass,
As heavy Mules are neither Horse nor Ass.
Those half-learn'd Witlings, num'rous in our Isle,
As half-form'd Insects on the Banks of Nile;

Unfinish'd Things, one knows not what to call,
Their Generation's so equivocal:
To tell 'em, wou'd a hundred Tongues require,
Or one vain Wit's, that might a hundred tire.
　　But you who seek to give and merit Fame,
And justly bear a Critick's noble Name,
Be sure your self and your own Reach to know,
How far your Genius, Taste, and Learning go;
Launch not beyond your Depth, but be discreet,
And mark that Point where Sense and Dulness meet.
　　Nature to all things fix'd the Limits fit,
And wisely curb'd proud Man's pretending Wit:
As on the Land while here the Ocean gains,
In other Parts it leaves wide sandy Plains;
Thus in the Soul while Memory prevails,
The solid Pow'r of Understanding fails;
Where Beams of warm Imagination play,
The Memory's soft Figures melt away.
One Science only will one Genius fit;
So vast is Art, so narrow Human Wit:
Not only bounded to peculiar Arts,
But oft in those, confin'd to single Parts.
Like Kings we lose the Conquests gain'd before,
By vain Ambition still to make them more:
Each might his sev'ral Province well command,
Wou'd all but stoop to what they understand.
　　First follow Nature, and your Judgment frame
By her just Standard, which is still the same:
Unerring Nature, still divinely bright,
One clear, unchang'd, and Universal Light,
Life, Force, and Beauty, must to all impart,
At once the Source, and End, and Test of Art.
Art from that Fund each just Supply provides,
Works without Show, and without Pomp presides:
In some fair Body thus th' informing Soul
With Spirits feeds, with Vigour fills the whole,
Each Motion guides, and ev'ry Nerve sustains;
It self unseen, but in th' Effects, remains.
Some, to whom Heav'n in Wit has been profuse,
Want as much more, to turn it to its use;
For Wit and Judgment often are at strife,
Tho' meant each other's Aid, like Man and Wife.
'Tis more to guide than spur the Muse's Steed;
Restrain his Fury, than provoke his Speed;
The winged Courser, like a gen'rous Horse,
Shows most true Mettle when you check his Course.

    Those Rules of old discover'd, not devis'd,
Are Nature still, but Nature Methodiz'd;
Nature, like Liberty, is but restrain'd
By the same Laws which first herself ordain'd.
    Hear how learn'd Greece her useful Rules indites,
When to repress, and when indulge our Flights:
High on Parnassus' Top her Sons she show'd,
And pointed out those arduous Paths they trod,
Held from afar, aloft, th' Immortal Prize,
And urg'd the rest by equal Steps to rise;
Just Precepts thus from great Examples giv'n,
She drew from them what they deriv'd from Heav'n.
The gen'rous Critick fann'd the Poet's Fire,
And taught the World, with Reason to Admire.
Then Criticism the Muse's Handmaid prov'd,
To dress her Charms, and make her more belov'd;
But following Wits from that Intention stray'd;
Who cou'd not win the Mistress, woo'd the Maid;
Against the Poets their own Arms they turn'd,
Sure to hate most the Men from whom they learn'd.
So modern Pothecaries, taught the Art
By Doctor's Bills to play the Doctor's Part,
Bold in the Practice of mistaken Rules,
Prescribe, apply, and call their Masters Fools.
Some on the Leaves of ancient Authors prey,
Nor Time nor Moths e'er spoil'd so much as they:
Some dryly plain, without Invention's Aid,
Write dull Receits how Poems may be made:
These leave the Sense, their Learning to display,
And those explain the Meaning quite away.
    You then whose Judgment the right Course wou'd steer,
Know well each Ancient's proper Character,
His Fable, Subject, Scope in ev'ry Page,
Religion, Country, Genius of his Age:
Without all these at once before your Eyes,
Cavil you may, but never Criticize.
Be Homer's Works your Study, and Delight,
Read them by Day, and meditate by Night,
Thence form your Judgment, thence your Maxims bring,
And trace the Muses upward to their Spring;
Still with It self compar'd, his Text peruse;
And let your Comment be the Mantuan Muse.
    When first young Maro in his boundless Mind
A Work t'outlast Immortal Rome design'd,
Perhaps he seem'd above the Critick's Law,
And but from Nature's Fountains scorn'd to draw:

But when t'examine ev'ry Part he came,
Nature and Homer were, he found, the same:
Convinc'd, amaz'd, he checks the bold Design, ⎫
And Rules as strict his labour'd Work confine, ⎬
As if the Stagyrite o'erlook'd each Line. ⎭
Learn hence for Ancient Rules a just Esteem;
To copy Nature is to copy Them.

   Some Beauties yet, no Precepts can declare,
For there's a Happiness as well as Care.
Musick resembles Poetry, in each ⎫
Are nameless Graces which no methods teach, ⎬
And which a Master-Hand alone can reach. ⎭
If, where the Rules not far enough extend,
(Since Rules were made but to promote their End)
Some Lucky Licence answers to the full
Th' Intent propos'd, that Licence is a Rule.
Thus Pegasus, a nearer way to take,
May boldly deviate from the common Track.
Great Wits sometimes may gloriously offend,
And rise to Faults true Criticks dare not mend;
From vulgar Bounds with brave Disorder part,
And snatch a Grace beyond the Reach of Art,
Which, without passing thro' the Judgment, gains
The Heart, and all its End at once attains.
In Prospects, thus, some Objects please our Eyes, ⎫
Which out of Nature's common Order rise, ⎬
The shapeless Rock, or hanging Precipice. ⎭
But tho' the Ancients thus their Rules invade,
(As Kings dispense with Laws Themselves have made)
Moderns, beware! Or if you must offend
Against the Precept, ne'er transgress its End,
Let it be seldom, and compell'd by Need,
And have, at least, Their Precedent to plead.
The Critick else proceeds without Remorse,
Seizes your Fame, and puts his Laws in force.

   I know there are, to whose presumptuous Thoughts
Those Freer Beauties, ev'n in Them, seem Faults:
Some Figures monstrous and mis-shap'd appear,
Consider'd singly, or beheld too near,
Which, but proportion'd to their Light, or Place,
Due Distance reconciles to Form and Grace.
A prudent Chief not always must display
His Pow'rs in equal Ranks, and fair Array,
But with th' Occasion and the Place comply,
Conceal his Force, nay seem sometimes to Fly.
Those oft are Stratagems which Errors seem,

Nor is it Homer Nods, but We that Dream.
　Still green with Bays each ancient Altar stands,
Above the reach of Sacrilegious Hands,
Secure from Flames, from Envy's fiercer Rage,
Destructive War, and all-involving Age.
See, from each Clime the Learn'd their Incense bring;
Hear, in all Tongues consenting Pæans ring!
In Praise so just, let ev'ry Voice be join'd,
And fill the Gen'ral Chorus of Mankind!
Hail Bards Triumphant! born in happier Days;
Immortal Heirs of Universal Praise!
Whose Honours with Increase of Ages grow,
As Streams roll down, enlarging as they flow!
Nations unborn your mighty Names shall sound,
And Worlds applaud that must not yet be found!
Oh may some Spark of your Cœlestial Fire
The last, the meanest of your Sons inspire,
(That on weak Wings, from far, pursues your Flights;
Glows while he reads, but trembles as he writes)
To teach vain Wits a Science little known,
T' admire Superior Sense, and doubt their own!

　Of all the Causes which conspire to blind
Man's erring Judgment, and misguide the Mind,
What the weak Head with strongest Byass rules,
Is Pride, the never-failing Vice of Fools.
Whatever Nature has in Worth deny'd,
She gives in large Recruits of needful Pride;
For as in Bodies, thus in Souls, we find
What wants in Blood and Spirits, swell'd with Wind;
Pride, where Wit fails, steps in to our Defence,
And fills up all the mighty Void of Sense!
If once right Reason drives that Cloud away,
Truth breaks upon us with resistless Day;
Trust not your self; but your Defects to know,
Make use of ev'ry Friend—and ev'ry Foe.
　A little Learning is a dang'rous Thing;
Drink deep, or taste not the Pierian Spring:
There shallow Draughts intoxicate the Brain,
And drinking largely sobers us again.
Fir'd at first Sight with what the Muse imparts,
In fearless Youth we tempt the Heights of Arts,
While from the bounded Level of our Mind,
Short Views we take, nor see the Lengths behind,
But more advanc'd, behold with strange Surprize
New, distant Scenes of endless Science rise!

So pleas'd at first, the towring Alps we try,
Mount o'er the Vales, and seem to tread the Sky;
Th' Eternal Snows appear already past,
And the first Clouds and Mountains seem the last:
But those attain'd, we tremble to survey
The growing Labours of the lengthen'd Way,
Th' increasing Prospect tires our wandring Eyes,
Hills peep o'er Hills, and Alps on Alps arise!
   A perfect Judge will read each Work of Wit
With the same Spirit that its Author writ,
Survey the Whole, nor seek slight Faults to find,
Where Nature moves, and Rapture warms the Mind;
Nor lose, for that malignant dull Delight,
The gen'rous Pleasure to be charm'd with Wit.
But in such Lays as neither ebb, nor flow,
Correctly cold, and regularly low,
That shunning Faults, one quiet Tenour keep;
We cannot blame indeed—but we may sleep.
In Wit, as Nature, what affects our Hearts
Is not th' Exactness of peculiar Parts;
'Tis not a Lip, or Eye, we Beauty call,
But the joint Force and full Result of all.
Thus when we view some well-proportion'd Dome,
(The World's just Wonder, and ev'n thine O Rome!)
No single Parts unequally surprize;
All comes united to th' admiring Eyes;
No monstrous Height, or Breadth, or Length appear;
The Whole at once is Bold, and Regular.
   Whoever thinks a faultless Piece to see,
Thinks what ne'er was, nor is, nor e'er shall be.
In ev'ry Work regard the Writer's End,
Since none can compass more than they Intend;
And if the means be just, the Conduct true,
Applause, in spite of trivial Faults, is due.
As Men of Breeding, sometimes Men of Wit,
T' avoid great Errors, must the less commit,
Neglect the Rules each Verbal Critick lays,
For not to know some Trifles, is a Praise.
Most Criticks, fond of some subservient Art,
Still make the Whole depend upon a Part,
They talk of Principles, but Notions prize,
And All to one lov'd Folly Sacrifice.
   Once on a time, La Mancha's Knight, they say,
A certain Bard encountring on the Way,
Discours'd in Terms as just, with Looks as Sage,
As e'er cou'd Dennis, of the Grecian Stage;
Concluding all were desp'rate Sots and Fools,

Who durst depart from Aristotle's Rules.
Our Author, happy in a Judge so nice,
Produc'd his Play, and beg'd the Knight's Advice,
Made him observe the Subject and the Plot,
The Manners, Passions, Unities, what not?
All which, exact to Rule were brought about,
Were but a Combate in the Lists left out.
What! Leave the Combate out? Exclaims the Knight;
Yes, or we must renounce the Stagyrite.
Not so by Heav'n (he answers in a Rage)
Knights, Squires, and Steeds, must enter on the Stage.
So vast a Throng the Stage can ne'er contain.
Then build a New, or act it in a Plain.

   Thus Criticks, of less Judgment than Caprice,
Curious, not Knowing, not exact, but nice,
Form short Ideas; and offend in Arts
(As most in Manners) by a Love to Parts.

   Some to Conceit alone their Taste confine,
And glitt'ring Thoughts struck out at ev'ry Line;
Pleas'd with a Work where nothing's just or fit;
One glaring Chaos and wild Heap of Wit:
Poets like Painters, thus, unskill'd to trace
The naked Nature and the living Grace,
With Gold and Jewels cover ev'ry Part,
And hide with Ornaments their Want of Art.
True Wit is Nature to Advantage drest,
What oft was Thought, but ne'er so well Exprest,
Something, whose Truth convinc'd at Sight we find,
That gives us back the Image of our Mind:
As Shades more sweetly recommend the Light,
So modest Plainness sets off sprightly Wit:
For Works may have more Wit than does 'em good,
As Bodies perish through Excess of Blood.

   Others for Language all their Care express,
And value Books, as Women Men, for Dress:
Their Praise is still—*The stile is excellent:*
The Sense, they humbly take upon Content.
Words are like Leaves; and where they most abound,
Much Fruit of Sense beneath is rarely found.
False Eloquence, like the Prismatic Glass,
Its gawdy Colours spreads on ev'ry place;
The Face of Nature we no more Survey,
All glares alike, without Distinction gay:
But true Expression, like th' unchanging Sun, ⎫
Clears, and improves whate'er it shines upon, ⎬
It gilds all Objects, but it alters none. ⎭
Expression is the Dress of Thought, and still

Appears more decent as more suitable;
A vile Conceit in pompous Words exprest,
Is like a Clown in regal Purple drest;
For diff'rent Styles with diff'rent Subjects sort,
As several Garbs with Country, Town, and Court.
Some by Old Words to Fame have made Pretence;
Ancients in Phrase, meer Moderns in their Sense!
Such labour'd Nothings, in so strange a Style,
Amaze th'unlearn'd, and make the Learned Smile.
Unlucky, as Fungoso in the Play,
These Sparks with aukward Vanity display   }
What the Fine Gentleman wore Yesterday!
And but so mimick ancient Wits at best,
As Apes our Grandsires in their Doublets drest.
In Words, as Fashions, the same Rule will hold;
Alike Fantastick, if too New, or Old;
Be not the first by whom the New are try'd,
Nor yet the last to lay the Old aside.
    But most by Numbers judge a Poet's Song,
And smooth or rough, with them, is right or wrong;
In the bright Muse tho' thousand Charms conspire,
Her Voice is all these tuneful Fools admire,
Who haunt Parnassus but to please their Ear,   }
Not mend their Minds; as some to Church repair,
Not for the Doctrine, but the Musick there.
These Equal Syllables alone require,
Tho' oft the Ear the open Vowels tire,
While Expletives their feeble Aid do join,
And ten low Words oft creep in one dull Line,
While they ring round the same unvary'd Chimes,
With sure Returns of still expected Rhymes.
Where-e'er you find *the cooling Western Breeze*,
In the next Line, it *whispers thro' the Trees*;
If *Chrystal Streams with pleasing Murmurs creep*,
the Reader's threaten'd (not in vain) with *Sleep*.
Then, at the last, and only Couplet fraught
With some unmeaning Thing they call a Thought,
A needless Alexandrine ends the Song,
That like a wounded Snake, drags its slow length along.
Leave such to tune their own dull Rhimes, and know
What's roundly smooth, or languishingly slow;
And praise the Easie Vigor of a Line,
Where Denham's Strength, and Waller's Sweetness join.
True Ease in Writing comes from Art, not Chance,
As those move easiest who have learn'd to dance.
'Tis not enough no Harshness gives Offence,

The Sound must seem an Eccho to the Sense.
Soft is the Strain when Zephyr gently blows,
And the smooth Stream in smoother Numbers flows;
But when loud Surges lash the sounding Shore,
The hoarse, rough Verse shou'd like the Torrent roar.
When Ajax strives, some Rock's vast Weight to throw,
The Line too labours, and the Words move slow;
Not so, when swift Camilla scours the Plain,
Flies o'er th'unbending Corn, and skims along the Main.
Hear how Timotheus' vary'd Lays surprize,
And bid Alternate Passions fall and rise!
While, at each Change, the Son of Lybian Jove
Now burns with Glory, and then melts with Love;
Now his fierce Eyes with sparkling Fury glow;
Now Sighs steal out, and Tears begin to flow:
Persians and Greeks like Turns of Nature found,
And the World's Victor stood subdu'd by Sound!
The Pow'r of Musick all our Hearts allow;
And what Timotheus was, is Dryden now.

   Avoid Extreams; and shun the Fault of such,
Who still are pleas'd too little, or too much.
At ev'ry Trifle scorn to take Offence,
That always shows Great Pride, or Little Sense;
Those Heads as Stomachs are not sure the best
Which nauseate all, and nothing can digest.
Yet let not each gay Turn thy Rapture move,
For Fools Admire, but Men of Sense Approve;
As things seem large which we thro' Mists descry,
Dulness is ever apt to Magnify.

   Some foreign Writers, some our own despise;
The Ancients only, or the Moderns prize:
(Thus Wit, like Faith, by each Man is apply'd
To one small Sect, and All are damn'd beside.)
Meanly they seek the Blessing to confine,
And force that Sun but on a Part to Shine;
Which not alone the Southern Wit sublimes,
But ripens Spirits in cold Northern Climes;
Which from the first has shone on Ages past,
Enlights the present, and shall warm the last:
(Tho' each may feel Increases and Decays,
And see now clearer and now darker Days)
Regard not then if Wit be Old or New,
But blame the False, and value still the True.

   Some ne'er advance a Judgment of their own,
But catch the spreading Notion of the Town;
They reason and conclude by Precedent,

And own stale Nonsense which they ne'er invent.
Some judge of Authors' Names, not Works, and then
Nor praise nor blame the Writings, but the Men.
Of all this Servile Herd the worst is He
That in proud Dulness joins with Quality,
A constant Critick at the Great-man's Board,
To fetch and carry Nonsense for my Lord.
What woful stuff this Madrigal wou'd be,
In some starv'd Hackny Sonneteer, or me?
But let a Lord once own the happy Lines,
How the Wit brightens! How the Style refines!
Before his sacred Name flies ev'ry Fault,
And each exalted Stanza teems with Thought!
    The Vulgar thus through Imitation err;
As oft the Learn'd by being Singular;
So much they scorn the Crowd, that if the Throng
By Chance go right, they purposely go wrong;
So Schismatics the plain Believers quit,
And are but damn'd for having too much Wit.
    Some praise at Morning what they blame at Night;
But always think the last Opinion right.
A Muse by these is like a Mistress us'd,
This hour she's idoliz'd, the next abus'd,
While their weak Heads, like Towns unfortify'd,
'Twixt Sense and Nonsense daily change their Side.
Ask them the Cause; *They're wiser still,* they say;
And still to Morrow's wiser than to Day.
We think our Fathers Fools, so wise we grow;
Our wiser Sons, no doubt, will think us so.
Once School-Divines this zealous Isle o'erspread;
Who knew most Sentences was deepest read;
Faith, Gospel, All, seem'd made to be disputed,
And none had Sense enough to be Confuted.
Scotists and Thomists, now, in Peace remain,
Amidst their kindred Cobwebs in Duck-Lane.
If Faith it self has diff'rent Dresses worn,
What wonder Modes in Wit shou'd take their Turn?
Oft, leaving what is Natural and fit,
The current Folly proves the ready Wit,
And Authors think their Reputation safe,
Which lives as long as Fools are pleas'd to Laugh.
    Some valuing those of their own Side, or Mind,
Still make themselves the measure of Mankind;
Fondly we think we honour Merit then,
When we but praise Our selves in Other Men.
Parties in Wit attend on those of State,

And publick Faction doubles private Hate.
Pride, Malice, Folly, against Dryden rose,
In various Shapes of Parsons, Criticks, Beaus;
But Sense surviv'd, when merry Jests were past;
For rising Merit will buoy up at last.
Might he return, and bless once more our Eyes,
New Blackmores and new Milbourns must arise;
Nay shou'd great Homer lift his awful Head,
Zoilus again would start up from the Dead.
Envy will Merit as its Shade pursue,
But like a Shadow, proves the Substance true;
For envy'd Wit, like Sol Eclips'd, makes known
Th' opposing Body's Grossness, not its own.
When first that Sun too powerful Beams displays,
It draws up Vapours which obscure its Rays;
Be ev'n those Clouds at last adorn its Way,
Reflect new Glories, and augment the Day.
   Be thou the first true Merit to befriend;
His Praise is lost, who stays till All commend;
Short is the Date, alas, of Modern Rhymes;
And 'tis but just to let 'em live betimes.
No longer now that Golden Age appears,
When Patriarch-Wits surviv'd a thousand Years;
Now Length of Fame (our second Life) is lost,
And bare Threescore is all ev'n That can boast:
Our Sons their Fathers' failing Language see,
And such as Chaucer is, shall Dryden be.
So when the faithful Pencil has design'd
Some bright Idea of the Master's Mind,
Where a new World leaps out at his command,
And ready Nature waits upon his Hand;
When the ripe Colours soften and unite,
And sweetly melt into just Shade and Light,
When mellowing Years their full Perfection give,
And each Bold Figure just begins to Live;
The treach'rous Colours the fair Art betray,
And all the bright Creation fades away!
   Unhappy Wit, like most mistaken Things,
Attones not for the Envy which it brings.
In Youth alone its empty Praise we boast,
But soon the Short-liv'd Vanity is lost!
Like some fair Flow'r the early Spring supplies,
That gaily Blooms, but ev'n in blooming Dies.
What is this Wit which must our Cares employ?
The Owner's Wife, that other Men enjoy,
Then most our Trouble still when most admir'd,

And still the more we give, the more requir'd;
Whose Fame with Pains we guard, but lose with Ease,
Sure some to vex, but never all to please;
'Tis what the Vicious fear, the Virtuous shun;
By Fools 'tis hated, and by Knaves undone!
　　If Wit so much from Ign'rance undergo,
Ah let not Learning too commence its Foe!
Of old, those met Rewards who cou'd excel,
And such were Prais'd who but endeavour'd well:
Tho' Triumphs were to Gen'rals only due,
Crowns were reserv'd to grace the Soldiers too.
Now, they who reach Parnassus' lofty Crown,
Employ their Pains to spurn some others down;
And while Self-Love each jealous Writer rules,
Contending Wits become the Sport of Fools:
But still the Worst with most Regret commend,
For each Ill Author is as bad a Friend.
To what base Ends, and by what abject Ways,
Are Mortals urg'd thro' Sacred Lust of Praise!
Ah ne'er so dire a Thirst of Glory boast,
Nor in the Critick let the Man be lost!
Good-Nature and Good-Sense must ever join;
To Err is Humane; to Forgive, Divine.
　　But if in Noble Minds some Dregs remain,
Not yet purg'd off, of Spleen and sow'r Disdain,
Discharge that Rage on more Provoking Crimes,
Nor fear a Dearth in these Flagitious Times.
No Pardon vile Obscenity should find,
Tho' Wit and Art conspire to move your Mind;
But Dulness with Obscenity must prove
As Shameful sure as Impotence in Love.
In the fat Age of Pleasure, Wealth, and Ease,
Sprung the rank Weed, and thriv'd with large Increase;
When Love was all an easie Monarch's Care;
Seldom at Council, never in a War:
Jilts rul'd the State, and Statesmen Farces writ;
Nay Wits had Pensions, and young Lords had Wit:
The Fair sate panting at a Courtier's Play,
And not a Mask went un-improv'd away:
The modest Fan was lifted up no more,
And Virgins smil'd at what they blush'd before—
The following Licence of a Foreign Reign
Did all the Dregs of bold Socinus drain;
Then Unbelieving Priests reform'd the Nation,
And Vice admir'd to find a Flatt'rer there!
Encourag'd thus, Witt's Titans brav'd the Skies,

And the Press groan'd with Licenc'd Blasphemies—
These Monsters, Criticks! with your Darts engage,
Here point your Thunder, and exhaust your Rage!
Yet shun their Fault, who, Scandalously nice,
Will needs mistake an Author into Vice;
All seems Infected that th' Infected spy,
As all looks yellow to the Jaundic'd Eye.

    Learn then what Morals Criticks ought to show,
For 'tis but half a Judge's Task, to Know.
'Tis not enough, Taste, Judgment, Learning, join;
In all you speak, let Truth and Candor Shine:
That not alone what to your Sense is due,
All may allow; but seek your Friendship too.
    Be silent always when you doubt your Sense;
And speak, tho' sure, with seeming Diffidence:
Some positive persisting Fops we know,
Who, if once wrong, will needs be always so;
But you, with Pleasure own your Errors past,
And make each Day a Critick on the last.
    'Tis not enough your Counsel still be true,
And taught more Pleasant Methods of Salvation;
Where Heav'ns Free Subjects might their Rights dispute,
Lest God himself shou'd seem too Absolute.
Pulpits their Sacred Satire learn'd to spare,
Blunt Truths more Mischief than nice Falshoods do;
Men must be taught as if you taught them not;
And Things unknown propos'd as Things forgot:
Without Good Breeding, Truth is disapprov'd;
That only makes Superior Sense belov'd.
    Be Niggards of Advice on no Pretence;
For the worst Avarice is that of Sense:
With mean Complacence ne'er betray your Trust,
Nor be so Civil as to prove Unjust; ·
Fear not the Anger of the Wise to raise;
Those best can bear Reproof, who merit Praise.
    'Twere well, might Criticks still this Freedom take;
But Appius reddens at each Word you speak,
And stares, Tremendous! with a threatning Eye,
Like some fierce Tyrant in Old Tapestry!
Fear most to tax an Honourable Fool,
Whose Right it is, uncensur'd to be dull;
Such without Wit are Poets when they please,
As without Learning they can take Degrees.
Leave dang'rous Truths to unsuccessful Satyrs,
And Flattery to fulsome Dedicators,

Whom, when they Praise, the World believes no more,
Than when they promise to give Scribling o'er.
'Tis best sometimes your Censure to restrain,
And charitably let the Dull be vain:
Your Silence there is better than your Spite,
For who can rail so long as they can write?
Still humming on, their drowzy Course they keep,
And lash'd so long, like Tops, are lash'd asleep.
False Steps but help them to renew the Race,
As after Stumbling, Jades will mend their Pace.
What Crouds of these, impenitently bold,
In Sounds and jingling Syllables grown old,
Still run on Poets in a raging Vein,
Ev'n to the Dregs and Squeezings of the Brain;
Strain out the last, dull dropping of their Sense,
And Rhyme with all the Rage of Impotence!
  Such shameless Bards we have; and yet 'tis true,
There are as mad, abandon'd Criticks too.
The Bookful Blockhead, ignorantly read,
With Loads of Learned Lumber in his Head,
With his own Tongue still edifies his Ears,
And always List'ning to Himself appears.
All Books he reads, and all he reads assails,
From Dryden's *Fables* down to Durfey's *Tales*.
With him, most Authors steal their Works, or buy;
Garth did not write his own Dispensary.
Name a new Play, and he's the Poet's Friend,
Nay show'd his Faults—but when wou'd Poets mend?
No Place so Sacred from such Fops is barr'd,
Nor is Paul's Church more safe than Paul's Church-yard:
Nay, fly to Altars; there they'll talk you dead;
For Fools rush in where Angels fear to tread.
Distrustful Sense with modest Caution speaks; }
It still looks home, and short Excursions makes; }
But ratling Nonsense in full Vollies breaks; }
And never shock'd, and never turn'd aside,
Bursts out, resistless, with a thundering Tyde!
  But where's the Man, who Counsel can bestow,
Still pleas'd to teach, and yet not proud to know?
Unbiass'd, or by Favour or by Spite;
Not dully prepossest, nor blindly right;
Tho' Learn'd, well-bred; and tho' well-bred, sincere;
Modestly bold, and Humanly severe?
Who to a Friend his Faults can freely show,
And gladly praise the Merit of a Foe?
Blest with a Taste exact, yet unconfin'd;

A Knowledge both of Books and Humankind;
Gen'rous Converse; a Soul exempt from Pride;
And Love to Praise, with Reason on his Side?
    Such once were Criticks, such the Happy Few,
Athens and Rome in better Ages knew.
The mighty Stagyrite first left the Shore,
Spread all his Sails, and durst the Deeps explore;
He steer'd securely, and discover'd far,
Led by the Light of the Mæonian Star.
Poets, a Race long unconfin'd and free,
Still fond and proud of Savage Liberty,
Receiv'd his Laws, and stood convinc'd 'twas fit
Who conquer'd Nature, shou'd preside o'er Wit.
    Horace still charms with graceful Negligence,
And without Method talks us into Sense,
Will like a Friend familiarly convey
The truest Notions in the easiest way.
He, who Supream in Judgment, as in Wit,
Might boldly censure, as he boldly writ,
Yet judg'd with Coolness, tho' he sung with Fire;
His Precepts teach but what his Works inspire.
Our Criticks take a contrary Extream,
They judge with Fury, but they write with Fle'me:
Nor suffers Horace more in wrong Translations
By Wits, than Criticks in as wrong Quotations.
    See Dionysius Homer's Thoughts refine,
And call new Beauties forth from ev'ry Line!
    Fancy and Art in gay Petronius please,
The Scholar's Learning, with the Courtier's Ease.
    In grave Quintilian's copious Work we find
The justest Rules, and clearest Method join'd;
Thus useful Arms in Magazines we place,
All rang'd in Order, and dispos'd with Grace,
But less to please the Eye, than arm the Hand,
Still fit for Use, and ready at Command.
    Thee, bold Longinus! all the Nine inspire,
And bless their Critick with a Poet's Fire.
An ardent Judge, who Zealous in his Trust,
With Warmth gives Sentence, yet is always Just;
Whose own Example strengthens all his Laws,
And Is himself that great Sublime he draws.
    Thus long succeeding Criticks justly reign'd,
Licence repress'd, and useful Laws ordain'd;
Learning and Rome alike in Empire grew,
And Arts still follow'd where her Eagles flew;
From the same Foes, at last, both felt their Doom,

And the same Age saw Learning fall, and Rome.
With Tyranny, then Superstition join'd,
As that the Body, this enslav'd the Mind;
Much was Believ'd, but little understood,
And to be dull was constru'd to be good;
A second Deluge Learning thus o'er-run,
And the Monks finish'd what the Goths begun.

   At length, Erasmus, that great, injur'd Name,
(The Glory of the Priesthood, and the Shame!)
Stemm'd the wild Torrent of a barb'rous Age,
And drove those Holy Vandals off the Stage.

   But see! each Muse, in Leo's Golden Days,
Starts from her Trance, and trims her wither'd Bays!
Rome's ancient Genius, o'er its Ruins spread,
Shakes off the Dust, and rears his rev'rend Head!
Then Sculpture and her Sister-Arts revive;
Stones leap'd to Form, and Rocks began to live;
With sweeter Notes each rising Temple rung;
A Raphael painted, and a Vida sung!
Immortal Vida! on whose honour'd Brow
The Poet's Bays and Critick's Ivy grow:
Cremona now shall ever boast thy Name,
As next in Place to Mantua, next in Fame!

   But soon by Impious Arms from Latium chas'd,
Their ancient Bounds the banish'd Muses past;
Thence Arts o'er all the Northern World advance;
But Critic Learning flourish'd most in France.
The Rules, a Nation born to serve, obeys,
And Boileau still in Right of Horace sways.
But we, brave Britons, Foreign Laws despis'd,
And kept unconquer'd, and unciviliz'd,
Fierce for the Liberties of Wit, and bold,
We still defy'd the Romans, as of old.
Yet some there were, among the sounder Few
Of those who less presum'd, and better knew,
Who durst assert the juster Ancient Cause,
And here restor'd Wit's Fundamental Laws.
Such was the Muse, whose Rules and Practice tell,
Nature's chief Master-piece is writing well.
Such was Roscomon—not more learn'd than good,
With Manners gen'rous as his Noble Blood;
To him the Wit of Greece and Rome was known,
And ev'ry Author's Merit, but his own.
Such late was Walsh,—the Muse's Judge and Friend,
Who justly knew to blame or to commend;
To Failings mild, but zealous for Desert;

The clearest Head, and the sincerest Heart.
This humble Praise, lamented Shade! receive,
This Praise at least a grateful Muse may give!
The Muse, whose early Voice you taught to Sing,
Prescrib'd her Heights, and prun'd her tender Wing,
(Her Guide now lost) no more attempts to rise,
But in low Numbers short Excursions tries:
Content, if hence th' Unlearn'd their Wants may view,
The Learn'd reflect on what before they knew:
Careless of Censure, nor too fond of Fame,
Still pleas'd to praise, yet not afraid to blame,
Averse alike to Flatter, or Offend,
Not free from Faults, nor yet too vain to mend.

THE ILIAD

THE PREFACE

Homer is universally allow'd to have had the greatest Invention of any Writer whatever. The Praise of Judgment Virgil has justly contested with him, and others may have their Pretensions as to particular Excellencies; but his Invention remains yet unrival'd. Nor is it a Wonder if he has ever been acknowledg'd the greatest of Poets, who most excell'd in That which is the very Foundation of Poetry. It is the Invention that in different degrees distinguishes all great Genius's: The utmost Stretch of human Study, Learning, and Industry, which masters every thing besides, can never attain to this. It furnishes Art with all her Materials, and without it Judgment itself can at best but steal wisely: For Art is only like a prudent Steward that lives on managing the Riches of Nature. Whatever Praises may be given to Works of Judgment, there is not even a single Beauty in them but is owing to the Invention: As in the most regular Gardens, however Art may carry the greatest Appearance, there is not a Plant or Flower but is the Gift of Nature. The first can only reduce the Beauties of the latter into a more obvious Figure, which the common Eye may better take in, and is therefore more entertain'd with. And perhaps the reason why most Criticks are inclin'd to prefer a judicious and methodical Genius to a great and fruitful one, is, because they find it easier for themselves to pursue their Observations through an uniform and bounded Walk of Art, than to comprehend the vast and various Extent of Nature.

Our Author's Work is a wild Paradise, where if we cannot see all the Beauties so distinctly as in an order'd Garden, it is only because the Number of them is infinitely greater. 'Tis like a copious Nursery which contains the Seeds and first Productions of every kind, out of which those who follow'd him have but selected some particular Plants, each according to his Fancy, to cultivate and beautify. If some things are too luxuriant, it is owing to the Richness of the Soil; and if others are not arriv'd to Perfection or Maturity, it is only because they are overrun and opprest by those of a stronger Nature.

It is to the Strength of this amazing Invention we are to attribute that unequal'd Fire and Rapture, which is so forcible in Homer, that no Man of a true Poetical Spirit is Master of himself while he reads him. What he writes is of the most animated Nature imaginable; every thing moves, every thing lives, and is put in Action. If a Council be call'd, or a Battle fought, you are not coldly inform'd of what was said or done as from a third Person; the Reader is hurry'd out of himself by the Force of the Poet's Imagination, and turns in one place to a Hearer, in another to a Spectator. The Course of his Verses resembles that of the Army he describes,

Οἱ δ' ἄρ' ἴσαν, ὡσεί τε πυρὶ χθὼν πᾶσα νέμοιτο.

They pour along like a Fire that sweeps the whole Earth before it. 'Tis however remarkable that his Fancy, which is every where vigorous, is not discover'd immediately at the beginning of his Poem in its fullest Splendor: It grows in the Progress both upon himself and others, and becomes on Fire like a Chariot-Wheel, by its own Rapidity. Exact Disposition, just Thought, correct Elocution, polish'd Numbers, may have been found in a thousand; but this Poetical Fire, this *Vivida vis animi,* in a very few. Even in Works where all those are imperfect or neglected, this can over-power Criticism, and make us admire even while we dis-approve. Nay, where this appears, tho' attended with Absurdities, it brightens all the Rubbish about it, 'till we see nothing but its own Splendor. This Fire is discern'd in Virgil, but discern'd as through a Glass, reflected, and more shining than warm, but every where equal and constant: In Lucan and Statius, it bursts out in sudden, short, and interrupted Flashes: In Milton, it glows like a Furnace kept up to an uncommon Fierceness by the Force of Art: In Shakespear, it strikes before we are aware, like an accidental Fire from Heaven: But in Homer, and in him only, it burns every where clearly, and every where irresistibly.

I shall here endeavour to show, how this vast Invention exerts itself in a manner superior to that of any Poet, thro' all the main constituent Parts of his Work, as it is the great and peculiar Characteristick which distinguishes him from all other Authors.

This strong and ruling Faculty was like a powerful Planet, which in the Violence of its Course, drew all things within its Vortex. It seem'd not enough to have taken in the whole Circle of Arts, and the whole Compass of Nature; all the inward Passions and Affections of Mankind to supply his Characters, and all the outward Forms and Images of Things for his Descriptions; but wanting yet an ampler Sphere to expatiate in, he open'd a new and boundless Walk for his Imagination, and created a World for himself in the Invention of Fable. That which Aristotle calls the *Soul of Poetry,* was first breath'd into it by Homer. I shall begin with considering him in this Part, as it is naturally the first, and I speak of it both as it means the Design of a Poem, and as it is taken for Fiction.

Fable may be divided into the *Probable,* the *Allegorical,* and the *Marvelous.* The *Probable Fable* is the Recital of such Actions as tho' they did not happen, yet might, in the common course of Nature: Or of such as tho' they did, become Fables by the additional Episodes and manner of telling them. Of this sort is the main Story of an Epic Poem, the Return of Ulysses, the Settlement of the Trojans in Italy, or the like. That of the *Iliad* is the Anger of Achilles, the most short and single Subject that ever was chosen by any Poet. Yet this he has supplied with a vaster Variety of Incidents and Events, and crouded with a greater Number of Councils, Speeches, Battles, and Episodes of all kinds, than are to be found even in those Poems whose Schemes are of the utmost Latitude and Irregularity. The Action is hurry'd on with the most vehement Spirit, and its whole Duration employs not so much as fifty Days. Virgil, for want of so warm a Genius, aided himself by taking in a more extensive Subject, as well as a greater Length of Time, and contracting the Design of both Homer's Poems into one, which is yet but a fourth part as large as his. The other Epic Poets have us'd the same Practice, but generally carry'd it so far as to superinduce a Multiplicity of Fables, destroy the Unity of Action, and lose their Readers in an unreasonable Length of Time. Nor is it only in the main Design that they have been unable to add to his Invention, but they have follow'd him in every Episode and Part of Story. If he has given a regular Catalogue of an Army, they all draw up their Forces in the same Order. If he has funeral Games for Patroclus, Virgil has the same for Anchises, and Statius (rather than omit them) destroys the Unity of his Action for those of Archemorus. If Ulysses visit the Shades, the Æneas of Virgil and Scipio of Silius are sent after him. If he be detain'd from his Return by the Allurements of Calypso, so is Æneas by Dido, and Rinaldo by Armida. If Achilles be absent from the Army on the Score of a Quarrel thro' half the Poem, Rinaldo must absent himself just as long, on the like account. If he gives his Heroe a Suit of celestial Armour, Virgil and Tasso make the same Present to theirs. Virgil has not only observ'd this close Imitation of Homer, but where he had not led the way, supply'd the Want from other Greek Authors. Thus the Story of Sinon and the Taking of Troy was copied (says Macrobius) almost word for word from Pisander, as the Loves of Dido and Æneas are taken from those of Medæa and Jason in Apollonius, and several others in the same manner.

To proceed to the *Allegorical Fable:* If we reflect upon those innumerable Knowledges, those Secrets of Nature and Physical Philosophy which Homer is generally suppos'd to have wrapt up in his Allegories, what a new and ample Scene of Wonder may this Consideration afford us? How fertile will that Imagination appear, which was able to cloath all the Properties of Elements, the Qualifications of the Mind, the Virtues and Vices, in Forms and Persons; and to introduce them into Actions agreeable to the Nature of the Things they shadow'd? This is a Field in which no succeeding Poets could dispute with Homer; and whatever Commendations have been allow'd them on this Head, are by no means for their Invention in having enlarg'd his Circle, but for their Judgment in having contracted it. For when the Mode of Learning chang'd in following Ages, and Science was deliver'd in a plainer manner, it then became as reasonable in the more modern Poets to lay it aside, as it was in Homer to make use of it. And perhaps it was no unhappy Circumstance for Virgil, that there was not in his Time that Demand upon him of so great an Invention, as might be capable of furnishing all those Allegorical Parts of a Poem.

The *Marvelous Fable* includes whatever is supernatural, and especially the Machines of the Gods. If Homer was not the first who introduc'd the Deities (as Herodotus imagines) into the Religion of Greece, he seems the first who brought them into a System of Machinery for Poetry, and such an one as makes its greatest Importance and Dignity. For we find those Authors who have been offended at the literal Notion of the Gods, constantly laying their Accusation against Homer as the undoubted Inventor of them. But whatever cause there might be to blame his Machines in a Philosophical or Religious View, they are so perfect in the Poetick, that Mankind have been ever since contented to follow them: None have been able to enlarge the Sphere of Poetry beyond the Limits he has set: Every Attempt of this Nature has prov'd unsuccessful; and after all the various Changes of Times and Religions, his Gods continue to this Day the Gods of Poetry.

We come now to the Characters of his Persons, and here we shall find no Author has ever drawn so many with so visible and surprizing a Variety, or given us such lively and affecting Impressions of them. Every one has something so singularly his own, that no Painter could have distinguish'd them more by their Features, than the Poet has by their Manners. Nothing can be more exact than the Distinctions he has observ'd in the different degrees of Virtues and Vices. The single Quality of Courage is wonderfully diversify'd in the several Characters of the *Iliad*. That of Achilles is furious and intractable; that of Diomede forward, yet list'ning to Advice and subject to Command: We see in Ajax an heavy and self-considering Valour, in Hector an active and vigilant one: The Courage of Agamemnon is inspirited by Love of Empire and Ambition, that of Menelaus mix'd with Softness and Tenderness for his People: We find in Idomeneus a plain direct Soldier, in Sarpedon a gallant and generous one. Nor is this judicious and astonishing Diversity to be found only in the principal Quality which constitutes the Main of each Character, but even in the Under-parts of it, to which he takes care to give a Tincture of that principal one. For Example, the main Characters of Ulysses and Nestor consist in Wisdom, and they are distinct in this; the Wisdom of one is artificial and various, of the other natural, open, and regular. But they have, besides, Characters of Courage; and this Quality also takes a different Turn in each from the difference of his Prudence: For one in the War depends still upon Caution, the other upon Experience. It would be endless to produce Instances of these Kinds. The Characters of Virgil are far from striking us in this open manner; they lie in a great degree hidden and undistinguish'd, and where they are mark'd most evidently, affect us not in proportion to those of Homer. His Characters of Valour are much alike; even that of Turnus seems no way peculiar but as it is in a superior degree; and we see nothing that differences the Courage of Mnestheus from that of Sergesthus, Cloanthus, or the rest. In like manner it may be remark'd of Statius's Heroes, that an Air of Impetuosity runs thro' them all; the same horrid and savage Courage appears in his Capaneus, Tydeus, Hippomedon, &c. They have a Parity of Character which makes them seem Brothers of one Family. I believe when the Reader is led into this Track of Reflection, if he will pursue it through the Epic and Tragic Writers, he will be convinced how infinitely superior in this Point the Invention of Homer was to that of all others.

The Speeches are to be consider'd as they flow from the Characters, being perfect or defective as they agree or disagree with the Manners of those who utter them. As there is more variety of Characters in the *Iliad*, so there is of Speeches, than in any other Poem. *Every thing in it has Manners* (as Aristotle expresses it) that is, every thing is acted or spoken. It is hardly credible in a Work of such length, how small a Number of Lines are employ'd in Narration. In Virgil the Dramatic Part is less in proportion to the Narrative; and the Speeches often consist of general Reflections or Thoughts, which might be equally just in any Person's Mouth upon the same Occasion. As many of his Persons have no apparent Characters, so many of his Speeches escape being apply'd and judg'd by the Rule of Propriety. We oftner think of the Author himself when we read Virgil, than when we are engag'd in Homer: All which are the Effects of a colder Invention, that interests us less in the Action describ'd: Homer makes us Hearers, and Virgil leaves us Readers.

If in the next place we take a View of the Sentiments, the same presiding Faculty is eminent in the Sublimity and Spirit of his Thoughts. Longinus has given his Opinion, that it was in this Part Homer principally excell'd. What were alone sufficient to prove the Grandeur and Excellence of his Sentiments in general, is that they have so remarkable a Parity with those of the Scripture: Duport, in his *Gnomologia Homerica,* has collected innumerable Instances of this sort. And it is with Justice an excellent modern Writer allows, that if Virgil has not so many Thoughts that are low and vulgar, he has not so many that are sublime and noble; and that the Roman Author seldom rises into very astonishing Sentiments where he is not fired by the *Iliad.*

If we observe his Descriptions, Images, and Similes, we shall find the Invention still predominant. To what else can we ascribe that vast Comprehension of Images of every sort, where we see each Circumstance and Individual of Nature summon'd together by the Extent and Fecundity of his Imagination; to which all things, in their various Views, presented themselves in an Instant, and had their Impressions taken off to Perfection at a Heat? Nay, he not only gives us the full Prospects of Things, but several unexpected Peculiarities and Side-Views, unobserv'd by any Painter but Homer. Nothing is so surprizing as the Descriptions of his Battels, which take up no less than half the *Iliad,* and are supply'd with so vast a Variety of Incidents, that no one bears a Likeness to another; such different Kinds of Deaths, that no two Heroes are wounded in the same manner; and such a Profusion of noble Ideas, that every Battel rises above the last in Greatness, Horror, and Confusion. It is certain there is not near that Number of Images and Descriptions in any Epic Poet; tho' every one has assisted himself with a great Quantity out of him: And it is evident of Virgil especially, that he has scarce any Comparisons which are not drawn from his Master.

If we descend from hence to the Expression, we see the bright Imagination of Homer shining out in the most enliven'd Forms of it. We acknowledge him the Father of Poetical Diction, the first who taught that Language of the Gods to Men. His Expression is like the colouring of some great Masters, which discovers itself to be laid on boldly, and executed with Rapidity. It is indeed the strongest and most glowing imaginable, and touch'd with the greatest Spirit. Aristotle had reason to say, He was the only Poet who had found out Living Words; there are in him more daring Figures and Metaphors than in any good Author whatever. An Arrow is impatient to be on the Wing, a Weapon thirsts to drink the Blood of an Enemy, and the like. Yet his Expression is never too big for the Sense, but justly great in proportion to it: 'Tis the Sentiment that swells and fills out the Diction, which rises with it, and forms itself about it. For in the same degree that a Thought is warmer, an Expression will be brighter; and as That is more strong, This will become more perspicuous: Like Glass in the Furnace which grows to a greater Magnitude, and refines to a greater Clearness, only as the Breath within is more powerful, and the Heat more intense.

To throw his Language more out of Prose, Homer seems to have affected the Compound-Epithets. This was a sort of Composition peculiarly proper to Poetry, not only as it heighten'd the Diction, but as it assisted and fill'd the Numbers with greater Sound and Pomp, and likewise conduced in some measure to thicken the Images. On this last Consideration I cannot but attribute these to the Fruitfulness of his Invention, since (as he has manag'd them) they are a sort of supernumerary Pictures of the Persons or Things they are join'd to. We see the Motion of Hector's Plumes in the Epithet Κορνθαίολος, the Landscape of Mount Neritus in that of Εἰνοσίφυλλος, and so of others; which particular Images could not have been insisted upon so long as to express them in a Description (tho' but of a single Line) without diverting the Reader too much from the principal Action or Figure. As a Metaphor is a short Simile, one of these Epithets is a short Description.

Lastly, if we consider his Versification, we shall be sensible what a Share of Praise is due to his Invention in that also. He was not satisfy'd with his Language as he found it settled in any of Part of Greece, but search'd thro' its differing Dialects with this particular View, to beautify and perfect his Numbers: He consider'd these as they had a greater Mixture of Vowels or Consonants, and accordingly employ'd them as the Verse requir'd either a greater Smoothness or Strength. What he most affected was the Ionic, which has a peculiar Sweetness from its never using Contractions, and from its Custom of resolving the Dipthongs into two Syllables; so as to make the Words open themselves with a more spreading and sonorous Fluency. With this he mingled the Attic Contractions, the broader Doric, and the feebler Æolic, which often rejects its Aspirate, or takes off its Accent; and compleated this Variety by altering some Letters with the License of Poetry. Thus his Measures, instead of being Fetters to his Sense, were always in readiness to run along with the Warmth of his Rapture; and even to give a farther Representation of his Notions, in the Correspondence of their Sounds to what they signify'd. Out of all these he has deriv'd that Harmony, which makes us confess he had not only the richest Head, but the finest Ear in the World. This is so great a Truth, that whoever will but consult the Tune of his Verses even without understanding them (with the same sort of Diligence as we daily see practis'd in the Case of Italian Opera's) will find more Sweetness, Variety, and Majesty of Sound, than in any other Language or Poetry. The Beauty of his Numbers is allow'd by the Criticks to be copied but faintly by Virgil himself, tho' they are so just to ascribe it to the Nature of the Latine Tongue. Indeed the Greek has some Advantages both from the natural Sound of its Words, and the Turn and Cadence of its Verse, which agree with the Genius of no other Language. Virgil was very sensible of this, and used the utmost Diligence in working up a more intractable Language to whatsoever Graces it was capable of, and in particular never fail'd to bring the Sound of his Line to a beautiful Agreement with its Sense. If the Grecian Poet has not been so frequently celebrated on this Account as the Roman, the only reason is, that fewer Criticks have understood one Language than the other. Dionysius of Halicarnassus has pointed out many of our Author's Beauties in this kind, in his *Treatise of the Composition of Words,* and others will be taken notice of the the Course of the Notes. It suffices at present to observe his Numbers, that they flow with so much ease, as to make one imagine Homer had no other care than to transcribe as fast as the Muses dictated; and at the same time with so much Force and inspiriting Vigour, that they awaken and raise us like the Sound of a Trumpet. They roll along as a plentiful River, always in motion, and always full; while we are born away by a Tide of Verse, the most rapid, and yet the most smooth imaginable.

Thus on whatever side we contemplate Homer, what principally strikes us is his Invention. It is that which forms the Character of each Part of his Work; and accordingly we find it to have made his Fable more extensive and copious than any other, his Manners more lively and strongly marked, his Speeches more affecting and transported, his Sentiments more warm and sublime, his Images and Descriptions more full and animated, his Expression more rais'd and daring, and his Numbers more rapid and various. I hope in what has been said of Virgil with regard to any of these Heads, I have no way derogated from his Character. Nothing is more absurd or endless, than the common Method of comparing eminent Writers by an Opposition of particular Passages in them, and forming a Judgment from thence of their Merit upon the whole. We ought to have a certain Knowledge of the principal Character and distinguishing Excellence of each: It is in that we are to consider him, and in proportion to his Degree in that we are to admire him. No Author or Man ever excell'd all the World in more than one Faculty, and as Homer has done this in Invention, Virgil has in Judgment. Not that we are to think Homer wanted Judgment, because Virgil had it in a more eminent degree; or that Virgil wanted Invention, because Homer possest a larger share of it: Each of these great Authors had more of both than perhaps any Man besides, and are only said to have less in Comparison with one another. Homer was the greater Genius, Virgil the better Artist. In one we most admire the Man, in the other the Work. Homer hurries and transports us with a commanding Impetuosity, Virgil leads us with an attractive Majesty: Homer scatters with a generous Profusion, Virgil bestows with a careful Magnificence: Homer like the Nile, pours out his Riches with a sudden Overflow; Virgil like a River in its Banks, with a gentle and constant Stream. When we behold their Battels, methinks the two Poets resemble the Heroes they celebrate: Homer, boundless and irresistible as Achilles, bears all before him, and shines more and more as the Tumult increases; Virgil calmly daring like Æneas, appears undisturb'd in the midst of the Action, disposes all about him, and conquers with Tranquillity: And when we look upon their Machines, Homer seems like his own Jupiter in his Terrors, shaking Olympus, scattering the Lightnings, and firing the Heavens; Virgil like the same Power in his Benevolence, counselling with the Gods, laying Plans for Empires, and regularly ordering his whole Creation.

But after all, it is with great Parts as with great Virtues, they naturally border on some Imperfection; and it is often hard to distinguish exactly where the Virtue ends, or the Fault begins. As Prudence may sometimes sink to Suspicion, so may a great Judgment decline to Coldness; and as Magnanimity may run up to Profusion or Extravagance, so may a great Invention to Redundancy or Wildness. If we look upon Homer in this View, we shall perceive the chief Objections against him to proceed from so noble a Cause as the Excess of this Faculty.

Among these we may reckon some of his Marvellous Fictions, upon which so much Criticism has been spent as surpassing all the Bounds of Probability. Perhaps it may be with great and superior Souls as with gigantick Bodies, which exerting themselves with unusual Strength, exceed what is commonly thought the due Proportion of Parts, to become Miracles in the whole; and like the old Heroes of that Make, commit something near Extravagance amidst a Series of glorious and inimitable Performances. Thus Homer has his speaking Horses, and Virgil his Myrtles distilling Blood, without so much as contriving the easy Intervention of a Deity to save the Probability.

It is owing to the same vast Invention that his Similes have been thought too exuberant and full of Circumstances. The Force of this Faculty is seen in nothing more, than its Inability to confine itself to that single Circumstance upon which the Comparison is grounded: It runs out into Embellishments of additional Images, which however are so manag'd as not to overpower the main one. His Similes are like Pictures, where the principal Figure has not only its proportion given agreeable to the Original, but is also set off with occasional Ornaments and Prospects. The same will account for his manner of heaping a Number of Comparisons together in one Breath, when his Fancy suggested to him at once so many various and correspondent Images. The Reader will easily extend this Observation to more Objections of the same kind.

If there are others which seem rather to charge him with a Defect or Narrowness of Genius, than an Excess of it; those seeming Defects will be found upon Examination to proceed wholly from the Nature of the Times he liv'd in. Such are his grosser Representations of the Gods, and the vicious and imperfect Manners of his Heroes, which will be treated of in the following Essay: But I must here speak a word of the latter, as it is a Point generally carried into Extreams both by the Censurers and Defenders of Homer. It must be a strange Partiality to Antiquity to think with Madam Dacier, 'that those Times and Manners are so much the more excellent, as they are more contrary to ours.' Who can be so prejudiced in their Favour as to magnify the Felicity of those Ages, when a Spirit of Revenge and Cruelty reign'd thro' the World, when no Mercy was shown but for the sake of Lucre, when the greatest Princes were put to the Sword, and their Wives and Daughters made Slaves and Concubines? On the other side I would not be so delicate as those modern Criticks, who are shock'd at the servile Offices and mean Employments in which we sometimes see the Heroes of Homer engag'd. There is a Pleasure in taking a View of that Simplicity in Opposition to the Luxury of succeeding Ages; in beholding Monarchs without their Guards, Princes tending their Flocks, and Princesses drawing Water from the Springs. When we read Homer, we ought to reflect that we are reading the most ancient Author in the Heathen World; and those who consider him in this Light, will double their

Pleasure in the Perusal of him. Let them think they are growing acquainted with Nations and People that are now no more; that they are stepping almost three thousand Years backward into the remotest Antiquity, and entertaining themselves with a clear and surprizing Vision of Things no where else to be found, and the only authentick Picture of that ancient World. By this means alone their greatest Obstacles will vanish; and what usually creates their Dislike, will become a Satisfaction.

This Consideration may farther serve to answer for the constant Use of the same Epithets to his Gods and Heroes, such as the *far-darting Phœbus*, the *blue-ey'd Pallas*, the *swift-footed Achilles*, &c. which some have censured as impertinent and tediously repeated. Those of the Gods depended upon the Powers and Offices then believ'd to belong to them, and had contracted a Weight and Veneration from the Rites and solemn Devotions in which they were us'd: They were a sort of Attributes that it was a Matter of Religion to salute them with on all Occasions, and an Irreverence to omit. As for the Epithets of great Men, Mons. Boileau is of Opinion; that they were in the Nature of Sir-Names, and repeated as such; for the Greeks having no Names deriv'd from their Fathers, were oblig'd when they mention'd any one to add some other Distinction; either naming his Parents expressly, or his Place of Birth, Profession, or the like: As Alexander Son of Philip, Herodotus of Halicarnassus, Diogenes the Cynic, &c. Homer therefore complying with the Custom of his Countrey, us'd such distinctive Additions as better agreed with Poetry. And indeed we have something parallel to these in modern Times, such as the names of *Harold Harefoot, Edmund Ironside, Edward Longshanks, Edward the black Prince*, &c. If yet this be thought to account better for the Propriety than for the Repetition, I shall add a farther Conjecture. Hesiod dividing the World into its Ages, has plac'd a fourth Age between the Brazen and the Iron one, of Heroes distinct from other Men, a divine Race, who fought at Thebes and Troy, are called Demi-Gods, and live by the Care of Jupiter in the Islands of the Blessed. Now among the divine Honours which were paid them, they might have this also in common with the Gods, not to be mention'd without the Solemnity of an Epithet, and such as might be acceptable to them by its celebrating their Families, Actions, or Qualities.

What other Cavils have been rais'd against Homer are such as hardly deserve a Reply, but will yet be taken notice of as they occur in the Course of the Work. Many have been occasion'd by an injudicious Endeavour to exalt Virgil; which is much the same, as if one should think to raise the Superstructure by undermining the Foundation: One would imagine by the whole Course of their Parallels, that these Criticks never so much as heard of Homer's having written first; a Consideration which whoever compares these two Poets ought to have always in his Eye. Some accuse him for the same things which they overlook or praise in the other; as when they prefer the Fable and Moral of the *Æneis* to those of the *Iliad*, for the same Reasons which might set the *Odysses* above the *Æneis*: as that the Heroe is a wiser Man; and the Action of the one more beneficial to his Countrey than that of the other: Or else they blame him for not doing what he never design'd; as because Achilles is not as good and

perfect a Prince as Æneas, when the very Moral of his Poem requir'd a contrary
Character. It is thus that Rapin judges in his Comparison of Homer and Virgil.
Others select those particular Passages of Homer which are not so labour'd as
some that Virgil drew out of them: This is the whole Management of Scaliger
in his Poetices. Others quarrel with what they take for low and mean
Expressions, sometimes thro' a false Delicacy and Refinement, oftner from an
Ignorance of the Graces of the Original; and then triumph in the Aukwardness
of their own Translations. This is the Conduct of Perault in his Parallels.
Lastly, there are others, who pretending to a fairer Proceeding, distinguish
between the personal Merit of Homer, and that of his Work; but when they
come to assign the Causes of the great Reputation of the *Iliad*, they found it
upon the Ignorace of his Times, and the Prejudice of those that followed. And
in pursuance of this Principle, they make those Accidents (such as the
Contention of the Cities, &c.) to be the Causes of his Fame, which were in
Reality the Consequences of his Merit. The same might as well be said of
Virgil, or any great Author, whose general Character will infallibly raise many
casual Additions to their Reputation. This is the Method of Mons. de la Motte;
who yet confesses upon the whole, that in whatever Age Homer had liv'd he
must have been the greatest Poet of his Nation, and that he may be said in this
Sense to be the Master even of those who surpass'd him.

In all these Objections we see nothing that contradicts his Title to the
Honour of the chief Invention; and as long as this (which is indeed the
Characteristic of Poetry itself) remains unequal'd by his Followers, he still
continues superior to them. A cooler Judgment may commit fewer Faults, and
be more approv'd in the Eyes of One Sort of Criticks: but that Warmth of Fancy
will carry the loudest and most universal Applauses which holds the Heart of
a Reader under the strongest Enchantment. Homer not only appears the
Inventor of Poetry, but excells all the Inventors of other Arts in this, that he has
swallow'd up the Honour of those who succeeded him. What he has done
admitted no Encrease, it only left room for Contraction or Regulation. He
shew'd all the Stretch of Fancy at once; and if he has fail'd in some of his
Flights, it was but because he attempted every thing. A Work of this kind
seems like a mighty Tree which rises from the most vigorous Seed, is improv'd
with Industry, flourishes, and produces the finest Fruit; Nature and Art have
conspir'd to raise it; Pleasure and Profit join'd to make it valuable: and they
who find the justest Faults, have only said, that a few Branches (which run
luxuriant thro' a Richness of Nature) might be lopp'd into Form to give it a
more regular Appearance.

Having now spoken of the Beauties and Defects of the Original, it remains
to treat of the Translation, with the same View to the chief Characteristic. As
far as that is seen in the main Parts of the Poem, such as the Fable, Manners,
and Sentiments, no Translator can prejudice it but by wilful Omissions or
Contractions. As it also breaks out in every particular Image, Description, and
Simile; whoever lessens or too much softens those, takes off from this chief
Character. It is the first grand Duty of an Interpreter to give his Author entire
and unmaim'd; and for the rest, the Diction and Versification only are his

proper Province; since these must be his own, but the others he is to take as he finds them.

It should then be consider'd what Methods may afford some Equivalent in our Language for the Graces of these in the Greek. It is certain no literal Translation can be just to an excellent Original in a superior Language: but it is a great Mistake to imagine (as many have done) that a rash Paraphrase can make amends for this general Defect; which is no less in danger to lose the Spirit of an Ancient, by deviating into the modern Manners of Expression. If there be sometimes a Darkness, there is often a Light in Antiquity, which nothing better preserves than a Version almost literal. I know no Liberties one ought to take, but those which are necessary for transfusing the Spirit of the Original, and supporting the Poetical Style of the Translation: and I will venture to say, there have not been more Men misled in former times by a servile dull Adherence to the Letter, than have been deluded in ours by a chimerical insolent Hope of raising and improving their Author. It is not to be doubted that the Fire of the Poem is what a Translator should principally regard, as it is most likely to expire in his managing: However it is his safest way to be content with preserving this to his utmost in the Whole, without endeavouring to be more than he finds his Author is, in any particular Place. 'Tis a great Secret in Writing to know when to be plain, and when poetical and figurative; and it is what Homer will teach us if we will but follow modestly in his Footsteps. Where his Diction is bold and lofty, let us raise ours as high as we can; but where his is plain and humble, we ought not to be deterr'd from imitating him by the fear of incurring the Censure of a meer English Critick. Nothing that belongs to Homer seems to have been more commonly mistaken than the just Pitch of his Style: Some of his Translators having swell'd into Fustian in a proud Confidence of the Sublime; others sunk into Flatness, in a cold and timorous Notion of Simplicity. Methinks I see these different Followers of Homer, some sweating and straining after him by violent Leaps and Bounds, (the certain Signs of false Mettle) others slowly and servilely creeping in his Train, while the Poet himself is all the time proceeding with an unaffected and equal Majesty before them. However of the two Extreams one could sooner pardon Frenzy than Frigidity: No Author is to be envy'd for such Commendations as he may gain by that Character of Style, which his Friends must agree together to call Simplicity, and the rest of the World will call Dulness. There is a graceful and dignify'd Simplicity, as well as a bald and sordid one, which differ as much from each other as the Air of a plain Man from that of a Sloven: 'Tis one thing to be tricked up, and another not to be dress'd at all. Simplicity is the Mean between Ostentation and Rusticity.

This pure and noble Simplicity is no where in such Perfection as in the Scripture and our Author. One may affirm with all respect to the inspired Writings, that the Divine Spirit made use of no other Words but what were intelligible and common to Men at that Time, and in that Part of the World; and as Homer is the Author nearest to those, his Style must of course bear a greater Resemblance to the sacred Books than that of any other Writer. This Consideration (together with what has been observ'd of the Parity of some of his Thoughts) may methinks induce a Translator on the one hand to give into several of those general Phrases and Manners of Expression, which have attain'd a Veneration even in our Language from their use in the Old Testament; as on the other, to avoid those which have been appropriated to the Divinity, and in a manner consign'd to Mystery and Religion.

For a farther Preservation of this Air of Simplicity, a particular Care should be taken to express with all Plainness those Moral Sentences and Proverbial Speeches which are so numerous in this Poet. They have something Venerable, and as I may say Oracular, in that unadorn'd Gravity and Shortness with which they are deliver'd: a Grace which would be utterly lost by endeavouring to give them what we call a more ingenious (that is a more modern) Turn in the Paraphrase.

Perhaps the Mixture of some Græcisms and old Words after the manner of Milton, if done without too much Affectation, might not have an ill Effect in a Version of this particular Work, which most of any other seems to require a venerable Antique Cast. But certainly the use of modern Terms of War and Government, such as Platoon, Campagne, Junto, or the like (which some of his Translators have fallen into) cannot be allowable; those only excepted, without which it is impossible to treat the Subjects in any living Language.

There are two Peculiarities in Homer's Diction that are a sort of Marks or Moles, by which every common Eye distinguishes him at first sight: Those who are not his greatest Admirers look upon them as Defects, and those who are seem pleased with them as Beauties. I speak of his Compound-Epithets and of his Repetitions. Many of the former cannot be done literally into English without destroying the Purity of our Language. I believe such should be retain'd as slide easily of themselves into an English-Compound, without Violence to the Ear or to the receiv'd Rules of Composition; as well as those which have receiv'd a Sanction from the Authority of our best Poets, and are become familiar thro' their use of them; such as the Cloud-compelling Jove, &c. As for the rest, whenever any can be as fully and significantly exprest in a single word as in a compounded one, the Course to be taken is obvious. Some that cannot be so turn'd as to preserve their full Image by one or two Words, may have Justice done them by Circumlocution; as the Epithet εἰνοσίφυλλος to a Mountain would appear little or ridiculous translated literally *Leaf-shaking*, but affords a majestic Idea in the Periphrasis: *The lofty Mountain shakes his waving Woods.* Others that admit of differing Significations, may receive an Advantage by a judicious Variation according to the Occasions on which they are introduc'd. For Example, the Epithet of Apollo, εκηβόλος, or *far-shooting*, is capable of two Explications; one literal in respect of the Darts and Bow, the Ensigns of that God, the other allegorical with regard to the Rays of the Sun: Therefore in such Places where Apollo is represented as a God in Person, I would use the former Interpretation, and where the Effects of the Sun are describ'd, I would make choice of the latter. Upon the whole, it will be necessary to avoid that perpetual Repetition of the same Epithets which we find in Homer, and which, tho' it might be accommodated (as has been already shewn) to the Ear of those Times, is by no means so to ours: But one may wait for Opportunities of placing them, where they derive an additional Beauty from the Occasions on which they are employed; and in doing this properly, a Translator may at once shew his Fancy and his Judgment.

As for Homer's Repetitions; we may divide them into three sorts; of whole Narrations and Speeches, of single Sentences, and of one Verse or Hemistich. I hope it is not impossible to have such a Regard to these, as neither to lose so known a Mark of the Author on the one hand, nor to offend the Reader too much on the other. The Repetition is not ungraceful in those Speeches where the Dignity of the Speaker renders it a sort of Insolence to alter his Words; as in the Messages from Gods to Men, or from higher Powers to Inferiors in Concerns of State, or where the Ceremonial of Religion seems to require it, in the solemn Forms of Prayers, Oaths, or the like. In other Cases, I believe the best Rule is to be guided by the Nearness, or Distance, at which the Repetitions are plac'd in the Original: When they follow too close one may vary the Expression, but it is a Question whether a profess'd Translator be authorized to omit any: If they be tedious, the Author is to answer for it.

It only remains to speak of the Versification. Homer (as has been said) is perpetually applying the Sound to the Sense, and varying it on every new Subject. This is indeed one of the most exquisite Beauties of Poetry, and attainable by very few: I know only of Homer eminent for it in the Greek, and Virgil in Latine. I am sensible it is what may sometimes happen by Chance, when a Writer is warm, and fully possest of his Image: however, it may be reasonably believed they design'd this, in whose Verse it so manifestly appears in a superior degree to all others. Few Readers have the Ear to be Judges of it, but those who have will see I have endeavour'd at this Beauty.

Upon the whole, I must confess my self utterly incapable of doing Justice to Homer. I attempt him in no other Hope but that which one may entertain without much Vanity, of giving a more tolerable Copy of him than any entire Translation in Verse has yet done. We have only those of Chapman, Hobbes, and Ogilby. Chapman has taken the Advantage of an immeasurable Length of Verse, notwithstanding which there is scarce any Paraphrase more loose and rambling than his. He has frequent Interpolations of four or six Lines, and I remember one in the thirteenth Book of the *Odysses*, ver. 312, where he has spun twenty Verses out of two. He is often mistaken in so bold a manner, that one might think he deviated on purpose, if he did not in other Places of his Notes insist so much upon Verbal Trifles. He appears to have had a strong Affectation of extracting new Meanings out of his Author, insomuch as to promise in his Rhyming Preface, a Poem of the Mysteries he had revealed in Homer; and perhaps he endeavoured to strain the obvious Sense to this End. His Expression is involved in Fustian, a Fault for which he was remarkable in his Original Writings, as in the Tragedy of *Bussy d'Amboise*, &c. In a word, the Nature of the Man may account for his whole Performance; for he appears from his Preface and Remarks to have been of an arrogant Turn, and an Enthusiast in Poetry. His own Boast of having finish'd half the *Iliad* in less than fifteen Weeks, shews with what Negligence his Version was performed. But that which is to be allowed him, and which very much contributed to cover his Defects, is a daring fiery Spirit that animates his Translation, which is something like what one might imagine Homer himself would have writ before he arriv'd to Years of Discretion. Hobbes has given us a correct Explanation of the Sense in general, but for Particulars and Circumstances he continually lopps them, and often omits the most beautiful. As for its being esteem'd a close Translation, I doubt not many have been led into that Error by the Shortness of it, which proceeds not from his following the Original Line by Line, but from the Contractions above-mentioned. He sometimes omits whole Similes and Sentences, and is now and then guilty of Mistakes which no Writer of his Learning could have fallen into, but thro' Carelessness. His Poetry, as well as Ogilby's, is too mean for Criticism.

It is a great Loss to the Poetical World that Mr. Dryden did not live to translate the *Iliad*. He has left us only the first Book and a small Part of the sixth; in which if he has in some Places not truly interpreted the Sense, or preserved the Antiquities, it ought to be excused on account of the Haste he was obliged to write in. He seems to have had too much Regard to Chapman, whose Words he sometimes copies, and has unhappily follow'd him in Passages where he wanders from the Original. However had he translated the whole Work, I would no more have attempted Homer after him than Virgil, his Version of whom (notwithstanding some human Errors) is the most noble and spirited Translation I know in any Language. But the Fate of great Genius's is like that of great Ministers, tho' they are confessedly the first in the Commonwealth of Letters, they must be envy'd and calumniated only for being at the Head of it.

That which in my Opinion ought to be the Endeavour of any one who translates Homer, is above all things to keep alive that Spirit and Fire which makes his chief Character. In particular Places, where the Sense can bear any Doubt, to follow the strongest and most Poetical, as most agreeing with that Character. To copy him in all the Variations of his Style, and the different Modulations of his Numbers. To preserve in the more active or descriptive Parts, a Warmth and Elevation; in the more sedate or narrative, a Plainness and Solemnity; in the Speeches a Fulness and Perspicuity; in the Sentences a Shortness and Gravity. Not to neglect even the little Figures and Turns on the Words, nor sometimes the very Cast of the Periods. Neither to omit or confound any Rites or Customs of Antiquity. Perhaps too he ought to include the whole in a shorter Compass, than has hitherto been done by an Translator who has tolerably preserved either the Sense or Poetry. What I would farther recommend to him, is to study his Author rather from his own Text than from any Commentaries, how learned soever, or whatever Figure they make in the Estimation of the World. To consider him attentively in Comparison with Virgil above all the Ancients, and with Milton above all the Moderns. Next these the Archbishop of Cambray's *Telemachus* may give him the truest Idea of the Spirit and Turn of our Author, and Bossu's admirable *Treatise of the Epic Poem* the justest Notion of his Design and Conduct. But after all, with whatever Judgment and Study a Man may proceed, or with whatever Happiness he may perform such a Work; he must hope to please but a few, those only who have at once a Taste of Poetry, and competent Learning. For to satisfy such as want either, is not in the Nature of this Undertaking; since a meer Modern Wit can like nothing that is not Modern, and a Pedant nothing that is not Greek.

What I have done is submitted to the Publick, from whose Opinions I am prepared to learn; tho' I fear no Judges so little as our best Poets, who are most sensible of the Weight of this Task. As for the worst, whatever they shall please to say, they may give me some Concern as they are unhappy Men, but none as they are malignant Writers. I was guided in this Translation by Judgments very different from theirs, and by Persons for whom they can have no Kindness, if an old Observation be true, that the strongest Antipathy in the World is that of Fools to Men of Wit. Mr. Addison was the first whose Advice determin'd me to undertake this Task, who was pleas'd to write to me upon that Occasion in such Terms as I cannot repeat without Vanity. I was obliged to Sir Richard Steele for a very early Recommendation of my Undertaking to the Publick. Dr. Swift promoted my Interest with that Warmth with which he always serves his Friend. The Humanity and Frankness of Sir Samuel Garth are what I never knew wanting on any Occasion. I must also acknowledge with infinite Pleasure the many friendly Offices as well as sincere Criticisms of Mr. Congreve, who had led me the way in translating some Parts of Homer, as I wish for the sake of the World he had prevented me in the rest. I must add the Names of Mr. Rowe and Dr. Parnell, tho' I shall take a farther Opportunity of doing Justice to the last, whose Good-nature (to give it a great Panegyrick) is no less extensive than his Learning. The Favour of these Gentlemen is not entirely undeserved by one who bears them so true an Affection. But what can I say of the Honour so many of the Great have done me, while the First Names of the Age appear as my Subscribers, and the most distinguish'd Patrons and Ornaments of Learning as my chief Encouragers. Among these it is a particular Pleasure to me to find, that my highest Obligations are to such who have done most Honour to the Name of Poet: That his Grace the Duke of Buckingham was not displeas'd I should undertake the Author to whom he has given (in his excellent Essay) the finest Praise he ever yet receiv'd.

> Read Homer once, and you can read no more;
> For all things else appear so mean and poor,
> Verse will seem Prose: yet often on him look,
> And you will hardly need another Book.

That the Earl of Halifax was one of the first to favour me, of whom it is hard to say whether the Advancement of the Polite Arts is more owing to his Generosity or his Example. That such a Genius as my Lord Bolingbroke, not more distinguished in the great Scenes of Business than in all the useful and entertaining Parts of Learning, has not refus'd to be the Critick of these Sheets, and the Patron of their Writer. And that so excellent an Imitator of Homer as the noble Author of the Tragedy of Heroic Love, has continu'd his Partiality to me from my writing Pastorals to my attempting the *Iliad*. I cannot deny my self the Pride of confessing, that I have had the Advantage not only of their Advice for the Conduct in general, but their Correction of several Particulars of this Translation.

I could say a great deal of the Pleasure of being distinguish'd by the Earl of Carnarvon, but it is almost absurd to particularize any one generous Action in a Person whose whole Life is a continued Series of them. The Right Honourable Mr. Stanhope, the present Secretary of State, will pardon my Desire of having it known that he was pleas'd to promote this Affair. The particular Zeal of Mr. Harcourt (the Son of the late Lord Chancellor) gave me a Proof of how much I am honour'd in a Share of his Friendship. I must attribute to the same Motive that of several others of my Friends, to whom all Acknowledgments are render'd unnecessary by the Privileges of a familiar Correspondence: And I am satisfy'd I can no way better oblige Men of their Turn, than by my Silence.

In short, I have found more Patrons than ever Homer wanted. He would have thought himself happy to have met the same Favour at Athens, that has been shewn me by its learned Rival, the University of Oxford. If my Author had the Wits of After-Ages for his Defenders, his Translator has had the Beauties of the present for his Advocates; a Pleasure too great to be changed for any Fame in Reversion. And I can hardly envy him those pompous Honours he receiv'd after Death, when I reflect on the Enjoyment of so many agreeable Obligations, and easy Friendships which make the Satisfaction of Life. This Distinction is the more to be acknowledg'd, as it is shewn to one whose Pen has never gratify'd the Prejudices of particular Parties, or the Vanities of particular Men. Whatever the Success may prove, I shall never repent of an Undertaking in which I have experienc'd the Candour and Friendship of so many Persons of Merit; and in which I hope to pass some of those Years of Youth that are generally lost in a Circle of Follies, after a manner neither wholly unuseful to others, nor disagreeable to my self.

An Epistle To
Dr. Arbuthnot

Shut, shut the door, good John! fatigu'd I said,
Tye up the knocker, say I'm sick, I'm dead,
The Dog-star rages! nay 'tis past a doubt,
All Bedlam, or Parnassus, is let out:
Fire in each eye, and Papers in each hand,
They rave, recite, and madden round the land.
    What Walls can guard me, or what Shades can hide?
They pierce my Thickets, thro' my Grot they glide,
By land, by water, they renew the charge,
They stop the Chariot, and they board the Barge.
No place is sacred, not the Church is free,
Ev'n Sunday shines no Sabbath-day to me:
Then from the Mint walks forth the Man of Ryme,
Happy! to catch me, just at Dinner-time.
    Is there a Parson, much be-mus'd in Beer,
A maudlin Poetess, a ryming Peer,
A Clerk, foredoom'd his Father's soul to cross,
Who pens a Stanza when he should engross?
Is there, who lock'd from Ink and Paper, scrawls
With desp'rate Charcoal round his darken'd walls?
All fly to Twit'nam, and in humble strain
Apply to me, to keep them mad or vain.
Arthur, whose giddy Son neglects the Laws,
Imputes to me and my damn'd work the cause:
Poor Cornus sees his frantic Wife elope,
And curses Wit, and Poetry, and Pope.
    Friend to my Life, (which did not you prolong,
The World had wanted many an idle Song)
What Drop or Nostrum can this Plague remove?
Or which must end me, a Fool's Wrath or Love?
A dire Dilemma! either way I'm sped,
If Foes, they write, if Friends, they read me dead.
Seiz'd and ty'd down to judge, how wretched I!
Who can't be silent, and who will not lye;
To laugh, were want of Goodness and of Grace,
And to be grave, exceeds all Pow'r of Face.
I sit with sad Civility, I read
With honest anguish, and an aking head;
And drop at last, but in unwilling ears,

This saving counsel, "Keep your Piece nine years."
    Nine years! cries he, who high in Drury-lane
Lull'd by soft Zephyrs thro' the broken Pane,
Rymes e're he wakes, and prints before Term ends,
Oblig'd by hunger and Request of friends:
"The Piece you think is incorrect; why take it,
"I'm all submission, what you'd have it, make it."
    Three things another's modest wishes bound,
My Friendship, and a Prologue, and ten Pound.
    Pitholeon sends to me: "You know his Grace,
"I want a Patron; ask him for a Place."
Pitholeon libell'd me—"but here's a Letter
"Informs you Sir, 'twas when he knew no better.
"Dare you refuse him? Curl invites to dine,
"He'll write a Journal, or he'll turn Divine."
    Bless me! a Packet.—"'Tis a stranger sues,
"A Virgin Tragedy, an Orphan Muse."
If I dislike it, "Furies, death and rage!"
If I approve, "Commend it to the Stage."
There (thank my Stars) my whole Commission ends,
The Play'rs and I are, luckily, no friends.
Fir'd that the House reject him, "'Sdeath I'll print it
"And shame the Fools—your Int'rest, Sir, with Lintot."
Lintot, dull rogue! will think your price too much.
"Not Sir, if you revise it, and retouch."
All my demurrs but double his attacks,
At last he whispers "Do, and we go snacks."
Glad of a quarrel, strait I clap the door,
Sir, let me see your works and you no more.
    'Tis sung, when Midas' Ears began to spring,
(Midas, a sacred Person and a King)
His very Minister who spy'd them first,
(Some say his Queen) was forc'd to speak, or burst.
And is not mine, my Friend, a sorer case,
When ev'ry Coxcomb perks them in my face?
"Good friend forbear! you deal in dang'rous things,
"I'd never name Queens, Ministers, or Kings;
"Keep close to Ears, and those let Asses prick,
"'Tis nothing"—Nothing? if they bite and kick?
Out with it, Dunciad! let the secret pass,
That Secret to each Fool, that he's an Ass:
The truth once told, (and wherefore shou'd we lie?)
The Queen of Midas slept, and so may I.
    You think this cruel? take it for a rule,
No creature smarts so little as a Fool.
Let Peals of Laughter, Codrus! round thee break,

Thou unconcern'd canst hear the mighty Crack.
Pit, Box and Gall'ry in convulsions hurl'd,
Thou stand'st unshook amidst a bursting World.
Who shames a Scribler? break one cobweb thro',
He spins the slight, self-pleasing thread anew;
Destroy his Fib, or Sophistry; in vain,
The Creature's at his dirty work again;
Thron'd in the Centre of his thin designs;
Proud of a vast Extent of flimzy lines.
Whom have I hurt? has Poet yet, or Peer,
Lost the arch'd eye-brow, or Parnassian sneer?
And has not Colly still his Lord, and Whore?
His Butchers Henley, his Free-masons Moor?
Does not one Table Bavius still admit?
Still to one Bishop Philips seem a Wit?
Still Sapho—"Hold! for God-sake—you'll offend:
"No Names—be calm—learn Prudence of a Friend:
"I too could write, and I am twice as tall,
"But Foes like these!"—One Flatt'rer's worse than all;
Of all mad Creatures, if the Learn'd are right,
It is the Slaver kills, and not the Bite.
A Fool quite angry is quite innocent;
Alas! 'tis ten times worse when they repent.

One dedicates, in high Heroic prose,
And ridicules beyond a hundred foes;
One from all Grubstreet will my fame defend,
And, more abusive, calls himself my friend.
This prints my Letters, that expects a Bribe,
And others roar aloud, "Subscribe, subscribe."
There are, who to my Person pay their court,
I cough like Horace, and tho' lean, am short,
Ammon's great Son one shoulder had too high,
Such Ovid's nose, and "Sir! you have an Eye—"
Go on, obliging Creatures, make me see
All that disgrac'd my Betters, met in me:
Say for my comfort, languishing in bed,
"Just so immortal Maro held his head:"
And when I die, be sure you let me know
Great Homer dy'd three thousand years ago.

Why did I write? what sin to me unknown
Dipt me in Ink, my Parents', or my own?
As yet a Child, nor yet a Fool to Fame,
I lisp'd in Numbers, for the Numbers came.
I left no Calling for this idle trade,

No Duty broke, no Father dis-obey'd.
The Muse but serv'd to ease some Friend, not Wife,
To help me thro' this long Disease, my Life,
To second, ARBUTHNOT! thy Art and Care,
And teach, the Being you preserv'd, to bear.

But why then publish? Granville the polite,
And knowing Walsh, would tell me I could write;
Well-natur'd Garth inflam'd with early praise,
And Congreve lov'd, and Swift endur'd my Lays;
The Courtly Talbot, Somers, Sheffield read,
Ev'n mitred Rochester would nod the head,
And St. John's self (great Dryden's friends before)
With open arms receiv'd one Poet more.
Happy my Studies, when by these approv'd!
Happier their Author, when by these belov'd!
From these the world will judge of Men and Books,
Not from the Burnets, Oldmixons, and Cooks.
Soft were my Numbers, who could take offence
While pure Description held the place of Sense?
Like gentle Fanny's was my flow'ry Theme,
A painted Mistress, or a purling Stream.
Yet then did Gildon draw his venal quill;
I wish'd the man a dinner, and sate still:
Yet then did Dennis rave in furious fret;
I never answer'd, I was not in debt:
If want provok'd, or madness made them print,
I wag'd no war with Bedlam or the Mint.
Did some more sober Critic come abroad?
If wrong, I smil'd; if right, I kiss'd the rod.
Pains, reading, study, are their just pretence,
And all they want is spirit, taste, and sense.
Comma's and points they set exactly right,
And 'twere a sin to rob them of their Mite.
Yet ne'r one sprig of Laurel grac'd these ribalds,
From slashing Bentley down to pidling Tibalds.
Each Wight who reads not, and but scans and spells,
Each Word-catcher that lives on syllables,
Ev'n such small Critics some regard may claim,
Preserv'd in Milton's or in Shakespear's name.
Pretty! in Amber to observe the forms
Of hairs, or straws, or dirt, or grubs, or worms;
The things, we know, are neither rich nor rare,
But wonder how the Devil they got there?
Were others angry? I excus'd them too;
Well might they rage; I gave them but their due.

A man's true merit 'tis not hard to find,
But each man's secret standard in his mind,
That Casting-weight Pride adds to Emptiness,
This, who can gratify? for who can guess?
The Bard whom pilf'red Pastorals renown,
Who turns a Persian Tale for half a crown,
Just writes to make his barrenness appear,
And strains from hard-bound brains eight lines a-year:
He, who still wanting tho' he lives on theft,
Steals much, spends little, yet has nothing left:
And he, who now to sense, now nonsense leaning,
Means not, but blunders round about a meaning:
And he, whose Fustian's so sublimely bad,
It is not Poetry, but Prose run mad:
All these, my modest Satire bad translate,
And own'd, that nine such Poets made a Tate.
How did they fume, and stamp, and roar, and chafe?
And swear, not Addison himself was safe.
    Peace to all such! but were there One whose fires
True Genius kindles, and fair Fame inspires,
Blest with each Talent and each Art to please,
And born to write, converse, and live with ease:
Shou'd such a man, too fond to rule alone,
Bear, like the Turk, no brother near the throne,
View him with scornful, yet with jealous eyes,
And hate for Arts that caus'd himself to rise;
Damn with faint praise, assent with civil leer,
And without sneering, teach the rest to sneer;
Willing to wound, and yet afraid to strike,
Just hint a fault, and hesitate dislike;
Alike reserv'd to blame, or to commend,
A tim'rous foe, and a suspicious friend,
Dreading ev'n fools, by Flatterers besieg'd,
And so obliging that he ne'er oblig'd;
Like Cato, give his little Senate laws,
And sit attentive to his own applause;
While Wits and Templers ev'ry sentence raise,
And wonder with a foolish face of praise.
Who but must laugh, if such a man there be?
Who would not weep, if Atticus were he!
    What tho' my Name stood rubric on the walls?
Or plaister'd posts, with Claps in capitals?
Or smoaking forth, a hundred Hawkers load,
On Wings of Winds came flying all abroad?
I sought no homage from the Race that write;
I kept, like Asian Monarchs, from their sight:

Poems I heeded (now be-rym'd so long)
No more than Thou, great GEORGE! a Birth- day Song.
I ne'r with Wits or Witlings past my days,
To spread about the Itch of Verse and Praise;
Nor like a Puppy daggled thro' the Town,
To fetch and carry Sing-song up and down;
Nor at Rehearsals sweat, and mouth'd, and cry'd,
With Handkerchief and Orange at my side:
But sick of Fops, and Poetry, and Prate,
To Bufo left the whole Castalian State.
   Proud, as Apollo on his forked hill,
Sate full-blown Bufo, puff'd by ev'ry quill;
Fed with soft Dedication all day long,
Horace and he went hand in hand in song.
His Library, (where Busts of Poets dead
And a true Pindar stood without a head)
Receiv'd of Wits an undistinguish'd race,
Who first his Judgment ask'd, and then a Place:
Much they extoll'd his Pictures, much his Seat,
And flatter'd ev'ry day, and some days eat:
Till grown more frugal in his riper days,
He pay'd some Bards with Port, and some with Praise,
To some a dry Rehearsal was assign'd,
And others (harder still) he pay'd in kind.
Dryden alone (what wonder?) came not nigh,
Dryden alone escap'd this judging eye:
But still the Great have kindness in reserve,
He help'd to bury whom he help'd to starve.
   May some choice Patron bless each gray goose quill!
May ev'ry Bavius have his Bufo still!
So, when a Statesman wants a Day's defence,
Or Envy holds a whole Week's war with Sense,
Or simple Pride for Flatt'ry makes demands;
May Dunce by Dunce be whistled off my hands!
Blest be the Great! for those they take away,
And those they left me—For they left me GAY,
Left me to see neglected Genius bloom,
Neglected die! and tell it on his Tomb;
Of all thy blameless Life the sole Return
My Verse, and QUEENSB'RY weeping o'er thy Urn!
Oh let me live my own! and die so too!
("To live and die is all I have to do:")
Maintain a Poet's Dignity and Ease,
And see what friends, and read what books I please.
Above a Patron, tho' I condescend
Sometimes to call a Minister my Friend:

I was not born for Courts or great Affairs,
I pay my Debts, believe, and say my Pray'rs,
Can sleep without a Poem in my head,
Nor know, if Dennis be alive or dead.
    Why am I ask'd, what next shall see the light?
Heav'ns! was I born for nothing but to write?
Has Life no Joys for me? or (to be grave)
Have I no Friend to serve, no Soul to save?
"I found him close with Swift"—"Indeed? no doubt"
(Cries prating Balbus) "something will come out."
'Tis all in vain, deny it as I will.
"No, such a Genius never can lye still,"
And then for mine obligingly mistakes
The first Lampoon Sir Will. or Bubo makes.
Poor guiltless I! and can I chuse but smile,
When ev'ry Coxcomb knows me by my Style?
    Curst be the Verse, how well soe'er it flow,
That tends to make one worthy Man my foe,
Give Virtue scandal, Innocence a fear,
Or from the soft-ey'd Virgin steal a tear!
But he, who hurts a harmless neighbour's peace,
Insults fal'n Worth, or Beauty in distress,
Who loves a Lye, lame slander helps about,
Who writes a Libel, or who copies out:
That Fop whose pride affects a Patron's name,
Yet absent, wounds an Author's honest fame;
Who can your Merit selfishly approve,
And show the Sense of it, without the Love;
Who has the Vanity to call you Friend,
Yet wants the Honour injur'd to defend;
Who tells whate'er you think, whate'er you say,
And, if he lye not, must at least betray:
Who to the Dean and silver Bell can swear,
And sees at Cannons what was never there:
Who reads but with a Lust to mis-apply,
Make Satire a Lampoon, and Fiction, Lye.
A Lash like mine no honest man shall dread,
But all such babling blockheads in his stead.
    Let Sporus tremble—"What? that Thing of silk,
"Sporus, that mere white Curd of Ass's milk?
"Satire or Sense alas! can Sporus feel?
"Who breaks a Butterfly upon a Wheel?"
Yet let me flap this Bug with gilded wings,
This painted Child of Dirt that stinks and stings;
Whose Buzz the Witty and the Fair annoys,
Yet Wit ne'er tastes, and Beauty ne'er enjoys,

So well-bred Spaniels civilly delight
In mumbling of the Game they dare not bite.
Eternal Smiles his Emptiness betray,
As shallow streams run dimpling all the way.
Whether in florid Impotence he speaks,
And, as the Prompter breathes, the Puppet squeaks;
Or at the Ear of Eve, familiar Toad,
Half Froth, half Venom, spits himself abroad,
In Puns, or Politicks, or Tales, or Lyes,
Or Spite, or Smut, or Rymes, or Blasphemies.
His Wit all see-saw between that and this,
Now high, now low, now Master up, now Miss,
And he himself one vile Antithesis.
Amphibious Thing! that acting either Part,
The trifling Head, or the corrupted Heart!
Fop at the Toilet, Flatt'rer at the Board,
Now trips a Lady, and now struts a Lord.
Eve's Tempter thus the Rabbins have exprest,
A Cherub's face, a Reptile all the rest;
Beauty that shocks you, Parts that none will trust,
Wit that can creep, and Pride that licks the dust.
    Not Fortune's Worshipper, nor Fashion's Fool,
Not Lucre's Madman, nor Ambition's Tool,
Not proud, nor servile, be one Poet's praise
That, if he pleas'd, he pleas'd by manly ways;
That Flatt'ry, ev'n to Kings, he held a shame,
And thought a Lye in Verse or Prose the same:
That not in Fancy's Maze he wander'd long,
But stoop'd to Truth, and moraliz'd his song:
That not for Fame, but Virtue's better end,
He stood the furious Foe, the timid Friend,
The damning Critic, half-approving Wit,
The Coxcomb hit, or fearing to be hit;
Laugh'd at the loss of Friends he never had,
The dull, the proud, the wicked, and the mad;
The distant Threats of Vengeance on his head,
The Blow unfelt, the Tear he never shed;
The Tale reviv'd, the Lye so oft o'erthrown;
Th' imputed Trash, and Dulness not his own;
The Morals blacken'd when the Writings scape;
The libel'd Person, and the pictur'd Shape;
Abuse on all he lov'd, or lov'd him, spread,
A Friend in Exile, or a Father, dead;
The Whisper that to Greatness still too near,
Perhaps, yet vibrates on his SOVEREIGN'S Ear—
Welcome for thee, fair Virtue! all the past:

For thee, fair Virtue! welcome ev'n the last!
  "But why insult the Poor, affront the Great?"
A Knave's a Knave, to me, in ev'ry State,
Alike my scorn, if he succeed or fail,
Sporus at Court, or Japhet in a Jayl,
A hireling Scribler, or a hireling Peer,
Knight of the Post corrupt, or of the Shire,
If on a Pillory, or near a Throne,
He gain his Prince's Ear, or lose his own.
  Yet soft by Nature, more a Dupe than Wit,
Sapho can tell you how this Man was bit:
This dreaded Sat'rist Dennis will confess
Foe to his Pride, but Friend to his Distress:
So humble, he has knock'd at Tibbald's door,
Has drunk with Cibber, nay has rym'd for Moor.
Full ten years slander'd, did he once reply?
Three thousand Suns went down on Welsted's Lye:
To please a Mistress, One aspers'd his life;
He lash'd him not, but let her be his Wife:
Let Budgel charge low Grubstreet on his quill,
And write whate'er he pleas'd, except his Will;
Let the Two Curls of Town and Court, abuse
His Father, Mother, Body, Soul, and Muse.
Yet why? that Father held it for a rule
It was a Sin to call our Neighbour Fool,
That harmless Mother thought no Wife a Whore,—
Hear this! and spare his Family, James More!
Unspotted Names! and memorable long,
If there be Force in Virtue, or in Song.
  Of gentle Blood (part shed in Honour's Cause,
While yet in Britain Honour had Applause)
Each Parent sprung—"What Fortune, pray?"—Their own,
And better got than Bestia's from the Throne.
Born to no Pride, inheriting no Strife,
Nor marrying Discord in a Noble Wife,
Stranger to Civil and Religious Rage,
The good Man walk'd innoxious thro' his Age.
No Courts he saw, no Suits would ever try,
Nor dar'd an Oath, nor hazarded a Lye:
Un-learn'd, he knew no Schoolman's subtle Art,
No Language, but the Language of the Heart.
By Nature honest, by Experience wise,
Healthy by Temp'rance and by Exercise:
His Life, tho' long, to sickness past unknown,
His Death was instant, and without a groan.
Oh grant me thus to live, and thus to die!

Who sprung from Kings shall know less joy than I.
  O Friend! may each Domestick Bliss be thine!
Be no unpleasing Melancholy mine:
Me, let the tender Office long engage
To rock the Cradle of reposing Age,
With lenient Arts extend a Mother's breath,
Make Languor smile, and smooth the Bed of Death,
Explore the Thought, explain the asking Eye,
And keep a while one Parent from the Sky!
On Cares like these if Length of days attend,
May Heav'n, to bless those days, preserve my Friend,
Preserve him social, chearful, and serene,
And just as rich as when he serv'd a QUEEN!
Whether that Blessing be deny'd, or giv'n,
Thus far was right, the rest belongs to Heav'n.

EPILOGUE TO THE SATIRES

Dialogue I

Fr.

Not twice a twelvemonth you appear in Print,
And when it comes, the Court see nothing in't.
You grow correct that once with Rapture writ,
And are, besides, too Moral for a Wit.
Decay of Parts, alas! we all must feel—
Why now, this moment, don't I see you steal?
'Tis all from Horace: Horace long before ye
Said, "Tories call'd him Whig, and Whigs a Tory;"
And taught his Romans, in much better metre,
"To laugh at Fools who put their trust in Peter."
But Horace, Sir, was delicate, was nice;
Bubo observes, he lash'd no sort of Vice:
Horace would say, Sir Billy serv'd the Crown,
Blunt could do Bus'ness, H—ggins knew the Town,
In Sappho touch the Failing of the Sex,
In rev'rend Bishops note some small Neglects,
And own, the Spaniard did a waggish thing,
Who cropt our Ears, and sent them to the King.
His sly, polite, insinuating stile
Could please at Court, and make AUGUSTUS smile:
An artful Manager, that crept between
His Friend and Shame, and was a kind of Screen.
But 'faith your very Friends will soon be sore;
Patriots there are, who wish you'd jest no more—
And where's the Glory? 'twill be only thought
The Great man never offer'd you a Groat.
Go see Sir ROBERT—

        P. See Sir ROBERT!—hum—
And never laugh—for all my life to come?
Seen him I have, but in his happier hour
Of Social Pleasure, ill-exchang'd for Pow'r;
Seen him, uncumber'd with the Venal tribe,
Smile without Art, and win without a Bribe.
Would he oblige me? let me only find,
He does not think me what he thinks mankind.
Come, come, at all I laugh He laughs, no doubt,
The only diff'rence is, I dare laugh out.

    F. Why yes: with Scripture still you may be free;
A Horse-laugh, if you please, at Honesty;
A Joke on JEKYL, or some odd Old Whig,
Who never chang'd his Principle, or Wig:
A Pariot is a Fool in ev'ry age,
Whom all Lord Chamberlains allow the Stage:
These nothing hurts; they keep their Fashion still,
And wear their strange old Virtue as they will.

    If any ask you, "Who's the Man, so near
"His Prince, that writes in Verse, and has his Ear?
Why answer LYTTELTON, and I'll engage
The worthy Youth shall ne'er be in a rage:
But were his Verses vile, his Whisper base,
You'd quickly find him in Lord Fanny's case.
Sejanus, Wolsey, hurt not honest FLEURY,
But well may put some Statesmen in a fury.

    Laugh then at any, but at Fools or Foes;
These you but anger, and you mend not those:
Laugh at your Friends, and if your Friends are sore,
So much the better, you may laugh the more.
To Vice and Folly to confine the jest,
Sets half the World, God knows, against the rest;
Did not the Sneer of more impartial men
At Sense and Virtue, balance all agen.
Judicious Wits spread wide the Ridicule,
And charitably comfort Knave and Fool.

    P. Dear Sir, forgive the Prejudice of Youth:
Adieu Distinction, Satire, Warmth, and Truth!
Come harmless Characters that no one hit,
Come Henley's Oratory, Osborn's Wit!
The Honey dropping from Favonio's tongue,
The Flow'rs of Bubo, and the Flow of Y—ng!
The gracious Dew of Pulpit Eloquence;
And all the well-whipt Cream of Courtly Sense,
That first was H—vy's, F—'s next, and then
The S—te's, and then H—vy's once agen.
O come, that easy Ciceronian stile,
So Latin, yet so English all the while,
As, tho' the Pride of Middleton and Bland,
All Boys may read, and Girls may understand!
Then might I sing without the least Offence,
And all I sung should be the Nation's Sense:
Or teach the melancholy Muse to mourn,

Hang the sad Verse on CAROLINA's Urn,
And hail her passage to the Realms of Rest,
All Parts perform'd, and all her Children blest!
So—Satire is no more—I feel it die—
No Gazeteer more innocent than I!
And let, a God's-name, ev'ry Fool and Knave
Be grac'd thro' Life, and flatter'd in his Grave.

    F. Why so? if Satire know its Time and Place,
You still may lash the Greatest—in Disgrace:
For Merit will by turns forsake them all;
Would you know when? exactly when they fall.
But let all Satire in all Changes spare
Immortal S—k, and grave De—re!
Silent and soft, as Saints remove to Heav'n,
All Tyes dissolv'd, and ev'ry Sin forgiv'n,
These, may some gentle, ministerial Wing
Receive, and place for ever near a King!
There, where no Passion, Pride, or Shame transport,
Lull'd with the sweet Nepenthe of a Court;
There, where no Father's, Brother's, Friend's Disgrace
Once break their Rest, or stir them from their Place;
But past the Sense of human Miseries,
All Tears are wip'd for ever from all Eyes;
No Cheek is known to blush, no Heart to throb,
Save when they lose a Question, or a Job.

    P.Good Heav'n forbid, that I shou'd blast their Glory,
Who know how like Whig-Ministers to Tory,
And when three Sov'reigns dy'd, could scarce be vext,
Consid'ring what a Gracious Prince was next.
Have I in silent wonder seen such things
As Pride in Slaves, and Avarice in Kings,
And at a Peer, or Peeress shall I fret,
Who starves a Sister, or forswears a Debt?
Virtue, I grant you, is an empty boast;
But shall the Dignity of Vice be lost?
Ye Gods! shall Cibber's Son, without rebuke
Swear like a Lord? or a Rich out-whore a Duke?
A Fav'rite's Porter with his Master vie,
Be brib'd as often, and as often lie?
Shall Ward draw Contracts with a Statesman's skill?
Or Japhet pocket, like his Grace, a Will?
Is it for Bond or Peter (paltry Things!)
To pay their Debts or keep their Faith like Kings?
If Blount dispatch'd himself, he play'd the man,

And so may'st Thou, Illustrious Passeran!
But shall a Printer, weary of his life,
Learn from their Books to hang himself and Wife?
This, this, my friend, I cannot, must not bear;
Vice thus abus'd, demands a Nation's care;
This calls the Church to deprecate our Sin,
And hurls the Thunder of the Laws on Gin.

  Let modest Foster, if he will, excell
Ten Metropolitans in preaching well;
A simple Quaker, or a Quaker's Wife,
Out-do Landaffe, in Doctrine—yea, in Life;
Let humble ALLEN, with an aukward Shame,
Do good by stealth, and blush to find it Fame.
Virtue may chuse the high or low Degree,
'Tis just alike to Virtue, and to me;
Dwell in a Monk, or light upon a King,
She's still the same, belov'd, contented thing.
Vice is undone, if she forgets her Birth,
And stoops from Angels to the Dregs of Earth:
But 'tis the Fall degrades her to a Whore;
Let Greatness own her, and she's mean no more:
Her Birth, her Beauty, Crowds and Courts confess,
Chaste Matrons praise her, and grave Bishops bless:
In golden Chains the willing World she draws,
And hers the Gospel is, and hers the Laws:
Mounts the Tribunal, lifts her scarlet head,
And sees pale Virtue carted in her stead!
Lo! at the Wheels of her Triumphal Car,
Old England's Genius, rough with many a Scar,
Dragg'd in the Dust! his Arms hang idly round,
His Flag inverted trails along the ground!
Our Youth, all liv'ry'd o'er with foreign Gold,
Before her dance; behind her crawl the Old!
See thronging Millions to the Pagod run,
And offer Country, Parent, Wife, or Son!
Hear her black Trumpet thro' the Land proclaim,
That "Not to be corrupted is the Shame."
In Soldier, Churchman, Patriot, Man in Pow'r,
'Tis Av'rice, all, Ambition is no more!
See, all our Nobles begging to be Slaves!
See, all our Fools aspiring to be Knaves!
The Wit of Cheats, the Courage of a Whore,
Are what ten thousand envy and adore.
All, all look up, with reverential Awe,
On Crimes that scape, or triumph o'er the Law:

While Truth, Worth, Wisdom, daily they decry—
"Nothing is Sacred now but Villany."

   Yet may this Verse (if such a Verse remain)
Show there was one who held it in disdain.

Giambattista Vico

1668–1744

Giambattista Vico was born on June 23, 1668. At the age of seven he fell down a flight of stairs, where he remained a good five hours without moving and deprived of consciousness. It was expected that the child would die or, if he survived, become an idiot; instead (as Vico proudly points out) the accident only served to foster within him "a nature melancholic and sharp, which must pertain to profound and ingenious men." (*Vita di G. Vico scritta da se medesimo,* in *Raccolta di opuscoli scientifici e filologici,* Venice, Zani, 1728, Vol. 1, p. 145.) In fact Vico became a brilliant student. His autobiography records his advanced studies as a child, and his wide reading. At the age of eighteen, while browsing in his father's bookshop, he fell into a conversation with one Monsignor Geronimo Rocca concerning the best method to teach jurisprudence. Impressed by Vico's rhetorical ability and his learning, Rocca (who was bishop of Ischia) had him appointed tutor to his nephews. Vico remained employed in this capacity nine years. It was in this period that he found the opportunity to extend his knowledge of classical and vulgar literature, reading Virgil, Horace, Dante, Boccaccio and Petrarch; his knowledge of Plato and Aristotle, however, seems to have come to him secondhand. At Vatolla he also completed his first work, the poem *Affetti di un disperato* (1692). Even though this poem expressed real spiritual torment according to conventional Baroque poetic norms, its philosophical outlook lay outside the framework of Catholic orthodoxy.

With regard to Vico's early religious doubts much has been written. Suffice it to say that his doctrinal orientation during the "formative" years of his life (the years before he started to compose and emend the different versions of the *Scienza Nuova* [1725, 1730, 1744]) was to say the least, equivocal. His discovery of Grotius is important in this respect. From the researches of the historian Arnaldo Momigliano we know that by 1713 Vico was reading Grotius' *De jure belli et pacis,* and had been requested to write the notes to an edition of Grotius for a Neapolitan printer. Vico refused to do so, claiming that it was not fitting for a man of Catholic faith to comment on the works of a heretic. (See A. Momigliano, "Vico's *Scienza Nuova:* Roman 'Bestioni' and Roman 'Eroi', *History and Theory,* V, 1(1966):3–23; reprinted in Momigliano, *Studies in Historiography,* Middletown, 1977, p. 260.) Behind Vico's refusal Momigliano sees an assertion of his claim to orthodoxy as a result of changed political conditions in Naples after 1719. Between 1717 (when he was asked to write the commentary on Grotius) and 1719, it is probable that Vico could find no suitable way to object formally to the "heretical" Grotius whose thought was to become so central to his own. It is probable that Vico's actual religious beliefs were more suspect from the point of view of the Church than his nominal objections to freethinking would suggest, given the fact that he associated with a circle of epicureans who ran afoul of the Holy Office around 1690.

Vico tended to turn away from both freethinking and the writing of verse sometime after his appointment to the Chair of Eloquence at the University of Naples in 1697. He was becoming more and more engrossed in the learned and antiquarian studies that were to culminate in the writing of his *magnum opus*. Plato and Tacitus among the ancients, and Bacon and Grotius among the moderns formed a kind of intellectual fraternity for the young professor. "In practice, Vico made little use of Plato and Tacitus: they remained pieces of classical scenery, the one contemplating man as he should be, the other as he is. But he sought his information in the learned books of the sixteenth and seventeenth centuries and derived his problems from them." (Momigliano, *op. cit.*, p. 258).

Vico felt more at home in the speculative reaches of Renaissance philosophy than in the arid Cartesian system that held sway over the thought of his day. He scornfully characterized the contemporary Neapolitan scene with observations that metaphysics had been put to rout, poetry constrained, and oratory in ruins. (See Michael Mooney, *Vico in the Tradition of Rhetoric*, Princeton, 1985). He opposed the latest methods of research into the past as well as the latest fashions in philosophy. For these reasons he preferred Spinoza over Descartes, and antiquarian speculation over the new craze for archeological excavations. His primary intellectual preoccupations included the chronologies of the ancient peoples, the secret wisdom of the pagans, the notion of Natural Law as expressed by Grotius, and, finally, the notion of a cyclic historical sequence culminating in the *ricorso,* which was ambiguously connected to the notion of Christian Providence. All of these issues, in one form or another, found their way into the editions of the *Scienza Nuova* which he put out from 1725 until his death in 1744.

THE NEW SCIENCE

BOOK II

Section II

Poetic Logic

That which is metaphysics insofar as it contemplates things in all the forms of their being, is logic insofar as it considers things in all the forms by which they may be signified. Accordingly, as poetry has been considered by us above as a poetic metaphysics in which the theological poets imagined bodies to be for the most part divine substances, so now that same poetry is considered as poetic logic, by which it signifies them.

401 "Logic" comes from *logos*, whose first and proper meaning was *fabula*, fable, carried over into Italian as *favella*, speech. In Greek the fable was also called *mythos*, myth, whence comes the Latin *mutus*, mute. For speech was born in mute times as mental [or sign] language, which Strabo in a golden passage [1.2.6] says existed before vocal or articulate [language]; whence *logos* means both word and idea. It was fitting that the matter should be so ordered by divine providence in religious times, for it is an eternal property of religions that they attach more importance to meditation than to speech. Thus the first language in the first mute times of the nations must have begun with signs, whether gestures or physical objects, which had natural relations to the ideas [to be expressed]. For this reason *logos*, or word, meant also deed to the Hebrews and thing to the Greeks, as Thomas Gataker observes in his *De instrumenti stylo*. Similarly, *mythos* came to be defined for us as *vera narratio*, or true speech, the natural speech which first Plato and then Iamblichus said had been spoken in the world at one time. But this was mere conjecture on their part, and Plato's effort to recover this speech in the *Cratylus* was therefore vain, and he was criticized for it by Aristotle and Galen. For that first language, spoken by the theological poets, was not a language in accord with the nature of the things it dealt with (as must have been the sacred language invented by Adam, to whom God granted divine onomathesia, the giving of names to things according to the nature of each), but was a fantastic speech making use of physical substances endowed with life and most of them imagined to be divine.

402 This is the way in which the theological poets apprehended Jove, Cybele or Berecynthia, and Neptune, for example, and, at first mutely pointing, explained them as substances of the sky, the earth, and the sea,

185

which they imagined to be animate divinities and were therefore true to their senses in believing them to be gods. By means of these three divinities, in accordance with what we have said above concerning poetic characters, they explained everything appertaining to the sky, the earth, and the sea. And similarly by means of the other divinities they signified the other kinds of things appertaining to each, denoting all flowers, for instance, by Flora, and all fruits by Pomona. We nowadays reverse this practice in respect of spiritual things, such as the faculties of the human mind, the passions, virtues, vices, sciences, and arts; for the most part the ideas we form of them are so many feminine personifications, to which we refer all the causes, properties, and effects that severally appertain to them. For when we wish to give utterance to our understanding of spiritual things, we must seek aid from our imagination to explain them and, like painters, form human images of them. But these theological poets, unable to make use of the understanding, did the opposite and more sublime thing: they attributed senses and passions, as we saw not long since, to bodies, and to bodies as vast as sky, sea, and earth. Later, as these vast imaginations shrank and the power of abstraction grew, the personifications were reduced to diminutive signs. Metonymy drew a cloak of learning over the prevailing ignorance of these origins of human institutions, which have remained buried until now. Jove becomes so small and light that he is flown about by an eagle. Neptune rides the waves in a fragile chariot. And Cybele rides seated on a lion.

403   Thus the mythologies, as their name indicates, must have been the proper languages of the fables; the fables being imaginative class concepts, as we have shown, the mythologies must have been the allegories corresponding to them. Allegory is defined as *diversiloquium* insofar as, by identity not of proportion but (to speak scholastically) of predicability, allegories signify the diverse species or the diverse individuals comprised under these genera. So that they must have a univocal signification connoting a quality common to all their species and individuals (as Achilles connotes an idea of valor common to all strong men, or Ulysses an idea of prudence common to all wise men); such that these allegories must be the etymologies of the poetic languages, which would make their origins all univocal, whereas those of the vulgar languages are more often analogical. We also have the definition of the word "etymology" itself as meaning *veriloquium*, just as fable was defined as *vera narratio*.

Corollaries concerning Poetic
Tropes, Monsters, and Metamorphoses

I

404   All the first tropes are corollaries of this poetic logic. The most luminous and therefore the most necessary and frequent is metaphor. It is most praised when it gives sense and passion to insensate things, in accordance with the metaphysics above discussed, by which the first poets attributed to bodies the being of animate substances, with capacities measured by their own, namely sense and passion, and in this way made fables of them. Thus every metaphor so formed is a fable in brief. This gives a basis for judging the time when metaphors made their appearance in the languages. All the metaphors conveyed by likenesses taken from bodies to signify the operations of abstract minds must date from times when philosophies were taking shape. The proof of this is that in every language the terms needed for the refined arts and recondite sciences are of rustic origin.

405 It is noteworthy that in all languages the greater part of the expressions relating to inanimate things are formed by metaphor from the human body and its parts and from the human senses and passions. Thus, head for top or beginning; the brow and shoulders of a hill; the eyes of needles and of potatoes; mouth for any opening; the lip of a cup or pitcher; the teeth of a rake, a saw, a comb; the beard of wheat; the tongue of a shoe; the gorge of a river; a neck of land; an arm of the sea; the hands of a clock; heart for center (the Latins used *umbilicus,* navel, in this sense); the belly of a sail; foot for end or bottom; the flesh of fruits; a vein of rock or mineral; the blood of grapes for wine; the bowels of the earth. Heaven or the sea smiles; the wind whistles; the waves murmur; a body groans under a great weight. The farmers of Latium used to say the fields were thirsty, bore fruit, were swollen with grain; and our rustics speak of plants making love, vines going mad, resinous trees weeping. Innumerable other examples could be collected from all languages. All of which is a consequence of our axiom that man in his ignorance makes himself the rule of the universe, for in the examples cited he has made of himself an entire world. So that, as rational metaphysics teaches that man becomes all things by understanding them (*homo intelligendo fit omnia*), this imaginative metaphysics shows that man becomes all things by *not* understanding them (*homo non intelligendo fit omnia*); and perhaps the latter proposition is truer than the former, for when man understands he extends his mind and takes in the things, but when he does not understand he makes the things out of himself and becomes them by transforming himself into them.

II

406 In such a logic, sprung from such a metaphysics, the first poets had to give names to things from the most particular and the most sensible ideas. Such ideas are the sources, respectively, of synechdoche and metonymy. Metonymy of agent for act resulted from the fact that names for agents were commoner than names for acts. Metonymy of subject for form and accident was due to inability to abstract forms and qualities from subjects. Certainly metonymy of cause for effect produced in each case a little fable, in which the cause was imagined as a woman clothed with her effects: ugly Poverty, sad Old Age, pale Death.

III

407 Synecdoche developed into metaphor as particulars were elevated into universals or parts united with the other parts together with which they make up their wholes. Thus the term "mortals" was originally and properly applied only to men, as the only beings whose mortality there was any occasion to notice. The use of "head" for man or person, so frequent in vulgar Latin, was due to the fact that in the forests only the head of a man could be seen from a distance. The word "man" itself is abstract, comprehending as in a philosophic genus the body and all its parts, the mind and all its faculties, the spirit and all its dispositions. In the same way, *tignum* and *culmen*, log and top, came to be used with entire propriety when thatching was the practice for rafter and thatch; and later, with the adornment of cities, they signified all the materials and trim of a building. Again, *tectum*, roof, came to mean a whole house because in the first times a covering sufficed for a house. Similarly, *puppis*, poop, for a ship, because it was the highest part and therefore the first to be seen by those on shore; as in the returned barbarian times a ship was called a sail. Similarly, *mucro*, point, for sword, because the latter is an abstract word and as in a genus comprehends pummel, hilt, edge, and point; and it was the point they felt which aroused their fear. Similarly, the material for the formed whole, as iron for sword, because they did not know how to abstract the form from the material. That bit of synecdoche and metonymy, *Tertia messis erat* ("It was the third harvest"), was doubtless born of a natural necessity, for it took more than a thousand years for the astronomical term "year" to rise among the nations; and even now the Florentine peasantry say, "We have reaped so many times," when they mean "so many years." And that knot of two synecdoches and a metonymy, *Post aliquot, mea regna videns, mirabor, aristas?* ("After a few harvests shall I wonder at seeing my kingdoms?") [Vergil, *Eclogue* 1.69], betrays only too well the poverty of expression of the first rustic times, in which the phrase "so many ears of wheat"—even more particular than harvests—was used for "so many years." And because of the excessive poverty of the expression, the grammarians have assumed an excess of art behind it.

IV

408 Irony certainly could not have begun until the period of reflection, because it is fashioned of falsehood by dint of a reflection which wears the mask of truth. Here emerges a great principle of human institutions, confirming the origin of poetry disclosed in this work: that since the first men of the gentile world had the simplicity of children, who are truthful by nature, the first fables could not feign anything false; they must therefore have been, as they have been defined above, true narrations.

V

409 From all this it follows that all the tropes (and they are all reducible to the four types above discussed), which have hitherto been considered ingenious invention of writers, were necessary modes of expression of all the first poetic nations, and had originally their full native propriety. But these expressions of the first nations later became figurative when, with the further development of the human mind, words were invented which signified abstract forms or genera comprising their species or relating parts with their wholes. And here begins the overthrow of two common errors of the grammarians: that prose speech is proper speech, and poetic speech improper; and that prose speech came first and afterward speech in verse.

VI

410 Poetic monsters and metamorphoses arose from a necessity of this first human nature, its inability to abstract forms or properties from subjects. By their logic they had to put subjects together in order to put their forms together, or to destroy a subject in order to separate its primary form from the contrary form which had been imposed upon it. Such a putting together of ideas created the poetic monsters. In Roman law, as Antoine Favre observes in his *Iurisprudentiae papinianeae scientia,* children born of prostitutes are called monsters because they have the nature of men together with the bestial characteristic of having been born of vagabond or uncertain unions. And it was as being monsters of this sort, we shall find, that children born of noble women without benefit of solemn nuptials were commanded by the Law of the Twelve Tables to be thrown into the Tiber.

VII

411 The distinguishing of ideas produced metamorphoses. Among other examples preserved by ancient jurisprudence is the heroic Latin phrase *fundum fieri,* to become ground of, used in place of *auctorem fieri,* to become author of, to authorize, to ratify; the explanation being that, as the ground supports the farm or soil and that which is sown, planted, or built thereon, so the ratifier supports an act which without his ratification would fail; and he does this by quitting the form of a being moving at will, which he is, and taking on the contrary form of a stable thing.

Corollaries concerning Speech by Poetic Characters among the First Nations

412 The poetic speech which our poetic logic has helped us to understand continued for a long time into the historical period, much as great and rapid rivers continue far into the sea, keeping sweet the waters borne on by the force of their flow. We have cited in the Axioms the statement of Iamblichus that the Egyptians attributed to Thrice-great Hermes all their discoveries useful to human life. And we confirmed this by another axiom: that "children, by the ideas and names of the men, women and things they have seen first, afterwards apprehend and name all the men, women and things that bear any resemblance or relation to the first." This we said was the great natural source of the poetic characters, with which the first peoples naturally thought and spoke. We also remarked that, if Iamblichus had reflected upon this nature of human institutions, bringing into relation with it the habit of the ancient Egyptians which he himself reports, he would certainly not have intruded into the mysteries of the vulgar wisdom of the Egyptians the sublime mysteries of his own Platonic wisdom.

413   Now in view of the nature of children and the custom of the first Egyptians, we assert that poetic speech, in virtue of the poetic characters it employs, can yield many important discoveries concerning antiquity.

I

414   Solon must have been a sage of vulgar wisdom, party leader of the plebs in the first times of the aristocratic commonwealth at Athens. This fact was indeed preserved by Greek history where it narrates that at first Athens was held by the optimates. In this work we shall show that such was universally the case in all the heroic commonwealths. The heroes or nobles, by a certain nature of theirs which they believed to be of divine origin, were led to say that the gods belonged to them, and consequently that the auspices of the gods were theirs also. By means of the auspices they kept within their own orders all the public and private institutions of the heroic cities. To the plebeians, whom they believed to be of bestial origin and consequently men without gods and hence without auspices, they conceded only the uses of natural liberty. (This is a great principle of institutions that are discussed through almost the whole of the present work.) Solon, however, had admonished the plebeians to reflect upon themselves and to realize that they were of like human nature with the nobles and should therefore be made equal with them in civil rights—unless, indeed, Solon was [a poetic character for] the Athenian plebeians themselves, considered under this aspect [of knowing themselves and demanding their rights].

415   The ancient Romans must also have had such a Solon among them. For the plebeians in the heroic struggles with the nobles, as ancient Roman history openly tells us, kept saying that the fathers of whom Romulus composed the Senate (and from whom these patricians were descended) *non esse caelo demissos*, "had not come down from heaven"; that is, that Jove was equal [just] to all. This is the civil history of the expression *Jupiter omnibus aequus*, into which the learned later read the tenet that all minds are equal and that the differences they take on arise from differences in the organization of their bodies and in their civil education. By this reflection the Roman plebeians began to achieve equality with the patricians in civil liberty, until they entirely changed the Roman commonwealth from an aristocratic to a popular form. We proposed this as a hypothesis in the Notes on the Chronological Table, where we considered the Publilian Law in idea; and we shall show that it occurred in fact not only in the Roman but in all the other ancient commonwealths. Both by reasons and by authority we shall demonstrate that the plebeians of the peoples universally, beginning with Solon's reflection, changed the commonwealths from aristocratic to popular.

416   Hence Solon was made the author of that celebrated saying, "Know thyself," which, because of the great civil utility it had had for the Athenian people, was inscribed in all the public places of the city. Later the learned preferred to regard it as having been intended for what in fact it is, a great counsel respecting metaphysical and moral things, and because of it Solon was reputed a sage in esoteric wisdom and made prince of the Seven Sages of Greece. In this way, because from this reflection there sprang up at Athens all the institutions and laws that shape a democratic commonwealth, and because of the first peoples' habit of thinking in poetic characters, these institutions and laws were all attributed by the Athenians to Solon, just as, by the Egyptians, all inventions useful to human civil life were attributed to Thrice-great Hermes.

II

417   In the same way all the laws concerning social classes must have been attributed to Romulus.

III

418   And to Numa, all those concerning sacred institutions and divine ceremonies, for which Roman religion was later conspicuous in its time of greatest pomp.

IV

419   To Tullus Hostilius, all the laws and institutions of military discipline.

V

420   To Servius Tullius, the census [tax], which is the foundation of democratic commonwealths, and other laws in great number having to do with popular liberty, so that he was acclaimed by Tacitus as *praecipuus sanctor legum*, "chief ordainer of laws." For the census of Servius Tullius was the basic institution of the aristocratic commonwealths by which the plebeians obtained from the nobles the bonitary ownership of the fields, which gave them occasion later for creating the tribunes of the plebs to defend for them this part of natural liberty, and the tribunes gradually led them to the attainment of full civil liberty. Thus the census of Servius Tullius, by affording the occasions and starting points, developed into a census which was the basic institution of the

Roman popular commonwealth. This was discussed by way of hypothesis in the Notes on the Publilian Law, and will later be shown to be true in fact.

VI

421 To Tarquinius Priscus, all the ensigns and devices with which the majesty of the Roman Empire was later resplendent in the most illustrious times of Rome.

VII

422 In the same way a great many laws enacted in later times were interpolated in the Twelve Tables. And (as was fully demonstrated in our *Principles of Universal Law*) since the sole purpose for which the decemvirs were created was the law by which the nobles extended quiritary ownership to the plebeians, and since this was the first law to be inscribed on a public tablet, all the laws making for equal liberty which were later inscribed on public tablets were attributed to the decemvirs because of their aspect of popular liberty. Take as a test case Greek luxury in the matter of funerals. Since the decemvirs would not have taught it to the Romans by prohibiting it, the prohibition must have come after the Romans had adopted it. But that cannot have been until after the wars with the Tarentines and with Pyrrhus, in which their acquaintance with the Greeks began. This explains the fact observed by Cicero that this law translated into Latin the very words in which it had been conceived in Athens.

VIII

423 It is the same with Draco, author of the laws written in blood at the time when Greek history tells us Athens was occupied by the optimates. This was in the time of the heroic aristocracies, in which Greek history also tells us the Heraclids were scattered through all Greece, even into Attica. They finally settled in the Peloponnesus and established their kingdom in Sparta, which was certainly an aristocratic commonwealth. Draco must have been one of the Gorgon's serpents nailed to the shield of Perseus, which signifies the rule of the laws. This shield with the frightful penalties it bore turned to stone those who looked upon it; just as in sacred history similar laws were called *leges sanguinis,* laws of blood, because of the exemplary punishments they carried. Minerva armed herself with this shield and was called Athena. And among the Chinese, who write in hieroglyphics to this day, a dragon is the ensign of the civil power. It is something to wonder at that two nations so distant from each other in space and time should think and express themselves in the same poetic manner. For in all Greek history nothing else is told of this Draco.

IX

424 This discovery of the poetic characters confirms us in placing Aesop considerably earlier than the Seven Sages of Greece. For this philological truth is confirmed for us by the following history of human ideas. The Seven Sages were admired because they began to impart precepts of morality or of civil doctrine in the forms of maxims like the famous "Know thyself" of Solon, who was their prince. This was a precept of civil doctrine, later carried over into metaphysics and morals. But Aesop had previously imparted such counsels in the form of comparisons, which the poets had still earlier used to express themselves. And the order of human ideas is to observe the similarities of things first to express oneself and later for purposes of proof. Proof, in turn, is first by example, for which a single likeness suffices, and finally by induction, for which more are required. Socrates, father of all the sects of philosophers, introduced by induction the dialectic which Aristotle later perfected with the syllogism, which cannot proceed without a universal. But to undeveloped minds it suffices to present a single likeness in order to persuade them; as, by a single fable of the sort invented by Aesop, the worthy Menenius Agrippa reduced the rebellious Roman plebs to obedience.

425 That Aesop was a poetic character of the *socii* or *famuli* of the heroes, is revealed to us with prophetic insight by the urbane Phaedrus in one of the prologues of his *Fables:*

> Attend me briefly while I now disclose
> How art of fable telling first arose.
> Unhappy slaves, in servitude confined,
> Dared not to their harsh masters show their mind,
> But under veiling of the fable's dress
> Contrived their thoughts and feelings to express,
> Escaping still their lords' affronted wrath.
> So Aesop did; I widen out his path,

as is clearly confirmed for us by his fable of the lion's share. For the plebeians were called *socii* of the heroic cities, and shared the hardships and dangers of war but not the spoils and the conquests. Hence Aesop was called a slave, because the plebeians were *famuli* of the heroes. And he was represented as ugly, because civil beauty was considered to come only from solemnized marriages, and only the heroes contracted such marriages. For the same reason Thersites was ugly, for he must have been a character of the plebeians who served the heroes in the Trojan War. He was beaten by Ulysses with the scepter of Agamemnon, just as the ancient Roman plebeians were beaten by the nobles with rods over their bare shoulders—*regium in morem,* in royal fashion, as Sallust puts it in St. Augustine's *City of God*—until the Porcian Law freed Roman shoulders from the rod.

426 Such counsels, then, dictated by natural reason as useful to free civil life, must have been sentiments cherished by the plebs of the heroic cities. Aesop was made a poetic character of these plebs in this respect. Later, fables having to do with moral philosophy were ascribed to him, and he was turned into the first moral philosopher, just as Solon, who by his laws made Athens a free commonwealth, was turned into a sage. And because Aesop counseled in fables, he was supposed to have lived before Solon, who counseled in maxims. These fables must have been conceived originally in heroic verse. There is a later tradition that they were conceived in iambic verse, which the Greek peoples spoke in a transitional period between heroic verse and prose. They were finally written in prose and have reached us in that form.

X

427   In this way the later discoveries of esoteric wisdom were attributed to the first authors of vulgar wisdom; and [poetic characters like] Zoroaster in the East, Thrice-great Hermes in Egypt, Orpheus in Greece, Pythagoras in Italy, originally lawgivers, were finally believed to have been philosophers, as Confucius is today in China. For certainly the Pythagoreans in Magna Graecia were so called in the sense of nobles, who, having tried to reduce all their commonwealths from popular to aristocratic, were all slain. And the Golden Verses of Pythagoras were an imposture, as were also the Oracles of Zoroaster, the *Poimander* of Thrice-great Hermes, and the *Orphics* or verses of Orpheus. There did not come down to the ancients any book on philosophy written by Pythagoras, and Philolaus was the first Pythagorean to write one, as Scheffer observes in his *De philosophia italica.*

Corollaries Concerning the
Origins of Languages and Letters

428   Now from the theology of the poets, or poetic metaphysics, by way of the poetic logic sprung from it, we go on to discover the origin of languages and letters. Concerning these there are as many opinions as there are scholars who have written on the subject. So that Gerard Jan Voss says in his *Grammatica:* "With regard to the invention of letters, many authors have brought together many things, in such profusion and confusion that you go away from them more uncertain than you came." And Herman Hugo in his *De prima scribendi origine* observes: "There is no other subject on which more numerous or more conflicting opinions are to be found than in the discussion of the origin of letters and writing. How many conflicts of opinion! What is one to believe? What not believe?" Not without reason, therefore, did Bernard von Mallinckrodt, in his *De natura et usu literarum,* conclude from the impossibility of understanding how they arose that they were divine inventions; in which view he was followed by Ingewald Eling in his *Historia linguae graecae.*

429   But the difficulty as to the manner of their origin was created by the scholars themselves, all of whom regarded the origin of letters as a separate question from that of the origin of languages, whereas the two were by nature conjoined. And they should have made out as much from the words "grammar" and "characters." From the former, because grammar is defined as the art of speaking, yet *grammata* are letters, so that grammar should have been defined as the art of writing. So, indeed, it was defined by Aristotle, and so in fact it originally was; for all nations began to speak by writing, since all were originally mute. "Character," on the other hand, means idea, form, model; and certainly poetic characters came before those of articulate sounds [that is, before alphabetic characters]. Josephus stoutly maintains that at the time of Homer the so-called vulgar letters had not yet been invented. Moreover, if these letters had been shaped to represent articulated sounds instead of being arbitrary signs, they would have been uniform among all nations, as the articulated sounds themselves are. Thus, in their hopeless ignorance of the way in which languages and letters began, scholars have failed to understand how the first nations thought in poetic characters, spoke in fables, and wrote in hieroglyphs. Yet these should have been the principles, which must by their nature be most certain, of philosophy in its study of human ideas and of philology in its study of human words.

430 Having now to enter upon a discussion of this matter, we shall give a brief sample of the opinions that have been held respecting it—opinions so uncertain, frivolous, inept, pretentious or ridiculous, and so numerous, that we need not relate them. By way of sample, then: because in the returned barbarian times Scandinavia by the conceit of the nations was called *vagina gentium* and was believed to be the mother of all other nations in the world, therefore by the conceit of scholars Johannes and Olaus Magnus were of opinion that their Goths had preserved from the beginning of the world the letters divinely invented by Adam. This dream was laughed at by all the scholars, but this did not keep Johannes van Gorp from following suit and going one better by claiming that his own Dutch language, which is not much different from Saxon, has come down from the Earthly Paradise and is the mother of all other languages. This claim was ridiculed by Joseph Justus Scaliger, Philipp Camerarius, Christian Becman, and Martin Schoock. And yet this conceit swelled to the bursting point in the *Atlantica* of Olof Rudbeck, who will have it that the Greek letters came from the runes; that the Phoenician letters, to which Cadmus gave the order and values of those of the Hebrews, were inverted runes: and that the Greeks finally straightened them here and rounded them there by rule and compass. And because the inventor is called Merkurssman among the Scandinavians, he will have it that the Mercury who invented letters for the Egyptians was a Goth. Such license in rendering opinions concerning the origins of letters should prepare the reader to receive the things we shall say of them here not merely with impartial readiness to see what they bring forward that is new, but with diligence to meditate upon them and to accept them for what they must be: namely, principles of all the human and divine knowledge of the gentile world.

431 The philosophers and philologians should all have begun to treat of the origins of languages and letters from the following principles. (1) That the first men of the gentile world conceived ideas of things by imaginative characters of animate and mute substances. (2) That they expressed themselves by means of gestures or physical objects which had natural relations with the ideas; for example, three ears of grain, or acting as if swinging a scythe three times, to signify three years. (3) That they thus expressed themselves by a language with natural significations. (Plato and Iamblichus said such a language had once been spoken in the world; it must have been the most ancient language of Atlantis, which scholars would have us believe expressed ideas by the nature of the things, that is, by their natural properties.) It is because the philosophers and philologians have treated separately these two things which are naturally conjoined [—the origins of languages and letters—] that the inquiry into the origins of letters has proved so difficult for them,—as difficult as that into the origins of languages, with which they have been either not at all or very little concerned.

432   At the outset of our discussion, then, we posit as our first principle the philological axiom that according to the Egyptians there had been spoken in their world in all preceding time three languages corresponding in number and order to the three ages that had elapsed in their world: the ages of gods, heroes, and men. The first language had been hieroglyphic, sacred or divine; the second, symbolic, by signs or by heroic devices; the third, epistolary, for men at a distance to communicate to each other the current needs of their lives. [Cf. Clement of Alexandria, *Miscellanies* 5.4.] Concerning these three languages there are two golden passages in Homer's *Iliad,* from which it clearly appears that the Greeks agreed with the Egyptians in this matter. In the first it is told how Nestor lived through three generations of men speaking different languages. Nestor must therefore have been a heroic character of the chronology determined by the thee languages corresponding to the three ages of the Egyptians; and the phrase "to live the years of Nestor" must have meant "to live the years of the world." The other passage is that in which Aeneas relates to Achilles that men of different language began to inhabit Ilium after Troy was moved to the seashore and Pergamum became its fortress. To this first principle we join the tradition, also Egyptian, that their Thoth or Mercury invented both law and letters.

433   Around this truth we assemble the following others. Among the Greeks "name" and "character" had the same meaning, so that the Church Fathers used indiscriminately the two expressions *de divinis characteribus* and *de divinis nominibus.* "Name" and "definition" have also the same meaning; thus, in rhetoric, under the head of *quaestio nominis* we find a search for definition of the fact, and in medicine the nomenclature of diseases is the head under which their nature is defined. Among the Romans "names" meant originally and properly houses branching into many families. And that the first Greeks also used "names" in this sense is shown by the patronymics, or names of fathers, which are so often used by the poets and above all by Homer. (According to Livy, a tribune of the plebs defined the patricians as those *qui possunt nomine ciere patrem,* "who can use the surnames of their fathers" [that is, who were born in lawful wedlock].) These patronymics later disappeared in the popular liberty of all the rest of Greece, but were preserved by the Heraclids in the aristocratic commonwealth of Sparta. In Roman law *nomen* signifies right. Similarly, in Greek *nomos* signifies law, and from *nomos* comes *nomisma,* money, as Aristotle notes; and according to etymologists, *nomos* becomes in Latin *nummus.* In French, *loi* means law, and *aloi* means money; and among the second barbarians the term "canon" was applied both to ecclesiastical law and to the annual rent paid by the feudal leaseholder to the lord of the land he held in fief. This uniformity of thinking perhaps explains why the Latins used the term *ius* both for law and for the fat of sacrificed animals, which was Jove's due; for Jove was originally called *Ious*, from which were later derived the genitives *Iovis* and *iuris*. Among the Hebrews also, of the three parts into which they divided the animal sacrificed as a peace offering, the fat was accounted God's due and burned on the altar. The Latin *praedia*, estates (a term which must have been applied to rustic earlier than to urban estates), were so called because the first cultivated fields were the first booty (*praeda*) in the world. The first taming was of such fields, which were therefore in ancient Roman law called *manucaptae* (whence *manceps* for one under real-estate bond to the public treasury); and in Roman law *iura praediorum* remained a term for the so-called real servitudes, which were attached to real estate. And lands referred to as *manucaptae* must at first have been called *mancipia;* and it is certainly in this sense that we must understand the article of the Law of the Twelve Tables, *Qui nexum faciet mancipiumque,* that is, "Whoever shall consign a bond, and shall consign thereby his manor . . .". The Italians, following the same line of thought as the ancient Romans, called the manors *poderi*, as having been acquired by force. Further evidence: the returned barbarians called the fields with their boundaries *presas terrarum*. The Spaniards call bold enterprises *prendas*. The Italians call family coats of arms *imprese*, and use *termini* in the sense of "words" (a usage surviving in scholastic dialectic). They also call family coats of arms *insegne*, from which is derived the verb *insegnare*, to teach. So Homer, in whose time so-called vulgar letters had not yet been invented, says Proetus's letter to Eurcia against Bellerophon was written in *sēmata,* signs.

434 To crown all these things, let the following three incontrovertible truths be added. (1) Since it has been demonstrated that the first gentile nations were all mute in their beginnings, they must have expressed themselves by gestures or by physical objects having natural relations with their ideas. (2) They must have used signs to fix the boundaries of their estates and to have enduring witnesses of their rights. (3) They all made use of money. All these truths will give us the origins of languages and letters, and thereby of hieroglyphs, laws, names, family coats of arms, medals, money, and of the language and writing in which the first natural law of the gentes was spoken and written.

435 In order to establish more firmly the principles of all this, we must here uproot the false opinion held by some of the Egyptians that the hieroglyphs were invented by philosophers to conceal in them their mysteries of lofty esoteric wisdom. For it was by a common natural necessity that all the first nations spoke in hieroglyphs. In Africa, to the case of Egypt already noted we may add, following Heliodorus in his *Aethiopica*, the Ethiopians, who used as hieroglyphs the tools of all the mechanical arts. In the East the magic characters of the Chaldeans must have been hieroglyphs. In northern Asia, Idanthyrsus, king of the Scythians (quite late in their extremely long history, in which they had conquered even the Egyptians, who boasted themselves the most ancient of all nations), used five real words to answer Darius the Great, who had declared war on him. These five were a frog, a mouse, a bird, a ploughshare, and a bow. The frog signified that he, Idanthyrsus, was born of the earth of Scythia as frogs are born of the earth in summer rains, so that he was a son of that land. The mouse signified that he, like a mouse, had made his home where he was born; that is, that he had established his nation there. The bird signified that there the auspices were his; that is, that he was subject to none but God. The ploughshare signified that he had reduced those lands to cultivation, and thus tamed and made them his own by force. And finally the bow signified that as supreme commander of the arms of Scythia he had the duty and the might to defend her. This explanation, so natural and necessary, is to be set against the ridiculous ones worked out by the counselors of Darius, according to St. Cyril [i.e., Clement of Alexandria in his *Miscellanies* 5.8]. Add to the interpretation of the Scythian hieroglyphics by Darius's counselors the far-fetched, artificial, and contorted interpretations by scholars of the Egyptian hieroglyphics, and it will be evident that in general the true and proper use made of hieroglyphics by the first peoples has hitherto not been understood. As for the Latins, Roman history has not left us without such a tradition; witness the mute heroic answer which Tarquinius Superbus sends to his son in Gabii, when in the presence of the messenger he cuts off the heads of poppies with the stick he has in his hands. In northern Europe, as Tacitus observes in describing their customs, the ancient Germans were not acquainted with the secrets of letters (*literarum secreta*); that is, they did not know how to write their hieroglyphics. This must have remained the case down to the times of Frederick the Swabian, indeed to those of Rudolph of Hapsburg, when they began to write state papers in vulgar German script. In northern France there was a hieroglyphic speech called rebus of Picardy, which must have been, as in Germany, a speech by physical things; that is, by the hieroglyphics of Idanthyrsus. Even in Ultima Thule, in fact in its remotest part, namely Scotland, as Hector Boece relates in his history of that nation, they wrote in hieroglyphics in ancient times. In the West Indies the Mexicans were found to write in hieroglyphics, and Jan de Laet in his description of the new India describes the hieroglyphics of the Indians as diverse heads of animals, plants, flowers, and fruits, and notes that they distinguish families by their totemic symbols [on boundary posts]; which is the same use that is made of family coats-of-arms in our world. In the East Indies the Chinese still write in hieroglyphics.

436   Thus is deflated the conceit of the scholars who came afterwards, a conceit to which that of the extremely conceited Egyptians dared not swell itself: namely, that the other sages of the world had learned from the Egyptians how to conceal their esoteric wisdom under hieroglyphics.

437   Having posited these principles of poetic logic and dissipated this conceit of the scholars, we return now to the three languages of the Egyptians. The first of these, that of gods, is attested for the Greeks by Homer, who, in five passages of his two poems, makes mention of a language more ancient than his own, which is certainly heroic, and calls it "language of the gods". Three of the passages are in the *Iliad:* the first where he tells that the creature called

Briareus by the gods was called Aegaeon by men; the second where he speaks of a bird called chalcis by the gods and cymindis by men; the third where he says the river of Troy is called Xanthus by the gods, Scamander by men. In the *Odyssey* there are two passages: one where he says what men call Scylla and Charybdis the gods call Planctae Petrae; the other where Mercury gives Ulysses a secret remedy against the enchantments of Circe, an herb called moly by the gods, knowledge of which is denied to men. Plato has many things to say about these passages [*Cratylus* 391Dff], but to no purpose; so that Dio Chrysostom later slanderously accuses Homer of pretending to understand the language of the gods, which naturally is denied to men. But it may be questioned whether in these Homeric passages we should not take "gods" to mean "heroes"; for the heroes took the name of gods over the plebeians of their cities, whom they called men (as in the returned barbarian times the vassals were called *homines,* to the astonishment of Hotman), and the great lords (as in the recourse of barbarism) made a vaunt of possessing marvelous medical secrets. Thus the differences referred to may have been no more than differences between noble and vulgar speech. Be that as it may, there can be no doubt that among the Latins Varro occupied himself with the language of the gods, for he had the diligence to collect thirty thousand of their names, which would have sufficed for a copious divine vocabulary, with which the peoples of Latium might express all their human needs, which in those simple and frugal times must have been few indeed, being only the things that were necessary to life. The Greeks too had gods to the number of thirty thousand, for they made a deity of every stone, spring, brook, plant, and offshore rock. Such deities included the dryads, hamadryads, oreads, and napeads. Just so the American Indians make a god of everything that exceeds their limited understanding. Thus the divine fables of the Greeks and Latins must have been the true first hieroglyphs, or sacred or divine characters, corresponding to those of the Egyptians.

438   The second kind of speech, corresponding to the age of heroes, was said by the Egyptians to have been spoken by symbols. To these may be reduced the heroic emblems, which must have been the mute comparisons which Homer calls *sēmata* (the signs in which the heroes wrote). In consequence they must have been metaphors, images, similitudes, or comparisons, which, having passed into articulate speech, supplied all the resources of poetic expression. For certainly Homer, if we accept the resolute denial of Josephus the Jew that there has come down to us any writer more ancient than he, was the first author of the Greek tongue; and, since we owe to the Greeks all that has reached us of the gentile world, he was the first author of that entire world. Among the Latins the earliest memorials of their tongue are the fragments of the Salian songs, and the first writer of whom there is mention is Livius Andronicus the poet. With the recourse of barbarism in Europe, new languages were born. The first language of the Spaniards was that called "*el romance,*" and consequently that of heroic poetry, for the *romanceros* were the heroic poets of the returned barbarian times. In France the first writer in vulgar French was Arnaut Daniel Pacca, the first of all the Provençal poets, who flourished in the eleventh century. And finally the first writers in Italy were the Florentine and Sicilian rhymers.

439   The epistolary speech of the Egyptians, suitable for expressing the needs of common everyday life in communication from a distance, must have been born of the lower classes of a dominant people in Egypt, which must have been that of Thebes (whose king Ramses extended his rule over all that great nation), because for the Egyptians that language corresponds to the age of men, the term used for the plebeians of the heroic peoples to differentiate them from the heroes. This language must be understood as having sprung up by their free consent, by this eternal property, that vulgar speech and writing are a right of the people. When the emperor Claudius found three additional letters necessary to the Latin language, the Roman people would not accept them; nor have the Italians accepted those devised by Giorgio Trissino, though their lack is felt in Italian.

440   The epistolary or vulgar language of the Egyptians must have been written with letters likewise vulgar. Since the vulgar letters of the Egyptians resemble those of the Phoenicians, it is necessary to suppose that one of these peoples borrowed from the other. Those who think that the Egyptians were the first discoverers of all the things necessary or useful to human society, must consequently hold that the Egyptians taught their letters to the Phoenicians. But Clement the Alexandrian, who must have been better informed than any other author in matters Egyptian, relates that Sanchuniathon or Sancuniates the Phoenician (who in the Chronological Table is placed in the heroic age of Greece) had written the history of Phoenicia in vulgar letters; and he therefore proposes him as the first author of the gentile world to have written in vulgar characters. In this connection is has to be said that the Phoenicians, certainly the first merchant people of the world, having entered Egypt for trading purposes, may well have carried thither their vulgar letters. But, entirely apart from argument or conjecture, vulgar tradition assures us that these same Phoenicians brought their letters to Greece. Tacitus, examining this tradition, suggests that they passed off as their own invention the letters invented by others, meaning the Egyptian hieroglyphics. But, to allow the popular tradition some ground of truth (as we have proved all such traditions must have), let us say that the Phoenicians brought to Greece hieroglyphics received from others, and that these could only have been the mathematical characters or geometric figures which they had received from the Chaldeans. The latter were beyond question the first mathematicians and especially the first astronomers of the nations; whence Zoroaster the Chaldean (whose name means "observer of the stars" according to Bochart) was the first sage of the gentile world. The Phoenicians used these Chaldean characters as notations for numbers in their mercantile business, in pursuit of which long before Homer's time they frequented the shores of Greece. This is made evident by Homer's own poems, and especially the *Odyssey*. For in Homer's time, as Josephus vigorously maintains against the Greek grammarian Apion, vulgar letters had not yet been invented by the Greeks. But the latter, with supreme genius, in which they certainly surpassed all nations, took over these geometric forms to represent the various articulated sounds, and shaped them into vulgar characters of letters with consummate beauty. These were later adopted by the Latins, whose letters, as Tacitus himself observes, resembled the most ancient Greek ones. Weighty proof of this is the fact that the Greeks for a long period, and the Latins down to their latest times, used capital letters to represent numbers. It must have been these letters that were taught to the Latins by Demaratus the Corinthian and by Carmenta, the wife of Evander the Arcadian. We shall explain later that in ancient times Greek colonies had been taken to Latium by sea and by land.

441   There is no merit in the contention of many scholars that, because the Hebrews and the Greeks give almost the same names to their vulgar letters, the Greeks must have got theirs from the Hebrews. It is more reasonable that the Hebrews should have imitated the Greek nomenclature than vice versa. For it is universally agreed that from the time that Alexander the Great conquered the empire of the East (which after his death was divided by his captains) Greek speech spread throughout Egypt and the East. And since it is also generally agreed that grammar was introduced quite late among the Hebrews, it follows necessarily that the Hebrew men of letters called their Hebrew letters by the Greek names. Moreover, since the elements [of anything] are very simple in nature, the Greeks must at first have called their letters by the simplest sounds [e.g., "ah" for α], and it must have been for that reason that the letters were called elements. The Latins, following suit, called them with the same gravity, and also kept the forms of the letters like the most ancient Greek ones. We must therefore conclude that calling the letters by complex names [e.g., "alpha" for α] was introduced late among the Greeks, and later still brought by the Greeks to the Hebrews in the East.

442   These arguments confute the opinion of those who would have it that Cecrops the Egyptian brought vulgar letters to the Greeks. Another opinion, that Cadmus the Phoenician must have brought them from Egypt into Greece because he founded a city there and named it Thebes after the capital of the greatest Egyptian dynasty, will be refuted later by the principles of Poetic Geography, by which it will appear that the Greeks who went to Egypt called the Egyptian capital Thebes because it bore a resemblance to their native city of that name. And finally we understand why cautious critics, cited by an anonymous English writer on the uncertainty of the sciences [Thomas Baker, *Reflections on Learning*], conclude from the too early date assigned to Sancuniates that he never existed. We, accordingly, not to put him out of the world entirely, judge that he must be set in a later age, certainly after Homer. And to allow the Phoenicians priority over the Greeks in the invention of the so-called vulgar letters (not failing, however, to take into account that the Greeks had more genius than the Phoenicians), it has to be said that Sancuniates must have lived a little before Herodotus, who was called the father of Greek history, which he wrote in the vulgar speech. For Sancuniates was called the historian of truth; that is, a writer of what Varro in his division of times calls the historic time. In that time, according to the Egyptian division of three languages corresponding to the three ages of the world that had elapsed before them, they spoke in the epistolary language written in vulgar characters.

443   Now, as the heroic or poetic language was founded by the heroes, so the vulgar languages were introduced by the vulgar, who were the plebs of the heroic peoples. By the Latins these languages were properly called vernacular. They could not, however, have been introduced by those *vernae* defined by the grammarians as slaves born at home of enslaved prisoners of war, for these naturally learn the languages of their parents' peoples. But the first and properly so-called *vernae* were the *famuli* of the heroes in the state of the families. These *famuli*, of whom the masses of the first plebs of the heroic cities were later composed, were precursors of the slaves later secured by the cities through war. All this is confirmed by the two languages of which Homer speaks: the one of gods, the other of men, which we have interpreted as the heroic and the vulgar language, respectively.

444   The philologians have all accepted with an excess of good faith the view that in the vulgar languages meanings were fixed by convention. On the contrary, because of their natural origins, they must have had natural significations. This is easy to observe in vulgar Latin (which is more heroic than vulgar Greek, and therefore as much more robust as the latter is more refined), which has formed almost all its words by metaphors drawn from natural objects according to their natural properties or sensible effects. And in general metaphor makes up the great body of the language among all nations. But the grammarians, encountering great numbers of words which give confused and indistinct ideas of things, and not knowing their origins, which had made them at first clear and distinct, have given peace to their ignorance by setting up the universal maxim that articulate human words have arbitrary significations. And they have dragged in Aristotle, Galen, and other philosophers, and armed them against Plato and Iamblichus.

445   There remains, however, the very great difficulty: How is it that there are as many different vulgar tongues as there are peoples? To solve it, we must here establish this great truth: that, as the peoples have certainly by diversity of climates acquired different natures, from which have sprung as many different customs, so from their different natures and customs as many different languages have arisen. For by virtue of the aforesaid diversity of their natures they have regarded the same utilities or necessities of human life from different points of view, and there have thus arisen so many national customs, for the most part differing from one another and at times contrary to one another; so and not otherwise there have arisen as many different languages as there are nations. An evident confirmation of this is found in the proverbs, which are maxims of human life, the same in substance but expressed from as many points of view as there are or have been different nations. Thus the same heroic origins, preserved in brief in the vulgar tongues, have given rise to the phenomenon so astonishing to biblical critics: that the names of the same kings appear in one form in sacred and in another in profane history. The reason is that the one perchance considers men with regard to their appearance or power, the other with regard to their customs, undertakings, or

whatever else it may have been. In the same way we still find the cities of
Hungary given one name by the Hungarians, another by the Greeks, another
by the Germans, another by the Turks. The German language, which is a
living heroic language, transforms almost all names from foreign languages
into its own. We may conjecture that the Latins and Greeks did the same when
we find them discussing so many barbarian matters with Greek and Latin
elegance. This must be the cause of the obscurity encountered in ancient
geography and in the natural history of fossils, plants, and animals. And for this
reason we excogitated, in the first edition of this work, an Idea of a Mental
Dictionary for assigning meanings to all the different articulate languages,
reducing them all to certain unities of ideas in substance, which, considered
from various points of view, have come to be expressed by different words in
each. We make continual use of this in working out the argument of our
Science. And we gave a very full example of it in which we showed that the
fathers of families, considered from fifteen different points of view in the state
of the families and of the first commonwealths, at the time when the languages
must have been taking form, were called by an equal number of different
names by fifteen nations ancient and modern. (And most weighty are those
arguments concerning the institutions of that time which are taken from the
original meanings of the words, as set forth in the Axioms.) This is one of the
three passages on account of which we do not regret the publication of that
book. The aforesaid Dictionary develops in a new way the argument presented
by Thomas Hayne in his dissertation on the kinship of languages and in his
others on languages in general and on the harmony of various languages.
From all this we infer the following corollary: that languages are more
beautiful in proportion as they are richer in these condensed heroic expressions; that they are more beautiful because they are more expressive; and that
because they are more expressive they are truer and more faithful. And that on
the contrary, in proportion as they are more crowded with words of unknown
origin, they are less delightful, because obscure and confused, and therefore
more likely to deceive and lead astray. The latter must be the case with
languages formed by the mixture of many barbarous tongues, the history of
whose original and metaphorical meanings has not come down to us.

446   To enter now upon the extremely difficult [question of the] way in
which these three kinds of languages and letters were formed, we must
establish this principle: that as gods, heroes, and men began at the same time
(for they were, after all, men who imagined the gods and believed their own
heroic nature to be a mixture of the divine and human natures), so these three
languages began at the same time, each having its letters which developed
along with it. They began, however, with these three very great differences:
that the language of gods was almost entirely mute, only very slightly
articulate; the language of heroes, an equal mixture of articulate and mute,
and consequently of vulgar speech and of the heroic characters used in writing
by the heroes, which Homer calls *sēmata*; the language of men, almost entirely
articulate and only very slightly mute, there being no vulgar language so
copious that there are not more things than it has words for. Thus necessarily

the heroic language was in the beginning disordered in the extreme; and this is a great source of the obscurity of the fables. The fable of Cadmus will serve as a signal example. Cadmus slays the great serpent, sows its teeth, armed men spring up from the furrows, he throws a great rock among them, they fight to the death, and finally Cadmus himself changes into a serpent. So ingenious was this Cadmus, who brought letters to the Greeks, by whom this fable was transmitted, that, as we shall explain presently, it contains several centuries of poetic history!

447 To follow up what has already been said: at the same time that the divine character of Jove took shape—the first human thought in the gentile world—articulate language began to develop by way of onomatopoeia, through which we still find children happily expressing themselves. By the Latins Jove was at first, from the roar of the thunder, called *Ious;* by the Greeks, from the whistle of the lightning, *Zeus;* by the Easterners, from the sound of burning fire, he must have been called *Ur,* whence came *Urim,* the power of fire; and from this same origin must have come the Greek *ouranos,* sky, and the Latin verb *uro,* to burn. From the whistle of the lightning must have also come the Latin *cel,* one of the monosyllables of Ausonius, pronounced however with the Spanish cedilla (ç), which is required to give point to Ausonius's own jesting line about Venus: *Nata salo, suscepta solo, patre edita caelo,* "Born of the sea, adopted by the soil, raised by her father to the sky." With respect to these origins it is to be noted that the same sublimity of invention evinced in the fable of Jove, which we have observed above, marks the beginning of poetic locution in onomatopoeia, which Dionysius Longinus [i.e., Demetrius *On Style* 2.94f] certainly includes among the sources of the sublime, and which he illustrates from Homer, citing the sizzling sound (*siz'*) emitted by the eye of Polyphemus when Ulysses pierces it with the fiery stake.

448 Human words were formed next from interjections, which are sounds articulated under the impetus of violent passions. In all languages these are monosyllables. Thus it is not beyond likelihood that, when wonder had been awakened in men by the first thunderbolts, these interjections of Jove should give birth to one produced by the human voice: *pa!;* and that this should then be doubled: *pape!* From this interjection of wonder was subsequently derived Jove's title of father of men and gods, and thus it came about presently that all the gods were fathers, and the goddesses, mothers; whence the Latin names *Iupiter, Diespiter, Marspiter, Juno genitrix.* The fables certainly tell us that Juno was sterile; and many other gods and goddesses did not marry among their kind. (Venus was called the concubine, not the wife, of Mars.) Nonetheless they were all called fathers. (On this point there are some verses of Lucilius which we have cited in the Notes to our *Universal Law.*) They were called fathers in the sense in which *patrare* originally meant to do or make, which is the prerogative of God. *Patrare* occurs thus even in Scripture, where, in the story of the creation of the world, it is said that on the seventh day God rested *ab opere quod patrarat,* from the work which he had done. Thence must have been derived the verb *impetrare,* as if for *impatrare.* The form used in the science of augury was *impetrire,* to obtain a good augury, concerning whose origin the Latin grammarians have written so much nonsense. This proves that the first interpretation (*interpretatio,* as if for *interpatratio*) was the interpretation of the divine laws declared by the auspices.

449 The strong men in the family state, from a natural ambition of human pride, arrogated to themselves this divine title of fathers (a fact which may have been the ground for the vulgar tradition that the first strong men on earth had caused themselves to be adored as gods); but, observing the piety they owed to the deities, they called the latter gods. Later, when the strong men of the first cities took the name of gods upon themselves, they were moved by the same piety to call the deities immortal gods, to differentiate them from themselves, the mortal gods. But in this may be observed the grossness of these giants, like that which travelers report of the Big Feet. A fair trace of it has remained in the ancient Latin words *pipulum* and *pipare,* in the sense of complaint and to complain, which must be derived from the interjection of lament, *pi, pi. Pipulum* in this sense in Plautus is generally interpreted as synonymous with *obvagulatio* in the Twelve Tables, which must come from *vagire,* which is properly the crying of children. A similar origin from the interjection of fear must be assigned to the Greek word *paian,* which begins with *pai.* Concerning this the Greeks have a very ancient golden tradition to the effect that when they were terrified by the great serpent called Python they invoked the aid of Apollo with the words *iō paiān.* Dazed with fear, they first pronounced them slowly three times, but then, when Apollo had slain the Python, they jubilantly pronounced them another three times quickly, dividing the omega into two omicrons and the dipthong *ai* into two syllables. Thus naturally was Greek heroic verse at first spondaic and then dactylic, and it has retained this eternal property, that it gives preference to the dactyl in every foot except the last. Song arose naturally, in the measure of heroic verse, under the impulse of most violent passions, even as we still observe men sing when moved by great passions, especially extreme happiness or grief. What has been said here will shortly be of much use when we discuss the origins of song and verse.

450 They went on to form pronouns; for interjections give vent to one's own passions, a thing which one can do even by oneself, but pronouns serve in sharing our ideas with others concerning things which we cannot name or whose names another may not understand. Pronouns are likewise in all languages, for the greater part, if not quite all, monosyllables. The first of them, or at least among the first, must have been the one which occurs in that golden passage of Ennius [Tragedies 351]: *Aspice hoc sublime cadens, quem omnes invocant Iovem* (Behold this sublime overhanging, which all invoke as Jove), where *hoc,* this, stands for *caelum,* the sky. It occurs also in vulgar Latin: *Luciscit hoc iam,* for *albescit caelum,* the sky grows light. And articles have from their birth this eternal property: that they go before the nouns to which they are attached.

451 Later were formed the particles, of which a great part are the prepositions, which also, in almost all languages, are monosyllables. These preserve in the name they bear this eternal property: that they go before the nouns which require them and the verbs with which they form compounds.

452   Gradually nouns were formed. In the chapter on the Origins of the Latin Language in the first edition of this work, we listed a great number of nouns which sprang up within Latium, beginning with the sylvan life of the Latins and continuing through their rural into their earliest city life; all of them formed as monosyllables, showing no trace of foreign origin, not even Greek, except for four words: *bous, sūs, mūs,* and *sēps,* the last of which means hedge in Latin and serpent in Greek. This is the second of the three passages in that work which we regard as adequate. It may serve as a model to scholars of other languages in investigating their origins to the great profit of the republic of letters. Certainly in the German language, for instance, which is a mother language (because foreign nations never entered that country to rule over it), the roots are all monosyllabic. And that nouns sprang up before verbs is proved by this eternal property: that there is no statement that does not begin with a noun, expressed or understood, which governs it.

453   Last of all, the authors of the languages formed the verbs, as we observe children expressing nouns and particles but leaving the verbs to be understood. For nouns awaken ideas which leave firm traces; particles, signifying modifications, do the same; but verbs signify motions, which involve past and future, which are measured from the indivisible present, which even philosophers find very hard to understand. Our assertion may be supported by a medical observation. There is a good man living among us who, after a severe apoplectic stroke, utters nouns but has completely forgotten verbs. Even the verbs which are genera of all the others—as *sum* is of being, to which are reduced all essences, which is as much as to say all metaphysical things; *sto* of rest and *eo* of motion, to which are reduced all physical things; *do, dico,* and *facio,* to which are reduced all feasible things, whether moral, economic, or civil—these verbs must have begun as imperatives. For in the state of the families, which was extremely poor in language, the fathers alone must have spoken and given commands to their children and *famuli,* who, under the terrors of patriarchal rule, as we shall soon see, must have executed the commands in silence and with blind obsequiousness. These imperatives are all monosyllables, as they have remained: *es, sta, i, da, dic, fac,* be, stand, go, give, say, make.

454   This [theory of the] genesis of languages is in conformity with the principles of universal nature, by which the elements of all things, out of which they are composed and into which they are bound to be resolved, are indivisible; and also with the principles of human nature in particular, according to the axiom that "children, even in the present copiousness of language into which they are born, and in spite of the extreme flexibility of the fibers of their organs for articulating words, begin with monosyllables". So much the more must we deem the first men of the nations to have done so, for their organs were extremely obdurate, and they had not yet heard a human voice. [Our theory] gives us, moreover, the order in which the parts of speech arose, and consequently the natural causes of syntax.

455 All this seems more reasonable than what Julius Caesar Scaliger and Francisco Sánchez have said with regard to the Latin language, reasoning from the principles of Aristotle, as if the peoples that invented the languages must first have gone to school to him!

Corollaries concerning the Origins of Poetic Style, Digression, Inversion, Rhythm, Song, and Verse

456 In this way the nations formed the poetic language, composed of divine and heroic characters, later expressed in vulgar speech, and finally written in vulgar characters. It was born entirely of poverty of language and need of expression. This is proved by the first lights of poetic style, which are vivid representations, images, similes, comparisons, metaphors, circumlocutions, phrases explaining things by their natural properties, descriptions gathered from their minuter or their more sensible effects, and, finally, emphatic and even superfluous adjuncts.

457 Digressions were born of the grossness of the heroic minds, unable to confine themselves to those essential features of things that were to the purpose in hand, as we see to be naturally the case with the feeble-minded and above all with women.

458 Inversions arose from the difficulty of completing statements with their verbs, which were the last part of speech to be invented. Thus the Greeks, who were more ingenious, used fewer inversions than the Latins, and the Latins fewer than the Germans.

459 Prose rhythm was understood late by the writers—in Greek by Gorgias of Leontini, and in Latin by Cicero—because earlier (according to Cicero himself [*Orator* 49.166f; *The Making of an Orator* 3.44.173ff]) they had given a rhythmic character to their orations by using certain poetic measures. This fact will presently be very useful when we discuss the origins of song and verse.

460 From all this it appears to have been demonstrated that, by a necessity of human nature, poetic style arose before prose style; just as, by the same necessity, the fables, or imaginative universals, arose before the rational or philosophic universals, which were formed through the medium of prose speech. For after the poets had formed poetic speech by associating particular ideas, as we have fully shown, the peoples went on to form prose speech by contracting into a single word, as into a genus, the parts which poetic speech had associated. Take for example the poetic phrase "the blood boils in my heart," based on a property natural, eternal, and common to all mankind. They took the blood, the boiling, and the heart, and made of them a single word, as it were a genus, called in Greek *stomachos,* in Latin *ira,* and in Italian *collera.* Following the same pattern, hieroglyphs and heroic letters [or emblems] were reduced to a few vulgar letters, as genera assimilating innumerable diverse articulate sounds; a feat requiring consummate genius. By means of these vulgar genera, both of words and letters, the minds of the peoples grew quicker and developed powers of abstraction, and the way was thus prepared for the coming of the philosophers, who formed intelligible genera. What has here been discussed is a small portion of the history of ideas. To such an extent has it been necessary, in seeking the origins of letters, to deal in the same breath with those of languages!

461 Concerning song and verse, since men are shown to have been originally mute, they must have uttered vowel sounds by singing, as mutes do; and later, like stammerers, they must have uttered articulate consonantal sounds, still by singing. This first singing of the peoples has left a great testimony in the diphthongs surviving in the languages. These must originally have been much more numerous, as the Greeks and the French, who passed prematurely from the poetic to the vulgar age, have left us a great many of them. The reason for this is that the vowels are easy to form and the consonants difficult, and, as has been shown, the first dull-witted men were moved to utterance only by very violent passions, which are naturally expressed in a very loud voice. And nature brings it about that when man greatly raises his voice, he breaks into diphthongs and song. Thus the first Greeks, in the time of their gods, formed the first spondaic heroic verse with the diphthong *pai,* employing twice as many vowels as consonants.

462 Again, this first song of the peoples sprang naturally from the difficulty of the first utterances, which can be demonstrated both from cause and from effect. From cause, since in these men the fibers of the organ for articulating sounds were quite hard, and there were very few sounds they could make; as on the other hand children, with very flexible fibers, born into our present plenty of words, are observed to pronounce consonants only with the greatest difficulty; and the Chinese, whose vulgar language has no more than three hundred articulate vocables, give them various modifications of pitch and time to match their one hundred and twenty thousand hieroglyphs, and thus speak by singing. And from effect, by the contraction of words, of which innumerable examples are observed in Italian poetry (in our "Origins of the Latin Language" we set forth a great number which must have begun short and been lengthened in the course of time); and on the other hand by redundancies, because stutterers use a syllable which they can more readily utter singing in such a way as to compensate for those they find it difficult to pronounce. Thus there was among us in my time an excellent tenor with this speech defect, who, when he stumbled over a word, would break into the sweetest song and so pronounce it. Certainly the Arabs begin almost all their words with *al-;* and it is said the Huns were so called because they began all theirs with *hun-.* Finally, that languages began with song is shown by what we have just said: that prior to Gorgias and Cicero the Greek and Latin prose writers used certain almost poetic rhythms, as in the returned barbarian times the Fathers of the Roman Church did (and, it will be found, those of the Greek Church did too), so that their prose seems made for chanting.

463 The first verse must have sprung up comformably to the language and time of the heroes; that is, it was heroic verse, the grandest of all, and the proper verse for heroic poetry; and it was born of the most violent passions of fear and joy, for heroic poetry has to do only with extremely perturbed passions. However, its spondaic origin was not from the great fear of the Python, as vulgar tradition relates; for such perturbation rather quickens ideas and words then retards them; whence in Latin *festinans* and *solicitus* connote fear. No, it was because of the slowness of mind and stiffness of tongue of the founders of the nations that heroic verse was born spondaic; and from that origin it retains the characteristic of never admitting anything but a spondee in the last foot. Later, as minds and tongues became quicker, the dactyl was introduced. Then, as both became still more practiced, there arose the iamb, the quick foot, as Horace calls it. Finally, when mind and tongue had reached the highest degree of celerity, there developed prose, which speaks, as it were, in intelligible genera. Iambic verse comes so near to prose that prose writers have often fallen into it inadvertently. Thus song went on growing swifter in its verse forms in proportion as ideas and tongues became quicker among the nations.

464 This philosophy is confirmed by history, which tells us of nothing more ancient than oracles and sybils. Thus, to signify that a thing was very old, there was the saying, "That is older than the sybil"; and the sybils, of whom a good dozen have come down to us, were scattered among all the first nations. There is a vulgar tradition to the effect that the sybils sang in heroic verse, and the oracles of all nations also gave their responses in heroic hexameters. For that reason the Greeks called this verse Pythian from their famous oracle of Pythian Apollo, who must have been so called from his slaying of the serpent called Python, which gave rise to the first spondaic verse. Heroic verse was called Saturnian by the Latins, as Festus attests [s.n. Saturnus]. It must have sprung up in Italy in the age of Saturn, which corresponds to the golden age of the Greeks, in which Apollo, like the other gods, had dealings on earth with men. And Ennius says, again according to Festus, that in this verse the fauns of Italy delivered their prophecies or oracles (which certainly among the Greeks, as we have just said, were delivered in hexameters). But later the term "Saturnian verses" was applied to iambic senarii, perhaps because by then it was as natural to speak in these Saturnian iambic verses as it had previously been to speak in Saturnian heroic verses.

465 Hebraists today are divided in their opinions on the question whether Hebrew poetry is metrical or merely rhythmical. However, Josephus, Philo, Origen, and Eusebius stand as favoring meter, and (what is most to our present purpose) St. Jerome holds [in his preface to it] that the Book of Job, which is older than the books of Moses, was composed in heroic verse from the beginning of the third chapter to the end of the forty-second.

466 The Arabs, ignorant of letters, as related by the anonymous author [Thomas Baker] of [a book on] the uncertainty of the sciences, preserved their language by the oral tradition of their poems until they overran the eastern provinces of the Greek empire.

467 The Egyptians inscribed memorials of their dead in verse on columns called syringes, from *sir*, which means song; whence the name of the Siren, a deity beyond doubt celebrated for her singing. Ovid [in his *Metamor-*

phoses 1.689ff] says the nymph Syrinx was equally celebrated for beauty and for song. By the same token, the Syrians and Assyrians, whose names are likewise derived from *sir*, must have spoken at first in verse.

468 Certainly the founders of Greek humanity were the theological poets, and these were heroes and sang in heroic verse.

469 The first authors of the Latin language were the Salii, who were sacred poets, from whom we have the fragments of the Salian verses, which have an air of heroic verse and are the oldest memorials of Latin speech. The conquering ancient Romans left memorials of their triumphs in a sort of heroic verse, like the *Duello magno dirimendo, regibus subigendis* of Lucius Aemilius Regillus, and the *Fundit, fugat, prosternit maximas legiones* of Acilius Glabrio, and others [in *Grammatici Latini* ed. Keil, 6.265]. In the fragments of the Law of the Twelve Tables, the articles seem upon close examination to end for the most part in Adonic verses, which are the concluding portions of heroic verses. Cicero must have imitated them in his own laws, which begin thus: *Deos caste adeunto. Pietatem adhibento.* ("They shall approach the gods in purity. They shall bring piety with them.") Whence the Roman custom mentioned by Cicero whereby the children learned the Law of the Twelve Tables by singing it *tanquam necessarium carmen*, as a required song. The Cretan children, we are told by Aelian [*Various History* 2.39], did likewise [with the laws of their country]. Certainly Cicero, famous as the inventor of prose rhythm among the Latins, as Gorgias of Leontini had been among the Greeks, must otherwise have shunned in his prose—prose of so weighty an argument—not merely verses so sonorous as these but even iambics (much as they resemble prose), for he guarded himself against the latter even in his familiar correspondence. Hence the vulgar traditions of [laws being given in] this kind of verse must be true: the first, according to Plato, that the laws of the Egyptians were poems of the goddess Isis; the second, according to Plutarch [*Lycurgus* 4.2–4], that Lycurgus gave his laws to the Spartans in verse, forbidding them in one particular law to acquire knowledge of letters; the third, according to Maximus of Tyre, that Jove had given the laws to Minos in verse; the fourth and last, cited by Suidas, that Draco, who by another vulgar tradition wrote his laws in blood, proclaimed them to the Athenians in verse.

470 We return now from the laws to history. Tacitus in his account of the customs of the ancient Germans relates that they preserved in verse the beginnings of their history, and Lipsius in his notes on this passage says the same of the American Indians. The examples of these two nations, of which the first was known only to the Romans, and to them very late, and the second discovered but two centuries ago by our Europeans, give us a strong argument for conjecturing the same of all other barbarous nations, both ancient and modern; and, conjecture aside, the authorities tell us that the Persians among the ancient nations, and the Chinese among those discovered in modern times, wrote their first histories in verse. And here let this important observation be made: that, if the peoples were established by laws, and if among all these peoples the laws were given in verse, and if the first institutions of these peoples were likewise preserved in verse, it necessarily follows that all the first peoples were poets.

471 We resume now the subject under discussion, concerning the origins of verse. According to Festus [s.n. Saturnus], the wars with Carthage were described in heroic verse by Naevius even before Ennius's time; and Livius Andronicus, the first Latin writer, wrote the *Romanidae,* a heroic poem containing the annals of the ancient Romans. In the returned barbarian times the Latin historians were heroic poets, like Gunther, William of Apulia, and others. The first writers in the modern languages of Europe were versemakers; and in Silesia, a province inhabited almost entirely by peasants, the people are born poets. And generally the German language preserves its heroic origins intact—even to excess—and this is the reason, though Adam Rechenberg is unaware of it, for the fact he attests, that Greek compound words can be happily rendered in German, especially in poetry. Bernegger compiled a catalog of these words and Georg Christoph Peisker has since been at pains to extend it in his *Index . . . pro graecae et germanicae linguae analogia.* The ancient Latin language has also left us many examples of compounds formed by combining whole words; and of these compounds the poets, as of their right, have continued to make use. For it must have been a common property of all the first languages that they were furnished first with nouns and only later with verbs, and so they had supplied the lack of verbs by putting nouns together. These must be the principles of what [G. D.] Morhofen has written in his *Unterricht von der teutschen Sprache und Poesie.* Let this stand as a proof that "if the scholars of the German language apply themselves to seeking its origins by these principles they will make marvelous discoveries."

472 All that has been here reasoned out seems clearly to confute the common error of the grammarians, who say that prose speech came first and speech in verse afterward. And within the origins of poetry, as they have been here disclosed, we have found the origins of languages and letters.

BOOK III

Section I

Introduction

780 Although our demonstration in the preceding book that poetic wisdom was the vulgar wisdom of the peoples of Greece, who were first theological and later heroic poets, should carry as a necessary consequence that the wisdom of Homer was not at all different in kind, yet, as Plato left firmly fixed the opinion that Homer was endowed with sublime esoteric wisdom (and all the other philosophers have followed in his train, with [pseudo-] Plutarch foremost, writing an entire book on the matter, we shall here examine particularly if Homer was ever a philosopher. On this question another complete book was written by Dionysius Longinus, which is mentioned by Diogenes Laertius in his life of Pyrrho [i.e., by Suidas in the article on Longinus].

The Esoteric Wisdom Attributed to Homer

781 Let us concede to Homer what certainly must be granted, that he had to conform to the quite vulgar feelings and hence the vulgar customs of the barbarous Greece of his day, for such vulgar feelings and vulgar customs provide the poets with their proper materials. Let us therefore concede to him what he narrates: that the gods are esteemed according to their strength, as by his supreme strength Jove attempts to show, in the fable of the great chain, that he is the king of men and gods. On the basis of this vulgar opinion he makes it credible that Diomed can wound Venus and Mars with the help of Minerva, who, in the contest of the gods, despoils Venus and strikes Mars with a rock (and Minerva forsooth was the goddess of philosophy in vulgar belief, and uses weapons so worthy of the wisdom of Jove!). Let us allow him to tell of the inhuman custom (so contrary to what the writers on the natural law of the gentes claim to have been eternally practiced among the nations) which then prevailed among the barbarous peoples of Greece (who are held to have spread humanity through the world): to wit, that of poisoning arrows (for Ulysses goes to Ephyra to seek poisonous herbs for this purpose), and further, that of denying burial to enemies slain in battle, leaving their unburied bodies instead as a prey to dogs and vultures (on which account the unhappy Priam found so costly the ransom of his son's body, though the naked corpse of Hector had already been dragged by Achille's chariot three times around the walls of Troy).

782 Nevertheless, if the purpose of poetry is to tame the ferocity of the vulgar whose teachers the poets are, it was not the part of a wise man, versed in such fierce feelings and customs, to arouse admiration of them in the vulgar in order that they should take pleasure in them and be confirmed in them by that pleasure. Nor was it the part of a wise man to arouse pleasure in the villainous vulgar at the villainies of the gods, to say nothing of the heroes. As, for example, we read of mars in the midst of the contest calling Minerva a dog-fly, and of Minerva punching Diana (i.e., Venus, and of Agememnon and Achilles, the latter the greatest of the Greek heroes and the former the head of the Greek league, and both of them kings, calling each other dogs, as servants in popular comedies would scarcely do nowadays.

783 But what name under heaven more appropriate than sheer stupidity can be given to the wisdom of his captain, Agamemnon? For he has to be compelled by Achilles to do his duty in restoring Chryseis to Chryses, her father, priest of Apollo, the god who, on account of this rape, was decimating the Greek army with a cruel pestilence. And then, holding himself offended, Agamemnon thought to regain his honor by an act of justice of a piece with his wisdom, by wrongfully stealing Briseis from Achilles, who bore in his person the fate of Troy, so that, on his withdrawing in anger with his men and ships, Hector might make short work of the Greeks still surviving the pestilence. Here is the Homer hitherto considered the architect of Greek polity or civility, starting with such an episode the thread with which he weaves the whole *Iliad*, the principal actors of which are such a captain [as Agamemnon] and such a hero as we have shown Achilles to be when we spoke of the Heroism of the First Peoples. Here is the Homer unrivaled in creating poetic characters, the greatest of which are so discordant with this civil human nature of ours, yet perfectly decorous in relation to the punctilious heroic nature.

784   What are we then to say of his representing his heroes as delighting so much in wine, and, whenever they are troubled in spirit, finding all their comfort, yes, and above all others the wise Ulysses, in getting drunk? Fine precepts for consolation, most worthy of a philosopher!

785   [J. C.] Scaliger [*Poetices* 5.3] is indignant at finding almost all his comparisons to be taken from beasts and other savage things. But even if we admit that they were necessary to Homer in order to make himself better understood by the wild and savage vulgar, nevertheless to attain such success in them—for his comparisons are incomparable—is certainly not characteristic of a mind chastened and civilized by any sort of philosophy. Nor could the truculent and savage style in which he describes so many, such varied, and such bloody battles, so many and such extravagantly cruel kinds of butchery as make up all the sublimity of the *Iliad* in particular, have originated in a mind touched and humanized by any philosophy.

786   The constancy, moreover, which is developed and fixed by the study of the wisdom of the philosophers, could not have depicted gods and heroes of such instability. For some, though deeply moved and distressed, are quieted and calmed by the slightest contrary suggestion; others, though boiling with violent wrath, if they chance to recall some sad event, break into bitter tears. (Just so, in the returned barbarism of Italy, at the end of which came Dante, the Tuscan Homer, who also sang only of history, we read of Cola di Rienzo, whose biography we said above exhibited vividly the customs of the Greek heroes as described by Homer, that when he spoke of the unhappy Roman state oppressed by the great of that time, both he and his hearers broke down in uncontrollable tears.) Others, conversely, when deep in grief, if some pleasant diversion offers itself, like the banquet of Alcinous in the case of the wise Ulysses, completely forget their troubles and give themselves over to hilarity. Others, quiet and calm, at some innocent remark which is not to their humor, react with such violence and fly into such a blind rage as to threaten the speaker with a frightful death. So it is with Achilles when he receives Priam in his tent on the afore-mentioned occasion when the latter, protected by Mercury, has come through the Greek camp by night and all alone in order to ransom the body of Hector. Achilles receives him at dinner and, because of a little phrase that does not please him and which has fallen inadvertently from the mouth of the unhappy father grieving for such a valorous son, flies into a rage. Forgetting the sacred laws of hospitality, unmindful of the simple faith in which Priam has come all alone to him because he trusts completely in him alone, unmoved by the many great misfortunes of such a king or by pity for such a father or by the veneration due to so old a man, heedless of the common lot which avails more than anything else to arouse compassion, he allows his bestial wrath to reach such a point as to thunder at him that he will cut off his head. The same Achilles, even while impiously determined not to forgive a private injury at the hands of Agamemnon (which, grave though it was, could not justly be avenged by the ruin of their fatherland and of their entire nation), is pleased—he who carries with him the fate of Troy—to see all the Greeks fall to ruin and suffer miserable defeat at Hector's hands; nor is he moved by love of country or by his nation's glory to bring them any aid. He does it, finally, only to satisfy a purely private grief, the slaying of his friend Patroclus by Hector. And not even in death is he placated for the loss of his Briseis until the unhappy beautiful royal maiden Polyxena, of the ruined house of the once rich and puissant Priam, but now become a miserable slave, has been sacrificed before his tomb, and his ashes, thirsting for vengeance, have drunk up the last drop of her blood [Euripides, *Hecuba* 37,220f]. To say nothing of what is really past understanding: that a philosopher's gravity and propriety of thought could have been possessed by a man who amused himself by inventing so many fables worthy of old women entertaining children, as those with which Homer stuffed his other poem, the *Odyssey*.

787   Such crude, course, wild, savage, volatile, unreasonable or unreasonably obstinate, frivolous, and foolish customs as we set forth in Book Two in the Corrollaries on the Heroic Nature, can pertain only to men who are like children in the weakness of their minds, like women in the vigor of their imaginations, and like violent youths in the turbulence of their passions; whence we must deny to Homer any kind of esoteric wisdom. These are the considerations which first gave rise to the doubts that put us under the necessity of seeking out the true Homer.

Homer's Fatherland

788   Such was the esoteric wisdom hitherto attributed to Homer; let us now examine his origin. Almost all the cities of Greece claimed to be his birthplace and there were not lacking those who asserted that he was an Italian Greek. To determine his native land Leo Allacci in his *De patria Homeri* spends much effort in vain. But since there has come down to us no writer more ancient than Homer, as Josephus stoutly maintains against the grammarian Apion, and since the writers came long after him, we are obliged to apply our metaphysical criticism, treating him as founder of a nation, as he has been held to be of Greece, and to discover the truth, both as to his age and as to his fatherland, from Homer himself.

789   Certainly, as regards the Homer who was author of the *Odyssey*, we are assured that he must have come from the west of Greece and a little toward the south, as evidenced by that golden passage in which Alcinous, king of the Phaeacians in what is now Corfu, offers to Ulysses, who is anxious to be on his way, a well-fitted ship manned by his vassals. These, he says, are expert mariners who could take the hero, if need were, as far as Euboea (now Negropont), which, by the report of those whom chance had taken thither, was a land far away, a sort of Ultima Thule of the Greeks. This passage shows clearly that the Homer of the *Odyssey* was not the same as the Homer of the *Iliad*, for Euboea was not far from Troy, which was situated in Asia near the shore of the Hellespont, on the narrow strait of which there are now two fortresses called the Dardanelles, a name recalling to this day its origin from that of Dardania, the ancient territory of Troy. And certainly we find in Seneca [*Shortness of Life* 13.2] that there was a celebrated debate among the grammarians as to whether the *Iliad* and the *Odyssey* were by the same author.

790 As for the contest among the Greek cities for the honor of claiming Homer as citizen, it came about because almost all of them observed in his poems words and phrases and bits of dialect that belonged to their own vernaculars.

791 What has been said here will serve for the discovery of the true Homer.

The Age of Homer

792 We find evidence regarding the age of Homer in the following passages of his poems.

I

793 For the funeral of Patroculs, Achilles causes to be played almost all the kinds of games that were later played in the Olympics when Greek civilization was at its height.

II

794 The arts of casting in low relief and of engraving on metals had already been invented, as is shown, among other examples, by the shield of Achilles. Painting had not yet been invented. For casting abstracts the surfaces of things along with some relief, and engraving does the same with some depth; but painting abstracts the surfaces absolutely, and this is a labor calling for the greatest ingenuity. Hence neither Homer nor Moses ever mentions anything painted, and this is an argument of their antiquity.

III

795 The delights of the gardens of Alcinous, the magnificence of his palace, and the sumptuousness of his banquets indicate to us that the Greeks had reached the stage of admiring luxury and pomp.

IV

796 The Phoenicians were already bringing to Greek shores ivory, purple, Arabian incense used to perfume the grotto of Venus; further, a linen finer than the outer skin of an onion, embroidered garments, and, among the gifts of the suitors, one [such garment] for the adornment of Penelope, draped on a frame contrived with such delicate springs that they stretched it out in the fuller places and drew it in the slender places. An invention worthy of the effeminacy of our day!

V

797 The coach of Priam, in which he drives to Achilles, is made of cedar wood, and the cave of Calypso is fragrant with its perfumes, which betrays a sensuous refinement that was still foreign to the pleasure of the Romans when they were most bent on wasting their substance in luxury in the days of Nero and Heliogabalus.

VI

798 We read of voluptuous baths in the dwelling of Circe.

VII

799 The youthful servants of the suitors are handsome, graceful, and blond-haired, even as the amenity of our present customs would demand.

VIII

800 The men care for their hair like women; this is a reproach brought against the effeminate Paris by Hector and Diomed.

IX

801 It is true that Homer describes his heroes as always eating roast meats. This is the simplest and easiest way of cooking them, since it requires nothing but live coals. This practice was retained in the case of sacrifices, and the Romans used the term *prosiicia* for the meat of the victims roasted on the altars, which was then cut up and divided among the guests. In later times, however, it was roasted on spits just like unconsecrated meat. So Achilles on the occasion of the dinner he gives Priam cuts up the lamb and Patroclus then roasts it [on a spit], prepares the table and puts bread upon it in serving baskets; for the heroes celebrated no banquets which were not sacrificial in nature, with themselves in the character of priests. Among the Latins these survived in the *epulae,* sumptuous banquets given usually by the great, in the *epulum,* a public feast for the people, and in the sacred banquet of which the priests called *epulones* partook. Agamemnon himself, accordingly, kills the two lambs whose sacrifice consecrates the terms of the war with Priam. Such was the magnificence at that time of an idea we would now associate with a butcher! Only after this stage must have come boiled meats, for in addition to fire they require water, a kettle, and along with it a tripod. Vergil has his heroes eat this kind of meat also, and he has them roast meat on spits. Last of all came seasoned foods, which, besides the things already mentioned, called also for condiments. Now, to get back to the heroic banquets of Homer, though he describes the most delicate food of the Greeks as made of flour, cheese, and honey, yet two of his similes are drawn from fishing. And Ulysses, when pretending to be poor and asking alms of one of the suitors, tells him that to hospitable kings, that is to those who are charitable to poor wanderers, the gods give seas abounding in fish, which are the greatest delight of the table.

X

802 Lastly (and what is more to our purpose), Homer seems to have appeared at a time when heroic law had already decayed in Greece and the period of popular liberty had begun, for his heroes contract marriages with foreigners, and bastards succeed to kingdoms. And so indeed it must have been, for, long since, Hercules, stained by the blood of the ugly centaur Nessus, had gone forth in madness and died, signifying the end of heroic law.

803 As therefore with regard to the age of Homer we are unwilling to scorn authority altogether, in all these matters gathered and noted from his poems themselves (not as much from the *Iliad* as from the *Odyssey*, which Dionysius Longinus holds was composed in Homer's old age), we confirm the opinion of those who place him long after the Trojan War. The interval runs to as much as 460 years, or until about the period of Numa. Indeed, we believe we are humoring them in not assigning him to a time even nearer our own. For they say it was after Numa's time that Psammeticus opened Egypt to the Greeks. Yet the Greeks, as appears from numerous passages particularly in the *Odyssey*, had long since opened their own country to commerce with the Phoenicians, whose tales no less than their merchandise the Greek peoples had come to delight in, just as Europeans do now in those of the Indies. There is thus no contradiction between these two facts: on the one hand that Homer never saw Egypt, and on the other that he recounts so many things of Egypt and Libya, of Phoenicia and Asia, and above all of Italy and Sicily; for these things had been related to the Greeks by the Phoenicians.

804 Yet we do not see how to reconcile so many refined customs with the many wild and savage ones which he attributes to his heroes at the same time, and particularly in the *Iliad*. So that, lest barbarous acts be confounded with gentle ones—*ne placidis coëant immitia*—we must suppose that the two poems were composed and compiled by various hands through the successive ages.

805 Thus, from what we have here said of the fatherland and of the age of Homer as he has hitherto been held to be, our doubts take courage for the search for the true Homer.

Homer's Matchless Faculty for Heroic Poetry

806 The complete absence of philosophy which we have shown in Homer, and our discoveries concerning his fatherland and his age, arouse in us a strong suspicion that he may perhaps have been quite simply a man of the people. This suspicion is confirmed by Horace's observation in his *Art of Poetry* concerning the desperate difficulty of creating fresh characters or persons of tragedy after Homer, on account of which he advises poets to take their characters from Homer's poems. Now this grave difficulty must be taken in conjunction with the fact that the personages of the New Comedy are all of artificial creation; indeed, there was an Athenian law requiring the New Comedy to appear on the stage with characters entirely fictitious, and the Greeks managed this so successfully that the Latins, for all their pride, despaired of competing, as Quintilian acknowledged in saying: *Cum graecis de comoedia non contendimus,* "We do not rival the Greeks in comedy."

807 To Horace's difficulty we must add two others of wider scope. For one thing, how is it that Homer, who came first, was such an inimitable heroic poet, while tragedy, which was born later, began with the crudeness familiar to everybody and which we shall later describe more in detail? And for another, how is it that Homer, who preceded philosophy and the poetic and critical arts, was yet the most sublime of all the sublime poets, and that after the invention of philosophies and of the arts of poetry and criticism there was no poet who could come within a long distance of competing with him? However, putting aside our two difficulties, that of Horace combined with what we have said of the New Comedy should have spurred scholars like Patrizzi, Scaliger, and Castelvetro and other valiant masters of the poetic art to investigate the reason for the difference.

808 The reason cannot be found elsewhere than in the origin of poetry, as discovered above in the Poetic Wisdom, and consequently in the discovery of the poetic characters in which alone consists the essence of poetry itself. For the New Comedy portrays our present human customs, on which the Socratic philosophy had meditated, and hence, from the latter's general maxims concerning human morals, the Greek poets, profoundly steeped in that doctrine (as was Menander for example, in comparison with whom Terence was called even by the Latins "half a Menander"), could create certain luminous examples of ideal human types, by the light and splendor of which they might awaken the vulgar, who are as quick to learn from convincing examples as they are incapable of understanding from reasoned maxims. The Old Comedy took arguments or subjects from real life and made plays of them just as they were, as the wicked Aristophanes once did with the good Socrates, thus bringing on his ruin. But tragedy puts on the scene heroic hatred, scorn, wrath, and revenge, which spring from sublime natures which naturally are the source of sentiments, modes of speech, and actions in general that are wild, crude, and terrible. Such arguments are clothed with an air of marvel, and all these matters are in closest conformity among themselves and uniform in their subjects. Such works the Greeks could produce only in the time of their heroism, at the end of which Homer must have come. This is shown by the following metaphysical criticism. The fables, which at their birth had come forth direct and proper, reached Homer distorted and perverted. As may be seen throughout the Poetic Wisdom above set forth, they were all at first true histories, which were gradually altered and corrupted, and in their corrupt form finally came down to Homer. Hence he must be assigned to the third age of the heroic poets. The first age invented the fables to serve as true narratives, the primary and proper meaning of the word *mythos*, as defined by the Greeks themselves, being "true narration". The second altered and corrupted them. The third and last, that of Homer, received them thus corrupted.

809 But, to return to our purpose, for the reason assigned to us by this effect, Aristotle in his *Poetics* says that only Homer knew how to invent poetic falsehoods. For his poetic characters, which are incomparable for the sublime appropriateness which Horace admires in them, were imaginative universals, as defined above in the Poetic Metaphysics, to which the peoples of Greece attached all the various particulars belonging to each genus. To Achilles, for example, who is the subject of the *Iliad*, they attached all the properties of heroic valor, and all the feelings and customs arising from these natural properties, such as those of quick temper, punctiliousness, wrathfulness, implacability, violence, the arrogation of all right to might, as they are summed up by Horace in his description of this character. To Ulysses, the subject of the *Odyssey*, they attached all the feelings and customs of heroic wisdom; that is, those of wariness, patience, dissimulation, duplicity, deceit, always preserving propriety of speech and indifference of action, so that others may of themselves fall into error and may be the causes of their own deception. And to these two characters, according to kind, they attached those actions of particular men which were conspicuous enough to arouse and move the still dull and stupid Greeks to note them and refer them to their kinds. These two characters, since they had been created by an entire nation, could only be conceived as naturally uniform (in which uniformity, agreeable to the common sense of an entire nation, alone consists the decorum or beauty and charm of a fable); and, since they were created by powerful imaginations, they could not be created as anything but sublime. Hence derive two eternal properties of poetry: one that poetic sublimity is inseparable from popularity, and the other that peoples who have first created heroic characters for themselves will afterward apprehend human customs only in terms of characters made famous by luminous examples.

Philosophical Proofs for
The Discovery of the True Homer

810 In view of what we have stated, the following philosophical proofs may be assembled.

I

811 First of all, the one numbered above among the axioms which states that men are naturally led to preserve the memories of the institutions and laws that bind them within their societies.

II

812 The truth understood by Castelvetro, that history must have come first and then poetry, for history is a simple statement of the true but poetry is an imitation besides. Yet this scholar, though otherwise most acute, failed to make use of this clue to discover the true principles of poetry by combining it with the other philosophical proof which follows next.

III

813 Inasmuch as the poets came certainly before the vulgar historians, the first history must have been poetic.

IV

814 The fables in their origin were true and severe narrations, whence *mythos*, fable, was defined as *vera narratio*. But because they were originally for the most part gross, they gradually lost their original meanings, were then altered, subsequently became improbable, after that obscure, then scandalous, and finally incredible. These are the seven sources of the difficulties of the fables, which can all easily be found throughout Book Two.

V

815 And, as we have shown in the same book, they were received by Homer in this corrupt and distorted form.

VI

816 The poetic characters, in which the essence of the fables consists, were born of the need of a nature incapable of abstracting forms and properties from subjects. Consequently they must have been the manner of thinking of entire peoples, who had been placed under this natural necessity in the times of their greatest barbarism. It is an eternal property of the fables always to enlarge the ideas of particulars. On this there is a fine passage in Aristotle [*Rhetoric* 2.21.1395b1–10] in which he remarks that men of limited ideas erect every particular into a maxim. The reason must be that the human mind, which is indefinite, being constricted by the vigor of the senses, cannot otherwise express its almost divine nature than by thus enlarging particulars in imagination. It is perhaps on this account that in both the Greek and the Latin poets the images of gods and heroes always appear larger than those of men, and that in the returned barbarian times the paintings particularly of the Eternal Father, of Jesus Christ, and of the Virgin Mary are exceedingly large.

VII

817   Since barbarians lack reflection, which, when ill used, is the mother of falsehood, the first heroic Latin poets sang true histories; that is, the Roman wars. And in the returned barbarian times, in virtue of this nature of barbarism, the Latin poets like Gunther, William of Apulia, and others again sang nothing but history, and the romancers of the same period thought they were writing true histories. Even Boiardo and Ariosto, who came in an age illuminated by philosophy, took the subjects of their poems from the history of Bishop Turpin of Paris. And in virtue of this same nature of barbarism, which for lack of reflection does not know how to feign (whence it is naturally truthful, open, faithful, generous, and magnanimous), even Dante, though learned in the loftiest esoteric knowledge, filled the scenes of his *Comedy* with real persons and portrayed real events in the lives of the dead. For that reason he gave the name *Comedy* to his poem, for the Old Comedy of the Greeks portrayed real persons in its plays. In this respect Dante was like the Homer of the *Iliad,* which Dionysius Longinus says is all dramatic or representative, as the *Odyssey* is all narrative. Francesco Petrarca too, though a most learned man, yet sang in Latin of the second Carthaginian war, and his *Trionfi,* in Tuscan, which have a heroic note, are nothing but a collection of histories. And here we have a luminous proof of the fact that the first fables were histories. For satire spoke ill of persons not only real but well known; tragedy took for its arguments characters of poetic history; the Old Comedy put into its plots famous living persons; the New Comedy, born in times of the most lively reflection, finally invented characters entirely fictitious (just as in the Italian language the New Comedy came in again only with the marvelously learned Cinquecento): and neither among the Greeks nor among the Latins was an entirely ficitious character ever the protagonist of a tragedy. Strong confirmation of this is found in the popular taste which will not accept musical dramas, the arguments of which are always tragic, unless they are taken from history, whereas it will tolerate fictitious plots in comedies because, since they deal with private life which is not public knowledge, it believes them true.

VIII

818   Since poetic characters are of this nature, their poetic allegories, as we have shown above throughout the Poetic Wisdom, must necessarily contain historical significations referring only to the earliest times of Greece.

IX

819   Such histories must naturally have been preserved in the memories of the communities of the peoples, in virtue of our first philosophical proof; for, as the children of the nations, they must have had marvelously strong memories. And this was not without divine providence, for up to the time of Homer and indeed somewhat afterward, common script had not yet been invented, on the authority of Josephus against Apion. In that human indigence, the peoples, who were almost all body and almost no reflection, must have been all vivid sensation in perceiving particulars, strong imagination in apprehending and enlarging them, sharp wit in referring them to their imaginative genera, and robust memory in retaining them. It is true that the faculties appertain to the mind, but they have their roots in the body and draw their strength from it. Hence memory is the same as imagination, which for that reason is called *memoria* in Latin. (In Terence [*Lady of Andros* 625], for example, we find *memorabile* in the sense of imaginable, and commonly we find *comminisci* for feigning, which is proper to the imagination, and thence *commentum* for a fiction.) Imagination is likewise taken for ingenuity or invention. (In the returned barbarian times an ingenious man was called imaginative, *fantastico;* so, for example, Cola di Rienzo is described by his contemporary biographer.) Memory thus has three different aspects: memory when it remembers things, imagination when it alters or imitates them, and invention when it gives them a new turn or puts them into proper arrangement and relationship. For these reasons the theological poets called Memory the mother of the Muses.

X

820 The poets must therefore have been the first historians of the nations. This is why Castelvetro failed to make use of his dictum for finding the true origins of poetry; for he and all others who have discussed the matter (from Plato and Aristotle on down) could easily have observed that all gentile histories have their beginnings in fables, as we set forth the Axioms and demonstrated in the Poetic Wisdom.

XI

821 By the very nature of poetry it is impossible for anyone to be at the same time a sublime poet and a sublime metaphysician, for metaphysics abstracts the mind from the senses, and the poetic faculty must submerge the whole mind in the senses; metaphysics soars up to universals, and the poetic faculty must plunge deep into particulars.

XII

822 In virtue of the axiom that he who has not the natural gift may by industry succeed in every [other] capacity, but that in poetry success by industry is completely denied to him who lacks the natural gift, the poetic and critical "arts" serve to make minds cultivated but not great. For delicacy is a small virtue and greatness naturally disdains all small things. Indeed, as a great rushing torrent cannot fail to carry turbid waters and roll stones and trunks along in the violence of its course, so his very greatness accounts for the low expressions we so often find in Homer.

XIII

823   But this does not make Homer any the less the father and prince of all sublime poets.

XIV

824   For we have seen that Aristotle regarded the Homeric lies as without equal, which is equivalent to Horace's opinion that his characers are inimitable.

XV

825   He is celestially sublime in his poetic sentences, which must be expressions of true passions, or in virtue of a burning imagination must make themselves truly felt by us, and they must therefore be individuated in those who feel them. Hence maxims of life, as being general, we defined as sentences of philosophers; and reflections on the passions themselves are the work of false and frigid poets.

XVI

826   The poetic comparisons taken from wild and savage things are certainly incomparable in Homer.

XVII

827   The frightfulness of the Homeric battles and deaths gives to the *Iliad* all its marvelousness.

XVIII

828   But these sentences, comparisons, and descriptions could not have been the natural product of a calm, cultivated, and gentle philosopher.

XIX

829   For in their customs the Homeric heroes are like boys in the frivolity of their minds, like women in the vigor of their imaginations, and like turbulent youths in the boiling fervor of their wrath, and therefore it is impossible that a philosopher should have conceived them so naturally and felicitously.

XX

830 The ineptitudes and indecencies are effects of the awkwardness with which Greek peoples had labored to express themselves in the extreme poverty of their language in its formative period.

XXI

831 And even if the Homeric poems contained the most sublime mysteries of esoteric wisdom, as we have shown in the Poetic Wisdom that they certainly do not, the form in which they are expressed could not have been conceived by a straighforward, orderly, and serious mind such as befits a philosopher.

XXII

832 The heroic language was a language of similes, images, and comparisons, born of the lack of genera and species, which are necessary for the proper definition of things, and hence born of a necessity of nature common to entire peoples.

XXIII

833 It was by a necessity of nature that the first nations spoke in heroic verse. Here too we must admire the providence which, in the time when the characters of common script were not yet invented, ordained that the nations should speak in verses so that their memories might be aided by meter and rhythm to preserve more easily the histories of their families and cities.

XXIV

834 These fables, sentences, and customs, this language and verse, were all called heroic, and were current in the times to which history has assigned the heroes, as has been fully shown above in the Poetic Wisdom.

XXV

835 Hence all the aforesaid were properties of entire peoples and consequently common to all the individual men of these peoples.

XXVI

836 In virtue, however, of the very nature from which sprang all the aforesaid properties, which made Homer the greatest of poets, we denied that he was ever a philosopher.

XXVII

837 Further we showed above in the Poetic Wisdom that the meanings of esoteric wisdom were intruded into the Homeric fables by the philosophers who came later.

XXVIII

838 But, as esoteric wisdom appertains to but few individual men, so we have just seen that the very decorum of the heroic poetic characters, in which consists all the essence of the heroic fables, cannot be achieved today by men most learned in philosophy, in the art of poetry, and in the art of criticism. It is for this decorum that Aristotle and Horace give the palm to Homer, the former saying that his lies are beyond equal and the latter that his characters are inimitable, which comes to the same thing.

Philological Proofs for
The Discovery of the True Homer

839 With this great number of philosophical proofs, resulting in large part from the metaphysical criticism of the founders of the gentile nations, among whom we must number Homer, since certainly we have no more ancient profane writer than he (as Josephus the Jew stoutly maintains), we may conjoin the following philological proofs.

I

840 All ancient profane histories have fabulous beginnings.

II

841 Barbarous peoples, cut off from all the other nations of the world, as were the Germans and the American Indians, have been found to preserve in verses the beginnings of their history.

III

842 It was the poets who began to write Roman history.

IV

843 In the returned barbarian times, the histories were written by the poets who wrote in Latin.

V

844 Manetho, high priest of the Egyptians, interpreted the ancient history of Egypt, written in hieroglyphics, as a sublime natural theology.

VI

845   In the Poetic Wisdom we showed that the Greek philosophers did the same with the early history of Greece recounted in fables.

VII

846   Wherefore above in the Poetic Wisdom we were obliged to reverse the path of Manetho and, stripping off the mystical interpretations, to restore to the fables their original historical meanings; and the naturalness and ease, free of violence, subterfuge, or distortion, with which we were able to do so, show that the historical allegories which they contained were proper to them.

VIII

847   All of which strongly confirms the assertion of Strabo, in a golden passage, that before Herodotus, or rather before Hecatacus of Miletus, the history of the peoples of Greece was all written by their poets.

IX

848   And in Book Two we showed that the first writers of both ancient and modern nations were poets.

X

849   There are two golden passages in the *Odyssey* in which it is said, in praise of a speaker who has told a story well, that he has told it like a musician or singer. Just such indeed were the Homeric rhapsodes, who were vulgar men, each preserving by memory some part of the Homeric poems.

XI

850   Homer left none of his poems in writing, according to the firm assertion of Flavius Josephus the Jew against Apion the Greek grammarian.

XII

851   The rhapsodes went about the cities of Greece singing the books of Homer at the fairs and festivals, some singing one of them, others another.

XIII

852   By the etymology of their name from the two words which compose it, rhapsodes were stitchers-together of songs, and these songs they must certainly have collected from none other than their own peoples. Similarly [the common noun] *homēros* is said to come from *homou*, together, and *eirein*, to link; thus signifying a guarantor, as being one who binds creditor and debtor together. This derivation is as farfetched and forced [when applied to a guarantor] as it is natural and proper when applied to our Homer as a binder or compiler of fables.

XIV

853 The Pisistratids, tyrants of Athens, divided and arranged the poems of Homer, or had them divided and arranged, into [two groups,] the *Iliad* and *Odyssey*. Hence we may understand what a confused mass of material they must have been before, when the difference we can observe between the styles of the two poems is infinite.

XV

854 The Pisistratids also ordered that from that time onward the poems should be sung by the rhapsodes at the Panathenaic festivals, as Cicero writes in his *On the Nature of the Gods* [i.e., *On the Orator* 3.34.137, or rather Plato in his *Hipparchus* 228B], and Aelian also [*Various History* 8.2], who is followed on this point by [his editor, Johann] Scheffer.

XVI

855 But the Pisistratids were expelled from Athens only a few years earlier than the Tarquins were from Rome. So, if we assume that Homer lived as late as the time of Numa, a long period must still have ensued after the Pisistratids during which the rhapsodes continued to preserve his poems by memory. This tradition takes away all credit from the other according to which it was at the time of the Pisistratids that Aristarchus purged, divided, and arranged the poems of Homer, for that could not have been done without vulgar writing, and so from then on there would have been no need of rhapsodes to sing the several parts of them from memory.

XVII

856 By this reasoning, Hesiod, who left his works in writing, would have to be placed after the Pisistratids, since we have no authority for supposing that he was preserved by the memory of the rhapsodes as Homer was, though the vain diligence of the chronologists has placed him thirty years before Homer. Like the Homeric rhapsodes, however, were the cyclic poets, who preserved all the fabulous history of Greece from the origins of their gods down to the return of Ulysses to Ithaca. These cyclic poets, so called from *kyklos*, circle, could have been no other than simple men who would sing the fables to the common people gathered in a circle around them on festive days. The circle is precisely the one alluded to by Horace in his *Art of Poetry* in the phrase *vilem patulumque orbem*, "the base and large circle," concerning which Dacier is not at all satisfied with the commentators who assert that Horace here means long episodes or digressions. And perhaps the reason for his dissatisfaction is this:

that it is not necessary that an episode in a plot be base simply because it is long. To cite examples, the episode of the joys of Rinaldo and Armida in the enchanted garden, and that of the conversation of the old shepherd with Erminia, are indeed long but are not therefore base; for the former is ornate and the latter tenuous and delicate, and both are noble. But in our present passage Horace, having advised the tragic poets to take their arguments from the poems of Homer, runs into the difficulty that in that case they would not be [creative] poets, since their plots would be those invented by Homer. So Horace answers them that the epic stories of Homer will become tragic plots of their own if they will bear three things in mind. The first is to refrain from making idle paraphrases, in the way we still see men read the *Orlando furioso* or the [*Orlando*] *innamorato* or some other rhymed romance to the "base and large circles" of idle people on feast days, and, after reciting each stanza, explain it to them in prose with more words. The second is not to be faithful translators. The third and last is not to be servile imitators, but, adhering to the characters that Homer attributes to his heroes, to bring forth from them new sentiments, speeches, and actions in conformity with them; thus on the same subjects they will be new poets in the style of Homer. So, in the same passage, Horace speaks of a "cyclical poet" as a trivial marketplace poet. Authors of this sort are ordinarily called *kyklioi* and *enkyklioi,* and their collective work was called *kyklos epikos, kyklia epē, poiēma enkyklikon,* and sometimes *kyklos* without qualification, as Gerard Langbaine observes in his preface to Dionysius Longinus. So in this way it may be that Hesiod, who contains all the fables of the gods, is earlier than Homer.

XVIII

857   For this reason the same may be said of Hippocrates, who left many great works, written not indeed in verse but in prose, so that they naturally could not have been preserved by memory; whence he is to be assigned to about the time of Herodotus.

XIX

858   From all this [it is evident that G. J.] Voss placed an excess of good faith in the three heroic inscriptions [reported by Herodotus 5.59ff] with which he thought he could confute Josephus. For these inscriptions, the first of Amphitryon, the second of Hippocoön, and the third of Laomedon [i.e., Laodamas], are impostures similar to those still committed by falsifiers of medals. Martin Schoock supports Josephus against Voss.

XX

859   We may add that Homer never mentions vulgar Greek letters, and the epistle written by Proetus to Eureia as a trap for Bellerophon is said by Homer to have been written in *sēmata.*

XXI

860 Though Aristarchus emended Homer's poems, they still retain a great variety of dialects and many improprieties of speech, which must have been idiomatic expressions of various peoples of Greece, and many licenses in meter besides.

XXII

861 The fatherland of Homer is not known.

XXIII

862 Almost all the cities of Greece laid claim to him.

XXIV

863 Above we have brought forward strong conjectures that the Homer of the *Odyssey* was from the west of Greece and toward the south, and that the Homer of the *Iliad* was from the east and toward the north.

XXV

864 Not even Homer's age is known.

XXVI

865 The opinions on this point are so numerous and so varied that the divergence extends to 460 years, the extreme estimates putting it as early as the Trojan War and as late as the time of Numa.

XXVII

866 Dionysius Longinus, being unable to ignore the great diversity in the styles of the two poems, says that Homer composed the *Iliad* in his youth and the *Odyssey* in his old age: a strange detail to be known about a man of whom we do not know the two most important historical facts, namely when and where he lived, regarding which history has left us in the dark in telling of the greatest luminary of Greece.

XXVIII

867 This consideration should destroy all faith in Herodotus or whoever was the author of the *Life of Homer,* in which so many delightful minor details are narrated as to fill an entire volume, and all trust as well in the *Life* of him written by Plutarch, who, being a philosopher, spoke of him with greater sobriety.

XXIX

868 But perhaps Longinus based his conjecture on the fact that in the *Iliad* Homer depicts the wrath and the pride of Achilles, which are properties of youth, while in the *Odyssey* he relates the wiles and stratagems of Ulysses, which are characteristics of the aged.

XXX

869 Tradition says that Homer was blind and that from his blindness he took his name, which in the Ionic dialect means blind.

XXXI

870 Homer himself describes as blind the poets who sing at the banquets of the great, such as the one who sings at the banquet given by Alcinous for Ulysses, and the one who sings at the feast of the suitors.

XXXII

871 It is a property of human nature that the blind have marvelously retentive memories.

XXXIII

872 And finally [tradition says] that he was poor and wandered through the market places of Greece singing his own poems.

Section II

Introduction

873 Now all these things reasoned out by us or related by others concerning Homer and his poems, without our having intentionally aimed at any such result—indeed, it had not even entered into our reflections when readers of the first edition of this *New Science* (which was not worked out on the same method as the present), men of acute minds and excelling in scholarship and learning, suspected that the Homer believed in up to now was not real—all these things, I say, now compel us to affirm that the same thing has happened in the case of Homer as in that of the Trojan War, of which the most judicious critics hold that though it marks a famous epoch in history it never in the world took place. And certainly if, as in the case of the Trojan War, there did not remain of Homer certain great vestiges in the form of his poems, the great difficulties would lead us to conclude that he was a purely ideal poet who never existed as a particular man in the world of nature. But the many great difficulties on the one hand, taken together with the surviving poems on the other, seem to force us to take the middle ground that Homer was an idea or a heroic character of Grecian men insofar as they told their histories in song.

The Improprieties and Improbabilities of Homer

874 In the light of this discovery, all the things in the speeches and in the narrative which are improprieties and improbabilities in the Homer hitherto believed in become proper and necessary in the Homer herein discovered. And first of all, those most important matters concerning Homer on which we are left in uncertainlty compel us to say:

I

875 That the reason why the Greek peoples so vied with each other for the honor of being his fatherland, and why almost all claimed him as citizen, is that the Greek peoples were themselves Homer.

II

876 That the reason why opinions as to his age vary so much is that our Homer truly lived on the lips and in the memories of the peoples of Greece throughout the whole period from the Trojan War down to the time of Numa, a span of 460 years.

III

877 And the blindness

IV

878 and the poverty of Homer were characteristics of the rhapsodes, who, being blind, whence each of them was called *homēros*, had exceptionally retentive memories, and, being poor, sustained life by singing the poems of Homer throughout the cities of Greece; and they were the authors of these poems inasmuch as they were a part of these peoples who had composed their histories in the poems.

V

879 Thus Homer composed the *Iliad* in his youth, that is, when Greece was young and consequently seething with sublime passions, such as pride, wrath, and lust for vengeance, passions which do not tolerate dissimulation but which love magnanimity; and hence this Greece admired Achilles, the hero of violence. But he wrote the *Odyssey* in his old age, that is, when the spirits of Greece had been somewhat cooled by reflection, which is the mother

of prudence, so that it admired Ulysses, the hero of wisdom. Thus in the time
of Homer's youth the peoples of Greece found pleasure in coarseness, villainy,
ferocity, savagery, and cruelty, while in the time of his old age they found
delight in the luxury of Alcinous, the joys of Calypso, the pleasures of Circe,
the songs of the Sirens, the pastimes of the suitors, and the attempts, nay the
siege and the assaults, on the chastity of Penelope: two sets of customs which,
conceived above as existing at the same time, seemed to us incompatible. This
difficulty was enough to cause the divine Plato to declare, in order to solve it,
that Homer had foreseen by inspiration these nauseating, morbid, and
dissolute customs. Yet in this way he merely made of Homer a stupid founder
of Greek civility, for, however much he may condemn, he nevertheless teaches
these corrupt and decadent customs which were to come long after the nations
of Greece had been founded, to the end that, by an acceleration of the natural
course of human institutions, the Greeks might hasten on toward corruption.

VI

880   In this fashion we show that the Homer who was the author of the
Iliad preceded by many centuries the Homer who was the author of the
Odyssey.

VII

881   And we show that it was from the northeastern part of Greece that
the Homer came who sang of the Trojan War, which took place in his country,
and that it was from the southwestern part of Greece that the Homer came
who sang of Ulysses, whose kingdom was in that region.

VIII

882   Thus Homer, lost in the crowd of the Greek peoples, is justified
against all the accusations leveled at him by the critics, and particularly
[against those made] on account of his

IX

883   base sentences,

X

884   vulgar customs,

XI

885   crude comparisons,

XII

886 local idioms,

XIII

887 licenses in meter,

XIV

888 variations in dialect,

XV

889 and his having made men of gods and gods of men.

890 These last-mentioned fables Dionysius Longinus does not trust himself to sustain save by the props of philosophical allegories, which amounts to admitting that, as they sounded when sung to the Greeks, they cannot have brought Homer the glory of having been the founder of Greek civility. The same difficulty recurs in Homer's case which we raised against Orpheus as the founder of Greek humanity. But the aforesaid properties and particularly the last all appertained to the Greek peoples themselves. For inasmuch as at their founding they were themselves pious, religious, chaste, strong, just, and magnanimous, they made their gods so also, as our natural theogony has demonstrated above; then later, in the long passage of the years, as the fables became obscure and customs decayed, from their own character they judged the gods too to be dissolute, as we have set forth at length in the Poetic Wisdom. This in virtue of the axiom that men naturally bend obscure or dubious laws to their own passions and utilities. For they feared that the gods would not be agreeable to their desires if they were not like them in customs.

XVI

891 But more than ever to Homer belong by right the two great pre-eminences which are really one: that poetic falsehoods, as Aristotle says, and heroic characters, as Horace says, could be created only by him. On this account Horace avows himself to be no poet because he lacks the skill or the wit to maintain what he calls the colors of works, *colores operum,* which means the same thing as the poetic untruths of Aristotle's phrase, for in Plautus [*Braggart Warrior* 186 variant] we find *obtinere colorem* in the sense of telling a lie that under every aspect has the appearance of truth, which is what a good fable must be.

892 In addition to these, all those other pre-eminences fall to him which have been ascribed to him by all the masters of the art of poetry, declaring him incomparable.

XVII

893 in his wild and savage comparisons,

XVIII

894   in his cruel and fearful descriptions of battles and deaths,

XIX

895   in his sentences filled with sublime passions,

XX

896   in the expressiveness and splendor of his style. All these were
properties of the heroic age of the Greeks, in which and throughout which
Homer was an incomparable poet, just because, in the age of vigorous
memory, robust imagination, and sublime invention, he was in no sense a
philosopher.

XXI

897   Wherefore neither philosophies, arts of poetry, nor arts of criticism,
which came later, could create a poet who could come anywhere near to
rivaling Homer.
898   And, what is more, his title is assured to the three immortal eulogies
that are given him:

XXII

899   first of having been the founder of Greek polity or civility;

XXIII

900   second, of having been the father of all other poets;

XXIV

901   and third, of having been the source of all Greek philosophies. None
of these eulogies could have been given to the Homer hitherto believed in. Not
the first, for, counting from the time of Deucalion and Pyrrha, Homer comes
eighteen hundred years after the institution of marriage had laid the first
foundations of Greek civility, as we have shown throughout the Poetic
Wisdom. Not the second, for it was certainly before Homer's time that the
theological poets flourished, such as Orpheus, Amphion, Linus, Musaeus, and
others, among whom the chronologists have placed Hesiod, putting him thirty
years before Homer. Cicero affirms in his *Brutus* that there were other heroic
poets before Homer, and Eusebius mentions some by name in his *Preparation
for the Gospel,* such as Philammon, Thamyris, Demodocus, Epimenides,
Aristaeus, and others. And, finally, not the third, for, as we have shown fully
and at length in the Poetic Wisdom, the philosophers did not discover their
philosophies in the Homeric fables but rather inserted them therein. But it was

poetic wisdom itself whose fables provided occasions for the philosophers to meditate their lofty truths, and supplied them also with means for expounding them, as we showed throughout Book Two in fulfillment of the promise made at its beginning.

The Poems of Homer Revealed as Two Great Treasure Stores of the Natural Law of the Gentes of Greece

902   But above all, in virtue of our discovery we may ascribe to Homer an additional and most dazzling glory:

XXV

903   that of having been the first historian of the entire gentile world who has come down to us.

XXVI

904   Wherefore his poems should henceforth be highly prized as being two great treasure stores of the customs of early Greece. But the same fate has befallen the poems of Homer as the Law of the Twelve Tables; for, just as the latter, having been held to be the laws given by Solon to the Athenians and subsequently taken over by the Romans, has up to now concealed from us the history of the natural law of the heroic gentes of Latium, so the Homeric poems, having been regarded as works thrown off by a particular man, a rare and consummate poet, have hitherto concealed from us the history of the natural law of the gentes of Greece.

Appendix

905   We have already shown above that there were three ages of poets before Homer. First came the age of the theological poets, who were themselves heroes and sang true and austere fables; second, that of the heroic poets, who altered and corrupted the fables; and third, the Homeric age, which received them in their altered and corrupted form. Now the same metaphysical criticism of the history of the obscurest antiquity, that is, the explanation of the ideas the earliest nations naturally formed, can illuminate and distinguish for us the history of the dramatic and lyric poets, on which the philosophers have written only in an obscure and confused fashion.

906   The philosophers class among the lyric poets Amphion [i.e., Arion] of Methymna, a most ancient poet of heroic times, and affirm that he discovered the dithyramb and therewith the chorus, and that he introduced satyrs singing in verses, and that the dithyramb was a chorus led about singing verses in praise of Bacchus. They say that noteworthy tragic poets flourished within the period of the lyric; and Diogenes Laertius affirms that in tragedy the chorus was at first the only actor. They say that Aeschylus was the first tragic poet, and Pausanias relates that he was commanded by Bacchus to write tragedies (although Horace says that Thespis was their originator, in that passage of his *Art of Poetry* where he begins his treatment of tragedy with satire, and that Thespis introduced satire [i.e., the satyr play] on carts at vintage time). Later, they say, came Sophocles, called by Polemon the Homer of the tragic poets; and the cycle was completed by Euripides, whom Aristotle [*Poetics* 13.10.1453a 29] calls *tragikōtatos,* the most tragic of them all. They say that in the same period came Aristophanes, who invented the Old Comedy and opened the way for the New (which was later traveled by Menander), with his play entitled *The Clouds,* which was the ruin of Socrates. Then some of them put Hippocrates in the time of the tragic poets, others in the lyric period. But Sophocles and Euripides lived somewhat before the time of the Law of the Twelve Tables, and the lyre poets came even later; which would seem to upset the chronology which puts Hippocrates in the age of the Seven Sages of Greece.

907 To solve this difficulty we must declare that there were two kinds of tragic poets and two kinds of lyric poets.

908 The ancient lyric poets must in the first place have been the authors of hymns in honor of the gods, like those attributed to Homer, composed in heroic verse. They must later have been the poets of that lyric vein in which Achilles sings to his lyre the praises of the heroes who have gone before. Similarly among the Latins the first poets were the authors of the Salian verses, which were hymns sung by the priests called Salii on the festival days of the gods. (The priests were perhaps so called from *salio,* to leap, even as the first Greek choruses danced in a circle.) The fragments of these verses are the most ancient memorials of the Latin language that have come down to us, and they have an air of heroic verse. All of which is in accord with the beginnings of the humanity of the nations, which in the first, or religious, period must have offered praise only to the gods (even as in the last barbarian times this religious custom returned, and the priests, the only literate men of the time, composed only sacred hymns); whereas later, in the heroic period, they must have admired and celebrated only the great deeds of the heroes, such as those sung by Achilles. It is to this kind of sacred lyric poets that Amphion [i.e., Arion] of Methymna must have belonged. He was also the originator of the dithyramb, which was the first rough beginning of tragedy, composed in heroic verse (the first kind of verse in which the Greeks sang). Thus the dithyramb of Amphion was the first satire, and it is with satire that Horace begins his discussion of tragedy.

909 The new lyric poets were the melic poets, whose prince is Pindar, and who wrote in verse what we in Italian call *arie per musica,* airs to be set to music. This sort of verse must have come later than the iambic, which in turn was the kind of verse in which the Greeks commonly spoke after the heroic verse. Thus Pindar came in the times of the pompous bravery of Greece admired at the Olympic games, at which these lyric poets sang. In the same way Horace came in the most sumptuous times of Rome, under the reign of Augustus; and among the Italians the melic period came in the times of the greatest softness and tenderness.

910 The tragic and comic poets ran their course between the following limits. Thespis in one part of Greece and Amphion [i.e, Arion] in another originated at vintage time the satire, or satyr play, the primitive form of tragedy, with satyrs for its characters. In the rough and simple fashion of those days they must have invented the first mask by covering their feet, legs, and thighs with goat skins which they must have had at hand, and painting their breasts and faces with the lees of wine and fitting their foreheads with horns (on which account, perhaps, in our own day the vintagers are still vulgarly called *cornuti,* horned). In this sense it may well be true that Bacchus, god of the vintage, commanded Aeschylus to compose tragedies. All of which accords well with the times when the heroes were asserting that the plebeians were monsters of two natures, half man, half goat. Thus there is strong ground for conjecture that tragedy had its beginnings in this chorus of satyrs and that it took its name from the primitive mask we have described, rather than from the award of a *tragos,* or goat, to the winner in a competition in this sort of verse. (Horace glances at this latter possibility without making anything of it, and calls the goat paltry.) And the satire preserved this eternal property with which it was born: that of expressing invective and insult; for the peasants, thus roughly masked and riding in the carts in which they carried the grapes, had the license—as the vintagers still have in our happy Campania (once called the dwelling of Bacchus)—of hurling abuse at their betters. Hence we may understand with how little truth the learned later inserted into the fable of Pan (since *pan* signifies "all") the philosophical mythology to the effect that he signifies the universe, and that the hairy nether parts mean the earth, the red breast and face the element of fire, and the horns the sun and the moon. The Romans, however, preserved for us the historical mythology concerning him in the word *satyra,* which, according to Festus, was a dish made of various kinds of foods. Hence the later expression *lex per satyram* for an omnibus law. So, in dramatic satire, which we are discussing here, according to Horace (for no examples of this form have come down to us either from the Greeks or from the Latins), various types of characters made their appearance, such as gods, heroes, kings, artisans, and slaves. But the satire that survived among the Romans does not treat of varied matters, since each poem is devoted to a separate argument.

911 Then Aeschylus brought about the transition from the Old Tragedy, that is, the satyr play, to Middle Tragedy by using human masks and by converting the dithyramb of Amphion [i.e., Arion], which was a chorus of satyrs, into a chorus of men. And Middle Tragedy must have been the origin of Old Comedy, in which great personages were portrayed and the chorus was therefore fitting. Afterward came first Sophocles and then Euripides, who left us the final form of tragedy. The Old Comedy ended with Aristophanes, because of the bad name it gave Socrates, and Menander bequeathed us the

New Comedy, built around private and fictitious personages, who could be fictitious because they were private and could therefore be believed to be real. Hence there was no longer any room for the chorus, which is a public that comments, and comments only on public matters.

912 In this way the satire was composed in heroic verse, as the Latins afterward preserved it, because the first peoples spoke in heroic verse. Later they spoke in iambic verse, so that tragedy was composed in iambic verse quite naturally, and comedy only by an empty adherence to precedent when the Greek peoples were already speaking in prose. The iambic meter was certainly appropriate to tragedy, for it is a verse born to give vent to anger, and its movement is that of what Horace calls a swift foot. Vulgar tradition says that it was invented by Archilochus to vent his wrath against Lycambes, who had refused to give him his daughter in marriage and that the bitterness of his verses drove father and daughter to hang themselves in desperation. This must have been a history of the heroic contest over *connubium,* in which the rebellious plebeians must have hanged the nobles along with their daughters.

913 So was born that monstrosity of poetic art by which the same violent, rapid, and excited verse is made to fit such grand poetry as that of tragedy, considered by Plato even more lofty than the epic, and at the same time such delicate poetry as that of comedy; and the same metric foot, well adapted, as we have said, to express wrath and rage, in which tragedy must break forth so fearfully, is considered equally good as a vehicle for jests, games, and sentimental love affairs, which must make up all the grace and charm of comedy.

914 As a result of the indiscriminate use of the terms "lyric" and "tragic," Hippocrates was placed in the time of the Seven Sages; but he should rather be put about the time of Herodotus, since he came at a time when men still spoke largely in fables (for his own life has a tinge of the fabulous, and Herodotus's *History* is largely narrated in the form of fables), yet not only had speech in prose been introduced but also writing in vulgar characters, in which Herodotus wrote his history and Hippocrates wrote the many works on medicine that have come down to us.

Henry Fielding

1707–1754

Henry Fielding is a figure of epic stature in the history of English literature. Byron referred to Fielding as a "prose Homer." Coleridge said that the wit of his comic-epic novel *Tom Jones* "surpassed Swift and Pope," and that *Joseph Andrews* was "the most perfect plot ever planned." And Sir Walter Scott first gave Fielding the title that literary history has since secured for him—"the father of the British novel."

Fielding was born into a wealthy English family in 1707. After an apparently comfortable and happy childhood in Somerset, he weathered the severity of Eton, where he cultivated a deep knowledge of the classics and a special affection for the satiric author Lucian. At the age of seventeen he went to London for the first time. There, for four years, he led the life of a young gentleman of leisure, which included the writing and production of a play and a failed attempt to elope with a wealthy heiress. He returned to the study of the classics at Leyden from 1728 to 1730, but then went back to London. Faced, he said, with the choice of being a hackneyed coachman or a hackneyed writer, Fielding decided to be a writer. Until just before his death in 1754 he occupied a central position in the literary, social, and political milieu of Enlightenment London.

Before he ever became famous for his novels, Fielding had already become notorious as a playwright, journalist, pamphleteer, and magistrate. Between 1730 and 1735, Fielding wrote 25 plays, many of which he produced himself as the manager of "The Little Theater in the Haymarket". Although they no longer hold the stage, his farces and burlesques scandalized and delighted London audiences of the time, and drew much lively scurrility from Pope and his Grub Street hacks. As Fielding's reputation grew, his dramas became more overtly political, openly attacking the corruption and ineptitude of the government. In 1735, in a play called *The Golden Rump*, Fielding so viciously satirized Walpole that the Prime Minister pushed through Parliament the Licensing Act, by which all new plays had to be approved by the Lord Chamberlain.

The Licensing Act, Fielding said, ended his career as a dramatist just when it should have begun. But he carried his war against vice and imposture into journalism, continuing to bait his old antagonists in numerous pamphlets and newspapers. He now also had time to earn a law degree. He was thus prepared when power shifted into the hands of his Opposition friends; in 1748 Fielding was rewarded with the position of Justice of the Peace, Magister of Bow Street.

As a magistrate, Fielding undertook the Herculean task of ridding

Middlesex of its infamous gangs, robbers, brothels, dancing halls, gaming houses, and libelous newspapers. Although his moralistic zeal as a man of justice seems incongruous with his lewdness as a man of letters, Fielding was by all accounts a fair and unusually effective magistrate. Whereas previous magistrates had earned as much as 11,000 pounds a month by complicating complaints and collecting extra fees, Fielding averaged only 1,300 because he preferred to settle complaints outside of court. He seems to have felt great compassion for the impoverished, weak, and infirm people who filled London's streets. His table, it was said, was open to anyone, and Fielding was known to be generous to a fault.

Meanwhile, the unparalleled success of Samuel Richardson's *Pamela* had made Fielding into a novelist. In 1741 *An Apology for the Life of Mrs "Shamela" Andrews* appeared, satirizing Richardson's sentimentality and prudish morality. Although Fielding never claimed authorship of this anonymously published novel, it was widely recognized as his work, by the infuriated Richardson and others. Fielding followed *Shamela* in 1742 with *The History & Adventures of Joseph Andrews, and of his friend Abraham Adams, Written in Imitation of the Manner of Cervantes, Author of Don Quixote.* This novel is recognized as a masterpiece of sustained irony and social criticism.

Weary and sick with gout, Fielding now stopped writing for two years. He took his beloved and admired wife to Bath in the hopes of curing her sickness, but she "caught a fever and died in his arms." Fielding's grief, according to his friends, "approached to frenzy." After another year, however, he regained his strength and, much to the delight of the Grub Street Hacks, married his wife's maid, Mary Daniel, who was pregnant. In 1749 he completed and published another masterpiece, *The History of Tom Jones.* He died four years later in Lisbon.

In the Preface to *Joseph Andrews,* Fielding makes a valuable contribution to the theory of comedy. He offers an original definition of "the ridiculous" as that brand of humor which stems from affectation. Fielding sees the exposure of affectations, especially those which give some men power over others, as the social and moral responsibility of comedy.

JOSEPH ANDREWS

PREFACE

As it is possible the mere English Reader may have a different Idea of Romance with the Author of these little Volumes;[1] and may consequently expect a kind of Entertainment, not be found, nor which was even intended, in the following Pages; it may not be improper to premise a few Words concerning this kind of Writing, which I do not remember to have seen hitherto attempted in our Language.

The Epic as well as the Drama is divided into Tragedy and Comedy. Homer, who was the Father of this Species of Poetry, gave us a Pattern of both these,[2] tho' that of the latter kind is entirely lost; which Aristotle tells us,[3] bore the same relation to Comedy which his *Iliad* bears to Tragedy. And perhaps, that we have no more Instances of it among the Writers of Antiquity, is owing to the Loss of this great Pattern, which, had it survived, would have found its Imitators equally with the other Poems of this great Original.

And farther, as this Poetry may be Tragic or Comic, I will not scruple to say it may be likewise either in Verse or Prose: for tho' it wants one particular, which the Critic enumerates in the constituent Parts of an Epic Poem, namely Metre; yet, when any kind of Writing contains all its other Parts, such as Fable, Action, Characters, Sentiments, and Diction, and is deficient in Metre only; it seems, I think, reasonable to refer it to the Epic; at least, as no Critic hath thought proper to range it under any other Head, nor to assign it a particular Name to itself.

Thus the *Telemachus*[4] of the Arch-Bishop of Cambray appears to me of the Epic Kind, as well as the *Odyssey* of Homer; indeed, it is much fairer and more reasonable to give it a Name common with that Species from which it differs only in a single Instance, than to confound it with those which it resembles in no other. Such are those voluminous Works commonly called Romances, namely, *Clelia, Cleopatra, Astræa, Cassandra,* the *Grand Cyrus,*[5] and innumerable others which contain, as I apprehend, very little Instruction or Entertainment.

Now a comic Romance is a comic Epic-Poem in Prose; differing from Comedy, as the serious Epic from Tragedy: its Action being more extended and comprehensive; containing a much larger Circle of Incidents, and introducing a greater Variety of Characters. It differs from the serious Romance in its Fable and Action, in this; that as in the one these are grave and solemn, so in the other they are light and ridiculous: it differs in its Characters, by introducing Persons of inferiour Rank, and consequently of inferiour Manners, whereas the grave Romance, sets the highest before us; lastly in its Sentiments and Diction, by preserving the Ludicrous instead of the Sublime. In the Diction I think, Burlesque itself may be sometimes admitted; of which many Instances will occur in this Work, as in the Descriptions of the Battles, and some other Places, not necessary to be pointed out to the Classical Reader; for whose Entertainment those Parodies or Burlesque Imitations are chiefly calculated.

But tho' we have sometimes admitted this in our Diction, we have carefully excluded it from our Sentiments and Characters: for there it is never properly introduced, unless in Writings of the Burlesque kind, which this is not intended to be. Indeed, no two Species of Writing can differ more widely than the Comic and the Burlesque: for as the latter is ever the Exhibition of what is monstrous and unnatural, and where our Delight, if we examine it, arises from the surprizing Absurdity, as in appropriating the Manners of the highest to the lowest, or *è converso;* so in the former, we should ever confine ourselves strictly to Nature from the just Imitation of which, will flow all the Pleasure we can this way convey to a sensible Reader. And perhaps, there is one Reason, why a Comic Writer should of all others be the least excused for deviating from Nature, since it may not be always so easy for a serious Poet to meet with the Great and the Admirable; but Life every where furnishes an accurate Observer with the Ridiculous.

I have hinted this little, concerning Burlesque; because, I have often heard that Name given to Performances, which have been truly of the Comic kind, from the Author's having sometimes admitted it in his Diction only; which as it is the Dress of Poetry, doth like the Dress of Men establish Characters, (the one of the whole Poem, and the other of the whole Man,) in vulgar Opinion, beyond any of their greater Excellencies: But surely, a certain Drollery in Style, where the Characters and Sentiments are perfectly natural, no more constitutes the Burlesque, than an empty Pomp and Dignity of Words, where every thing else is mean and low, can entitle any Performance to the Appellation of the true Sublime.

And I apprehend, my Lord Shaftesbury's Opinion of mere Burlesque[6] agrees with mine, when he asserts, 'There is no such Thing to be found in the Writings of the Antients.' But perhaps, I have less Abhorrence than he professes for it: and that not because I have had some little Success on the Stage this way;[7] but rather, as it contributes more to exquisite Mirth and Laughter than any other; and these are probably more wholesome Physic for the Mind, and conduce better to purge away Spleen, Melancholy and ill Affections, than is generally imagined. Nay, I will appeal to common Observation, whether the same Companies are not found more full of Good-Humour and Benevolence, after they have been sweeten'd for two or three Hours with Entertainments of this kind, than when soured by a Tragedy or a grave Lecture.

But to illustrate all this by another Science, in which, perhaps, we shall see the Distinction more clearly and plainly: Let us examine the Works of a Comic History-Painter, with those Performances which the Italians call *Caricatura;* where we shall find the true Excellence of the former, to consist in the exactest copying of Nature; insomuch, that a judicious Eye instantly rejects any thing *outré;* any Liberty which the Painter hath taken with the Features of that *Alma Mater.*—Whereas in the *Caricatura* we allow all

Licence. Its Aim is to exhibit Monsters, not Men; and all Distortions and Exaggerations whatever are within its proper Province.

Now what *Caricatura* is in Painting, Burlesque is in Writing; and in the same manner the Comic Writer and Painter correlate to each other. And here I shall observe, that as in the former, the Painter seems to have the Advantage; so it is in the latter infinitely on the side of the Writer: for the Monstrous is much easier to paint than describe, and the Ridiculous to describe than paint.

And tho' perhaps this latter Species doth in either Science so strongly affect and agitate the Muscles as the other; yet it will be owned, I believe, that a more rational and useful Pleasure arises to us from it. He who should call the Ingenious Hogarth[8] a Burlesque Painter, would, in my Opinion, do him very little Honour: for sure it is much easier, much less the Subject of Admiration, to paint a Man with a Nose, or any other Feature of a preposterous Size, or to expose him in some absurd or monstrous Attitude, than to express the Affections of Men on Canvas. It hath been thought a vast Commendation of a Painter, to say his Figures seem to breathe; but surely, it is a much greater and nobler Applause, that they appear to think.

But to return—The Ridiculous only, as I have before said, falls within my Province in the present Work.—Nor will some Explanation of this Word be thought impertinent by the Reader, if he considers how wonderfully it hath been mistaken, even by Writers who have profess'd it: for to what but such a Mistake, can we attribute the many Attempts to ridicule the blackest Villanies; and what is yet worse, the most dreadful Calamities? What could exceed the Absurdity of an Author, who should write the Comedy of Nero, with the merry Incident of ripping up his Mother's Belly;[9] or what would give a greater Shock to Humanity, than an Attempt to expose the Miseries of Poverty and Distress to Ridicule? And yet, the Reader will not want much Learning to suggest such Instances to himself.

Besides, it may seem remarkable, that Aristotle, who is so fond and free of Definitions, hath not thought proper to define the Ridiculous. Indeed, where he tells us it is proper to Comedy, he hath remarked that Villany is not its Object:[10] but he hath not, as I remember, positively asserted what is. Nor doth the Abbé Bellegarde, who hath writ a Treatise on this Subject,[11] tho' he shews us many Species of it, once trace it to its Fountain.

The only Source of the true Ridiculous (as it appears to me) is Affectation.[12] But tho' it arises from one Spring only, when we consider the infinite Streams into which this one branches, we shall presently cease to admire at the copious Field it affords to an Observer. Now Affectation proceeds from one of these two Causes, Vanity, or Hypocrisy: for as Vanity puts us on affecting false Characters, in order to purchase Applause; so Hypocrisy sets us on an Endeavour to avoid Censure by concealing our Vices under an Appearance of their opposite Virtues. And tho' these two Causes are often confounded, (for there is some Difficulty in distinguishing them) yet, as they proceed from very different Motives, so they are clearly distinct in their Operations: for indeed, the Affectation which arises from Vanity is nearer to Truth than the other; as it hath not that violent Repugnancy of Nature to struggle with, which that of the Hypocrite hath. It may be likewise noted, that Affectation doth not imply an absolute Negation of those Qualities which are affected: and therefore, tho', when it proceeds from Hypocrisy, it be nearly allied to Deceit; yet when it comes from Vanity only, it partakes of the Nature of Ostentation: for instance, the Affectation of Liberality in a vain Man, differs visibly from the same Affectation in the Avaricious; for tho' the vain Man is not what he would appear, or hath not the Virtue he affects, to the degree he would be thought to have it; yet it sits less aukwardly on him than on the avaricious Man, who is the very Reverse of what he would seem to be.

From the Discovery of this Affectation arises the Ridiculous—which always strikes the Reader with Surprize and Pleasure; and that in a higher and stronger Degree when the Affectation arises from Hypocrisy, than when from Vanity: for to discover any one to be the exact Reverse of what he affects, is more surprizing, and consequently more ridiculous, than to find him a little deficient in the Quality he desires the Reputation of. I might observe that our Ben Johnson,[13] who of all Men understood the Ridiculous the best, hath chiefly used the hypocritical Affectation.

Now from Affectation only, the Misfortunes and Calamities of Life, or the Imperfections of Nature, may become the Objects of Ridicule. Surely he hath a very ill-framed Mind, who can look on Ugliness, Infirmity, or Poverty, as ridiculous in themselves: nor do I believe any Man living who meets a dirty Fellow riding through the Streets in a Cart, is struck with an Idea of the Ridiculous from it; but if he should see the same Figure descend from his Coach and Six, or bolt from his Chair with his Hat under his Arm, he would then begin to laugh, and with justice. In the same manner, were we to enter a poor House, and behold a wretched Family shivering with Cold and languishing with Hunger, it would not incline us to Laughter, (at least we must have very diabolical Natures, if it would:) but should we discover there a Grate, instead of Coals, adorned with Flowers, empty Plate or China Dishes on the Side-board, or any other Affectation of Riches and Finery either on their Persons or in their Furniture; we might then indeed be excused, for ridiculing so fantastical an Appearance. Much less are natural Imperfections the Objects of Derision: but when Ugliness aims at the Applause of Beauty, or Lameness endeavours to display Agility; it is then that these unfortunate Circumstances, which at first moved our Compassion, tend only to raise our Mirth.[14]

The Poet[15] carries this very far;

> None are for being what they are in Fault,
> But for not being what they would be thought.

Where if the Metre would suffer the Word Ridiculous to close the first Line, the Thought would be rather more proper. Great Vices are the proper Objects of our Detestation, smaller Faults of our Pity: but Affectation appears to me the only true Source of the Ridiculous.

But perhaps it may be objected to me, that I have against my own Rules introduced Vices, and of a very black Kind into this Work. To which I shall answer: First, that it is very difficult to pursue a Series of human Actions and keep clear from them. Secondly, That the Vices to be found here, are rather the accidental Consequences of some human Frailty, or Foible, than Causes habitually existing in the Mind. Thirdly, That they are never set forth as the Objects of Ridicule but Detestation. Fourthly, That they are never the principal Figure at that Time on the Scene; and lastly, they never produce the intended Evil.

Having thus distinguished *Joseph Andrews* from the Productions of Romance Writers on the one hand, and Burlesque Writers on the other, and given some few very short Hints (for I intended no more) of this Species of writing, which I have affirmed to be hitherto unattempted in our Language; I shall leave to my good natur'd Reader to apply my Piece to my Observations, and will detain him no longer than with a Word concerning the Characters in this Work.

And here I solemnly protest, I have no Intention to vilify or asperse any one: for tho' every thing is copied from the Book of Nature, and scarce a Character or Action produced which I have not taken from my own Observations and Experience, yet I have used the utmost Care to obscure the Persons by such different Circumstances, Degrees, and Colours, that it will be impossible to guess at them with any degree of Certainty; and if it ever happens otherwise, it is only where the Failure characterized is so minute, that it is a Foible only which the Party himself may laugh at as well as any other.

As to the Character of Adams, as it is the most glaring in the whole, so I conceive it is not to be found in any Book now extant. It is designed a Character of perfect Simplicity; and as the Goodness of his Heart will recommend him to the Good-natur'd; so I hope it will excuse me to the Gentlemen of his Cloth; for whom, while they are worthy of their sacred Order, no Man can possibly have a greater Respect. They will therefore excuse me, notwithstanding the low Adventures in which he is engaged, that I have made him a Clergyman; since no other Office could have given him so many Opportunities of displaying his worthy Inclinations.

NOTES

1. *Joseph Andrews* was originally published in two volumes.
2. The *Margites*, a satirical epic having a fool (*margos*) as hero, was attributed to Homer by both Aristotle and Zeno.
3. *Poetics*, iv. 12. (References to the *Poetics* are to the Loeb Classical Library translation [London, 1927].)
4. *Les Avantures de Télémaque fils d'Ulysse* (1699), a popular prose epic having as its theme the education of a prince, was written by the French theologian, François de Salignac de la Mothe-Fénelon (1651–1715). Fénelon was named Archbishop of Cambrai in 1695.

5. These voluminous French romances were translated into English during the seventeenth century by John Davies, Sir Charles Cotterel, and others, and were very much in vogue; Mr. Spectator discovered them in the library of the fashionable Leonora (*Spectator*, no. 37 [12 April 1711]). *Astrée*, the several parts of which were issued 1607–28, is by Honoré d'Urfé (1567–1625); *Cassandre* (1644–50) in 10 vols. and *Cléopâtre* (1647–56) in 12 vols. are by Gauthier de Costes de la Calprenède (1614–63); *Clélie* (1654–60) and *Artamène, ou le Grand Cyrus* (1649–53), both in 10 vols., are by Mlle Madeleine de Scudéry (1607–1701).

6. Anthony Ashley Cooper, third Earl of Shaftesbury (1671–1713). In Part I, Section 4, of *Sensus Communis: An Essay on the Freedom of Wit and Humour* (first published in 1709 and later included in the *Characteristics* [1711]), Shaftesbury remarks that buffoonery and burlesque flourish best in those countries where tyranny prohibits the free expression of serious thought; thus the Italians surpass the English in ridicule and raillery. In Section 5 he continues: ''Tis for this reason, I verily believe, that the Antients discover so little of this Spirit, and that there is hardly such a thing found as mere *Burlesque* in any Authors of the politer Ages' (5th ed. [1732], i. 73).

7. Fielding's burlesque dramas include *Tom Thumb* (1730), *The Covent-Garden Tragedy* (1732), and *Tumble-Down Dick; or, Phaeton in the Suds* (1736). The first of these, a brilliant travesty of heroic tragedy, had an initial run of 'upwards of Forty Nights, to the politest Audiences'. (Preface to *The Tragedy of Tragedies; or, The Life and Death of Tom Thumb the Great* [1731].)

8. Fielding's good friend, William Hogarth (1697–1764), is the 'History-Painter' to whose work Fielding refers in distinguishing between comic art and caricature. Hogarth himself illustrated the difference in *Characters and Caricaturas* (1743), and returned Fielding's compliment with this advice to the curious: 'For a farther explanation of the difference betwixt *Character and Caricatura*, see ye Preface to Jo^h Andrews.' (John Ireland, *A Supplement to Hogarth Illustrated* [1798], p. 342.) Fielding's great admiration for Hogarth's work may be seen in this passage from *The Champion*, 10 June 1740: 'I esteem the ingenious Mr. Hogarth as one of the most useful Satyrists any Age hath produced. In his excellent Works you see the delusive Scene exposed with all the Force of Humour, and, on casting your Eyes on another Picture, you behold the dreadful and fatal Consequence. I almost dare affirm that those two Works of his, which he calls the *Rake's* and the *Harlot's Progress*, are calculated more to serve the Cause of Virtue, and for the Preservation of Mankind, than all the Folio's of Morality which have been ever written; and a sober Family should no more be without them, than without the *Whole Duty of Man* in their House.' In *Tom Jones*, Fielding directs his readers to specific paintings by Hogarth to clarify the description of Bridget Allworthy (I. xi), Mrs. Partridge (II. iii), and Thwackum (III. vi). Other complimentary references to Hogarth or his works occur in *The Vernoniad, An Essay on Conversation, Amelia, The Covent-Garden Journal*, and *The Journal of a Voyage to Lisbon*. Appropriately, it is to Hogarth that we owe the only known portrait of Fielding, drawn as the frontispiece to Arthur Murphy's edition of the *Works* (1762).

9. In A.D. 59 Nero (A.D. 37–68) ordered the assassination of his mother Agrippina, who, in a gesture of repudiation of her son, preferred her womb to the sword and was stabbed to death. (See Tacitus, *Annals*, XIII. 8.) In *The Jacobite's Journal* (26 March 1748) Fielding used the same illustration in declaring his intention to abandon ridicule as a weapon against the Jacobites who were trying to overthrow the government: 'To consider such Attempts as these in a ludicrous Light, would be as absurd as the Conceit of a Fellow in *Bartholomew-Fair*, who exhibited the comical Humours of Nero ripping up his Mother's Belly. . . . '

10. *Poetics*, v. 1–2.

11. *Reflexions sur le ridicule, et sur les moyens de l' éviter* (1696) by Jean Baptiste Morvan de Bellegarde (1648–1734). Affectation, vanity, and imposture are among the varieties of ridiculous behaviour which the Abbé Bellegarde warns his readers to avoid. When Fielding resumed discussion of this subject in *The Covent-Garden Journal* (18 and 25 July 1752), he praised 'the judicious Abbé Bellegarde' and earnestly recommended his 'excellent Lessons on the Ridiculous'.

12. Though he seems to imply as much, Fielding is by no means the first, even among his more immediate contemporaries, to analyse the Ridiculous. To mention only two of many precursors: 'A Dissertation upon Laughter' had appeared anonymously in *The Publick Register: or, The Weekly Magazine, etc.* during January 1741, in which we are said to laugh because of the incongruity between our expectations of how a person will behave and his actual behaviour; earlier, in two essays in *Common Sense* (3 and 10 September 1737), the writer follows La Rochefoucauld in tracing the Ridiculous to its causes in affectation and vanity (but not in hypocrisy, which is said to provoke indignation rather than amusement).

Fielding himself had attempted to locate the sources of the Ridiculous before he wrote the Preface, and he returned to the subject more than once. In *The Champion* (15 April 1740) he stated that 'Vanity is the true Source of Ridicule,' and in the leader for 20 November 1739 he had found much ridiculous behaviour to arise from a common vice, hypocrisy. Toward the end of his career he devoted space in *The Covent-Garden Journal* to a fresh consideration of the subject: at this time he attributed the Ridiculous to the triumph of 'Humour' over good-breeding, which is in turn simply the observance of 'the most golden of all Rules' (18 July 1752); and, he continued, one of the chief reasons for such behaviour is the lack of proper methods of education (25 July 1752).

13. Fielding greatly admired Ben Jonson (1572–1637). In stating his later view that humours are the source of the Ridiculous, Fielding quotes at length from a relevant passage in *Every Man Out of His Humour* (*Covent-Garden Journal*, 18 July 1752).

14. Cf. the first of William Wycherly's 'Maxims and Moral Reflections' in *Posthumous Works* (1728), p. 9: 'Our Natural Imperfections are never more our Shame, than when by Art we endeavour to hide them, or improve them into Perfections: For we are pitied, while we go lame because we can't help it; but laugh'd at for pretending to dance, when we are oblig'd to hobble.'

15. William Congreve (1670–1729). The verses are from his poem, 'Of Pleasing; An Epistle to Sir Richard Temple', ll. 63–64.

Oliver Goldsmith

1728–1774

Oliver Goldsmith, one of the greatest authors of the Restoration, was born into a prominent Anglo-Irish family. As a child, Goldsmith was exposed to Irish folk culture through his tutor, Elizabeth Delap. He thus became familiar with the banshees, fairy rides, elfin kings, and fierce heroes of Irish lore; he also spoke Gaelic fluently. Though a Protestant, and of ancient Saxon stock, he was more Irish than the Irish.

As a boy Goldsmith was frequently the butt of raillery and coarse humor. From the start he cut a blundering, awkward figure; to the end (we have Johnson's word on this) this greatest of English comic storytellers appeared ridiculous in conversation, and behaved as if he were a half-wit. He was often flogged as a dunce by his schoolmaster. In 1744, at the age of sixteen, Goldsmith, the ungainly villager, was sent off to Trinity College in Dublin. There he cut a more ridiculous figure than ever. While frittering away his time at Trinity in revel and dissipation, his father died, leaving him virtually penniless. He tried his hand at five or six professions, failing signally in all of them. When a generous relation gave him fifty pounds, he immediately squandered all of it gambling. He then got it into his head to become a doctor; going up to Edinburgh, he was soon sent packing to Leyden. On the Continent he wandered about aimlessly, playing the flute. He lived at the gates of convents in Italy. Once he claimed to have been present at a conversation between Voltaire and Fontenelle, which supposedly took place in Paris when Goldsmith was visiting that city. Scholars have shown that Goldsmith was hundreds of miles away from Paris at the time at which he claimed the conversation took place. Given the fact that Goldsmith was nothing short of an habitual liar, this story, like so many others, is of dubious authenticity.

Upon his return to London, Goldsmith lived by his pen, writing anonymous articles and reviews, among which are essays under the title of *The Bee* and the *Life of Beau Nash*. He was beginning to acquire something of a reputation among the booksellers. Before long he was a companion of Burke and Johnson, Reynolds and Boswell. The circumstances of the sale of his only novel, *The Vicar of Wakefield,* are interesting enough, though probably apocryphal. Around 1764 Goldsmith had been living in a pitiful garret without having paid his rent for many months. Having no other recourse, his landlady summoned the sheriff. Goldsmith duly dispatched a messenger to Samuel Johnson with an urgent plea for help. Johnson sent back the messenger with a guinea, promising to follow as soon as he was able. Lumbering towards Goldsmith's hovel, Johnson soon discovered that his needy friend had used the guinea to buy a bottle of Madeira, and was involved in an extended harangue with the landlady. Johnson quietly stoppered the bottle and asked his friend how he was going to obtain the funds necessary to pacify her and to avoid debtor's prison. Goldsmith replied by handing Johnson the manuscript of the *Vicar of Wakefield*. Perusing it briefly, Johnson found it satisfactory, left immediately and returned from the booksellers with sixty pounds. In this way what proved to be one of the most popular English novels ever written came to be published, and Goldsmith's rent was (this one time at least) paid in full.

In the opinion of most critics this novel is poorly constructed; but almost everyone who has read it agrees it is extraordinarily funny. The earlier chapters have all the sweetness of pastoral poetry, together with all the vivacity of comedy. Moses and his spectacles, the vicar and his monogamy, the sharper and his cosmogony, the squire proving from Aristotle that relatives are related, Olivia preparing herself for the arduous task of converting a rakish lover by studying the controversy between Robinson Crusoe and Friday, the great ladies with their scandal about Sir Tomkyn's amours and Dr. Burdock's verses, and Mr. Burchell with his "Fudge," have caused as much harmless mirth as had ever been caused by matter packed into so small a number of pages.

With the success of his *Vicar*, Goldsmith turned to writing for the stage. His first play, *The Good Natur'd Man*, did not fare as well as it should have. It was not until 1773, when *She Stoops to Conquer* was put on at the Covent Garden, that Goldsmith came into his own. This play came to fix the comic genius of Goldsmith in the firmament of English comedy. An uproarious farce which packed the house night after night, it helped Goldsmith as much as his occasional journalism, insipid conversation, and perilous finances could harm him.

Nevertheless, by his fortieth year the spendthrift author owed up to two thousand pounds to a growing army of creditors. His health began to fail; he did not survive his forty-sixth year. Those friends who had made it their habit to poke fun at their wayward friend were sincerely grieved. Burke is reported to have burst out into tears upon hearing of the death of Goldsmith. He was buried in an unmarked grave; his friends had a cenotaph erected in Westminster Abbey.

ESSAYS

ON THE ORIGIN OF POETRY

The study of polite literature is generally supposed to include all the liberal arts of poetry, painting, sculpture, music, eloquence, and architecture. All these are founded on imitation; and all of them mutually assist and illustrate each other. But as painting, sculpture, music, and architecture, cannot be perfectly attained without long practice of manual operation, we shall distinguish them from poetry and eloquence, which depend entirely on the faculties of the mind; and on these last, as on the arts which immediately constitute the Belles-Lettres, employ our attention in the present inquiry: or, if it should run to a greater length than we propose, it shall be confined to poetry alone; a subject that comprehends in its full extent the province of taste, or what is called polite literature, and differs essentially from eloquence, both in its end and origin.

Poetry sprang from ease, and was consecrated to pleasure; whereas eloquence arose from necessity, and aims at conviction. When we say poetry sprang from ease, perhaps we ought to except that species of it, which owed its rise to inspiration and enthusiasm, and properly belonged to the culture of religion. In the first ages of mankind, and even in the original state of nature, the unlettered mind must have been struck with sublime conceptions, with admiration and awe, by those great phenomena, which, though every day repeated, can never be viewed without internal emotion. Those would break forth in exclamations expressive of the passion produced, whether surprise or gratitude, terror or exultation. The rising, the apparent course, the setting, and seeming renovation of the sun; the revolution of light and darkness; the splendor, change, and circuit of the moon, and the canopy of heaven bespangled with stars, must have produced expressions of wonder and adoration. "O glorious luminary! great eye of the world, source of that light which guides my steps! of that heat which warms me when chilled with cold! of that influence which cheers the face of nature! whither dost thou retire every evening with the shades? Whence dost thou spring every morning with renovated lustre, and never-fading glory? Art thou not the ruler, the creator, the God, of all that I behold? I adore thee, as thy child, thy slave, thy suppliant! I crave thy protection, and the continuance of thy goodness! Leave me not to perish with cold, or to wander solitary in utter darkness! Return, return, after thy wonted absence: drive before thee the gloomy clouds that would obscure the face of nature. The birds begin to warble, and every animal is filled with gladness at thy approach: even the trees, the herbs, and the flowers, seem to rejoice with fresher beauties, and send forth a grateful incense to thy power, whence their origin is derived!" A number of individuals, inspired with the same ideas, would join in these orisons, which would be accompanied with corresponding gesticulations of the body. They would be improved by practice, and grow regular from repetition. The sounds and gestures would naturally fall into measured cadence. Thus, the song and dance would be produced; and a system of worship being formed, the Muse would be consecrated to the purposes of religion.

Hence those forms of thanksgivings, and litanies of supplication, with which the religious rites of all nations, even the most barbarous, are at this day celebrated in every quarter of the known world. Indeed this is a circumstance in which all nations surprisingly agree, how much soever they may differ in every other article of laws, customs, manners and religion. The ancient Egyptians celebrated the festivals of their god Apis with hymns and dances. The superstition of the Greeks, partly derived from the Egyptians, abounded with poetical ceremonies, such as choruses and hymns, sung and danced at their apotheoses, sacrifices, games, and divinations. The Romans had their *carmen seculare,* and Salian priests, who on certain festivals sung and danced through the streets of Rome. The Israelites were famous for this kind of exultation: "And Miriam, the prophetess, the sister of Aaron, took a timbrel in her hand, and all the women went out after her, with timbrels and with dances, and Miriam answered them, Sing ye to the Lord," &c.—"And David danced before the Lord with all his might." The psalms composed by this monarch, the songs of Deborah and Isaiah, are further confirmations of what we have advanced.

From the Phœnicians the Greeks borrowed the cursed Orthyan song, when they sacrificed their children to Diana. The poetry of the bards constituted great part of the religious ceremonies among the Gauls and Britons, and the carousals of the Goths were religious institutions, celebrated with songs of triumph. The Mahometan Dervise dances to the sound of the flute, and whirls himself round until he grows giddy, and falls into a trance. The Marabous compose hymns in praise of Allah. The Chinese celebrate their grand festivals with processions of idols, songs, and instrumental music. The Tartars, Samoieds, Laplanders, Negroes, even the Caffres called Hottentots, solemnize their worship, such as it is, with songs and dancing; so that we may venture to say, poetry is the universal vehicle, in which all nations have expressed their most sublime conceptions.

Poetry was, in all appearance, previous to any concerted plan of worship, and to every established system of legislation. When certain individuals, by dint of superior prowess or understanding, had acquired the veneration of their fellow-savages, and erected themselves into divinities on the ignorance and superstition of mankind; then mythology took place, and such a swarm of deities arose, as produced a religion replete with the most shocking absurdities. Those whom their superior talents had deified, were found to be still actuated by the most brutal passions of human nature; and, in all probability, their votaries were glad to find such examples, to countenance their own vicious inclinations. Thus fornication, incest, rape, and even bestiality, were sanctified by the amours of Jupiter, Pan, Mars, Venus, and Apollo. Theft was patronized by Mercury, drunkenness by Bacchus, and cruelty by Diana. The same heroes and legislators, those who delivered their country, founded cities, established societies, invented useful arts, or contributed in any eminent degree to the security and happiness of their fellow-creatures, were inspired by the same lusts and appetites which domineered among the inferior classes of mankind; therefore, every vice incident to human nature was celebrated in the worship of one or other of these divinities, and every infirmity consecrated by public feast and solemn sacrifice.

In these institutions the poet bore a principal share. It was his genius that contrived the plan, that executed the form of worship, and recorded in verse the origin and adventures of their gods and demi-gods. Hence the impurities and horrors of certain rites, the groves of Paphos and Baal-Peor, the orgies of Bacchus, the human sacrifices to Moloch and Diana. Hence the theogony of Hesiod, the theology of Homer, and those innumerable maxims scattered through the ancient poets, inviting mankind to gratify their sensual appetites, in imitation of the gods, who were certainly the best judges of happiness. It is well known, that Plato expelled Homer from his commonwealth, on account of the infamous characters by which he has distinguished his deities, as well as for some depraved sentiments which he found diffused through the course of the Iliad and Odyssey. Cicero enters into the spirit of Plato, and exclaims, in his first book, De Naturá Deorum:—"Nec multa absurdiora sunt ea, quæ, poetarum vocibus fusa, ipsa suavitate nocuerunt: qui, et irâ inflammatos, et libidine furentes, induxerunt Deos, feceruntque ut eorum bella, pugnas, prælia, vulnera videremus: odia præterea, dissidia, discordias, ortus, interritus, querelas, lamentationes, effusas in omni intemperantiâ libidines, adulteria, vincula, cum humano genere concubitus, mortalesque ex immortali procreatos." "Nor are those things much more absurd which, flowing from the poet's tongue, have done mischief even by the sweetness of his expression. The poets have introduced gods inflamed with anger and enraged with lust; and even produced before our eyes their wars, their wrangling, their duels, and their wounds. They have exposed, besides, their antipathies, animosities, and dissensions; their origin and death; their complaints and lamentations; their appetites indulged to all manner of excess; their adulteries, their fetters, their amorous commerce with the human species, and from immortal parents derived a mortal offspring."

As the festivals of the gods necessarily produced good cheer, which often carried to riot and debauchery, mirth of consequence prevailed; and this was always attended with buffoonery. Taunts and jokes, and raillery and repartee, would necessarily ensue; and individuals would contend for the victory in wit and genius. These contests would in time be reduced to some regulations, for the entertainment of the people thus assembled, and some prize would be decreed to him who was judged to excel his rivals. The candidates for fame and profit being thus stimulated, would task their talents, and naturally recommend these alternate recriminations to the audience, by clothing them with a kind of poetical measure, which should bear a near resemblance to prose. Thus, as the solemn service of the day was composed in the most sublime species of poetry, such as the ode or hymn, the subsequent altercation was

carried on in iambics, and gave rise to satire. We are told by the Stagirite, that
the highest species of poetry was employed in celebrating great actions, but the
humbler sort used in this kind of contention; and that in the ages of antiquity
there were some bards that professed heroics, and some that pretended to
iambics only. Οἱ μὲν ἡροïχῶν οἱ δὲ ἰάμβων ποιῆται.

To these rude beginnings we not only owe the birth of satire, but likewise the origin of dramatic poetry. Tragedy herself, which afterwards attained
to such dignity as to rival the epic muse, was at first no other than a trial
of crambo, or iambics, between two peasants, and a goat was the prize, as
Horace calls it, *vile certamen ob hircum,* "a mean contest for a he-goat."
Hence, the name τραγῳ δὶα, signifying the goat-song, from τράγος *hircus,*
and ὠδη *carmen.*

> *Carmine qui tragico vilem certavit ob hircum,*
> *Mox etiam agrestes satyros nudavit, et asper*
> *Incolumi gravitate jocum tentavit, eò quòd*
> *Illecebris erat et gratâ novitate morandus*
> *Spectator functusque sacris, et potus et exlex.*

> The tragic bard, who for a worthless prize,
> Bid naked satyrs in his chorus rise;
> His muse severe, secure, and undismay'd,
> The rustic joke in solemn strain convey'd;
> For novelty alone, he knew, could charm
> A lawless crowd, with wine and feasting warm.

Satire then was originally a clownish dialogue in loose iambics, so called
because the actors were disguised like satyrs, who not only recited the praises
of Bacchus, or some other deity, but interspersed their hymns with sarcastic
jokes and altercation. Of this kind is the Cyclop of Euripides, in which Ulysses
is the principal actor. The Romans also had their Atellanæ or interludes of the
same nature, so called from the city of Atella, where they were first acted; but
these were highly polished in comparison of the original entertainment, which
was altogether rude and innocent. Indeed the Cyclop itself, though composed
by the accomplished Euripides, abounds with such impurity as ought not to
appear on the stage of any civilized nation.

It is very remarkable, that the Atellanæ, which were in effect tragi-
comedies, grew into such esteem among the Romans, that the performers in
these pieces enjoyed several privileges which were refused to the ordinary
actors. They were not obliged to unmask, like the other players, when their
action was disagreeable to the audience. They were admitted into the army,
and enjoyed the privileges of free citizens, without incurring that disgrace
which was affixed to the characters of other actors. The poet Laberius, who
was of the equestrian order, being pressed by Julius Cæsar to act a part in his
own performance, complied with great reluctance, and complained of the
dishonor he had incurred, in his proverb preserved by Macrobius, which is one
of the most elegant morsels of antiquity.

Tragedy and comedy flowed from the same fountain, though their streams were soon divided. The same entertainment which, under the name of *tragedy*, was rudely exhibited by clowns, for the prize of a goat, near some rural altar of Bacchus, assumed the appellation of *comedy* when it was transferred into cities, and represented with a little more decorum in a cart or wagon that strolled from street to street, as the name χωμῳδία implies, being derived from χώμη a street, and ὠδὴ a poem. To this origin Horace alludes in these lines:

> *Dicitur et plaustris vexisse poemata Thespis,*
> *Quæ canerent agerentque peruncti fœcibus ora.*

> Thespis, inventor of dramatic art,
> Convey'd his vagrant actors in a cart:
> High o'er the crowd the mimic tribe appear'd,
> And play'd and sung, with lees of wine besmear'd.

Thespis is called the inventor of the dramatic art, because he raised the subject from clownish altercation to the character and exploits of some hero: he improved the language and versification, and relieved the chorus by the dialogue of two actors. This was the first advance towards that consummation of genius and art, which constitutes what is now called a perfect tragedy. The next great improver was Æschylus, of whom the same critic says:

> *Post hunc personæ pallæque repertor honestæ*
> *Æschylus, et modicis instravit pulpita tignis;*
> *Et docuit magnumque loqui, nitique cothurno.*

> Then Æschylus a decent vizard us'd;
> Built a low stage; the flowing robe diffus'd.
> In language more sublime two actors rage,
> And in the graceful buskin tread the stage.

The dialogue which Thespis introduced was called the *episode*, because it was an addition to the former subject, namely, the praises of Bacchus; so that now tragedy consisted of two distinct parts, independent of each other; the old recitative, which was the chorus, sung in honor of the gods; and the episode, which turned upon the adventures of some hero. This episode being found very agreeable to the people, Æschylus, who lived about half a century after Thespis, still improved the drama, united the chorus to the episode, so as to make them both parts or members of one fable, multiplied the actors, contrived the stage, and introduced the decorations of the theatre; so that Sophocles, who succeeded Æschylus, had but one step to surmount in order to bring the drama to perfection. Thus tragedy was gradually detached from its original institution, which was entirely religious. The priests of Bacchus loudly complained of this innovation by means of the episode, which was foreign to the intention of the chorus: and hence arose the proverb of *Nihil ad*

Dionysium, "Nothing to the purpose." Plutarch himself mentions the episode, as a perversion of tragedy from the honor of the gods to the passions of men. But, notwithstanding all opposition, the new tragedy succeeded to admiration; because it was found the most pleasing vehicle of conveying moral truths, of meliorating the heart, and extending the interests of humanity.

Comedy, according to Aristotle, is the younger sister of tragedy. As the first originally turned upon the praises of the gods, the latter dwelt on the follies and vices of mankind. Such, we mean, was the scope of that species of poetry which acquired the name of comedy, in contradiction to the tragic muse; for in the beginning they were the same. The foundation upon which comedy was built, we have already explained to be the practice of satirical repartee or altercation, in which individuals exposed the follies and frailties of each other on public occasions of worship and festivity.

The first regular plan of comedy is said to have been the Margites of Homer, exposing the idleness and folly of a worthless character; but of this performance we have no remains. That division which is termed the ancient comedy, belongs to the labors of Eupolis, Cratinus, and Aristophanes, who were contemporaries, and flourished at Athens about four hundred and thirty years before the Christian era. Such was the license of the muse at this period, that far from lashing vice in general characters, she boldly exhibited the exact portrait of every individual who had rendered himself remarkable or notorious by his crimes, folly, or debauchery. She assumed every circumstance of his external appearance, his very attire, air, manner, and even his name; according to the observation of Horace,

> *Poetæ*
> ———*quorum comœdia prisca virorum est:*
> *Si quis erat dignus describi, quòd malus, aut fur,*
> *Quòd mœchus foret, aut sicarius, aut alioqui*
> *Famosus, multâ cum libertate notabant.*
>
> The comic poets, in its earliest age,
> Who form'd the manners of the Grecian stage—
> Was there a villain who might justly claim
> A better right of being damn'd to fame,
> Rake, cut-throat, thief, whatever was his crime,
> They boldly stigmatiz'd the wretch in rhyme."

Eupolis is said to have satirized Alcibiades in this manner, and to have fallen a sacrifice to the resentment of that powerful Athenian; but others say he was drowned in the Hellespont, during a war against the Lacedemonians; and that in consequence of this accident the Athenians passed a decree, that no poet should ever bear arms.

The comedies of Cratinus are recommended by Quintilian for their eloquence; and Plutarch tells us, that even Pericles himself could not escape the censure of this poet.

Aristophanes, of whom there are eleven comedies still extant, enjoyed such a pre-eminence of reputation, that the Athenians by a public decree honored him with a crown made of a consecrated olive-tree, which grew in the citadel, for his care and success in detecting and exposing the vices of those who governed the commonwealth. Yet this poet, whether impelled by mere wantonness of genius, or actuated by malice and envy, could not refrain from employing the shafts of his ridicule against Socrates, the most venerable character of Pagan antiquity. In the comedy of the "Clouds," this virtuous philosopher was exhibited on the stage under his own name, in a cloak exactly resembling that which Socrates wore, in a mask modelled from his features, disputing publicly on the nature of right and wrong. This was undoubtedly an instance of the most flagrant licentiousness; and what renders it the more extraordinary, the audience received it with great applause, even while Socrates himself sat publicly in the theatre. The truth is, the Athenians were so fond of ridicule, that they relished it even when employed against the gods themselves, some of whose characters were very roughly handled by Aristophanes and his rivals in reputation.

We might here draw a parallel between the inhabitants of Athens and the natives of England, in point of constitution, genius, and disposition. Athens was a free state like England, that piqued itself upon the influence of the democracy. Like England, its wealth and strength depended upon its maritime power; and it generally acted as umpire in the disputes that arose among its neighbors. The people of Athens, like those of England, were remarkably ingenious, and made great progress in the arts and sciences. They excelled in poetry, history, philosophy, mechanics, and manufactures; they were acute, discerning, disputatious, fickle, wavering, rash, and combustible, and, above all other nations in Europe, addicted to ridicule; a character which the English inherit in a very remarkable degree.

If we may judge from the writings of Aristophanes, his chief aim was to gratify the spleen and excite the mirth of his audience; of an audience too, that would seem to have been uninformed by taste, and altogether ignorant of decorum; for his pieces are replete with the most extravagant absurdities, virulent slander, impiety, impurities, and low buffoonery. The comic muse, not contented with being allowed to make free with the gods and philosophers, applied her scourge so severely to the magistrates of the commonwealth, that it was thought proper to restrain her within bounds by a law, enacting, that no person should be stigmatized under his real name; and thus the chorus was silenced. In order to elude the penalty of this law, and gratify the taste of the people, the poets began to substitute fictitious names, under which they exhibited particular characters in such lively colors, that the resemblance could not possibly be mistaken or overlooked. This practice gave rise to what is called the *middle comedy*, which was but of short duration; for the legislature, perceiving that the first law had not removed the grievance against which it was provided, issued a second ordinance, forbidding, under severe penalities, any real or family occurrences to be represented. This restriction was the immediate cause of improving comedy into a general mirror, held forth to reflect the various follies and foibles incident to human nature; a species of writing called the *new comedy,* introduced by Diphilus and Menander, of whose works nothing but a few fragments remain.

ON POETRY
AS DISTINGUISHED FROM OTHER WRITING

Having communicated our sentiments touching the origin of poetry, by tracing tragedy and comedy to their common source, we shall now endeavor to point out the criteria by which poetry is distinguished from every other species of writing. In common with other arts, such as statuary and painting, it comprehends imitation, invention, composition, and enthusiasm. Imitation is, indeed, the basis of all the liberal arts: invention and enthusiasm constitute genius, in whatever manner it may be displayed. Eloquence of all sorts admits of enthusiasm. Tully says, an orator should be "vehemens ut procella, excitatus ut torrens, incensus ut fulmen; tonat, fulgurat, et rapidis eloquentiæ fluctibus cuncta proruit et proturbat." "Violent as a tempest, impetuous as a torrent, and glowing intense like the red bolt of heaven: he thunders, lightens, overthrows, and bears down all before him, by the irresistible tide of eloquence." This is the *mens divinior atque os magna sanaturum* of Horace. This is the talent,

> ——*Meum qui pectus inaniter angit,*
> *Irritat, mulcet, falsis terroribus implet:*
> *Ut magus.*

> With passions not my own who fires my heart;
> Who with unreal terrors fills my breast,
> As with a magic influence possess'd."

We are told, that Michael Angelo Buonaroti used to work at his statues in a fit of enthusiasm, during which he made the fragments of the stone fly about him with surprising violence. The celebrated Lulli being one day blamed for setting nothing to music but the languid verses of Quinault, was animated with the reproach, and running in a fit of enthusiasm to his harpsichord, sung in recitative, and accompanied four pathetic lines from the Iphigenia of Racine, with such expression as filled the hearers with astonishment and horror.

Though versification be one of the criteria that distinguish poetry from prose, yet it is not the sole mark of distinction. Were the histories of Polybius and Livy simply turned into verse, they would not become poems; because they would be destitute of those figures, embellishments, and flights of imagination, which display the poet's art and invention. On the other hand, we have many productions that justly lay claim to the title of poetry, without having the advantage of versification; witness the Psalms of David, the Song of Solomon, with many beautiful hymns, descriptions, and rhapsodies, to be found in different parts of the Old Testament, some of them the immediate productions of divine inspiration; witness the Celtic fragments which have lately appeared in the English language, and are certainly replete with poetical merit. But though good versification alone will not constitute poetry, bad versification alone will certainly degrade and render disgustful the sublimest sentiments and finest flowers of imagination. This humiliating power of bad verse appears in many translations of the ancient poets; in Ogilby's Homer, Trapp's Virgil, and frequently in Creech's Horace. This last indeed is not wholly devoid of spirit; but it seldom rises above mediocrity, and, as Horace says,

> ——*Mediocribus esse poetis*
> *Non homines, non Di, non concessere columnæ.*

> But gods, and men, and letter'd post denies,
> That poets ever are of middling size.

How is that beautiful ode, beginning with "Justum et tenacem propositi virum," chilled and tamed by the following translation;

> He who by principle is sway'd,
>   In truth and justice still the same,
> Is neither of the crowd afraid,
>   Though civil broils the state inflame;
> Nor to a haughty tyrant's frown will stoop,
> Nor to a raging storm, when all the winds are up.
> Should nature with convulsions shake,
>   Struck with the fiery bolts of Jove,
> The final doom and dreadful crack
>   Cannot his constant courage move.

That long Alexandrine—"Nor to a raging storm, when all the winds are up," is drawling, feeble, swollen with a pleonasm or tautology, as well as deficient in the rhyme; and as for the "dreadful crack," in the next stanza, instead of exciting terror, it conveys a low and ludicrous idea. How much more elegant and energetic is this paraphrase of the same ode, inserted in one of the volumes of Hume's History of England.

> The man whose mind on virtue bent,
> Pursues some greatly good intent
>   With undiverted aim,
> Serene beholds the angry crowd;
> Nor can their clamors fierce and loud
>   His stubborn honor tame.

> Nor the proud tyrant's fiercest threat,
> Nor storms that from their dark retreat
>   The lawless surges wake;
> Nor Jove's dread bolt, that shakes the pole,

> The firmer purpose of his soul
>   With all its powers can shake.
>
> "Should nature's frame in ruins fall,
> And Chaos o'er the sinking ball
>   Resume primeval sway,
> His courage chance and fate defies,
> Nor feels the wreck of earth and skies
>   Obstruct its destin'd sway."

If poetry exists independent of versification, it will naturally be asked, how then is it to be distinguished? Undoubtedly, by its own peculair expression: it has a language of its own, which speaks so feelingly to the heart, and so pleasingly to the imagination, that its meaning cannot possibly be misunderstood by any person of delicate sensations. It is a species of painting with words, in which the figures are happily conceived, ingeniously arranged, affectingly expressed, and recommended with all the warmth and harmony of coloring: it consists of imagery, description, metaphors, similes, and sentiments, adapted with propriety to the subject, so contrived and executed as to soothe the ear, surprise and delight the fancy, mend and melt the heart, elevate the mind, and please the understanding. According to Flaccus:

> *Aut prodesse volunt, aut delectare poetæ;*
> *Aut simul et jucunda et idonea dicere vitæ.*
>
> Poets would profit or delight mankind,
> And with th' amusing show th' instructive join'd.
>
> *Omne tulit punctum, qui miscuit utile dulci*
> *Lectorem delectando, pariterque monendo*
>
> Profit and pleasure mingled thus with art,
> To soothe the fancy and improve the heart.

Tropes and figures are likewise liberally used in rhetoric; and some of the most celebrated orators have owned themselves much indebted to the poets. Theophrastus expressly recommends the poets for this purpose. From their source, the spirit and energy of the pathetic, the sublime, and the beautiful, are derived. But these figures must be more sparingly used in rhetoric than in poetry, and even then mingled with argumentation, and a detail of facts altogether different from poetical narration. The poet, instead of simply relating the incident, strikes off a glowing picture of the scene, and exhibits it in the most lively colors to the eye of the imagination. "It is reported that Homer was blind," says Tully in his Tusculan Questions, "yet his poetry is no other than painting. What country, what climate, what ideas, battles, commotions, and contests of men, as well as wild beasts, has he not painted in such a manner as to bring before our eyes those very scenes, which he himself could not behold!" We cannot, therefore, subscribe to the opinion of some ingenious critics, who have blamed Mr. Pope for deviating in some instances from the simplicity of Homer, in his translation of the Iliad and Odyssey. For example, the Grecian bard says simply, the sun rose; and his translator gives us a beautiful picture of the sun rising. Homer mentions a person who played upon the lyre; the translator sets him before us warbling to the silver strings. If this be a deviation, it is at the same time an improvement. Homer himself, as Cicero observes above, is full of this kind of painting, and particularly fond of description, even in situations where the action seems to require haste. Neptune, observing from Samothrace the discomfiture of the Grecians before Troy, flies to their assistance, and might have been wafted thither in half a line: but the bard describes him, first, descending the mountain on which he sat; secondly, striding towards his palace at Ægæ, and yoking his horses; thirdly, he describes him putting on his armor; and lastly, ascending his car, and driving along the surface of the sea. Far from being disgusted by these delays, we are delighted with the particulars of the description. Nothing can be more sublime than the circumstance of the mountain's trembling beneath the footsteps of an immortal

> ——Τρέμε δ' οὔρεα μακρὰ καὶ ὕλη
> Ποσσὶν ὑπ' ἀθανάτοισι Ποσειδάωνος ἰόντος.

But this passage to the Grecian fleet is altogether transporting.

> Βῆ δ' ἐλάαν ἐπὶ κύματ, κ. τ. λ.

> He mounts the car, the golden scourge applies,
> He sits superior, and the chariot flies;
> His whirling wheels the glassy surface sweep:
> Th' enormous monsters, rolling o'er the deep,
> Gamble around him on the watery way,
> And heavy whales in awkward measures play:
> The sea subsiding spreads a level plain,
> Exults and crowns the monarch of the main:
> The parting waves before his coursers fly,
> The wond'ring waters leave his axle dry.——

With great veneration for the memory of Mr. Pope, we cannot help objecting to some lines of this translation. We have no idea of the sea's exulting and crowning Neptune, after it had subsided into a level plain. There is no such image in the original. Homer says, the whales exulted, and knew or owned their king; and that the sea parted with joy: γηθοσύνη δὲ θάλασσα διίστατο. Neither is there a word of the wondering waters: we therefore think the lines might be thus altered to advantage.

> They knew and own'd the monarch of the main:
> The sea subsiding spreads a level plain:
> The curling waves before his coursers fly;
> The parting surface leaves his brazen axle dry.

Besides the metaphors, similes, and allusions of poetry, there is an infinite variety of tropes, or turns of expression, occasionally disseminated through works of genius, which serve to animate the whole, and distinguish the glowing effusions of real inspiration from the cold efforts of mere science. These tropes consist of a certain happy choice and arrangement of words, by which ideas are artfully disclosed in a great variety of attitudes, of epithets, and compound epithets; of sounds collected in order to echo the sense conveyed; of apostrophes; and above all, the enchanting use of the prosopopœia, which is a kind of magic, by which the poet gives life and motion to every inanimate part of nature. Homer, describing the wrath of Agamemnon, in the first book of the Iliad, strikes off a glowing image in two words:

ὄσσε δ' οἱ πυρὶ λαμπετο ουντι ἐΐκτην.

And from his eye-balls *flash'd the living fire.*

This indeed is a figure, which has been copied by Virgil, and almost all the poets of every age—*oculis* micat *acribus ignis*—ignescunt iræ: *auris dolor ossibus* ardet. Milton, describing Satan in Hell, says,

> With head uplift above the wave, and eye
> That *sparkling blaz'd!*

> He spake: and to confirm his words out flew
> Milions of flaming swords, drawn from the thighs
> Of mighty cherubim. The sudden *blaze*
> Far round *illumin'd* Hell——

There are certain words in every language particularly adapted to the poetical expression; some from the image or idea they convey to the imagination; and some from the effect they have upon the ear. The first are truly *figurative;* and others may be called *emphatical.* Rollin observes, that Virgil has upon many occasions poetized (if we may be allowed the expression) a whole sentence by means of the same word, which is *pendere.*

> *Ite meæ, felix quondam pecus, ite capellæ,*
> *Non ego vos posthac, viridi projectus in antro,*
> *Dumosâ pendere procul de rupe videbo.*

> At ease reclin'd beneath the verdant shade,
> No more shall I behold my happy flock
> Aloft *hang* browsing on the tufted rock.

Here the word *pendere* wonderfully improves the landscape, and renders the whole passage beautifully picturesque. The same figurative verb we meet with in many different parts of the Æneid.

> *Hi summo in fluctu pendent, his unda dehiscens*
> *Terram inter fluctus aperit.*

> These on the mountain billow *hung;* to those
> The *yawning waves* the yellow sand disclose.

In this instance, the words *pendent* and *dehiscens, hung* and *yawning,* are equally poetical. Addison seems to have had this passage in his eye, when he wrote his Hymn, which is inserted in the Spectator:

> For though in dreadful whirls we *hung,*
> High on the broken wave.

And in another piece of a like nature, in the same collection:

> Thy providence my life sustain'd
> And all my wants redress'd,
> When in the silent womb I lay,
> And *hung* upon the breast.

Shakspeare, in his admired description of Dover cliff, uses the same expression:

> half way down
> *Hangs* one that gathers samphire—dreadful trade!

Nothing can be more beautiful than the following picture, in which Milton has introduced the same expressive tint

> he, on his side,
> Leaning half rais'd, with looks of cordial love
> *Hung* over her enamor'd.

We shall give one example from Virgil, to show in what a variety of scenes it may appear with propriety and effect. In describing the progress of Dido's passion for Æneas, the Poet says,

> *Iliacos iterùm demens audire labores*
> *Exposcit, pendetque iterùm narrantis ab ore.*

> The woes of Troy once more she begg'd to hear;
> Once more the mournful tale employed his tongue,
> While in fond rapture on his lips she *hung.*

The reader will perceive in all these instances, that no other word could be substituted with equal energy; indeed no other word could be used without degrading the sense, and defacing the image.

There are many other verbs of poetical import fetched from nature and from art, which the poet uses to advantage, both in a literal and metaphorical sense; and these have been always translated for the same purpose from one language to another; such as *quasso, concutio, cio, suscito, lenio, sævio, mano, fluo, ardeo, mico, aro,* to shake, to wake, to rouse, to soothe, to rage, to flow, to shine or blaze, to plough.—Quassantia *tectum limina—Æneas, casu* concussus *acerbo—Ære ciere viros, Martemque* accendere *cantu—Æneas* acuit Martem *et se* suscitat *irâ—Impium* lenite *clamorem.* Lenibat *curas—Ne* sævi *magna sacerdos—Sudor ad imos* manabat *solos—Suspensæque diu lachrymæ* fluxere *per ora—Juvenali* ardebat *amore—*Micat *æreus ensis—Nullum maris æquor* arandum. It will be unnecessary to insert examples of the same nature from the English poets.

The words we term *emphatical,* are such as by their sound express the sense they are intended to convey; and with these the Greek abounds, above all other languages, not only from its natural copiousness, flexibility, and significance, but also from the variety of its dialects, which enables a writer to vary his terminations occasionally as the nature of the subject requires, without offending the most delicate ear, or incurring the imputation of adopting vulgar provincial expressions. Every smatterer in Greek can repeat

Βῆ ἀκέων παρὰ Θῖνα πολυφλοίσβοῖο Θαλάσσης,

in which the two last words wonderfully echo to the sense, conveying the idea of the sea dashing on the shore. How much more significant in sound than that beautiful image of Shakspeare—

The sea that on th' unnumber'd pebbles beats.

And yet, if we consider the strictness of propriety, this last expression would seem to have been selected on purpose to concur with the other circumstances which are brought together to ascertain the vast height of Dover cliff; for the poet adds, "cannot be heard so high." The place where Gloster stood was so high above the surface of the sea, that the φλοίσβος, or *dashing,* could not be heard; and therefore an enthusiastic admirer of Shakspeare might with some plausibility affirm, the poet had chosen an expression in which that sound is not at all conveyed.

In the very same page of Homer's Iliad we meet with two other striking instances of the same sort of beauty; Apollo, incensed at the insults his priest had sustained, descends from the top of Olympus, with his bow and quiver rattling on his shoulder as he moved along:

Ἔκλαγξαν δ' ἄρ' οἴστω ἐπ' ὤμων.

Here the sound of the word Ἔχλαγξαν admirably expresses the clanking of armor; as the third line after this surprisingly imitates the twanging of a bow.

Δεινή δὲ κλαγγή γένετ' ἀργυρέοιο βιοῖο.

In shrill-toned murmurs sung the twanging bow.

Many beauties of the same kind are scattered through Homer, Pindar, and Theocritus, such as the βομβεῦσα μέλισσα, *susurrans apicula;* the ἁδὺ ψιθύρισμα, *dulcem susurrum;* and the μελίσδεται, for the sighing of the pine.

The Latin language teems with sounds adapted to every situation, and the English is not destitute of this significant energy. We have the *cooing* turtle, the *sighing* reed, the *warbling* rivulet, the *sliding* stream, the *whispering* breeze, the glance, the gleam, the flash, the *bickering* flame, the *dashing* wave, the *gushing* spring, the *howling* blast, the *rattling* storm, the *pattering* shower, the *crimp* earth, the *mouldering* tower, the *twanging* bowstring, the *clanging* arms, the *clanking* chains, the *twinkling* stars, the *tinkling* chords, the *trickling* drops, the *twittering* swallow, the *cawing* rook, the *screeching* owl; and a thousand other words and epithets, wonderfully suited to the sense they imply.

Among the select passages of poetry which we shall insert by way of illustration, the reader will find instances of all the different tropes and figures which the best authors have adopted in the variety of their poetical works, as well as of the apostrophe, abrupt transition, repetition, and prosopopæia.

In the mean time it will be necessary still farther to analyze those principles which constitute the essence of poetical merit; to display those delightful parterres that teem with the fairest flowers of imagination; and distinguish between the gaudy offspring of a cold insipid fancy, and the glowing progeny, diffusing sweets, produced and invigorated by the sun of genius.

ON THE USE OF METAPHORS

Of all the implements of poetry, the Metaphor is the most generally and successfully used, and indeed may be termed the Muse's caduceus, by the power of which she enchants all nature. The metaphor is a shorter simile, or rather a kind of magical coat, by which the same idea assumes a thousand different appearances. Thus the word *plough,* which originally belongs to agriculture, being metaphorically used, represents the motion of a ship at sea, and the effects of old age upon the human countenance—

—Plough'd the bosom of the deep—
And time had plough'd his venerable front.

Almost every verb, noun substantive, or term of art in any language, may be in this manner applied to a variety of subjects with admirable effect; but the danger is in sowing metaphors too thick, so as to distract the imagination of the reader, and incur the imputation of deserting nature, in order to hunt after conceits. Every day produces poems of all kinds so inflated with metaphor, that they may be compared to the gaudy bubbles blown up from a solution of soap. Longinus is of opinion, that a multitude of metaphors is never excusable, except in those cases when the passions are roused, and like a winter torrent rush down impetuous, sweeping them with collective force along. He brings an instance of the following quotation from Demosthenes: "Men," says he, "profligates, miscreants, and flatterers, who having severally preyed upon the bowels of their country, at length betrayed her liberty, first to Philip, and now again to Alexander; who, placing the chief felicity of life in the indulgence of infamous lusts and appetites, overturned in the dust that freedom and independence which was the chief aim and end of all our worthy ancestors."

Aristotle and Theophrastus seem to think it is rather too bold and hazardous to use metaphors so freely, without interposing some mitigating phrase, such as, "If I may be allowed the expression," or some equivalent excuse. At the same time, Longinus finds fault with Plato for hazarding some metaphors, which indeed appear to be equally affected and extravagant, when he says, "the government of a state should not resemble a bowl of hot fermenting wine, but a cool and moderate beverage *chastised by the sober deity*,"—a metaphor that signifies nothing more than "mixed or lowered with water." Demetrius Phalereus justly observes, that "though a judicious use of metaphors wonderfully raises, sublimes, and adorns oratory or elocution, yet they should seem to flow naturally from the subject; and too great a redundancy of them inflates the discourse to a mere rhapsody." The same observation will hold in poetry; and the more liberal or sparing use of them will depend in a great measure on the nature of the subject.

Passion itself is very figurative, and often bursts out into metaphors; but in touching the pathos, the poet must be perfectly well acquainted with the emotions of the human soul, and carefully distinguish between those metaphors which rise glowing from the heart, and those cold conceits which are engendered in the fancy. Should one of these last unfortunately intervene, it will be apt to destroy the whole effect of the most pathetical incident or situation. Indeed, it requires the most delicate taste, and a consummate knowledge of propriety, to employ metaphors in such a manner as to avoid what the ancients call the τὸ ψυχϱὸν, the *frigid,* or false sublime. Instances of this kind were frequent even among the correct ancients. Sappho herself is blamed for using the hyperbole λευχοτέϱοι χιόνος, *whiter than snow.* Demetrius is so nice as to be disgusted at the simile of *swift as the wind;* though in speaking of a race-horse, we know from experience that this is not even an hyperbole. He would have had more reason to censure that kind of metaphor which Aristotle styles χατ᾽ ἐνέϱγειαν, exhibiting things inanimate as endued with sense and reason; such as that of the sharp-pointed arrow, *eager* to take wing among the crowd. Ὁ᾽ ξυβελὴς χαϑ᾽ ὅμιλον ἐπιπτέσϑαι μενεαίνων. Not but that, in descriptive poetry, this figure is often allowed and admired. The *cruel* sword, the *ruthless* dagger, the *ruffian* blast, are epithets which frequently occur. The *faithful* bosom of the earth, the *joyous* boughs, the trees that *admire their images* reflected in the stream, and many other examples of this kind, are found disseminated through the works of our best modern poets: yet still they must be sheltered under the privilege of the *poetica licentïa;* and, except in poetry, they would give offence.

More chaste metaphors are freely used in all kinds of writing; more sparingly in history, and more abundantly in rhetoric: we have seen that Plato indulges in them even to excess. The orations of Demosthenes are animated and even inflamed with metaphors, some of them so bold as even to entail upon him the censure of the critics. Τότε τῷ Πυϑωνι τῷ ϱήτοϱι ἔοντι χαϑ᾽ ὁμῶη.—"Then I did not yield to Python the orator, when he *overflowed* you with a tide of eloquence." Cicero is still more liberal in the use of them; he ransacks all nature, and pours forth a redundancy of figures, even with a lavish hand. Even the chaste Xenophon, who generally illustrates his subject by way of simile, sometimes ventures to produce an expressive metaphor, such as, "part of the phalanx *fluctuated* in the march;" and indeed nothing can be more significant than this word ἐξεχύμηνε, to represent a body of men staggered, and on the point of giving way. Armstrong has used the word *fluctuate* with admirable efficacy, in his philosophical poem, entitled, "The Art of Preserving Health."

> O when the growling winds contend, and all
> The sounding forest *fluctuates* in the storm,
> To sink in warm repose, and hear the din
> Howl o'er the steady battlements

The word *fluctuate* on this occasion not only exhibits an idea of struggling, but also echoes to the sense like the ἔφριξεν δὲ μαχὴ of Homer; which, by the by, it is impossible to render into English, for the verb φρίσσω signifies not only to stand erect like prickles, as a grove of lances, but also to make a noise like the crashing of armor, the hissing of javelins, and the splinters of spears.

Over and above an excess of figures, a young author is apt to run into a confusion of mixed metaphors, which leave the sense disjointed, and distract the imagination. Shakspeare himself is often guilty of these irregularities. The soliloquy in Hamlet, which we have so often heard extolled in terms of admiration, is, in our opinion, a heap of absurdities, whether we consider the situation, the sentiment, the argumentation, or the poetry. Hamlet is informed by the Ghost, that his father was murdered, and therefore he is tempted to murder himself, even after he had promised to take vengeance on the usurper, and expressed the utmost eagerness to achieve this enterprise. It does not appear that he had the least reason to wish for death; but every motive which may be supposed to influence the mind of a young prince, concurred to render life desirable—revenge towards the usurper; love for the fair Ophelia; and the ambition of reigning. Besides, when he had an opportunity of dying without being accessary to his own death; when he had nothing to do but, in obedience to his uncle's command, to allow himself to be conveyed quietly to England, where he was sure of suffering death; instead of amusing himself with meditations on mortality, he very wisely consulted the means of self-preservation, turned the tables upon his attendants, and returned to Denmark. But granting him to have been reduced to the lowest state of despondence, surrounded with nothing but horror and despair, sick of this life and eager to tempt futurity, we shall see how far he argues like a philosopher.

In order to support this general charge against an author so universally held in veneration, whose very errors have helped to sanctify his character among the multitude, we will descend to particulars, and analyze this famous soliloquy.

Hamlet, having assumed the disguise of madness, as a cloak under which he might the more effectually revenge his father's death upon the murderer and usurper, appears alone upon the stage in a pensive and melancholy attitude, and communes with himself in these words:

> To be, or not to be? that is the question:—
> Whether 'tis nobler in the mind, to suffer

The slings and arrows of outrageous fortune,
Or to take arms against a sea of troubles,
And by opposing, end them?—To die,—to sleep,—
No more; and, by a sleep, to say we end
The heart-ache, and the thousand natural shocks
That flesh is heir to,—'tis a consummation
Devoutly to be wish'd. To die;—to sleep;—
To sleep! perchance to dream;—ay, there's the rub;
For in that sleep of death what dreams may come,
When we have shuffled off this mortal coil,
Must give us pause.——There's the respect
That makes calamity of so long life;
For who would bear the whips and scorns of time,
The oppressor's wrong, the proud man's contumely,
The pangs of despis'd love, the law's delay,
The insolence of office, and the spurns
That patient merit of the unworthy takes,
When he himself might his *quietus* make
With a bare bodkin? Who would fardels bear,
To groan and sweat under a weary life,
But that the dread of something after death,—
That undiscover'd country, from whose bourne
No traveller returns,—puzzles the will;
And makes us rather bear those ills we have,
Than fly to others that we know not of?
Thus conscience does make cowards of us all;
And thus the native hue of resolution
Is sicklied o'er with the pale cast of thought;
And enterprises of great pith and moment,
With this regard, their currents turn awry,
And lose the name of action.

We have already observed, that there is not any apparent circumstance in the fate or situation of Hamlet, that should prompt him to harbor one thought of self-murder; and therefore these expressions of despair imply an impropriety in point of character. But supposing his condition was truly desperate, and he saw no possibility of repose but in the uncertain harbor of death, let us see in what manner he argues on that subject. The question is, "To be, or not to be;" to die by my own hand, or live and suffer the miseries of life. He proceeds to explain the alternative in these terms, "Whether 'tis nobler in the mind to suffer, or endure, the frowns of fortune, or to take arms, and by opposing, end them." Here he deviates from his first proposition, and death is no longer the question. The only doubt is, whether he will stoop to misfortune, or exert his faculties in order to surmount it. This surely is the obvious meaning, and indeed the only meaning that can be implied in these words,

> Whether 'tis nobler in the mind, to suffer
> The slings and arrows of outrageous fortune,
> Or to take arms against a sea of troubles,
> And by opposing, end them.

He now drops this idea, and reverts to his reasoning on death, in the course of which he owns himself deterred from suicide by the thoughts of what may follow death:

> ——the dread of something after death,—
> That undiscover'd country, from whose bourne
> No traveller returns.

This might be a good argument in a Heathen or Pagan, and such indeed Hamlet really was; but Shakspeare has already represented him as a good Catholic, who must have been acquainted with the truths of revealed religion, and says expressly in this very play,

> ——had not the Everlasting fix'd
> His canon 'gainst self-murder."

Moreover, he had just been conversing with his father's spirit, piping hot from purgatory, which we would presume is not within the *bourne* of this world. The dread of what may happen after death, says he,

> Makes us rather bear those ills we have,
> Than fly to others that we know not of.

This declaration at least implies some knowledge of the other world, and expressly asserts, that there must be *ills* in that world, though what kind of *ills* they are, we do not know. The argument, therefore, may be reduced to this lemma: this world abounds with *ills* which I feel; the other world abounds with *ills*, the nature of which I do not know; therefore, I will rather bear those *ills* I have, "than fly to *others* which I know not of;" a deduction amounting to a certainty, with respect to the only circumstance that should create a doubt, namely, whether in death he should rest from his misery; and if he was certain there were evils in the next world, as well as in this, he had no room to reason at all about the matter. What alone could justify his thinking on the subject, would have been the hope of flying from the ills of this world, without encountering any *others* in the next.

Nor is Hamlet more accurate in the following reflection:

> Thus conscience does make cowards of us all.

A bad conscience will make us cowards; but a good conscience will make us brave. It does not appear that any thing lay heavy on his conscience; and from the premises we cannot help inferring, that conscience in this case was entirely out of the question. Hamlet was deterred from suicide by a full conviction, that, in flying from one sea of troubles which he did know, he should fall into another which he did not know.

His whole chain of reasoning, therefore, seems inconsistent and incongruous. "I am doubtful whether I should live, or do violence upon my own life; for I know not whether it is more honorable to bear misfortune patiently, than to exert myself in opposing misfortune, and by opposing, end it." Let us throw it into the form of a syllogism, it will stand thus: "I am oppressed with ills; I know not whether it is more honorable to bear those ills patiently, or to end them by taking arms against them; *ergo,* I am doubtful whether I should slay myself or live. To die, is no more than to sleep; and to *say* that by a sleep we end the heartache," &c., "'tis a consummation devoutly to be wished." Now to *say it,* was of no consequence unless it had been true." "I am afraid of the dreams that may happen in that sleep of death; and I choose rather to bear those ills I have in this life, than to fly to *other ills* in that undiscovered country, from whose bourne no traveller ever returns. I have ills that are almost insupportable in this life. I know not what is in the next, because it is an undiscovered country: *ergo,* I had rather bear those ills I have, than fly to others which I know not of." Here the conclusion is by no means warranted by the premises. "I am sore afflicted in this life; but I will rather bear the afflictions of this life, than plunge myself in the afflictions of another life; *ergo,* conscience makes cowards of us all." But this conclusion would justify the logician in saying, *negatur consequens;* for it is entirely detached from the major and minor proposition.

This soliloquy is not less exceptionable in the propriety of expression, than in the chain of argumentation. "To die—to sleep—no more," contains an ambiguity, which all the art of punctuation cannot remove; for it may signify that "to die," is to sleep no more; or the expression "no more," may be considered as an abrupt apostrophe in thinking, as if he meant to say "no more of that reflection."

"Ay, there's the rub," is a vulgarism beneath the dignity of Hamlet's character, and the words that follow leave the sense imperfect

> For in that sleep of death what dreams may come,
> When we have shuffled off this mortal coil,
> Must give us pause.

Not the dreams that might come, but the fear of what dreams might come, occasioned the pause or hesitation. Respect in the same line may be allowed to pass for consideration: but

> The oppressor's wrong, the proud man's contumely,

according to the invariable acceptation of the words wrong and contumely, can signify nothing but the wrongs sustained by the oppressor, and the contumely or abuse thrown upon the proud man; though it is plain that Shakspeare used them in a different sense: neither is the word spurn a substantive, yet as such he has inserted it in these lines:

> The insolence of office, and the spurns
> That patient merit of the unworthy takes.

If we consider the metaphors of the soliloquy, we shall find them jumbled together in a strange confusion.

If the metaphors were reduced to painting, we should find it a very difficult task, if not altogether impracticable, to represent, with any propriety, outrageous fortune using her slings and arrows, between which indeed there is no sort of analogy in nature. Neither can any figure be more ridiculously absurd than that of a man taking arms against the sea, exclusive of the incongruous medley of slings, arrows, and seas, justled within the compass of one reflection. What follows is a strange rhapsody of broken images of sleeping, dreaming, and shifting off a *coil,* which last conveys no idea that can be represented on canvas. A man may be exhibited shuffling off his garments or his chains; but how he should shuffle off a *coil,* which is another term for noise and tumult, we cannot comprehend. Then we have "long-lived calamity," and "time armed with whips and scorns;" and "patient merit spurned at by unworthiness," and "misery with a bare bodkin going to make his own *quietus,*" which at best is but a mean metaphor. These are followed by figures "sweating under fardels of burdens," "puzzled with doubts," "shaking with fears," and "flying from evils." Finally, we see "resolution sicklied o'er with pale thought," a conception like that of representing health by sickness; and a "current of pith turned awry so as to lose the name of action," which is both an error in fancy, and a solecism in sense. In a word, this soliloquy may be compared to the "*Ægri somnia,*" and the "*Tabula, cujus vanæ finguntur species.*"

But while we censure the chaos of broken, incongruous metaphors, we ought also to caution the young poet against the opposite extreme, of pursuing a metaphor until the spirit is quite exhausted in a succession of cold conceits; such as we see in the following letter, said to be sent by Tamerlane to the Turkish Emperor Bajazet. "Where is the monarch that dares oppose our arms? Where is the potentate who doth not glory in being numbered among our vassals? As for thee, descended from a Turcoman mariner, since the vessel of thy unbounded ambition hath been wrecked in the gulf of thy self-love, it would be proper that thou shouldest furl the sails of thy temerity, and cast the anchor of repentance in the port of sincerity and justice, which is the harbor of safety; lest the tempest of our vengeance make thee perish in the sea of that punishment thou hast deserved."

But if these labored conceits are ridiculous in poetry, they are still more inexcusable in prose: such as we find them frequently occur in Strada's Bellum Belgicum. "Vix descenderat à prætoria navi Cæsar, cùm fæda ilico exorta in portu tempestas; classem impetu disjecit, prætoriam hausit; quasi non vecturam ampliùs Cæsarem Cæsarisque fortunam." "Cæsar had scarcely set his feet on shore, when a terrible tempest arising, shattered the fleet even in the harbor, and sent to the bottom the prætorian ship, as if he resolved it should no longer carry Cæsar and his fortunes."

Yet this is modest in comparison of the following flowers: "Alii, pulsis è tormento catenis discerpti sectique, dimidiato corpore pugnabant sibi superstites, ac peremptæ partis ultores." "Others, dissevered and cut in twain by chain-shot, fought with one-half of their bodies that remained, in revenge of the other half that was slain."

Homer, Horace, and even the chaste Virgil, is not free from conceits. The latter, speaking of a man's hand cut off in battle, says:

> *Te decisa suum, Laride, dextera quærit;*
> *Semianimesque micant digiti, ferrumque retractant,*

> Thy hand, poor Laris, sought its absent lord,
> Thy dying fingers, quiv'ring on the plain,
> With starts convulsive grasp the steel in vain
> *Dryden.*

thus enduing the amputated hand with sense and volition. This, to be sure, is a violent figure, and hath been justly condemned by some accurate critics; but we think they are too severe in extending the same censure to some other passages in the most admired authors. Virgil, in his sixth Eclogue, says:

> *Omnia quæ, Phœbo quondam meditante, beatus*
> *Audiit Eurotas, jussitque ediscere lauros,*
> *Ille canit.*

> Whate'er, when Phœbus bless'd the Arcadian plain,
> Eurotas heard and taught his bays the strain,
> The senior sung—

And Pope has copied the conceit in his Pastorals:

> Thames heard the numbers as he flow'd along,
> And bade his willows learn the moving song.

Vida thus begins his first Eclogue:

> *Dicite, vos musæ, et juvenum memorate querelas;*
> *Dicite: nam motas ipsas ad carmina cautes,*
> *Et requiêsse suos perhibent vaga flumina cursus.*

> Say, heavenly muse, their youthful frays rehearse;
> Begin, ye daughters of immortal verse;
> Exulting rocks have own'd the power of song,
> And rivers listen'd as they flow'd along."

Racine adopts the same bold figure in his Phædra:

> Le flot qui l'apporta recule epouvanté:

> The wave that bore him, backwards shrunk appall'd.

Even Milton has indulged himself in the same license of expression:

> ——As when to them who sail
> Beyond the Cape of Hope, and now are past

> Mozambic, off at sea north-east winds blow
> Sabæan odor from the spicy shore
> Of Araby the blest; with such delay
> Well pleas'd they slack their course, and many a league,
> Cheer'd with the grateful smell, old Ocean smiles.

Shakspeare says:

> ——I've seen
> Th' ambitious ocean swell, and rage, and foam,
> To be exalted with the threat'ning clouds."

And indeed more correct writers, both ancient and modern, abound with the same kind of figure, which is reconciled to propriety, and even invested with beauty, by the efficacy of the prosopopœia, which personifies the object. Thus, when Virgil says Enipeus heard the songs of Apollo, he raises up, as by enchantment, the idea of a river god crowned with sedges, his head raised above the stream, and in his countenance the expression of pleased attention. By the same magic we see, in the couplet quoted from Pope's Pastorals, old father Thames leaning upon his urn, and listening to the poet's strain.

Thus, in the regions of poetry all nature, even the passions and affections of the mind, may be personified into picturesque figures for the entertainment of the reader. Ocean smiles or frowns, as the sea is calm or tempestuous; a Triton rules on every angry billow; every mountain has its Nymph, every stream its Naiad, every tree its Hamadryad, and every art its Genius. We cannot, therefore, assent to those who censure Thomson as licentious for using the following figure:

> O vale of bliss! O softly swelling hills!
> On which the power of cultivation lies,
> And joys to see the wonders of his toil.

We cannot conceive a more beautiful image than that of the genius of agriculture distinguished by the implements of his art, imbrowned with labor, glowing with health, crowned with a garland of foliage, flowers, and fruit, lying stretched at ease on the brow of a gentle swelling hill, and contemplating with pleasure the happy effects of his own industry.

Neither can we join issue against Shakspeare for his comparison, which hath likewise incurred the censure of the critics:

> ——The noble sister of Poplicola,
> The moon of Rome; chaste as the icicle
> That's curdled by the frost from purest snow,
> And hangs on Dian's temple

This is no more than illustrating a quality of the mind, by comparing it with a sensible object. If there is no impropriety in saying such a man is true as steel, firm as a rock, inflexible as an oak, unsteady as the ocean; or in describing a disposition cold as ice, or fickle as the wind; and these expressions are justified by constant practice; we shall hazard an assertion, that the comparison of a chaste woman to an icicle is proper and picturesque, as it obtains only in the circumstances of cold and purity: but that the addition of its being curdled from the purest snow, and hanging on the temple of Diana, the patroness of virginity, heightens the whole into a most beautiful simile, that gives a very respectable and amiable idea of the character in question.

The simile is no more than an extended metaphor, introduced to illustrate and beautify the subject; it ought to be apt, striking, properly pursued, and adorned with all the graces of poetical melody. But a simile of this kind ought never to proceed from the mouth of a person under any great agitation of spirit; such as a tragic character overwhelmed with grief, distracted by contending cares, or agonizing in the pangs of death. The language of passion will not admit simile, which is always the result of study and deliberation. We will not allow a hero the privilege of a dying swan, which is said to chant its approaching fate in the most melodious strain; and therefore, nothing can be more ridiculously unnatural, than the representation of a lover dying upon the stage with a labored simile in his mouth.

The orientals, whose language was extremely figurative, have been very careless in the choice of their similes; provided the resemblance obtained in one circumstance, they minded not whether they disagreed with the subject in every other respect. Many instances of this defect in congruity, may be culled from the most sublime parts of Scripture.

Homer has been blamed for the bad choice of his similes on some particular occasions. He compares Ajax to an ass in the Iliad, and Ulysses to a steak broiling on the coals in the Odyssey. His admirers have endeavored to excuse him, by reminding us of the simplicity of the age in which he wrote; but they have not been able to prove that any ideas of dignity or importance were, even in those days, affixed to the character of an ass, or the quality of a beef-collop; therefore, they were very improper illustrations for any situation in which a hero ought to be represented.

Virgil has degraded the wife of king Latinus, by comparing her, when she was actuated by the Fury, to a top which the boys lash for diversion. This, doubtless, is a low image, though in other respects the comparison is not destitute of propriety; but he is much more justly censured for the following simile, which has no sort of reference to the subject. Speaking of Turnus, he says:

>——*medio dux agmine Turnus*
>*Vertitur arma tenens, et toto vertice suprà est,*
>*Ceu septem surgens sedatis amnibus altus*
>*Per tacitum Ganges: aut pingui flumine Nilus*
>*Cum refluit campis, et jam se condidit alveo.*

>But Turnus, chief amidst the warrior train,
>In armor towers the tallest on the plain,
>The Ganges thus by seven rich streams supplied,

A mighty mass devolves in silent pride:
Thus Nilus pours from his prolific urn,
When from the fields o'erflow'd his vagrant streams return.

These, no doubt, are majestic images; but they bear no sort of resemblance to a hero glittering in armor at the head of his forces.

Horace has been ridiculed by some shrewd critics for this comparison, which, however, we think is more defensible than the former. Addressing himself to Munatius Plancus, he says:

> Albus ut obscuro deterget nubila cœlo
>   Sæpe Notus, neque parturit imbres
> Perpetuos; sic tu sapiens finire memento
>   Tristitiam, vitæque labores
> Molli, Plance, mero.

As Notus often, when the welkin lowers,
Sweeps off the clouds, nor teems perpetual showers,
So let thy wisdom, free from anxious strife,
In mellow wine dissolve the cares of life.

DUNKIN

The analogy, it must be confessed, is not very striking; but nevertheless, it is not altogether void of propriety. The poet reasons thus: as the south wind, though generally attended with rain, is often known to dispel the clouds, and render the weather serene; so do you, though generally on the rack of thought, remember to relax sometimes, and drown your cares in wine. As the south wind is not always moist, so you ought not always to be dry.

A few instances of inaccuracy, or mediocrity, can never derogate from the superlative merit of Homer and Virgil, whose poems are the great magazines, replete with every species of beauty and magnificence, particularly abounding with similes, which astonish, delight, and transport the reader.

Every simile ought not only to be well adapted to the subject, but also to include every excellence of description, and to be colored with the warmest tints of poetry. Nothing can be more happily hit off than the following in the Georgics, to which the poet compares Orpheus lamenting his lost Eurydice.

> *Qualis populeâ mœrens Philomela sub umbrâ*
> *Amissos queritur fœtus, quos durus arator*
> *Observans nido implumes detraxit; at illa*
> *Flet noctem, ramoque sedens miserabile carmen*
> *Integrat, et mœstis latè loca questibus implet.*

So Philomela, from th' umbrageous wood,
In strains melodious mourns her tender brood,
Snatch'd from the nest by some rude ploughman's hand,
On some lone bough the warbler takes her stand;

The live-long night she mourns the cruel wrong,
And hill and dale resound the plaintive song.

Here we not only find the most scrupulous propriety, and the happiest choice, in comparing the Thracian bard to Philomel the poet of the grove; but also the most beautiful description, containing a fine touch of the pathos, in which last particular indeed Virgil, in our opinion, excels all other poets, whether ancient or modern.

One would imagine that nature had exhausted itself, in order to embellish the poems of Homer, Virgil, and Milton, with similes and metaphors. The first of these very often uses the comparison of the wind, the whirlwind, the hail, the torrent, to express the rapidity of his combatants; but when he comes to describe the velocity of the immortal horses that drew the chariot of Juno, he raises his ideas to the subject, and, as Longinus observes, measures every leap by the whole breadth of the horizon.

> Ὅσσον δ᾽ ἠεροειδὲς ἀνὴρ ἴδεν ὀφθαλμοῖσιν
> Ἥμενος ἐν σκοπιῃ, λεύσσων ἐπὶ οἴνοπα πόντον,
> Τόσσον ἐπιθρώσκουσι θεῶν ὑψεχέες ἵπποι.

For as a watchman from some rock on high
O'er the wide main extends his boundless eye;
Through such a space of air with thund'ring sound
At ev'ry leap th' immortal coursers bound.

The celerity of this goddess seems to be a favorite idea with the poet; for in another place, he compares it to the thought of a traveller revolving in his mind the different places he had seen, and passing through them in imagination more swift than the lightning flies from east to west.

Homer's best similes have been copied by Virgil, and almost every succeeding poet, howsoever they may have varied in the manner of expression. In the third book of the Iliad, Menelaus seeing Paris, is compared to a hungry lion espying a hind or goat:

> Ωσε λέων ἐχάρη μεγάλῳ ἐπὶ σώματι κύρσας
> Εὑρὼν ἢ ἔλαφον κεραὸν, ἢ ἄγριον αἴγα, &c.

So joys the lion, if a branching deer
Or mountain goat his bulky prize appear;
In vain the youths oppose, the mastiffs bay,
The lordly savage rends the panting prey.
Thus fond of vengeance, with a furious bound
In clanging arms he leaps upon the ground.

The Mantuan bard, in the tenth book of the Æneid, applies the same simile to Mezentius, when he beholds Acron in the battle.

> *Impastus stabulâ altâ leo ceu sæpe peragrans*
> *(Suadet enim vesana fames), si fortè fugacem*
> *Conspexit capream, aut surgentem in cornua cervum;*

Gaudet hians immanè, comasque arrexit, et hæret
Visceribus super accumbens: lavit improba teter
Ora cruor.

Then as a hungry lion, who beholds
A gamesome goat who frisks about the folds,
Or beamy stag that grazes on the plain;
He runs, he roars, he shakes his rising mane:
He grins, and opens wide his greedy jaws,
The prey lies panting underneath his paws;
He fills his famish'd maw, his mouth runs o'er
With unchew'd morsels, while he churns the gore.

DRYDEN

The reader will perceive that Virgil has improved the simile in one particular, and in another fallen short of his original. The description of the lion shaking his mane, opening his hideous jaws distained with the blood of his prey, is great and picturesque; but on the other hand, he has omitted the circumstance of devouring it without being intimidated, or restrained by the dogs and the youths that surround him; a circumstance that adds greatly to our ideas of his strength, intrepidity, and importance.

ON THE USE OF HYPERBOLE

Of all the figures in poetry, that called the Hyperbole is managed with the greatest difficulty. The hyperbole is an exaggeration with which the muse is indulged for the better illustration of her subject, when she is warmed into enthusiasm. Quintilian calls it an ornament of the bolder kind. Demetrius Phalereus is still more severe. He says the hyperbole is of all forms of speech the most frigid; Μάλιστα δὲ ἡ Ὑπεϱβολὴ ψυχϱ̣ τατσν πάντων; but this must be understood with some grains of allowance. Poetry is animated by the passions; and all the passions exaggerated. Passion itself is a magnifying medium. There are beautiful instances of the hyperbole in the Scripture, which a reader of sensibility cannot read without being strongly affected. The difficulty lies in choosing such hyperboles as the subject will admit of; for, according to the definition of Theophrastus, the frigid in style is that which exceeds the expression suitable to the subject. The judgment does not revolt against Homer for representing the horses of Ericthonius running over the standing corn without breaking off the heads, because the whole is considered as a fable, and the north wind is represented as their sire; but the imagination is a little startled, when Virgil, in imitation of this hyperbole, exhibits Camilla as flying over it without even touching the tops.

Illa vel intactæ segetis per summa volaret
Gramina

[Outstripp'd the winds in speed upon the plain,
Flew o'er the fields, nor hurt the bearded grain]
DRYDEN

This elegant author, we are afraid, has upon some other occasions degenerated into the frigid, in straining to improve upon his great master.

Homer, in the Odyssey, a work which Longinus does not scruple to charge with bearing the marks of old age, describes a storm in which all the four winds were concerned together.

Σὺν δ' Εὐρός τε, Νοτός τ' ἔπεσε, Ζεφυρός τε δυσαὴς,
Καὶ Βορέης αἰθρηγένετης μέγα λῦμα κυλίνδων.

We know that such a contention of contrary blasts could not possibly exist in nature; for even in hurricanes the winds blow alternately from different points of the compass. Nevertheless, Virgil adopts the description, and adds to its extravagance

Incubuêre mari, totumque à sedibus imis
Unà Eurusque Notusque ruunt, creberque procellis
Africus.

Here the winds not only blow together, but they turn the whole body of the ocean topsy-turvy:

East, west, and south, engage with furious sweep
And from its lowest bed upturn the foaming deep.

The north wind, however, is still more mischievous:

——Stridens aquilone procella
Velum adversa ferit, fluctusque ad sidera tollit.

The sail then Boreas rends with hideous cry,
And whirls the madd'ning billows to the sky.

The motion of the sea between Scylla and Charybdis is still more magnified; and Ætna is exhibited as throwing out volumes of flame, which brush the stars. Such expressions as these are not intended as a real representation of the thing specified; they are designed to strike the reader's imagination; but they generally serve as marks of the author's sinking under his own ideas, who, apprehensive of injuring the greatness of his own conception, is hurried into excess and extravagance.

Quintilian allows the use of hyperbole, when words are wanting to express any thing in its just strength or due energy: then, he says, it is better to exceed in expression than fall short of the conception; but he likewise observes, that there is no figure or form of speech so apt to run into fustian. Nec aliâ magris viâ in χαχοξηλιαν itur.

If the chaste Virgil has thus trespassed upon poetical probability, what can we expect from Lucan but hyperboles even more ridiculously extravagant? He represents the winds in contest, the sea in suspense, doubting to which it shall give way. He affirms, that its motion would have been so violent as to produce a second deluge, had not Jupiter kept it under by the clouds; and as to the ship during this dreadful uproar, "the sails touch the clouds, while the keel strikes the ground."

Nubila tanguntur velis, et terra carinâ.

This image of dashing water at the stars, Sir Richard Blackmore has produced in colors truly ridiculous. Describing spouting whales in his Prince Arthur, he makes the following comparison:

Like some prodigious water engine made
To play on heaven, if fire should heaven invade.

The great fault in all these instances is a deviation from propriety, owing to the erroneous judgment of the writer, who, endeavoring to captivate the admiration with novelty, very often shocks the understanding with extravagance. Of this nature is the whole description of the Cyclops, both in the Odyssey of Homer, and the Æneid of Virgil. It must be owned, however, that the Latin poet, with all his merit, is more apt than his great original to dazzle us with false fire, and practise upon the imagination with gay conceits, that will not bear the critic's examination. There is not in any of Homer's works now subsisting such an example of the false sublime, as Virgil's description of the thunderbolts forging under the hammers of the Cyclops.

Tres imbris torti radios, tres nubis aquosæ
Addiderant, rutili tres ignis et alitis Austri.

Three rays of writhen rain, of fire three more,
Of winged southern winds and cloudy store,
As many parts, the dreadful mixture frame.
DRYDEN

This is altogether a fantastic piece of affectation, of which we can form no sensible image, and serves to chill the fancy, rather than warm the admiration of a judging reader.

Extravagant hyperbole is a weed that grows in great plenty through the works of our admired Shakspeare. In the following description, which hath been much celebrated, one sees he has had an eye to Virgil's thunderbolts.

O, then I see queen Mab hath been with you.
She is the fairies' midwife; and she comes
In shape no bigger than an agate-stone
On the fore-finger of an alderman,
Drawn with a team of little atomies
Athwart men's noses as they lie asleep;
Her wagon-spokes made of long spinner's legs;

The cover, of the wings of grasshoppers;
The traces, of the smallest spider's web;
The collars, of the *moonshine's wat'ry beams*," &c.

Even in describing fantastic beings there is a propriety to be observed; but surely nothing can be more revolting to common sense, than this numbering of the *moonbeams* among the other implements of queen Mab's harness, which though extremely slender and diminutive, are nevertheless objects of the touch, and may be conceived capable of use.

The ode and satire admit of the boldest hyperboles; such exaggerations suit the impetuous warmth of the one; and in the other have a good effect in exposing folly, and exciting horror against vice. They may be likewise successfully used in comedy, for moving and managing the powers of ridicule.

Edmund Burke

1729–1797

Edmund Burke was born in Dublin, Ireland, in 1729, of a Protestant father and a Roman Catholic mother. Due to an early bout with one of the epidemics which raged through Ireland in these years, Burke limped from boyhood, and remained thin and delicate throughout his life. A distant relative of the poet Edmund Spenser, Burke spent his happiest boyhood days on the same green and misty estate which helped to inspire *The Faerie Queene*. It was there that he developed his love for Ireland's landscape and its rich mythical heritage—an affection which he later expressed in passionate defenses of the Irish before the English parliament. Sensitive, serious, and diligent in his studies, Burke was admitted to Trinity College in 1744 and went to London in 1750 to study at Middle Temple.

In England, Burke finally broke free of his domineering father. In 1757, he openly defied his father by marrying Jane Nugent, the daughter of an Irish Catholic doctor. Within the year they had two sons, and they remained devoted to each other for the rest of their long lives. Burke also defied his father at this time by deciding to pursue his literary ambitions rather than entering law school. In an effort to gain recognition as a writer, Burke revised a manuscript he had written in Ireland when he was nineteen. He published it with the title *A Philosophic Enquiry into the Origin of Our Ideas of The Sublime and The Beautiful*. The essay was widely read and highly praised. It earned Burke a secure place in the literary society of Johnson, Goldsmith, Garrick, and Reynolds, and it attracted the attention of such continental luminaries as Diderot, Kant, and Lessing. Burke subsequently devoted all his efforts to political thinking, but his theory of the sublime exercized a profound influence on English poetry—most notably in the work of William Wordsworth.

At the heart of Burke's essay is his contention that the sublime may be distinguished from the beautiful on the grounds that sublimity includes an element of terror. Beauty, Burke suggests, pleases us because it touches our genial instincts toward "society"—it "induces in us a state of affection or tenderness . . . " Sublimity moves us more powerfully, he argues, because it has a strong threat of danger within it and thus activates our strongest instinct—self preservation. Although this idea is not original with Burke, he can be said to have articulated it anew for the next generation of poets. Whether he learned it from Burke or Milton, this distinction greatly influenced Wordsworth's poetics. Much of *The Prelude* can be read in Burkean terms as a movement through beauty toward sublimity followed by a return to the more genial landscape now enhanced in the mind of the poet by the experience of terror. Toward the end of the poem, Wordsworth speaks of his youthful attraction to the sublime in terms which directly echo Burke, and Milton: "Still to the very going out of youth / I too exclusive only esteemed that beauty, which, as Milton says, / Hath terror in it".

Burke was better known, indeed renowned, as a political figure. During a time dominated by the radical rationalist spirit of the French Revolution, Burke emerged as an eloquent critic of Jacobinism, and as a defender of tradition, continuity, and respect for the past. Although he recognized the necessity of change and reform, Burke was skeptical of radical abstract solutions externally imposed upon a society. He preferred a vision of organic development evolving from within, consistent with the country's unique character and history. Never a dogmatic conservative, however, Burke defended the American Revolution as consistent with and necessary to the nation's growth and identity. He also fiercely defended the Irish and the Indians, and he worked to limit the power of the King. He prophesied the excesses of the French Revolution in a series of famous addresses to Parliament between 1765 and 1795. It was the publication of Burke's *Reflections on The Revolution in France* which provoked Thomas Paine to publish his famous *Rights of Man*.

Burke's organic view of society provided Wordsworth, among others, with a powerful alternative to the theories of Rousseau with which he had become disillusioned. He retired from Parliament in 1794. Always extremely sensitive and emotionally explosive, he was often the victim of bouts of melancholia, and his last years were heavily clouded with the death of his great friend Johnson and the death of his son. He died in 1797, but in the 1850 version of *The Prelude* Wordsworth immortalized him:

> Genius of Burke! forgive the pen seduced
> By specious wonders . . .
> I see him, old, but vigourous in age,—
> Stand like an oak . . .
> While he forewarns, denounces, launches forth,
> Against all systems built on abstract rights,
> Keen ridicule, the majesty proclaims
> Of Institutes and Laws, hallowed by time;
> Declares the vital power of social ties
> Endeared by Custom; and with high disdain,
> Exploding upstart Theory, insists
> Upon the allegiance to which men are born—

ON THE SUBLIME AND BEAUTIFUL

FROM
Part I

Of the Sublime

W hatever is fitted in any sort to excite the ideas of pain and danger, that is to say, whatever is in any sort terrible, or is conversant about terrible objects, or operates in a manner analogous to terror, is a source of the *sublime;* that is, it is productive of the strongest emotion which the mind is capable of feeling. I say the strongest emotion, because I am satisfied the ideas of pain are much more powerful than those which enter on the part of pleasure. Without all doubt, the torments which we may be made to suffer are much greater in their effect on the body and mind, than any pleasures which the most learned voluptuary could suggest, or than the liveliest imagination, and the most sound and exquisitely sensible body, could enjoy. Nay, I am in great doubt whether any man could be found, who would earn a life of the most perfect satisfaction at the price of ending it in the torments, which justice inflicted in a few hours on the late unfortunate regicide in France. But as pain is stronger in its operation than pleasure, so death is in general a much more affecting idea than pain; because there are very few pains, however exquisite, which are not preferred to death: nay, what generally makes pain itself, if I may say so, more painful, is, that it is considered as an emissary of this king of terrors. When danger or pain press too nearly, they are incapable of giving any delight, and are simply terrible; but at certain distances, and with certain modifications, they may be, and they are, delightful, as we every day experience. The cause of this I shall endeavor to investigate hereafter. . . .

Of Beauty

The passion which belongs to generation, merely as such, is lust only. This is evident in brutes, whose passions are more unmixed, and which pursue their purposes more directly than ours. The only distinction they observe with regard to their mates, is that of sex. It is true, that they stick severally to their own species in preference to all others. But this preference, I imagine, does not arise from any sense of beauty which they find in their species, as Mr. Addison supposes, but from a law of some other kind, to which they are subject; and this we may fairly conclude, from their apparent want of choice amongst those objects to which the barriers of their species have confined them. But man, who is a creature adapted to a greater variety and intricacy of relation, connects with the general passion the idea of some *social* qualities, which direct and heighten the appetite which he has in common with all other animals; and as he is not designed like them to live at large, it is fit that he should have something to create a preference, and fix his choice; and this in general should be some sensible quality; as no other can so quickly, so powerfully, or so surely produce its effect. The object therefore of this mixed passion, which we call love, is the *beauty* of the *sex*. Men are carried to the sex in general, as it is the sex, and by the common law of nature; but they are attached to particulars by personal *beauty*. I call beauty a social quality; for where women and men, and not only they, but when other animals give us a sense of joy and pleasure in beholding them (and there are many that do so), they inspire us with sentiments of tenderness and affection towards their persons; we like to have them near us, and we enter willingly into a kind of relation with them, unless we should have strong reasons to the contrary. But to what end, in many cases, this was designed, I am unable to discover; for I see no greater reason for a connection between man and several animals who are attired in so engaging a manner, than between him and some others who entirely want this attraction, or possess it in a far weaker degree. But it is probable that Providence did not make even this distinction, but with a view to some great end; though we cannot perceive distinctly what it is, as his wisdom is not our wisdom, nor our ways his ways. . . .

Sympathy

It is by the first of these passions that we enter into the concerns of others; that we are moved as they are moved, and are never suffered to be indifferent spectators of almost anything which men can do or suffer. For sympathy must be considered as a sort of substitution, by which we are put into the place of another man, and affected in many respects as he is affected: so that this passion may either partake of the nature of those which regard self-preservation, and turning upon pain may be a source of the sublime; or it may turn upon ideas of pleasure; and then whatever has been said of the social affections, whether they regard society in general, or only some particular modes of it, may be applicable here. It is by this principle chiefly that poetry, painting, and other affecting arts, transfuse their passions from one breast to another, and are often capable of grafting a delight on wretchedness, misery, and death itself. It is a common observation, that objects which in the reality would shock, are in tragical, and such like representations, the source of a very high species of pleasure. This, taken as a fact, has been the cause of much reasoning. The satisfaction has been commonly attributed, first, to the comfort we receive in considering that so melancholy a story is no more than a fiction; and, next, to the contemplation of our own freedom from the evils which we see represented. I am afraid it is a practice much too common in inquiries of this nature, to attribute the cause of feelings which merely arise from the mechanical structure of our bodies, or from the natural frame and constitution of our minds, to certain conclusions of the reasoning faculty on the objects presented to us; for I should imagine, that the influence of reason in producing our passions is nothing near so extensive as it is commonly believed.

The Effects of Sympathy
In the Distresses of Others

To examine this point concerning the effect of tragedy in a proper manner, we must previously consider how we are affected by the feelings of our fellow-creatures in circumstances of real distress. I am convinced we have a degree of delight, and that no small one, in the real misfortunes and pains of others; for let the affection be what it will in appearance, if it does not make us shun such objects, if on the contrary it induces us to approach them, if it makes us dwell upon them, in this case I conceive we must have a delight or pleasure of some species or other in contemplating objects of this kind. Do we not read the authentic histories of scenes of this nature with as much pleasure as romances or poems, where the incidents are fictitious? The prosperity of no empire, nor the grandeur of no king, can so agreeably affect in the reading, as the ruin of the state of Macedon, and the distress of its unhappy prince. Such a catastrophe touches us in history as much as the destruction of Troy does in fable. Our delight, in cases of this kind, is very greatly heightened, if the sufferer be some excellent person who sinks under an unworthy fortune. Scipio and Cato are both virtuous characters; but we are more deeply affected by the violent death of the one, and the ruin of the great cause he adhered to, than with the deserved triumphs and uninterrupted prosperity of the other: for terror is a passion which always produces delight when it does not press too closely; and pity is a passion accompanied with pleasure, because it arises from love and social affection. Whenever we are formed by nature to any active purpose, the passion which animates us to it is attended with delight, or a pleasure of some kind, let the subject-matter be what it will; and as our Creator has designed that we should be united by the bond of sympathy, he has strengthened that bond by a proportionable delight; and there most where our sympathy is most wanted,—in the distresses of others. If this passion was simply painful, we would shun with the greatest care all persons and places that could excite such a passion; as some, who are so far gone in indolence as not to endure any strong impression, actually do. But the case is widely different with the greater part of mankind; there is no spectacle we so eagerly pursue, as that of some uncommon and grievous calamity; so that whether the misfortune is before our eyes, or whether they are turned back to it in history, it always touches with delight. This is not an unmixed delight, but blended with no small uneasiness. The delight we have in such things hinders us from shunning scenes of misery; and the pain we feel prompts us to relieve ourselves in relieving those who suffer; and all this antecedent to any reasoning, by an instinct that works us to its own purposes without our concurrence.

Of the Effects of Tragedy

It is thus in real calamities. In imitated distresses the only difference is the pleasure resulting from the effects of imitation; for it is never so perfect, but we can perceive it is imitation, and on that principle are somewhat pleased with it. And indeed in some cases we derive as much or more pleasure from that source than from the thing itself. But then I imagine we shall be much mistaken if we attribute any considerable part of our satisfaction in tragedy to the consideration that tragedy is a deceit, and its representations no realities. The nearer it approaches the reality, and the further it removes us from all idea of fiction, the more perfect is its power. But be its power of what kind it will, it never approaches to what it represents. Choose a day on which to represent the most sublime and affecting tragedy we have; appoint the most favorite actors; spare no cost upon the scenes and decorations; unite the greatest efforts of poetry, painting, and music; and when you have collected your audience, just at the moment when their minds are erect with expectation, let it be reported that a state criminal of high rank is on the point of being executed in the adjoining square; in a moment the emptiness of the theatre would demonstrate the comparative weakness of the imitative arts, and proclaim the triumph of the real sympathy. I believe that this notion of our having a simple pain in the reality, yet a delight in the representation, arises from hence, that we do not sufficiently distinguish what we would by no means choose to do, from what we should be eager enough to see if it was once done. We delight in seeing things, which so far from doing, our heartiest wishes would be to see redressed. This noble capital, the pride of England and of Europe, I believe no man is so strangely wicked as to desire to see destroyed by a conflagration or an earthquake, though he should be removed himself to the greatest distance from the danger. But suppose such a fatal accident to have happened, what numbers from all parts would crowd to behold the ruins, and amongst them many who would have been content never to have seen London in its glory! Nor is it, either in real or fictitious distresses, our immunity from them which produces our delight; in my own mind I can discover nothing like it. I apprehend that this mistake is owing to a sort of sophism, by which we are frequently imposed upon; it arises from our not distinguishing between what is indeed a necessary condition to our doing or suffering anything in general, and what is the *cause* of some particular act. If a man kills me with a sword, it is a necessary condition to this that we should have been both of us alive before the fact; and yet it would be absurd to say that our being both living creatures was the cause of his crime and of my death. So it is certain that it is absolutely necessary my life should be out of any imminent hazard, before I can take a delight in the sufferings of others, real or imaginary, or indeed in anything else from any cause whatsoever. But then it is a sophism to argue from thence that this immunity is the cause of my delight either on these or on any occasions. No one can distinguish such a cause of satisfaction in his own mind, I believe; nay, when we do not suffer any very acute pain, nor are exposed to any imminent danger of our lives, we can feel for others, whilst we suffer ourselves; and often then most when we are softened by affliction; we see with pity even distresses which we would accept in the place of our own. . . .

The Recapitulation

To draw the whole of what has been said into a few distinct points:—The passions which belong to self-preservation turn on pain and danger; they are simply painful when their causes immediately affect us; they are delightful when we have an idea of pain and danger, without being actually in such circumstances; this delight I have not called pleasure, because it turns on pain, and because it is different enough from any idea of positive pleasure. Whatever excites this delight, I call *sublime*. The passions belonging to self-preservation are the strongest of all the passions.

The second head to which the passions are referred with relation to their final cause, is society. There are two sorts of societies. The first is, the society of sex. The passion belonging to this is called love, and it contains a mixture of lust; its object is the beauty of women. The other is the great society with man and all other animals. The passion subservient to this is called likewise love, but it has no mixture of lust, and its object is beauty; which is a name I shall apply to all such qualities in things as induce in us a sense of affection and tenderness, or some other passion the most nearly resembling these. The passion of love has its rise in positive pleasure; it is, like all things which grow out of pleasure, capable of being mixed with a mode of uneasiness, that is, when an idea of its object is excited in the mind with an idea at the same time of having irretrievably lost it. This mixed sense of pleasure I have not called *pain*, because it turns upon actual pleasure, and because it is, both in its cause and in most of its effects, of a nature altogether different.

Next to the general passion we have for society, to a choice in which we are directed by the pleasure we have in the object, the particular passion under this head called sympathy has the greatest extent. The nature of this passion is, to put us in the place of another in whatever circumstance he is in, and to affect us in a like manner; so that this passion may, as the occasion requires, turn either on pain or pleasure; but with the modifications mentioned in some cases in Sect. 11. As to imitation and preference, nothing more need be said.

The Conclusion

I believed that an attempt to range and methodize some of our most leading passions would be a good preparative to such an inquiry as we are going to make in the ensuing discourse. The passions I have mentioned are almost the only ones which it can be necessary to consider in our present design; though the variety of the passions is great, and worthy, in every branch of that variety, of an attentive investigation. The more accurately we search into the human mind, the stronger traces we everywhere find of His wisdom who made it. If a discourse on the use of the parts of the body may be considered as a hymn to the Creator; the use of the passions, which are the organs of the mind, cannot be barren of praise to him, nor unproductive to ourselves of that noble and uncommon union of science and admiration, which a contemplation of the works of infinite wisdom alone can afford to a rational mind; whilst, referring to him whatever we find of right or good or fair in ourselves, discovering his strength and wisdom even in our own weakness and imperfection, honoring them where we discover them clearly, and adoring their profundity where we are lost in our search, we may be inquisitive without impertinence, and elevated without pride; we may be admitted, if I may dare to say so, into the counsels of the Almighty by a consideration of his works. The elevation of the mind ought to be the principal end of all our studies; which, if they do not in some measure effect, they are of very little service to us. But, besides this great purpose, a consideration of the rationale of our passions seems to me very necessary for all who would effect them upon solid and sure principles. It is not enough to know them in general; to affect them after a delicate manner, or to judge properly of any work designed to affect them, we should know the exact boundaries of their several jurisdictions; we should pursue them through all their variety of operations, and pierce into the inmost, and what might appear inaccessible parts of our nature,

Quod latet arcanâ non enarrabile fibrâ.

Without all this it is possible for a man, after a confused manner sometimes to satisfy his own mind of the truth of his work; but he can never have a certain determinate rule to go by, nor can he ever make his propositions sufficiently clear to others. Poets, and orators, and painters, and those who cultivate other branches of the liberal arts, have, without this critical knowledge, succeeded well in their several provinces, and will succeed: as among artificers there are many machines made and even invented without any exact knowledge of the principles they are governed by. It is, I own, not uncommon to be wrong in theory, and right in practice: and we are happy that it is so. Men often act right from their feelings, who afterwards reason but ill on them from principle; but as it is impossible to avoid an attempt at such reasoning, and equally impossible to prevent its having some influence on our practice, surely it is worth taking some pains to have it just, and founded on the basis of sure experience. We might expect that the artists themselves would have been our surest guides; but the artists have been too much occupied in the practice: the philosophers have done little; and what they have done, was mostly with a view to their own schemes and systems; and as for those called critics, they have generally sought the rule of the arts in the wrong place; they sought it among poems, pictures, engravings, statues, and buildings. But art can never give the rules that make an art. This is, I believe, the reason why artists in general, and poets, principally, have been confined in so narrow a circle: they have been rather imitators of one another than of nature; and this with so faithful an uniformity, and to so remote an antiquity, that it is hard to say who gave the first model. Critics follow them, and therefore can do little as guides. I can judge but poorly of anything, whilst I measure it by no other standard than itself. The true standard of the arts is in every man's power; and an easy observation of the most common, sometimes of the meanest things in nature, will give the truest lights, where the greatest sagacity and industry, that slights such observation, must leave us in the dark, or, what is worse, amuse and mislead us by false lights. In an inquiry it is almost everything to be once in a right road. I am satisfied I have done but little by these observations considered in themselves; and I never should have taken the pains to digest them, much less should I have ever ventured to publish them, if I was not convinced that nothing tends more to the corruption of science than to suffer it to stagnate. These waters must be troubled, before they can exert their virtues. A man who works beyond the surface of things, though he may be wrong himself, yet he clears the way for others, and may chance to make even his errors subservient to the cause of truth. In the following parts I shall inquire what things they are that cause in us the affections of the sublime and beautiful, as in this I have considered the affections themselves. I only desire one favor,—that no part of this discourse may be judged of by itself, and independently of the rest; for I am sensible I have not disposed my materials to abide the test of a captious controversy, but of a sober and even forgiving examination; that they are not armed at all points for battle, but dressed to visit those who are willing to give a peaceful entrance to truth.

FROM

Part II

Of the Passion Caused by the Sublime

The passion caused by the great and sublime in *nature*, when those causes operate most powerfully, is astonishment: and astonishment is that state of the soul in which all its motions are suspended, with some degree of horror. In this case the mind is so entirely filled with its object, that it cannot entertain any other, nor by consequence reason on that object which employs it. Hence arises the great power of the sublime, that, far from being produced by them, it anticipates our reasonings, and hurries us on by an irresistible force. Astonishment, as I have said, is the effect of the sublime in its highest degree; the inferior effects are admiration, reverence, and respect.

Terror

No passion so effectually robs the mind of all its powers of acting and reasoning as *fear*. For fear being an apprehension of pain or death, it operates in a manner that resembles actual pain. Whatever therefore is terrible, with regard to sight, is sublime too, whether this cause of terror be endued with greatness of dimensions or not; for it is impossible to look on anything as trifling, or contemptible, that may be dangerous. There are many animals, who, though far from being large, are yet capable of raising ideas of the sublime, because they are considered as objects of terror. As serpents and poisonous animals of almost all kinds. And to things of great dimensions, if we annex an adventitious idea of terror, they become without comparison greater. A level plain of a vast extent on land, is certainly no mean idea; the prospect of such a plain may be as extensive as a prospect of the ocean; but can it ever fill the mind with anything so great as the ocean itself? This is owing to several causes; but it is owing to none more than this, that the ocean is an object of no small terror. Indeed terror is in all cases whatsoever, either more openly or latently, the ruling principle of the sublime. Several languages bear a strong testimony to the affinity of these ideas. They frequently use the same word to signify indifferently the modes of astonishment or admiration and those of terror. Θάμβος is in Greek either fear or wonder; δεινός is terrible or respectable; αἰδέω, to reverence or to fear. *Vereor* in Latin is what αἰδέω is in Greek. The Romans used the verb *stupeo,* a term which strongly marks the state of an astonished mind, to express the effect either of simple fear, or of astonishment; the word *attonitus* (thunder-struck) is equally expressive of the alliance of these ideas; and do not the French *étonnement,* and the English *astonishment* and *amazement,* point out as clearly the kindred emotions which attend fear and wonder? They who have a more general knowledge of languages, could produce, I make no doubt, many other and equally striking examples.

Obscurity

To make anything very terrible, obscurity seems in general to be necessary. When we know the full extent of any danger, when we can accustom our eyes to it, a great deal of the apprehension vanishes. Every one will be sensible of this, who considers how greatly night adds to our dread, in all cases of danger, and how much the notions of ghosts and goblins, of which none can form clear ideas, affect minds which give credit to the popular tales concerning such sorts of beings. Those despotic governments which are founded on the passions of men, and principally upon the passion of fear, keep their chief as much as may be from the public eye. The policy has been the same in many cases of religion. Almost all the heathen temples were dark. Even in the barbarous temples of the Americans at this day, they keep their idol in a dark part of the hut, which is consecrated to his worship. For this purpose too the Druids performed all their ceremonies in the bosom of the darkest woods, and in the shade of the oldest and most spreading oaks. No person seems better to have understood the secret of heightening, or of setting terrible things, if I may use the expression, in their strongest light, by the force of a judicious obscurity than Milton. His description of death in the second book is admirably studied; it is astonishing with what a gloomy pomp, with what a significant and expressive uncertainty of strokes and coloring, he has finished the portrait of the king of terrors:

> The other shape,
> If shape it might be called that shape had none
> Distinguishable, in member, joint, or limb;
> Or substance might be called that shadow seemed;
> For each seemed either; black he stood as night;
> Fierce as ten furies; terrible as hell;
> And shook a deadly dart. What seemed his head
> The likeness of a kingly crown had on.

In this description all is dark, uncertain, confused, terrible, and sublime to the last degree.

Of the Difference Between Clearness and Obscurity With Regard to the Passions

It is one thing to make an idea clear, and another to make it *affecting* to the imagination. If I make a drawing of a palace, or a temple, or a landscape, I present a very clear idea of those objects; but then (allowing for the effect of imitation which is something) my picture can at most affect only as the palace, temple, or landscape, would have affected in the reality. On the other hand, the most lively and spirited verbal description I can give raises a very obscure and imperfect *idea* of such objects; but then it is in my power to raise a stronger *emotion* by the description than I could do by the best painting. This experience constantly evinces. The proper manner of conveying the *affections* of the mind from one to another is by words; there is a great insufficiency in all other methods of communication; and so far is a clearness of imagery from being absolutely necessary to an influence upon the passions, that they may be considerably operated upon, without presenting any image at all, by certain sounds adapted to that purpose; of which we have a sufficient proof in the acknowledged and powerful effects of instrumental music. In reality, a great clearness helps but little towards affecting the passions, as it is in some sort an enemy to all enthusiasms whatsoever.

The Same Subject Continued

There are two verses in Horace's *Art of Poetry* that seem to contradict this opinion; for which reason I shall take a little more pains in clearing it up. The verses are,

> *Segnius irritant animos demissa per aures,*
> *Quam quæ sunt oculis subjecta fidelibus.*

On this the Abbé du Bos founds a criticism, wherein he gives painting the preference to poetry in the article of moving the passions; principally on account of the greater *clearness* of the ideas it represents. I believe this excellent judge was led into this mistake (if it be a mistake) by his system; to which he found it more conformable than I imagine it will be found to experience. I know several who admire and love painting, and yet who regard the objects of their admiration in that art with coolness enough in comparison of that warmth with which they are animated by affecting pieces of poetry or rhetoric. Among the common sort of people, I never could perceive that painting had much influence on their passions. It is true that the best sorts of painting, as well as the best sorts of poetry, are not much understood in that sphere. But it is most certain that their passions are very strongly roused by a fanatic preacher, or by the ballads of Chevy Chase, or the Children in the Wood, and by other little popular poems and tales that are current in that rank of life. I do not know of any paintings, bad or good, that produce the same effect. So that poetry, with all its obscurity, has a more general, as well as a more powerful dominion over the passions, than the other art. And I think there are reasons in nature, why the obscure idea, when properly conveyed, should be more affecting than the clear. It is our ignorance of things that causes all our admiration, and chiefly excites our passions. Knowledge and acquaintance make the most striking causes affect but little. It is thus with the vulgar; and all men are as the vulgar in what they do not understand. The ideas of eternity, and infinity, are among the most affecting we have: and yet perhaps there is nothing of which we really under-stand so little, as of infinity and eternity. We do not anywhere meet a more sublime description than this justly-celebrated one of Milton, wherein he gives the portrait of Satan with a dignity so suitable to the subject:

> He above the rest
> In shape and gesture proudly eminent
> Stood like a tower; his form had yet not lost
> All her original brightness, nor appeared
> Less than archangel ruined, and th' excess
> Of glory obscured: as when the sun new risen
> Looks through the horizontal misty air
> Shorn of his beams; or from behind the moon
> In dim eclipse disastrous twilight sheds
> On half the nations; and with fear of change
> Perplexes monarchs.

Here is a very noble picture; and in what does this poetical picture consist? In images of a tower, an archangel, the sun rising through mists, or in an eclipse, the ruin of monarchs and the revolutions of kingdoms. The mind is hurried out of itself, by a crowd of great and confused images; which affect because they are crowded and confused. For separate them, and you lose much of the greatness; and join them, and you infallibly lose the clearness. The images raised by poetry are always of this obscure kind; though in general the effects of poetry are by no means to be attributed to the images it raises; which point we shall examine more at large hereafter. But painting, when we have allowed for the pleasure of imitation, can only affect simply by the images it presents; and even in painting, a judicious obscurity in some things contributes to the effect of the picture; because the images in painting are exactly similar to those in nature; and in nature, dark, confused, uncertain images have a greater power on the fancy to form the grander passions, than those have which are more clear and determinate. But where and when this observation may be applied to practice, and how far it shall be extended, will be better deduced from the nature of the subject, and from the occasion, than from any rules that can be given.

I am sensible that this idea has met with opposition, and is likely still to be rejected by several. But let it be considered that hardly anything can strike the mind with its greatness, which does not make some sort of approach towards infinity; which nothing can do whilst we are able to perceive its bounds; but to see an object distinctly, and to perceive its bounds, is one and the same thing. A clear idea is therefore another name for a little idea. There is a passage in the book of Job amazingly sublime, and this sublimity is principally due to the terrible uncertainty of the thing described: *In thoughts from the visions of the night, when deep sleep falleth upon men, fear came upon me and trembling, which made all my bones to shake. Then a spirit passed before my face. The hair of my flesh stood up. It stood still,* but I could not discern the form thereof; *an image was before mine eyes; there was silence; and I heard a voice,—Shall mortal man be more just than God?* We are first prepared with the utmost solemnity for the vision; we are first terrified, before we are let even into the obscure cause of our emotion: but when this grand cause of terror makes its appearance, what is it? Is it not wrapt up in the shades of its own incomprehensible darkness, more awful, more striking, more terrible, than the liveliest description, than the clearest painting, could possibly represent it? When painters have attempted to give us clear representations of these very fanciful and terrible ideas, they have, I think, almost always failed; insomuch that I have been at a loss, in all the pictures I have seen of hell, to determine whether the painter did not intend something ludicrous. Several painters have handled a subject of this kind, with a view of assembling as many horrid phantoms as their imagination could suggest; but all the designs I have chanced to meet of the temptations of St. Anthony were rather a sort of odd, wild grotesques, than anything capable of producing a serious passion. In all these subjects poetry is very happy. Its apparitions, its chimeras, its harpies, its allegorical figures, are grand and affecting; and though Virgil's Fame and Homer's Discord are obscure, they are magnificent figures. These figures in painting would be clear enough, but I fear they might become ridiculous. . . .

FROM

Part III

Of Beauty

It is my design to consider beauty as distinguished from the sublime; and, in the course of the inquiry, to examine how far it is consistent with it. But previous to this, we must take a short review of the opinions already entertained of this quality; which I think are hardly to be reduced to any fixed principles; because men are used to talk of beauty in a figurative manner, that is to say, in a manner extremely uncertain, and indeterminate. By beauty, I mean that quality, or those qualities in bodies, by which they cause love, or some passion similar to it. I confine this definition to the merely sensible qualities of things, for the sake of preserving the utmost simplicity in a subject, which must always distract us whenever we take in those various causes of sympathy which attach us to any persons or things from secondary considerations, and not from the direct force which they have merely on being viewed. I likewise distinguish love, (by which I mean that satisfaction which arises to the mind upon contemplating anything beautiful, of whatsoever nature it may be,) from desire or lust; which is an energy of the mind, that hurries us on to the possession of certain objects, that do not affect us as they are beautiful, but by means altogether different. We shall have a strong desire for a woman of no remarkable beauty; whilst the greatest beauty in men, or in other animals, though it causes love, yet excites nothing at all of desire. Which shows that beauty, and the passion caused by beauty, which I call love, is different from desire, though desire may sometimes operate along with it; but it is to this latter that we must attribute those violent and tempestuous passions, and the consequent emotions of the body which attend what is called love in some of its ordinary acceptations, and not to the effects of beauty merely as it is such. . . .

Fitness Not the Cause of Beauty

It is said that the idea of utility, or of a part's being well adapted to answer its end, is the cause of beauty, or indeed beauty itself. If it were not for this opinion, it had been impossible for the doctrine of proportion to have held its ground very long; the world would be soon weary of hearing of measures which related to nothing, either of a natural principle, or of a fitness to answer some end; the idea which mankind most commonly conceive of proportion, is the suitableness of means to certain ends, and, where this is not the question, very seldom trouble themselves about the effect of different measures of things. Therefore it was necessary for this theory to insist that not only artifical, but natural objects took their beauty from the fitness of the parts for their several purposes. But in framing this theory, I am apprehensive that experience was not sufficiently consulted. For, on that principle, the wedge-like snout of a swine, with its tough cartilage at the end, the little sunk eyes, and the whole make of the head, so well adapted to its offices of digging and rooting, would be extremely beautiful. The great bag hanging to the bill of a pelican, a thing highly useful to this animal, would be likewise as beautiful in our eyes. The hedge-hog, so well secured against all assaults by his prickly hide, and the porcupine with his missile quills, would be then considered as creatures of no small elegance. There are few animals whose parts are better contrived than those of a monkey: he has the hands of a man, joined to the springy limbs of a beast; he is admirably calculated for running, leaping, grappling, and climbing; and yet there are few animals which seem to have less beauty in the eyes of all mankind. I need say little on the trunk of the elephant, of such various usefulness, and which is so far from contributing to his beauty. How well fitted is the wolf for running and leaping! how admirably is the lion armed for battle! but will any one therefore call the elephant, the wolf, and the lion, beautiful animals? I believe nobody will think the form of a man's leg so well adapted to running, as those of a horse, a dog, a deer, and several other creatures; at least they have not that appearance: yet, I believe, a well-fashioned human leg will be allowed to far exceed all these in beauty. If the fitness of parts was what constituted the loveliness of their form, the actual employment of them would undoubtedly much augment it; but this, though it is sometimes so upon another principle, is far from being always the case. A bird on the wing is not so beautiful as when it is perched; nay, there are several of the domestic fowls which are seldom seen to fly, and which are nothing the less beautiful on that account; yet birds are so extremely different in their form from the beast and human kinds, that you cannot, on the principle of fitness, allow them anything agreeable, but in consideration of their parts being designed for quite other purposes. I never in my life chanced to see a peacock fly; and yet before, very long before I considered any aptitude in his form for the aërial life, I was struck with the extreme beauty which raises that bird above many of the best flying fowls in the world; though, for anything I saw, his way of living was much like that of the swine, which fed in the farm-yard along with him. The same may be said of cocks, hens, and the like; they are of the flying kind in figure; in their manner of moving not very different from men and beasts. To leave these foreign examples; if beauty in our own species was annexed to use, men would be much more lovely than women; and strength and agility would be considered as the only beauties. But to call strength by the name of beauty, to have but one denomination for the qualities of a Venus and Hercules, so totally different in almost all respects, is surely a strange confusion of ideas, or abuse of words. The cause of the confusion, I imagine, proceeds from our frequently perceiving the parts of the human and other animal bodies to be at once very beautiful, and very well adapted to their purposes; and we are deceived by a sophism, which makes us take that for a cause which is only a concomitant: this is the sophism of the fly; who imagined he raised a great dust, because he stood upon the chariot that really raised it. The stomach, the lungs, the liver, as well as other parts, are incomparably well adapted to their purposes; yet they are far from having any beauty. Again, many things are very beautiful, in which it is impossible to discern any idea of use. And I appeal to the first and most natural feelings of mankind, whether on beholding a beautiful eye, or a well-fashioned mouth, or a well-turned leg, any ideas of their being well fitted for seeing, eating, or running, ever present themselves. What idea of use is it that flowers excite, the most beautiful part of the vegetable world? It is true that the infinitely wise and good Creator has, of his bounty, frequently joined beauty to those things which he has made useful to us; but this does not prove that an idea of use and beauty are the same thing, or that they are any way dependent on each other. . . .

Perfection Not the Cause of Beauty

There is another notion current, pretty closely allied to the former; that *perfection* is the constituent cause of beauty. This opinion has been made to extend much further than to sensible objects. But in these, so far is perfection, considered as such, from being the cause of beauty; that this quality, where it is highest, in the female sex, almost always carries with it an idea of weakness and imperfection. Women are very sensible of this; for which reason they learn to lisp, to totter in their walk, to counterfeit weakness, and even sickness. In all this they are guided by nature. Beauty in distress is much the most affecting beauty. Blushing has little less power; and modesty in general, which is a tacit allowance of imperfection, is itself considered as an amiable quality, and certainly heightens every other that is so. I know it is in every body's mouth, that we ought to love perfection. This is to me a sufficient proof, that it is not the proper object of love. Who ever said we *ought* to love a fine woman, or even any of these beautiful animals which please us? Here to be affected, there is no need of the concurrence of our will. . . .

The Sublime and Beautiful Compared

On closing this general view of beauty, it naturally occurs that we should compare it with the sublime; and in this comparison there appears a remarkable contrast. For sublime objects are vast in their dimensions, beautiful ones comparatively small; beauty should be smooth and polished; the great, rugged and negligent: beauty should shun the right line, yet deviate from it insensibly; the great in many cases loves the right line; and when it deviates, it often makes a strong deviation: beauty should not be obscure; the great ought to be dark and gloomy: beauty should be light and delicate; the great ought to be solid, and even massive. They are indeed ideas of a very different nature, one being founded on pain, the other on pleasure; and, however they may vary afterwards from the direct nature of their causes, yet these causes keep up an eternal distinction between them, a distinction never to be forgotten by any whose business it is to affect the passions. In the infinite variety of natural combinations, we must expect to find the qualities of things the most remote imaginable from each other united in the same object. We must expect also to find combinations of the same kind in the works of art. But when we consider the power of an object upon our passions, we must know that when anything is intended to affect the mind by the force of some predominant property, the affection produced is like to be the more uniform and perfect, if all the other properties or qualities of the object be of the same nature, and tending to the same design as the principal.

> If black and white blend, soften, and unite
> A thousand ways, are there no black and white?

If the qualities of the sublime and beautiful are sometimes found united, does this prove that they are the same; does it prove that they are any way allied;

does it prove even that they are not opposite and contradictory? Black and white may soften, may blend; but they are not therefore the same. Nor, when they are so softened and blended with each other, or with different colors, is the power of black as black, or of white as white, so strong as when each stands uniform and distinguished.

FROM
Part V

Of Words

Natural objects affect us by the laws of that connection which Providence has established between certain motions and configurations of bodies, and certain consequent feelings in our mind. Painting affects in the same manner, but with the superadded pleasure of imitation. Architecture affects by the laws of nature and the law of reason; from which latter result the rules of proportion, which make a work to be praised or censured, in the whole or in some part, when the end for which it was designed is or is not properly answered. But as to words; they seem to me to affect us in a manner very different from that in which we are affected by natural objects, or by painting or architecture; yet words have as considerable a share in exciting ideas of beauty and of the sublime as many of those, and sometimes a much greater than any of them; therefore an inquiry into the manner by which they excite such emotions is far from being unnecessary in a discourse of this kind.

The Common Effects of Poetry, Not by Raising Ideas of Things

The common notion of the power of poetry and eloquence, as well as that of words in ordinary conversation, is, that they affect the mind by raising in it ideas of those things for which custom has appointed them to stand. To examine the truth of this notion, it may be requisite to observe that words may be divided into three sorts. The first are such as represent many simple ideas *united by nature* to form some one determinate composition, as man, horse, tree, castle, &c. These I call *aggregate words*. The second are they that stand for one simple idea of such compositions, and no more; as red, blue, round, square, and the like. These I call *simple abstract* words. The third are those which are formed by an union, an *arbitrary* union of both the others, and of the various relations between them in greater or lesser degrees of complexity; as virtue, honor, persuasion, magistrate, and the like. These I call *compound abstract* words. Words, I am sensible, are capable of being classed into more curious distinctions; but these seem to be natural, and enough for our purpose; and they are disposed in that order in which they are commonly taught, and in which the mind gets the ideas they are substituted for. I shall begin with the third sort of words; compound abstracts, such as virtue, honor, persuasion, docility. Of these I am convinced, that whatever power they may have on the passions, they do not derive it from any representation raised in the mind of the things for which they stand. As compositions, they are not real essences, and hardly cause, I think, any real ideas. Nobody, I believe, immediately on hearing the sounds, virtue, liberty, or honor, conceives any precise notions of the particular modes of action and thinking, together with the mixed and simple ideas, and the several relations of them for which these words are substituted; neither has he any general idea compounded of them; for if he had, then some of those particular ones, though indistinct perhaps, and confused, might come soon to be perceived. But this, I take it, is hardly ever the case. For, put yourself upon analyzing one of these words, and you must reduce it from one set of general words to another, and then into the simple abstracts and aggregates, in a much longer series than may be at first imagined, before any real idea emerges to light, before you come to discover anything like the first principles of such compositions; and when you have made such a discovery of the original ideas, the effect of the composition is utterly lost. A train of thinking of this sort is much too long to be pursued in the ordinary ways of conversation; nor is it at all necessary that it should. Such words are in reality but mere sounds; but they are sounds which being used on particular occasions, wherein we receive some good, or suffer some evil; or see others affected with good or evil; or which we hear applied to other interesting things or events; and being applied in such a variety of cases, that we know readily by habit to what things they belong, they produce in the mind, whenever they are afterwards mentioned, effects similar to those of their occasions. The sounds being often used without reference to any particular occasion, and carrying still their first impressions, they at last utterly lose their connection with the particular occasions that gave rise to them; yet the sound, without any annexed notion, continues to operate as before.

General Words Before Ideas

Mr. Locke has somewhere observed, with his usual sagacity, that most general words, those belonging to virtue and vice, good and evil especially, are taught before the particular modes of action to which they belong are presented to the mind; and with them, the love of the one, and the abhorrence of the other; for the minds of children are so ductile, that a nurse, or any person about a child, by seeming pleased or displeased with anything, or even any word, may give the disposition of the child a similar turn. When, afterwards, the several occurrences in life come to be applied to these words, and that which is pleasant often appears under the name of evil; and what is disagreeable to nature is called good and virtuous; a strange confusion of ideas and affections arises in the minds of many; and an appearance of no small contradiction between their notions and their actions. There are many who love virtue and who detest vice, and this not from hypocrisy or affectation, who notwithstanding very frequently act ill and wickedly in particulars without the least remorse; because these particular occasions never came into view, when the passions on the side of virtue were so warmly affected by certain words heated originally by the breath of others; and for this reason, it is hard to repeat certain sets of words, though owned by themselves unoperative, without being in some degree affected; especially if a warm and affecting tone of voice accompanies them, as suppose,

> Wise, valiant, generous, good, and great.

These words, by having no application, ought to be unoperative; but when words commonly sacred to great occasions are used, we are affected by them even without the occasions. When words which have been generally so applied are put together without any rational view, or in such a manner that they do not rightly agree with each other, the style is called bombast. And it requires in several cases much good sense and experience to be guarded against the force of such language; for when propriety is neglected, a greater number of these affecting words may be taken into the service, and a greater variety may be indulged in combining them.

The Effect of Words

If words have all their possible extent of power, three effects arise in the mind of the hearer. The first is, the *sound;* the second, the *picture,* or representation of the thing signified by the sound; the third is, the *affection* of the soul produced by one or by both of the foregoing. *Compounded abstract* words, of which we have been speaking, (honor, justice, liberty, and the like,) produce the first and the last of these effects, but not the second. *Simple abstracts* are used to signify some one simple idea without much adverting to others which may chance to attend it, as blue, green, hot, cold, and the like; these are capable of affecting all three of the purposes of words; as the *aggregate* words, man, castle, horse, &c. are in a yet higher degree. But I am of opinion, that the most general effect, even of these words, does not arise from their forming pictures of the several things they would represent in the imagination; because, on a very diligent examination of my own mind, and getting others to consider theirs, I do not find that once in twenty times any such picture is formed, and when it is, there is most commonly a particular effort of the imagination for that purpose. But the aggregate words operate, as I said of the compound-abstracts, not by presenting any image to the mind, but by having from use the same effect on being mentioned, that their original has when it is seen. Suppose we were to read a passage to this effect: "The river Danube rises in a moist and mountainous soil in the heart of Germany, where, winding to and fro, it waters several principalities, until, turning into Austria, and laving the walls of Vienna, it passes into Hungary; there with a vast flood, augmented by the Save and the Drave, it quits Christendom, and rolling through the barbarous countries which border on Tartary, it enters by many mouths in the Black Sea." In this description many things are mentioned, as mountains, rivers, cities, the sea, &c. But let anybody examine himself, and see whether he has had impressed on his imagination any pictures of a river, mountain, watery soil, Germany, &c. Indeed it is impossible, in the rapidity and quick succession of words in conversation, to have ideas both of the sound of the word, and of the thing represented; besides, some words, expressing real essences, are so mixed with others of a general and nominal import, that it is impracticable to jump from sense to thought, from particulars to generals, from things to words, in such a manner as to answer the purposes of life; nor is it necessary that we should.

Examples That Words May Affect Without Raising Images

I find it very hard to persuade several that their passions are affected by words from whence they have no ideas; and yet harder to convince them that in the ordinary course of conversation we are sufficiently understood without raising any images of the things concerning which we speak. It seems to be an odd subject of dispute with any man, whether he has ideas in his mind or not. Of this, at first view, every man, in his own forum, ought to judge without appeal. But, strange as it may appear, we are often at a loss to know what ideas we have of things, or whether we have any ideas at all upon some subjects. It even requires a good deal of attention to be thoroughly satisfied on this head. Since I wrote these papers, I found two very striking instances of the possibility there is, that a man may hear words without having any idea of the things which they represent, and yet afterwards be capable of returning them to others, combined in a new way, and with great propriety, energy, and instruction. The first instance is that of Mr. Blacklock, a poet blind from his birth. Few men blessed with the most perfect sight can describe visual objects with more spirit and justness than this blind man; which cannot possibly be attributed to his having a clearer conception of the things he describes than is common to other persons. Mr. Spence, in an elegant preface which he has written to the works of this poet, reasons very ingeniously, and, I imagine, for the most part, very rightly, upon the cause of this extraordinary phenomenon; but I cannot altogether agree with him, that some improprieties in language and thought, which occur in these poems, have arisen from the blind poet's imperfect conception of visual objects, since such improprieties, and much greater, may be found in writers even of a higher class than Mr. Blacklock, and who, notwithstanding, possessed the faculty of seeing in its full perfection. Here is a poet doubtless as much affected by his own descriptions as any that reads them can be; and yet he is affected with this strong enthusiasm by things of which he neither has, nor can possibly have, any idea further than that of a bare sound: and why may not those who read his works be affected in the same manner that he was; with as little of any real ideas of the things described? The second instance is of Mr. Saunderson, professor of mathematics in the University of Cambridge. This learned man had acquired great knowledge in natural philosophy, in astronomy, and whatever sciences depend upon mathematical skill. What was the most extraordinary and the most to my purpose, he gave excellent lectures upon light and colors; and this man taught others the theory of those ideas which they had, and which he himself undoubtedly had not. But it is probable that the words red, blue, green, answered to him as well as the ideas of the colors themselves; for the ideas of greater or lesser degrees of refrangibility being applied to these words, and the blind man being instructed in what other respects they were found to agree or to disagree, it was as easy for him to reason upon the words as if he had been fully master of the ideas. Indeed it must be owned he could make no new discoveries in the way of experiment. He did nothing but what we do every day in common discourse. When I wrote this last sentence, and used the words *every day* and *common discourse,* I had no images in my mind of any succession of time; nor of men in conference with each other; nor do I imagine that the reader will have any such ideas on reading it. Neither when I spoke of red, or blue, and green, as well as refrangibility, had I these several colors, or the rays of light passing into a different medium, and there diverted from their course, painted before me in the way of images. I know very well that the mind possesses a faculty of raising such images at pleasure; but then an act of the will is necessary to this; and in ordinary conversation or reading it is very rarely that any image at all is excited in the mind. If I say, "I shall go to Italy next summer," I am well understood. Yet I believe nobody has by this painted in his imagination the exact figure of the speaker passing by land or by water, or both; sometimes on horseback, sometimes in a carriage: with all the particulars of the journey. Still less has he any idea of Italy, the country to which I proposed to go; or of the greenness of the fields, the ripening of the fruits, and the warmth of the air, with the change to this from a different season, which are the ideas for which the word *summer* is substituted; but least of all has he any image from the word *next;* for this word stands for the idea of many summers, with the exclusion of all but one: and surely the man who says *next summer* has no images of such a succession, and such an exclusion. In short, it is not only of those ideas which are commonly called abstract, and of which no image at all can be formed, but even of particular, real beings, that we converse without having any idea of them excited in the imagination; as will certainly appear on a diligent examination of our own minds. Indeed, so little does poetry depend for its effect on the power of raising sensible images, that I am convinced it would lose a very considerable part of its energy, if this were the necessary result of all description. Because that union of affecting words, which is the most powerful of all poetical instruments, would frequently lose its force along with its propriety and consistency, if the sensible images were always excited. There is not, perhaps, in the whole Æneid a more grand and labored passage than the description of Vulcan's cavern in Etna, and the works that are there carried on. Virgil dwells particularly on the formation of the thunder which he describes unfinished under the hammers of the Cyclops. But what are the principles of this extraordinary composition?

Tres imbris torti radios, tres nubis aquosæ
Addiderant; rutili tres ignis, et alitis austri:
Fulgores nunc terrificos, sonitumque, metumque
Miscebant operi, flammisque sequacibus iras.

This seems to me admirably sublime: yet if we attend coolly to the kind of sensible images which a combination of ideas of this sort must form, the chimeras of madmen cannot appear more wild and absurd than such a picture. *"Three rays of twisted showers, three of watery clouds, three of fire, and three of the winged south wind; then mixed they in the work terrific lightnings, and sound, and fear, and anger, with pursuing flames."* This strange composition is formed into a gross body; it is hammered by the Cyclops, it is in part polished, and partly continues rough. The truth is, if poetry gives us a noble assemblage of words corresponding to many noble ideas, which are connected by circumstances of time or place, or related to each other as cause and effect, or associated in any natural way, they may be moulded together in any form, and perfectly answer their end. The picturesque connection is not demanded; because no real picture is formed; nor is the effect of the description at all the less upon this account. What is said of Helen by Priam and the old men of his council, is generally thought to give us the highest possible idea of that fatal beauty.

Οὐ νέμεσις, Τρῶας καὶ ἐϋκνήμιδας Ἀχαιοὺς
Τοιῇδ' ἀμφὶ γυναικὶ πολὺν χρόνον ἄλγεα πάσχειν
Αἰνῶς ἀθανάτῃσι Θεῇς εἰς ὦπα ἔοικεν.

They cried, No wonder such celestial charms
For nine long years have set the world in arms;
What winning graces! what majestic mien!
She moves a goddess, and she looks a queen.

                                                                               Pope

Here is not one word said of the particulars of her beauty; nothing which can in the least help us to any precise idea of her person; but yet we are much more touched by this manner of mentioning her, than by those long and labored descriptions of Helen, whether handed down by tradition, or formed by fancy, which are to be met with in some authors. I am sure it affects me much more than the minute description which Spenser has given of Belphebe; though I own that there are parts, in that description, as there are in all the descriptions of that excellent writer, extremely fine and poetical. The terrible picture which Lucretius has drawn of religion in order to display the magnanimity of his philosophical hero in opposing her, is thought to be designed with great boldness and spirit:—

Humana ante oculos fœdè cum vita jaceret,
In terris, oppressa gravi sub religione,
Quæ caput e cœli regionibus ostendebat
Horribili super aspectu mortalibus instans;

Primus Graius homo mortales tollere contra
Est oculos ausus.

What idea do you derive from so excellent a picture? none at all, most certainly: neither has the poet said a single word which might in the least serve to mark a single limb or feature of the phantom, which he intended to represent in all the horrors imagination can conceive. In reality, poetry and rhetoric do not succeed in exact description so well as painting does; their business is, to affect rather by sympathy than imitation; to display rather the effect of things on the mind of the speaker, or of others, than to present a clear idea of the things themselves. This is their most extensive province, and that in which they succeed the best.

Poetry Not Strictly an Imitative Art

Hence we may observe that poetry, taken in its most general sense, cannot with strict propriety be called an art of imitation. It is indeed an imitation so far as it describes the manners and passions of men which their words can express; where *animi motus effert interprete lingua.* There it is strictly imitation; and all merely *dramatic* poetry is of this sort. But *descriptive* poetry operates chiefly by *substitution;* by the means of sounds, which by custom have the effect of realities. Nothing is an imitation further than as it resembles some other thing; and words undoubtedly have no sort of resemblance to the ideas for which they stand.

How Words Influence the Passions

Now, as words affect, not by any original power, but by representation, it might be supposed, that their influence over the passions should be but light; yet it is quite otherwise; for we find by experience, that eloquence and poetry are as capable, nay indeed much more capable, of making deep and lively impressions than any other arts, and even than nature itself in very many cases. And this arises chiefly from these three causes. First, that we take an extraordinary part in the passions of others, and that we are easily affected and brought into sympathy by any tokens which are shown of them; and there are no tokens which can express all the circumstances of most passions so fully as words; so that if a person speaks upon any subject, he can not only convey the subject to you, but likewise the manner in which he is himself affected by it. Certain it is, that the influence of most things on our passions is not so much from the things themselves, as from our opinions concerning them; and these again depend very much on the opinions of other men, conveyable for the most part by words only. Secondly, there are many things of a very affecting nature, which can seldom occur in the reality, but the words that represent them often do; and thus they have an opportunity of making a deep impression and taking root in the mind, whilst the idea of the reality was transient; and to some perhaps never really occurred in any shape, to whom it is notwithstanding very affecting, as war, death, famine, &c. Besides many ideas have never been at all presented to the senses of any men but by words, as God, angels, devils, heaven, and hell, all of which have however a great influence over the passions. Thirdly, by words we have it in our power to make such *combinations* as we cannot possibly do otherwise. By this power of combining we are able, by the addition of well-chosen circumstances, to give a new life and force to the simple object. In painting we may represent any fine figure we please; but we never can give it those enlivening touches which it may receive from words. To represent an angel in a picture, you can only draw a beautiful young man winged: but what painting can furnish out anything so grand as the addition of one word, "the angel of the *Lord*"? It is true, I have here no clear idea; but these words affect the mind more than the sensible image did; which is all I contend for. A picture of Priam dragged to the altar's foot, and there murdered, if it were well executed, would undoubtedly be very moving; but there are very aggravating circumstances, which it could never represent:

Sanguine fœdantem quos ipse sacraverat ignes.

As a further instance, let us consider those lines of Milton, where he describes the travels of the fallen angels through their dismal habitation:

O'er many a dark and dreary vale
They passed, and many a region dolorous;
O'er many a frozen, many a fiery Alp;
Rocks, caves, lakes, fens, bogs, dens, and shades of death,
A universe of death.

Here is displayed the force of union in

Rocks, caves, lakes, dens, bogs, fens, and shades;

which yet would lose the greatest part of their effect, if they were not the

Rocks, caves, lakes, dens, bogs, fens, and shades—of *Death*.

This idea or this affection caused by a word, which nothing but a word could annex to the others, raises a very great degree of the sublime, and this sublime is raised yet higher by what follows, a "*universe of death*." Here are again two ideas not presentable but by language, and an union of them great and amazing beyond conception; if they may properly be called ideas which present no distinct image to the mind; but still it will be difficult to conceive how words can move the passions which belong to real objects, without representing these objects clearly. This is difficult to us, because we do not sufficiently distinguish, in our observations upon language, between a clear expression and a strong expression. These are frequently confounded with each other, though they are in reality extremely different. The former regards the understanding, the latter belongs to the passions. The one describes a thing as it is, the latter describes it as it is felt. Now, as there is a moving tone of voice, an impassioned countenance, an agitated gesture, which affect independently of the things about which they are exerted, so there are words, and certain dispositions of words, which being peculiarly devoted to passionate subjects, and always used by those who are under the influence of any passion, touch and move use more than those which far more clearly and distinctly express the subject-matter. We yield to sympathy what we refuse to description. The truth is, all verbal description, merely as naked description, though never so exact, conveys so poor and insufficient an idea of the thing described, that it could scarcely have the smallest effect, if the speaker did not call in to his aid those modes of speech that mark a strong and lively feeling in himself. Then, by the contagion of our passions, we catch a fire already kindled in another, which probably might never have been struck out by the object described. Words, by strongly conveying the passions by those means which we have already mentioned, fully compensate for their weakness in other respects. It may be observed, that very polished languages, and such as are praised for their superior clearness and perspicuity, are generally deficient in strength. The French language has that perfection and that defect. Whereas the Oriental tongues, and in general the languages of most unpolished people, have a great force and energy of expression, and this is but natural. Unculti-vated people are but ordinary observers of things, and not critical in distin-guishing them; but, for that reason they admire more, and are more affected with what they see, and therefore express themselves in a warmer and more passionate manner. If the affection be well conveyed, it will work its effect without any clear idea, often without any idea at all of the thing which has originally given rise to it.

It might be expected, from the fertility of the subject, that I should consider poetry, as it regards the sublime and beautiful, more at large; but it must be observed, that in this light it has been often and well handled already. It was not my design to enter into the criticism of the sublime and beautiful in any art, but to attempt to lay down such principles as may tend to ascertain, to distinguish, and to form a sort of standard for them; which purposes I thought might be best effected by an inquiry into the properties of such things in nature, as raise love and astonishment in us; and by showing in what manner they operated to produce these passions. Words were only so far to be considered as to show upon what principle they were capable of being the representatives of these natural things, and by what powers they were able to affect us often as strongly as the things they represent, and sometimes much more strongly.

Denis Diderot

1713–1784

Denis Diderot, one of history's most famous freethinkers, was born into an extremely pious bourgeois family in Langue, France, in 1713. His mother was the daughter of a tanner, and his father was a cutler—a master craftsman who enjoyed a reputation for excellent workmanship and personal integrity. Although Diderot later became estranged from his family, he expressed admiration for both parents throughout his life, saying that there were but two or three honest men and women in the world, and Providence, or good luck, had sent them to him. He also greatly loved his youngest sister, Angelique, whose death in a convent at the age of 28 inspired his later exposé of convent life in his novel *The Nun*.

By the time he was ten years old, Diderot had already entered the Jesuit college at Langue. There he benefited from a rigorous classical training, showing himself extremely quick in his studies and winning many prizes. For a brief time he showed interest in learning his father's trade, but he was a disaster in the shop—"spoiling everything he touched." At age thirteen he became an abbé in preparation for the priesthood. Despite his eventual notorious atheism, it seems that until he met his wife at age twenty-eight Diderot often considered pursuing an ecclesiastical career. For a time he even fasted, wore a hair shirt, and slept on straw.

When he was fifteen, Diderot went to Paris to complete his studies. Although not much is known about the next fourteen years of his life, it is clear that he spent them in Paris and that they were characterized more by dissolution than asceticism. It is also clear that Diderot spent a good deal of his time at the theatre. Thinking about becoming an actor himself, Diderot memorized speeches and attended as many plays as he could afford, sometimes putting his hands over his ears as he watched in order to concentrate on the actors' gestures and movements, and sometimes closing his eyes in order to concentrate on the diction, meter, and intonation of spoken poetry.

Diderot returned to Langue briefly in 1741 to request his father's permission to marry Anne Toinette Champion. His father violently objected. He had Diderot arrested and incarcerated in a monastery while he attempted to sway him from his plan. Diderot escaped, however, returned to Paris, and was secretly married. Presently the father of a daughter (the first of four), Diderot began a long and illustrious career as France's most eminent man of letters—chief among the *philosophes*.

In addition to editing the first *Encyclopedie,* Diderot was an extraordinarily prolific writer. Between 1745 and his death in 1784, he wrote significant and often highly controversial works in a variety of fields. Among the most important, his *Philosophical Thoughts* of 1746 asserted the existence of a natural morality independent of the influence of the Church and appealed for religious toleration. *An Essay on Blindness,* published in 1749, contained a proposal to teach the blind to read by the sense of touch, as well as a daring doctrine of materialist atheism which anticipated Darwin and for which Diderot was arrested. *Thoughts on the Interpretation of Nature* outlined a Baconian empiricist dialectic which became the philosophic method of the age. Diderot also wrote many of the articles for the *Encyclopedie,* as well as numerous essays, three novels, and several plays. Throughout his work Diderot advocated the spirit of science and freethinking against the authority of the Church.

Diderot's criticism, which has become increasingly influential, develops from his empiricism and naturalism. In an essay *On the Beautiful* in the *Encyclopedie* he argues that there is no internal, absolute sense of beauty; the basis of the beautiful is rather the perception of relationships. Thus the artist, like the scientist, must seek for reality in the external world. *The Letter on the Deaf and Dumb* reflects upon the mysterious relationship of sound to meaning in poetry, and suggests that poetic language can be understood as "hieroglyphic"—speculations later taken up and employed by Baudelaire, the Symbolists, and Wallace Stevens. And in his *Discourse on Dramatic Poetry* of 1758, Diderot anticipates Ibsen in his call for greater realism on the stage and new type of "bourgeois tragedy."

In *The Paradox of the Actor,* Diderot uses characteristic dialogue form to argue that the actor, like the poet or the scientist, cannot rely on his emotions or "sensibility," but rather must observe and imitate nature as it shows itself in human gestures. The greatest actor or the greatest poet, Diderot suggests, is not necessarily the man of greatest passion, but rather the man who most capably masters the technique of representing passion. The actor can become everything, Diderot argues, because he is himself nothing. Without being rigidly Neoclassical, Diderot here offers a provocative alternative to Romantic idealizations of the artist. This essay may also be read as a proto-Lacanian commentary on the psychological problem of self identity.

THE PARADOX OF ACTING

The First Speaker. Let us talk no more of that.

The Second Speaker. Why?

The First. It is the work of a friend of yours.[1]

The Second. What does that matter?

The First. A good deal. What is gained by accepting the alternatives of holding his talent or my judgment cheap, of going back on the good opinion you hold either of him or of me?

The Second. That will not be the result; and were it so it would make no hole in my friendship for both of you, founded as it is on firmer grounds.

The First. May be.

The Second. It is so. Do you know of what you just now remind me? Of an author I know who fell on his knees to a woman he loved to beg her not to go to the first night of a piece of his.

The First. A modest man, and a prudent.

The Second. He was afraid that her affection might hang on the amount of his literary fame.

The First. Like enough.

The Second. That a public check might lessen him somewhat in his mistress's eyes.

The First. That loss of love would follow on loss of reputation. That strikes you as absurd?

The Second. It was thought to be so. The box was taken; he had a complete success; and you may guess how he was embraced, made much of, caressed.

The First. He would have been made all the more of if the piece had been hissed.

The Second. I am sure I am right.

The First. And I hold to my view.

The Second. Hold to it by all means; but remember that I at least am not a woman, and that I am anxious you should explain yourself.

The First. Absolutely?

The Second. Absolutely.

The First. I should find it much easier to say nothing than to veil what I really think.

The Second. Of course.

The First. I shall be uncompromising.

The Second. That is just what my friend would like you to be.

The First. Well then, as I must speak—his work, crabbed, obscure, complicated, bombastic as it is in style, is yet full of commonplace. A great dramatic artist will not be a bit the better, a poor actor not a bit the less inefficient, for reading it. It is Nature who bestows personal gifts—appearance,

309

voice, judgment, tact. It is the study of the great models, the knowledge of the human heart, the habit of society, earnest work, experience, close acquaintance with the boards, which perfect Nature's gifts. The actor who is merely a mimic can count upon being always tolerable; his playing will call neither for praise nor for blame.

The Second. Or else for nothing but blame.

The First. Granted. The actor who goes by Nature alone is often detestable, sometimes excellent. But in whatever line, beware of a level mediocrity. No matter how harshly a beginner is treated, one may easily foretell his future success. It is only the incapables who are stifled by cries of 'Off! off!'[2] How should Nature without Art make a great actor when nothing happens on the stage exactly as it happens in nature, and when dramatic poems are all composed after a fixed system of principles? And how can a part be played in the same way by two different actors when, even with the clearest, the most precise, the most forceful of writers, words are no more, and never can be more, than symbols, indicating a thought, a feeling, or an idea; symbols which need action, gesture, intonation, expression, and a whole context of circumstance, to give them their full significance? When you have heard these words—

> *'Que fait là votre main?'*
> *'Je tâte votre habit, l'étoffe en est moelleuse'*
> ['Your hand—what does it there?'
> 'It feels your robe; 'tis soft and pleasant to the touch']

what do you know of their meaning? Nothing. Weigh well what follows, and remember how often and how easily it happens that two speakers may use the same words to express entirely different thoughts and matters. The instance I am going to cite is a very singular one; it is the very work of your friend that we have been discussing. Ask a French actor what he thinks of it; he will tell you that every word of it is true. Ask an English actor, and he will swear that, *'By God*, there's not a sentence to change! It is the very gospel of the stage!' However, since there is nothing in common between the way of writing comedy and tragedy in England, and the way of writing stage poems in France; since, according to Garrick himself, an actor who will play you a scene of Shakespeare to perfection is ignorant of the first principles of declamation needed for Racine; since, entwined by Racine's musical lines as if by so many serpents whose folds compress his head, his feet, his hands, his legs, and his arms, he would, in attempting these lines, lose all liberty of action; it follows obviously that the French and the English actors, entirely at one as to the soundness of your author's principles, are yet at variance, and that the technical terms of the stage are so broad and so vague that men of judgment, and of diametrically opposite views, yet find in them the light of conviction. Now hold closer than ever to your maxim, *'Avoid explanation if what you want is a mutual understanding.'*[3]

The Second. You think that in every work, and especially in this, there are two distinct meanings, both expressed in the same terms, one understood in London, the other in Paris?

The First. Yes; and that these terms express so clearly the two meanings that your friend himself has fallen into a trap. In associating the names of English with those of French actors, applying to both the same precepts, giving to both the same praise and the same reproofs, he has doubtless imagined that what he said of the one set was equally true of the other.

The Second. According to this, never before was author so wrong-headed.

The First. I am sorry to admit that this is so, since he uses the same words to express one thing at the Cross-roads of Bussy and another thing at Drury Lane. Of course I may be wrong. But the important point on which your author and I are entirely at variance concerns the qualities above all necessary to a great actor. In my view he must have a deal of judgment. He must have in himself an unmoved and disinterested onlooker. He must have, consequently, penetration and no sensibility; the art of mimicking everything, or, which comes to the same thing, the same aptitude for every sort of character and part.

The Second. No sensibility?

The First. None. I have not yet arranged my ideas logically, and you must let me tell them to you as they come to me, with the same want of order that marks your friend's book. If the actor were full, really full, of feeling, how could he play the same part twice running with the same spirit and success? Full of fire at the first performance, he would be worn out and cold as marble at the third. But take it that he is an attentive mimic and thoughtful disciple of Nature, then the first time he comes on the stage as Augustus, Cinna, Orosmanes, Agamemnon, or Mahomet, faithful copying of himself and the effects he has arrived at, and constantly observing human nature, will so prevail that his acting, far from losing in force, will gather strength with the new observations he will make from time to time. He will increase or moderate his effects, and you will be more and more pleased with him. If he is himself while he is playing, how is he to stop being himself? If he wants to stop being himself, how is he to catch just the point where he is to stay his hand?

What confirms me in this view is the unequal acting of players who play from the heart. From them you must expect no unity. Their playing is alternately strong and feeble, fiery and cold, dull and sublime. To-morrow they will miss the point they have excelled in to-day; and to make up for it will excel in some passage where last time they failed.[4] On the other hand, the actor who plays from thought, from study of human nature, from constant imitation of some ideal type, from imagination, from memory, will be one and the same at all performances, will be always at his best mark; he has considered, combined, learnt and arranged the whole thing in his head; his diction is neither monotonous nor dissonant. His passion has a definite course—it has bursts, and it has reactions; it has a beginning, a middle, and an end. The accents are the same, the positions are the same, the movements are the same; if there is any difference between two performances, the latter is generally the better. He will be invariable; a looking-glass, as it were, ready to reflect realities, and to reflect them ever with the same precision, the same strength, and the same truth. Like the poet he will dip for ever into the inexhaustible treasure-house of Nature, instead of coming very soon to an end of his own poor resources.

What acting was ever more perfect than Clairon's?[5] Think over this, study it; and you will find that at the sixth performance of a given part she has every detail of her acting by heart, just as much as every word of her part. Doubtless she has imagined a type, and to conform to this type has been her first thought; doubtless she has chosen for her purpose the highest, the greatest, the most perfect type her imagination could compass. This type, however, which she has borrowed from history, or created as who should create some vast spectre in her own mind, is not herself. Were it indeed bounded by her own dimensions, how paltry, how feeble would be her playing! When, by dint of hard work, she has got as near as she can to this idea, the thing is done; to preserve the same nearness is a mere matter of memory and practice. If you were with her while she studied her part how many times you would cry out, *That is right!* and how many times she would answer, *You are wrong!*

Just so a friend of Le Quesnoy's[6] once cried, catching him by the arm, 'Stop! you will make it worse by bettering it—you will spoil the whole thing!' 'What I have done,' replied the artist, panting with exertion, 'you have seen; what I have got hold of and what I mean to carry out to the very end you cannot see.'

I have no doubt that Clairon goes through just the same struggles as Le Quesnoy in her first attempts at a part; but once the struggle is over, once she has reached the height she has given to her spectre, she has herself well in hand, she repeats her efforts without emotion. As it will happen in dreams, her head touches the clouds, her hands stretch to grasp the horizon on both sides; she is the informing soul of a huge figure, which is her outward casing, and in which her efforts have enclosed her. As she lies careless and still on a sofa with folded arms and closed eyes she can, following her memory's dream, hear herself, see herself, judge herself, and judge also the effects she will produce. In such a vision she has a double personality; that of the little Clairon and of the great Agrippina.

The Second. According to you the likest thing to an actor, whether on the boards or at his private studies, is a group of children who play at ghosts in a graveyard at dead of night, armed with a white sheet on the end of a broomstick, and fending forth from its shelter hollow groans to frighten wayfarers.

The First. Just so, indeed. Now with Dumesnil[7] it is a different matter: she is not like Clairon. She comes on the stage without knowing what she is going to say; half the time she does not know what she is saying: but she has one sublime moment. And pray, why should the actor be different from the poet, the painter, the orator, the musician? It is not in the stress of the first burst that characteristic traits come out; it is in moments of stillness and self-command; in moments entirely unexpected. Who can tell whence these traits have their being? They are a sort of inspiration. They come when the man of genius is hovering between nature and his sketch of it, and keeping a watchful eye on both. The beauty of inspiration, the chance hits of which his work is full, and of which the sudden appearance startles himself, have an importance, a success, a sureness very different from that belonging to the first fling. Cool reflection must bring the fury of enthusiasm to its bearings.

The extravagant creature who loses his self-control has no hold on us; this is gained by the man who is self-controlled. The great poets, especially the great dramatic poets, keep a keen watch on what is going on, both in the physical and the moral world.

The Second. The two are the same.

The First. They dart on everything which strikes their imagination; they make, as it were, a collection of such things. And from these collections, made all unconsciously, issue the grandest achievements of their work.

Your fiery, extravagant, sensitive fellow, is for ever on the boards; he acts the play, but he gets nothing out of it. It is in him that the man of genius finds his model. Great poets, great actors, and, I may add, all great copyists of Nature, in whatever art, beings gifted with fine imagination, with broad judgment, with exquisite tact, with a sure touch of taste, are the least sensitive of all creatures. They are too apt for too many things, too busy with observing, considering, and reproducing, to have their inmost hearts affected with any liveliness. To me such an one always has his portfolio spread before him and his pencil in his fingers.

It is we who feel; it is they who watch, study, and give us the result.[8] And then . . . well, why should I not say it? Sensibility is by no means the distinguishing mark of a great genius. He will have, let us say, an abstract love of justice, but he will not be moved to temper it with mercy. It is the head, not the heart, which works in and for him. Let some unforeseen opportunity arise, the man of sensibility will lose it; he will never be a great king, a great minister, a great commander, a great advocate, a great physician. Fill the front of a theatre with tearful creatures, but I will none of them on the boards. Think of women, again. They are miles beyond us in sensibility; there is no sort of comparison between their passion and ours. But as much as we are below them in action, so much are they below us in imitation. If a man who is really manly drops a tear, it touches us more nearly than a storm of weeping from a woman. In the great play, the play of the world, the play to which I am constantly recurring, the stage is held by the fiery souls, and the pit is filled with men of genius. The actors are in other words madmen; the spectators, whose business it is to paint their madness, are sages. And it is they who discern with a ready eye the absurdity of the motley crowd, who reproduce it for you, and who make you laugh both at the unhappy models who have bored you to death and at yourself. It is they who watch you, and who give you the mirth-moving picture of the tiresome wretch and of your own anguish in his clutches.[9]

You may prove this to demonstration, and a great actor will decline to acknowledge it; it is his own secret. A middling actor or a novice is sure to contradict you flatly; and of some others it may be said that they believe they feel, just as it has been said of some pious people that they believe they believe; and that without faith in the one case and without sensibility in the other there is no health.

This is all very well, you may reply; but what of these touching and sorrowful accents that are drawn from the very depth of a mother's heart and that shake her whole being? Are these not the result of true feeling? are these not the very inspiration of despair? Most certainly not. The proof is that they are all planned; that they are part of a system of declamation; that, raised or lowered by the twentieth part of a quarter of a tone, they would ring false; that they are in subjection to a law of unity; that, as in harmony, they are arranged in chords and in discords; that laborious study is needed to give them completeness; that they are the elements necessary to the solving of a given problem; that, to hit the right mark once, they have been practised a hundred times; and that, despite all this practice, they are yet found wanting. Look you, before he cries 'Zaïre vous pleurez,' or 'Vous y serez ma fille,' the actor has listened over and over again to his own voice. At the very moment when he touches your heart he is listening to his own voice; his talent depends not, as you think, upon feeling, but upon rendering so exactly the outward signs of feeling, that you fall into the trap. He has rehearsed to himself every note of his passion. He has learnt before a mirror every particle of his despair. He knows exactly when he must produce his handkerchief and shed tears; and you will see him weep at the word, at the syllable, he has chosen, not a second sooner or later. The broken voice, the half-uttered words, the stifled or prolonged notes of agony, the trembling limbs, the faintings, the bursts of fury—all this is pure mimicry, lessons carefully learned, the grimacing of sorrow, the magnificent aping which the actor remembers long after his first study of it, of which he was perfectly conscious when he first put it before the public, and which leaves him, luckily for the poet, the spectator, and himself, a full freedom of mind. Like other gymnastics, it taxes only his bodily strength. He puts off the sock or the buskin; his voice is gone; he is tired; he changes his dress, or he goes to bed; and he feels neither trouble, nor sorrow, nor depression, nor weariness of soul. All these emotions he has given to you. The actor is tired, you are unhappy; he has had exertion without feeling, you feeling without exertion. Were it otherwise the player's lot would be the most wretched on earth: but he is not the person he represents; he plays it, and plays it so well that you think he is the person; the deception is all on your side; he knows well enough that he is not the person.

For diverse modes of feeling arranged in concert to obtain the greatest effect, scored orchestrally, played *piano* and played *forte*, harmonised to make an individual effect—all that to me is food for laughter. I hold to my point, and I tell you this: 'Extreme sensibility makes middling actors; middling sensibility makes the ruck of bad actors; in complete absence of sensibility is the possibility of a sublime actor.' The player's tears come from his brain, the sensitive being's from his heart; the sensitive being's soul gives unmeasured trouble to his brain; the player's brain gives sometimes a touch of trouble to his soul: he weeps as might weep an unbelieving priest preaching of the Passion;

as a seducer might weep at the feet of a woman whom he does not love, but on whom he would impose; like a beggar in the street or at the door of a church—a beggar who substitutes insult for vain appeal; or like a courtesan who has no heart, and who abandons herself in your arms.

Have you ever thought on the difference between the tears raised by a tragedy of real life and those raised by a touching narrative? You hear a fine piece of recitation; by little and little your thoughts are involved, your heart is touched, and your tears flow. With the tragedy of real life the thing, the feeling and the effect, are all one; your heart is reached at once, you utter a cry, your head swims, and the tears flow. These tears come of a sudden, the others by degrees. And here is the superiority of a true effect of nature over a well-planned scene. It does at one stroke what the scene leads up to by degrees, but it is far more difficult to reproduce its effect; one incident ill given would shatter it. Accents are more easily mimicked than actions, but actions go straighter to the mark. This is the basis of a canon to which I believe there is no exception. If you would avoid coldness you must complete your effect by action and not by talk.

So, then, have you no objection to make? Ah! I see! You give a recitation in a drawing-room; your feelings are stirred; your voice fails you; you burst into tears. You have, as you say, felt, and felt deeply. Quite so; but had you made up your mind to that? Not at all. Yet you were carried away, you surprised and touched your hearers, you made a great hit. All this is true enough. But now transfer your easy tone, your simple expression, your every-day bearing, to the stage, and, I assure you, you will be paltry and weak. You may cry to your heart's content, and the audience will only laugh. It will be the tragedy outside a booth at a fair.[10] Do you suppose that the dialogue of Corneille, of Racine, of Voltaire, or, let me add, of Shakespeare, can be given with your ordinary voice and with your fireside tone? No; not a bit more than you would tell a fireside story with the open-mouthed emphasis fit for the boards.

The Second. Perhaps Racine and Corneille, great names as they are, did nothing of account.

The First. Oh, blasphemy! Who could dare to say it? Who to endorse it? The merest word Corneille wrote cannot be given in everyday tone.

But, to go back, it must have happened to you a hundred times that at the end of your recitation, in the very midst of the agitation and emotion you have caused in your drawing-room audience, a fresh guest has entered, and wanted to hear you again. You find it impossible, you are weary to the soul. Sensibility, fire, tears, all have left you. Why does not the actor feel the same exhaustion? Because there is a world of difference between the interests excited by a flattering tale and by your fellow-man's misfortune. Are you Cinna? Have you ever been Cleopatra, Merope, Agrippina? Are these same personages on the stage ever historical personages? Not at all. They are the vain images of poetry. No, nor even that. They are the phantoms fashioned from this or that poet's special fantasy. They are well enough on the stage, these hippogriffs, so to call them, with their actions, their bearing, their intonations. They would make but a sorry figure in history; they would raise laughter in society. People would whisper to each other, 'Is this fellow mad? Where in the world does this Don Quixote come from? Who is the inventor of all this stuff? In what world do people talk like this?'

The Second. And why are they not intolerable on the stage?

The First. Because there is such a thing as stage convention. As old a writer as Æschylus laid this down as a formula—it is a protocol three thousand years old.

The Second. And will this protocol go on much longer?

The First. That I cannot tell you. All I know is that one gets further away from it as one gets nearer to one's own time and country. Find me a situation closer to that of Agamemnon in the first scene of *Iphigenia* than that of *Henri IV.*: when, beset by fears only too well founded, he said to those around him, 'They will kill me; there is nothing surer; they will kill me!' Suppose that great man, that superb and hapless monarch, troubled in the night-watches with this deadly presentiment, got up and knocked at the door of Sully, his minister and friend—is there, think you, a poet foolish enough to make Henri say—

> '*Oui, c'est Henri, s'est ton roi qui t'éveille;*
> *Viens, reconnais la voix qui frappe ton oreille?*'
> (Ay, it is Agamemnon [Henri], 'tis thy King
> That wakes thee; his the voice that strikes thine ear.)

Or to make Sully reply—

> '*C'est vous-même, seigneur? Quel important besoin*
> *Vous a fait devancer l'aurore de si loin?*
> *A peine un faible jour vous éclaire et me guide,*
> *Vos yeux seuls et les miens sont ouverts. . . .*'[11]
> [Is't thou indeed, my lord? What grave concern
> Has made thee leave thy couch before the dawn?
> A feeble light scarce lets me see thy face,
> No eyes but ours are open yet in Aulis. . . .]

The Second. Perhaps Agamemnon really talked like that.

The First. No more than Henri IV. did. Homer talks like that; Racine talks like that; poetry talks like that; and this pompous language can only be used by unfamiliar personages, spoken from poetical lips, with poetical tone. Reflect a little as to what, in the language of the theatre, is *being true*. Is it showing things as they are in nature? Certainly not. Were it so the true would be the commonplace. What then, is truth for stage purposes? It is the conforming of action, diction, face, voice, movement, and gesture, to an ideal type invented by the poet, and frequently enhanced by the player. That is the strange part of it. This type not only influences the tone, it alters the actor's very walk and bearing. And hence it is that the player in private and the player on the boards are two personages, so different that one can scarce recognise the player in private. The first time I saw Mlle. Clairon in her own house I exclaimed, by a natural impulse, 'Ah, mademoiselle, I thought you were at least a head taller!'

An unhappy, a really unhappy woman, may weep and fail to touch you; worse than that, some trivial disfigurement in her may incline you to laughter; the accent which is apt to her is to your ears dissonant and vexatious; a movement which is habitual to her makes her grief show ignobly and sulkily to you; almost all the violent passions lend themselves to grimaces which a tasteless artist will copy but too faithfully, and which a great actor will avoid. In the very whirlwind of passion we would have a man preserve his manly dignity. And what is the effect of this heroic effort? To give relief and temperance to sorrow. We would have this heroine fall with a becoming grace, that hero die like a gladiator of old in the midst of the arena to the applause of the circus, with a noble grace, with a fine and picturesque attitude. And who will execute this design of ours? The athlete who is mastered by pain, shattered by his own sensibility, or the athlete who is trained, who has self-control, who, as he breathes his last sigh, remembers the lessons of the gymnasium? Neither the gladiator of old nor the great actor dies as people die in their beds; it is for them to show us another sort of death, a death to move us; and the critical spectator will feel that the bare truth, the unadorned fact, would seem despicable and out of harmony with the poetry of the rest.

Not, mark you, that Nature unadorned has not her moments of sublimity; but I fancy that if there is any one sure to give and preserve their sublimity it is the man who can feel it with his passion and his genius, and reproduce it with complete self-possession.

I will not, however, deny that there is a kind of acquired or factitious sensibility; but if you would like to know what I think about it, I hold it to be nearly as dangerous as natural sensibility. By little and little it leads the actor into mannerism and monotony. It is an element opposed to the variety of a great actor's functions. He must often strip it from him; and it is only a head of iron which can make such a self-abnegation. Besides, it is far better for the ease and success of his study, for the catholicity of his talent and the perfection of his playing, that there should be no need of this strange parting of self from self. Its extreme difficulty, confining each actor to one single line, leads perforce to a numerous company, where every part is ill played; unless, indeed, the natural order of things is reversed, and the pieces are made for the actors. To my thinking the actors, on the contrary, ought to be made for the pieces.[12]

The Second. But if a crowd of people collected in the street by some catastrophe begin of a sudden, and each in his own way, and without any concert, to exhibit a natural sensibility, they will give you a magnificent show, and display you a thousand types, valuable for sculpture, music, and poetry.

The First. True enough. But will this show compare with one which is the result of a pre-arranged plan, with the harmony which the artist will put into it when he transfers it from the public way to his stage or canvas? If you say it will, then I shall make you this answer: What is this boasted magic of art if it only consists in spoiling what both nature and chance have done better than art? Do you deny that one can improve on nature? Have you never, by way of praising a woman, said she is as lovely as one of Raphael's Madonnas? Have you never cried, on seeing a fine landscape, 'It's as good as a description in a novel?' Again, you are talking to me of a reality. I am talking to you of an imitation. You are talking to me of a passing moment in Nature. I am talking to you of a work of Art, planned and composed—a work which is built up by degrees, and which lasts. Take now each of these actors; change the scene in the street as you do on the boards, and show me your personages left successively to themselves, two by two or three by three. Leave them to their own swing; make them full masters of their actions; and you will see what a monstrous discord will result. You will get over this by making them rehearse together. Quite so. And then good-bye to their natural sensibility; and so much the better.

A play is like any well-managed association, in which each individual sacrifices himself for the general good and effect. And who will best take the measure of the sacrifice? The enthusiast or the fanatic? Certainly not. In society, the man of judgment; on the stage, the actor whose wits are always about him. Your scene in the street has the same relation to a scene on the stage that a band of savages has to a company of civilised men.

Now is the time to talk to you of the disastrous influence which a middling associate has on a first-rate player. This player's conception is admirable; but he has to give up his ideal type in order to come down to the level of the poor wretch who is playing with him. Then he says farewell to his study and his taste. As happens with talks in the street or at the fireside, the principal speaker lowers his tone to that of his companion. Or if you would like another illustration, take that of whist, where you lose a deal of your own skill if you cannot rely on your partner. More than this, Clairon will tell you, if you ask her, that Le Kain[13] would maliciously make her play badly or inadequately, and that she would avenge herself by getting him hissed. What, then, are two players who mutually support each other? Two personages whose types are, in due proportion, either equal, or else in them the subordination demanded by the circumstances, as laid down by the poet, is observed. But for this there would be an excess, either of strength or of weakness; and such a want of harmony as this is avoided more frequently by the strong descending to the weak than by its raising the weak to its own level. And pray, do you know the reason of the numberless rehearsals that go on? They are to strike the balance between the different talents of the actors, so as to establish a general unity in playing. When the vanity of an individual interferes with this balance the result is to injure the effect and to spoil your enjoyment; for it is seldom that the excellence of one actor can atone for the mediocrity, which it brings into relief, of his companions. I have known a great actor suffer from his temperament in this way. The stupid public said he was extravagant, instead of discerning that his associate was inadequate.

Come, you are a poet; you have a piece for the stage; and I leave you to choose between actors with the soundest judgments and the coolest heads and actors of sensibility. But before you make up your mind let me ask you one question. What is the time of life for a great actor? The age when one is full of fire, when the blood boils in the veins, when the slightest check troubles one to the soul, when the wit blazes at the veriest spark? I fancy not. The man whom Nature stamps an actor does not reach his topmost height until he has had a long experience, until the fury of the passions is subdued, until the head is cool and the heart under control. The best wine is harsh and crude in its fermenting. It is by long lying in the cask that it grows generous. Cicero, Seneca, and Plutarch, I take to represent the three ages of composition in men. Cicero is often but a blaze of straw, pretty to look at; Seneca a fire of vine-branches, hurtful to look at; but when I stir old Plutarch's ashes I come upon the great coals of a fire that gives me a gentle warmth.

Baron, when sixty years old, played the Earl of Essex, Xiphares, Britannicus, and played them well. Gaussin,[14] at fifty, bewitched her audiences in *L'Oracle et la Pupille*.

The Second. She cannot have looked the part.

The First. No; and here you hit perhaps an insurmountable obstacle to getting a perfect stage performance. For that your player must have trod the boards many years, and sometimes a part calls for the blush of youth.[15] If there ever has been an actress who at seventeen could play Monimia, Dido, Pulcheria, Hermione, why then that is a miracle which will not be repeated.[16] However, an old player does not become ridiculous until his strength has quite left him, or until his fine art will not avail to outweigh the contrast between his real and his supposed age. As on the stage, so is it in the world, where people never fall foul of a woman's conduct unless she has neither talent nor other kind of merit enough to veil her failing.

In our days Clairon and Molé[17] played when they first appeared like automata; afterwards they became fine players.[18] Why was this? Did they, think you, acquire more soul, sensibility, heart, in proportion as they grew older?

It is not long since, after ten years' absence from the stage, Clairon consented to a reappearance. If she played but moderately, was it that she had lost her soul, her sensibility, her heart? Not at all; what she had lost was the memory of her methods. I appeal to the future to confirm me.

The Second. What! you believe she will come back to the stage?

The First. Or die of boredom. What substitute is there for the great passions and the house's plaudits?

If such or such an actor or actress were as deeply moved as people suppose, tell me if the one would think of casting an eye round the boxes, the other of smiling to some one at the wing, and, as almost all of them do, speaking straight to the pit; and if the call-boy would have to go to the greenroom and interrupt a third player in a hearty fit of laughter by telling him that it's time to go and stab himself?

Come, I will sketch you a scene between an actor and his wife who detested each other; a scene of tender and passionate love; a scene publicly played on the boards, just as I am going to rehearse it, or maybe a trifle better; a scene in which both players surpassed themselves—in which they excited continual bursts of applause from pit and boxes; a scene interrupted half-a-score of times with our clapping of hands and exclamations of delight. Their triumph was won in the third scene of the fourth act of Molière's *Le Dépit Amoureaux*. The actor plays Eraste, Lucile's lover. The actor's wife plays Lucile, Eraste's adored.

THE ACTOR

Non, non, ne croyez pas, madame,
Que je revienne encor vous parler de ma flamme.
  (THE ACTRESS. *I just advise you.*)
C'en est fait.
  (*I hope so.*)
                    Je me veux guérir et connais bien,
Ce que de votre cœur a possédé le mien.
  (*More than you deserved.*)
Un courroux si constant pour l'ombre d'une offense,
  (*You offend me! You flatter yourself.*)
M'a trop bien éclairci de votre indifférence:
Et je dois vous montrer que les traits du mépris,
  (*Yes, the deepest contempt.*)
Sont sensibles surtout aux généreux esprits
  (*Yes, to generous minds.*)
Je l'avouerai, mes yeux observaient dans les vôtres,
Des charmes qu'ils n'ont point trouvés dans tous les autres.
  (*Not for want of looking.*)
Et le ravissement où j'étais de mes fers
Les aurait préférés à des sceptres offerts.
  (*You have made a better bargain.*)
Je vivais tout en vous;
  (*That's not the case; you tell a lie.*)
                          Et je l'avouerai même
Peut-être qu'après tout j'aurai quoique outragé,
Assez de peine encore à m'en voir dégagé.
  (*That would be a bore.*)
Possible que malgré la cure qu'elle essaie
Mon âme saignera longtemps de cette plaie.
  (*Don't be afraid—mortification has set in.*)
Et qu'affranchi d'un joug qui faisait tout mon bien,
Il faudra me résoudre à n'aimer jamais rien.
  (*You'll find a way out of that.*)
Mais enfin il n'importe; et puisque votre haine,
Chasse un cœur tant de fois que l'amour vous ramène,
C'est la dernière ici des importunités
Que vous aurez jamais de mes vœux rebutés.

THE ACTRESS

Vous pouvez faire aux miens la grâce tout entière,
Monsieur, et m'épargner encor cette dernière.

(THE ACTOR. *Sweetheart, you are an insolent baggage, and you shall live to repent this.*)

THE ACTOR

Eh bien, madame! eh bien! ils seront satisfaits,
Je romps avecque vous, et j'y romps pour jamais,
Puisque vous le voulez, que je perde la vie,
Lorsque de vous parler je reprendrai l'envie.

THE ACTRESS

Taint mieux, c'est m'obliger.

THE ACTOR

Non, non, n'ayez pas peur

(THE ACTRESS. *Afraid of you? Not I!*)

Que je fausse parole! Eussé-je un faible cœur,
Jusques à n'en pouvoir effacer votre image,
Croyez que vous n'aurez jamais cet avantage
    (*Ill-luck, you mean.*)
De me voir revenir.

THE ACTRESS

Ce serait bien en vain.

(THE ACTOR. *My darling, you are an arrant wretch; but I'll teach you to behave.*)

THE ACTOR

Moi-même de cent coups je percerais mon sein.
    (THE ACTRESS. *I wish to Heaven you would!*)
Si j'avais jamais fait cette bassesse insigne.
    (*Why not, after so many others?*)
De vous revoir après traitement indigne.

THE ACTRESS

Soit; n'en parlons donc plus.[19]

And so on, and so on. After this double scene—one of love, the other of marriage—as Eraste led his adored Lucile to the wing he squeezed her arm so hard as to tear his sweet wife's flesh, and answered her complaints with the bitterest insults.

The Second. If I had heard these two simultaneous scenes I don't think I should ever have set foot in a playhouse again.

The First. If you think this actor and actress were moved, let me ask you, was it in the lovers' scene, or the husband and wife's scene, or both? Now listen to another scene between the same actress and another player—her lover. While he is speaking his lines the actress says of her husband, '*He is a brute. He called me . . . I cannot repeat what he called me.*'

While she, in turn, gives her lines, her lover replies, '*Aren't you accustomed to it by this time?*'

And so on from speech to speech. 'Do we sup together to-night?' 'By all means; but how can we escape observation?' 'That you must manage.' 'If he finds out?' 'It will make no odds; and we shall have a quiet evening.' 'Whom shall we ask?' 'Whom you like.' 'The Chevalier, to begin with; he is our mainstay.' 'Talking of him, do you know I could easily get up a jealousy of him?' 'And I could as easily give you cause for it.'

Thus, then, these sensitive creatures seemed to you to be heart and soul in the speeches spoken out loud, which you heard, while really they were immersed in the speeches spoken under their breath, which you did not hear. You exclaimed to yourself, 'It must be admitted that she is a charming actress; no one listens so well as she does; and she plays with an intelligence, a grace, a conviction, a fine touch, a sensibility, by no means common.' I meanwhile laughed at your exclamations.

Well, this actress plays her husband false with another actor, plays this other actor false with the Chevalier, and plays the Chevalier false with yet another person, with whom the Chevalier catches her. The Chevalier plots a mighty vengeance. He takes his place in the lowest part of the stageseats[20] (the Comte de Lauraguais had not then rid our stage of this arrangement). Stationed thus he looked forward to disconcerting the faithless wretch by his presence, and by his contemptuous looks to completely upsetting her, and getting her hooted by the pit. The piece begins; the traitress appears; she sees the Chevalier, and without any disturbance to her acting she says to him, with a smile, 'Ah! silly fellow, making a fuss for nothing!' The Chevalier smiles in his turn, and she goes on: 'You are coming to-night?' He makes no answer, and she continues: 'Let us make an end of this foolish quarrel; and do you order up your carriage.' And do you know in what scene she put in all this? It was in one of the most touching scenes of La Chaussée,[21] a scene in which the actress was convulsed with sobs and made us drop scalding tears. This startles you; yet it is an exact statement of fact.

The Second. It's enough to sicken one of the stage.

The First. And why, pray? If this kind of people could not achieve such feats, what business would they have on the stage? Now I will tell you a thing I have actually seen.

Garrick[22] will put his head between two folding-doors, and in the course of five or six seconds his expression will change successively from wild delight to temperate pleasure, from this to tranquillity, from tranquillity to surprise, from surprise to blank astonishment, from that to sorrow, from sorrow to the air of one overwhelmed, from that to fright, from fright to horror, from horror to despair, and thence he will go up again to the point from which he started. Can his soul have experienced all these feelings, and played this kind of scale in concert with his face? I don't believe it; nor do you. If you ask this famous man, who in himself is as well worth a visit to England as the ruins of Rome are worth a visit to Italy; if you ask him, I say, for the scene of the Pastrycook's Boy he will play it for you; if you asked him directly afterwards for the great scene in *Hamlet* he would play it for you. He was as ready to cry over the tarts in the gutter as to follow the course of the air-drawn dagger.[23] Can one laugh or cry at will? One shall make a show of doing so as well or ill as one can, and the completeness of the illusion varies as one is or is not Garrick.

I play the fool in this sort sometimes, and with success enough to take in men who have knocked about the world a great deal. When I go distracted over the pretended death of my sister in the scene with the Norman lawyer; when in the scene with the First Clerk of the Admiralty I confess to the paternity of the child of a captain's wife; I seem exactly as if I suffered grief and shame: but do I suffer either? Not a bit more now that the thing is in definite stage shape than originally in private company, where I invented these two parts before putting them into a stage play.[24] What, then, is a great actor? A man who, having learnt the words set down for him by the author, fools you thoroughly, whether in tragedy or comedy.

Sedaine produces the *Philosophe sans le Savoir*. I took more interest in the piece's success than he did; envy of others' talents is not among my vices; I have enough indeed without it. I may call to witness all my brothers in literature, if, whenever they have deigned to consult me as to their work, I have not done all I could to give a fitting answer to this high mark of esteem. The *Philosophe sans le Savoir* trembles in the balance at the first and second performances, and I am very sorry for it; at the third it goes like wildfire, and I am delighted. The next morning I jump into a coach and rush to find Sedaine. It was winter and horribly cold, but I went everywhere where I could hope to find him. I am told he is in the depths of the Faubourg St. Antoine, and my driver takes me there. I rush up to him, I throw my arms round his neck, my voice fails me, and tears run down my cheeks. There you have the man of sensibility, the middling man. Sedaine, reserved and still, looks at me and says, 'Ah! Monsieur Diderot, you are splendid!' There you have the man of observation—the man of genius.

I told this story one day at table in the house of a man whose high talents marked him for the greatest place in the State—in the house of M. Necker.[25] There were many men of letters there; amongst them Marmontel, who is my friend as I am his. He said to me with an ironical air, 'Then, if Voltaire is overcome by the mere narrative of a pathetic incident, and Sedaine is undisturbed by the sight of a friend in tears, Voltaire is the ordinary man and Sedaine the man of genius.' This apostrophe put me out, and reduced me to silence, because the man of sensibility, like me, is wrapped up in the objection to his argument, loses his head, and does not find his answer until he is leaving the house. A cold and self-possessed person might have replied to Marmontel, 'Your observation would come better from other lips than yours, for you feel no more than Sedaine, and you too turn out fine work. You, being in the same line with him, might have left it to some one else to be an impartial judge of his talent. But, without preferring Sedaine to Voltaire, or Voltaire to Sedaine, can you tell me what would have come out of the brains of the author of the *Philosophe sans le Savoir*, of the *Déserteur*, and of *Paris Sauvé*, if, instead of passing thirty-five years of his life in damping plaster and cutting stone, he had spent all this time, like Voltaire, like you and me, in reading and thinking on Homer, Virgil, Tasso, Cicero, Demosthenes, and Tacitus? We could never learn to see things as he does; he might have learnt to tell them as we do. I look upon him as one of the latest posterity of Shakespeare; of Shakespeare, whom I shall compare neither to the Apollo Belvedere nor to the Gladiator, nor to Antinous, nor to the Farnese Hercules, but rather to the Saint Christopher in

Notre Dame—a shapeless Colossus, coarsely sculptured, if you will. Yet we might all walk between his legs and never a head reach to his thighs.'

Now here is another instance of a man reduced at one moment to flat stupidity by sensibility, and the next rising to sublimity by the self-possession following the stifling of his sensibility.

A man of letters, whose name I will hold back, had fallen into great poverty.[26] He had a wealthy brother, a theologian. I asked the poor brother why the rich one did not help him. 'Because,' he replied, 'he thinks very ill of me.' I obtained his leave to go and see the theologian. I went, was announced, and told the theologian I had come to talk about his brother. He took me by the hand, made me sit down, and then pointed out that a man of sense takes care to know the client whose case he takes up. Then he said, with some liveliness, 'Do you know my brother?' 'I think so.' 'Do you know his conduct to me?' 'I think so.' 'You do? Then you know . . . ' and herewith my theologian sets off to tell me, with astonishing rapidity and energy, a whole chain of infamies, the one more revolting than the other. My senses feel confused; I am over-whelmed; I lack courage to plead for so vile a wretch as is presented to my view. Luckily the theologian, growing prolix in his philippic, gave me time to recover. By degrees the man of sensibility disappeared, and made way for the man of eloquence; for I may venture to say that on this occasion I was eloquent. 'Sir,' said I coldly to the theologian, 'your brother has done worse than this, and I admire you for concealing the worst of his infamies.' 'I conceal nothing.' 'To all you have told me you might have added that one night, as you left your house to go to matins, he caught you by the throat, and drawing a dagger from beneath his dress was about to plunge it in your bosom.' 'He is quite capable of it; but I have not accused him of it because he never did it.' Then rising suddenly, and fixing a firm, stern look on my theologian, I cried in accents of thunder, and with all the force and emphasis indignation can give, 'And had he done it, would that be a reason for refusing your brother bread?' The theologian, overborne, overwhelmed, confounded, held his peace, walked about the room, came back to me, and granted me an annual allowance for his brother.

Is it at the moment when you have just lost your friend or your adored one that you set to work at a poem on your loss? No! ill for him who at such a moment takes pleasure in his talent. It is when the storm of sorrow is over, when the extreme of sensibility is dulled, when the event is far behind us, when the soul is calm, that one remembers one's eclipsed happiness, that one is capable of appreciating one's loss, that memory and imagination unite, one to retrace the other to accentuate, the delights of a past time: then it is that one regains self-possession and expression. One writes of one's falling tears, but they do not fall while one is hunting a strong epithet that always escapes one; one writes of one's falling tears, but they do not fall while one is employed in polishing one's verse; or if the tears do flow the pen drops from the hand: one falls to feeling, and one ceases writing.

Again, it is with intense pleasure as with intense pain—both are dumb. A tender-hearted and sensitive man sees again a friend he has missed during a long absence; the friend makes an unexpected reappearance, and the other's heart is touched; he rushes to him, he embraces him, he would speak, but cannot; he stammers and trips over his words; he says he knows not what, he does not hear the answer: if he could see that the delight is not mutual, how hurt he would be! Judge, this picture being true, how untrue are the stage meetings, where both friends are so full of intelligence and self-control. What could I not say to you of the insipid and eloquent disputes as to who is to die, or rather who is not to die, but that this text, on which I should enlarge for ever, would take us far from our subject? Enough has been said for men of true and fine taste; what I could add would teach nothing to the rest. Now, who is to come to the rescue of these absurdities so common on the stage? The actor? and what actor?

The circumstances in which sensibility is as hurtful in society as on the stage are a thousand to one. Take two lovers, both of whom have their declaration to make. Who will come out of it best? Not I, I promise you. I remember that I approached the beloved object with fear and trembling; my heart beat, my ideas grew confused, my voice failed me, I mangled all I said; I cried *yes* for *no;* I made a thousand blunders; I was illimitably inept; I was absurd from top to toe, and the more I saw it, the more absurd I became. Meanwhile, under my very eyes, a gay rival, light-hearted and agreeable, master of himself, pleased with himself, losing no opportunity for the finest flattery, made himself entertaining and agreeable, enjoyed himself; he implored the touch of a hand which was at once given him, he sometimes caught it without asking leave, he kissed it once and again. I the while, alone in a corner, avoiding a sight which irritated me, stifling my sighs, cracking my fingers with grasping my wrists, plunged in melancholy, covered with a cold sweat, I could neither show nor conceal my vexation. People say of love that it robs witty men of their wit, and gives it to those who had none before: in other words, makes some people sensitive and stupid, others cold and adventurous.

The man of sensibility obeys the impulse of Nature, and gives nothing more or less than the cry of his very heart; the moment he moderates or strengthens this cry he is no longer himself, he is an actor.

The great actor watches appearances; the man of sensibility is his model; he thinks over him, and discovers by after-reflection what it will be best to add or cut away. And so from mere argument he goes to action.

At the first performance of *Inès de Castro,* and at the point where the children appear, the pit fell to laughing. Duclos,[27] who was playing Inez, was angered, and cried to the pit: 'Laugh, you blockheads, at the finest point in the piece!' The pit listened, and was silent; the actress went on with her part, and her tears and the spectators' flowed together. Tell me now, Can one pass and repass in this way from one deep feeling to another, from sorrow to anger, from anger to sorrow? I cannot think it; what I can very well think is, that Duclos's anger was real, her sorrow pretended.

Quinault-Dufresne[28] plays the part of Severus in *Polyeucte.* Sent by the Emperor to harry the Christians, he confides to a friend his real feeling about the calumniated sect. Common sense demanded that this confidence, which might cost him the prince's favour, his honours, his fortune, his liberty, perhaps his life, should be uttered in a low tone. The pit called out, 'Speak louder!' He replied, 'And do you, Sirs, speak less loud!' Had he really been Severus, could he so quickly have again become Quinault? No, I tell you, no. Only the man of self-possession, such as he no doubt had, the exceptional actor, the player who is before all a player, can so drop and again assume his mask.

Lekain-Ninias[29] enters his father's tomb, and there cuts his mother's throat; he comes out with blood-stained hands. He is horror-stricken; his limbs tremble, his eyes roll wildly, his hair stands on end. So does yours to see him; terror seizes on you, you are as lost as he is. However, Lekain-Ninias sees a diamond drop which has fallen from an actress's ear, and pushes it towards the wing with his foot. And this actor feels? Impossible. You will not call him a bad actor? Of course not. What, then, is Lekain-Ninias? A cold man, who is without feeling, but who imitates it excellently. It is all very well for him to cry out, 'Where am I?' I answer, 'Where are you? You know well enough. You are on the boards, and you are in the act of kicking a diamond drop off the stage.'

An actor has a passion for an actress; they come together by chance in a stage scene of jealousy. If the actor is poor the scene will be improved; if he is a real player it will lose: in such a case the fine actor becomes himself, and is no longer the grand and ideal type of a jealous man that he has striven for. The proof that if this be so the actor and actress lower themselves to everyday life is, that if they kept to their stilts they would laugh in each other's faces; the bombastic jealousy of tragedy would seem to them a mere clowning of their own.

The Second. All the same there are truths of Nature.

The First. Yes, as in a statue by a sculptor who has given a close transcript of a bad model. You may admire the exactitude, but the whole effect is poor and wretched.

I will go further. A sure way to act in a cramped, mean style, is to play one's own character. You are, let us say, a tartufe, a miser, a misanthrope; you may play your part well enough, but you will not come near what the poet has done. He has created *the* Tartufe, *the* Miser, *the* Misanthrope.

The Second. And how do you make out the difference between *a* tartufe and *the* Tartufe?

The First. Billard, the clerk, is a tartufe; Grizel, the abbé, is a tartufe, but he is not *the* Tartufe. Toinard, the banker, was a miser, but he was not *the* Miser. *The* Miser, *the* Tartufe, were drawn from the Toinards and Grizels in the world; they contain their broadest and most marked features, but there is in them no exact portrait of a given individual; and that is why the real people don't recognise themselves in their types. The comedy that depends on 'go,' even the comedy of character, is an exaggeration. The fun of society is a light froth, which evaporates on the stage; the fun of the stage is an edged tool which would cut deep in society. For imaginary beings we have not the consideration we are bound to have for real beings.

Satire deals with *a* tartufe; comedy with *the* Tartufe. Satire attacks the vicious; comedy attacks a vice. If there had been only one or two *Précieuses ridicules* in the world they would have afforded matter for a satire, but not for a comedy.

Go to La Grenée,[30] and ask him for a picture of *Painting;* he will think he has done what you want when he has put on his canvas a woman before an easel with her thumb through a palette and a brush in her hand. Ask him for *Philosophy;* he will think he has given it you by producing a woman in careless attire resting her elbow on a desk by lamplight, dishevelled and thoughtful, reading or meditating. Ask him for *Poetry;* he will paint the same woman with a laurel-wreath round her brows and a roll of manuscript in her hand. For *Music,* you shall see the same woman with a lyre instead of the roll. Ask him for *Beauty;* ask the same from a cleverer man than him; and, unless I am much mistaken, he will be persuaded that all you want from his art is a picture of a handsome woman. The same fault is common to your actor and to this painter; and I would say to them, 'Your picture, your acting, are mere portraits of individuals far below the general idea traced by the poet and the ideal type of which I hoped to have a representation. This lady of yours is as handsome as you like; but she is not Beauty. There is the same difference between your work and your model as between your model and the type.'

The Second. But, after all, this ideal type may be a phantom!

The First. No.

The Second. But since it is ideal it is not real; and you cannot understand a thing that is impalpable.

The First. True. But let us take an art, say sculpture, at its beginning. It copied the first model that came to hand. Then it saw that there were better models, and took them for choice. Then it corrected first their obvious, then their less obvious fault, until by dint of long study it arrived at a figure which was no longer nature.

The Second. Why, pray?

The First. Because the development of a machine so complex as the human body cannot be regular. Go to the Tuileries or the Champs Elysées on a fête-day; look at all the women in the walks, and you will not find one in whom the two corners of the mouth are exactly alike. Titian's Danaë is a portrait; the Love at the foot of the couch is an ideal. In a picture of Raphael's, which went from M. de Thiers' collection to Catherine the Second's, St. Joseph is a common-place man; the Virgin is a real and a beautiful woman; the infant Christ is an ideal. But if you would like to know more as to these speculative principles of art I will send you my *Salons.*

The Second. I have heard the work praised by a man of fine taste and keen discernment.

The First. M. Suard.

The Second. And by a woman who combines an angel's purity with the finest taste.

The First. Madame Necker.

The Second. Let us go back to our subject.

The First. By all means; though I would rather sing the praises of virtue than discuss somewhat idle questions.

The Second. Quinault-Dufresne, a boaster by nature, played the Boaster[31] splendidly.

The First. You are right; but how do you know that he was playing his own self? And why should not Nature have made a boaster very near the line between the fine real and the fine ideal, the line on which the different schools find their exercise-ground?

The Second. I do not understand you.

The First. I have explained myself more fully in my *Salons*, in which I commend to your notice the passage on Beauty in general. Meanwhile tell me this: Is Quinault-Dufresne Orosmanes? No. However, who has taken his place, or ever will take his place, in this part? Was he the man for the *Préjugé à la Mode*? No. Yet with how much truth he played it!

The Second. According to you the great actor is everything and nothing.

The First. Perhaps it is just because he is nothing that he is before all everything. His own special shape never interferes with the shapes he assumes.

Among all those who have practised the fine and valuable profession of actors or lay preachers, one of the most sterling characters, one who showed it the most in his physiognomy, his tone, his bearing, the brother of the *Diable Boiteux* of Gil Blas, of the *Bachelier de Salamanque*, Montmesnil[32]. . . .

The Second. Son of Le Sage, the father of the illustrious family you have named.

The First. . . . played, with equal success, Aristides in the *Pupille*, Tartufe in the comedy so named, Mascarille in the *Fourberies de Scapin*, the lawyer, or M. Guillaume, in the farce of *Patelin*.

The Second. I have seen him.

The First. And to your astonishment, for all these different parts he had a fitting visage. This did not come by Nature, for Nature had given him but one, his own; the others he drew from Art.

Is there such a thing as artificial sensibility? Consider, sensibility, whether acquired or inborn, is not in place in all characters. What, then, is the quality acquired which makes an actor great in *l'Avare, le Joueur, le Flatteur, le Grondeur, le Médecin malgré lui* (the least sensitive or moral personage yet devised by a poet), *le Bourgeois Gentilhomme, le Malade Imaginaire, le Cœur Imaginaire*—in Nero, in Mithridates, in Atreus, in Phocas, in Sertorius, and in a host of other characters, tragic and comic, where sensibility is diametrically opposed to the spirit of the part? It is the faculty of knowing and imitating all natures. Believe me, we need not multiply causes when one cause accounts for all appearances.

Sometimes the poet feels more deeply than the actor; sometimes, and perhaps oftener, the actor's conception is stronger than the poet's; and there is nothing truer than Voltaire's exclamation, when he heard Clairon in a piece of his, '*Did I really write that?*' Does Clairon know more about it than Voltaire? Anyhow, at that moment the ideal type in the speaking of the part went well beyond the poet's ideal type in the writing of it. But this ideal type was not Clairon. Where, then, lay her talent? In imagining a mighty shape, and in copying it with genius. She imitated the movement, the action, the gesture, the whole embodiment of a being far greater than herself. She had learnt that Æschines, repeating a speech of Demosthenes, could never reproduce 'the roar of the brute.' He said to his disciples, 'If this touches you, or nearly, what would have been the effect *si audivissetis bestiam mugientem* [had you heard the roaring beast]?' The poet had engendered the monster, Clairon made it roar.

It would be a strange abuse of language to give the name of sensibility to this faculty of reproducing all natures, even ferocious natures. Sensibility, according to the only acceptation yet given of the term, is, as it seems to me, that disposition which accompanies organic weakness, which follows on easy affection of the diaphragm, on vivacity of imagination, on delicacy of nerves, which inclines one to being compassionate, to being horrified, to admiration, to fear, to being upset, to tears, to faintings, to rescues, to flights, to exclamations, to loss of self-control, to being contemptuous, disdainful, to having no clear notion of what is true, good, and fine, to being unjust, to going mad. Multiply souls of sensibility, and you will multiply in the same proportion good and bad actions of every kind, extravagant praise and extravagant blame.

Work, poets, for a nation given to vapours, and sensitive; content yourselves with the tender, harmonious, and touching elegies of Racine; this nation would flee the butcheries of Shakespeare; its feeble spirit cannot stand violent shocks; beware of offering it too vigorous a picture; rehearse to it, if you will,

> '*Le fils tout dégouttant du meurtre de son père,*
> *Et sa tête à la main, demandant son salaire.*'
> [The son all bloodied from the murder of his sire,
> Bearing the severed head and clamant for his hire.]

But go no further. If you dared to say with Homer, 'Whither goest thou, unhappy one? Thou know'st not, then, that it is to me Heaven sends the children of ill-fated fathers; thou wilt not receive thy mother's last embraces; e'en now I see thee stretched on the earth; the birds of prey, grouped round thy corpse, tear out thine eyes, flapping their wings with delight'—If you said this all the women, turning away their heads, would cry, 'Oh! horrible!' . . . And it would be all the worse if this speech, delivered by a great actor, had all the strength of truthful accent.

The Second. I am tempted to interrupt you to ask what you think of the bowl presented to Gabrielle de Vergy,[33] who saw in it her lover's bleeding heart.

The First. I shall answer you that we must be consistent, and if we are revolted at this spectacle neither must we permit Œdipus to show himself with his eyes torn out, while we must drive Philoctetes, tormented by his wound, and expressing his pain with inarticulate cries, off the stage. The ancients had, as I think, an idea of tragedy different from ours; and these ancients—

that is the Greeks, that is the Athenians, this fine people, who have left us models in every direction of art unequalled by other nations—Æschylus, I say, Sophocles, Euripides, were not at work for years together to produce the trifling passing impressions which disappear in the gaiety of a supper-party. It was their object to rouse a deep grief for the lot of the ill-fated; it was their object not only to amuse their fellow-citizens but also to make them better. Were they wrong? Were they right? To produce their effect they made the Eumenides rush on the scene, tracking the parricide and guided by the scent of blood in their nostrils. They had too much taste to approve the imbroglios, the jugglings with daggers, which are fit only for children. A tragedy is, to my thinking, nothing but a fine page of history divided into a certain number of marked periods. Thus, we are waiting for the sheriff.[34] He arrives. He questions the squire of the village. He proposes apostasy to him. The other refuses. He condemns him to death. He sends him to prison. The daughter implores mercy for her father. The sheriff will grant it; but on a revolting condition. The squire is put to death. The inhabitants rush on the sheriff. He flies before them. The lover of the squire's daughter strikes him dead with one dagger thrust, and the abominable fanatic dies cursed by all around him. A poet does not need much more material for a great work. Suppose the daughter goes to her mother's tomb to learn her duty to the author of her being; suppose that she is in doubt about the sacrifice of honour demanded from her; that in this doubt she keeps her lover aloof, and will not hear the language of his passion; that she obtains leave to visit her father in prison; that her father wishes to marry her and her lover, and she refuses; that she does sacrifice her honour, and her father is put to death the while; that you are unaware of her fate until her lover, when she is distracted with grief at her father's death, learns what she has done to save him; that then the sheriff comes in hunted by the mob and is struck down by the lover. There you have part of the details of such a work.

The Second. Part?

The First. Yes, part. Will not the young lovers propose flight to the squire? Will not the villagers propose to him to exterminate the sheriff and his satellites? Will there not be a priest who preaches toleration? And in the midst of this terrible day will the lover be idle? And cannot one suppose certain ties between these characters, and make something out of such ties? Why should not the sheriff have been a suitor of the squire's daughter? Why should he not return with vengeance in his heart against the squire, who has turned him out of the place, and the daughter, who has scorned his suit? What important incidents one can get out of the simplest subject if one has patience to think it over! What colour one can give them if one is eloquent! And you cannot be a dramatic poet without being eloquent. And do you suppose I shan't have a fine stage effect? The sheriff's interrogatory, for instance, will be given with all the pomp of circumstance. No, leave the staging to me, and so an end to this digression.

I take thee to witness, Roscius of England, celebrated Garrick; thee, who by the unanimous consent of all existing nations art held for the greatest actor they have known! Now render homage to truth. Hast thou not told me that, despite thy depth of feeling, thy action would be weak if, whatever passion or character thou hadst to render, thou couldst not raise thyself by the power of thought to the grandeur of a Homeric shape with which thou soughtest to identify thyself? When I replied that it was not then from thine own type thou didst play, confess thine answer. Didst not avow avoiding this with care, and say that thy playing was astounding only because thou didst constantly exhibit a creature of the imagination which was not thyself?

The Second. A great actor's soul is formed of the subtle element with which a certain philosopher filled space, an element neither cold nor hot, heavy nor light, which affects no definite shape, and, capable of assuming all, keeps none.

The First. A great actor is neither a pianoforte, nor a harp, nor a spinnet, nor a violin, nor a violoncello; he has no key peculiar to him; he takes the key and the tone fit for his part of the score, and he can take up any. I put a high value on the talent of a great actor; he is a rare being—as rare as, and perhaps greater than, a poet.

He who in society makes it his object, and unluckily has the skill, to please every one, is nothing, has nothing that belongs to him, nothing to distinguish him, to delight some and weary others. He is always talking, and always talking well; he is an adulator by profession, he is a great courtier, he is a great actor.

The Second. A great courtier, accustomed since he first drew breath to play the part of a most ingenious puppet,[35] takes every kind of shape at the pull of the string in his master's hands.

The First. A great actor is also a most ingenious puppet, and his strings are held by the poet, who at each line indicates the true form he must take.

The Second. So then a courtier, an actor, who can take only one form, however beautiful, however attractive it may be, are a couple of wretched pasteboard figures?

The First. I have no thought of calumniating a profession I like and esteem—I mean, the actor's. I should be in despair if a misunderstanding of my observations cast a shade of contempt on men of a rare talent and a true usefulness, on the scourges of absurdity and vice, on the most eloquent preachers of honesty and virtue, on the rod which the man of genius wields to chastise knaves and fools. But look around you, and you will see that people of never-failing gaiety have neither great faults nor great merits; that as a rule people who lay themselves out to be agreeable are frivolous people, without any sound principle; and that those who, like certain persons who mix in our society, have no character, excel in playing all.

Has not the actor a father, a mother, a wife, children, brothers, sisters, acquaintances, friends, a mistress? If he were endowed with that exquisite sensibility which people regard as the thing principally needed for his profession, harassed and struck like us with an infinity of troubles in quick succession, which sometimes wither and sometimes tear our hearts, how many days would he have left to devote to our amusement? Mighty few. The Groom of the Chambers would vainly interpose his sovereignty, the actor's state would often make him answer, 'My lord, I cannot laugh to-day,' or, 'It is over cares other than Agamemnon's that I would weep.' It is now known, however, that the troubles of life, common to actors as to us, and far more opposed to the free exercise of their calling, often interrupt them.

In society, unless they are buffoons, I find them polished, caustic, and cold; proud, light of behaviour, spendthrifts, self-interested; struck rather by our absurdities than touched by our misfortunes; masters of themselves at the spectacle of an untoward incident or the recital of a pathetic story; isolated, vagabonds, at the command of the great; little conduct, no friends, scarce any of those holy and tender ties which associate us in the pains and pleasures of another, who in turn shares our own. I have often seen an actor laugh off the stage; I do not remember to have ever seen one weep. What do they, then, with this sensibility that they arrogate and that people grant them? Do they leave it on the stage at their exit, to take it up again at their next entrance?

What makes them slip on the sock or the buskin? Want of education, poverty, a libertine spirit. The stage is a resource, never a choice. Never did actor become so from love of virtue, from desire to be useful in the world, or to serve his country or family; never from any of the honourable motives which might incline a right mind, a feeling heart, a sensitive soul, to so fine a profession.

I myself, in my young days, hesitated between the Sorbonne and the stage. In the bitterest depth of winter I used to go and recite aloud parts in Molière and in Corneille in the solitary alleys of the Luxembourg. What was my project? To gain applause? Perhaps. To mix on intimate terms with actresses whom I found charming, and who I knew were not straitlaced? Certainly. I know not what I would not have done to please Gaussin, who was then making her first appearance, and was beauty itself; or Dangeville,[36] who on the stage was so full of charm.

It has been said that actors have no character, because in playing all characters they lose that which Nature gave them, and they become false just as the doctor, the surgeon, and the butcher, become hardened. I fancy that here cause is confounded with effect, and that they are fit to play all characters because they have none.

The Second. A person does not become cruel because he is an executioner; but an executioner because he is cruel.

The First. It is all very well for me to look into these persons' characters; I see nothing in them to distinguish them from their fellow-citizens except a vanity which might be termed insolence, a jealousy which fills their company with trouble and hatred. Perhaps of all associations there is not one where the associates' common interest and that of the public is more constantly and more clearly sacrificed to wretched little pretensions. Envy is worse among them that among authors: this is saying a good deal, but it is true. One poet more easily forgives another the success of a piece than one actress forgives another the applause which marks her out for some illustrious or rich debauchee. You find them great on the stage because, as you say, they have soul; I find them little and mean in society because they have none: with the words and the tone of Camille or the elder Horace they have ever the conduct of Frosine or Sganarelle. Now, to estimate what is at the bottom of their hearts, must I rely on the borrowed reports that are so admirably tricked out, or on the nature of actors and the tenor of their life?

The Second. But of old Molière, the Quinaults, Montmesnil, and to-day Brisart[37] and Caillot,[38] who is equally at home in great and little company, to whose keeping you would fearlessly confide your secrets and your purse, to whom you would trust your wife's honour and your daughter's innocence, with much more security than you would to this or that great gentleman of the Court or this or that venerated priest of our altar . . .

The First. The praise is not overcharged. What annoys me is, that I do not hear you cite a greater number of actors who deserve or have deserved it. What annoys me is, that among all these possessors *ex-officio* of one quality, which is the valuable and fruitful source of so many others, an actor who is a man of honour, an actress who is a woman of virtue, are such rare phenomena.

Let us conclude from this that it is untrue that they have an exclusive claim to this quality, and that the sensibility which would overcome them in private life as on the stage, if they were endowed with it, is neither the basis of their character nor the cause of their success; that it belongs to them neither more nor less than to any other class of people; and one sees so few great actors because parents do not bring up their children for the stage; because people do not prepare for it by an education begun in youth; and a company of actors is not—as it would have to be among a people who attached the due importance, honour, and recompense to the function of speaking to assembled multitudes who come to be taught, amused, and corrected—a corporation formed like other commonwealths, of persons chosen from every kind of good family, and led to the stage as to the services, the law, or the church, by taste or choice, and with the approval of their natural guardians.

The Second. The degradation of modern actors is, it seems to me, an unlucky heritage from the old actors.

The First. I think so.

The Second. If plays had been invented in these days, when people have more sensible notions, perhaps . . . But you are not listening: what are you thinking of?

The First. I am following up my first idea, and thinking of the influence plays might have on good taste and morals if players were people of position and their profession an honoured one. Where is the poet would dare propose to men of birth to publicly repeat coarse or stupid speeches?—to women, of character not much lighter than the women we know, to impudently utter before a quantity of listeners such things as they would blush to hear in private at their fireside? If the conditions were altered our playwriters would soon attain to a purity, a delicacy, a grace, that they are further from than perhaps they think. Can you doubt that it would re-act upon the national tone?

The Second. One might perhaps object that the pieces, old and new, which your well-behaved players would exclude from their repertory, are the very ones we play in private theatricals.

The First. And what difference does it make if our fellow-citizens lower themselves to the level of the most wretched players? Would it be the less useful, the less desirable, that our actors should raise themselves to the level of the best citizens?

The Second. The change is not easy.

The First. When I gave the *Père de Famille,* the magistrate of police exhorted me to follow the career.

The Second. Why did you not?

The First. Because, not having achieved the success which I had promised myself with it, and not flattering myself that I could do much better, I grew disgusted with a calling for which I thought I had not enough talent.

The Second. And why did this piece, which nowadays fills the house before half-past four, and which the players always put up when they want a thousand crowns, have so lukewarm a welcome at first?

The First. Some said that our habits were too factitious to suit themselves to a style so simple; too corrupt to taste a style so virtuous.

The Second. That was not without a show of truth.

The First. But experience has shown that it was not true, for we have grown no better. Besides, the true, the honest has such an ascendency over us, that if a poet's work includes two characters in this kind, and if he has genius, his success will be only the more assured. It is, above all, when all is false that we love the true; it is, above all, when all is corrupt that the stage becomes purest. The citizen who presents himself at the door of a theatre leaves his vices there, and only takes them up again as he goes out. There he is just, impartial, a good friend, a lover of virtue; and I have often seen by my side bad fellows deeply indignant at actions which they would not have failed to commit had they found themselves in the same circumstances in which the poet had placed the personage they abhorred. If I did not succeed at first it was because the style was new to audience and actors; because there was a strong prejudice, still existing, against what people call tearful comedy; because I had a crowd of enemies at court, in town, among magistrates, among Churchmen, among men of letters.

The Second. And how did you incur so much enmity?

The First. Upon my word I don't know, for I have not written satires on great or small, and I have crossed no man on the path of fortune and dignities. It is true that I was one of the people called Philosophers, who were then viewed as dangerous citizens, and on whom the Government let loose two or three wretched subalterns without virtue, without insight, and, what is worse, without talent. But enough of that.

The Second. To say nothing of the fact that these philosophers had made things more difficult for poets and men of letters in general, it was no longer possible to make oneself distinguished by knowing how to turn out a madrigal or a nasty couplet.

The First. That may be. A young rake, instead of sedulously haunting the studio of the painter, the sculptor, the artist who has adopted him, has wasted the best years of his life, and at twenty he has no resources and no talent. What is he to become? A soldier or an actor. You find him, then, enrolled in a country company. He strolls it until he can promise himself an appearance in the capital. An unhappy creature has wallowed in gutter debauchery; tired of the most abject of conditions, that of a low courtesan, she learns a few parts by heart; she goes one morning to Clairon, as the slave of old used to go to the ædile or the prætor. Clairon takes her by the hand, makes her turn round, touches her with her wand, and says to her, 'Go and make the gaping crowd laugh or cry.'

They are excommunicated. The public, which cannot do without them, despises them. They are slaves, constantly dreading the rod of another slave. Think you that the marks of so continual a degradation can fail to have effect, and that under the burden of shame the soul can be strong enough to reach the heights of Corneille?

The despotism that people practise to them they practise in turn to authors, and I know not which is the meaner, the insolent actor or the author who endures him.

The Second. People like to have their plays acted.

The First. On whatever condition. Give your money at the door, and they will weary of your presence and your applause. Well enough off with the small boxes, they have been on the point of deciding either that the author should give up his profits or that his piece should not be accepted.

The Second. But this project involved nothing less than the extinction of the dramatic author's career.

The First. What does that matter to them?

The Second. You have, I think, but little more to say.

The First. You are mistaken. I must now take you by the hand and lead you to the presence of Clairon, that incomparable enchantress.

The Second. She, at least, was proud of her calling.

The First. As will be all who excel in it. The stage is despised by those actors only who have been hissed off the boards. I must show you Clairon in the real transports of anger. If in them she happened to preserve the bearing, the accent, the action of the stage, with all its artifice and emphasis, would you not hold your sides? could you contain your laughter? What, then, would you tell me? Do you not roundly assert that true sensibility and assumed sensibility are two very different things? You laugh at what you would have admired on the stage; and why, pray? The fact is, that Clairon's real anger resembles simulated anger, and you are able to distinguish between the personality and the passion which that personality assumes. The likeness of passion on the stage is not then its true likeness; it is but extravagant portraiture, caricature on a grand scale, subject to conventional rules. Well, interrogate yourself, ask yourself what artist will confine himself most strictly within the limits of these rules? What kind of actor will most successfully lay hold on this regulated bombast—the man dominated by his own character, or the man born without character, or the man who strips himself of his own to put on another greater, more noble, more fiery, more elevated? One is one's self by nature; one becomes some one else by imitation; the heart one is supposed to have is not the heart one has. What, then, is the true talent? That of knowing well the outward symptoms of the soul we borrow, of addressing ourselves to the sensations of those who hear and see us, of deceiving them by the imitation of these symptoms, by an imitation which aggrandises everything in their imagination, and which becomes the measure of their judgment; for it is impossible otherwise to appreciate that which passes inside us. And after all, what does it matter to us whether they feel or do not feel, so long as we know nothing about it?

He, then, who best knows and best renders, after the best conceived ideal type, these outward signs, is the greatest actor.

The Second. He, then, who leaves least to the imagination of the great actor is the greatest poet.

The First. I was just going to say so. When by long stage habit one keeps a stage accent in private life, and brings into it Brutus, Cinna, Mithridates, Cornelius, Merope, Pompey, do you know what he does? He couples with a soul small or great, exactly as Nature has cut its measure, the outward signs of an exalted and gigantic soul that is not his own. The result of this is ridicule.

The Second. What a cruel satire is this, innocent or of malice prepense, on actors and authors!

The First. How so?

The Second. Any one, I imagine, may have a great and strong soul; any one, I imagine, may have the bearing, the manner, the action, appropriate to his soul; and I do not think that the expression of true grandeur can ever be ridiculous.

The First. What follows then?

The Second. Ah, you rogue! you dare not say it, and I shall have to incur the general indignation on your behalf. It follows that true tragedy is yet to seek, and that, with all their faults, the ancients came nearer to it than we do.

The First. It is true that it delights me to hear Philoctetes say with such simple strength to Neoptolemus, who brings him back the arrows of Hercules, which he stole at Ulysses's instigation,—'See what a deed you had done! Without knowing it, you had condemned an unhappy wretch to perish of grief and hunger. Your crime is another's, your repentance your own. No; never would you have thought of doing a deed so shameful had you been left to yourself. See then, my child, how important is it for your time of life to keep only honest company. This is what you got by associating with a rascal. And why have aught to do with a man of this character? Would your father have chosen him for your companion and friend? Your good father, who never let any but the first men in the army come near him, what would he say if he saw you with a Ulysses?'

Is there anything is this discourse which you might not address to my son, or I to yours?

The Second. No.

The First. Yet it is finely said.

The Second. Certainly.

The First. And would the tone in which this discourse would be given on the stage differ from the tone in which one would give it in society?

The Second. I do not think so.

The First. And would this tone be ridiculous in private life?

The Second. Not at all.

The First. The stronger the action, the simpler the language, the more I admire it. I am much afraid that for a hundred years on end we have taken the rodomontade of Madrid for the heroism of Rome, and mixed up the tone of the Tragic with that of the Epic Muse.

The Second. Our Alexandrine verse is too harmonious, and is too noble for dialogue.

The First. And our verse of ten syllables too futile and too light. However this may be, I would like you never to go to a performance of one of Corneille's Roman pieces, but when you are fresh from reading Cicero's letters to Atticus. How bombastic our dramatic authors seem to me, how repulsive are their declamations, when I recall the simplicity and strength of Regulus's discourse dissuading the Senate and the Roman people from an exchange of prisoners! Thus he expresses himself in an ode, a poem which includes a good deal more of fire, spirit, and exaltation, than a tragic monologue,—He says:—

'I have seen our ensigns hanging in the temples of Carthage. I have seen Roman soldiers stripped of their arms, unstained with one drop of blood. I have seen liberty forgotten, citizens with their arms bound behind their backs. I have seen the town gates wide open, and the harvest thick on the fields we ravaged. And you think that, brought back, they will return braver. You add loss to shame. Virtue once driven from a degraded soul never returns. Hope nothing from him who might have died and has let himself be strangled. O Carthage, how great and proud thou art in our shame!'

Such was his discourse, such his conduct. He refuses the embraces of his wife and children; he feels himself unworthy of them, like a vile slave. He keeps his eyes moodily fixed on the ground, and scorns the tears of his friends until he has brought the senators to a determination he alone could have proposed, and until he is allowed to go back to his exile.

The Second. That is simple and splendid, but the really heroic moment was afterwards.

The First. You are right.

The Second. He knew well the torture the savage foe was preparing for him. However, recovering his serenity, he disengages himself from his kinsmen, who seek to put off his return, as easily as in former times he disengaged himself from the crowd of his clients to go and shake off the fatigue of business in his fields at Venafrum or his campaign at Tarentum.

The First. Very good. Now lay your hand on your heart and tell me if our poets contain many passages of a tone proper for so grand yet so domestic a virtue, and how from such lips as Regulus's would sound either our tender jeremiades or most of our brave words in Corneille's manner. How many things do I not dare to confide to you! I should be stoned in the streets were I known to be guilty of such blasphemy; and I am not anxious for any kind of a martyr's crown. If the day comes when a man of genius dare give his characters the simple tone of antique heroism, the actor's art will assume a new difficulty, for declamation will cease to be a kind of sing-song.[39]

For the rest, in saying that sensibility was the mark of a good heart and a middling genius I made no common confession; for if Nature ever moulded a sensitive soul that soul is mine. The man of sensibility is too much at the mercy of his diaphragm to be a great king, a great politician, a great magistrate, a just man, or a close observer, and, consequently, an admirable imitator of Nature—unless, indeed, he can forget himself, distract himself from himself, and, with the aid of a strong imagination, make for himself certain shapes which serve him for types, and on which he keeps his attention fixed, with the aid of a tenacious memory. Only then it is not his own self that is concerned; it is another's mind and will that master him.

Here I should stop; but you will more readily forgive me the misplacing than the omission of an observation. This phenomenon must surely sometimes have struck you. A budding actor, or let us say a budding actress, asks you to come and see her quietly to form an opinion of her talent. You grant that she has soul, sensibility, passion. You cover her with praises, and leave her when you depart in hope of the greatest success. But what happens? She appears, she is hissed, and you acknowledge that the hisses are deserved. Why is this? Has she lost her soul, her sensibility, her passion, between the morning and the evening? No; but in her ground-floor room you were both on the same low level; you listened to her regardless of convention; she was face-to-face with you; between you there was no model for purposes of comparison; you were satisfied with her voice, her gesture, her expression, her bearing; all was in proportion to the audience and the space; there was nothing that called for exaltation. On the boards all the conditions were changed: there a different impersonation was needed, since all the surroundings were enlarged.

In private theatricals, in a drawing-room, where the spectator is almost on a level with the actor, the true dramatic impersonation would have struck you as being on an enormous, a gigantic scale, and at the end of the performance you would have said confidentially to a friend, 'She will not succeed; she is too extravagant'; and her success on the stage would have astonished you. Let me repeat it, whether for good or ill, the actor says nothing and does nothing in private life in the same way as on the stage: it is a different world.

But there is a decisive fact, which was told me by an accurate person of an original and attractive turn of mind, the Abbé Galiani, and which I have since heard confirmed by another accurate person, also of an original and attractive turn of mind, the Marquis de Caraccioli, ambassador of Naples at Paris. This is, that at Naples, the native place of both, there is a dramatic poet whose chief care is not given to composing his piece.

The Second. Yours, the *Père de Famille,* had a great success there.

The First. Four representations running were given before the King. This was contrary to court etiquette, which lays down that there shall be as many plays as days of performance. The people were delighted. However, the Neapolitan poet's care is to find in society persons of the age, face, voice, and character fitted to fill his parts. People dare not refuse him, because the Sovereign's amusement is concerned. And when, think you, do the company begin really to act, to understand each other, to advance towards the point of perfection he demands? It is when the actors are worn out with constant rehearsals, are what we call 'used up.' From this moment their progress is surprising; each identifies himself with his part; and it is at the end of this hard work that the performances begin and go on for six months on end, while the Sovereign and his subjects enjoy the highest pleasure that can be obtained from a stage illusion. And can this illusion, as strong, as perfect at the last as at the first performance, be due in your opinion to sensibility? For the rest, the question I am diving into was once before started between a middling man of letters, Rémond de Sainte-Albine,[40] and a great actor, Riccoboni.[41] The man of letters pleaded the cause of sensibility; the actor took up my case. The story is one which has only just come to my knowledge.

I have spoken, you have heard me, and now I ask you what you think of it.

The Second. I think that that arrogant, decided, dry, hard little man, to whom one would attribute a large allowance of contemptuousness if he had only a quarter as much as prodigal Nature has given him of self-sufficiency, would have been a little more reserved in his judgment if you had had the condescension to put your arguments before him and he the patience to listen to you. Unluckily he knows everything, and as a man of universal genius he thinks himself absolved from listening.

The First. Well, the public pays him out for it. Do you know Madame Riccoboni?[42]

The Second. Who does not know the author of a great number of charming works, full of intelligence, of purity, of delicacy, and grace?

The First. Would you call her a woman of sensibility?

The Second. She has proved it, not only by her works, but by her conduct. There was an incident in her life which led her to the brink of the tomb. After an interval of twenty years she has not ceased to weep; the source of her tears is not yet dry.

The First. Well, this woman, one of the most sensitive that Nature ever made, was one of the worst actresses that ever appeared on the stage. No one talks better on dramatic art; no one plays worse.

The Second. Let me add that she is aware of it, and that she has never complained of being unjustly hissed.

The First. And why with this exquisite sensibility, which, according to you, is the actor's chief requirement, is Mme. Riccoboni so bad?

The Second. It must be that other requirements fail her to such an extent that the chief one cannot make up for their absence.

The First. But she is not ill-looking; she has her wits about her; she has a tolerable bearing; her voice has nothing discordant about it. She possesses all the good qualities that education can give. In society there is no repellent point about her. You see her with no feeling of pain; you listen to her with the greatest pleasure.

The Second. I don't understand it at all; all I know is, that the public has never been able to make up its quarrel with her, and that for twenty years on end she has been the victim of her calling.

The First. And of her sensibility, out of which she could never raise herself; and it is because she has always remained herself that the public has consistently rejected her.

The Second. Now come, do you not know Caillot?

The First. Very well.

The Second. Have you ever talked with him of this?

The First. No.

The Second. In your place I should be glad to have his opinion.

The First. I have it.

The Second. What is it?

The First. Your own and your friend's.

The Second. There is a tremendous authority against you.

The First. I admit it.

The Second. And how did you know Caillot's opinion?

The First. Through a woman full of intellect and keenness, the Princess de Galitzin. Caillot was playing the Deserter,[43] and was still on the spot where he had just gone through the agonies which she, close by, had shared, of an unhappy man resigned to lose his mistress and his life. Caillot draws near the Princess's box, and with the smile you know on his face makes some lively, well-bred, and courteous remarks. The Princess, astonished, says to him, 'What! You are not dead? I, who was only a spectator of your anguish, have only just come to myself.' 'No, Madam, I am not dead. My lot would be indeed pitiable if I died so often.' 'Then you feel nothing?' 'Ah, pardon me.' And so they engaged in a discussion which ended as this of ours will end—I shall keep to my opinion and you to yours. The Princess could not remember Caillot's arguments, but she had noticed that this great imitator of Nature at the very moment of his agony, when he was on the point of being dragged to execution, seeing that the chair on which he would have to lay down the fainting Louise was badly placed, rearranged it as he cried in a moribund voice, *Louise comes not, and my hour is nigh!*[44]

The Second. I am going to propose a compromise; to keep for the actor's natural sensibility those rare moments in which he forgets himself, in which he no longer sees the play, in which he forgets that he is on a stage, in which he is at Argos, or at Mycenæ, in which he is the very character he plays. He weeps . . .

The First. In proper time?

The Second. Yes. He exclaims . . .

The First. With proper intonation?

The Second. Yes. He is tormented, indignant, desperate; he presents to my eyes the real image, and conveys to my ears and heart the true accents of the passion which shakes him, so that he carries me away and I forget myself, and it is no longer Brizart or Le Kain, but Agamemnon or Nero that I hear. All other moments of the part I give up to art. I think it is perhaps then with Nature as with the slave who learns to move freely despite his chain. The habit of carrying it takes from it its weight and constraint.

The First. An actor of sensibility may perhaps have in his part one or two of these impulses of illusion; and the finer their effect the more they will be out of keeping with the rest. But tell me, when this happens does not the play cease to give you pleasure and become a cause of suffering?

The Second. Oh, no!

The First. And will not this figment of suffering have a more powerful effect than the every-day and real spectacle of a family in tears around the death-bed of a loved father or an adored mother?

The Second. Oh, no!

The First. Then you and the actor have not so completely forgotten yourselves?

The Second. You have already pushed me hard, and I doubt not you could push me yet harder; but I think I could shake you if you would let me enlist an ally. It is half-past four; they play *Dido;* let us go and see Mademoiselle Raucourt: she can answer you better than I can.

The First. I wish it may be so, but I scarce hope it. Do you think she can do what neither Lecouvreur,[45] nor Duclos, nor Deseine,[46] nor Balincourt,[47] nor Clairon, nor Dumesnil has accomplished? I dare tell you this, that if our young beginner is still far from perfect, it is because she is too much of a novice to avoid feeling;[48] and I predict that if she continues to feel, to remain herself, and to prefer the narrow instinct of nature to the limitless study of art, she will never rise to the height of the actresses I have named. She will have fine moments, but she will not be fine. It will be with her as with Gaussin and many others, who all their lives have been mannered, weak, and monotonous, only because they have never got out of the narrow limits which their natural sensibility imposed upon them. You are still bent on marshalling Mademoiselle Raucourt against me?

The Second. Certainly.

The First. As we go I will tell you a thing which has a close enough connexion with the subject of our talk. I knew Pigalle;[49] his house was open to me. One morning I go there; I knock; the artist opens the door with his roughing-chisel in his hand; then stopping me on the threshold of the studio he says, 'Before I let you pass, assure me you will not be alarmed at a beautiful woman without a rag of clothes on.' I smiled and walked in. He was working at his monument to Marshal Saxe, and a very handsome model was standing to him for the figure of France. But how do you suppose she struck me among the colossal figures around her? She seemed poor, small, mean—a kind of frog; she was overwhelmed by them, and I should have had to take the artist's word for it that the frog was a beautiful woman, if I had not waited for the end of the sitting and seen her on the same level with myself, my back turned to the gigantic figures which reduced her to nothingness. I leave it to you to apply this curious experience to Gaussin, to Riccoboni, to all actresses who have been unable to attain to greatness on the stage.

If by some impossible chance an actress were endowed with a sensibility comparable in degree to that which the most finished art can simulate, the stage offers so many different characters for imitation, one leading part brings in so many opposite situations that this rare and tearful creature, incapable of playing two different parts well, would at best excel in certain passages of one part; she would be the most unequal, the narrowest, the least apt actress you can imagine. If it happened that she attempted a great flight, her predominant sensibility would soon bring her down to mediocrity. She would be less like a strong steed at the gallop than a poor hack taking the bit in its teeth. Then one instant of energy, momentary, sudden, without gradation or preparation, would strike you as an attack of madness.

Sensibility being after all the mate of Sorrow and Weakness, tell me if a gentle, weak, sensitive creature is fit to conceive and express the self-possession of Léontine, the jealous transports of Hermione, the fury of Camilla, the maternal tenderness of Merope, the delirium and remorse of Phædra, the tyrannical pride of Agrippina, the violence of Clytemnestra? Leave your ever tearful one to one of our elegiac arts, and do not take her out of it.

The fact is, that to have sensibility is one thing, to feel is another. One is a matter of soul, the other of judgment. One may feel strongly and be unable to express it; one may alone, or in private life, at the fireside, give expression, in reading or acting, adequate for a few listeners, and give none of any account on the stage. On the stage, with what we call sensibility, soul, passion, one may give one or two tirades well and miss the rest. To take in the whole extent of a great part, to arrange its light and shade, its forts and feebles; to maintain an equal merit in the quiet and in the violent passages; to have variety both in harmonious detail and in the broad effect; to establish a system of declamation which shall succeed in carrying off every freak of the poet's—this is matter for a cool head, a profound judgment, an exquisite taste,—a matter for hard work, for long experience, for an uncommon tenacity of memory. The rule, *Qualis ab incepto processerit et sibi constet* [Let it continue as it began, harmonious with itself], rigorous enough for the poet, is fixed down to the minutest point for the actor. He who comes out from the wing without having his whole scheme of acting in his head, his whole part marked out, will all his life play the part of a beginner. Or if endowed with intrepidity, self-sufficiency, and spirit, he relies on his quickness of wit and the habit of his calling, he will bear you down with his fire and the intoxication of his emotions, and you will applaud him as an expert of painting might smile at a free sketch, where all was indicated and nothing marked. This is the kind of prodigy which may be seen sometimes at a fair or at Nicolet's.[50] Perhaps such people do well to remain as they are— mere roughed-out actors. More study would not give them what they want, and might take from them what they have. Take them for what they are worth, but do not compare them to a finished picture.

The Second. I have only one more question to ask you.

The First. Ask it.

The Second. Have you ever seen a whole piece played to perfection?

The First. On my word I can't remember it. Stop a bit—yes, sometimes— a middling piece by middling actors.

Our two talkers went to the playhouse, but as there were no places to be had they turned off to the Tuileries. They walked for some time in silence. They seemed to have forgotten that they were together, and each talked to himself as if he were alone, the one out loud, the other so low that he could not be heard, only at intervals letting out words, isolated but distinct, from which it was easy to guess that he did not hold himself defeated.

The thoughts of the man with the paradox are the only ones of which I can give an account, and here they are, disconnected as they must be when one omits in a soliloquy the intermediate parts which serve to hang it together. He said: Put an actor of sensibility in his place, and see how he will get out of the mess. What did this man do, however? He puts his foot on the balustrade, refastens his garter, and answers the courtier he despises with his head turned on his shoulder; and thus an incident which would have disconcerted any one but this cold and great actor is suddenly adapted to the surroundings and becomes a trait of genius.[51]

[He spoke, I think, of Baron, in the tragedy of the *Comte d'Essex*. He added with a smile:]

Yes; he will tell you she feels when, her head in her confidante's bosom, almost at the point of death, her eyes turned to the third tier of boxes, she suddenly sees an old Justice, who is dissolved in tears, and whose grief expresses itself in ludicrous grimaces, when she exclaims, 'Look up there! there's a fine face for you!' muttering the words under her breath, like the end of some inarticulate moan. Tell me no such stuff!

If I remember right, this was Gaussin in *Zaïre*.

And this third, whose end was so tragic. I knew him; I knew his father, who asked me sometimes to talk to him through his ear-trumpet.

[Here we are evidently dealing with the excellent Montmesnil.]

He was candour and honour itself. What was there in common between his character and that of Tartufe, which he played so well? Nothing. Where did he find the stiff neck, the strange roll of the eyes, the honeyed tone, and all the other fine touches in the hypocrite's part? Take care how you answer; I have you.

In a profound imitation of Nature.

In a profound imitation of Nature?

And you will note that the inward signs which chiefly mark the simplicity of the soul are not so much to be seen in Nature as the outward signs of hypocrisy. You cannot study them there, and an actor of great talent will find more difficulty in seizing on and examining the one than the other. And if I maintained that of all the qualities of the soul sensibility is the easiest to counterfeit, since there is scarce a man alive so cruel, so inhuman, that there is no germ of it in his heart, and that he has never felt it—a thing which cannot be safely said of all the other passions, such as avarice, distrust? But an excellent instrument . . . ?

Ah, I understand you. Between him who counterfeits sensibility and him who feels there will always be the difference between an imitation and a reality.

And so much the better; so much the better, I tell you. In the first case the actor has no trouble about separating himself from himself; he will arrive at one blow, at one bound, at the height of his ideal type . . .

At one blow, at one bound!

You are pettifogging over an expression. I mean that, never being brought back to the little type before him, he will be as great, as astonishing, as perfect an imitator of sensibility as of avarice, hypocrisy, duplicity—of every character that is not his own, of every passion that he does not feel. What the person of natural sensibility shows me will be little; the other's imitation will be strong; or, if the copies should be of equal strength, which I by no means grant you, the one, master of himself, playing entirely by study and judgment, will be, as daily experience shows us, more of a piece than the one who plays part from nature, part from study, part from a type, part from himself. However cleverly the two imitations may be fused together, a keen spectator will discriminate between them even more easily than a great artist will discern in a statue the line which marks off either two different styles or a front taken from one model and a back from another. . . . Let a consummate actor leave off playing from his head, let him forget himself, let his heart be involved, let sensibility possess him, let him give himself up to it . . .

He will intoxicate us.

Perhaps.

He will transport us with admiration.

It is not impossible; but it will be on condition of not breaking through his system of declamation; of not injuring the unity of the performance; otherwise you will say that he has gone mad. Yes, on this supposition you will, I admit, have a fine moment; but would you rather have a fine moment than a fine part? If that is your choice it is not mine.

Here the man with the paradox was silent. He walked with long strides, not seeing where he went; he would have knocked up against those who met him right and left if they had not got out of his way. Then, suddenly stopping, and catching his antagonist tight by the arm, he said, with a dogmatic and quiet tone, 'My friend, there are three types—Nature's man, the poet's man, the actor's man. Nature's is less great than the poet's, the poet's less great than the great actor's, which is the most exalted of all. This last climbs on the shoulders of the one before him and shuts himself up inside a great basket-work figure of which he is the soul. He moves this figure so as to terrify even the poet, who no longer recognises himself; and he terrifies us, as you have very well put it, just as children frighten each other by tucking up their little skirts and putting them over their heads, shaking themselves about, and imitating as best they can the croaking lugubrious accents of the spectre that they counterfeit. Have you not seen engravings of children's sports?[52] Have you not observed an urchin coming forward under a hideous old man's mask, which hides him from head to foot? Behind this mask he laughs at his little companions, who fly in terror before him. This urchin is the true symbol of the actor; his comrades are the symbol of the audience. If the actor has but middling sensibility, and if that is his only merit, will you not call him a middling man? Take care, for this is another trap I am laying for you. And if he is endowed with extreme sensibility what will come of it?—What will come of it? That he will either play no more, or play ludicrously ill; yes, ludicrously; and to prove it you can see the same thing in me when you like. If I have a recital of some pathos to give, a strange trouble arises in my heart and head; my tongue trips, my voice changes, my ideas wander, my speech hangs fire. I babble; I perceive it; tears course down my cheeks; I am silent. But with this I make an effect—in private life; on the stage I should be hooted.

Why?

Because people come not to see tears, but to hear speeches that draw tears; because this truth of nature is out of tune with the truth of convention. Let me explain myself: I mean that neither the dramatic system, nor the action, nor the poet's speeches, would fit themselves to my stifled, broken, sobbing declamation. You see that it is not allowable to imitate Nature, even at her best, or Truth too closely; there are limits within which we must restrict ourselves.

And who has laid down those limits?

Good sense, which will not play off one talent at the expense of another. The actor must sometimes sacrifice himself to the poet.

But if the poet's composition lent itself to that style?

Then you would have a sort of tragedy very different from what you have here.

And where would be the harm?

I do not know what you would gain, but I know very well what you would lose.

Here the man with the paradox came near his antagonist for the second or third time, and said to him,—

The saying is gross, but it is amusing, and it was said by an actress as to whose talent there are no two opinions. It is a pendant to the speech and situation of Gaussin: she, too, has her head on the breast of Pillot-Pollux; she is dying, at least I think so, and she says to him in a low tone, 'Ah, Pillot, que tu pues!' ['Oh, Pillot, how you do stink!'] This was Arnould playing Télaïre. At this moment was Arnould really Télaïre? No; she was Arnould, consistently Arnould.[53] You will never bring me to praise the intermediate degrees of a quality which, if it were carried to its fullest extent, and the actor were mastered by it, would spoil all. But let me suppose that the poet has written a scene to be declaimed on the stage as I should recite it in private life, who would play such a scene? No one: no, no one; not even an actor most completely master of his actions; for once that he came well out of it he would miss it a thousand times. Success, then, hangs on so little! This last argument strikes you as not very cogent? So be it, but not the less shall I deduct from it a little bursting of some bubbles, a lowering of some stilts by a few notches, and the leaving things pretty much as they are. For one poet of genius who attained this prodigious truth to nature there would be a vast number of flat and insipid imitators. It is not allowable, under pain of becoming insipid, awkward, and detestable, to go one line below the simplicity of Nature. Don't you think so?

The Second. I don't think anything. I did not hear what you said.

The First. What? We have not been continuing our dispute?

The Second. No.

The First. Then what the deuce were you doing? And of what were you dreaming?

The Second. That an English actor, called, I think, Macklin (I was at the playhouse that day), having to make his excuses to the pit for his temerity in playing I know not what part in Shakespeare's *Macbeth* after Garrick, said, amongst other things, that the impressions which subjugated actors and submitted them to the poet's genius and inspiration were very hurtful to them. I do not remember the reasons he gave for it, but they were very good, and they were felt and applauded. For the rest, if you are curious about it you will find them in a letter inserted in the *St. James's Chronicle,* over the signature of 'Quintilian.'[54]

The First. So, then, I have been talking all alone all this long time?

The Second. Very likely—just as long as I have been dreaming all alone. You know that of old actors played women's parts?

The First. I know it.

The Second. Aulus Gellius recounts in his *Attic Nights* that a certain Paulus, robed in the lugubrious trappings of Electra, instead of presenting himself on the stage with the urn of Orestes, appeared holding in his arms the urn containing the ashes of his own son whom he had just lost; and then it was no vain representation, no petty sorrow of the stage: but the house rang with real shrieks and groans.

The First. And you believe that Paulus at this moment spoke on the stage as he would have spoken at his fireside? No, no. This prodigious effect, as to which I entertain no doubt, depended neither on Euripides's verse nor on the declamation of the actor, but on the spectacle of a desolate father who bathed with his tears the urn holding his own son's ashes. This Paulus was perhaps only a middling actor; no better than that Æsopus of whom Plutarch reports, that, 'playing one day to a full house the part of Atreus, deliberating with himself how he shall avenge himself on his brother Thyestes, there was one of the servants who wished to run suddenly past him, and he (Æsopus) being beside himself with the vehement emotion and the ardour he threw into representing to the life the furious passion of King Atreus, gave him such a blow on the head with the sceptre he held in his hand that he killed him on the spot.' He was a madman, and the tribune ought to have sent him straight off to the Tarpeian rock.

The Second. Probably he did.

The First. I doubt it. The Romans attached so much importance to the life of a great actor, and so little to the life of a slave.

But they say an actor is all the better for being excited, for being angry. I deny it. He is best when he imitates anger. Actors impress the public not when they are furious, but when they play fury well. In tribunals, in assemblies, everywhere where a man wishes to make himself master of others' minds, he feigns now anger, now fear, now pity, now love, to bring others into these divers states of feeling. What passion itself fails to do, passion well imitated accomplishes.

Do not people talk in society of a man being a great actor? They do not mean by that that he feels, but that he excels in simulating, though he feels nothing—a part much more difficult than that of the actor; for the man of the world has to find dialogue besides, and to fulfil two functions, the poet's and the actor's. The poet on the stage may be more clever than the actor of private life, but is it to be believed that an actor on the stage can be deeper, cleverer in feigning joy, sadness, sensibility, admiration, hate, tenderness, than an old courtier?

But it is late. Let us go sup.

NOTES

1. The work referred to was *Garrick, ou les Acteurs Anglais,* a translation by Antonio Fabio Sticotti of an English pamphlet. The translation appeared in Paris in 1769. Sticotti was one of the *Comédiens du Roi de la Troupe Italienne,* was famous in the parts both of Pierrot and of Pantalon, and was popular in private life. A most interesting account of the Italian company in Paris, and of how by degrees they came to act in French and to play French pieces, will be found in M. Campardon's book, *Les Comédiens du Roi de la Troupe Italienne.* (Paris: Berger-Levrault et Cie.)

I have, with considerable trouble, procured a copy of Sticotti's work in a second edition published, without his name on the title-page, in Paris by 'J.P. Costard, Libraire, Rue Saint Jean-de-Beauvais. M.DCC. LXX.' It is a free version, with many additions, of *The Actor, or a Treatise on the Art of Playing.* (London: Printed for R. Griffiths, at the Dunciad in Pater-noster Row. MDCCLV.)

2. Cf. Lord Beaconsfield's 'You *shall* hear me one day,' at the end of his first unsuccessful and derided speech in the House of Commons.

3. This was a favourite aphorism of Grimm, to whom the first sketch of the *Paradoxe* was addressed *à propos* of *Garrick, ou les Acteurs Anglais.* It is given in vol. viii. of M. Assézat's edition. (Paris: Garnier frères.)

4. This was, according to good authority, the case with Talma in his earlier days; and was certainly so with M. Mounet Sully in his earlier days. Both actors learnt by experience the unwisdom of relying upon inspiration alone.

5. Mlle. Clairon was born in Condé in 1723, and received her first impulse to go on the stage from seeing Mlle. Dangeville taking a dancing lesson in a room of which the windows were opposite to those of the attic in which Clairon's ill-natured mother had locked her up. She made her first appearance with the Italian company at the age of thirteen; then made a great success in comedy parts in the provinces; and at the age of eighteen came back to Paris. Here she appeared first at the Opera; then, in September 1743, at the Français, where she took every one by surprise by choosing to play Phèdre, and playing it with complete success. For twenty years from this time onwards she remained queen of the French stage. She left the stage in 1788 and died in 1803.

6. This is a mistake of Diderot's. The person referred to is Duquesnoy the Belgian sculptor.

7. Mlle. Dumesnil was born in 1713—not, as M. de Manne says in his *La Troupe de Voltaire,* in 1711. She came to Paris from the provinces in 1737, and made her first appearance at the Français in the same year as Clytemnestra in *Iphigénie en Aulide.* She was admitted the following year, left the stage in 1776, and died in year XI. of the Republic.

8. This was so with Goethe, to take an instance; and not improbably so with Shakespeare.

9. Cf. *inter alia* Horace, *Satires,* Book I., Sat. IX.; and *Les Fâcheux.*

10. '*Ce ne sera pas une tragédie, ce sera une parade tragique que vous joucrez.*' [It will be not a tragedy that you enact, but samples of a tragicomedy.]

Parade tragique is the brief sketch of a tale of horror given by strolling players outside their booth by way of tempting spectators to the fuller performance to be given inside.

11. There were believers in poets quite foolish enough for this long after Diderot's time. It was precisely because this sort of diction was dropped for a more natural one in *Hernani* that the play, from its first scene, raised such a storm among the classicists—as he who will may read in the pages of Théophile Gautier. The lines quoted are from the speeches of Agamemnon and Arcas in the opening of Racine's *Iphigénie,* the name Henri being substituted for Agamemnon. The English version is from *The Dramatic Works of Jean Racine: A Metrical English Version,* by Robert Bruce Boswell (London: George Bell and Sons, 1901).

12. Note by the publishers of the small popular edition in Paris:—'Our modern authors have ended in always writing their pieces for this or that actor. Hence the short life which their productions will have.' The practice, I may add, is, unfortunately, by no means unknown in England.

13. Le Kain made his first appearance at the Français in September 1750, as Titus in Voltaire's *Brutus.* His success was gained in spite of natural disadvantages in voice and personal appearance. He owed much to Clairon, but more to unceasing study and application. What helped him in the first instance to please critical taste was that, like Garrick, he was the first to venture on varying the conventional sing-song of declamation. Later he and Clairon reformed the stage costume. Much of interest will be found about him in the lately published pamphlet, *Talma on the Actor's Art.* He was great as a tragedian; good as a comedian. He died in February 1778.

14. Mlle. Gaussin was the daughter of Antoine Gaussin, Baron's coachman, and Jeanne Pollet, cook to Adrienne Lecouvreur. She made her *début* at the Comédie Française in 1731. She appeared in *Zaïre* and in *Alzire,* but she is best remembered in the part of Inès in *Inès de Castro,* a tragedy by the innovator La Motte, which was much laughed at at the time, though it made even the Regent weep. Mlle. Clairon thus described her sister-comédienne: 'Mlle. Gaussin had the loveliest head, the most touching voice. She had a noble presence, and all her movements had a childish grace which was irresistible; but she was Mlle. Gaussin in everything.' After a brilliant career, on the stage and in the world, this once famous actress, who counted statesmen, poets, and philosophers among her lovers, married an opera-dancer, who ill-treated her, and she died without a friend in 1767.

15. Baron, when eighty years old, came back to the stage to play Rodrigue in the *Cid.* All went well until he had to say,—

> '*Je suis jeune, il est vrai, mais aux âmes bien nées*
> *La valeur n'attend pas le nombre des années.*'

[My years are few, but, Count, in high-born souls
Valor and youth full oft united are.
          The Cid, translated into English blank verse by
       Florence Kendrick Cooper (D. Appleton & Co., 1901)]

The pit laughed once and twice. Baron came to the front and said: 'Gentlemen, I am about to begin again a third time; but I warn you, that if any one laughs I shall leave the stage and never come back again.' After this all went well, except that when he knelt to Chimène he could not get up again.

16. This is an allusion to Mlle. Raucourt's first appearances in 1772. She was, as a matter of fact, nineteen at the time. The publishers of the French popular edition have this note on the passage: 'The instance of Rachel has given a triumphant lie to Diderot's assertion.' It may, however, be supposed that the annotators did not mean that Rachel had nothing of her art to learn at seventeen. In our own times, and in England, a very distinguished actor was in the habit of saying that no man could possibly play Romeo until he was past fifty, and that then he might perhaps be a little old for the part.

17. Molé, born in Paris in November 1734, made his first appearance at the Français in 1754. He was an example, like Mrs. Siddons, of a player who triumphed completely over a first failure. Collé wrote of him in his *Journal,* judging him from his first appearances, that he had a good appearance and nothing more; no passion, no art, no ease, no grace. He was not admitted at first, but he went into the provinces, came back in 1760, and appeared successfully as Andronicus in Campistron's tragedy. From that date his success was assured. He was extremely versatile, and there is a story of him which tells for 'the man with the paradox.' Lemercier relates how he was carried away by Molé's acting, and rushed to congratulate him. Molé replied, 'I was not pleased with myself. I let myself go too much; I felt the situation too deeply; I became the personage instead of the actor playing it; I lost my self-control. I was true to Nature as I might be in private; the perspective of the stage demands something different. The piece is to be played again in a few days; come and see it then.' Lemercier went, and just before the great scene Molé turned to him and said, 'Now I have got my self-control: wait and see.' Never, Lemercier adds, were art and art's effect more striking. Molé died in 1802.

18. This was so, as many people well remember, in the case of Signor Mario, who, beginning by being a stick, ended by being so fine an actor that even without his exquisite voice and method of singing he would have been a great artist.

19. The subjoined rendering is from *The Dramatic Works of Molière,* rendered into English by Henri Van Laun (New York: A. W. Lovering, publisher, n. d.). The asterisks indicate the points at which Diderot places the actress's interjections.

Eraste. No, no, madam, do not think that I have come to speak to you again of my passion; * it is all over; * I am resolved to cure myself. I know how little share I have in your heart. * A resentment kept up so long for a slight offence * shows me your indifference but too plainly, and I must tell you that contempt, * above all things, wounds a lofty mind. * I confess I saw in you charms which I never found in any other; * the delight I took in my chains would have made me prefer them to sceptres, had they been offered to me. * . . . My life was centred in you; * I will even own that, though I am insulted, I shall still perhaps have difficulty enough to free myself. * Maybe, notwithstanding the cure I am attempting, my heart may for a long time smart with this wound. * Freed from a yoke which I was happy to bend under, I shall take a resolution never to love again. * But no matter, since your hatred repulses a heart which love brings back to you, this is the last time you shall ever be troubled by the man you so much despise.

Lucile. You might have made the favour complete, sir, and spared me also this last trouble. *

Eraste. Very well, madam, very well, you shall be satisfied. I here break off all acquaintance with you, and break it off for ever, since you wish it; may I lose my life if ever again I desire to converse with you!

Lucile. So much the better, you will oblige me.

Eraste. No, no, do not be afraid that I shall break my word! * For, though my heart may be weak enough not to be able to efface your image, be assured you shall never have the pleasure of seeing me return. *

Lucile. You may save yourself the trouble. *

Eraste. I would pierce my breast a hundred times * should I ever be so mean as to see you again, after this unworthy treatment. *

Lucile. Be it so; let us talk no more about it.

20. 'Aux balcons, sur les gradins les plus bas.' The meaning of the phrase may be best explained by the following quotation from Alfred de Musset's essay on Tragedy, written in 1838:—'How is it that the tragedies of Racine, fine as they are, appear, as it must be confessed they do, cold and formal, like stately statues half vivified? It is because, in 1759, the Count de Lauraguais procured the removal of seats for the audience from the stage, at a cost of thirty thousand francs. Now-a-days Andromache and Monimia stand alone in their vast peristyles, and have an area of sixty feet to walk about in. There are no more marquises to surround the actress and crack a joke with her after every tirade, to pick up Hermione's fan and criticise Theseus's stockings.'

21. Nivelle de la Chaussée, born in 1692, is looked upon as the founder of *drames* in France. Schlegel, speaking of Voltaire's *Enfant Prodigue* and *Nanine*, says that 'the affecting drama had been before attempted in France by La Chaussée.' Piron characteristically described La Chaussée's plays as 'Les Homélies du Révérend Père La Chaussée.' Among his best plays are *Le Préjugé à la Mode* (to which Mlle. Quinault is said to have contributed an act), *Mélanide*, and *La Gouvernante*. La Chaussée died in 1754.

22. Garrick spent six months in Paris in the winter of 1764–5, when Diderot made his acquaintance.

23. Here is an odd slip on the part of Diderot, who seems to have mixed up Hamlet with Macbeth, and to have left the mistake uncorrected.

24. This refers to the *Plan d'un Divertissement Domestique*, to *La Pièce et le Prologue*, and to the final form in which Diderot put the ideas of the rough sketch and the little piece, that final form being the play, *Est-il Bon, est-il Méchant?* The words are a close description of the part of M. Hardouin, in which Diderot sketched his own character. Baudelaire and M. Champfleury tried, many years ago, to get the play acted, the one at the Gaîté, the other at the Théâtre Français. It seems obvious from the text that Diderot, before either *La Pièce et le Prologue* or *Est-il Bon, est-il Méchant?* was written, was in the habit, as many people are now-a-days, of giving little dramatic sketches in private life, and that he himself played M. Hardouin in *Est-il Bon, est-il Méchant?* in private theatricals.

25. Necker was not Director-General of Finance till 1777. M. Assézat, the admirable editor of the *Œuvres complètes de Diderot*, points out that the reference proves that *Le Paradoxe sur le Comédien*, written in 1773, must have been afterwards retouched. It was not published until 1830.

26. This is the recital of an actual incident. Mme. de Vandeul in her *Memoirs* gives the names and some additional circumstances.

27. Mlle. Duclos was born in 1670. Her first appearances were made, without much success, on the lyric stage at the Royal Academy of Music in Paris. In October

1693, she appeared at the Français as Justine in *Geta*, a tragedy by Péchantré. In 1696 she was definitely installed as understudy for Mlle. de Champmeslé in the leading tragic parts. She left the stage in 1733, and died in 1748.

28. Quinault-Dufresne was born in 1693, and made his first appearance at the Français as Orestes in Crébillon's *Electra*, in October 1712. In the month of December following he became an actor of leading parts, both in tragedy and comedy. He left the stage in March 1741, and died in 1759. One of his great parts on the stage was Le Glorieux, and in private life he was in the habit of strutting into the Café Procope and there enlarging upon his genius and his beauty. He married Mlle. Deseine, and it is told of him that after he left the stage he said to his wife, 'I, Quinault-Dufresne, who have conquered the world in the characters of Cæsar and Alexander, my name, alas, is only known to my parrot!'

29. That is, of course, Le Kain as Ninias in *Sémiramis*.

30. A fashionable painter of the time, whose history, curious as it was, need not here be enlarged upon.

31. Le Glorieux.

32. Montménil, son of the celebrated Le Sage, made his first appearance at the Français in May 1726, as Mascarille in *L'Etourdi*. He gained some success, but his fellow-actors counselled him to work in the provinces. This he did, reappearing in Paris in 1728 as Hector in *Le Joueur*. Thenceforward his success was not doubtful. Montménil, Le Mazurier says, played capitally *L'Avocat Patelin*, *Turcaret*, the Valet in *Les Bourgeoises à la Mode*, M. Delorme in *Les Trois Cousines*, 'et en général tous les paysans [and uncultivated characters generally].' He died suddenly in September 1743.

33. The troubadour story of Gabrielle de Vergy is told, with the lady's name given as Margaret de Roussillon, in chap. xxix. of Scott's *Anne of Geierstein*.

34. All this talk about *Le Shérif* refers directly to one of Diderot's *scenarios* for plays which he never actually wrote. The *scenario* of *Le Shérif* is published in the eighth volume of M. Assézat's edition of the *Œuvres complètes de Diderot* (Garnier, Paris). It would, so far as I can see, have made a curiously bad play.

35. *Pantin.* A figure cut out in card, with strings attached to it. I have used the word puppet to avoid roundabout expression.

36. Mlle. Dangeville was born in Paris in 1714. Daughter of a ballet-master and an actress, she made her first appearance at the Français at the age of seven and a half. Her official first appearance was made in 1730, as Lisette in Destouches's *Médisant*. She was admitted two months afterwards, remained on the stage till 1763, and died in 1796. The editor of the *Mémoires Secrets*, echoing public opinion, wrote of her: 'You alone, inimitable Dangeville, never grow old. So fresh, so novel are you, that each time we see you we take to be the first time. Nature has showered her gifts on you, as though Art had refused to endow you; and Art has hastened to enrich you with her perfection as though Nature had granted you nought.' Her first appearances were so successful that it was said of her at the time that she began where great actresses left off.

37. Brizard was born in April 1721, and began his career as an actor by playing in comedy in the provinces. He made his first appearance at the Français in July 1757, as Alphonse in La Motte's tragedy, *Inès de Castro*. He was admitted in the following year, left the stage in 1786, and died in 1791. The *Mémoires Secrets* describe him thus: 'He has the majesty of the king, the sublimity of the pontiff, the tenderness or sternness of the father. He is a very great actor, who combines force with pathos, fire with feeling.'

38. An account of the great actor Caillot will be found later on in a note on a passage referring to him in greater detail.

39. It did, in fact, so cease with Le Kain; at least one gathers as much from all that

can be learnt of his method in other authors. This is so much the case that it is at first sight startling to find in one part of Diderot's work a full reference to Le Kain, and in another an implication that no actor had yet ventured to vary the conventional sing-song. But Diderot was as capable of making a slip as Homer.

40. Author of *Le Comédien*. 1747.

41. Riccoboni was born at Mantua in 1707, and came to France with his parents in 1716. In 1726 he made his first appearance, with success, at the Comédie Italienne, as the lover in Marivaux's *Surprise de l'Amour*. He twice left and twice rejoined the company. In 1749 he made what seemed a third and definitive retreat; but in 1759 he reappeared again as a member of the Troupe Italienne. He died in 1772. Baron Grimm describes him as a cold and pretentious actor. He was the author of various pieces, alone and in collaboration, and published a work called *Pensées sur la Déclamation*.

42. Mme. Riccoboni, wife of the actor at the Comédie Italienne, made her first appearance on that stage in August 1734. She went on acting for forty-six years, and was, according to all accounts, a very clever and interesting woman, and a bad actress. She left the stage in 1760 and died in 1792.

43. *Le Déserteur*, a pretty and interesting 'melodrama,' in the old sense of the word, by Sedaine.

44. Caillot was born in 1733 in Paris, in the Rue St. Honoré, where his father carried on a jeweller's business. In 1743 he was admitted under the name of Dupuis to the king's private band of musicians. In 1752 he took to acting in the provinces, and in 1760 he made his first appearance with the Troupe Italienne as Colas, in Favart's *Ninette à la Cour*. His success was instant, and increased as his career went on. He was admirable both as a singer and as an actor. Among his greatest successes was Blaise in *Lucile* (Marmontel's words to Grétry's music). In this it was thought unusual daring on his part to appear on the stage in a real peasant's dress, with really dusty boots, and with a really bald head. Grimm wrote of this performance: 'Caillot's playing of the part of Blaise is, I believe, one of the most interesting things that can be seen on any stage. This charming actor puts into his performance so much fineness, so much perfection, that it is impossible to imagine anything better. I defy Garrick, the great Garrick, to play the part better. . . . Caillot in all his parts carries truth in nature and in costume very far. I do not know how he has managed to have just the bald head that Blaise should have.' As a matter of fact, Caillot in Blaise, like Charles Mathews in Affable Hawk, appeared for the first time with his own bald head uncovered by a wig. Of his presence of mind on the stage there is a story parallel to Diderot's. In *Sylvain* he had to fall at his father's feet and catch him by the knees. The other actor, misunderstanding the movement, drew back, so that Caillot fell face forwards on the stage; but he managed the fall so cleverly that it was taken for a fine stroke of art. He left the stage in 1772, but occasionally returned to fill the place of a sick comrade.

45. Mlle. Le Couvreur, born at Fismes (Marne) in 1690, made her first appearance at the Français in May 1717, as Electra in Crébillon's tragedy. She was admitted the same month. She died in 1730, and the fact that she was refused Christian burial in Paris in the same year in which Mrs. Oldfield was buried with all pomp in Westminster Abbey is well known. Le Mazurier, who gives the outlines of the story concerning her on which the play of *Adrienne Lecouvreur* was founded, has also a full and most interesting account of her acting, from which some brief extracts may here be given. She was of a medium height, with sparkling eyes, fine features, and much distinction of manner. Her voice had naturally few tones, but she had learnt to give them infinite variety. Her diction was extremely natural, and this told greatly in her favour, as all her predecessors, except Floridor and Baron, had adopted a stilted enunciation. She and

Baron were said to be the most loyal members of the company. They both avoided the practice of 'starring' in the provinces, a practice which of late years has given rise to much disturbance at the Français. The excellence of her acting in scenes where she had to listen instead of speaking was especially remarkable. In all scenes her acting was full of nature and fire. She had every merit that Clairon had, with an amount of feeling that Clairon never possessed. She played many parts in comedy and played them well, but it was as a tragedian that she was unrivalled. Her death was felt as a public misfortune.

46. Mlle. Deseine, who afterwards married Quinault-Dufresne, made her first appearance at Fontainebleau before Louis XV. as Hermione in *Andromaque*. Her success was so marked that the king made her a present of a magnificent Roman dress, and she was at once admitted by special ordinance. She appeared as Hermione at the Français in 1725, left the stage in 1732, returned to it in 1733, and quitted it definitely in 1736. She died in 1759. That she was a great actress would be evident, if from nothing else, from the unreserved praise which Clairon bestows on her in her *Memoirs*.

47. Mlle. Balicourt (so Le Mazurier spells it) made her first appearance at the Français in 1727 as Cléopâtre in *Rodogune*. A month later she was admitted. Her great success was in parts demanding a queenly presence. All that was against her in these was her youth, and this Le Mazurier says, with a peculiarly French touch, the pit forgave her with more readiness than it forgave Duclos for remaining on the boards when she was sixty. She left the stage in 1738 and died in 1743.

48. A very distinguished English actor of our own day says of a part in which he has won much well-deserved fame, and which is full of feeling, that his great difficulty was to get over the feeling with which it naturally impressed him. He had to learn the words like a parrot before he could trust himself to give any meaning to them. When he first played it he was still a little liable to be carried away by its emotion, and he notes that 'whenever I began really to cry the audience left off crying.'

49. Pigalle was born in 1714 and died in 1785. Voltaire called him the French Phidias, and in return Pigalle executed perhaps the worst statue of Voltaire extant. His *Mercury* gained him his election to the Academy, and led to his visit to Frederick the Great. He presented himself at the Palace at Berlin as *l'auteur du Mercure,* and was told that His Majesty would give him twenty-four hours to leave the kingdom. Frederick's poems had been maltreated in the *Mercure de France*, and he took Pigalle for the critic.

50. Nicolet was, as may be judged from the context, one of the greatest managers of the *Théâtres de Foire*. He combated desperately, and had not a little to do with upsetting the exclusive rights claimed by the *Comédiens du Roi*, which rights were so skilfully eluded by Piron in his *Arlequin Deucalion*. The whole story, which is given in M. Bonnassies's *Spectacles Forains* (Paris: Dentu), affords a curious parallel to the similar struggle in England.

51. The same story of the accidental unfastening of a garter being turned to excellent account by an actor of great presence of mind has in later days been referred, probably by confusion with Diderot's story, to the scene in *Ruy Blas,* in which Don Salluste, disguised as a lackey, gives his commands to Ruy Blas disguised as Prime Minister.

52. For special instances of such plates M. Assézat refers us to *Les Jeux des Anciens*, by M. Becq de Fouquières (in 8vo. Reinwald, 1869).

53. Sophie Arnould, the most famous singer of her day, was born in 1740 and died in 1802. She first attracted notice by singing, when little more than a child, before Mme. de Pompadour, and she made her first appearance at the Opera at the age of seventeen. Mlle. Fel taught her singing, Clairon taught her acting. For details

concerning her romantic history readers may be referred to MM. de Goncourt's compilation, *Sophie Arnould d'après sa Correspondance* (Paris, Dentu). The scene related by Diderot took place in the opera of *Castor et Pollux*.

54. On this remarkable passage the usually irrefragable M. Assézat has a note which is perhaps equally remarkable, and of which I append a translation. The Italics are my own. 'The fact here recorded is another assistance to fixing approximately the date of Diderot's work. The quarrel between Macklin and Garrick lasted several years, but it was not till 1773 that Macklin took up Garrick's parts, notably that of Macbeth. As he had formerly been the moving spirit of a cabal against Garrick, which, despite his talent, went the length of rotten apples and bad eggs, so now, it is said, Garrick fostered a cabal against Macklin. Less lucky than his compeer, *or, unlike him, being unprovided with a sufficing gang of bruisers,* Macklin had to give up the boards. It was before he played Macbeth for the first time that he made a speech, in accordance with English stage custom, bespeaking the indulgence of the audience.'

Diderot has made a hopeless confusion between Garrick's quarrel with Macklin (as to which Macklin published a pamphlet in 1743) and the riotous proceedings which took place on Macklin's third performance of Macbeth at Covent Garden in 1773. These were due to Coleman's simultaneous engagement of William Smith and Macklin, both of whom claimed an exclusive right to acting certain characters, Macbeth amongst them. Full particulars will be found in Kirkman's *Life of Macklin*.

Thomas Gray

1716–1771

Thomas Gray, the most substantial poetic figure of the mid-eighteenth century, was a character who, much in the same manner as Blake, stood outside all the commonly-understood categories of his time. The traditional portrait of him as a sort of proto-Romantic—Coleridge disguised as Alexander Pope—does not really work, for it fails to take account of the very real differences that separated him from the circle of Wordsworth and Keats. A scholar and academic, Gray moved in a world that was both highly structured and remote, and the ornate, bleak texture of his verse distances him equally from the coffee-house chatter of the Neoclassicists and the bucolic soliloquies of the Romantics.

Born on December 26, 1716, Gray endured a domestic life made miserable by his father's brutal fits of rage and aggression. From an early age, he was supported almost exclusively by his mother, who was able to provide him with a sumptuous education (Eton, then Cambridge) by running a millinery shop. At Eton, he formed close friendships with Horace Walpole, Richard West, and Thomas Ashton; the members of this "Quadruple Alliance" came together as a result of their common literary interests and mutual distaste for athletics. Walpole, in particular, remained especially close to Gray throughout his life, and made an extensive tour of the Continent with him upon leaving Cambridge in 1739.

On his return to England in 1741, Gray settled once more in Cambridge, where he took up residence at his old college (Peterhouse) as a "fellow-commoner." He devoted most of his time to studying Greek and writing. His first well-known poems—works such as "To Spring" and "Ode on a Prospect of Eton College"—were composed around this time. By and large, they are fairly straightforward Neoclassical productions: carefully put together and highly derivative. Particularly remarkable from this period is Gray's beautiful "Sonnet on the Death of Richard West," composed in memory of his friend, who had died suddenly of shock upon learning of his mother's infidelities.

In 1751 Gray composed his "Elegy Written in a Country Church-yard." Although he had wished to make revisions to the work, a pirated edition soon appeared in print and Gray was forced to publish. The poem was immensely popular, and remains to this day one of the most frequently-quoted pieces of verse in the English language. It is highly representative of Gray's work, insofar as it contains, within a deceptively simple framework, numerous subtle allusions to other poets and works. Many have seen the "Elegy"—with its quiet, meditative tone and homely setting—as a prefiguration of Wordsworth's *Prelude* or *Tintern Abbey*.

In his later years, Gray became increasingly interested in Scandinavian and Celtic language and folklore, the influence of which may be seen in such works as "Two Norse Odes" and "The Descent of Odin." It is in these works especially that Gray is seen as a precursor of the Romantics, both in terms of poetic style and subject-matter. He spent his last years writing and studying at Pembroke College, Cambridge, where he collapsed and died during dinner on July 30, 1771. He was buried, fittingly enough, beside his beloved mother in the church-yard of Stoke Poges, Buckinghamshire, the setting of his "Elegy."

One of the most telling aspects of Gray's literary career was that he exerted great influence, both among his contemporaries and upon succeeding generations, through a remarkably small corpus of work. He wrote little, and agonized a great deal over even that small amount. Shy and extremely sensitive to criticism, he was entirely unequipped for the sort of public life required of man of letters in his period. The narrowly circumscribed world of academe provided him with a happy milieu in which to pursue his literary and intellectual interests, but it is quite plausible that it may have acted as a kind of *cul-de-sac* for his creative development. Gray was an innovator: his admiration of the Middle Ages, his interest in ballads and folk-verse, his affection for such locales as the Swiss Alps and the English Lake District—all were unorthodox for a man of his period. Had he moved in closer proximity to Grub Street, he would have been forced to defend himself, to expand upon his ideas. As it was, he was never required to carry his literary notions to their logical end, and thus his "romanticism" (if such it may be called) remained dormant, obscured by silence and preoccupation.

Observations on English Metre

Though I would not with Mr. Urry, the Editor of Chaucer, insert words and syllables, unauthorized by the oldest manuscripts, to help out what seems lame and defective in the measure of our ancient writers, yet as I see those manuscripts, and the first printed editions, so extremely inconstant in their manner of spelling one and the same word as to vary continually, and often in the compass of two lines, and seem to have no fixed orthography, I cannot help thinking it probable, that many great inequalities in the metre are owing to the neglect of transcribers, or that the manner of reading made up for the defects which appear in the writing. Thus the *y* which we often see prefixed to participles passive, *y*cleped, *y*hewe, &c. is not a mere arbitrary insertion to fill up the verse, but is the old Anglo-Saxon augment, always prefixed formerly to such participles, as *ge*lufod (loved) from lufian (to love), *ge*ræd, from rædan (to read), &c. which augment, as early as Edward the Confessor's time, began to be written with a *y,* or an *i,* as *y*lufod, *i*seld, for *ge*lufod, *ge*seld, (loved, sold,) as Dr. Hickes informs us in his Anglo-Saxon Grammar, C. 22, p. 136. This syllable, though (I suppose) then out of use in common speech, our poets inserted, where it suited them, in verse. The same did they by the final syllable of verbs, as bren*nin,* correc*tin,* dron*kin,* &c. (to burn, correct, drink,) which was also Saxon, all the infinitives in that tongue ending with an *an,* or *eon,* as *bebyrige*an, to bury, *mag*an, to be able, *gefe*on, to rejoice, and most of the participles passive, and the plural persons terminating with the same letter, as, *gefund*en, found, *beswung*en, beaten, &c.; and *we, ge, hi, miht*on, (we, he, they, might,) we *wold*on, we would; we *sceold*on, we should; we *ar*on, we are, &c. This termination began to be omitted after the Danes were settled among us; for in the Cimbrick tongue the verbs usually finished in *a,* as greip*a,* to gripe, hab*a,* to have, which in the Saxon were greip*an,* hab*an*; the transition is very apparent thence to the English, which we now speak. As then our writers inserted these initial and final letters, or omitted them; and, where we see them written, we do not doubt that they were meant to fill up the measure; it follows, that these Poets had an ear not insensible to defects in metre; and where the verse seems to halt, it is very probably occasioned by the transcriber's neglect, who, seeing a word spelt differently from the manner then customary, changed or omitted a few letters without reflecting on the injury done to the measure. The case is the same with the genitive case singular and the nominative plural of many nouns, which by the Saxon inflection had an additional syllable, as *word,* a word, *wordis,* of a word: *smith,* a smith, *smithis,* of a smith, *smithas,* smith, which, as Hickes observes, is the origin of the formation of those cases in our present tongue; but we now have reduced them, by our pronunciation, to an equal number of syllables with their nominatives singular. This was commonly done too, I imagine, in Chaucer's and Lydgate's time; but, in verse, they took the liberty either to follow the old language in pronouncing the final syllable, or to sink the vowel and abridge it, as was usual, according to the necessity of their versification. For example, they would read either vĭŏlēttĕs with four syllables, or violets with three; ban*kis*, or banks; triūmphys, or triūmphs, indifferently. I have mentioned (in some remarks on the verses of Lydgate) the *e* mute, and their use of it in words derived from the French, and I imagine that they did the same in many words of true English origin, which the Danes had before robbed of their final consonant, writing *bute* for the Saxon *butan* (without), *bifora* for *biforan* (before), *ondrede* for *ondreadan* (to dread), *gebringe* for *gebringan* (to bring), *doeme* for *deman* (to deem), and abundance of other words. Here we may easily conceive, that though the *n* was taken away, yet the *e* continued to be pronounced faintly, and though in time it was quite dropped in conversation, yet when the poet thought fit to make a syllable of it, it no more offended their ears than it now offends those of a Frenchman to hear it so pronounced, in verse.

Puttenham, in his *Art of Poetry*, addressed to Queen Elizabeth in 1587, tell us, L. 2, C. 4, that "Chaucer, Lydgate, and others used *Cesures* either very seldom, or not at all, or else very licentiously; and many times made their meetres (they called them *riding Ryme*) of such unshapely words as would allow no convenient cesure; and therefore did let their rymes run out at length, and never staid till they came to the end; which manner, though it were not to be misliked in some sort of meetre, yet in every long verse the cesure ought to be kept precisely, if it were but to serve as a law to correct the licentiousness of Rymers. Besides that, it pleaseth the eare better, and sheweth more cunning in the maker by following the rule of his restraint, for a Rymer that will be tied by no rules at all, but range as he list, may utter what he will; but such manner of Poesy is called in our Vulgar, '*Ryme Dogrell*,' with which rebuke we will that in no case our Maker shall be touched."

Then Puttenham gives rules for the Cesura, which he tells us, "In a verse of twelve syllables should always divide it exactly in the middle; in one of ten, it should fall on the fourth, in one of eight on the same, in one of seven on the same, or on none at all," &c. I mention no more than these, as they are now the only measures ádmitted into our serious poetry, and I shall consider how his rules hold in modern practice.

Alexandrines, or verses of twelve syllables, it is true, though Spenser sometimes does otherwise, must, if they would strike the ear agreeably, have their pause in the middle, as,

> And after toilsome days | a soft repose at night.

Or,

> He both her warlike Lords | outshined in Helen's eyes.

And this uniformity in the cesura is just the reason why we no longer use them but just to finish a lyric stanza: they are also sometimes interspersed arbitrarily among verses of ten syllables. This is an odd custom, but it is confirmed by the sanction which Dryden and Pope have given to it, for they soon tire the ear with this sameness of sound; and the French seemed to have judged ill in making them their heroic measure.

Verses of *eight* syllables are so far from being obliged to have their cesura on the fourth, that Milton, the best example of an exquisite ear that I can produce, varies it continually, as,

> To live with her, | and live with thee.　.　.　.On the 4th.
> In unreproved | pleasure free .　.　.　.　.　.　″　 ″　 5th.
> To hear the lark | begin his flight.　.　.　.　″　 ″　 4th.
> And singing | startle the dŭll nīght .　.　.　″　 ″　 3d.
> Whēre thĕ grēat sūn | bĕgīns hĭs stāte .　.　″　 ″　 4th.
> The clouds | in thousand liveries dight .　.　″　 ″　 2d.
> With masque | and antique pageantry .　.　″　 ″　 2d.

The more we attend to the composition of Milton's harmony, the more we shall be sensible how he loved to vary his pauses, his measures, and his feet, which gives that enchanting air of freedom and wildness to his versification, unconfined by any rules but those which his own feeling and the nature of his subject demanded. Thus he mixes the line of eight syllables with that of seven, the Trochee and the Spondee with the Iambic foot, and the single rhyme with the double. He changes the cesura as frequently in the heptasyllabic measure, as,

> Oft ŏn ă plāt | of rising ground   (Octosyll.)　　　.
> I hear | the far-off curfew sound,   (Oct:—) On the 2d.
> Ovĕr sōme | wide-water'd shore.　.　.　.　.　 ″　 ″　 3d.
> Swinging slow | with sullen roar:　.　.　.　.　″　 ″　 3d.
> Or if the air | will not permit, &c.　(Oct:—)　″　 ″　 4th.
> Far from all resort | of mirth.　.　.　.　.　.　″　 ″　 5th.
> Save the cricket | on the hearth .　.　.　.　″　 ″　 4th.
> Or the bellman's | drowsy charm .　.　.　.　″　 ″　 4th.

But the greatest confinement which Puttenham would lay on our verse is that of making the Cæsura constantly fall on the fourth syllable of our decasyllabic measure, which is now become our only heroic metre for all poems of any length. This restraint Wyatt and Lord Surrey submitted to, though here and there you find an instance of their breaking through it, though rarely. So,

> From these hye hilles | as when a spring doth falle,
> It trilleth down | with still and subtle course,
> Of this and that | it gathers aye, and shall
> Till it have just | downe flowed to stream and force:
> So fareth Love, | when he hath ta'en a course;

> Rage is his raine; | resistance 'vaileth none;
> The first eschue | is remedy alone.
>   Wyatt

And these verses of Surrey:

> In active games | of nimbleness and strength
> Where we did strain, | trained with swarms of youth,
> Our tender limbs, | which yet shot up in length:
> The secret groves, | which oft we made resound
> Of plesaunt plaint, | and of our Lady's praise,
> Recording oft, | what grace each one had found,
> What hope of speed, | what dread of long delays;
> The wild forèst, | the clothed holts with green,
> With reines availed, | and swift-ybreathed horse,
> With cry of hound, | and merry blasts between,
> Where we did chase | the fearful hart of force, &c.

But our poets have long since got loose from these fetters. Spenser judiciously shook them off; Milton, in his *Paradise Lost,* is ever changing and mingling his pauses, and the greatest writers after him have made it their study to avoid what Puttenham regarded as a rule of perfect versification.

These reflections may serve to shew us, that Puttenham, though he lived within about one hundred and fifty years of Chaucer's time, must have been mistaken with regard to what the old writers called their *Riding Rhyme;* for the *Canterbury Tales,* which he gives as an example of it, are as exact in their measure and in their pause as in the *Troilus and Cresseide,* where he says, "*the metre is very grave and stately;*" and this not only in the Knight's Tale, but in the comic Introduction and Characters; as,

> A monke ther was | fair for the maistery,
> An outrider | that loved venery,
> A manly man, | to ben an abbot able,
> Many a dainty horse | had he in stable;   (On the 6th.)
> And when he rode, | men might his bridle heare,
> Gingiling in a whistling wind, | as cleare   (On the 8th.)
> And eke as loud, as doth the chapell-bell, &c.

I conclude, that he was misled by the change which words had undergone in their accents since the days of Chaucer, and by the seeming defects of measure which frequently occur in the printed copies. I cannot pretend to say what it was they called *Riding Rhyme,* but perhaps it might be such as we see in the Northern Tale of Sir Thopas in Chaucer.

> Sir Thopas was | a doughty swaine,
> White was his face, | as pain de maine,
> His lippis red as rose, |
> His rudd is like | scarlet in graine,

And I you tell | in gode certaine
He had a seemly nose. | &c.

But nothing can be more regular than this sort of stanza, the pause always falling just in the middle of those verses which are of eight syllables, and at the end of those of six. I imagine that it was this very regularity which seemed so tedious to *mine host of the Tabbarde,* as to make him interrupt Chaucer in the middle of his story, with

No more of this for Goddis dignitè—
Mine earès akin of thy draftie speeche,
Now such a rime the Devil I beteeche,
This may well be clepe *Rime Dogrell,* quoth he, &c.

Hence too we see that Puttenham is mistaken in the sense of *Rhyme Dogrell,* for so far was it *from being tied to no rule at all,* that it was consistent with the greatest exactness in the Cæsura and in the Measure; but as he himself has said very well in another place, (B. ii. ch. 9,) "the over busie and too speedie returne of one manner of tune doth too much annoy and, as it were, glut the eare, unless it be in small and popular musickes, sung by these Cantabanqui upon benches and barrels-heads, where they have none other audience than boys and country fellows, that pass by them in the street; or else by blind harpers or such like tavern-minstrels, that give a fit of mirth for a groat; and their matters being for the most part stories of old time, as the Tale of Sir Thopas, the Reportes of Bevis of Southampton, Adam Bell, and Clymme of the Clough, and such other old romances and historical rhymes, made on purpose for the recreation of the common people at Christmas dinners and bride-ales in taverns and ale-houses, and such other places of base resort," &c. This was therefore *Dogrell,* whose frequent return of rhyme and similarity of sound easily imprinted it in the memory of the vulgar; and, by being applied of old to the meanest uses of poetry, it was grown distasteful to the ears of the better sort.

But the *Riding Rhyme* I rather take to be that which is confined to one measure, whatever that measure be, but not to one rhythm; having sometimes more, sometimes fewer syllables, and the pause hardly distinguishable, such as the Prologue and History of Beryn, found in some MSS. of Chaucer, and the Cook's Tale of Gamelyn, where the verses have twelve, thirteen, or fourteen syllables, and the Cæsura on the sixth, seventh, or eighth, as it happens. This having an air of rusticity, Spenser has very well adapted it to pastoral poetry, and in his hands it has an admirable effect, as in the Eclogue called March, which is in the same metre as Chaucer's Tale of Sir Thopas; and in February and May, where the two fables of the Oak and Bryer, and the Fox and Kid, for humour and expression are equal to any thing in our language. The measure, like our usual verse of eight syllables, is Dimeter-Iambic, but admits of a Trochee, Spondee, Amphybrachys, Anapæst, &c. in almost every place. Thus,

Sēĕst hŏw brāg you bullock bears . . .	Trochee in the 1st.
So smirk, so smooth, his pricked ears? .	Pure Iambic
His horns bĕen ăs brāde, as rainbow bent,	Anapæst in the 2d.
Hīs dēwlăp ăs līthe, as Lass of Kent! . .	The same.
Seē hōw hĕ vēntĕth īntŏ thĕ wīnd . . .	Anapæst in the last.
Wēenĕst, ŏf lōve is not his mind? &c. . .	Trochee in the 1st.

And,

Though marked him, with melting eyes,   Pure Iambic.

A thrilling throb frŏm hĕr heārt did rise,   Anapæst in the 4th.

And īntĕrrūptĕd ăll hĕr ŏthĕr spēech   { Amphibrachys in the 2d. Tribra- chys in the 3d.

Wīth sōme ōld sōrrŏw, thăt māde ă nĕw brēach,

Sēemĕd shĕ sāw ĭn hĕr yōunglĭng's fāce,   { Trochee in the 1st. Anapæst in the 3d.

The' ōld līnĕămēnts ŏf hīs Fāther's grace.   { Anapæst in 2d and 3d.

In these last six lines, the first has eight syllables, and the second nine, the third and fourth ten, the fifth nine, and the last ten: and this is the only English measure which has such a liberty of choice allowed in its feet, of which Milton has taken some little advantage, in using here and there a Trochee in his octosyllabics, and in the first foot only of his heroic verses. There are a very few instances of his going farther for the sake of some particular expression, as in that line,

Būrnt āftĕr thēm tŏ thĕ bōttŏmlĕss pīt,

where there is a Spondee in the first place, a Pyrrhic in the third, and a Trochee in the fourth, and that line,

Wīth īmpētŭoūs recoil and jarring sound,

with an Anapæst in the first place, &c.

Spenser has also given an instance of the decasyllabic measure with an unusual liberty in its feet, in the beginning of his Pastoral called August, thus,

Thĕn lŏ, Pērĭgōt, thĕ plēdge whĭch I plīght,
Ă māzĕr ÿwroūght ŏf thĕ māplĕ wāre,
Whĕreīn ĭs ĕnchāsĕd māný ă faĭr sīght
Ŏf beārs ănd tÿgĕrs, thāt mākĕn fiĕrce wār, &c.,

where there are Trochees, &c. in every foot but the last. I do not doubt that he had some ancient examples of this rhythm in his memory, when he wrote it. Bishop Douglas, in his Prologue to the eighth Æneid, written about eighty years before Spenser's Calendar, has something of the same kind.

I make no mention of the Hexameter, Sapphic, and other measures which Sir Philip Sidney and his friends attempted to introduce in Queen Elizabeth's reign, because they soon dropped into oblivion. The same thing had happened in France a little before, where, in 1553, Etienne Jodelle began to write in this way, and was followed by Baïf, Passerat, Nicholas Rapin, and others, but without success. (See Pasquier, Recherches, l. vii. c. 12.) And in Italy this was attempted by Claudio Tolomei, and other men of learning, to as little purpose. (See Crescimbeni Comment. vol. i. p. 21.)

Edward Young

1683–1765

Edward Young, an eighteenth-century critic and dramatist whose modest output and quietly unorthodox opinions have safeguarded for the last 200 years the obscurity he enjoyed during his own lifetime, deserves to be remembered as one of the more iconoclastic literary theorists of the Augustan Age. Although much of his writing never surpassed the level of hack-work, he managed nonetheless to formulate a radically new approach to literary composition that ran directly counter to prevailing attitudes, and provided, if not a blueprint, at least a major starting point for the Romantic movement.

Born in July 1683, Young studied first at Winchester, then at New College and Corpus Christi, Oxford. At Oxford he cultivated the friendship of the *literati* who were later to help him establish himself as a playwright in London, where he moved among the scribes and wits of Addison's circle. His earliest literary efforts were largely encomia written as a means of winning patronage; works—such as the *Epistle to the Right Honorable George Lord Landsdowne* or the *Elegy on the Death of Queen Anne,* whose nature and scope can be fairly accurately gauged by their titles. The latter work, written in 1714, contained a rather lavish paean to the new king, George I, who, in the best Hanoverian style, took no notice of it whatever. George II, however, seems to have possessed better manners, for upon his accession to the throne in 1726, he awarded Young a pension, and in 1728 he secured him a position as royal chaplain.

Young had been far from dormant in the intervening years. His first play, *Busiris, King of Egypt,* was produced in London in 1719. He continued to write drama throughout most of his life, plays that were consistently (if not spectacularly) popular during his own day, but which have since fallen into obscurity. Even *The Revenge,* written in 1721 and generally considered his finest play, is almost never performed today.

Shortly after Young started writing for the theatre, he published a series of satires composed in heroic couplets. Over a period of three years (1725–28) seven such pieces appeared; they were eventually collected into a single volume entitled *The Love of Fame.* These satires display the characteristic marks of Young's style—the discursive subject matter, the ability to construct a well-turned phrase, the rambling, slack organization—that both enhanced and dulled his reputation. They served as a model for Alexander Pope when he wrote his *Moral Essays.*

A series of deaths in Young's family—including that of his wife in 1741—prompted the composition of *The Complaint; or, Night Thoughts,* a blank-verse dramatic monologue of nearly 10,000 lines. Essentially a meditation on death, it was quite popular in Young's time, although most critical opinion has faulted it for being too long, badly organized, and frequently trite. Samuel Johnson's judgement of it as "a wilderness of thought in which the fertility of fancy scatters flowers of every hue" is a fair example of the stance taken—both in the eighteenth-century and today—by most literary exegetes.

Young's only known work of criticism, *Conjectures on Original Composition,* was written as a letter to his friend Samuel Richardson in 1759. Though Richardson's reaction to the thoughts expressed therein is not known, the public reception granted to the work in England was generally cool. Young's stance is ultimately an enthusiastic one: he objects to the overriding importance the Neoclassicists grant to precedent and imitation. His desire is to relax the formal restraints in literary composition, and give freer play to "genius."

As a theorist, Young antedates Wordsworth and Coleridge by nearly half a century, so it is not surprising that he found little audience for such ideas in England during his lifetime. *Conjectures* was translated into German, however, and enjoyed a far greater currency there than it did at home. Ironically, it was only through the discovery of the German Romantics that Young's theories were to exercise a significant influence in Britain, when they were adopted and expanded upon by the English Romantics.

Young's last years were spent in Hertfordshire, where he served as Rector of Welwyn. He died on April 5, 1765.

Conjectures on Original Composition

We confess the follies of youth without a blush; not so, those of age. However, keep me a little in countenance, by considering, that age wants amusements more, though it can justify them less, than the preceding periods of life. How you may relish the pastime here sent you, I know not. It is miscellaneous in its nature, somewhat licentious in its conduct; and, perhaps, not over-important in its end. However, I have endeavoured to make some amends, by digressing into subjects more important, and more suitable to my season of life. A serious thought standing single, among many of a lighter nature, will sometimes strike the careless wanderer after amusement only, with useful awe: as monumental marbles scattered in a wide pleasure-garden (and such there are) will call to recollection those who would never have sought it in a church-yard walk of mournful yews.

To one such monument I may conduct you, in which is a hidden lustre, like the sepulchral lamps of old; but not like those will this be extinguished, but shine the brighter for being produced, after so long concealment, into open day.

You remember that your worthy patron, and our common friend, put some questions on the serious drama, at the same time when he desired our sentiments on original and on moral composition. Though I despair of breaking through the frozen obstructions of age, and care's incumbent cloud, into that flow of thought and brightness of expression which subjects so polite require, yet will I hazard some conjectures on them.

I begin with original composition; and the more willingly, as it seems an original subject to me, who have seen nothing hitherto written on it: but, first, a few thoughts on composition in general. Some are of opinion, that its growth, at present, is too luxuriant, and that the press is overcharged. Overcharged, I think, it could never be, if none were admitted, but such as brought their *imprimatur* from sound understanding, and the public good. Wit, indeed, however brilliant, should not be permitted to gaze self-enamoured on its useless charms, in that fountain of fame, (if so I may call the press,) if beauty is all that it has to boast; but, like the first Brutus, it should sacrifice its most darling offspring to the sacred interests of virtue, and real service of mankind.

This restriction allowed, the more composition the better. To men of letters and leisure, it is not only a noble amusement, but a sweet refuge; it improves their parts, and promotes their peace; it opens a back-door out of the bustle of this busy and idle world, into a delicious garden of moral and intellectual fruits and flowers, the key of which is denied to the rest of mankind. When stung with idle anxieties, or teazed with fruitless imperti-nence, or yawning over insipid diversions, then we perceive the blessings of a lettered recess. With what a gust do we retire to our disinterested and immortal friends in our closet, and find our minds, when applied to some favourite theme, as naturally and as easily quieted and refreshed as a peevish child (and peevish children are we all till we fall asleep) when laid to the breast! Our happiness no longer lives on charity; nor bids fair for a fall, by leaning on that most precarious and thorny pillow, another's pleasure, for our repose. How independent of the world is he, who can daily find new acquaintance that at once entertain and improve him, in the little world, the minute but fruitful creation of his own mind!

These advantages composition affords us, whether we write ourselves, or in more humble amusement peruse the works of others. While we bustle through the thronged walks of public life, it gives us a respite, at least, from care; a pleasing pause of refreshing recollection. If the country is our choice or fate, there it rescues us from sloth and sensuality, which, like obscene vermin, are apt gradually to creep unperceived into the delightful bowers of our retirement, and to poison all its sweets. Conscious guilt robs the rose of its scent, the lily of its lustre; and makes an Eden a deflowered and dismal scene.

Moreover, if we consider life's endless evils, what can be more prudent, than to provide for consolation under them? A consolation under them the wisest of men have found in the pleasures of the pen: witness, among many more, Thucydides, Xenophon, Tully, Ovid, Seneca, Pliny the younger, who says, *In uxoris infirmitate, et amicorum periculo, aut morte turbatus, ad studia, unicum doloris levamentum, confugio.* And why not add to these their modern equals, Chaucer, Raleigh, Bacon, Milton, Clarendon, under the same shield, unwounded by misfortune, and nobly smiling in distress?

Composition was a cordial to these under the frowns of fortune; but evils there are which her smiles cannot prevent or cure. Among these are the languors of old age. If these are held honourable who in a hand benumbed by time have grasped the just sword in defence of their country, shall they be less esteemed whose unsteady pen vibrates to the last in the cause of religion, of virtue, of learning? Both these are happy in this, that, by fixing their attention on objects most important, they escape numberless little anxieties, and that *tædium vitæ* which often hangs so heavy on its evening hours. May not this insinuate some apology for my spilling ink, and spoiling paper, so late in life?

But there are who write with vigour and success, to the world's delight and their own renown. These are the glorious fruits where genius prevails. The mind of a man of genius is a fertile and pleasant field; pleasant as Elysium, and fertile as Tempe; it enjoys a perpetual spring. Of that spring originals are the fairest flowers: imitations are of quicker growth, but fainter bloom. Imitations are of two kinds; one of nature, one of authors: the first we call "originals," and confine the term "imitation" to the second. I shall not enter into the curious inquiry of what is, or is not, strictly speaking, original, content with what all must allow, that some compositions are more so than others; and the more they are so, I say, the better. Originals are, and ought to be, great favourites, for they are great benefactors; they extend the republic of letters, and add a new province to its dominion: imitators only give us a sort of duplicates of what we had, possibly much better, before; increasing the mere drug of books, while all that makes them valuable, knowledge and genius, are at a stand. The pen of an original writer, like Armida's wand, out of a barren waste calls a blooming spring: out of that blooming spring an imitator is a transplanter of laurels, which sometimes die on removal, always languish in a foreign soil.

But suppose an imitator to be most excellent, (and such there are,) yet still he but nobly builds on another's foundation; his debt is, at least, equal to his glory; which therefore, on the balance, cannot be very great. On the contrary, an original, though but indifferent (its originality being set aside,) yet has something to boast; it is something to say with him in Horace,—

Meo sum pauper in ære;

and to share ambition with no less than Cæsar, who declared he had rather be the first in a village than the second at Rome.

Still farther: an imitator shares his crown, if he has one, with the chosen object of his imitation; an original enjoys an undivided applause. An original may be said to be of a vegetable nature, it rises spontaneously from the vital root of genius; it grows, it is not made: imitations are often a sort of manufacture wrought up by those mechanics, art and labour, out of pre-existent materials not their own.

Again: we read imitation with somewhat of his languor who listens to a twice-told tale: our spirits rouse at an original: that is a perfect stranger, and all throng to learn what news from a foreign land; and though it comes, like an Indian prince, adorned with feathers only, having little of weight, yet of our attention it will rob the more solid, if not equally new. Thus every telescope is lifted at a new discovered star: it makes a hundred astronomers in a moment, and denies equal notice to the sun. But if an original, by being as excellent as new, adds admiration to surprise, then are we at the writer's mercy; on the strong wing of his imagination we are snatched from Britain to Italy, from climate to climate, from pleasure to pleasure; we have no home, no thought of our own, till the magician drops his pen; and then, falling down into ourselves, we awake to flat realities, lamenting the change, like the beggar who dreamt himself a prince.

It is with thoughts as it is with words, and with both as with men: they may grow old, and die. Words tarnished, by passing through the mouths of the vulgar, are laid aside as inelegant and obsolete. So thoughts, when become too common, should lose their currency; and we should send new metal to the mint, that is, new meaning to the press. The division of tongues at Babel did not more effectually debar men from "making themselves a name" (as the scripture speaks) than the too great concurrence or union of tongues will do for ever. We may as well grow good by another's virtue, or fat by another's food, as famous by another's thought. The world will pay its debt of praise but once, and, instead of applauding, explode a second demand as a cheat.

If it is said, that most of the Latin classics, and all the Greek, except, perhaps, Homer, Pindar, and Anacreon, are in the number of imitators, yet receive our highest applause; our answer is, that they, though not real, are accidental originals; the works they imitated, few excepted, are lost; they, on their fathers' decease, enter as lawful heirs on their estates in fame: the fathers of our copyists are still in possession; and secured in it, in spite of Goths and flames, by the perpetuating power of the press. Very late must a modern imitator's fame arrive, if it waits for their decease.

An original enters early on reputation: Fame, fond of new glories, sounds her trumpet in triumph at its birth; and yet how few are awakened by it into the noble ambition of like attempts! Ambition is sometimes no vice in life; it is always a virtue in composition. High in the towering Alps is the fountain of the Po: high in fame, and in antiquity, is the foutain of an imitator's undertaking: but the river, and the imitation, humbly creep along the vale. So few are our originals, that, if all other books were to be burnt, the lettered world would resemble some metropolis in flames, where a few incombustible buildings, a fortress temple, or tower, lift their heads, in melancholy grandeur, amid the mighty ruin. Compared with this conflagration, old Omar lighted up but a small bonfire when he heated the baths of the barbarians, for eight months together, with the famed Alexandrian library's inestimable spoils, that no profane book might obstruct the triumphant progress of his holy Alcoran round the globe.

But why are originals so few? Not because the writer's harvest is over, the great reapers of antiquity having left nothing to be gleaned after them; nor because the human mind's teeming time is past, or because it is incapable of putting forth unprecedented births; but because illustrious examples engross, prejudice, and intimidate. They *engross* our attention, and so prevent a due inspection of ourselves; they *prejudice* our judgment in favour of their abilities, and so lessen the sense of our own; and they *intimidate* us with the splendour of their renown and thus under diffidence bury our strength. Nature's impossibilities, and those of diffidence, lie wide asunder.

Let it not be suspected, that I would weakly insinuate any thing in favour of the moderns, as compared with ancient authors; no, I am lamenting their great inferiority. But I think it is no necessary inferiority; that it is not from Divine destination, but from some cause far beneath the moon. I think that human souls, through all periods, are equal; that due care and exertion would set us nearer our immortal predecessors than we are at present; and he who questions and confutes this, will show abilities not a little tending toward a proof of that equality which he denies.

After all, the first ancients had no merit in being originals: they could not be imitators. Modern writers have a choice to make, and therefore have a merit in their power. They may soar in the regions of liberty, or move in the soft fetters of easy imitation; and imitation has as many plausible reasons to urge as pleasure had to offer to Hercules. Hercules made the choice of an hero, and so became immortal.

Yet let not assertors of classic excellence imagine, that I deny the tribute it so well deserves. He that admires not ancient authors betrays a secret he would conceal, and tells the world that he does not understand them. Let us be as far from neglecting, as from copying, their admirable compositions: sacred be their rights, and inviolable their fame. Let our understanding feed on theirs; they afford the noblest nourishment; but let them nourish, not annihilate, our own. When we read, let our imagination kindle at their charms; when we write, let our judgment shut them out of our thoughts; treat even Homer himself as his royal admirer was treated by the cynic,—bid him stand aside, nor shade our composition from the beams of our own genius; for nothing original can rise, nothing immortal can ripen, in any other sun.

"Must we then," you say, "not imitate ancient authors?" Imitate them by all means; but imitate aright. He that imitates the divine Iliad does not imitate Homer; but he who takes the same method which Homer took for arriving at a capacity of accomplishing a work so great. Tread in his steps to the sole fountain of immortality; drink where he drank, at the true Helicon, that is, at the breast of nature. Imitate; but imitate not the composition, but the man. For may not this paradox pass into a maxim?—namely, "The less we copy the renowned ancients, we shall resemble them the more."

But possibly you may reply, that you must either imitate Homer, or depart from nature. Not so: for suppose you was to change place, in time, with Homer, then, if you write naturally, you might as well charge Homer with an imitation of you. Can you be said to imitate Homer for writing so as you would have written, if Homer had never been? As far as a regard to nature and sound sense will permit a departure from your great predecessors, so far ambitiously depart from them; the farther from them in similitude, the nearer are you to them in excellence; you rise by it into an original; become a noble collateral, not an humble descendant from them. Let us build our compositions with the spirit, and in the taste, of the ancients; but not with their materials: thus will they resemble the structures of Pericles at Athens, which Plutarch commends for having had an air of antiquity as soon as they were built. All eminence and distinction lies out of the beaten road, excursion and deviation are necessary to find it; and the more remote your path from the highway, the more reputable, if, like poor Gulliver, (of whom anon,) you fall not into a ditch in your way to glory.

What glory to come near, what glory to reach, what glory (presumptuous thought!) to surpass, our predecessors! And is that, then, in nature absolutely impossible? or is it not, rather, contrary to nature to fail in it? Nature herself sets the ladder, all wanting is our ambition to climb. For, by the bounty of nature, we are as strong as our predecessors, and by the favour of time (which is but another round in nature's scale) we stand on higher ground. As to the first, were they more than men? or are we less? Are not our minds cast in the same mould with those before the flood? The flood affected matter; mind escaped. As to the second, though we are moderns, the world is an ancient; more ancient far than when they whom we most admire filled it with their fame. Have we not their beauties, as stars, to guide; their defects, as rocks, to be shunned; the judgment of ages on both, as a chart to conduct, and a sure helm to steer, us in our passage to greater perfection than theirs? And shall we be stopped in our rival pretensions to fame by this just reproof?

Stat contra, dicitque tibi tua pagina, Fur es.
                                   MART.

It is by a sort of noble contagion, from a general familiarity with their writings, and not by any particular sordid theft, that we can be the better for those who went before us. Hope we from plagiarism any dominion in literature, as that of Rome arose from a nest of thieves?

Rome was a powerful ally to many states; ancient authors are our powerful allies; but we must take heed that they do not succour, till they enslave, after the manner of Rome. Too formidable an idea of their superiority, like a spectre, would fright us out of a proper use of our wits, and dwarf our understanding, by making a giant of theirs. Too great awe for them lays genius under restraint, and denies it that free scope, that full elbow-room, which is requisite for striking its most masterly strokes. Genius is a master-workman, learning is but an instrument; and an instrument, though most valuable, yet not always indispensable. Heaven will not admit of a partner in the accomplishment of some favourite spirits; but, rejecting all human means, assumes the whole glory to itself. Have not some, though not famed for erudition, so written, as almost to persuade us that they shone brighter and soared higher for escaping the boasted aid of that proud ally?

Nor is it strange; for what, for the most part, mean we by genius, but the power of accomplishing great things without the means generally reputed necessary to that end? A genius differs from a good understanding, as a magician from a good architect; that raises his structure by means invisible, this by the skilful use of common tools. Hence genius has ever been supposed to partake of something Divine. *Nemo unquam vir magnus fuit, sine aliquo afflatu divino.*

Learning, destitute of this superior aid, is fond and proud of what has cost it much pains; is a great lover of rules, and boaster of famed examples. As beauties less perfect, who owe half their charms to cautious art, learning inveighs against natural unstudied graces and small harmless inaccuracies, and sets rigid bounds to that liberty to which genius often owes its supreme glory, but the no-genius its frequent ruin. For unprescribed beauties, and unexampled excellence, which are characteristics of genius, lie without the pale of learning's authorities and laws; which pale, genius must leap to come at them: but by that leap, if genius is wanting, we break our necks, we lose that little credit which possibly we might have enjoyed before. For rules, like crutches, are a needful aid to the lame, though an impediment to the strong. A Homer casts them away, and, like his Achilles,

Jura negat sibi nata, nihil non arrogat,
                                   HORAT.

by native force of mind. There is something in poetry beyond prose reason; there are mysteries in it not to be explained, but admired, which render mere prose-men infidels to their divinity. And here pardon a second paradox: namely, "Genius often then deserves most to be praised when it is most sure to be condemned; that is, when its excellence, from mounting high, to weak eyes is quite out of sight."

If I might speak farther of learning and genius, I would compare genius to virtue, and learning to riches. As riches are most wanted where there is least virtue, so learning where there is least genius. As virtue without much riches can give happiness, so genius without much learning can give renown. As it is said, in Terence. *Pecuniam negligere interdum maximum est lucrum,* so, to neglect of learning genius sometimes owes its greater glory. Genius, therefore, leaves but the second place, among men of letters, to the learned. It is their merit and ambition to fling light on the works of genius, and point out its charms. We most justly reverence their informing radius for that favour; but we must much more admire the radiant stars pointed out by them.

A star of the first magnitude among the moderns was Shakspeare; among the ancients, Pindar; who, as Vossius tells us, boasted of his no-learning, calling himself the eagle, for his flight above it. And such genii as these may, indeed, have much reliance on their own native powers. For genius may be compared to the natural strength of the body; learning to the superinduced accoutrements of arms. If the first is equal to the proposed exploit, the latter rather encumbers, than assists; rather retards, than promotes, the victory. *Sacer nobis inest Deus,* says Seneca. With regard to the moral world, conscience—with regard to the intellectual, genius—is that god within. Genius can set us right in composition without the rules of the learned, as conscience sets us right in life without the laws of the land; this, singly, can make us good, as men; that, singly, as writers, can sometimes make us great.

I say, "sometimes," because there is a genius which stands in need of learning to make it shine. Of genius there are two species, an earlier, and a later; or call them infantine, and adult. An adult genius comes out of nature's hand; as Pallas out of Jove's head, at full growth, and mature; Shakspeare's genius was of this kind: on the contrary, Swift stumbled at the threshold, and set out for distinction on feeble knees. His was an infantine genius; a genius which, like other infants, must be nursed and educated, or it will come to nought. Learning is its nurse and tutor; but this nurse may overlay with an indigested load, which smothers common sense; and this tutor may mislead with pedantic prejudice, which vitiates the best understanding. As too great admirers of the fathers of the church have sometimes set up their authority against the true sense of scripture, so too great admirers of the classical fathers have sometimes set up their authority, or example, against reason.

Neve minor, neu sit quinto productior actu fabula.

So says Horace, so says ancient example. But reason has not subscribed. I know but one book that can justify our implicit acquiescence in it; and, by the way, on that book a noble disdain of undue deference to prior opinion has lately cast, and is still casting, a new and inestimable light.

But, superstition for our predecessors set aside, the classics are for ever our rightful and revered masters in composition, and our understandings bow before them. But when? When a master is wanted; which sometimes, as I have shown, is not the case. Some are pupils of nature only, nor go farther to school. From such we reap often a double advantage; they not only rival the reputation of the great ancient authors, but also reduce the number of mean ones among the moderns. For, when they enter on subjects which have been in former hands, such is their superiority, that, like a tenth wave, they overwhelm and bury in oblivion all that went before; and thus not only enrich and adorn, but remove a load, and lessen the labour, of the lettered world.

"But," you say, "since originals can arise from genius only, and since genius is so very rare, it is scarce worth while to labour a point so much, from which we can reasonably expect so little." To show that genius is not so very rare as you imagine, I shall point out strong instances of it, in a far distant quarter from that mentioned above. The minds of the schoolmen were almost as much cloistered as their bodies; they had but little learning, and few books; yet may the most learned be struck with some astonishment at their so singular natural sagacity, and most exquisite edge of thought. Who would expect to find Pindar and Scotus, Shakspeare and Aquinas, of the same party? Both equally show an original, unindebted energy; the *vigor igneus,* and *cœlestis origo,* burn in both; and leave us in doubt whether genius is more evident in the sublime flights and beauteous flowers of poetry, or in the profound penetrations, and marvellously keen and minute distinctions, called the "thorns of the schools." There might have been more able consuls called from the plough than ever arrived at that honour; many a genius, probably, there has been, which could neither write nor read. So that genius, that supreme lustre of literature, is less rare than you conceive.

By the praise of genius we detract not from learning; we detract not from the value of gold by saying that a diamond has greater still. He who disregards learning, shows that he wants its aid; and he that overvalues it, shows that its aid has done him harm. Over-valued, indeed, it cannot be, if genius as to composition is valued more. Learning we thank, genius we revere; that gives us pleasure, this gives us rapture; that informs, this inspires, and is itself inspired; for genius is from heaven, learning from man: this sets us above the low and illiterate; that, above the learned and polite. Learning is borrowed knowledge; genius is knowledge innate, and quite our own. Therefore, as Bacon observes, it may take a nobler name, and be called "wisdom;" in which sense of wisdom, some are born wise.

But here a caution is necessary against the most fatal of errors in those automaths, those "self-taught philosophers" of our age, who set up genius, and often mere fancied genius, not only above human learning, but Divine truth. I have called genius "wisdom;" but let it be remembered that, in the most renowned ages of the most refined Heathen wisdom, (and theirs is not Christian,) "the world by wisdom knew not God; and it pleased God, by the foolishness of preaching, to save those that believed." In the fairyland of fancy, genius may wander wild; there it has a creative power, and may reign arbitrarily over its own empire of chimeras. The wide field of nature, also, lies open before it, where it may range unconfined, make what discoveries it can, and sport with its infinite objects uncontrolled, as far as visible nature extends, painting them as wantonly as it will. But what painter of the most unbounded and exalted genius can give us the true portrait of a seraph? He can give us only what by his own, or others' eyes, has been seen; though that indeed infinitely compounded, raised, burlesqued, dishonoured, or adorned. In like manner, who can give us Divine truth unrevealed? Much less should any presume to set aside Divine truth when revealed, as incongruous to their own sagacities. Is this too serious for my subject? I shall be more so before I close.

Having put-in a caveat against the most fatal of errors, from the too great indulgence of genius, return we now to that too great suppression of it, which is detrimental to composition, and endeavour to rescue the writer, as well as the man. I have said, that some are born wise; but they, like those that are born rich, by neglecting the cultivation and produce of their own possessions, and by running in debt, may be beggared at last; and lose their reputations, as younger brothers estates, not by being born with less abilities than the rich heir, but at too late an hour.

Many a great man has been lost to himself and the public, purely because great ones were born before him. Hermias, in his Collections on Homer's blindness, says that Homer, requesting the gods to grant him a sight of Achilles, that hero rose, but in armour so bright, that it struck Homer blind with the blaze. Let not the blaze of even Homer's muse darken us to the discernment of our own powers, which may possibly set us above the rank of imitators; who, though most excellent, and even immortal, (as some of them are,) yet are still but *Dii minorum gentium,* nor can expect the largest share of incense, the greatest profusion of praise, on their secondary altars.

But farther still: a spirit of imitation hath many ill effects; I shall confine myself to three. First, it deprives the liberal and politer arts of an advantage which the mechanic enjoy: in these, men are ever endeavouring to go beyond their predecessors; in the former, to follow them. And since copies surpass not their originals, as streams rise not higher than their spring, rarely so high; hence, while arts mechanic are in perpetual progress and increase, the liberal are in retrogradation and decay. These resemble pyramids,—are broad at bottom, but lessen exceedingly as they rise; those resemble rivers which, from a small fountain-head, are spreading ever wider and wider as they run. Hence it is evident that different portions of understanding are not (as some imagine) allotted to different periods of time; for we see, in the same period, under-standing rising in one set of artists, and declining in another. Therefore, nature stands absolved, and our inferiority in composition must be charged on ourselves.

Nay, so far are we from complying with a necessity, which nature lays us under, that, Secondly, by a spirit of imitation we counteract nature, and thwart her design. She brings us into the world all originals. No two faces, no two minds, are just alike; but all bear nature's evident mark of separation on them. Born originals, how comes it to pass that we die copies? That meddling ape imitation, as soon as we come to years of indiscretion, (so let me speak,) snatches the pen, and blots out nature's mark of separation, cancels her kind intention, destroys all mental individuality. The lettered world no longer consists of singulars: it is a medley, a mass; and a hundred books, at bottom, are but one. Why are monkeys such masters of mimickry? Why receive they such a talent at imitation? Is it not as the Spartan slaves received a licence for ebriety,—that their betters might be ashamed of it?

The Third fault to be found with a spirit of imitation is, that, with great incongruity, it makes us poor and proud; makes us think little, and write much; gives us huge folios, which are little better than more reputable cushions to promote our repose. Have not some sevenfold volumes put us in mind of Ovid's sevenfold channels of the Nile at the conflagration?

> *Ostia septem*
> *Pulverulenta vacant septem sine flumine valles.*

Such leaden labours are like Lycurgus's iron money, which was so much less in value than in bulk, that it required barns for strong boxes, and a yoke of oxen to draw five hundred pounds.

But, notwithstanding these disadvantages of imitation, imitation must be the lot (and often an honourable lot it is) of most writers. If there is a famine of invention in the land, like Joseph's brethren, we must travel far for food; we must visit the remote and rich ancients. But an inventive genius may safely stay at home; that, like the widow's cruse, is divinely replenished from within, and affords us a miraculous delight. Whether our own genius be such or not, we diligently should inquire, that we may not go a-begging with gold in our purse; for there is a mine in man, which must be deeply dug ere we can conjecture its contents. Another often sees that in us which we see not ourselves; and may there not be that in us which is unseen by both? That there may, chance often discovers, either by a luckily-chosen theme, or a mighty premium, or an absolute necessity of exertion, or a noble stroke of emulation from another's glory; as that on Thucydides, from hearing Herodotus repeat part of his history at the Olympic games. Had there been no Herodotus, there might have been no Thucydides, and the world's admiration might have begun at Livy for excellence in that province of the pen. Demosthenes had the same stimulation on hearing Callistratus; or Tully might have been the first of consummate renown at the bar.

Quite clear of the dispute concerning ancient and modern learning, we speak not of performance, but powers. The modern powers are equal to those before them: modern performance in general is deplorable short. How great are the names just mentioned! yet who will dare affirm, that as great may not rise up in some future or even in the present age? Reasons there are why talents may not *appear*, none why they may not *exist*, as much in one period as another. An evocation of vegetable fruits depends on rain, air, and sun; an evocation of the fruits of genius no less depends on externals. What a marvellous crop bore it in Greece and Rome! and what a marvellous sunshine did it there enjoy! what encouragement from the nature of their governments, and the spirit of their people! Virgil and Horace owed their divine talents to

Heaven, their immortal works to men: thank Mæcenas and Augustus for them. Had it not been for these, the genius of those poets had lain buried in their ashes. Athens expended on her theatre, painting, sculpture, and architecture, a tax levied for the support of a war. Cæsar dropped his papers when Tully spoke; and Philip trembled at the voice of Demosthenes. And has there arisen but one Tully, one Demosthenes, in so long a course of years? The powerful eloquence of them both in one stream should never bear me down into the melancholy persuasion, that several have not been born, though they have not emerged. The sun as much exists in a cloudy day as in a clear: it is outward, accidental circumstances, that, with regard to genius either in nation or age,

> *Collectas que fugat nubes, solemque reducit*
> Virg.

As great, perhaps greater than those mentioned, (presumptuous as it may sound,) may possibly arise; for who hath fathomed the mind of man? Its bounds are as unknown as those of the creation; since the birth of which, perhaps, not one has so far exerted, as not to leave his possibilities beyond his attainments, his powers beyond his exploits. Forming our judgments altogether by what has been done, without knowing, or at all inquiring, what possibly might have been done, we naturally enough fall into too mean an opinion of the human mind. If a sketch of the divine Iliad, before Homer wrote, had been given to mankind, by some superior being, or otherwise, its execution would, probably, have appeared beyond the power of man. Now, to surpass it, we think impossible. As the first of these opinions would evidently have been a mistake, why may not the second be so too? Both are founded on the same bottom,—on our ignorance of the possible dimensions of the mind of man.

Nor are we only ignorant of the dimensions of the human mind in general, but even of our own. That a man may be scarce less ignorant of his own powers than an oyster of its pearl, or a rock of its diamond; that he may possess dormant, unsuspected abilities, till awakened by loud calls, or stung-up by striking emergencies; is evident from the sudden eruption of some men out of perfect obscurity into public admiration, on the strong impulse of some animating occasion; not more to the world's great surprise than their own. Few authors of distinction but have experienced something of this nature, at the first beamings of their yet unsuspected genius on their hitherto dark composition. The writer starts at it, as at a lucid meteor in the night, is much surprised, can scarce believe it true. During his happy confusion, it may be said to him, as to Eve at the lake,

> What there thou seest, fair creature, is thyself.
> Milton

Genius, in this view, is like a dear friend in our company under disguise; who, while we are lamenting his absence, drops his mask, striking us at once with equal surprise and joy. This sensation, which I speak of in a writer, might favour, and so promote, the fable of poetic inspiration. A poet of a strong imagination and a stronger vanity, on feeling it, might naturally enough realize the world's mere compliment, and think himself truly inspired: which is not improbable; for enthusiasts of all kinds do no less.

Since it is plain that men may be strangers to their own abilities, and by thinking meanly of them without just cause may possibly lose a name, perhaps a name immortal, I would find some means to prevent these evils. Whatever promotes virtue, promotes something more, and carries its good influence beyond the moral man: to prevent these evils, I borrow two golden rules from ethics, which are no less golden in composition than in life: 1. "Know thyself;" 2. "Reverence thyself." I design to repay ethics in a future letter, by two rules from rhetoric for its service.

1. "Know thyself." Of ourselves it may be said, as Martial says of a bad neighbour,—

Nil tam propè, tam proculque nobis.

Therefore dive deep into thy bosom; learn the depth, extent, bias, and full fort of thy mind; contract full intimacy with the stranger within thee; excite and cherish every spark of intellectual light and heat, however smothered under former negligence, or scattered through the dull, dark mass of common thoughts; and, collecting them into a body, let thy genius rise (if a genius thou hast) as the sun from chaos; and if I should then say, like an Indian, "Worship it," (though too bold,) yet should I say little more than my second rule enjoins; namely, "Reverence thyself."

That is, Let not great examples or authorities browbeat thy reason into too great a diffidence of thyself: thyself so reverence, as to prefer the native growth of thy own mind to the richest import from abroad: such borrowed riches make us poor. The man who thus reverences himself will soon find the world's reverence to follow his own. His works will stand distinguished; his the sole property of them; which property alone can confer the noble title of an author; that is, of one who, to speak accurately, thinks and composes; while other invaders of the press, how voluminous and learned soever, (with due respect be it spoken,) only read and write.

This is the difference between those two luminaries in literature, the well-accomplished scholar, and the divinely-inspired enthusiast: the first is, as the bright morning star; the second, as the rising sun. The writer who neglects those two rules above, will never stand alone: he makes one of a group, and thinks in wretched unanimity with the throng. Incumbered with the notions of others, and impoverished by their abundance, he conceives not the least embryo of new thought; opens not the least vista, through the gloom of ordinary writers, into the bright walks of rare imagination and singular design. While the true genius is crossing all public roads into fresh untrodden ground, he, up to the knees in antiquity, is treading the sacred footsteps of great examples, with the blind veneration of a bigot saluting the papal toe; comfortably hoping full absolution for the sins of his own understanding, from the powerful charm of touching his idol's infallibility.

Such meanness of mind, such prostration of our own powers, proceeds from too great admiration of others. Admiration has, generally, a degree of two very bad ingredients in it,—of ignorance, and of fear; and does mischief in composition and in life. Proud as the world is, there is more superiority in it given than assumed; and its grandees of all kinds owe more of their elevation to the littleness of others' minds, than to the greatness of their own. Were not prostrate spirits their voluntary pedestals, the figure they make among mankind would not stand so high. Imitators and translators are somewhat of the pedestal-kind, and sometimes rather raise their original's reputation, by showing him to be by them inimitable, than their own. Homer has been translated into most languages; Ælian tells us, that the Indians (hopeful tutors!) have taught him to speak their tongue. What expect we from them? Not Homer's Achilles, but something which, like Patroclus, assumes his name, and, at its peril, appears in his stead: nor expect we Homer's Ulysses gloriously bursting out of his cloud into royal grandeur, but an Ulysses under disguise, and a beggar to the last. Such is that inimitable father of poetry, and oracle of all the wise, whom Lycurgus transcribed; and for an annual public recital of whose works Solon enacted a law, that, it is much to be feared that his so numerous translations are but as the published testimonials of so many nations and ages, that this author, so divine, is untranslated still.

But here,

> *Cynthius aurem*
> *Vellit;*
> VIRG.

and demands justice for his favourite, and ours. Great things he has done; but he might have done greater. What a fall is it from Homer's numbers, free as air, lofty and harmonious as the spheres, into childish shackles and tinkling sounds! But, in his fall, he is still great;

> Nor appears
> Less than archangel ruin'd, and the excess
> Of glory obscured.
> MILTON

Had Milton never wrote, Pope had been less to blame; but when in Milton's genius Homer, as it were, personally rose to forbid Britons doing him that ignoble wrong, it is less pardonable, by that effeminate decoration, to put Achilles in petticoats a second time. How much nobler had it been, if his numbers had rolled on in full flow, through the various modulations of masculine melody, into those grandeurs of solemn sound which are indispensably demanded by the native dignity of heroic song! How much nobler, if he had resisted the temptation of that Gothic demon, which modern poesy, tasting, became mortal! O how unlike the deathless, divine harmony of three great names, (how justly joined!) of Milton, Greece, and Rome! His verse, but for this little speck of mortality, in its extreme parts, as his hero had in his heel, like him, had been invulnerable and immortal. But, unfortunately, that was undipped in Helicon, as this in Styx. Harmony, as well as eloquence, is essential to poesy; and a murder of his music is putting half Homer to death. "Blank" is a term of diminution: what we mean by "blank verse," is, verse unfallen, uncursed; verse reclaimed, re-inthroned in the true language of the gods: who never thundered, nor suffered their Homer to thunder, in rhyme; and therefore, I beg you, my friend, to crown it with some nobler term; nor let the greatness of the thing lie under the defamation of such a name.

But, supposing Pope's Iliad to have been perfect in its kind, yet it is a translation still; which differs as much from an original, as the moon from the sun.

> *Phœben alieno jusserat igne*
> *Impleri, solemque suo.*
>
> CLAUD

But as nothing is more easy than to write originally wrong, originals are not here recommended but under the strong guard of my first rule,—"Know thyself." Lucian, who was an original, neglected not this rule, if we may judge by his reply to one who took some freedom with him. He was, at first, an apprentice to a statuary; and when he was reflected on as such, by being called Prometheus, he replied, "I am, indeed, the inventor of a new work, the model of which I owe to none: and if I do not execute it well, I deserve to be torn by twelve vultures, instead of one."

If so, O Gulliver, dost thou not shudder at thy brother Lucian's vultures hovering over thee? Shudder on! They cannot shock thee more than decency has been shocked by thee. How have thy Houynhunms thrown thy judgment from its seat, and laid thy imagination in the mire! In what ordure hast thou dipped thy pencil! What a monster hast thou made of the "human face divine!" This writer has so satirised human nature, as to give a demonstration in himself, that it deserves to be satirised. "But," say his wholesale admirers, "few *could* so have written." True, and fewer *would*. If it required great abilities to commit the fault, greater still would have saved him from it. But whence arise such warm advocates for such a performance? From hence, namely, Before a character is established, merit makes fame; afterwards fame makes merit. Swift is not commended for this piece, but this piece for Swift. He has given us some beauties which deserve all our praise; and our comfort is, that his faults will not become common; for none can be guilty of them but who have wit as well as reputation to spare. His wit had been less wild, if his temper had not jostled his judgment. If his favourite Houynhunms could write, and Swift had been one of them, every horse with him would have been an ass, and he would have written a panegyric on mankind, saddling with much reproach the present heroes of his pen: on the contrary, being born amongst men, and, of consequence, piqued by many, and peevish at more, he has blasphemed a nature little lower than that of angels, and assumed by far higher than they. But surely the contempt of the world is not a greater virtue, than the contempt of mankind is a vice. Therefore I wonder that, though forborne by others, the laughter-loving Swift was not reproved by the venerable dean, who could sometimes be very grave.

For I remember, as I and others were taking with him an evening's walk, about a mile out of Dublin, he stopped short: we passed on; but, perceiving that he did not follow us, I went back, and found him fixed as a statue, and earnestly gazing upward at a noble elm, which in its uppermost branches was much withered and decayed. Pointing at it, he said, "I shall be like that tree: I shall die at top." As in this he seemed to prophesy like the Sybils: if, like one of them, he had burnt part of his works, especially this blasted branch of a noble genius, like her, too, he might have risen in his demand for the rest.

Would not his friend Pope have succeeded better in an original attempt? Talents untried are talents unknown. All that I know is, that, contrary to these sentiments, he was not only an avowed professor of imitation, but a zealous recommender of it also. Nor could he recommend any thing better, except emulation, to those who write. One of these all writers must call to their aid; but aids they are of unequal repute. Imitation is inferiority confessed, emulation is superiority contested or denied; imitation is servile, emulation generous; that fetters, this fires; that may give a name, this a name immortal. This made Athens to succeeding ages the rule of taste, and the standard of perfection. Her men of genius struck fire against each other; and kindled, by conflict, into glories, which no time shall extinguish. We thank Æschylus for Sophocles, and Parrhasius for Zeuxis, emulation for both. That bids us fly the general fault of imitators; bids us not to be struck with the loud report of former fame as with a knell, which damps the spirits, but as with a trumpet, which inspires ardour to rival the renowned. Emulation exhorts us, instead of learning our discipline for ever, like raw troops, under ancient leaders in composition, to put those laurelled veterans in some hazard of losing their superior posts in glory.

Such is Emulation's high-spirited advice, such her immortalizing call. Pope would not hear, pre-engaged with Imitation, which blessed him with all her charms. He chose rather, with his namesake of Greece, to triumph in the old world, than to look out for a new. His taste partook the error of his religion,—it denied not worship to saints and angels; that is, to writers who, canonized for ages, have received their apotheosis from established and universal fame. True poesy, like true religion, abhors idolatry; and though it honours the memory of the exemplary, and takes them willingly (yet cautiously) as guides in the way to glory, real (though unexampled) excellence is its only aim; nor looks it for any inspiration less than divine.

Though Pope's noble muse may boast her illustrious descent from Homer, Virgil, Horace, yet is an original author more nobly born. As Tacitus says of Curtius Rufus, an original author is born of himself, is his own progenitor, and will probably propagate a numerous offspring of imitators, to eternise his glory; while mule-like imitators die without issue. Therefore, though we stand much obliged for his giving us an Homer, yet had he doubled our obligation by giving us—a Pope. Had he a strong imagination, and the true sublime? That granted, we might have had two Homers instead of one, if longer had been his life; for I heard the dying swan talk over an epic plan a few weeks before his decease.

Bacon, under the shadow of whose great name I would shelter my present attempt in favour of originals, says, "Men seek not to know their own stock and abilities, but fancy their possessions to be greater, and their abilities less, than they really are." Which is, in effect, saying, that we ought to exert more than we do; and that, on exertion, our probability of success is greater than we conceive.

Nor have I Bacon's opinion only, but his assistance too, on my side. His mighty mind travelled round the intellectual world, and, with a more than eagle's eye, saw and has pointed out blank spaces or dark spots in it, on which the human mind never shone: some of these have been enlightened since; some are benighted still.

Moreover, so boundless are the bold excursions of the human mind, that, in the vast void beyond real existence, it can call forth shadowy beings and unknown worlds, as numerous, as bright, and perhaps as lasting as the stars: such quite-original beauties we may call paradisiacal,—

> *Natos sine semine flores.*
> Ovid

When such an ample area for renowned adventure in original attempts lies before us, shall we be as mere leaden pipes, conveying to the present age small streams of excellence from its grand reservoir in antiquity, and those too, perhaps, mudded in the pass? Originals shine like comets, have no peer in their path, are rivalled by none, and the gaze of all: all other compositions, if they shine at all, shine in clusters, like the stars in the galaxy; where, like bad neighbours, all suffer from all; each particular being diminished, and almost lost in the throng.

If thoughts of this nature prevailed,—if ancients and moderns were no longer considered as masters and pupils, but as hard-matched rivals for renown,—then moderns, by the longevity of their labours, might one day become ancients themselves; and old Time, that best weigher of merits, to keep his balance even, might have the golden weight of an Augustan age in both his scales; or, rather, our scale might descend; and that of antiquity (as a modern match for it strongly speaks) might kick the beam.

And why not? For, consider,—since an impartial Providence scatters talents indifferently, as through all orders of persons, so through all periods of time;—since a marvellous light, unenjoyed of old, is poured on us by revelation, with larger prospects extending our understanding, with brighter objects enriching our imagination, with an inestimable prize setting our passions on fire, thus strengthening every power that enables composition to shine;—since there has been no fall in man on this side Adam, who left no works, and the works of all other ancients are our auxiliars against themselves, as being perpetual spurs to our ambition, and shining lamps in our path to fame;—since this world is a school, as well for intellectual as moral advance, and the longer human nature is a school, the better scholar it should be;—since, as the moral world expects its glorious millennium, the world intellectual may hope, by the rules of analogy, for some superior degrees of excellence to crown her later scenes; nor may it only hope, but must enjoy them too; for Tully, Quintilian, and all true critics allow, that virtue assists genius, and that the writer will be more able, when better is the man:—all these particulars (I say) considered, why should it seem altogether impossible, that Heaven's latest editions of the human mind may be the most correct and fair; that the day may come when the moderns may proudly look back on the comparative darkness of former ages, on the children of antiquity, reputing Homer and Demosthenes as the dawn of divine genius, and Athens as the cradle of infant-fame? What a glorious revolution would this make in the rolls of renown!

"What a rant," say you, "is here!" I partly grant it: yet, consider, my friend, knowledge physical, mathematical, moral, and Divine, increases; all arts and sciences are making considerable advance; with them, all the accommodations, ornaments, delights, and glories of human life; and these are new food to the genius of a polite writer; these are as the root, and composition as the flower; and as the root spreads and thrives, shall the flower fail? As well may a flower flourish when the root is dead. It is prudence to read, genius to relish, glory to surpass, ancient authors; and wisdom to try our strength, in an attempt in which it would be no great dishonour to fail.

Why condemned Maro his admirable epic to the flames? Was it not because his discerning eye saw some length of perfection beyond it? And what he saw, may not others reach? And who bid fairer than our countrymen for that glory? Something new may be expected from Britons particularly; who seem not to be more severed from the rest of mankind by the surrounding sea, than by the current in their veins; and of whom little more appears to be required, in order to give us originals, than a consistency of character, and making their compositions of a piece with their lives. May our genius shine, and proclaim us in that noble view,—

minimá contentos nocte Britannos!
JUVENAL

And so it does; for in polite composition, in natural and mathematical knowledge, we have great originals already: Bacon, Boyle, Newton, Shakspeare, Milton, have showed us, that all the winds cannot blow the British flag farther than an original spirit can convey the British fame. Their names go round the world; and what foreign genius strikes not as they pass? Why should not their posterity embark in the same bold bottom of new enterprise, and hope the same success? Hope it they may: or you must assert, either that those originals, which we already enjoy, were written by angels, or deny that we are men. As Simonides said to Pausanias, reason should say to the writer, "Remember thou art a man." And for man not to grasp at all which is laudable within his reach, is a dishonour to human nature, and a disobedience to the Divine; for as Heaven does nothing in vain, its gift of talents implies an injunction of their use.

A friend of mine has obeyed that injunction: he has relied on himself; and with a genius, as well moral as original, (to speak in bold terms,) has cast out evil spirits; has made a convert to virtue of a species of composition, once most its foe: as the first Christian emperors expelled demons, and dedicated their temples to the living God.

But you, I know, are sparing in your praise of this author: therefore I will speak of one which is sure of your applause. Shakspeare mingled no water with his wine, lowered his genius by no vapid imitation. Shakspeare gave us a Shakspeare; nor could the first in ancient fame have given us more. Shakspeare is not their son, but brother; their equal, and that in spite of all his faults. Think you this too bold? Consider, in those ancients what is it the world admires? Not the fewness of their faults, but the number and brightness of their beauties; and if Shakspeare is their equal (as he doubtless is) in that which in them is admired, then is Shakspeare as great as they; and not impotence, but some other cause, must be charged with his defects. When we are setting the great men in competition, what but the comparative size of their genius is the subject of our inquiry? And a giant loses nothing of his size, though he should chance to trip in his race. But it is a compliment to those heroes of antiquity to suppose Shakspeare their equal only in dramatic powers; therefore, though his faults had been greater, the scale would still turn in his favour. There is at least as much genius on the British as on the Grecian stage, though the former is not swept so clean; so clean from violations not only of the dramatic, but moral, rule; for an honest Heathen, on reading some of our celebrated scenes, might be seriously concerned to see, that our obligations to the religion of nature were cancelled by Christianity.

Jonson, in the serious drama, is as much an imitator, as Shakspeare is an original. He was very learned, as Samson was very strong, to his own hurt. Blind to the nature of tragedy, he pulled down all antiquity on his head, and buried himself under it. We see nothing of Jonson, nor indeed of his admired (but also murdered) ancients; for what shone in the historian is a cloud on the poet; and Catiline might have been a good play, if Sallust had never writ.

Who knows whether Shakspeare might not have thought less, if he had read more? Who knows if he might not have laboured under the load of Jonson's learning, as Enceladus under Ætna? His mighty genius, indeed, through the most mountainous oppression would have breathed out some of his inextinguishable fire; yet, possibly, he might not have risen up into that giant, that much more than common man, at which we now gaze with amazement and delight. Perhaps he was as learned as his dramatic province required; for, whatever other learning he wanted, he was master of two books, unknown to many of the profoundly read, though books which the last conflagration alone can destroy,—the book of nature, and that of man. These he had by heart, and has transcribed many admirable pages of them into his immortal works. These are the fountain-head, whence the Castalian streams of original composition flow; and these are often muddled by other waters,—though waters, in their distinct channel, most wholesome and pure: as two chemical liquors, separately clear as crystal, grow foul by mixture, and offend the sight. So that he has not only as much learning as his dramatic province required, but, perhaps, as it could safely bear. If Milton had spared some of his learning, his muse would have gained more glory than he would have lost by it.

Dryden, destitute of Shakspeare's genius, had almost as much learning as Jonson, and, for the buskin, quite as little taste. He was a stranger to the pathos; and, by numbers, expression, sentiment, and every other dramatic cheat, strove to make amends for it; as if a saint could make amends for the want of conscience, a soldier for the want of valour, or a vestal of modesty! The noble nature of tragedy disclaims an equivalent: like virtue, it demands the heart; and Dryden had none to give. Let epic poets think: the tragedian's point is rather to feel: such distant things are a tragedian and a poet, that the latter, indulged, destroys the former. Look on Barnwell, and Essex, and see how, as to these distant characters, Dryden excels and is excelled. But the strongest demonstration of his no-taste for the buskin are his tragedies fringed with rhyme; which, in epic poetry, is a sore disease, in the tragic absolute death. To Dryden's enormity, Pope's was a light offence. As lacemen are foes to mourning, these two authors, rich in rhyme, were no great friends to those solemn ornaments which the noble nature of their works required.

"Must rhyme, then," say you, "be banished?" I wish the nature of our language could bear its entire expulsion; but our lesser poetry stands in need of a toleration for it: it raises that, but sinks the great; as spangles adorn children, but expose men. Prince Henry bespangled all over in his eyelet-hole suit, with glittering pins, and an Achilles, or an Almanzor, in his Gothic array, are very much on a level, as to the majesty of the poet and the prince. Dryden had a great, but a general capacity; and as for a general genius, there is no such thing in nature. A genius implies the rays of the mind concentred, and determined to some particular point: when they are scattered widely, they act feebly, and strike not with sufficient force to fire or dissolve the heart. As what comes from the writer's heart reaches ours; so what comes from his head sets our brains at work, and our hearts at ease. It makes a circle of thoughtful circles, not of distressed patients; and a passive audience is what tragedy requires. Applause is not to be given, but extorted; and the silent lapse of a single tear does the writer more honour than the rattling thunder of a thousand hands. Applauding hands and dry eyes (which during Dryden's theatrical reign often met) are a satire on the writer's talent and the spectator's taste. When by such judges the laurel is blindly given, and by such a poet proudly received, they resemble an intoxicated host, and his tasteless guests, over some sparkling adulteration, commending their champagne.

But Dryden has his glory, though not on the stage. What an inimitable original is his ode! A small one, indeed, but of the first lustre, and without a flaw; and, amid the brightest boasts of antiquity, it may find a foil.

Among the brightest of the moderns, Mr. Addison must take his place. Who does not approach his character with great respect? They who refuse to close with the public in his praise, refuse at their peril. But, if men will be fond of their own opinions, some hazard must be run. He had, what Dryden and Jonson wanted, a warm and feeling heart; but, being of a grave and bashful nature, through a philosophic reserve, and a sort of moral prudery, he concealed it, where he should have let loose all his fire, and have showed the most tender sensibilities of heart. At his celebrated "Cato," few tears are shed, but Cato's own; which, indeed, are truly great, but unaffecting, except to the noble few who love their country better than themselves. The bulk of mankind want virtue enough to be touched by them. His strength of genius has reared up one glorious image, more lofty and truly golden than that in the plains of Dura, for cool admiration to gaze at, and warm patriotism (how rare!) to worship: while those two throbbing pulses of the drama, by which alone it is shown to live, terror and pity, neglected through the whole, leave our unmolested hearts at perfect peace. Thus the poet, like his hero, through mistaken excellence, and virtue overstrained, becomes a sort of suicide; and that which is most dramatic in the drama dies. All his charms of poetry are but as funeral flowers which adorn—all his noble sentiments but as rich spices which embalm—the tragedy deceased.

Of tragedy, pathos is not only the life and soul, but the soul inextinguishable: it charms us through a thousand faults. Decorations, which in this author abound, though they might immortalize other poesy, are the *splendida peccata* which damn the drama; while, on the contrary, the murder of all other beauties is a venial sin, nor plucks the laurel from the tragedian's brow. Was it otherwise, Shakspeare himself would run some hazard of losing his crown.

Socrates frequented the plays of Euripides; and what living Socrates would decline the theatre, at the representation of Cato? Tully's assassins found him in his litter, reading the "Medea" of the Grecian poet, to prepare himself for death. Part of "Cato" might be read to the same end. In the weight and dignity of moral reflection, Addison resembles that poet who was called "the dramatic philospher;" and is himself, as he says of Cato, "ambitiously sententious." But as to the singular talent, so remarkable in Euripides, at melting down hearts into the tender streams of grief and pity, there the resemblance fails. His beauties sparkle, but do not warm; they sparkle as stars in a frosty night. There is, indeed, a constellation in his play; there is the philosopher, patriot, orator, and poet; but where is the tragedian? And, if that is wanting,

> *Cur in theatrum, Cato severe, venisti?*
> Martial

And, when I recollect what passed between him and Dryden, in relation to this drama, I must add the next line,—

> *An ideò tantùm veneras, ut exires?*

For, when Addison was a student at Oxford, he sent up this play to his friend Dryden, as a proper person to recommend it to the theatre, if it deserved it; who returned it with very great commendation, but with his opinion, that, on the stage, it could not meet with its deserved success. But though the performance was denied in the theatre, it brought its author on the public stage of life. For, persons in power inquiring soon after of the head of his college for a youth of parts, Addison was recommended, and readily received, by means of the great reputation which Dryden had just then spread of him above.

There is this similitude between the poet and the play: as this is more fit for the closet than the stage, so that shone brighter in private conversation than on the public scene. They both had a sort of local excellency, as the Heathen gods a local divinity; beyond such a bound they unadmired, and these unadored. This puts me in mind of Plato, who denied "Homer" to the public; that "Homer" which, when in his closet, was rarely out of his hand. Thus, though "Cato" is not calculated to signalize himself in the warm emotions of the theatre, yet we find him a most amiable companion, in our calmer delights of recess.

Notwithstanding what has been offered, this, in many views, is an exquisite piece. But there is so much more of art than nature in it, that I can scarce forbear calling it an exquisite piece of statuary,

> Where the smooth chisel all its skill has shown,
> To soften into flesh the rugged stone.
>
> ADDISON

That is, where art has taken great pains to labour undramatic matter into dramatic life; which is impossible. However, as it is, like Pygmalion, we cannot but fall in love with it, and wish it was alive. How would a Shakspeare or an Otway have answered our wishes? They would have outdone Prometheus, and, with their heavenly fire, have given him not only life, but immortality. At their dramas (such is the force of nature) the poet is out of sight, quite hid behind his Venus, never thought of, till the curtain falls. Art brings our author forward, he stands before his piece; splendidly, indeed, but unfortunately, for the writer must be forgotten by his audience, during the representation, if for ages he would be remembered by posterity. In the theatre, as in life, delusion is the charm; and we are undelighted the first moment we are undeceived. Such demonstration have we, that the theatre is not yet opened in which solid happiness can be found by man; because none are more than comparatively good; and folly has a corner in the heart of the wise.

A genius fond of ornament should not be wedded to the tragic muse, which is in mourning: we want not to be diverted at an entertainment, where our greatest pleasure arises from the depth of our concern. But whence (by the way) this odd generation of pleasure from pain? The movement of our melancholy passions is pleasant, when we ourselves are safe; we love to be at once miserable and unhurt: so are we made; and so made, perhaps, to show us the Divine goodness; to show that none of our passions were designed to give us pain, except when being pained is for our advantage on the whole; which is evident from this instance, in which we see that passions the most painful administer greatly, sometimes, to our delight. Since great names have accounted otherwise for this particular, I wish this solution, though to me probable, may not prove a mistake.

To close our thoughts on "Cato:" He who sees not much beauty in it has no taste for poetry; he who sees nothing else, has no taste for the stage. Whilst it justifies censure, it extorts applause. It is much to be admired, but little to be felt. Had it not been a tragedy, it had been immortal; as it is a tragedy, its uncommon fate somewhat resembles his who, for conquering gloriously, was condemned to die. Both shone, but shone fatally; because in breach of their respective laws, the laws of the drama, and the laws of arms. But how rich in reputation must that author be, who can spare a "Cato" without feeling the loss!

That loss by our author would scarce be felt; it would be but dropping a single feather from a wing, that mounts him above his contemporaries. He has a more refined, decent, judicious, and extensive genius, than Pope or Swift. To distinguish this triumvirate from each other, and, like Newton, to discover the different colours in these genuine and meridian rays of literary light, Swift is a singular wit, Pope a correct poet, Addison a great author. Swift looked on wit as the *jus divinum* to dominion and sway in the world, and considered as usurpation all power that was lodged in persons of less sparkling understandings. This inclined him to tyranny in wit. Pope was somewhat of his opinion, but was for softening tyranny into lawful monarchy; yet were there some acts of severity in his reign. Addison's crown was elective: he reigned by the public voice:

> *Volentes*
> *Per populos dat jura, viamque affectat Olympo.*
> Virg

But as good books are the medicine of the mind, if we should dethrone these authors, and consider them, not in their royal, but their medicinal, capacity, might it not then be said—that Addison prescribed a wholesome and pleasant regimen, which was universally relished, and did much good;—that Pope preferred a purgative of satire, which, though wholesome, was too painful in its operation;—and that Swift insisted on a large dose of ipecacuanha, which, though readily swallowed, from the fame of the physician, yet, if the patient had any delicacy of taste, he threw up the remedy, instead of the disease?

Addison wrote little in verse, much in sweet, elegant, Virgilian prose; so let me call it, since Longinus calls Herodotus most Homeric, and Thucydides is said to have formed his style on Pindar. Addison's compositions are built with the finest materials, in the taste of the ancients, and (to speak his own language) on truly classic ground; and though they are the delight of the present age, yet am I persuaded that they will receive more justice from posterity. I never read him but I am stuck with such a disheartening idea of perfection, that I drop my pen. And, indeed, far superior writers should forget his compositions, if they would be greatly pleased with their own.

And yet, (perhaps you have not observed it,) what is the common language of the world, and even of his admirers, concerning him? They call him an elegant writer: that elegance which shines on the surface of his compositions seems to dazzle their understanding, and render it a little blind to the depth of sentiment which lies beneath: thus (hard fate!) he loses reputation with them, by doubling his title to it. On subjects the most interesting and important, no author of his age has written with greater, I had almost said with equal, weight; and they who commend him for his elegance pay him such a sort of compliment, by their abstemious praise, as they would pay to Lucretia, if they should commend her only for her beauty.

But you say, that you know his value already.—You know, indeed, the value of his writings, and close with the world in thinking them immortal; but, I believe, you know not that his name would have deserved immortality, though he had never written; and *that*, by a better title than the pen can give. You know, too, that his life was amiable; but, perhaps, you are still to learn that his death was triumphant. That is a glory granted to very few; and the paternal hand of Providence, which sometimes snatches home its beloved children in a moment, must convince us, that it is a glory of no great consequence to the dying individual; that, when it is granted, it is granted chiefly for the sake of the surviving world, which may profit by his pious example, to whom is indulged the strength and opportunity to make his virtue shine out brightest at the point of death. And here permit me to take notice, that the world will, probably, profit more by a pious example of lay-extraction, than by one born of the church; the latter being usually taxed with an abatement of influence by the bulk of mankind: therefore, to smother a bright example of this superior good influence, may be reputed a sort of murder injurious to the living, and unjust to the dead.

Such an example have we in Addison; which, though hitherto suppressed, yet, when once known, is unsuppressible, of a nature too rare, too striking to be forgotten. For, after a long and manly, but vain, struggle with his distemper, he dismissed his physicians, and with them all hopes of life. But with his hopes of life he dismissed not his concern for the living; but sent for a youth nearly related, and finely accomplished, yet not above being the better for good impressions from a dying friend. He came; but, life now glimmering in the socket, the dying friend was silent. After a decent and proper pause, the youth said, "Dear sir, you sent for me: I believe, and I hope, that you have some commands; I shall hold them most sacred." May distant ages not only hear, but feel, the reply! Forcibly grasping the youth's hand, he softly said, "See in what peace a Christian can die!" He spoke with difficulty, and soon expired. Through grace Divine, how great is man! Through Divine mercy, how stingless death! Who would not thus expire?

What an inestimable legacy were those few dying words to the youth beloved! what a glorious supplement to his own valuable fragment on the truth of Christianity! what a full demonstration, that his fancy could not feign beyond what his virtue could reach! For when he would strike us most strongly with the grandeur of Roman magnanimity, his dying hero is ennobled with this sublime sentiment:—

> While yet I live, let me not live in vain.
>
> Cato

But how much more sublime is that sentiment when realized in life; when dispelling the languors, and appeasing the pains, of a last hour, and brightening with illustrious action the dark avenue and all-awful confines of an eternity! When his soul scarce animated his body, strong faith and ardent charity animated his soul into Divine ambition of saving more than his own. It is for our honour and our advantage to hold him high in our esteem; for the better men are, the more they will admire him; and the more they admire him, the better will they be.

By undrawing the long-closed curtain of his death-bed, have I not showed you a stranger in him whom you knew so well? Is not this of your favourite author,

> *notá major imago?*
>
> Virg

His compositions are but a noble preface; the grand work is his death: that is a work which is read in heaven. How has it joined the final approbation of angels to the previous applause of men! How gloriously had he opened a splendid path, through fame immortal, into eternal peace! How hath he given religion to triumph amidst the ruins of his nature; and, stronger than death, risen higher in virtue when breathing his last!

If all our men of genius had so breathed their last,—if all our men of genius, like him, had been men of genius for eternals,—then had we never been pained by the report of a latter end—O, how unlike to this! But a little to balance our pain, let us consider, that such reports as make us at once adore and tremble, are of use, when too many these are who must tremble before they will adore; and who convince us, to our shame, that the surest refuge of our endangered virtue is in the fears and terrors of the disingenuous human heart.

"But reports," you say, "may be false;" and you farther ask me, "If all reports were true, how came an anecdote of so much honour to human nature as mine to lie so long unknown? What inauspicious planet interposed to lay its lustre under so lasting and so surprising an eclipse?"

The fact is indisputably true; nor are you to rely on me for the truth of it. My report is but a second edition; it was published before, though obscurely, and with a cloud before it. As clouds before the sun are often beautiful, so this of which I speak. How finely pathetic are those two lines, which this so solemn and affecting scene inspired!—

> He taught us how to live; and, O, too high
> A price for knowledge, taught us how to die.
>
> TICKELL

With truth wrapped in darkness, so sung our oracle to the public, but explained himself to me. He was present at his patron's death; and that account of it here given, he gave to me before his eyes were dry. By what means Addison taught us how to die, the poet left to be made known by a late and less able hand; but one more zealous for his patron's glory: zealous and impotent, as the poor Egyptian, who gathered a few splinters of a broken boat, as a funeral pile for the great Pompey, studious of doing honour to so renowned a name. Yet had not this poor plank (permit me here so to call this imperfect page) been thrown out, the chief article of his patron's glory would probably have been sunk for ever, and late ages have received but a fragment of his fame: a fragment glorious indeed, for his genius how bright! But to commend him for composition, though immortal, is detraction now, if there our encomium ends; let us look farther to that concluding scene, which spoke human nature not unrelated to the Divine. To that let us pay the long and large arrear of our greatly posthumous applause.

This you will think a long digression; and justly: if that may be called a digression, which was my chief inducement for writing at all. I had long wished to deliver up to the public this sacred deposit, which by Providence was lodged in my hands; and I entered on the present undertaking partly as an introduction to that which is more worthy to see the light; of which I gave an intimation in the beginning of my letter: for this is the monumental marble there mentioned, to which I promised to conduct you; this is the sepulchral lamp, the long-hidden lustre of our accomplished countryman, who now rises, as from his tomb, to receive the regard so greatly due to the dignity of his death: a death to be distinguished by tears of joy; a death which angels beheld with delight.

And shall that which would have shone conspicuous amid the resplendent lights of Christianity's glorious morn, by these dark days be dropped into oblivion? Dropped it is; and dropped by our sacred, august, and ample register of renown, which has entered in its marble-memoirs the dim splendour of far inferior worth. Though so lavish of praise, and so talkative of the dead, yet is it silent on a subject, which (if any) might have taught its unlettered stones to speak. If powers were not wanting, a monument more durable than those of marble should proudly rise in this ambitious page, to the new and far nobler Addison, than that which you and the public have so long and so much admired. Nor this nation only; for it is Europe's Addison, as well as ours; though Europe knows not half his title to her esteem; being as yet unconscious that the dying Addison far outshines her Addison immortal. Would we resemble him? Let us not limit our ambition to the least illustrious part of his character; heads, indeed, are crowned on earth; but hearts only are crowned in heaven: a truth which, in such an age of authors, should not be forgotten.

It is piously to be hoped, that this narrative may have some effect, since all listen when a death-bed speaks; and regard the person departing as an actor of a part which the great Master of the drama has appointed us to perform to-morrow. This was a Roscius on the stage of life; his exit how great! Ye lovers of virtue, *plaudite;* and let us, my friend, ever "remember his end, as well as our own, that we may never do amiss."

I am, dear Sir,
　　Your most obliged humble servant.

P.S. How far Addison is an original, you will see in my next; where I descend from this consecrated ground into his sublunary praise: and great is the descent, though into noble heights of intellectual power.

Samuel Johnson

1709–1784

Samuel Johnson was born at Lichfield, in Staffordshire, on the 18th of September, 1709. Johnson was a sickly child, afflicted at an early age by scrofula, or the "king's evil." When still an infant he was brought before Queen Anne to receive the royal touch; his condition only worsened. Nearly blind in one eye, his face was pitted and scarred, prone to involuntary twitching and violent convulsions, he suffered the effects of lack of proper treatment in his infancy for the rest of his life.

From childhood as well Johnson was haunted by melancholy. Added to this were uncommonly well-developed powers of observation and memory, insatiable curiosity, and a tendency to read everything he could lay his hands on. In his father's bookshop he encountered literature for the first time. Boswell recounts that once, while searching for some apples, he came upon a large folio of Petrarch, "whom he had seen mentioned, in some preface, as one of the restorers of learning. His curiosity having been thus excited, he sat down with avidity, and read a greater part of the book." Such stories, apocryphal or not, nevertheless convey something of the real enthusiasm with which Johnson as a youngster was drawn to books.

By the time he was sixteen or eighteen, Johnson had become an accomplished Latinist. He was trained in this language by the undermaster of Lichfield school, one Mr. Hawkins, and by the more exigent headmaster Mr. Hunter, who quite literally whipped his Latin grammar into him. In his later years Johnson came to approve of corporal punishment as a method to teach children, asserting that only severe measures could suffice to make diligent scholars out of lay-abouts like himself.

While Johnson was maturing, the fortunes of his family steadily declined. By the time he was ready for Oxford, his father's finances had reached such a sorry state that the younger Johnson had to have his tuition paid by a generous neighbor. The indigent scholar had so little money that he could not afford to clothe himself adequately.

At Oxford Johnson continued on his irregular ramble through ancient and modern literature. "He told me, that from his earliest years he loved to read poetry, but hardly ever read any poem to an end; that he read Shakespeare at a period so early that the speech of Ghost in Hamlet terrified him when he was alone; that Horace's Odes were the compositions in which he took most delight, and was long before he liked his Epistles and Satires. He told me what he read *solidly* at Oxford was Greek; not the Grecian historians, but Homer and Euripides, and now and then a little Epigram; that the study of which he was most fond was Metaphysicks, but he had not read much, in that way."

(BOSWELL, *Life of Johnson*, A.D. 1709–27.) Nevertheless, Boswell also records having seen marginalia in Johnson's books that indicate a regular and methodical study of Virgil, Ovid, Theocritus, and Juvenal, in addition to Euripides and Horace.

In 1731 Johnson, more destitute than ever, could no longer support himself at Oxford, and was obliged to leave without taking a degree. He quartered with old friends; attempted unsuccessfully to sell, by subscription, an edition of the poems of Politian; he even found work translating from the French the Abyssinian travels of one Father Lobo. (This work would later provide him with a source for *Rasselas*.) The most important event of Johnson's early manhood was his marriage, on July 9, 1735, to a prosperous widow named Elizabeth Porter, who he knew affectionately as "Tetty" and to whom he became absolutely devoted. At this point he found it expedient to supplement his income by giving Latin lessons. One of his first pupils was David Garrick, later to become the most celebrated actor in London, manager of the Drury Lane Theatre, and the producer of Johnson's verse tragedy *Irene*.

Johnson began his literary career as a journalist in the employ of Edward Cave, editor of the *Gentleman's Magazine*. His first task was to report on the debates in parliament. While thus engaged in writing the so-called "Reports on the Debates of the Senate of Lilliput," he first came in contact with politics, an experience that left him a stalwart Tory. Boswell remarks that from his infancy Johnson exhibited Tory leanings, illustrating this contention with the probably apocryphal story of his enthusiastic approbation, at the age of three, of the Tory preacher Sacheverell.

Johnson brought off his first successful literary *coup* with the anonymous publication of his satire *London*, a work in imitation of Juvenal's third satire, in May 1738. "It is remarkable," wrote Boswell, "that it [*London*] came out on the same morning with Pope's satire entitled *1738*; so that England had at once its Juvenal and Horace as poetical monitors. . . . Everybody was delighted with it; and there being no name to it, the first buzz of the literary circles was 'here is an unknown poet, greater than Pope'." *The Gentleman's Magazine* recorded that *London* had required a second edition before the week was out; and Pope, upon being told that Johnson was "some obscure man", is reputed to have said, "He will soon be deterré" (i.e., unearthed).

London was a *tour de force*, a poem that sooner or later put Johnson's name on everybody's lips. It not only managed to capture the essence of London life in its most sordid aspects; it did this with wit, detachment, and a felicitous combination of direct observation of the life of the city and close familiarity with Juvenal's original. What emerges is wholly new, an evocative, pithy, eminently vital satire that showed London to London with incomparable effect:

> Here malice, rapine, accident, conspire
> And now a rabble rages, now a fire
> Their ambush here relentless ruffians lay
> And here the fell attorney prowls for prey;

Here falling houses thunder on your head;
And here a female atheist talks you dead.

At the time that Johnson wrote *London*, his knowledge of the poverty and squalor of the more destitute inhabitants of literary London was painfully acute. All he had to do was record the pathetic circumstances of his own life and of the lives of his companions. Among Johnson's associates at this time may be mentioned Boyse, who, when his shirts were pledged, scrawled Latin verses sitting up in bed with his arms through two holes in his blanket, who composed very respectable sacred poetry when he was sober, and who was at last run over by a hackney coach when he was drunk; Hoole, surnamed the metaphysical tailor, who, instead of attending to his measures, used to trace geometrical diagrams on the board where he sat cross-legged; and the penitent impostor, George Psalmanazar, who was an accomplished Hebraist and no less accomplished devourer of opium, and claimed to come from the island of Formosa, although he was French. But of all of these characters surely the most memorable is the poet Richard Savage. Surly, poor to the point of raggedness, vociferous, unkempt, full of anecdotes, he was fond of hurling imprecations at former patrons whose money he had squandered and was, by the time Johnson met him, thoroughly habituated to living on nothing at all in the streets of London and in the countryside. His was a positively abject life, which had previously enjoyed the company of princes; Johnson came to share his every misery, and to know the lowest places he frequented in all their wretchedness. The precise date of Johnson's first acquaintance with Savage is unknown. What is certain is that Savage died in prison after he departed from London for Wales in 1743. The two of them had lived through the filth, danger and privation in the whore-ridden back streets of the city, which had revealed its seamier side to the one who had known better days, and the other who could only hope to know them. But it was precisely as a result of their friendship that Johnson's fame became so well-established. Working with the fund of anecdotes he gathered from Savage during their nocturnal wanderings, Johnson created in his *Life of Savage* (the first of his literary biographies) a unique specimen of this genre. Educated London had never seen the likes of such a life described with such verisimilitude and eloquence. Sir Joshua Reynolds' reaction is typical of the fascination that the *Life of Savage* held for readers who had been bored by the commonplaces of previous literary biographies: "Sir Joshua Reynolds told me, that upon his return from Italy he met with it (i.e., the *Life of Savage*) in Devonshire, knowing nothing of its author, and began to read it while he was standing with his arm leaning against a chimney-piece. It seized his attention so strongly, that, not being able to lay down the book till he had finished it, when he attempted to move, he found his arm totally benumbed." (BOSWELL, *op. cit.*, Aetat. 35.)

Although Johnson had published this work anonymously, all of literary London immediately knew him to be its author. His fame began to spread; by 1747 he was well enough known so that he could not only publish a proposal for his *Dictionary of the English Language*, but also plan to bring out *Irene*, a tragedy he begun to compose several years before. With the help of his old pupil and fellow Lichfield man Garrick, *Irene* was staged at the Drury Lane Theater in the winter of 1749. The play did well (it ran for nine consecutive nights, a respectable showing by eighteenth-century standards), so well that Johnson managed to secure a profit of three hundred pounds, making himself more prosperous than he had ever been before.

It was typical of Johnson to underestimate the length of time necessary to complete his long-term literary projects. Added to this was his inability to save money; both of these facts combined to make Johnson a very unhappy man in the early 1750s. Work on his dictionary proceeded so slowly that it did not appear until 1755. Having frittered away the profits of *Irene* years before that, he found himself chronically in debt. To make matters worse, Tetty's health was failing. He needed to secure a reliable source of weekly income, and had to find an effective way to overcome his deep-seated tendency to procrastinate. His answer to both of these dilemmas was to found a periodical that came out twice a week, on Tuesdays and Saturdays: the *Rambler*.

The *Rambler* proved to be an excellent way to spur Johnson on to write often and for cash. A biweekly review such as he envisioned—inspired by the urbane social commentary of Addison and Steele's *Spectator*—had a good chance of succeeding. As it turned out, the essays he wrote did not lack wit or sophistication. Nevertheless, Johnson's characteristically dignified style, his measured, ciceronian cadences, bore little resemblance to the style of Addison and Steele. The public, eager for diversion, complained that Johnson's approach was insufficiently amusing. In this connection James Clifford's remarks are apposite:

> The Rambler is often thought of as predominately a sober, sonorous, moral work, with only flashes of humor. There are a fair number of light, amusing essays, and Johnson's style sometimes is the source of the humor. He was quite willing to laugh at himself. There are scores of amusing commentaries on the use of philosophic words, disappointments of marriage, faulty education, disappointed fortune hunters, and other topics. If Johnson cannot ever quite catch the light touch of Addison and Steele, he does at times come close.
>
> (*Dictionary Johnson: Samuel Johnson's Middle Years*, 1979, p. 84)

Though the style departed from that of his models, the subject matter was on the whole at least as variable. Topics ranged from the impotence of wealth to the vanity of stoicism, and from the relation of the sound of Milton's poetry to its sense to the misfortunes of a prostitute named Misella, one of Johnson's many acquaintances from the night streets of London. The first number came out on March 10, 1750, the two-hundred and eighth, on March 4, 1753, when Tetty's condition had deteriorated to such an extent that Johnson had to lay down his pen.

Tetty died in the early hours of March 18, 1752. Johnson was inconsolable. Throughout the spring and summer he was incapable of work, overwhelmed as he was by grief. It was only the following September that brought some change. He began to cast about for a new occupation, which soon took the form of a new periodical, more light-hearted than the *Rambler:* the *Adventurer.* Two thirds of the essays were written by his friends John Hawkesworth and Bonnell Thornton. On November 7, 1752, the first number came out, and proved to more successful than its more sober precursor. Enjoying the success of his latest enterprise, freed from the responsibility of writing all of the contributions, Johnson could at last concentrate on bringing his much-awaited dictionary to completion.

By April 3, 1753, he had begun the second volume, which he worked on at a feverish pace, so that by the spring of the following year the bulk of his lexicographical material for the entire work was ready for one final correction. Warton arranged for Johnson to receive an honorary degree from Oxford before the *Dictionary* reached final form. On April 15, 1755 Johnson—for the first time Samuel Johnson, A.M.—published his dictionary, dedicating it not to Lord Chesterfield (as was expected), but to no other sovereign power save that of his labor, prodigious erudition, and the workings of Providence.

The *Dictionary* was a milestone in the history of lexicography. It was not the first work of its kind in the English language. Its etymologies were haphazard and, at times, wholly incorrect. Its philological method was approximate at best. Nevertheless, it was the most learned and comprehensive of all the dictionaries then available; it was the first attempt to "provide as accurately (as possible) all the various shades of meaning of a single word;" and it was "the first [dictionary] in England to combine the various functions we now demand of a dictionary." (CLIFFORD, *op. cit.*, p. 145.) Moreover, the range of citation from poets, philosophers and divines was unprecedented in its extensiveness and is still astonishing. Thomas Carlyle assessed Johnson's achievement aptly: "Had Johnson left nothing but the *Dictionary,* one might have traced there a great intellect, a genuine man."

After the publication of his *magnum opus* Johnson enjoyed a greater renown than ever before. He was named acting editor of a leading political journal, the *Literary Magazine,* in 1761, and convinced the skeptical publisher Jacob Tonson to resuscitate plans for a complete edition of Shakespeare that had lain dormant since 1745, when Johnson was still a relatively obscure hack writer. Johnson's journalistic output for the *Literary Magazine* revealed his anticommerical and anticolonial stance so strongly that scholars believe that he was considered too much of a nuisance to the regime then in power to retain his editorial position for very long. His indignant remarks concerning England's involvement in colonial wars in America were not well received by the proprietors of the magazine; within a year he was out of the political workshop, and back into the literary. He had begun to work on the new edition of Shakespeare which he had promised to Tonson by the Christmas of 1757.

As it turned out, the eight volumes, complete with preface, line-by-line emendations of crucial passages, and general critical commentaries, took Johnson not one and a half, but nine years to complete. Of all his undertakings it was this one that most tried the patience of his friends, nearly disgraced his reputation, and sorely vexed his publisher. The polemicist

Churchill finally shamed Johnson into completing the task he had set out for himself. Calling Johnson "Pomposo," he ridiculed Johnson's credulity in the recent affair of the "Cock Lane Ghost" (an eleven year old girl had managed to deceive many of the great minds of London into believing she was haunted), and accused him of soliciting subscriptions at a healthy fee for goods that would never be delivered. Johnson buckled under and finally succeeded in completing his mammoth project by October of 1765, preserving his reputation and his friendship with many of his subscribers.

By the time he finished his Shakespeare project, his mother had died, *Rasselas* had been written to defray the expense of her funeral, one-hundred and four numbers of the *Idler* had come and gone, and Dr. Johnson, royal pensioner, recipient of three hundred pounds sterling per annum, had made the acquaintance of a rather unprepossessing Scots lawyer by the name of James Boswell. Their meeting, in the back-parlour of Tom Davie's bookshop, led to the creation of the most memorable biography in all of English literature.

If Johnson was a hopeless case when it came to finishing his long-term projects on time, he more than made up for this defect when writing short compositions. In this connection Boswell recounts the following anecdote: "Mr. Langton remembers Johnson, when on a visit to Oxford, asking him one evening how long it was till the post went out; and on being told about an half an hour, he exclaimed, 'then we shall do very well.' He upon this instantly sat down and finished an Idler, which it was necessary should be in London the next day. Mr. Langton having signified a wish to read it, "Sir, (said he) you shall not do more than I have done myself." He then folded it up, and sent it off. (BOSWELL, *op. cit., Aetat.* 49).

Financially independent for the first time in his life, Johnson at last began to enjoy some measure of self-confidence and to display (as the previous story indicates) powers hitherto untapped. It was in these years immediately following the granting of his pension and the publication of his edition of Shakespeare that the persona of Johnson as indefatigable conversationalist became firmly established. He would lie abed until midday or later, to be awakened by a constant stream of visitors of all kinds, to whose queries he gave critical responses as memorable as they were spontaneous. In the afternoons he repaired to the coffeehouses to carouse well into the night. He gave free rein to that species of indolence that only great men can turn to their advantage. Too lazy to put pen to paper, his conversation overflowed with all the brilliance of wit and learning that had graced his writing. His moral fervor and eloquence were perfected and intensified by talk. He was never so completely, and so freely, himself as when he was giving himself to others in conversation. In 1764, with Reynolds, Goldsmith, Burke, and others, he founded the Club, where he could indulge his gifts of conversation with other men of parts and learning.

It was in these years that Boswell gathered most of his material for his life of Johnson. The late 1760s were for Johnson a period of intense social activity at the expense of his literary pursuits. In 1765, around the time he completed his Shakespeare, he became acquainted with Hester Lynch Thrale, a friendship which gave the aging and infirm man of letters the solace, amusement, and affection only feminine company could provide for him. Keeping a house on Fleet Street that was populated by as odd an assortment of characters as ever were associated with a literary man, he also regularly frequented the luxurious spas at Bath in the company of the Thrales.

In 1773, having been interested by reports of a region of the British Isles where life had not changed considerably since medieval times, Johnson, along with Boswell, undertook a journey to the Hebrides. Two years later his *Journey to the Hebrides* was published. The critical reception of this volume in England was nothing short of unanimously positive; in Scotland, however, it was greeted with a mixture of subdued affability, granite indifference, and violent scorn.

With the exception of an unfortunate episode surrounding the publication of a political pamphlet concerning the unrest in the American colonies, the late 1770s saw Johnson working assiduously on a project that was as well executed as it was universally well received. In 1777 a deputation of forty men representing the most influential of the London booksellers asked Johnson to contribute biographical prefaces to a new edition of English poets that began with Cowley. Johnson was the logical choice for such an enterprise. His knowledge of biographical and literary minutiae, anecdotes, and of the refinements of criticism after the Restoration was without parallel. In the opinion of Macaulay,

> The *Lives of the Poets*, is, on the whole, the best of Johnson's works. The narratives are as entertaining as any novel. The remarks on life and on human nature are eminently shrewd and profound. The criticisms are often excellent, and, even when grossly and provokingly unjust, well deserve to be studied. *Savage's Life* Johnson reprinted nearly as it had appeared in 1744. Whoever, after reading that life, will proceed to the other lives will be struck by the difference of the style.

Macaulay, no mean stylist himself, goes on to explain that years of cultivated talk and educated leisure gave the mature Johnson a diction that "frequently had a colloquial ease which it formerly wanted." Pointing to the change of style that is perceptible in the *Journey to the Hebrides*, the great Victorian man of letters, who made a point of asserting that Johnson's conversation was better than anything he ever wrote, nevertheless implies in his praise of the *Lives* that its style, tone, and diction were closer than Johnson's other writings to the virtues of his speech.

Johnson's life of literary effort had come full circle with the publication of his last great work. Having captured the attention and admiration of the literate classes over thirty years earlier with his *Life of Savage,* a work that bears the mark of painful and difficult literary apprenticeship, Johnson crowned his career with a general survey of all that is great in English literature from Shakespeare to his own times. In this way he secured his position as the greatest critic of English literature in the eighteenth century, and among the greatest the world may ever produce.

Johnson died on December 13, 1784, at Bolt Court, London and was buried with much fanfare at Westminster Abbey.

AN ESSAY ON EPITAPHS

Though criticism has been cultivated in every age of learning, by men of great abilities and extensive knowledge, till the rules of writing are become rather burdensome than instructive to the mind; though almost every species of composition has been the subject of particular treatises, and given birth to definitions, distinctions, precepts and illustrations; yet no critic of note that has fallen within my observation has hitherto thought sepulchral inscriptions worthy of a minute examination, or pointed out with proper accuracy their beauties and defects.

The reasons of this neglect it is useless to inquire, and perhaps impossible to discover; it might be justly expected that this kind of writing would have been the favourite topic of criticism, and that self-love might have produced some regard for it, in those authors that have crowded libraries with elaborate dissertations upon Homer; since to afford a subject for heroic poems is the privilege of very few, but every man may expect to be recorded in an epitaph, and therefore, finds some interest in providing that his memory may not suffer by an unskilful panegyric.

If our prejudices in favour of antiquity deserve to have any part in the regulation of our studies, epitaphs seem entitled to more than common regard, as they are probably of the same age with the art of writing. The most ancient structures in the world, the pyramids, are supposed to be sepulchral monuments, which either pride or gratitude erected, and the same passions which incited men to such laborious and expensive methods of preserving their own memory, or that of their benefactors, would doubtless incline them not to neglect any easier means by which the same ends might be obtained. Nature and reason have dictated to every nation that to preserve good actions from oblivion is both the interest and duty of mankind; and therefore we find no people acquainted with the use of letters that omitted to grace the tombs of their heroes and wise men with panegyrical inscriptions.

To examine, therefore, in what the perfection of epitaphs consists, and what rules are to be observed in composing them, will be at least of as much use as other critical inquiries; and for assigning a few hours to such disquisitions, great examples at least, if not strong reasons, may be pleaded.

An epitaph, as the word itself implies, is an inscription on a tomb, and in its most extensive import may admit indiscriminately satire or praise. But as malice has seldom produced monuments of defamation, and the tombs hitherto raised have been the work of friendship and benevolence, custom has contracted the original latitude of the word, so that it signifies in the general acceptation an inscription engraven on a tomb in honour of the person deceased.

As honours are paid to the dead in order to incite others to the imitation of their excellences, the principal intention of epitaphs is to perpetuate the examples of virtue, that the tomb of a good man may supply the want of his presence, and veneration for his memory produce the same effect as the observation of his life. Those epitaphs are, therefore, the most perfect which set virtue in the strongest light, and are best adapted to exalt the reader's ideas, and to rouse his emulation.

To this end it is not always necessary to recount the actions of a hero, or enumerate the writings of a philosopher; to imagine such informations necessary is to detract from their characters, or to suppose their works mortal, or their achievements in danger of being forgotten. The bare name of such men answers every purpose of a long inscription.

Had only the name of Sir Isaac Newton been subjoined to the design upon his monument, instead of a long detail of his discoveries, which no philosopher can want, and which none but a philosopher can understand, those by whose direction it was raised had done more honour both to him and to themselves.

This, indeed, is a commendation which it requires no genius to bestow, but which can never become vulgar or contemptible, if bestowed with judgment; because no single age produces many men of merit superior to panegyric. None but the first names can stand unassisted against the attacks of time, and if men raised to reputation by accident or caprice have nothing but their names engraved on their tombs, there is danger lest in a few years the inscription require an interpreter. Thus have their expectations been disappointed who honoured Picus of Mirandola with this pompous epitaph:

> Hic situs est Picus Mirandola, caetera norunt
> Et Tagus et Ganges, forsan et Antipodes.[1]

His name then celebrated in the remotest corners of the earth is now almost forgotten; and his works, then studied, admired, and applauded, are now mouldering in obscurity.

Next in dignity to the bare name is a short character simple and unadorned, without exaggeration, superlatives, or rhetoric. Such were the inscriptions in use among the Romans, in which the victories gained by their emperors were commemorated by a single epithet; as Caesar Germanicus, Caesar Dacicus, Germanicus, Illyricus. Such would be this epitaph, *Isaacus Newtonus, naturae legibus investigatis, hic quiescit.*[2]

But to far the greatest part of mankind a longer encomium is necessary for the publication of their virtues, and the preservation of their memories; and, in the composition of these it is that art is principally required, and precepts, therefore, may be useful.

In writing epitaphs, one circumstance is to be considered which affects no other composition; the place in which they are now commonly found restrains them to a particular air of solemnity, and debars them from the admission of all lighter or gayer ornaments. In this, it is that the style of an epitaph necessarily differs from that of an elegy. The customs of burying our dead either in or near our churches, perhaps originally founded on a rational design of fitting the mind for religious exercises, by laying before it the most affecting proofs of the uncertainty of life, makes it proper to exclude from our epitaphs all such allusions as are contrary to the doctrines for the propagation of which the churches are erected, and to the end for which those who peruse the monuments must be supposed to come thither. Nothing is, therefore, more ridiculous than to copy the Roman inscriptions, which were engraven on stones by the highway, and composed by those who generally reflected on mortality only to excite in themselves and others a quicker relish of pleasure, and a more luxurious enjoyment of life, and whose regard for the dead extended no farther than a wish that *the earth might be light upon them*.

All allusions to the heathen mythology are, therefore, absurd, and all regard for the senseless remains of a dead man impertinent and superstitious. One of the first distinctions of the primitive Christians was their neglect of bestowing garlands on the dead, in which they are very rationally defended by their apologist in Minutius Felix.[3] 'We lavish no flowers nor odours on the dead,' says he, 'because they have no sense of fragrance or beauty.' We profess to reverence the dead, not for their sake, but for our own. It is therefore always with indignation or contempt that I read the epitaph on Cowley, a man whose learning and poetry were his lowest merits.

> *Aurea dum late volitant tua scripta per orbem,*
> *Et fama eternum vivis, divine poeta,*
> *Hic placida jaceas requie, custodiat urnam*
> *Cana fides, vigilentque perenni lampade musae!*
> *Sit sacer ille locus, nec quis temerarius ausit*
> *Sacrilega turbare manu venerabile bustum.*
> *Intacti maneant, maneant per saecula dulces*
> *Coweleii cineres, serventque immobile saxum.*[4]

To pray that the ashes of a friend may lie undisturbed, and that the divinities that favoured him in his life may watch for ever round him, to preserve his tomb from violation, and drive sacrilege away, is only rational in him who believes the soul interested in the repose of the body, and the powers which he invokes for its protection able to preserve it. To censure such expressions, as contrary to religion, or as remains of heathen superstition, would be too great a degree of severity. I condemn them only as uninstructive and unaffecting, as too ludicrous for reverence or grief, for Christianity and a temple.

That the designs and decorations of monuments ought, likewise, to be formed with the same regard to the solemnity of the place, cannot be denied; it is an established principle that all ornaments owe their beauty to their propriety. The same glitter of dress that adds graces to gaiety and youth would make age and dignity contemptible. Charon with his boat is far from heightening the awful grandeur of the universal judgment, though drawn by Angelo[5] himself; nor is it easy to imagine a greater absurdity than that of gracing the walls of a Christian temple with the figure of Mars leading a hero to battle, or Cupids sporting round a virgin. The pope who defaced the statues of the deities at the tomb of Sannazarius[6] is, in my opinion, more easily to be defended than he that erected them.

It is, for the same reason, improper to address the epitaph to the passenger, a custom which in injudicious veneration for antiquity introduced again at the revival of letters, and which, among many others, Passeratius suffered to mislead him in his epitaph upon the heart of Henry, king of France, who was stabbed by Clement the monk, which yet deserves to be inserted, for the sake of showing how beautiful even improprieties may become in the hands of a good writer.

> *Adsta, viator, et dole regum vices.*
> *Cor regis isto conditur sub marmore,*
> *Qui jura Gallis, jura Sarmatis dedit,*
> *Tectus cucullo hunc sustulit sicarius.*
> *Abi, viator, et dole regum vices.*[7]

In the monkish ages, however ignorant and unpolished, the epitaphs were drawn up with far greater propriety than can be shown in those which more enlightened times have produced.

> Orate pro anima——miserrimi peccatoris[8]

was an address to the last degree striking and solemn, as it flowed naturally from the religion then believed, and awakened in the reader sentiments of benevolence for the deceased, and of concern for his own happiness. There was nothing trifling or ludicrous, nothing that did not tend to the noblest end, the propagation of piety, and the increase of devotion.

It may seem very superfluous to lay it down as the first rule for writing epitaphs that the name of the deceased is not to be omitted; nor should I have thought such a precept necessary, had not the practice of the greatest writers shown that it has not been sufficiently regarded. In most of the poetical epitaphs, the names for whom they were composed may be sought to no purpose, being only prefixed on the monument. To expose the absurdity of this omission, it is only necessary to ask how the epitaphs which have outlived the stones on which they were inscribed would have contributed to the information of posterity had they wanted the names of those whom they celebrated.

In drawing the character of the deceased, there are no rules to be observed which do not equally relate to other compositions. The praise ought not to be general, because the mind is lost in the extent of any indefinite idea, and cannot be affected with what it cannot comprehend. When we hear only of a good or great man, we know not in what class to place him, nor have any notion of his character, distinct from that of a thousand others; his example can have no effect upon our conduct, as we have nothing remarkable or eminent to propose to our imitation. The epitaph composed by Ennius for his own tomb has both the faults last mentioned.

> *Nemo me decoret lacrumis, nec funera fletu*
> *Faxit. Cur?—Volito vivu' per ora virum.*[9]

The reader of this epitaph receives scarce any idea from it; he neither conceives any veneration for the man to whom it belongs, nor is instructed by what methods this boasted reputation is to be obtained.

Though a sepulchral inscription is professedly a panegyric, and, therefore, not confined to historical impartiality, yet it ought always to be written with regard to truth. No man ought to be commended for virtues which he never possessed, but whoever is curious to know his faults must inquire after them in other places; the monuments of the dead are not intended to perpetuate the memory of crimes, but to exhibit patterns of virtue. On the tomb of Maecenas his luxury is not to be mentioned with his munificence, nor is the proscription to find a place on the monument of Augustus.

The best subject for epitaphs is private virtue; virtue exerted in the same circumstances in which the bulk of mankind are placed, and which, therefore, may admit of many imitators. He that has delivered his country from oppression, or freed the world from ignorance and error, can recite the emulation of a very small number; but he that has repelled the temptations of poverty, and disdained to free himself from distress at the expense of his virtue, may animate multitudes, by his example, to the same firmness of heart and steadiness of resolution.

Of this kind I cannot forbear the mention of two Greek inscriptions;[10] one upon a man whose writings are well known, the other upon a person whose memory is preserved only in her epitaph, who both lived in slavery, the most calamitous estate in human life:

Ζωσιμη ἡ πριν ἐουσα μονω τω Σωματι δουλη,
  Και πω σωματι νυν εὑρεν ἐλευθεριην.

Zosima, quae solo fuit olim corpore serva,
  Corpore nunc etiam libera facta fuit.

Zosima, who, in her life, could only have her body enslaved,
  now finds her body, likewise, set at liberty.

It is impossible to read this epitaph without being animated to bear the evils of life with constancy, and to support the dignity of human nature under the most pressing afflictions, both by the example of the heroine, whose grave we behold, and the prospect of that state in which, to use the language of the inspired writers, *The poor cease from their labours, and the weary be at rest.*[11]

The other is upon Epictetus, the Stoic philosopher:

Δουλος 'Επικτητος γενομην, και Σωμ' ἀναπηρος,
  Και πενιην 'Ιρος, και φιλος 'Αθανατοις.

Servus Epictetus, mutilatus corpore, vixi
  Pauperieque Irus, curaque prima deum.

Epictetus, who lies here, was a slave and a cripple, poor as
  the beggar in the proverb, and the favourite of heaven.

In this distich is comprised the noblest panegyric and the most important instruction. We may learn from it that virtue is impracticable in no condition, since Epictetus could recommend himself to the regard of heaven, amidst the temptations of poverty and slavery; slavery, which has always been found so destructive to virtue that in many languages a slave and a thief are expressed by the same word. And we may be likewise admonished by it not to lay any stress on a man's outward circumstances in making an estimate of his real value, since Epictetus the beggar, the cripple, and the slave, was the favourite of heaven.

NOTES

1. 'Here lies Pico de Mirandola; the rest of his story is known by the Tagus and the Ganges, even the Antipodes.'

2. 'Here rests Isaac Newton, who searched out the laws of nature.'

3. (Also spelled Minucius.) An early Roman Christian, who wrote his dialogue *Octavius* in defence of Christianity against its pagan enemies. Johnson's quotation is from chapter xxxviii.

4. 'While your golden writings fly far and wide throughout the world, and you live eternally in fame, divine poet, may you lie here in peaceful rest; may grey-haired Faith guard your urn, and the Muses keep watch over it with their eternal torch! May this place be holy, and may no one be so bold as to venture to disturb this venerable bust with sacrilegious hand. Let the ashes of Cowley remain untouched, remain through kindly ages, and keep the tombstone unmoved.'

5. The reference is to Michelangelo's great painting of the Last Judgement in the Sistine Chapel, where Charon and his boat do indeed appear (they also appear in Dante's *Inferno*).

6. The tomb of the Renaissance poet Sannazaro in the church of Santa Maria del Parto in Naples was 'defaced' by the addition of the names 'David' and 'Judith' to the pedestals of the flanking statues of Apollo and Minerva.

7. 'Stay, wayfarer, and mourn the fates of kings. Buried beneath this marble is the heart of a king who gave laws to the French and to the Poles. A murderer hidden beneath a cowl laid him low. Go, wayfarer, and mourn the fates of kings.'

8. 'Pray for the soul of X, a most miserable sinner.' The blank is to be filled with the name of the deceased.

9. 'Let no one honour me with tears, nor have buried me with weeping. Why? I fly alive through the mouths of men.' Ennius was famed as the earliest Roman epic poet.

10. Johnson has translated these two epitaphs from the *Anthology* into Latin elegiacs as well as English prose. The Greek in the *GM* has some breathings (which have been regularized here), but no accents.

11. Matthew 11:28, 'Come unto me, all ye that labour and are heavy laden, and I will give you rest'; Job 3: 17, 'There the wicked cease from troubling, and there the weary be at rest.'

THE RAMBLER

Number 4

Saturday, March 31, 1750[1]

Simul et jucunda et idonea dicere vitae.
Horace, *Ars poetica*, I. 334

And join both profit and delight in one.
Creech

The works of fiction, with which the present generation seems more particularly delighted, are such as exhibit life in its true state, diversified only by accidents that daily happen in the world, and influenced by passions and qualities which are really to be found in conversing with mankind.

This kind of writing may be termed not improperly the comedy of romance, and is to be conducted nearly by the rules of comic poetry. Its province is to bring about natural events by easy means, and to keep up curiosity without the help of wonder: it is therefore precluded from the machines and expedients of the heroic romance, and can neither employ giants to snatch away a lady from the nuptial rites, nor knights to bring her back from captivity; it can neither bewilder its personages in desarts, nor lodge them in imaginary castles.[2]

I remember a remark made by Scaliger upon Pontanus, that all his writings are filled with the same images; and that if you take from him his lillies and his roses, his satyrs and his dryads, he will have nothing left that can be called poetry.[3] In like manner, almost all the fictions of the last age will vanish, if you deprive them of a hermit and a wood, a battle and a shipwreck.

Why this wild strain of imagination found reception so long, in polite and learned ages, it is not easy to conceive; but we cannot wonder that, while readers could be procured, the authors were willing to continue it: for when a man had by practice gained some fluency of language, he had no further care than to retire to his closet, let loose his invention, and heat his mind with incredibilities; a book was thus produced without fear of criticism, without the toil of study, without knowledge of nature, or acquaintance with life.

The task of our present writers is very different; it requires, together with that learning which is to be gained from books, that experience which can never be attained by solitary diligence, but must arise from general converse, and accurate observation of the living world. Their performances have, as Horace expresses it, *plus oneris quantum veniae minus,*[4] little indulgence, and therefore more difficulty. They are engaged in portraits of which every one

407

knows the original, and can detect any deviation from exactness of resemblance. Other writings are safe, except from the malice of learning, but these are in danger from every common reader; as the slipper ill executed was censured by a shoemaker who happened to stop in his way at the Venus of Apelles.[5]

But the fear of not being approved as just copiers of human manners, is not the most important concern that an author of this sort ought to have before him. These books are written chiefly to the young, the ignorant, and the idle, to whom they serve as lectures of conduct, and introductions into life. They are the entertainment of minds unfurnished with ideas, and therefore easily susceptible of impressions; not fixed by principles, and therefore easily following the current of fancy; not informed by experience, and consequently open to every false suggestion and partial account.

That the highest degree of reverence should be paid to youth, and that nothing indecent should be suffered to approach their eyes or ears; are precepts extorted by sense and virtue from an ancient writer, by no means eminent for chastity of thought.[6] The same kind, tho' not the same degree of caution, is required in every thing which is laid before them, to secure them from unjust prejudices, perverse opinions, and incongruous combinations of images.

In the romances formerly written, every transaction and sentiment was so remote from all that passes among men, that the reader was in very little danger of making any application to himself; the virtues and crimes were equally beyond his sphere of activity; and he amused himself with heroes and with traitors, deliverers and persecutors, as with beings of another species, whose actions were regulated upon motives of their own, and who had neither faults nor excellencies in common with himself.

But when an adventurer is levelled with the rest of the world, and acts in such scenes of the universal drama, as may be the lot of any other man; young spectators fix their eyes upon him with closer attention, and hope by observing his behaviour and success to regulate their own practices, when they shall be engaged in the like part.

For this reason these familiar histories may perhaps be made of greater use than the solemnities of professed morality, and convey the knowledge of vice and virtue with more efficacy than axioms and definitions. But if the power of example is so great, as to take possession of the memory by a kind of violence, and produce effects almost without the intervention of the will, care ought to be taken that, when the choice is unrestrained, the best examples only should be exhibited; and that which is likely to operate so strongly, should not be mischievous or uncertain in its effects.

The chief advantage which these fictions have over real life is, that their authors are at liberty, tho' not to invent, yet to select objects, and to cull from the mass of mankind, those individuals upon which the attention ought most to be employ'd; as a diamond, though it cannot be made, may be polished by art, and placed in such a situation, as to display that lustre which before was buried among common stones.

It is justly considered as the greatest excellency of art to imitate nature; but it is necessary to distinguish those parts of nature, which are most proper for imitation: greater care is still required in representing life, which is so often discoloured by passion, or deformed by wickedness. If the world be promiscuously described, I cannot see of what use it can be to read the account; or why it may not be as safe to turn the eye immediately upon mankind, as upon a mirror which shows all that presents itself without discrimination.

It is therefore not a sufficient vindication of a character, that it is drawn as it appears, for many characters ought never to be drawn; nor of a narrative, that the train of events is agreeable to observation and experience, for that observation which is called knowledge of the world, will be found much more frequently to make men cunning than good. The purpose of these writings is surely not only to show mankind, but to provide that they may be seen hereafter with less hazard; to teach the means of avoiding the snares which are laid by Treachery for Innocence, without infusing any wish for that superiority with which the betrayer flatters his vanity; to give the power of counteracting fraud, without the temptation to practise it; to initiate youth by mock encounters in the art of necessary defence, and to increase prudence without impairing virtue.

Many writers, for the sake of following nature, so mingle good and bad qualities in their principal personages, that they are both equally conspicuous; and as we accompany them through their adventures with delight, and are led by degrees to interest ourselves in their favour, we lose the abhorrence of their faults, because they do not hinder our pleasure, or, perhaps, regard them with some kindness for being united with so much merit.

There have been men indeed splendidly wicked, whose endowments threw a brightness on their crimes, and whom scarce any villainy made perfectly detestable, because they never could be wholly divested of their excellencies; but such have been in all ages the great corrupters of the world, and their resemblance ought no more to be preserved, than the art of murdering without pain.

Some have advanced, without due attention to the consequences of this notion, that certain virtues have their correspondent faults, and therefore that to exhibit either apart is to deviate from probability. Thus men are observed by Swift to be "grateful in the same degree as they are resentful."[7] This principle, with others of the same kind, supposes man to act from a brute impulse, and persue a certain degree of inclination, without any choice of the object; for, otherwise, though it should be allowed that gratitude and resentment arise from the same constitution of the passions, it follows not that they will be equally indulged when reason is consulted; yet unless that consequence be admitted, this sagacious maxim becomes an empty sound, without any relation to practice or to life.

Nor is it evident, that even the first motions to these effects are always in the same proportion. For pride, which produces quickness of resentment, will obstruct gratitude, by unwillingness to admit that inferiority which obligation implies; and it is very unlikely, that he who cannot think he receives a favour will acknowledge or repay it.

It is of the utmost importance to mankind, that positions of this tendency should be laid open and confuted; for while men consider good and evil as springing from the same root, they will spare the one for the sake of the other, and in judging, if not of others at least of themselves, will be apt to estimate their virtues by their vices. To this fatal error all those will contribute, who confound the colours of right and wrong, and instead of helping to settle their boundaries, mix them with so much art, that no common mind is able to disunite them.

In narratives, where historical veracity has no place, I cannot discover why there should not be exhibited the most perfect idea of virtue; of virtue not angelical, nor above probability, for what we cannot credit we shall never imitate, but the highest and purest that humanity can reach, which, exercised in such trials as the various revolutions of things shall bring upon it, may, by conquering some calamities, and enduring others, teach us what we may hope, and what we can perform. Vice, for vice is necessary to be shewn, should always disgust; nor should the graces of gaiety, or the dignity of courage, be so united with it, as to reconcile it to the mind. Wherever it appears, it should raise hatred by the malignity of its practices, and contempt by the meanness of its stratagems; for while it is supported by either parts or spirit, it will be seldom heartily abhorred. The Roman tyrant was content to be hated, if he was but feared;[8] and there are thousands of the readers of romances willing to be thought wicked, if they may be allowed to be wits. It is therefore to be steadily inculcated, that virtue is the highest proof of understanding, and the only solid basis of greatness; and that vice is the natural consequence of narrow thoughts, that it begins in mistake, and ends in ignominy.

Number 60

Saturday, October 13, 1750

Quid sit pulchrum, quid turpe, quid utile, quid non,
Plenius et melius Chrysippo et Crantore dicit.
                    Horace, *Epistles*, I.2.3–4

Whose works the beautiful and base contain;
Of vice and virtue more instructive rules,
Than all the sober sages of the schools.

                                            Francis

All joy or sorrow for the happiness or calamities of others is produced by an act of the imagination, that realises the event however fictitious, or approximates it however remote, by placing us, for a time, in the condition of him whose fortune we contemplate; so that we feel, while the deception lasts, whatever motions would be excited by the same good or evil happening to ourselves.

Our passions are therefore more strongly moved, in proportion as we can more readily adopt the pains or pleasures proposed to our minds, by recognising them as once our own, or considering them as naturally incident to our state of life. It is not easy for the most artful writer to give us an interest in happiness or misery, which we think ourselves never likely to feel, and with which we have never yet been made acquainted. Histories of the downfall of kingdoms, and revolutions of empires, are read with great tranquillity; the imperial tragedy pleases common auditors only by its pomp of ornament, and grandeur of ideas; and the man whose faculties have been engrossed by business, and whose heart never fluttered but at the rise or fall of stocks, wonders how the attention can be seized, or the affection agitated by a tale of love.

Those parallel circumstances, and kindred images, to which we readily conform our minds, are, above all other writings, to be found in narratives of the lives of particular persons; and therefore no species of writing seems more worthy of cultivation than biography, since none can be more delightful or more useful, none can more certainly enchain the heart by irresistible interest, or more widely diffuse instruction to every diversity of condition.

The general and rapid narratives of history, which involve a thousand fortunes in the business of a day, and complicate innumerable incidents in one great transaction, afford few lessons applicable to private life, which derives its comforts and its wretchedness from the right or wrong management of things which nothing but their frequency makes considerable, *Parva, si non fiant quotidie,* says Pliny,[9] and which can have no place in those relations which never descend below the consultation of senates, the motions of armies, and the schemes of conspirators.

I have often thought that there has rarely passed a life of which a judicious and faithful narrative would not be useful. For, not only every man has, in the mighty mass of the world, great numbers in the same condition with himself, to whom his mistakes and miscarriages, escapes and expedients, would be of immediate and apparent use; but there is such an uniformity in the state of man, considered apart from adventitious and separable decorations and disguises, that there is scarce any possibility of good or ill, but is common to human kind. A great part of the time of those who are placed at the greatest distance by fortune, or by temper, must unavoidably pass in the same manner; and though, when the claims of nature are satisfied, caprice, and vanity, and accident, begin to produce discriminations and peculiarities, yet the eye is not very heedful, or quick, which cannot discover the same causes still terminating their influence in the same effects, though sometimes accelerated, sometimes retarded, or perplexed by multiplied combinations. We are all prompted by the same motives, all deceived by the same fallacies, all animated by hope, obstructed by danger, entangled by desire, and seduced by pleasure.

It is frequently objected to relations of particular lives, that they are not distinguished by any striking or wonderful vicissitudes. The scholar who passed his life among his books, the merchant who conducted only his own affairs, the priest, whose sphere of action was not extended beyond that of his duty, are considered as no proper objects of publick regard, however they might have excelled in their several stations, whatever might have been their learning, integrity, and piety. But this notion arises from false measures of excellence and dignity, and must be eradicated by considering, that, in the esteem of uncorrupted reason, what is of most use is of most value.

It is, indeed, not improper to take honest advantages of prejudice, and to gain attention by a celebrated name; but the business of the biographer is often to pass slightly over those performances and incidents, which produce vulgar greatness, to lead the thoughts into domestick privacies, and display the minute details of daily life, where exterior appendages are cast aside, and men excel each only by prudence and by virtue. The account of Thuanus is, with great propriety, said by its author to have been written, that it might lay open to posterity the private and familiar character of that man, *cujus ingenium et candorem ex ipsius sciptis sunt olim semper miraturi,* whose candour and genius will to the end of time be by his writing preserved in admiration.[10]

There are many invisible circumstances which, whether we read as enquirers after natural or moral knowledge, whether we intend to enlarge our science, or increase our virtue, are more important than publick occurrences. Thus Salust, the great master of nature, has not forgot, in his account of Catiline, to remark that "his walk was now quick, and again slow," as an indication of a mind revolving something with violent commotion.[11] Thus the story of Melancthon affords a striking lecture on the value of time, by informing us, that when he made an appointment, he expected not only the hour, but the minute to be fixed, that the day might not run out in the idleness of suspense;[12] and all the plans and enterprizes of De Witt are now of less importance to the world, than that part of his personal character which represents him as "careful of his health, and negligent of his life."[13]

But biography has often been allotted to writers who seem very little acquainted with the nature of their task, or very negligent about the performance. They rarely afford any other account than might be collected from publick papers, but imagine themselves writing a life when they exhibit a chronological series of actions or preferments; and so little regard the manners or behaviour of their heroes, that more knowledge may be gained of a man's real character, by a short conversation with one of his servants, than from a formal and studied narrative, begun with his pedigree, and ended with his funeral.

If now and then they condescend to inform the world of particular facts, they are not always so happy as to select the most important. I know not well what advantage posterity can receive from the only circumstance by which Tickell has distinguished Addison from the rest of mankind, "the irregularity of his pulse"[14]: nor can I think myself overpaid for the time spent in reading the life of Malherb, by being enabled to relate, after the learned biographer, that Malherb had two predominant opinions; one, that the looseness of a single woman might destroy all her boast of ancient descent; the other, that the French beggars made use very improperly and barbarously of the phrase "noble Gentleman," because either word included the sense of both.[15]

There are, indeed, some natural reasons why these narratives are often written by such as were not likely to give much instruction or delight, and why most accounts of particular persons are barren and useless. If a life be delayed till interest and envy are at an end, we may hope for impartiality, but must expect little intelligence; for the incidents which give excellence to biography are of a volatile and evanescent kind, such as soon escape the memory, and are rarely transmitted by tradition. We know how few can portray a living acquaintance, except by his most prominent and observable particularities, and the grosser features of his mind; and it may be easily imagined how much of this little knowledge may be lost in imparting it, and how soon a succession of copies will lose all resemblance of the original.

If the biographer writes from personal knowledge, and makes haste to gratify the publick curiosity, there is danger lest his interest, his fear, his gratitude, or his tenderness, overpower his fidelity, and tempt him to conceal, if not to invent. There are many who think it an act of piety to hide the faults or failings of their friends, even when they can no longer suffer by their detection; we therefore see whole ranks of characters adorned with uniform panegyrick, and not to be known from one another, but by extrinsick and casual circumstances. "Let me remember," says Hale, "when I find myself inclined to pity a criminal, that there is likewise a pity due to the country."[16] If we owe regard to the memory of the dead, there is yet more respect to be paid to knowledge, to virtue, and to truth.

Number 93

Tuesday, February 5, 1751

Experiar quid concedatur in illos
Quorum Flaminiâ tegitur cinis atque Latinâ.
Juvenal, I.170–71

More safely truth to urge her claim presumes,
On names now found alone on books and tombs.

There are few books on which more time is spent by young students, than on treatises which deliver the characters of authors; nor any which oftener deceive the expectation of the reader, or fill his mind with more opinions which the progress of his studies and the encrease of his knowledge oblige him to resign.

Baillet has introduced his collection of the decisions of the learned, by an enumeration of the prejudices which mislead the critick, and raise the passions in rebellion against the judgment.[17] His catalogue, though large, is imperfect; and who can hope to complete it? The beauties of writing have been observed to be often such as cannot in the present state of human knowledge be evinced by evidence, or drawn out into demonstrations; they are therefore wholly subject to the imagination, and do not force their effects upon a mind preoccupied by unfavourable sentiments, nor overcome the counteraction of a false principle or of stubborn partiality.

To convince any man against his will is hard, but to please him against his will is justly pronounced by Dryden to be above the reach of human abilities.[18] Interest and passion will hold out long against the closest siege of diagrams and syllogisms, but they are absolutely impregnable to imagery and sentiment; and will for ever bid defiance to the most powerful strains of Virgil or Homer, though they may give way in time to the batteries of Euclid or Archimedes.

In trusting therefore to the sentence of a critick, we are in danger not only from that vanity which exalts writers too often to the dignity of teaching what they are yet to learn, from that negligence which sometimes steals upon the most vigilant caution, and that fallibility to which the condition of nature has subjected every human understanding; but from a thousand extrinsick and accidental causes, from every thing which can excite kindness or malevolence, veneration or contempt.

Many of those who have determined with great boldness, upon the various degrees of literary merit, may be justly suspected of having passed sentence, as Seneca remarks of Claudius,

> *Una tantum parte audita,*
> *Saepe et nulla,*
>   Apocolocyntosis,
>   XII.11–12

without much knowledge of the cause before them; for it will not easily be imagined of Langbaine, Borrichitus or Rapin, that they had very accurately perused all the books which they praise or censure; or that, even if nature and learning had qualified them for judges, they could read for ever with the attention necessary to just criticism. Such performances, however, are not wholly without their use; for they are commonly just echoes to the voice of fame, and transmit the general suffrage of mankind when they have no particular motives to suppress it.

Criticks, like all the rest of mankind, are very frequently misled by interest. The bigotry with which editors regard the authors whom they illustrate or correct, has been generally remarked. Dryden was known to have written most of his critical dissertations only to recommend the work upon which he then happened to be employed; and Addison is suspected to have denied the expediency of poetical justice, because his own Cato was condemned to perish in a good cause.[19]

There are prejudices which authors, not otherwise weak or corrupt, have indulged without scruple; and perhaps some of them are so complicated with our natural affections, that they cannot easily be disintangled from the heart. Scarce any can hear with impartiality a comparison between the writers of his own and another country; and though it cannot, I think, be charged equally on all nations, that they are blinded with this literary patriotism, yet there are none that do not look upon their authors with the fondness of affinity, and esteem them as well for the place of their birth, as for their knowledge or their wit. There is, therefore, seldom much respect due to comparative criticsm, when the competitors are of different countries, unless the judge is of a nation equally indifferent to both. The Italians could not for a long time believe, that there was any learning beyond the mountains; and the French seem generally persuaded, that there are no wits or reasoners equal to their own. I can scarcely conceive that if Scaliger had not considered himself allied to Virgil, by being born in the same country, he would have found his works so much superior to those of Homer, or have thought the controversy worthy of so much zeal, vehemence, and acrimony.

There is, indeed, one prejudice, and only one, by which it may be doubted whether it is any dishonour to be sometimes misguided. Criticism has so often given occasion to the envious and ill-natured of gratifying their malignity, that some have thought it necessary to recommend the virtue of candour without restriction, and to preclude all future liberty of censure. Writers possessed with this opinion are continually enforcing civility and decency, recommending to criticks the proper diffidence of themselves, and inculcating the veneration due to celebrated names.

I am not of opinion that these professed enemies of arrogance and severity, have much more benevolence or modesty than the rest of mankind; or that they feel in their own hearts, any other intention than to distinguish themselves by their softness and delicacy. Some are modest because they are timorous, and some are lavish of praise because they hope to be repaid.

There is indeed some tenderness due to living writers, when they attack none of those truths which are of importance of the happiness of mankind, and have committed no other offence than that of betraying their own ignorance or dulncss. I should think it cruelty to crush an insect who had provoked me only by buzzing in my ear; and would not willingly interrupt the dream of harmless stupidity, or destroy the jest which makes its author laugh. Yet I am far from thinking this tenderness universally necessary; for he that writes may be considered as a kind of general challenger, whom every one has a right to attack; since he quits the common rank of life, steps forward beyond the lists, and offers his merit to the publick judgment. To commence author is to claim praise, and no man can justly aspire to honour, but at the hazard of disgrace.

But whatever be decided concerning contemporaries, whom he that knows the treachery of the human heart, and considers how often we gratify our own pride or envy under the appearance of contending for elegance and propriety, will find himself not much inclined to disturb; there can surely be no exemptions pleaded to secure them from criticism, who can no longer suffer by reproach, and of whom nothing now remains but their writings and their names. Upon these authors the critick is, undoubtedly, at full liberty to exercise the strictest severity, since he endangers only his own fame, and, like Æneas when he drew his sword in the infernal regions, encounters phantoms which cannot be wounded. He may indeed pay some regard to established reputation; but he can by that shew of reverence consult only his own security, for all other motives are now at an end.

The faults of a writer of acknowledged excellence are more dangerous, because the influence of his example is more extensive; and the interest of learning requires that they should be discovered and stigmatized, before they have the sanction of antiquity conferred upon them, and become precedents of indisputable authority.

It has, indeed, been advanced by Addison, as one of the characteristicks of a true critick, that he points out beauties rather than faults.[20] But it is rather natural to a man of learning and genius, to apply himself chiefly to the study of writers who have more beauties than faults to be displayed: for the duty of criticism is neither to depreciate, nor dignify by partial representations, but to hold out the light of reason, whatever it may discover; and to promulgate the determinations of truth, whatever she shall dictate.

Number 106

Saturday, March 23, 1751

Opinionum commenta delet dies, naturae judicia confirmat.
Cicero, *De Natura Deorum*, II.2.5

Time obliterates the fictions of opinion, and confirms the decisions of nature.

It is necessary to the success of flattery, that it be accommodated to particular circumstances or characters, and enter the heart on that side where the passions stand ready to receive it. A lady seldom listens with attention to any praise but that of her beauty; a merchant always expects to hear of his influence at the bank, his importance on the exchange, the height of his credit, and the extent of his traffick: and the author will scarcely be pleased without lamentations of the neglect of learning, the conspiracies against genius, and the slow progress of merit, or some praises of the magnanimity of those who encounter poverty and contempt in the cause of knowledge, and trust for the reward of their labours to the judgment and gratitude of posterity.

An assurance of unfading laurels, and immortal reputation, is the settled reciprocation of civility between amicable writers. To raise "monuments more durable than brass, and more conspicuous than pyramids,"[21] has been long the common boast of literature; but among the innumerable architects that erect columns to themselves, far the greater part, either for want of durable materials, or of art to dispose them, see their edifices perish as they are towering to completion, and those few that for a while attract the eye of mankind, are generally weak in the foundation, and soon sink by the saps of time.

No place affords a more striking conviction of the vanity of human hopes, than a publick library; for who can see the wall crouded on every side by mighty volumes, the works of laborious meditation, and accurate enquiry, now scarcely known but by the catalogue,[22] and preserved only to encrease the pomp of learning, without considering how many hours have been wasted in vain endeavours, how often imagination has anticipated the praises of futurity, how many statues have risen to the eye of vanity, how many ideal converts have elevated zeal, how often wit has exulted in the eternal infamy of his antagonists, and dogmatism has delighted in the gradual advances of his authority, the immutability of his decrees, and the perpetuity of his power?

> *Non unquam dedit*
> *Documenta fors majora, quàm[n] fragili loco*
> *Starent superbi.*
>   Seneca, *Troades*, II. 4–6

Insulting chance ne'er call'd with louder voice,
On swelling mortals to be proud no more.

Of the innumerable authors whose performances are thus treasured up in magnificent obscurity, most are forgotten, because they never deserved to be remembered, and owed the honours which they once obtained, not to judgment or to genius, to labour or to art, but to the prejudice of faction, the stratagem of intrigue, or the servility of adulation.

Nothing is more common than to find men whose works are now totally neglected, mentioned with praises by their contemporaries, as the oracles of their age, and the legislators of science. Curiosity is naturally excited, their volumes after long enquiry are found, but seldom reward the labour of the search. Every period of time has produced these bubbles of artificial fame, which are kept up a while by the breath of fashion, and then break at once and are annihilated. The learned often bewail the loss of ancient writers whose characters have survived their works; but, perhaps, if we could now retrieve them, we should find them only the Granvilles, Montagues, Stepneys, and Sheffields of their time, and wonder by what infatuation or caprice they could be raised to notice.

It cannot, however, be denied, that many have sunk into oblivion, whom it were unjust to number with this despicable class. Various kinds of literary fame seem destined to various measures of duration. Some spread into exuberance with a very speedy growth, but soon wither and decay; some rise more slowly, but last long. Parnassus has its flowers of transient fragrance, as well as its oaks of towering height, and its laurels of eternal verdure.

Among those whose reputation is exhausted in a short time by its own luxuriance, are the writers who take advantage of present incidents or characters which strongly interest the passions, and engage universal attention.[23] It is not difficult to obtain readers, when we discuss a question which every one is desirous to understand, which is debated in every assembly, and has divided the nation into parties; or when we display the faults or virtues of

him whose public conduct has made almost every man his enemy or his friend.
To the quick circulation of such productions all the motives of interest and
vanity concur; the disputant enlarges his knowledge, the zealot animates his
passion, and every man is desirous to inform himself concerning affairs so
vehemently agitated and variously represented.

It is scarcely to be imagined, through how many subordinations of
interest, the ardour of party is diffused; and what multitudes fancy themselves
affected by every satire or panegyrick on a man of eminence. Whoever has, at
any time, taken occasion to mention him with praise or blame, whoever
happens to love or hate any of his adherents, as he wishes to confirm his
opinion, and to strengthen his party, will diligently peruse every paper from
which he can hope for sentiments like his own. An object, however small in
itself, if placed near to the eye, will engross all the rays of light; and a
transaction, however trivial, swells into importance, when it presses immediately on our attention. He that shall peruse the political pamphlets of any past
reign, will wonder why they were so eagerly read, or so loudly praised. Many
of the performances which had power to inflame factions, and fill a kingdom
with confusion, have now very little effect upon a frigid critick, and the time is
coming, when the compositions of later hirelings shall lie equally despised. In
proportion, as those who write on temporary subjects, are exalted above their
merit at first, they are afterwards depressed below it; nor can the brightest
elegance of diction, or most artful subtilty of reasoning, hope for much esteem
from those whose regard is no longer quickened by curiosity or pride.

It is, indeed, the fate of controvertists, even when they contend for
philosophical or theological truth, to be soon laid aside and slighted. Either the
question is decided, and there is no more place for doubt and opposition; or
mankind despair of understanding it, and grow weary of disturbance, content
themselves with quiet ignorance, and refuse to be harrassed with labours
which they have no hopes of recompensing with knowledge.

The authors of new discoveries may surely expect to be reckoned among
those, whose writings are secure of veneration: yet it often happens that the
general reception of a doctrine obscures the books in which it was delivered.
When any tenet is generally received and adopted as an incontrovertible
principle, we seldom look back to the arguments upon which it was first
established, or can bear that tediousness of deduction, and multiplicity of
evidence, by which its author was forced to reconcile it to prejudice, and fortify
it in the weakness of novelty against obstinacy and envy.

It is well known how much of our philosophy is derived from Boyle's
discovery of the qualities of the air; yet of those who now adopt or enlarge his
theory, very few have read the detail of his experiments. His name is, indeed,
reverenced; but his works are neglected; we are contented to know, that he
conquered his opponents, without enquiring what cavils were produced
against him, or by what proofs they were confuted.

Some writers apply themselves to studies boundless and inexhaustible, as
experiments and natural philosophy. These are always lost in successive
compilations, as new advances are made, and former observations become

more familiar. Others spend their lives in remarks on language, or explanations of antiquities, and only afford materials for lexicographers and commentators, who are themselves overwhelmed by subsequent collectors, that equally destroy the memory of their predecessors by amplification, transposition, or contraction. Every new system of nature gives birth to a swarm of expositors, whose business is to explain and illustrate it, and who can hope to exist no longer than the founder of their sect preserves his reputation.

There are, indeed, few kinds of composition from which an author, however learned or ingenious, can hope a long continuance of fame. He who has carefully studied human nature, and can well describe it, may with most reason flatter his ambition. Bacon, among all his pretensions to the regard of posterity, seems to have pleased himself chiefly with his essays, "which come home to mens business and bosoms," and of which, therefore, he declares his expectation, that they "will live as long as books last."[24] It may, however, satisfy an honest and benevolent mind to have been useful, though less conspicuous; nor will he that extends his hope to higher rewards, be so much anxious to obtain praise, as to discharge the duty which Providence assigns him.

Number 121

Tuesday, May 14, 1751

O imitatores, servum pecus!
Horace, *Epistles*, I.19.19

Away, ye imitators, servile herd!
Elphinston

I have been informed by a letter, from one of the universities, that among the youth from whom the next swarm of reasoners is to learn philosophy, and the next flight of beauties to hear elegies and sonnets, there are many, who, instead of endeavouring by books and meditation to form their own opinions, content themselves with the secondary knowledge, which a convenient bench in a coffee-house can supply; and, without any examination or distinction, adopt the criticisms and remarks, which happen to drop from those, who have risen, by merit or fortune, to reputation and authority.

These humble retailers of knowledge my correspondent stigmatizes with the name of Echoes; and seems desirous, that they should be made ashamed of lazy submission, and animated to attempts after new discoveries, and original sentiments.

It is very natural for young men to be vehement, acrimonious, and severe. For, as they seldom comprehend at once all the consequences of a position, or perceive the difficulties by which cooler and more experienced reasoners are restrained from confidence, they form their conclusions with great precipitance. Seeing nothing that can darken or embarrass the question, they expect to find their own opinion universally prevalent, and are inclined to impute uncertainty and hesitation to want of honesty, rather than of knowledge. I may, perhaps, therefore be reproached by my lively correspondent, when it shall be found, that I have no inclination to persecute these collectors of fortuitous knowledge with the severity required; yet, as I am now too old to be much pained by hasty censure, I shall not be afraid of taking into protection those whom I think condemned without a sufficient knowledge of their cause.

He that adopts the sentiments of another, whom he has reason to believe wiser than himself, is only to be blamed, when he claims the honours which are not due but to the author, and endeavours to deceive the world into praise and veneration; for, to learn, is the proper business of youth; and whether we encrease our knowledge by books, or by conversation, we are equally indebted to foreign assistance.

The greater part of students are not born with abilities to construct systems, or advance knowledge; nor can have any hope beyond that of becoming intelligent hearers in the schools of art, of being able to comprehend what others discover, and to remember what others teach. Even those to whom Providence has allotted greater strength of understanding, can expect only to improve a single science. In every other part of learning, they must be content to follow opinions, which they are not able to examine; and, even in that which they claim as peculiarly their own, can seldom add more than some small particle of knowledge, to the hereditary stock devolved to them from ancient times, the collective labour of a thousand intellects.

In science, which being fixed and limited, admits of no other variety than such as arises from new methods of distribution, or new arts of illustration, the necessity of following the traces of our predecessors is indisputably evident; but there appears no reason, why imagination should be subject to the same restraint.[25] It might be conceived, that of those who profess to forsake the narrow paths of truth every one may deviate towards a different point, since though rectitude is uniform and fixed, obliquity may be infinitely diversified. The roads of science are narrow, so that they who travel them, must either follow or meet one another; but in the boundless regions of possibility, which fiction claims for her dominion, there are surely a thousand recesses unexplored, a thousand flowers unplucked, a thousand fountains unexhausted, combinations of imagery yet unobserved, and races of ideal inhabitants not hitherto described.[26]

Yet, whatever hope may persuade, or reason evince, experience can boast of very few additions to ancient fable. The wars of Troy, and the travels of Ulysses, have furnished almost all succeeding poets with incidents, characters, and sentiments.[27] The Romans are confessed to have attempted little more than to display in their own tongue the inventions of the Greeks. There is, in all their writings, such a perpetual recurrence of allusions to the tales of the fabulous age, that they must be confessed often to want that power of giving pleasure which novelty supplies; nor can we wonder, that they excelled so much in the graces of diction, when we consider how rarely they were employed in search of new thoughts.

The warmest admirers of the great Mantuan poet can extol him for little more than the skill with which he has, by making his hero both a traveller and a warrior, united the beauties of the Iliad and Odyssey in one composition: yet his judgment was perhaps sometimes overborn by his avarice of the Homeric treasures; and, for fear of suffering a sparkling ornament to be lost, he has inserted it where it cannot shine with its original splendor.

When Ulysses visited the infernal regions, he found, among the heroes that perished at Troy, his competitor Ajax, who, when the arms of Achilles were adjudged to Ulysses, died by his own hand in the madness of disappointment. He still appeared to resent, as on earth, his loss and disgrace. Ulysses endeavoured to pacify him with praises and submission; but Ajax walked away without reply. This passage has always been considered as eminently beautiful; because Ajax, the haughty chief, the unlettered soldier, of unshaken courage, of immoveable constancy, but without the power of recommending his own virtues by eloquence, or enforcing his assertions by any other argument than the sword, had no way of making his anger known, but by gloomy sullenness, and dumb ferocity. His hatred of a man whom he conceived to have defeated him only by volubility of tongue, was therefore naturally shewn by silence more contemptuous and piercing than any words that so rude an orator could have found, and by which he gave his enemy no opportunity of exerting the only power in which he was superior.

When Æneas is sent by Virgil to the shades, he meets Dido the queen of Carthage, whom his perfidy had hurried to the grave; he accosts her with tenderness and excuses; but the lady turns away like Ajax in mute disdain. She turns away like Ajax, but she resembles him in none of those qualities which give either dignity or propriety to silence. She might, without any departure from the tenour of her conduct, have burst out like other injured women into clamour, reproach, and denunciation; but Virgil had his imagination full of Ajax, and therefore could not prevail on himself to teach Dido any other mode of resentment.

If Virgil could be thus seduced by imitation, there will be little hope, that common wits should escape; and accordingly we find, that besides the universal and acknowledged practice of copying the ancients, there has prevailed in every age a particular species of fiction. At one time all truth was conveyed in allegory; at another, nothing was seen but in a vision; at one period, all the poets followed sheep, and every event produced a pastoral; at another they busied themselves wholly in giving directions to a painter.

It is indeed easy to conceive why any fashion should become popular, by which idleness is favoured, and imbecility assisted; but surely no man of genius can much applaud himself for repeating a tale with which the audience is already tired, and which could bring no honour to any but its inventor.

There are, I think, two schemes of writing, on which the laborious wits of the present time employ their faculties. One is the adaptation of sense to all the rhymes which our language can supply to some word, that makes the burden of the stanza; but this, as it has been only used in a kind of amorous burlesque, can scarcely be censured with much acrimony. The other is the imitation of

Spenser, which, by the influence of some men of learning and genius, seems likely to gain upon the age, and therefore deserves to be more attentively considered.

To imitate the fictions and sentiments of Spenser can incur no reproach, for allegory is perhaps one of the most pleasing vehicles of instruction. But I am very far from extending the same respect to his diction or his stanza. His stile was in his own time allowed to be vicious, so darkened with old words and peculiarities of phrase, and so remote from common use, that Johnson [Ben Jonson] boldly pronounces him "to have written no language."[28] His stanza is at once difficult and unpleasing; tiresome to the ear by its uniformity, and to the attention by its length. It was at first formed in imitation of the Italian poets, without due regard to the genius of our language. The Italians have little variety of termination, and were forced to contrive such a stanza as might admit the greatest number of similar rhymes; but our words end with so much diversity, that it is seldom convenient for us to bring more than two of the same sound together. If it be justly observed by Milton,[29] that rhyme obliges poets to express their thoughts in improper terms, these improprieties must always be multiplied, as the difficulty of rhyme is encreased by long concatenations.

The imitators of Spenser are indeed not very rigid censors of themselves, for they seem to conclude, that when they have disfigured their lines with a few obsolete syllables, they have accomplished their design, without considering that they ought not only to admit old words,[30] but to avoid new. The laws of imitation are broken by every word introduced since the time of Spenser, as the character of Hector is violated by quoting Aristotle in the play.[31] It would indeed by difficult to exclude from a long poem all modern phrases, though it is easy to sprinkle it with gleanings of antiquity. Perhaps, however, the stile of Spenser might by long labour be justly copied; but life is surely given us for higher purposes than to gather what our ancestors have wisely thrown away, and to learn what is of no value, but because it has been forgotten.

Number 176

Saturday, Nov. 23, 1751

Naso suspendere adunco.
Horace, *Satires*, I.65

On me you turn the nose—

There are many vexatious accidents and uneasy situations which raise little compassion for the sufferer, and which no man but those whom they immediately distress, can regard with seriousness. Petty mischiefs, that have no influence on futurity, nor extend their effects to the res of life, are always seen with a kind of malicious pleasure. A mistake or embarrasment, which for the present moment fills the face with blushes, and the mind with confusion, will have no other effect upon those who observe it than that of convulsing them with irresistible laughter. Some circumstances of misery are so powerfully ridiculous, that neither kindness nor duty can withstand them; they bear down love, interest, and reverence, and force the friend, the dependent, or the child, to give way to instantaneous motions of merriment.

Among the principal of comick calamities, may be reckoned the pain which an author, not yet hardened into insensibility, feels at the onset of a furious critick, whose age, rank or fortune gives him confidence to speak without reserve; who heaps one objection upon another, and obtrudes his remarks, and enforces his corrections without tenderness or awe.

The author, full of the importance of his work, and anxious for the justification of every syllable, starts and kindles at the slightest attack; the critick, eager to establish his superiority, triumphing in every discovery of failure, and zealous to impress the cogency of his arguments, pursues him from line to line without cessation or remorse. The critick, who hazards little, proceeds with vehemence, impetuosity and fearlessness; the author, whose quiet and fame, and life and immortality are involved in the controversy, tries every art of subterfuge and defence; maintains modestly what he resolves never to yield, and yields unwillingly what cannot be maintained. The critick's purpose is to conquer, the author only hopes to escape; the critick therefore knits his brow, and raises his voice, and rejoices whenever he perceives any tokens of pain excited by the pressure of his assertions, or the point of his sarcasms. The author, whose endeavour is at once to mollify and elude his persecutor, composes his features, and softens his accent, breaks the force of assault by retreat, and rather steps aside than flies or advances.

As it very seldom happens that the rage of extemporary criticism inflicts fatal or lasting wounds, I know not that the laws of benevolence entitle this distress to much sympathy. The diversion of baiting an author has the sanction of all ages and nations, and is more lawful than the sport of teizing other animals, because for the most part he comes voluntarily to the stake, furnished, as he imagines, by the patron powers of literature, with resistless weapons, and impenetrable armour, with the mail of the boar of Erymanth, and the paws of the lion of *Nemea*.[32]

But the works of genius are sometimes produced by other motives than vanity; and he whom necessity or duty enforces to write, is not always so well satisfied with himself, as not to be discouraged by censorious imprudence. It may therefore be necessary to consider how they whom publication lays open to the insults of such as their obscurity secures against reprisals, may extricate themselves from unexpected encounters.

Vida, a man of considerable skill in the politicks of literature, directs his pupil wholly to abandon his defence, and even when he can irrefragably refute all objections, to suffer tamely the exultations of his antagonist.[33]

This rule may perhaps be just, when advice is asked, and severity solicited, because no man tells his opinion so freely as when he imagines it received with implicit veneration; and critics ought never to be consulted but while errors may yet be rectified or insipidity suppressed. But when the book has once been dismissed into the world, and can be no more retouched, I know not whether a very different conduct should be prescribed, and whether firmness and spirit may not sometimes be of use to overpower arrogance and repel brutality. Softness, dissidence and moderation will often be mistaken for imbecility and dejection; they lure cowardice to the attack by the hopes of easy victory, and it will soon be found that he whom every man thinks he can conquer, shall never be at peace.

The animadversions of criticks are commonly such as may easily provoke the sedatest writer to some quickness of resentment and asperity of reply. A man who by long consideration has familiarised a subject to his own mind, carefully surveyed the series of his thoughts, and planned all the parts of his composition into a regular dependance on each other, will often start at the sinistrous interpretations, or absurd remarks of haste and ignorance, and wonder by what infatuation they have been led away from the obvious sense, and upon what peculiar principles of judgment they decide against him.

The eye of the intellect, like that of the body, is not equally perfect in all, nor equally adapted in any to all objects; the end of criticism is to supply its defects; rules are the instruments of mental vision, which may indeed assist our faculties when properly used, but produce confusion and obscurity by unskilful application.

Some seem always to read with the microscope of criticism, and employ their whole attention upon minute elegance, or faults scarcely visible to common observation. The dissonance of a syllable, the recurrence of the same sound, the repetition of a particle, the smallest deviation from propriety, the slightest defect in construction or arrangement, swell before their eyes into enormities. As they discern with great exactness, they comprehend but a narrow compass, and know nothing of the justness of the design, the general spirit of the performance, the artifice of connection, or the harmony of the parts; they never conceive how small a proportion that which they are busy in contemplating bears to the whole, or how the petty inaccuracies with which they are offended, are absorbed and lost in general excellence.

Others are furnished by criticsm with a telescope. They see with great clearness whatever is too remote to be discovered by the rest of mankind, but are totally blind to all that lies immediately before them. They discover in every passage some secret meaning, some remote allusion, some artful allegory, or some occult imitation which no other reader ever suspected; but they have no perception of the cogency of arguments, the force of pathetick sentiments, the various colours of diction, or the flowery embellishments of fancy; of all that engages the attention of others, they are totally insensible, while they pry into worlds of conjecture, and amuse themselves with phantoms in the clouds.

In criticism, as in every other art, we fail sometimes by our weakness, but more frequently by our fault. We are sometimes bewildered by ignorance, and sometimes by prejudice, but we seldom deviate far from the right, but when we deliver ourselves up to the direction of vanity.

NOTES

1. This paper was occasioned by the popularity of Smollett's *Roderick Random* (1748) and Fielding's *Tom Jones* (1749).

2. Cf. *Preface to Shakespeare*, par. 13 (" . . . as the writers of barbarous romances invigorated the reader by a giant and a dwarf"). For Johnson's attraction to romances, see the account told Boswell by Bishop Percy (*Life*, I.49). Cf. *Life*, IV.17.

3. Scaliger's *Poetics*, VI.4.

4. *Epistles*, II.1.70.

5. Pliny, *Natural History*, XXXV.36.85.

6. Juvenal, XIV.

7. Swift-Pope *Miscellanies* (1727), II.354.

8. Suetonius, *Lives*, "Caligula," 30.1.

9. *Epistles*, III.1.

10. *Historiarum Sui Temporis* (1733). VII, pt. IV, p. 3, n. (col.2), printing the commentary of Nicolaus Rigaltius. A few days before his death, Johnson told John Nichols he "seriously entertained the thought of translating Thuanus" (*Life*, IV.410).

11. *De Coniuratione Catilinae*, XV.5.

12. Joachim Camerarius (1500–1574), *Vita Melanchthonis* (1777), p. 62.

13. Sir William Temple, "Essay on the Cure of Gout," *Works* (1770), III.244.

14. Preface, Addison,*Works* (1721), I.xvi.

15. Honorat de Bueil, Marquis de Racan, "Mémoirs pour la vie de Malherbe," *Oeuvres Complètes* (1857), I.258–59, 265.

16. Gilbert Burnet, *Life and Death of Sir Matthew Hale* (1805), p. 39.

17. *Jugemens des Scavans* (1685–86), I. Pt. 2, chs. 1–14.

18. See Hill's note in "Congreve," *Lives*, II.217, n. 4. SJ is probably thinking of Congreve's lines, in the Epilogue to *The Way of the World:* "And sure he must have more than mortal skill/ Who pleases anyone against his will." Or (as Miss Mary Lascelles suggests to us) was he perhaps recalling Dryden's words, in the Preface to *Absalom and Achitophel*, " . . . no man can be heartily angry with him, who pleases him against his will"?

19. *Spectator* 40, Cf. "Addison," *Lives*, II.134–35 (pars. 140–41).

20. *Spectator* 291.

21. Horace, *Odes*, III.30.

22. Cf. *Rambler* 2 (pars. 13–15).

23. Cf. SJ on Butler's *Hudibras*, *Idler* 59 (par. 7), and *Lives*, I.213f. (pars. 41–2).

24. Dedication to the *Essays*.

25. Cf. *Ramblers* 23 (par. 6) and 125 (par. 2).

26. Cf. *Ramblers* 124 (par. 9), 129 (final par.), and the close of *Adventurer* 95.

27. Cf. on Homer, *Preface to Shakespeare* (par. 3).

28. *Timber, or Discoveries*, ed. F. E. Schelling (1892), p. 57.

29. Preface to *Paradise Lost*.

30. Cf. "Gay" and "Collins," *Lives*, II.269 (par. 4); III.341 (par. 17), and on Thomas Warton, *Life*, III.158–59.

31. *Troilus and Cressida*, II.2.166.

32. These formidable creatures were destroyed by Hercules.

33. Cf. M. Hieronymus Vida *Ars poetica* 3. 469–72.

THE ADVENTURER

Number 95

Tuesday, 2 October 1753

Dulcique animos novitate tenebo.
Ovid, Metamorphoses, IV.284

And with sweet novelty your soul detain.

It is often charged upon writers, that with all their pretensions to genius and discoveries, they do little more than copy one another; and that compositions obtruded upon the world with the pomp of novelty, contain only tedious repetitions of common sentiments, or at best exhibit a transposition of known images, and give a new appearance to truth only by some slight difference of dress and decoration.

The allegation of resemblance between authors is indisputably true; but the charge of plagiarism, which is raised upon it, is not to be allowed with equal readiness.[1] A coincidence of sentiment may easily happen without any communication, since there are many occasions in which all reasonable men will nearly think alike. Writers of all ages have had the same sentiments, because they have in all ages had the same objects of speculation; the interests and passions, the virtues and vices of mankind, have been diversified in different times, only by unessential and casual varieties; and we must, therefore, expect in the works of all those who attempt to describe them, such a likeness as we find in the pictures of the same person drawn in different periods of his life.

It is necessary, therefore, that before an author be charged with plagiarism, one of the most reproachful, though, perhaps, not the most atrocious of literary crimes, the subject on which he treats should be carefully considered. We do not wonder, that historians, relating the same facts, agree in their narration; or that authors delivering the elements of science, advance the same theorems, and lay down the same definitions: yet it is not wholly without use to mankind, that books are multiplied, and that different authors lay out their labours on the same subject; for there will always be some reason why one should on particular occasions, or to particular persons, be preferable to another; some will be clear where others are obscure, some will please by their stile and others by their method, some by their embellishments and others by their simplicity, some by closeness and others by diffusion.

The same indulgence is to be shewn to the writers of morality: right and wrong are immutable; and those, therefore, who teach us to distinguish them, if they all teach us right, must agree with one another. The relations of social life, and the duties resulting from them, must be the same at all times and in all nations: some petty differences may be, indeed, produced, by forms of government or arbitrary customs; but the general doctrine can receive no alteration.

Yet it is not to be desired, that morality should be considered as interdicted to all future writers: men will always be tempted to deviate from their duty, and will, therefore, always want a monitor to recall them; and a new book often seizes the attention of the public, without any other claim than that it is new. There is likewise in composition, as in other things, a perpetual vicissitude of fashion; and truth is recommended at one time to regard, by appearances which at another would expose it to neglect: the author, therefore, who has judgement to discern the taste of his contemporaries, and skill to gratify it, will have always an opportunity to deserve well of mankind, by conveying instruction to them in a grateful vehicle.

There are likewise many modes of composition, by which a moralist may deserve the name of an original writer: he may familiarise his system by dialogues after the manner of the ancients, or subtilize it into a series of syllogistic arguments; he may enforce his doctrine by seriousness and solemnity, or enliven it by sprightliness and gayety; he may deliver his sentiments in naked precepts, or illustrate them by historical examples; he may detain the studious by the artful concatenation of a continued discourse, or relieve the busy by short strictures and unconnected essays.

To excel in any of these forms of writing, will require a particular cultivation of the genius; whoever can attain to excellence, will be certain to engage a set of readers, whom no other method would have equally allured; and he that communicates truth with success, must be numbered among the first benefactors to mankind.

The same observation may be extended likewise to the passions: their influence is uniform, and their effects nearly the same in every human breast:[2] a man loves and hates, desires and avoids, exactly like his neighbour; resentment and ambition, avarice and indolence, discover themselves by the same symptoms, in minds distant a thousand years from one another.

Nothing, therefore, can be more unjust, than to charge an author with plagiarism, merely because he assigns to every cause its natural effect; and makes his personages act, as others in like circumstances have always done. There are conceptions in which all men will agree, though each derives them from his own observation: whoever has been in love, will represent a lover impatient of every idea that interrupts his meditations on his mistress, retiring to shades and solitude that he may muse without disturbance on his approaching happiness, or associating himself with some friend that flatters his passion, and talking away the hours of absence upon his darling subject. Whoever has been so unhappy as to have felt the miseries of long continued hatred, will, without any assistance from antient volumes, be able to relate how the passions are kept in perpetual agitation, by the recollection of injury and meditations of revenge; how the blood boils at the name of the enemy, and life is worn away in contrivances of mischief.

Every other passion is alike simple and limited, if it be considered only with regard to the breast which it inhabits: the anatomy of the mind, as that of the body, must perpetually exhibit the same appearances; and though by the continued industry of successive inquirers, new movements will be from time to time discovered, they can affect only the minuter parts and are commonly of more curiosity than importance.

It will now be natural to inquire, by what arts are the writers of the present and future ages to attract the notice and favour of mankind. They are to observe the alterations which time is always making in the modes of life, that they may gratify every generation with a picture of themselves. Thus love is uniform, but courtship is perpetually varying; the different arts of gallantry, which beauty has inspired, would of themselves be sufficient to fill a volume; sometimes balls and serenades, sometimes tournaments and adventures have been employed to melt the hearts of ladies, who in another century have been sensible of scarce any other merit than that of riches, and listened only to jointures and pin money. Thus the ambitious man has at all times been eager of wealth and power; but these hopes have been gratified in some countries by supplicating the people, and in others by flattering the prince: honour in some states has been only the reward of military atchievements, in others it has been gained by noisy turbulence and popular clamours. Avarice has worn a different form, as she actuated the usurer of Rome, and the stock jobber of England; and idleness itself, how little soever inclined to the trouble of invention, has been forced from time to time to change its amusements, and contrive different methods of wearing out the day.

Here then is the fund, from which those who study mankind may fill their compositions with an inexhaustible variety of images and allusions; and he must be confessed to look with little attention upon scenes thus perpetually changing, who cannot catch some of the figures before they are made vulgar by reiterated descriptions.

It has been discovered by Sir Isaac Newton,[3] that the distinct and primogenial colours are only seven; but every eye can witness, that from various mixtures in various proportions, infinite diversifications of tints may be produced. In like manner, the passions of the mind, which put the world in motion, and produce all the bustle and eagerness of the busy crouds that swarm upon the earth; the passions, from whence arise all the pleasures and pains that we see and hear of, if we analize the mind of man, are very few; but those few agitated and combined, as external causes shall happen to operate, and modified by prevailing opinions and accidental caprices, make such frequent alterations on the surface of life, that the show while we are busied in delineating it, vanishes from the view, and a new set of objects succeeds, doomed to the same shortness of duration with the former: thus curiosity may always find employment, and the busy part of mankind will furnish the contemplative with the materials of speculation to the end of time.

The complaint, therefore, that all topics are preoccupied, is nothing more than the murmur of ignorance or idleness, by which some discourage others and some themselves: the mutability of mankind will always furnish writers with new images, and the luxuriance of fancy may always embellish them with new decorations.

NOTES

1. Cf. *Rambler* 143 (pars. 1–3).

2. Cf. *Rambler* 36 (last par.): "Poetry has to do rather with the passions of men, which are uniform, than their customs, which are changeable."

3. First stated by Newton in *Philosophical Transactions*, No. 80 (1672), p. 3082: "There are . . . two sorts of colours . . . The original or primary colours are, Red, Yellow, Green, Blew, and a Violet-purple, together with Orange, Indico, and an indefinite variety of intermediate gradations"; and later in *Opticks* (1704), Bk. I, pt. ii: prop. 2, theor. 2, p. 88; prop. 3, exper. 7, p. 92; *et passim*. Johnson used "primogenial" for "primigenial"; but in his *Dictionary* he noted that the word should have been written "primigenial."

THE IDLER

Number 44

Saturday, February 17, 1759

Memory is, among the faculties of the human mind, that of which we make the most frequent use, or rather that of which the agency is incessant or perpetual. Memory is the primary and fundamental power, without which there could be no other intellecutal operation. Judgment and ratiocination suppose something already known, and draw their decisions only from experience. Imagination selects ideas from the treasures of remembrance, and produces novelty only by varied combinations. We do not even form conjectures of distant, or anticipations of future events, but by concluding what is possible from what is past.

The two offices of memory are collection and distribution; by one images are accumulated, and by the other produced for use. Collection is always the employment of our first years, and distribution commonly that of our advanced age.

To collect and reposite the various forms of things, is far the most pleasing part of mental occupation. We are naturally delighted with novelty, and there is a time when all that we see is new. When first we enter into the world, withersoever we turn our eyes, they meet knowledge with pleasure at her side; each diversity of nature pours ideas in upon the soul; neither search nor labour are necessary; we have nothing more to do than to open our eyes, and curiosity is gratified.

Much of the pleasure which the first survey of the world affords, is exhausted before we are conscious of our own felicity, or able to compare our condition with some other possible state. We have therefore few traces of the joy of our earliest discoveries; yet we all remember a time when nature had so many untasted gratifications, that every excursion gave delight which can now be found no longer, when the noise of a torrent, the rustle of a wood, the song of the birds, or the play of lambs, had power to fill the attention, and suspend all perception of the course of time.

But these easy pleasures are soon at an end; we have seen in a very little time so much, that we call out for new objects of observation, and endeavour to find variety in books and life. But study is laborious, and not always satisfactory; and conversation has its pains as well as pleasures; we are willing to learn, but not willing to be taught; we are pained by ignorance, but pained yet more by another's knowledge.

From the vexation of pupillage men commonly set themselves free about the middle of life, by shutting up the avenues of intelligence, and resolving to rest in their present state; and they, whose ardour of enquiry continues longer, find themselves insensibly forsaken by their instructors. As every man advances in life, the proportion between those that are younger, and that are older than himself, is continually changing; and he that has lived half a century, finds few that do not require from him that information which he once expected from those that went before him.

Then it is that the magazines of memory are opened, and the stores of accumulated knowledge are displayed by vanity or benevolence, or in honest commerce of mutual interest. Every man wants others, and is therefore glad when he is wanted by them. And as few men will endure the labour of intense meditation without necessity, he that has learned enough for his profit or his honour, seldom endeavours after further acquisitions.

The pleasure of recollecting speculative notions would not be much less than that of gaining them, if they could be kept pure and unmingled with the passage of life; but such is the necessary concatenation of our thoughts, that good and evil are linked together, and no pleasure recurs but associated with pain. Every revived idea reminds us of a time when something was enjoyed that is now lost, when some hope was yet not blasted, when some purpose had yet not languished into sluggishness or indifference.

Whether it be that life has more vexations than comforts, or, what is in the event just the same, that evil makes deeper impression than good, it is certain that few can review the time past without heaviness of heart. He remembers many calamities incurred by folly, many opportunities lost by negligence. The shades of the dead rise up before him, and he laments the companions of his youth, the partners of his amusements, the assistants of his labours, whom the hand of death has snatched away.

When an offer was made to Themistocles of teaching him the art of memory, he answered, that he would rather wish for the art of forgetfulness.[1] He felt his imagination haunted by phantoms of misery which he was unable to suppress, and would gladly have calmed his thoughts with some "oblivious antidote."[2] In this we all resemble one another; the hero and the sage are, like vulgar mortals, overburthened by the weight of life, all shrink from recollection, and all wish for an art of forgetfulness.

Number 59

Saturday, June 2, 1759

In the common enjoyments of life, we cannot very liberally indulge the present hour, but by anticipating part of the pleasure which might have relieved the tediousness of another day; and any uncommon exertion of strength, or preservance in labour, is succeeded by a long interval of languor and weariness. Whatever advantage we snatch beyond the certain portion allotted us by nature, is like money spent before it is due, which at the time of regular payment will be missed and regretted.

Fame, like all other things which are supposed to give or to encrease happiness, is dispensed with the same equality of distribution. He that is loudly praised will be clamorously censured; he that rises hastily into fame will be in danger of sinking suddenly into oblivion.

Of many writers who filled their age with wonder, and whose names we find celebrated in the books of their cotemporaries, the works are now no longer to be seen, or are seen only amidst the lumber of libraries which are seldom visited, where they lie only to shew the deceitfulness of hope, and the uncertainty of honour.

Of the decline of reputation many causes may be assigned. It is commonly lost because it never was deserved, and was conferred at first, not by the suffrage of criticism, but by the fondness of friendship, or servility of flattery. The great and popular are very freely applauded, but all soon grow weary of echoing to each other a name which has no other claim to notice, but that many mouths are pronouncing it at once.

But many have lost the final reward of their labours, because they were too hasty to enjoy it. They have laid hold on recent occurrences, and eminent names, and delighted their readers with allusions and remarks, in which all were interested, and to which all therefore were attentive. But the effect ceased with its cause; the time quickly came when new events drove the former from memory, when the vicissitudes of the world brought new hopes and fears, transferred the love and hatred of the public to other agents, and the writer whose works were no longer assisted by gratitude or resentment, was left to the cold regard of idle curiosity.

He that writes upon general principles, or delivers universal truths, may hope to be often read, because his work will be equally useful at all times and in every country, but he cannot expect it to be received with eagerness, or to spread with rapidity, because desire can have no particular stimulation; that which is to be loved long must be loved with reason rather than with passion. He that lays out his labours upon temporary subjects, easily finds readers, and quickly loses them; for what should make the book valued when its subject is no more.

These observations will shew the reason why the poem of *Hudibras* is almost forgotten however embellished with sentiments and diversified with allusions, however bright with wit, and however solid with truth. The hypocrisy which it detected, and the folly which it ridiculed, have long vanished from public notice.[3] Those who had felt the mischiefs of discord, and the tyranny of usurpation, read it with rapture, for every line brought back to memory something known, and gratified resentment, by the just censure of something hated. But the book which was once quoted by princes, and which supplied conversation to all the assemblies of the gay and witty, is now seldom mentioned, and even by those that affect to mention it, is seldom read. So vainly is wit lavished upon fugitive topics, so little can architecture secure duration when the ground is false.

Number 60

Saturday, June 9, 1759

Criticism is a study by which men grow important and formidable at very small expence. The power of invention has been conferred by nature upon few, and the labour of learning those sciences which may, by mere labour, be obtained, is too great to be willingly endured; but every man can exert such judgment as he has upon the works of others; and he whom nature has made weak, and idleness keeps ignorant, may yet support his vanity by the name of a critick.

I hope it will give comfort to great numbers who are' passing thro' the world in obscurity, when I inform them how easily distinction may be obtained. All the other powers of literature are coy and haughty, they must be long courted, and at last are not always gained; but criticism is a goddess easy of access and forward of advance, who will meet the slow and encourage the timerous; the want of meaning she supplies with words, and the want of spirit she recompenses with malignity.

This profession has one recommendation peculiar to itself, that it gives vent to malignity without real mischief. No genius was every blasted by the breath of criticks.[4] The poison which, if confined, would have burst the heart, fumes away in empty hisses, and malice is set at ease with very little danger to merit. The critick is the only man whose triumph is without another's pain, and whose greatness does not rise upon another's ruin.

To a study at once so easy and so reputable, so malicious and so harmless, it cannot be necessary to invite my readers by a long or laboured exhortation; it is sufficient, since all would be criticks if they could, to shew by one eminent example that all can be criticks if they will.

Dick Minim,[5] after the common course of puerile studies, in which he was no great proficient, was put apprentice to a brewer, with whom he had lived two years, when his uncle died in the city, and left him a large fortune in the stocks. Dick had for six months before used the company of the lower players, of whom he had learned to scorn a trade, and being now at liberty to follow his genius, he resolved to be a man of wit and humour. That he might be properly initiated in his new character, he frequented the coffee-houses near the theatres, where he listened very diligently day, after day, to those who talked of language and sentiments, and unities and catastrophes, till by slow degrees he began to think that he understood something of the stage, and hoped in time to talk himself.

But he did not trust so much to natural sagacity, as wholly to neglect the help of books. When the theatres were shut, he retired to Richmond with a few select writers, whose opinions he impressed upon his memory by unwearied diligence; and when he return with other wits to the town, was able to tell, in very proper phrases, that the chief business of art is to copy nature; that a perfect writer is not to be expected, because genius decays as judgment increases; that the great art is the art of blotting,[6] and that according to the rule of Horace every piece should be kept nine years.[7]

Of the great authors he now began to display the characters, laying down as an universal position that all had beauties and defects. His opinion was, that Shakespear, committing himself wholly to the impulse of nature, wanted that correctness which learning would have given him; and that Johnson [Ben Jonson], trusting to learning, did not sufficiently cast his eye on nature. He blamed the stanza of Spenser, and could not bear the hexameters of Sidney. Denham and Waller he held the first reformers of English numbers, and thought that if Waller could have obtained the strength of Denham, or Denham the sweetness of Waller, there had been nothing wanting to complete a poet.[8] He often expressed his commiseration of Dryden's poverty, and his indignation at the age which suffered him to write for bread; he repeated with rapture the first lines of *All for Love,* but wondered at the corruption of taste which could bear any thing so unnatural as rhyming tragedies. In Otway he found uncommon powers of moving the passions, but was disgusted by his general negligence, and blamed him for making a conspirator his hero; and never concluded his disquisition, without remarking how happily the sound of the clock is made to alarm the audience. Southern would have been his favourite, but that he mixes comick with tragick scenes, intercepts the natural course of the passions, and fills the mind with a wild confusion of mirth and melancholy. The versification of Rowe he thought too melodious for the stage, and too little varied in different passions. He made it the great fault of Congreve, that all his persons were wits, and that he always wrote with more art than nature.[9] He considered *Cato* rather as a poem than a play, and allowed Addison to be the complete master of allegory and grave humour, but paid no great deference to him as a critick. He thought the chief merit of Prior was in his easy tales and lighter poems, tho' he allowed that his *Solomon* had many noble sentiments elegantly expressed. In Swift he discovered an inimitable vein of irony, and an easiness which all would hope and few would attain. Pope he was inclined to degrade from a poet to a versifier, and thought his numbers rather luscious than sweet. He often lamented the neglect of *Phaedra and Hippolitus,*[10] and wished to see the stage under better regulations.

These assertions passed commonly uncontradicted; and if now and then an opponent started up, he was quickly repressed by the suffrages of the company, and Minim went away from every dispute with elation of heart and increase of confidence.

He now grew conscious of his abilities, and began to talk of the present state of dramatick poetry; wondered what was become of the comick genius which supplied our ancestors with wit and pleasantry, and why no writer could be found that durst now venture beyond a farce. He saw no reason for thinking that the vein of humour was exhausted, since we live in a country where liberty suffers every character to spread itself to its utmost bulk, and which therefore produces more originals than all the rest of the world together. Of tragedy he concluded business to be the soul, and yet often hinted that love predominates too much upon the modern stage.

He was now an acknowledged critick, and had his own seat in the coffee-house, and headed a party in the pit. Minim has more vanity than ill-nature, and seldom desires to do much mischief; he will perhaps murmur a little in the ear of him that sits next him, but endeavours to influence the audience to favour, by clapping when an actor exclaims "ye Gods," or laments the misery of his country.

By degrees he was admitted to rehearsals, and many of his friends are of opinion, that our present poets are indebted to him for their happiest thoughts; by his contrivance the bell was rung twice in *Barbarossa*,[11] and by his persuasion the author of *Cleone*[12] concluded his play without a couplet; for what can be more absurd, said Minim, than that part of a play should be rhymed, and part written in blank verse? and by what acquisition of faculties is the speaker who never could find rhymes before, enabled to rhyme at the conclusion of an act!

He is the great investigator of hidden beauties, and is particularly delighted when he finds "the sound an echo to the sense."[13] He has read all our poets with particular attention to this delicacy of versification, and wonders at the supineness with which their works have been hitherto perused, so that no man has found the sound of a drum in this distich,

> When pulpit, drum ecclesiastic,
> Was beat with fist instead of a stick;[14]

and that the wonderful lines upon honour and a bubble have hitherto passed without notice.

> Honour is like the glassy bubble,
> Which costs philosophers such trouble,
> Where one part crack'd, the whole does fly,
> And wits are crack'd to find out why.[15]

In these verses, says Minim, we have two striking accommodations of the sound to the sense. It is impossible to utter the two lines emphatically without an act like that which they describe; "bubble" and "trouble" causing a momentary inflation of the cheeks by the retention of the breath, which is afterwards forcibly emitted, as in the practice of "blowing bubbles." But the greatest excellence is in the third line, which is "crack'd" in the middle to express a crack, and then shivers into monosyllables. Yet has this diamond lain neglected with common stones, and among the innumerable admirers of *Hudibras* the observation of this superlative passage has been reserved for the sagacity of Minim.

Number 61

Saturday, June 16, 1759

Mr. Minim had now advanced himself to the zenith of critical reputation; when he was in the pit, every eye in the boxes was fixed upon him, when he entered his coffeehouse, he was surrounded by circles of candidates, who passed their noviciate of literature under his tuition; his opinion was asked by all who had no opinion of their own, and yet loved to debate and decide; and no composition was supposed to pass in safety to posterity, till it had been secured by Minim's approbation.

Minim professes great admiration of the wisdom and munificence by which the academies of the continent were raised, and often wishes for some standard of taste, for some tribunal, to which merit may appeal from caprice, prejudice, and malignity.[16] He has formed a plan for an academy of criticism, where every work of imagination may be read before it is printed, and which shall authoritatively direct the theatres what pieces to receive or reject, to exclude or to revive.

Such an institution would, in Dick's opinion, spread the fame of English literature over Europe, and make London the metropolis of elegance and politeness, the place to which the learned and ingenious of all countries would repair for instruction and improvement, and where nothing would any longer be applauded or endured that was not conformed to the nicest rules, and finished with the highest elegance.

Till some happy conjunction of the planets shall dispose our princes or ministers to make themselves immortal by such an academy, Minim contents himself to preside four nights in a week in a critical society elected by himself, where he is heard without contradiction, and whence his judgment is disseminated through the great vulgar and the small.[17]

When he is placed in the chair of criticism, he declares loudly for the noble simplicity of our ancestors, in opposition to the petty refinements, and ornamental luxuriance. Sometimes he is sunk in despair, and perceives false delicacy daily gaining ground, and sometimes brightens his countenance with a gleam of hope, and predicts the revival of the true sublime. He then fulminates his loudest censures against the monkish barbarity of rhyme;[18] wonders how beings that pretend to reason can be pleased with one line always ending like another; tells how unjustly and unnaturally sense is sacrificed to sound; how often the best thoughts are mangled by the necessity of confining or extending them to the dimensions of a couplet; and rejoices that genius has, in our days, shaken off the shackles which had encumbered it so long. Yet he allows that rhyme may sometimes be borne, if the lines be often broken, and the pauses judiciously diversified.

From blank verse he makes an easy transition to Milton, whom he produces as an example of the slow advance of lasting reputation. Milton is the only writer whose books Minim can read for ever without weariness. What cause it is that exempts this pleasure from satiety he has long and diligently enquired, and believes it to consist in the perpetual variation of the numbers, by which the ear is gratified and the attention awakened. The lines that are commonly thought rugged and unmusical, he conceives to have been written to temper the melodious luxury of the rest, or to express things by a proper cadence: for he scarcely finds a verse that has not this favourite beauty; he declares that he could shiver in a hothouse when he reads that

> the ground
> Burns frore, and cold performs th' effect of fire.[19]

And that when Milton bewails his blindness, the verse

So thick a drop serene has quench'd these orbs,[20]

has, he knows not how, something that strikes him with an obscure sensation like that which he fancies would be felt from the sound of darkness.

Minim is not so confident of his rules of judgment as not very eagerly to catch new light from the name of the author. He is commonly so prudent as to spare those whom he cannot resist, unless, as will sometimes happen, he finds the publick combined against them. But a fresh pretender to fame he is strongly inclined to censure, 'till his own honour requires that he commend him. 'Till he knows the success of a composition, he intrenches himself in general terms; there are some new thoughts and beautiful passages, but there is likewise much which he would have advised the author to expunge. He has several favourite epithets, of which he has never settled the meaning, but which are very commodiously applied to books which he has not read, or cannot understand. One is "manly," another is "dry," another "stiff," and another "flimzy"; sometimes he discovers delicacy of style, and sometimes meets with "strange expressions."

He is never so great, or so happy, as when a youth of promising parts is brought to receive his directions for the prosecution of his studies. He then puts on a very serious air; he advises the pupil to read none but the best authors, and, when he finds one congenial to his own mind, to study his beauties, but avoid his faults, and, when he sits down to write, to consider how his favourite author would think[21] at the present time on the present occasion. He exhorts him to catch those moments when he finds his thoughts expanded and his genius exalted, but to take care lest imagination hurry him beyond the bounds of nature. He holds diligence the mother of success, yet enjoins him, with great earnestness, not to read more than he can digest, and not to confuse his mind by pursuing studies of contrary tendencies. He tells him, that every man has his genius,[22] and that Cicero could never be a poet. The boy retires illuminated, resolves to follow his genius, and to think how Milton would have thought; and Minim feasts upon his own beneficence till another day brings another pupil.

Number 65

Saturday, July 14, 1759

The sequel of Clarendon's history,[23] at last happily published, in an accession to English literature equally agreeable to the admirers of elegance and the lovers of truth; many doubtful facts may now be ascertained, and many questions, after long debate, may be determined by decisive authority. He that records transactions in which himself was engaged, has not only an opportunity of knowing innumerable particulars which escape spectators, but has his natural powers exalted by that ardour which always rises at the remembrance of our own importance, and by which every man is enabled to relate his own actions better than another's.

The difficulties thro' which this work has struggled into light, and the delays with which our hopes have been long mocked, naturally lead the mind to the consideration of the common fate of posthumous compositions.

He who sees himself surrounded by admirers, and whose vanity is hourly feasted with all the luxuries of studied praise, is easily persuaded that his influence will be extended beyond his life; that they who cringe in his presence will reverence his memory, and that those who are proud to be numbered among his friends, will endeavour to vindicate his choice by zeal for his reputation.

With hopes like these, to the executors of Swift was committed the history of the last years of Queen Anne,[24] and to those of Pope the works which remained unprinted in his closet. The performances of Pope were burnt by those whom he had perhaps selected from all mankind as most likely to publish them;[25] and the history had likewise perished, had not a straggling transcript fallen into busy hands.

The papers left in the closet of Peiresc supplied his heirs with a whole winter's fuel,[26] and many of the labours of the learned Bishop Lloyd were consumed in the kitchen of his descendants.[27]

Some works, indeed, have escaped total destruction, but yet have had reason to lament the fate of orphans exposed to the frauds of unfaithful guardians. How Hale would have borne the mutilations which his *Pleas of the Crown* have suffered from the editor,[28] they who know his character will easily conceive.

The original copy of Burnet's history, tho' promised to some publick[29] library, has been never given; and who then can prove the fidelity of the publication, when the authenticity of Clarendon's history, tho' printed with the sanction of one of the first universities of the world, had not an unexpected manuscript been happily discovered, would, with the help of factious credulity, have been brought into question by the two lowest of all human beings,[30] a scribbler for a party, and a commissioner of excise?

Vanity is often no less mischievous than negligence or dishonesty. He that possesses a valuable manuscript, hopes to raise its esteem by concealment, and delights in the distinction which he imagines himself to obtain by keeping the key of a treasure which he neither uses nor imparts. From him it falls to some other owner, less vain but more negligent, who considers it as useless lumber, and rids himself of the incumbrance.

Yet there are some works which the authors must consign unpublished to posterity, however uncertain be the event, however hopeless be the trust. He that writes the history of his own times, if he adheres steadily to truth, will write that which his own times will not easily endure. He must be content to reposite his book till all private passions shall cease, and love and hatred give way to curiosity.

But many leave the labour of half their life to their executors and to chance, because they will not send them abroad unfinished, and are unable to finish them, having prescribed to themselves such a degree of exactness as human diligence scarcely can attain. "Lloyd," says Burnet, "did not lay out his learning with the same diligence as he laid it in."[31] He was always hesitating and enquiring, raising objections and removing them, and waiting for clearer light and fuller discovery. Baker, after many years past in biography, left his manuscripts to be buried in a library, because that was imperfect which could never be perfected.[32]

Of these learned men let those who aspire to the same praise, imitate the diligence and avoid the scrupulosity. Let it be always remembered that life is short, that knowledge is endless, and that many doubts deserve not to be cleared. Let those whom nature and study have qualified to teach mankind, tell us what they have learned while they are yet able to tell it, and trust their reputation only to themselves. No complaint is more frequently repeated among the learned, than that of the waste made by time among the labours of antiquity. Of those who once filled the civilized world with their renown nothing is now left but their names, which are left only to raise desires that never can be satisfied, and sorrow which never can be comforted.

Had all the writings of the ancients been faithfully delivered down from age to age, had the Alexandrian library been spared, and the Palatine repositories remained unimpaired, how much might we have known of which we are now doomed to be ignorant; how many laborious enquiries, and dark conjectures, how many collations of broken hints and mutilated passages might have been spared. We should have known the successions of princes, the revolutions of empire, the actions of the great, and opinions of the wise, the laws and constitutions of every state, and the arts by which public grandeur and happiness are acquired and preserved. We should have traced the progress of life, seen colonies from distant regions take possession of European deserts, and troops of savages settled into communities by the desire of keeping what they had acquired; we should have traced the gradations of civility, and travelled upward to the original of things by the light of history, till in remoter times it had glimmered in fable, and at last sunk into darkness.

If the works of imagination had been less diminished, it is likely that all future times might have been supplied with inexhaustible amusement by the fictions of antiquity. The tragedies of Sophocles and Euripides would have shewn all the stronger passions in all their diversities, and the comedies of Menander would have furnished all the maxims of domestic life. Nothing would have been necessary to moral wisdom but to have studied these great masters, whose knowledge would have guided doubt, and whose authority would have silenced cavils.

Such are the thoughts that rise in every student, when his curiosity is eluded, and his searches are frustrated; yet it may perhaps be doubted, whether our complaints are not sometimes inconsiderate, and whether we do not imagine more evil than we feel. Of the ancients, enough remains to excite our emulation, and direct our endeavours. Many of the works which time has left us, we know to have been those that were most esteemed, and which antiquity itself considered as models; so that having the originals, we may without much regret lose the imitations. The obscurity which the want of contemporary writers often produces, only darkens single passages, and those commonly of slight importance. The general tendency of every piece may be known, and tho' that diligence deserves praise which leaves nothing unexamined, yet its miscarriages are not much to be lamented; for the most useful truths are always universal, and unconnected with accidents and customs.

Such is the general conspiracy of human nature against contemporary merit; that if we had inherited from antiquity enough to afford employment for the laborious, and amusement for the idle, I know not what room would have been left for modern genius or modern industry; almost every subject would have been preoccupied, and every style would have been fixed by a precedent from which few would have ventured to depart. Every writer would have had a rival, whose superiority was already acknowledged, and to whose fame his work would, even before it was seen, be marked out for a sacrifice.

We see how little the united experience of mankind have been able to add to the heroic characters displayed by Homer, and how few incidents the fertile imagination of modern Italy has yet produced, which may not be found in the Iliad and Odyssey.[33] It is likely, that if all the works of the Athenian philosophers had been extant, Malbranche and Locke would have been condemned to be silent readers of the ancient metaphysicians; and it is apparent, that if the old writers had all remained, the Idler could not have written a disquisition on the loss.

Number 94

Saturday, February 2, 1760

It is common to find young men ardent and diligent in the pursuit of knowledge, but the progress of life very often produces laxity and indifference; and not only those who are at liberty to chuse their business and amusements, but those likewise whose professions engaged them in literary enquiries pass the latter part of their time without improvement, and spend the day rather in any other entertainment than that which they might find among their books.

This abatement of the vigour of curiosity is sometimes imputed to the insufficiency of learning. Men are supposed to remit their labours, because they find their labours to have been vain; and to search no longer after truth and wisdom, because they at last despair of finding them.

But this reason is for the most part very falsely assigned. Of learning, as of virtue, it may be affirmed, that it is at once honoured and neglected.[34] Whoever forsakes it will for ever look after it with longing, lament the loss which he does not endeavour to repair, and desire the good which he wants resolution to seize and keep. The idler never applauds his own idleness, nor does any man repent of the diligence of his youth.

So many hindrances may obstruct the aquisition of knowledge, that there is little reason for wondering that it is in a few hands. To the greater part of mankind the duties of life are inconsistent with much study, and the hours which they would spend upon letters must be stolen from their occupations and their families. Many suffer themselves to be lured by more spritely and luxurious pleasures from the shades of contemplation, where they find seldom more than a calm delight, such as, though greater than all others, if its certainty and its duration be reckoned with its power of gratification, is yet easily quitted for some extemporary joy, which the present moment offers, and another perhaps will put out of reach.

It is the great excellence of learning that it borrows very little from time or place; it is not confined to season or to climate, to cities or to the country, but may be cultivated and enjoyed where no other pleasure can be obtained. But this quality, which constitutes much of its value, is one occasion of neglect; what may be done at all times with equal propriety, is deferred from day to day, till the mind is gradually reconciled to the omission, and the attention is turned to other objects. Thus habitual idleness gains too much power to be conquered, and the soul shrinks from the idea of intellectual labour and intenseness of meditation.

That those who profess to advance learning sometimes obstruct it, cannot be denied; the continual multiplication of books not only distracts choice but disappoints enquiry. To him that has moderately stored his mind with images, few writers afford any novelty; or what little they had to add to the common stock of learning is so buried in the mass of general notions, that, like silver mingled with the oar of lead, it is too little to pay for the labour of separation; and he that has often been deceived by the promise of a title, at last grows weary of examining, and is tempted to consider all as equally fallacious.

There are indeed some repetitions always lawful, because they never deceive. He that writes the history of past times, undertakes only to decorate known facts by new beauties of method or of style, or at most to illustrate them by his own reflections. The author of a system, whether moral or physical, is obliged to nothing beyond care of selection and regularity of disposition. But there are others who claim the name of authors merely to disgrace it, and fill the world with volumes only to bury letters in their own rubbish. The traveller who tells, in a pompous folio, that he saw the Pantheon at Rome, and the Medicean Venus at Florence; the natural historian who, describing the productions of a narrow island, recounts all that it has in common with every other part of the world; the collector of antiquities, that accounts every thing a curiosity which the ruins of Herculaneum happen to emit, though an instrument already shewn in a thousand repositories, or a cup common to the ancients, the moderns, and all mankind, may be justly censured as the persecutors of students, and the thieves of that time which never can be restored.

Number 103

Saturday, April 5, 1760

Respicere ad longae jussit spatia ultima vitae.
Juvenal, x.275

Much of the pain and pleasure of mankind arises from the conjectures which every one makes of the thoughts of others; we all enjoy praise which we do not hear, and resent contempt which we do not see. The Idler may therefore be forgiven, if he suffers his imagination to represent to him what his readers will say or think when they are informed that they have now his last paper in their hands.

Value is more frequently raised by scarcity than by use. That which lay neglected when it was common, rises in estimation as its quantity becomes less. We seldom learn the true want of what we have till it is discovered that we can have no more.

This essay will, perhaps, be read with care even by those who have not yet attended to any other; and he that finds this late attention recompensed, will not forbear to wish that he had bestowed it sooner.

Though the Idler and his readers have contracted no close friendship they are perhaps both unwilling to part. There are few things not purely evil, of which we can say, without some emotion of uneasiness, "this is the last." Those who never could agree together, shed tears when mutual discontent has determined them to final separation; of a place which has been frequently visited, tho' without pleasure, the last look is taken with heaviness of heart; and the Idler, with all his chilness of tranquility, is not wholly unaffected by the thought that his last essay is now before him.

This secret horrour of the last is inseparable from a thinking being whose life is limited, and to whom death is dreadful.[35] We always make a secret comparison between a part and the whole; the termination of any period of life reminds us that life itself has likewise its termination; when we have done any thing for the last time, we involuntarily reflect that a part of the days allotted us is past, and that as more is past there is less remaining.

It is very happily and kindly provided, that in every life there are certain pauses and interruptions, which force consideration upon the careless, and seriousness upon the light; points of time where one course of action ends and another begins; and by vicissitude of fortune, or alteration of employment, by change of place, or loss of friendship, we are forced to say of something, "this is the last."

An even and unvaried tenour of life always hides from our apprehension the approach of its end. Succession is not perceived but by variation; he that lives to-day as he lived yesterday, and expects that, as the present day is, such will be the morrow, easily conceives time as running in a circle and returning to itself. The uncertainty of our duration is impressed commonly by dissimilitude of condition; it is only by finding life changeable that we are reminded of its shortness.

This conviction, however forcible at every new impression, is every moment fading from the mind; and partly by the inevitable incursion of new images, and partly by voluntary exclusion of unwelcome thoughts, we are again exposed to the universal fallacy; and we must do another thing for the last time, before we consider that the time is nigh when we shall do no more.

As the last *Idler* is published in that solemn week[36] which the Christian world has always set apart for the examination of the conscience, the review of life, the extinction of earthly desires and the renovation of holy purposes, I hope that my readers are already disposed to view every incident with seriousness, and improve it by meditation; and that when they see this series of trifles brought to a conclusion, they will consider that by outliving the *Idler*, they have past weeks, months, and years which are now no longer in their power; that an end must in time be put to every thing great as to every thing little; that to life must come its last hour, and to this system of being its last day, the hour at which probation ceases, and repentance will be vain; the day in which every work of the hand, and imagination of the heart shall be brought to judgment, and an everlasting futurity shall be determined by the past.

NOTES

1. Simonides made the offer. Cicero, *De finibus* II.32.104.
2. *Macbeth*, v.3.43. Johnson cites the passage in the Dictionary ("oblivious").
3. Cf. "Butler," *Lives*, I.213–14 (pars. 41–42); *Life*, II.369–70.
4. For similar remarks, see *Life*, II.61–62, n. 4.
5. From *minimus*—i.e. the least or smallest particle in size, value, or both. But this portrait is by no means wholly unfavorable.
6. Johnson is here echoing clichés from Alexander Pope's *Essay on Criticism* (ll. 68, 253–54, 56–57) and *Imitations of Horace* (II.1.281). Cf. *Rambler* 23 (par. 6).
7. *Ars poetica* l.388.
8. Johnson, as Hill notes, echoes consecutively here Pope's *Imitations of Horace* (II.1.279), Collins' *Epistle to Hanmer* (l.55), Pope's *Imitations of Horace* (II.1.98), Dryden's *Preface to the Fables* (par. 11), and Pope's *Essay on Criticism* (l.361); in the remarks on Otway immediately below, *Imitations of Horace* (II.1.278) and *Spectator* 39. The remark on the Spenserian stanza echoes Johnson's own opinion (*Rambler* 121, par. 14).
9. Minim expresses Johnson's own sentiments. Cf. "Congreve," *Lives*, II.218–19, 228 (pars. 16 and 33).
10. *Phaedra and Hippolytus*, by Edmund Smith (1707). Cf. Johnson's discussion of it in "Smith," *Lives*, II.16 (par. 49), and Addison's belief that the play was undeservedly neglected (*Spectator* 18).
11. *Barbarossa*, by Dr. John Brown (1754). Cf. Johnson's criticism that "the use of a bell is unknown to the Mahometans" (*Life*, II.131, n. 2).
12. By Robert Dodsley (1758). Cf. Johnson's remark that in it "there is more blood than brains" (*Life*, IV.20).
13. Pope, *Essay on Criticism*, l.365, the implications of which Johnson discusses in detail in *Ramblers* 92 and 94, and "Pope," *Lives*, III.230–32 (pars. 330–34).

14. *Hudibras,* I.1.11–12.

15. Ibid., II.2.385–88.

16. For Johnson's antagonism to the idea of an English academy, see "Roscommon," *Lives,* I.232–33 (pars. 13–18).

17. Johnson echoes the opening of Cowley's translation of Horace's *Odes,* III.1.

18. Minim echoes Milton's Preface to *Paradise Lost* and Edmund Smith on the "constraint of monkish rhyme" ("To the Memory of Mr. John Philips," 1.68).

19. *Paradise Lost,* II.594–95.

20. Ibid., III.25.

21. Johnson echoes Longinus, trans. William Smith (1739), pp. 38f.

22. Cf. Johnson's frequent statements to the contrary (e.g. *Rambler* 25, above, n.5)

23. *The Life of Edward, Earl of Clarendon . . . Being a Continuation of the History of the Grand Rebellion* (1759). The editor is still unknown.

24. Recounted in the Advertisement written by Charles Lucas to Swift's *History of the Four Last Years of the Queen's Reign* (1758). Cf. "Swift," *Lives,* II.27–28 (par. 65).

25. Cf. "Pope," *Lives,* III.192 (par. 249).

26. Johnson apparently refers to the account of Gilles Ménage: "On me disoit . . . que la sottise d'une nièce de M. de Peiresc nous avoit fait perdre un très-grand nombre de ces lettres: elle en avoit un cabinet plein, et les brûloit pour allumer son feu" (*Ménagiana,* 1693, par. 1, in *Ana, ou Collection de bons mots,* ed. B. de la Monnoye, 1799, II.2). They were letters to Peiresc; according to Pierre Gassendi, Peiresc's own manuscripts were carefully catalogued and bound, partly with the help of his brother and his nephew (*Mirrour of True Nobility . . . the Life of . . . Peiresk,* 1657, pp. 294–95). See also Johnson's life of Browne (par. 42).

27. A. T. Hart (*William Lloyd,* 1952, p. 146) cites Johnson himself, who may have heard it at Lichfield, as the authority for the story. Isaac Disraeli (*Miscellanies,* 1840, I.80) also apparently relied directly on Johnson.

28. See Gilbert Burnet, *Life and Death of Sir Matthew Hale* (1682) p. 186, on Hale's unwillingness to have his unpublished works printed after his death for fear they be changed. The mutilations of the first edition of the *Pleas of the Crown* (1678) are described in a preface to the 5th edition (1716). A correspondent in the *Gentleman's Magazine,* June 1760, comments on these publications.

29. "It would be proper to reposite, in some publick place, the manuscript of Clarendon, which has not escaped all suspicion of unfaithful publication" (Johnson's note, added in 1761).

30. John Oldmixon (1673–1742) and George Duckett (d. 1732). For details see "Smith," *Lives,* II.18–20 (pars. 57–71).

31. *History of His Own Time* (1840), I.130.

32. Thomas Baker (1656–1740), who intended to write an *Athenae Cantabrigienses* similar to Anthony Wood's work relating to Oxford. Of the forty-two folio volumes, twenty-three ended in the Harleian collection, and the rest in the university library at Cambridge. Other papers went to St. John's College. For a description see *Biographia Britannica,* 2nd ed. (1778), I.521–25 n.

33. Cf. *Preface to Shakespeare,* par 3.

34. Juvenal, Satire I.74, "Virtue is praised but neglected."

35. "The whole of life is but keeping away the thoughts of it" (*Life,* II. 93); cf. III.153, 188, 294–95. Boswell referred specifically to this number of the *Idler* in his journal, 3 October 1762 (*London Journal,* de luxe ed., 1951, pp. 67–68).

36. On Holy Saturday.

THE DICTIONARY

PREFACE

It is the fate of those who toil at the lower employments of life, to be rather driven by the fear of evil, than attracted by the prospect of good; to be exposed to censure, without hope of praise; to be disgraced by miscarriage, or punished for neglect, where success would have been without applause, and diligence without reward.

Among these unhappy mortals is the writer of dictionaries; whom mankind have considered, not as the pupil, but the slave of science, the pionier of literature, doomed only to remove rubbish and clear obstructions from the paths through which Learning and Genius press forward to conquest and glory, without bestowing a smile on the humble drudge that facilitates their progress. Every other authour may aspire to praise; the lexicographer can only hope to escape reproach, and even this negative recompense has been yet granted to very few.

I have, notwithstanding this discouragement, attempted a dictionary of the English language, which, while it was employed in the cultivation of every species of literature, has itself been hitherto neglected; suffered to spread, under the direction of chance, into wild exuberance; resigned to the tyranny of time and fashion; and exposed to the corruptions of ignorance, and caprices of innovation.

When I took the first survey of my undertaking, I found our speech copious without order, and energetick without rules: wherever I turned by view, there was perplexity to be disentangled, and confusion to be regulated; choice was to be made out of boundless variety, without any established principle of selection; adulterations were to be detected, without a settled test of purity; and modes of expression to be rejected or received, without the suffrages of any writers of classical reputation or acknowledged authority.

Having therefore no assistance but from general grammar, I applied myself to the perusal of our writers; and noting whatever might be of use to ascertain or illustrate any word or phrase, accumulated in time the materials of a dictionary, which, by degrees, I reduced to method, establishing to myself, in the progress of the work, such rules as experience and analogy suggested to me; experience, which practice and observation were continually increasing; and analogy, which, though in some words obscure, was evident in others.

In adjusting the Orthography, which has been to this time unsettled and fortuitous, I found it necessary to distinguish those irregularities that are inherent in our tongue, and perhaps coeval with it, from others which the ignorance or negligence of later writers has produced. Every language has its anomalies, which, though inconvenient, and in themselves once unnecessary, must be tolerated among the imperfections of human things, and which

445

require only to be registered, that they may not be increased, and ascertained, that they may not be confounded: but every language has likewise its improprieties and absurdities, which it is the duty of the lexicographer to correct or proscribe.

As language was at its beginning merely oral, all words of necessary or common use were spoken before they were written; and while they were unfixed by any visible signs, must have been spoken with great diversity, as we now observe those who cannot read catch sounds imperfectly, and utter them negligently. When this wild and barbarous jargon was first reduced to an alphabet, every penman endeavoured to express, as he could, the sounds which he was accustomed to pronounce or to receive, and vitiated in writing such words as were already vitiated in speech. The powers of the letters, when they were applied to a new language, must have been vague and unsettled, and therefore different hands would exhibit the same sound by different combinations.

From this uncertain pronunciation arise in a great part the various dialects of the same country, which will always be observed to grow fewer, and less different, as books are multiplied; and from this arbitrary representation of sounds by letters, proceeds that diversity of spelling observable in the Saxon remains, and I suppose in the first books of every nation, which perplexes or destroys analogy, and produces anomalous formations, that, being once incorporated, can never be afterward dismissed or reformed.

Of this kind are the derivatives *length* from *long, strength* from *strong, darling* from *dear, breadth* from *broad,* from *dry, drought,* and from *high, height,* which Milton, in zeal for analogy, writes *highth; Quid te exempta juvat spinis de pluribus una* [What does it avail to pluck out from many errors merely one?];[1] to change all would be too much, and to change one is nothing.

This uncertainty is most frequent in the vowels, which are so capriciously pronounced, and so differently modified, by accident or affectation, not only in every province, but in every mouth, that to them, as is well known to etymologists, little regard is to be shewn in the deduction of one language from another.

Such defects are not errours in orthography, but spots of barbarity impressed so deep in the English language, that criticism can never wash them away: these, therefore, must be permitted to remain untouched; but many words have likewise been altered by accident, or depraved by ignorance, as the pronunciation of the vulgar has been weakly followed; and some still continue to be variously written, as authours differ in their care or skill: of these it was proper to enquire the true orthography, which I have always considered as depending on their derivation, and have therefore referred them to their original languages: thus I write *enchant, enchantment, enchanter,* after the French, and *incantation* after the Latin; thus *entire* is chosen rather than *intire,* because it passed to us not from the Latin *integer,* but from the French *entier.*

Of many words it is difficult to say whether they were immediately received from the Latin or the French, since at the time when we had dominions in France, we had Latin service in our churches. It is, however, my opinion, that the French generally supplied us; for we have few Latin words, among the terms of domestick use, which are not French; but many French, which are very remote from Latin.

Even in words of which the derivation is apparent, I have been often obliged to sacrifice uniformity to custom; thus I write, in compliance with a numberless majority, *convey* and *inveigh, deceit* and *receipt, fancy* and *phantom;* sometimes the derivative varies from the primitive, as *explain* and *explanation, repeat* and *repetition.*

Some combinations of letters having the same power are used indifferently without any discoverable reason of choice, as in *choak, choke; soap, sope; fewel, fuel,* and many others; which I have sometimes inserted twice, that those who search for them under either form, may not search in vain.

In examining the orthography of any doubtful word, the mode of spelling by which it is inserted in the series of the dictionary, is to be considered as that to which I give, perhaps not often rashly, the preference. I have left, in the examples, to every authour his own practice unmolested, that the reader may balance suffrages, and judge between us: but this question is not always to be determined by reputed or by real learning; some men, intent upon greater things, have thought little on sounds and derivations; some, knowing in the ancient tongues, have neglected those in which our words are commonly to be sought. Thus Hammond writes *fecibleness* for *feasibleness,* because I suppose he imagined it derived immediately from the Latin; and some words, such as *dependant, dependent; dependance, dependence,* vary their final syllable, as one or another language is present to the writer.

In this part of the work, where caprice has long wantoned without controul, and vanity sought praise by petty reformation, I have endeavoured to proceed with a scholar's reverence for antiquity, and a grammarian's regard to the genius of our tongue. I have attempted few alterations, and among those few, perhaps the greater part is from the modern to the ancient practice; and I hope I may be allowed to recommend to those, whose thoughts have been perhaps employed too anxiously on verbal singularities, not to disturb, upon narrow views, or for minute propriety, the orthography of their fathers. It has been asserted, that for the law to be known, is of more importance than to be right. Change, says Hooker, is not made without inconvenience, even from worse to better.[2] There is in constancy and stability a general and lasting advantage, which will always overbalance the slow improvements of gradual correction. Much less ought our written language to comply with the corruptions of oral utterance, or copy that which every variation of time or place makes different from itself, and imitate those changes, which will again be changed, while imitation is employed in observing them.

This recommendation of steadiness and uniformity does not proceed from an opinion, that particular combinations of letters have much influence on human happiness; or that truth may not be successfully taught by modes of spelling fanciful and erroneous: I am not yet so lost in lexicography, as to forget that words are the daughters of earth, and that things are the sons of heaven.[3]

Language is only the instrument of science, and words are but the signs of ideas: I wish, however, that the instrument might be less apt to decay, and that signs might be permanent, like the things which they denote.

In settling the orthography, I have not wholly neglected the pronunciation, which I have directed, by printing an accent upon the acute or elevated syllable. It will sometimes be found, that the accent is placed by the authour quoted, on a different syllable from that marked in the alphabetical series; it is then to be understood, that custom has varied, or that the authour has, in my opinion, pronounced wrong. Short directions are sometimes given where the sound of letters is irregular; and if they are sometimes omitted, defect in such minute observations will be more easily excused, than superfluity.

In the investigation both of the orthography and signification of words, their Etymology was necessarily to be considered, and they were therefore to be divided into primitives and derivatives. A primitive word, is that which can be traced no further to any English root; thus *circumspect, circumvent, circumstance, delude, concave,* and *complicate,* though compounds in the Latin, are to us primitives. Derivatives are all those that can be referred to any word in English of greater simplicity.

The derivatives I have referred to their primitives, with an accuracy sometimes needless; for who does not see that *remoteness* comes from *remote, lovely* from *love, concavity* from *concave,* and *demonstrative* from *demonstrate?* but this grammatical exuberance the scheme of my work did not allow me to repress. It is of great importance in examining the general fabrick of a language, to trace one word from another, by noting the usual modes of derivation and inflection; and uniformity must be preserved in systematical works, though sometimes at the expence of particular propriety.

Among other derivatives I have been careful to insert and elucidate the anomalous plurals of nouns and preterites of verbs, which in the Teutonick dialects are very frequent, and though familiar to those who have always used them, interrupt and embarrass the learners of our language.

The two languages from which our primitives have been derived are the Roman and Teutonick: under the Roman I comprehend the French and provincial tongues; and under the Teutonick range the Saxon, German, and all their kindred dialects. Most of our polysyllables are Roman, and our words of one syllable are very often Teutonick.

In assigning the Roman original, it has perhaps sometimes happened that I have mentioned only the Latin, when the word was borrowed from the French; and considering myself as employed only in the illustration of my own language, I have not been very careful to observe whether the Latin word be pure or barbarous, or the French elegant or obsolete.

For the Teutonick etymologies, I am commonly indebted to Junius and Skinner,[4] the only names which I have forborn to quote when I copied their books; not that I might appropriate their labours or usurp their honours, but that I might spare a perpetual repetition by one general acknowledgment. Of these, whom I ought not to mention but with the reverence due to instructors and benefactors, Junius appears to have excelled in extent of learning, and

Skinner in rectitude of understanding. Junius was accurately skilled in all the northern languages, Skinner probably examined the ancient and remoter dialects only by occasional inspection into dictionaries; but the learning of Junius is often of no other use than to show him a track by which he may deviate from his purpose, to which Skinner always presses forward by the shortest way. Skinner is often ignorant, but never ridiculous: Junius is always full of knowledge; but his variety distracts his judgment, and his learning is very frequently disgraced by his absurdities.

The votaries of the northern muses will not perhaps easily restrain their indignation, when they find the name of Junius thus degraded by a disadvantageous comparison; but whatever reverence is due to his diligence, or his attainments, it can be no criminal degree of censoriousness to charge that etymologist with want of judgment, who can seriously derive *dream* from *drama*, because life is a drama, and a drama is a dream; and who declares with a tone of defiance, that no man can fail to derive *moan* from μόνος, *monos*, *single* or *solitary*, who considers that grief naturally loves to be alone.[5]

Our knowledge of the northern literature is so scanty, that of words undoubtedly Teutonick the original is not always to be found in any ancient language; and I have therefore inserted Dutch or German substitutes, which I consider not as radical but parallel, not as the parents, but sisters of the English.

The words which are represented as thus related by descent or cognation, do not always agree in sense; for it is incident to words, as to their authours, to degenerate from their ancestors, and to change their manners when they change their country. It is sufficient, in etymological enquiries, if the senses of kindred words be found such as may easily pass into each other, or such as may both be referred to one general idea.

The etymology, so far as it is yet known, was easily found in the volumes where it is particularly and professedly delivered; and, by proper attention to the rules of derivation, the orthography was soon adjusted. But to collect the words of our language was a task of greater difficulty: the deficiency of dictionaries was immediately apparent; and when they were exhausted, what was yet wanting must be sought by fortuitous and unguided excursions into books, and gleaned as industry should find, or chance should offer it, in the boundless chaos of a living speech. My search, however, has been either skilful or lucky; for I have much augmented the vocabulary.

As my design was a dictionary, common or appellative, I have omitted all words which have relation to proper names; such as *Arian, Socinian, Calvinist, Benedictine, Mahometan;* but have retained those of a more general nature, as *Heathen, Pagan.*

Of the terms of art I have received such as could be found either in books of science or technical dictionaries; and have often inserted, from philosophical writers, words which are supported perhaps only by a single authority, and which being not admitted into general use, stand yet as candidates or probationers, and must depend for their adoption on the suffrage of futurity.

The words which our authours have introduced by their knowledge of foreign languages, or ignorance of their own, by vanity or wantonness, by compliance with fashion or lust of innovation, I have registered as they occurred, though commonly only to censure them, and warn others against the folly of naturalizing useless foreigners to the injury of the natives.

I have not rejected any by design, merely because they were unnecessary or exuberant; but have received those which by different writers have been differently formed, as *viscid,* and *viscidity, viscous,* and *viscosity.*

Compounded or double words I have seldom noted, except when they obtain a signification different from that which the components have in their simple state. Thus *highwayman, woodman,* and *horsecourser,* require an explanation; but of *thieflike* or *coachdriver* no notice was needed, because the primitives contain the meaning of the compounds.

Words arbitrarily formed by a constant and settled analogy, like diminutive adjectives in *ish,* as *greenish, bluish,* adverbs in *ly,* as *dully, openly,* substantives in *ness,* as *vileness, faultiness,* were less diligently sought, and sometimes have been omitted, when I had no authority that invited me to insert them; not that they are not genuine and regular offsprings of English roots, but because their relation to the primitive being always the same, their signification cannot be mistaken.

The verbal nouns in *ing,* such as the *keeping* of the *castle,* the *leading* of the *army,* are always neglected, or placed only to illustrate the sense of the verb, except when they signify things as well as actions, and have therefore a plural number, as *dwelling, living;* or have an absolute and abstract signification, as *colouring, painting, learning.*

The participles are likewise omitted, unless, by signifying rather habit or quality than action, they take the nature of adjectives; as a *thinking* man, a man of prudence; a *pacing* horse, a horse that can pace: these I have ventured to call *participial adjectives.* But neither are these always inserted, because they are commonly to be understood, without any danger of mistake, by consulting the verb.

Obsolete words are admitted, when they are found in authours not obsolete, or when they have any force or beauty that may deserve revival.

As composition is one of the chief characteristicks of a language, I have endeavoured to make some reparation for the universal negligence of my predecessors, by inserting great numbers of compounded words, as may be found under *after, fore, new, night, fair,* and many more. These, numerous as they are, might be multiplied, but that use and curiosity are here satisfied, and the frame of our language and modes of our combination amply discovered.

Of some forms of composition, such as that by which *re* is prefixed to note *repetition,* and *un* to signify *contrariety* or *privation,* all the examples cannot be accumulated, because the use of these particles, if not wholly arbitrary, is so little limited, that they are hourly affixed to new words as occasion requires, or is imagined to require them.

There is another kind of composition more frequent in our language than perhaps in any other, from which arises to foreigners the greatest difficulty. We modify the signification of many verbs by a particle subjoined; as to *come off,* to escape by a fetch; to *fall on,* to attack; to *fall off,* to apostatize; to *break off,* to stop abruptly; to *bear out,* to justify; to *fall in,* to comply; to *give over,* to cease; to *set off,* to embellish; to *set in,* to begin a continual tenour; to *set out,* to begin a course or journey; to *take off,* to copy; with innumerable expressions of the same kind of which some appear wildly irregular, being so far distant from the sense of the simple words, that no sagacity will be able to trace the steps by which they arrived at the present use. These I have noted with great care; and though I cannot flatter myself that the collection is complete, I believe I have so far assisted the students of our language, that this kind of phraseology will be no longer insuperable; and the combinations of verbs and particles, by chance omitted, will be easily explained by comparison with those that may be found.

Many words yet stand supported only by the name of Bailey, Ainsworth, Philips,[6] or the contracted *Dict.* for *Dictionaries* subjoined; of these I am not always certain that they are read in any book but the works of lexicographers. Of such I have omitted many, because I had never read them; and many I have inserted, because they may perhaps exist, though they have escaped my notice: they are, however, to be yet considered as resting only upon the credit of former dictionaries. Others, which I considered as useful, or know to be proper, though I could not at present support them by authorities, I have suffered to stand upon my own attestation, claiming the same privilege with my predecessors of being sometimes credited without proof.

The words, thus selected and disposed, are grammatically considered; they are referred to the different parts of speech; traced, when they are irregularly inflected, through their various terminations; and illustrated by observations, not indeed of great or striking importance, separately considered, but necessary to the elucidation of our language, and hitherto neglected or forgotten by English grammarians.

That part of my work on which I expect malignity most frequently to fasten, is the *Explanation;* in which I cannot hope to satisfy those, who are perhaps not inclined to be pleased, since I have not always been able to satisfy myself. To interpret a language by itself is very difficult; many words cannot be explained by synonimes, because the idea signified by them has not more than one appellation; nor by paraphrase, because simple ideas cannot be described. When the nature of things is unknown, or the notion unsettled and indefinite, and various in various minds, the words by which such notions are conveyed, or such things denoted, will be ambiguous and perplexed. And such is the fate of hapless lexicography, that not only darkness, but light, impedes and distresses it; things may be not only too little, but too much known, to be happily illustrated. To explain, requires the use of terms less abstruse than that which is to be explained, and such terms cannot always be found; for as nothing can be proved but by supposing something intuitively known, and evident without proof, so nothing can be defined but by the use of words too plain to admit a definition.

Other words there are, of which the sense is too subtle and evanescent to be fixed in a paraphrase; such are all those which are by the grammarians termed expletives, and, in dead languages, are suffered to pass for empty sounds, of no other use than to fill a verse, or to modulate a period, but which are easily perceived in living tongues to have power and emphasis, though it be sometimes such as no other form of expression can convey.

My labour has likewise been much increased by a class of verbs too frequent in the English language, of which the signification is so loose and general, the use so vague and indeterminate, and the senses detorted so widely from the first idea, that it is hard to trace them through the maze of variation, to catch them on the brink of utter inanity, to circumscribe them by any limitations, or interpret them by any words of distinct and settled meaning; such are *bear, break, come, cast, full, get, give, do, put, set, go, run, make, take, turn, throw.* If of these the whole power is not accurately delivered, it must be remembered, that while our language is yet living, and variable by the caprice of every one that speaks it, these words are hourly shifting their relations, and can no more be ascertained in a dictionary, than a grove, in the agitation of a storm, can be accurately delineated from its picture in the water.

The particles are among all nations applied with so great latitude, that they are not easily reducible under any regular scheme of explication: this difficulty is not less, nor perhaps greater, in English, than in other languages. I have laboured them with diligence, I hope with success; such at least as can be expected in a task, which no man, however, learned or sagacious, has yet been able to perform.

Some words there are which I cannot explain, because I do not understand them; these might have been omitted very often with little inconvenience, but I would not so far indulge my vanity as to decline this confession: for when Tully owns himself ignorant whether *lessus,* in the twelve tables, means a *funeral song,* or *mourning garment;* and Aristotle doubts whether οὑρεύς in the Iliad, signifies a *mule,* or *muleteer,*[7] I may surely, without shame, leave some obscurities to happier industry, or future information.

The rigour of interpretative lexicography requires that the explanation, and the word explained, should be always reciprocal; this I have always endeavoured, but could not always attain. Words are seldom exactly synonimous; a new term was not introduced, but because the former was thought inadequate: names, therefore, have often many ideas, but few ideas have many names. It was then necessary to use the proximate word, for the deficiency of single terms can very seldom be supplied by circumlocution; nor is the inconvenience great of such mutilated interpretations, because the sense may easily be collected entire from the examples.

In every word of extensive use, it was requisite to mark the progress of its meaning, and show by what gradations of intermediate sense it has passed from its primitive to its remote and accidental signification; so that every foregoing explanation should tend to that which follows, and the series be regularly concatenated from the first notion to the last.

This is specious, but not always practicable; kindred senses may be so interwoven, that the perplexity cannot be disentangled, nor any reason be assigned why one should be ranged before the other. When the radical idea branches out into parallel ramifications, how can a consecutive series be formed of senses in their nature collateral? The shades of meaning sometimes pass imperceptibly into each other; so that though on one side they apparently differ, yet it is impossible to mark the point of contact. Ideas of the same race, though not exactly alike, are sometimes so little different, that no words can express the dissimilitude, though the mind easily perceives it, when they are exhibited together; and sometimes there is such a confusion of acceptations, that discernment is wearied, and distinction puzzled, and perseverance herself hurries to an end, by crouding together what she cannot separate.

These complaints of difficulty will, by those that have never considered words beyond their popular use, be thought only the jargon of a man willing to magnify his labours, and procure veneration to his studies by involution and obscurity. But every art is obscure to those that have not learned it: this uncertainty of terms, and commixture of ideas, is well known to those who have joined philosophy with grammar; and if I have not expressed them very clearly, it must be remembered that I am speaking of that which words are insufficient to explain.

The original sense of words is often driven out of use by their metaphorical acceptations, yet must be inserted for the sake of a regular origination. Thus I know not whether *ardour* is used for *material heat,* or whether *flagrant,* in English, ever signifies the same with *burning;* yet such are the primitive ideas of these words, which are therefore set first, though without examples, that the figurative senses may be commodiously deduced.

Such is the exuberance of signification which many words have obtained, that it was scarcely possible to collect all their senses; sometimes the meaning of derivatives must be sought in the mother term, and sometimes deficient explanations of the primitive may be supplied in the train of derivation. In any case of doubt or difficulty, it will be always proper to examine all the words of the same race; for some words are slightly passed over to avoid repetition, some admitted easier and clearer explanation than others, and all will be better understood, as they are considered in greater variety of structures and relations.

All the interpretations of words are not written with the same skill, or the same happiness: things equally easy in themselves, are not all equally easy to any single mind. Every writer of a long work commits errours, where there appears neither ambiguity to mislead, nor obscurity to confound him; and in a search like this, many felicities of expression will be casually overlooked, many convenient parallels will be forgotten, and many particulars will admit improvement from a mind utterly unequal to the whole performance.

But many seeming faults are to be imputed rather to the nature of the undertaking, than the negligence of the performer. Thus some explanations are unavoidably reciprocal or circular, as *hind, the female of the stag; stag, the male of the hind:* sometimes easier words are changed into harder, as *burial* into *sepulture* or *interment, drier* into *desiccative, dryness* into *siccity* or *aridity, fit* into *paroxysm;* for the easiest word, whatever it be, can never be translated into one more easy. But easiness and difficulty are merely relative, and if the present prevalence of our language should invite foreigners to this dictionary, many will be assisted by those words which now seem only to increase or produce obscurity. For this reason I have endeavoured frequently to join a Teutonick and Roman interpretation, as to cheer, to gladden, or exhilarate, that every learner of English may be assisted by his own tongue.

The solution of all difficulties, and the supply of all defects, must be sought in the examples, subjoined to the various senses of each word, and ranged according to the time of their authours.

When first I collected these authorities, I was desirous that every quotation should be useful to some other end than the illustration of a word; I therefore extracted from philosophers principles of science; from historians remarkable facts; from chymists complete processes; from divines striking exhortations; and from poets beautiful descriptions. Such is design, while it is yet at a distance from execution. When the time called upon me to range this accumulation of elegance and wisdom into an alphabetical series, I soon discovered that the bulk of my volumes would fright away the student, and was forced to depart from my scheme of including all that was pleasing or useful in English literature, and reduce my transcripts very often to clusters of words, in which scarcely any meaning is retained; thus to the weariness of copying, I was condemned to add the vexation of expunging. Some passages I have yet spared, which may relieve the labour of verbal searches, and intersperse with verdure and flowers the dusty desarts of barren philology.

The examples, thus mutilated, are no longer to be considered as conveying the sentiments or doctrine of their authours; the word for the sake of which they are inserted, with all its appendant clauses, has been carefully preserved; but it may sometimes happen, by hasty detruncation, that the general tendency of the sentence may be changed: the divine may desert his tenets, or the philosopher his system.

Some of the examples have been taken from writers who were never mentioned as masters of elegance or models of stile; but words must be sought where they are used; and in what pages, eminent for purity, can terms of manufacture or agriculture be found? Many quotations serve no other purpose, than that of proving the bare existence of words, and are therefore selected with less scrupulousness than those which are to teach their structures and relations.

My purpose was to admit no testimony of living authors, that I might not be misled by partiality, and that none of my cotemporaries might have reason to complain; nor have I departed from this resolution, but when some performance of uncommon excellence excited my veneration, when my memory supplied me, from late books, with an example that was wanting, or when my heart, in the tenderness of friendship, solicited admission for a favourite name.

So far have I been from any care to grace my pages with modern decorations, that I have studiously endeavoured to collect examples and authorities from the writers before the restoration, whose works I regard as the wells of English undefiled, as the pure sources of genuine diction. Our language for almost a century, has, by the concurrence of many causes, been gradually departing from its original Teutonick character, and deviating towards a Gallick structure and phraseology, from which it ought to be our endeavour to recal it, by making our ancient volumes the ground-work of stile, admitting among the additions of later times, only such as may supply real deficiencies, such as are readily adopted by the genius of our tongue, and incorporate easily with our native idioms.

But as every language has a time of rudeness antecedent to perfection, as well as of false refinement and declension, I have been cautious lest my zeal for antiquity might drive me into times too remote, and croud my book with words now no longer understood. I have fixed Sidney's work for the boundary, beyond which I make a few excursions. From the authours, which rose in the time of Elizabeth, a speech might be formed adequate to all the purposes of use and elegance. If the language of theology were extracted from Hooker and the translation of the Bible; the terms of natural knowledge from Bacon; the phrases of policy, war, and navigation from Raleigh; the dialect of poetry and fiction from Spenser and Sidney; and the diction of common life from Shakespeare, few ideas would be lost to mankind, for want of English words, in which they might be expressed.

It is not sufficient that a word is found, unless it be so combined as that its meaning is apparently determined by the tract and tenour of the sentence; such passages I have therefore chosen, and when it happened that any author gave a definition of a term, or such an explanation as is equivalent to a definition, I have placed his authority as a supplement to my own, without regard to the chronological order, that is otherwise observed.

Some words, indeed, stand unsupported by any authority, but they are commonly derivative nouns or adverbs, formed from their primitives by regular and constant analogy, or names of things seldom occurring in books, or words of which I have reason to doubt the existence.

There is more danger of censure from the multiplicity than paucity of examples; authorites will sometimes seem to have been accumulated without necessity or use, and perhaps some will be found, which might, without loss, have been omitted. But a work of this kind is not hastily to be charged with superfluities: those quotations, which to careless or unskilful perusers appear only to repeat the same sense, will often exhibit, to a more accurate examiner, diversities of signification, or, at least, afford different shades of the same meaning: one will shew the word applied to persons, another to things; one will express an ill, another a good, and a third a neutral sense; one will prove the expression genuine from an ancient author; another will shew it elegant from a modern: a doubtful authority is corroborated by another of more credit; an ambiguous sentence is ascertained by a passage clear and determinate; the word, how often soever repeated, appears with new associates and in different combinations, and every quotation contributes something to the stability or enlargement of the language.

When words are used equivocally, I receive them in either sense; when they are metaphorical, I adopt them in their primitive acceptation.

I have sometimes, though rarely, yielded to the temptation of exhibiting a genealogy of sentiments, by shewing how one authour copied the thoughts and diction of another: such quotations are indeed little more than repetitions, which might justly be censured, did they not gratify the mind, by affording a kind of intellectual history.

The various syntactical structures occurring in the examples have been carefully noted; the licence or negligence with which many words have been hitherto used, has made our stile capricious and indeterminate; when the different combinations of the same word are exhibited together, the preference is readily given to propriety, and I have often endeavoured to direct the choice.

Thus have I laboured by settling the orthography, displaying the analogy, regulating the structures, and ascertaining the signification of English words, to perform all the parts of a faithful lexicographer: but I have not always executed my own scheme, or satisfied my own expectations. The work, whatever proofs of diligence and attention it may exhibit, is yet capable of many improvements: the orthography which I recommend is still controvertible, the etymology which I adopt is uncertain, and perhaps frequently erroneous; the explanations are sometimes too much contracted, and sometimes too much diffused, the significations are distinguished rather with subtilty than skill, and the attention is harrassed with unnecessary minuteness.

The examples are too often injudiciously truncated, and perhaps sometimes, I hope very rarely, alleged in a mistaken sense; for in making this collection I trusted more to memory, than, in a state of disquiet and embarrassment, memory can contain, and purposed to supply at the review what was left incomplete in the first transcription.

Many terms appropriated to particular occupations, though necessary and significant, are undoubtedly omitted; and of the words most studiously considered and exemplified, many senses have escaped observation.

Yet these failures, however frequent, may admit extenuation and apology. To have attempted much is always laudable, even when the enterprize is above the strength that undertakes it: To rest below his own aim is incident to every one whose fancy is active, and whose views are comprehensive; nor is any man satisfied with himself because he has done much, but because he can conceive little. When first I engaged in this work, I resolved to leave neither words nor things unexamined, and pleased myself with a prospect of the hours which I should revel away in feasts of literature, with the obscure recesses of northern learning, which I should enter and ransack, the treasures with which I expected every search into those neglected mines to reward my labour, and the triumph with which I should display my acquisitions to mankind. When I had thus enquired into the original of words, I resolved to show likewise my attention to things; to pierce deep into every science, to enquire the nature of every substance of which I inserted the name, to limit every idea by definition strictly logical, and exhibit every production of art or nature in an accurate description, that my book might be in place of all other dictionaries whether appellative or technical. But these were the dreams of a poet doomed at last to wake a lexicographer. I soon found that it is too late to look for instruments, when the work calls for execution, and that whatever abilities I brought to my task, with those I must finally perform it. To deliberate whenever I doubted, to enquire whenever I was ignorant, would have protracted the undertaking without end, and, perhaps, without much improvement; for I did not find by my first experiments, that what I had not of my own was easily to be obtained: I saw that one enquiry only gave occasion to another, that book referred to book, that to search was not always to find, and to find was not always to be informed; and that thus to pursue perfection, was, like the first inhabitants of Arcadia, to chace the sun, which, when they had reached the hill where he seemed to rest, was still beheld at the same distance from them.

I then contracted my design, determining to confide in myself, and no longer to solicit auxiliaries, which produced more incumbrance than assistance: by this I obtained at least one advantage, that I set limits to my work, which would in time be ended, though not completed.

Despondency has never so far prevailed as to depress me to negligence; some faults will at last appear to be the effects of anxious diligence and persevering activity. The nice and subtle ramifications of meaning were not easily avoided by a mind intent upon accuracy, and convinced of the necessity of disentangling combinations, and separating similitudes. Many of the distinctions which to common readers appear useless and idle, will be found real and important by men versed in the school philosophy, without which no dictionary shall ever be accurately compiled, or skilfully examined.

Some senses however there are, which, though not the same, are yet so nearly allied, that they are often confounded. Most men think indistinctly, and therefore cannot speak with exactness; and consequently some examples might be indifferently put to either signification: this uncertainty is not to be imputed to me, who do not form, but register the language; who do not teach men how they should think, but relate how they have hitherto expressed their thoughts.

The imperfect sense of some examples I lamented, but could not remedy, and hope they will be compensated by innumerable passages selected with propriety, and preserved with exactness; some shining with sparks of imagination, and some replete with treasures of wisdom.

The orthography and etymology, though imperfect, are not imperfect for want of care, but because care will not always be successful, and recollection or information come too late for use.

That many terms of art and manufacture are omitted, must be frankly acknowledged; but for this defect I may boldly allege that it was unavoidable: I could not visit caverns to learn the miner's language, nor take a voyage to perfect my skill in the dialect of navigation, nor visit the warehouses of merchants, and shops of artificers, to gain the names of wares, tools and operations, of which no mention is found in books; what favourable accident, or easy enquiry brought within my reach, has not been neglected; but it had been a hopeless labour to glean up words, by courting living information, and contesting with the sullenness of one, and the roughness of another.

To furnish the academicians *della Crusca*[8] with words of this kind, a series of comedies called *la Fiera,* or *the Fair,* was professedly written by Buonaroti; but I had no such assistant, and therefore was content to want what they must have wanted likewise, had they not luckily been so supplied.

Nor are all words which are not found in the vocabulary, to be lamented as omissions. Of the laborious and mercantile part of the people, the diction is in a great measure casual and mutable; many of their terms are formed for some temporary or local convenience, and though current at certain times and places, are in others utterly unknown. This fugitive cant, which is always in a state of increase or decay, cannot be regarded as any part of the durable materials of a language, and therefore must be suffered to perish with other things unworthy of preservation.

Care will sometimes betray to the appearance of negligence. He that is catching opportunities which seldom occur, will suffer those to pass by unregarded, which he expects hourly to return; he that is searching for rare and remote things, will neglect those that are obvious and familiar: thus many of the most common and cursory words have been inserted with little illustration, because in gathering the authorities, I forbore to copy those which I thought likely to occur whenever they were wanted. It is remarkable that, in reviewing my collection, I found the word sea unexemplified.

Thus it happens, that in things difficult there is danger from ignorance, and in things easy from confidence; the mind, afraid of greatness, and disdainful of littleness, hastily withdraws herself from painful searches, and passes with scornful rapidity over tasks not adequate to her powers, sometimes too secure for caution, and again too anxious for vigorous effort; sometimes idle in a plain path, and sometimes distracted in labyrinths, and dissipated by different intentions.

A large work is difficult because it is large, even though all its parts might singly be performed with facility; where there are many things to be done, each must be allowed its share of time and labour, in the proportion only which it bears to the whole; nor can it be expected, that the stones which form the dome of a temple, should be squared and polished like the diamond of a ring.

Of the event of this work, for which, having laboured it with so much application, I cannot but have some degree of parental fondness, it is natural to form conjectures. Those who have been persuaded to think well of my design, will require that it should fix our language, and put a stop to those alterations which time and chance have hitherto been suffered to make in it without opposition. With this consequence I will confess that I flattered myself for a while; but now begin to fear that I have indulged expectation which neither reason nor experience can justify. When we see men grow old and die at a certain time one after another, from century to century, we laugh at the elixir that promises to prolong life to a thousand years; and with equal justice may the lexicographer be derided, who being able to produce no example of a nation that has preserved their words and phrases from mutability, shall imagine that his dictionary can embalm his language, and secure it from corruption and decay, that it is in his power to change sublunary nature, and clear the world at once from folly, vanity, and affectation.

With this hope, however, academies have been instituted, to guard the avenues of their languages, to retain fugitives, and repulse intruders; but their vigilance and activity have hitherto been vain; sounds are too volatile and subtile for legal restraints; to enchain syllables, and to lash the wind, are equally the undertakings of pride, unwilling to measure its desires by its strength. The French language has visibly changed under the inspection of the academy; the stile of Amelot's translation of Father Paul is observed by Le Courayer to be *un peu passé;*[9] and no Italian will maintain that the diction of any modern writer is not perceptibly different from that of Boccace, Machiavel, or Caro.

Total and sudden transformations of a language seldom happen; conquests and migrations are now very rare: but there are other causes of change, which, though slow in their operation, and invisible in their progress, are perhaps as much superiour to human resistance, as the revolutions of the sky, or intumescence of the tide. Commerce, however necessary, however lucrative, as it depraves the manners, corrupts the language; they that have frequent intercourse with strangers, to whom they endeavour to accommodate themselves, must in time learn a mingled dialect, like the jargon which serves the traffickers on the Mediterranean and Indian coasts. This will not always be confined to the exchange, the warehouse, or the port, but will be communicated by degrees to other ranks of the people, and be at last incorporated with the current speech.

There are likewise internal causes equally forcible. The language most likely to continue long without alteration, would be that of a nation raised a little, and but a little above barbarity, secluded from strangers, and totally employed in procuring the conveniencies of life; either without books, or, like some of the Mahometan countries, with very few: men thus busied and unlearned, having only such words as common use requires, would perhaps long continue to express the same notions by the same signs. But no such constancy can be expected in a people polished by arts, and classed by subordination, where one part of the community is sustained and accommodated by the labour of the other. Those who have much leisure to think, will always be enlarging the stock of ideas, and every increase of knowledge, whether real or fancied, will produce new words, or combinations of words. When the mind is unchained from necessity, it will range after convenience; when it is left at large in the fields of speculation, it will shift opinions; as any custom is disused, the words that expressed it must perish with it; as any opinion grows popular, it will innovate speech in the same proportion as it alters practice.

As by the cultivation of various sciences, a language is amplified, it will be more furnished with words deflected from original sense: the geometrician will talk of a courtier's zenith, or the eccentrick virtue of a wild hero, and the physician of sanguine expectations and phlegmatick delays. Copiousness of speech will give opportunities to capricious choice, by which some words will be preferred, and others degraded; vicissitudes of fashion will enforce the use of new, or extend the signification of known terms. The tropes of poetry will make hourly encroachments, and the metaphorical will become the current sense: pronunciation will be varied by levity or ignorance, and the pen must at length comply with the tongue; illiterate writers will at one time or other, by publick infatuation, rise into renown, who, not knowing the original import of words, will use them with colloquial licentiousness, confound distinction, and forget propriety. As politeness increases, some expressions will be considered as too gross and vulgar for the delicate, others as too formal and ceremonious for the gay and airy; new phrases are therefore adopted, which must, for the same reasons, be in time dismissed. Swift, in his petty treatise on the English language,[10] allows that new words must sometimes be introduced, but proposes that none should be suffered to become obsolete. But what makes a word obsolete, more than general agreement to forbear it? and how shall it be continued, when it conveys an offensive idea, or recalled again into the mouths of mankind, when it has once become unfamiliar by disuse, and unpleasing by unfamiliarity?

There is another cause of alteration more prevalent than any other, which yet in the present state of the world cannot be obviated. A mixture of two languages will produce a third distinct from both, and they will always be mixed, where the chief part of education, and the most conspicuous accomplishment, is skill in ancient or in foreign tongues. He that has long cultivated another language, will find its words and combinations croud upon his memory; and haste and negligence, refinement and affectation, will obtrude borrowed terms and exotick expressions.

The great pest of speech is frequency of translation. No book was ever turned from one language into another, without imparting something of its native idiom; this is the most mischievous and comprehensive innovation; single words may enter by thousands, and the fabrick of the tongue continue the same, but new phraseology changes much at once; it alters not the single stones of the building, but the order of the columns. If an academy should be established for the cultivation of our stile, which I, who can never wish to see dependance multiplied, hope the spirit of English liberty will hinder or destroy, let them, instead of compiling grammars and dictionaries, endeavour, with all their influence, to stop the licence of translatours, whose idleness and ignorance, if it be suffered to proceed, will reduce us to babble a dialect of France.

If the changes that we fear be thus irresistible, what remains but to acquiesce with silence, as in the other insurmountable distresses of humanity? it remains that we retard what we cannot repel, that we palliate what we cannot cure. Life may be lengthened by care, though death cannot be ultimately defeated: tongues, like governments, have a natural tendency to degeneration; we have long preserved our constitution, let us make some struggles for our language.

In hope of giving longevity to that which its own nature forbids to be immortal, I have devoted this book, the labour of years, to the honour of my country, that we may no longer yield the palm of philology, without a contest, to the nations of the continent. The chief glory of every people arises from its authours: whether I shall add any thing by my own writings to the reputation of English literature, must be left to time: much of my life has been lost under the pressures of disease; much has been trifled away; and much has always been spent in provision for the day that was passing over me; but I shall not think my employment useless or ignoble, if by my assistance foreign nations, and distant ages, gain access to the propagators of knowledge, and understand the teachers of truth; if my labours afford light to the repositories of science, and add celebrity to Bacon, to Hooker, to Milton, and to Boyle.

When I am animated by this wish, I look with pleasure on my book, however defective, and deliver it to the world with the spirit of a man that has endeavoured well. That it will immediately become popular I have not promised to myself: a few wild blunders, and risible absurdities, from which no work of such multiplicity was ever free, may for a time furnish folly with laughter, and harden ignorance in contempt; but useful diligence will at last prevail, and there never can be wanting some who distinguish desert; who will consider that no dictionary of a living tongue ever can be perfect, since while it is hastening to publication, some words are budding, and some falling away; that a whole life cannot be spent upon syntax and etymology, and that even a whole life would not be sufficient; that he, whose design includes whatever language can express, must often speak of what he does not understand; that a writer will sometimes be hurried by eagerness to the end, and sometimes faint with weariness under a task, which Scaliger compares to the labours of the anvil and the mine; that what is obvious is not always known, and what is known is not always present; that sudden fits of inadvertency will surprize vigilance, slight avocations will seduce attention, and casual eclipses of the mind will darken learning; and that the writer shall often in vain trace his memory at the moment of need, for that which yesterday he knew with intuitive readiness, and which will come uncalled into his thoughts tomorrow.

In this work, when it shall be found that much is omitted, let it not be forgotten that much likewise is performed; and though no book was ever spared out of tenderness to the authour, and the world is little solicitous to know whence proceeded the faults of that which it condemns; yet it may gratify curiosity to inform it, that the *English Dictionary* was written with little assistance of the learned, and without any patronage of the great; not in the soft obscurities of retirement, or under the shelter of academick bowers, but amidst inconvenience and distraction, in sickness and in sorrow. It may repress the triumph of malignant criticism to observe, that if our language is not here fully displayed, I have only failed in an attempt with no human powers have hitherto completed. If the lexicons of ancient tongues, now immutably fixed, and comprised in a few volumes, be yet, after the toil of successive ages, inadequate and delusive; if the aggregated knowledge, and co-operating diligence of the Italian academicians, did not secure them from the censure of Beni; if the embodied cricks of France, when fifty years had been spent upon their work, were obliged to change its oeconomy, and give their second edition another form, I may surely be contented without the praise of perfection, which, if I could obtain, in this gloom of solitude, what would it avail me? I have protracted by work till most of those whom I wished to please have sunk into the grave,[11] and success and miscarriage are empty sounds: I therefore dismiss it with frigid tranquillity, having little to fear or hope from censure or from praise.

NOTES

1. Horace *Epistles* 2. 2. 212.

2. Richard Hooker, *Of the Laws of Ecclesiastical Polity,* 4. 14.

3. A paraphrase of a line in Samuel Madden, *Boulter's Monument* (1745); Johnson had been hired to revise this poem.

4. The seventeenth-century scholars Francis Junius and Stephen Skinner were still the received authorities on etymology.

5. A rather long footnote by Johnson has here been prescinded; in it he supplies additional instances of the "etymological extravagance" of Junius.

6. For Bailey see headnote. Robert Ainsworth published a Latin *Thesaurus* in 1736, and Edward Phillips *A New World of English Words* in 1658.

7. Cf. Cicero *De legibus* 2. 23. 59, and Aristotle *Poetics* 25. 16.

8. The Italian Academy was established in 1582 and published a dictionary in 1612.

9. The French Academy published its dictionary in 1694. A. N. Amelot's translation of Fr. Paulo Sarpi's *History of the Council of Trent* had appeared eleven years before, in 1683, while P. F. LeCourayer provided in 1736 a fresh translation of the same work.

10. *A Proposition for Correcting, Improving, and Ascertaining the English Tongue* (1712).

11. Johnson's wife had died three years before.

FROM

THE PLAYS OF WILLIAM SHAKESPEARE

PREFACE

That praises are without reason lavished on the dead, and that the honours due only to excellence are paid to antiquity, is a complaint likely to be always continued by those, who, being able to add nothing to truth, hope for eminence from the heresies of paradox; or those, who, being forced by disappointment upon consolatory expedients, are willing to hope from posterity what the present age refuses, and flatter themselves that the regard which is yet denied by envy, will be at last bestowed by time.

Antiquity, like every other quality that attracts the notice of mankind, has undoubtedly votaries that reverence it, not from reason, but from prejudice. Some seem to admire indiscriminately whatever has been long preserved, without considering that time has sometimes co-operated with chance; all perhaps are more willing to honour past than present excellence; and the mind contemplates genius through the shades of age, as the eye surveys the sun through artificial opacity. The great contention of criticism is to find the faults of the moderns, and the beauties of the ancients. While an authour is yet living we estimate his powers by his worst performance, and when he is dead we rate them by his best.

To works, however, of which the excellence is not absolute and definite, but gradual and comparative; to works not raised upon principles demonstrative and scientifick, but appealing wholly to observation and experience, no other test can be applied than length of duration and continuance of esteem. What mankind have long possessed they have often examined and compared, and if they persist to value the possession, it is because frequent comparisons have confirmed opinion in its favour. As among the works of nature no man can properly call a river deep or a mountain high, without the knowledge of many mountains and many rivers; so in the productions of genius, nothing can be stiled excellent till it has been compared with other works of the same kind. Demonstration immediately displays its power, and has nothing to hope or fear from the flux of years; but works tentative and experimental must be estimated by their proportion to the general and collective ability of man, as it is discovered in a long succession of endeavours. Of the first building that was raised, it might be with certainty determined that it was round or square, but whether it was spacious or lofty must have been referred to time. The Pythagorean scale of numbers was at once discovered to be perfect;[1] but the poems of Homer we yet know not to transcend the common limits of human intelligence, but by remarking, that nation after nation, and century after century, has been able to do little more than transpose his incidents, new name his characters, and paraphrase his sentiments.

The reverence due to writings that have long subsisted arises therefore not from any credulous confidence in the superior wisdom of past ages, or gloomy persuasion of the degeneracy of mankind, but is the consequence of acknowledged and indubitable positions, that what has been longest known has been most considered, and what is most considered is best understood.

The Poet, of whose works I have undertaken the revision, may now begin to assume the dignity of an ancient, and claim the privilege of established fame and prescriptive veneration. He has long outlived his century, the term commonly fixed as the test of literary merit.[2] Whatever advantages he might once derive from personal allusions, local customs, or temporary opinions, have for many years been lost; and every topick of merriment or motive of sorrow, which the modes of artificial life afforded him, now only obscure the scenes which they once illuminated. The effects of favour and competition are at an end; the tradition of his friendships and his enmities has perished; his works support no opinion with arguments, or supply any faction with invectives; they can neither indulge vanity nor gratify malignity, but are read without any other reason than the desire of pleasure, and are therefore praised only as pleasure is obtained; yet, thus unassisted by interest or passion, they have past through variations of taste and changes of manners, and, as they devolved from one generation to another, have received new honours at every transmission.

But because human judgment, though it be gradually gaining upon certainty, never becomes infallible; and approbation, though long continued, may yet be only the approbation of prejudice or fashion; it is proper to inquire, by what peculiarities of excellence Shakespeare has gained and kept the favour of his countrymen.

Nothing can please many, and please long, but just representations of general nature. Particular manners can be known to few, and therefore few only can judge how nearly they are copied. The irregular combinations of fanciful invention may delight a-while, by that novelty of which the common satiety of life sends us all in quest; but the pleasures of sudden wonder are soon exhausted, and the mind can only repose on the stablity of truth.

Shakespeare is above all writers, at least above all modern writers, the poet of nature; the poet that holds up to his readers a faithful mirrour of manners and of life. His characters are not modified by the customs of particular places, unpractised by the rest of the world; by the peculiarities of studies or professions, which can operate but upon small numbers; or by the accidents of transient fashions or temporary opinions: they are the genuine progeny of common humanity, such as the world will always supply, and observation will always find. His persons act and speak by the influence of those general passions and principles by which all minds are agitated, and the whole system of life is continued in motion. In the writings of other poets a character is too often an individual; in those of Shakespeare it is commonly a species.[3]

It is from this wide extension of design that so much instruction is derived.

It is this which fills the plays of Shakespeare with practical axioms and domestick wisdom. It was said of Euripides, that every verse was a precept;[4] and it may be said of Shakespeare, that from his works may be collected a system of civil and oeconomical prudence. Yet his real power is not shown in the splendour of particular passages, but by the progress of his fable, and the tenour of his dialogue; and he that tries to recommend him by select quotations, will succeed like the pedant in Hierocles,[5] who, when he offered his house to sale, carried a brick in his pocket as a specimen.

It will not easily be imagined how much Shakespeare excells in accommodating his sentiments to real life, but by comparing him with other authours. It was observed of the ancient schools of declamation, that the more diligently they were frequented, the more was the student disqualified for the world, because he found nothing there which he should ever meet in any other place. The same remark may be applied to every stage but that of Shakespeare. The theatre, when it is under any other direction, is peopled by such characters as were never seen, conversing in a language which was never heard, upon topicks which will never arise in the commerce of mankind. But the dialogue of this authour is often so evidently determined by the incident which produces it, and is pursued with so much ease and simplicity, that it seems scarcely to claim the merit of fiction, but to have been gleaned by diligent selection out of common conversation, and common occurrences.[6]

Upon every other stage the universal agent is love, by whose power all good and evil is distributed, and every action quickened or retarded. To bring a lover, a lady and a rival into the fable; to entangle them in contradictory obligations, perplex them with oppositions of interest, and harrass them with violence of desires inconsistent with each other; to make them meet in rapture and part in agony; to fill their mouths with hyperbolical joy and outrageous sorrow; to distress them as nothing human ever was distressed; to deliver them as nothing human ever was delivered, is the business of a modern dramatist. For this probablity is violated, life is misrepresented, and language is depraved. But love is only one of many passions, and as it has no great influence upon the sum of life, it has little operation in the dramas of a poet, who caught his ideas from the living world, and exhibited only what he saw before him. He knew, that any other passion, as it was regular or exorbitant, was a cause of happiness or calamity.

Characters thus ample and general were not easily discriminated and preserved, yet perhaps no poet ever kept his personages more distinct from each other. I will not say, with Pope, that every speech may be assigned to the proper speaker,[7] because many speeches there are which have nothing characteristical; but, perhaps, though some may be equally adapted to every person, it will be difficult to find, any that can be properly transferred from the present possessor to another claimant. The choice is right, when there is reason for choice.

Other dramatists can only gain attention by hyperbolical or aggravated characters, by fabulous and unexampled excellence or depravity, as the writers of barbarous romances invigorated the reader by a giant and a dwarf; and he that should form his expectations of human affairs from the play, or from the tale, would be equally deceived. Shakespeare has no heroes; his scenes are occupied only by men, who act and speak as the reader thinks that he should himself have spoken or acted on the same occasion: Even where the agency is supernatural the dialogue is level with life. Other writers disguise the most natural passions and most frequent incidents; so that he who contemplates them in the book will not know them in the world: Shakespeare approximates the remote, and familiarizes the wonderful; the event which he represents will not happen, but if it were possible, its effects would probably be such as he has assigned; and it may be said, that he has not only shewn human nature as it acts in real exigences, but as it would be found in trials, to which it cannot be exposed.

This therefore is the praise of Shakespeare, that his drama is the mirrour of life; that he who has mazed his imagination, in following the phantoms which other writers raise up before him, may here be cured of his delirious extasies, by reading human sentiments in human language; by scenes from which a hermit may estimate the transactions of the world, and a confessor predict the progress of the passions.

His adherence to general nature has exposed him to the censure of criticks, who form their judgments upon narrower principles. Dennis and Rhymer think his Romans not sufficiently Roman; and Voltaire censures his kings as not completely royal. Dennis is offended, that Menenius, a senator of Rome, should play the buffoon; and Voltaire perhaps thinks decency violated when the Danish Usurper is represented as a drunkard.[8] But Shakespeare always makes nature predominate over accident; and if he preserves the essential character, is not very careful of distinctions superinduced and adventitious. His story requires Romans or kings, but he thinks only on men. He knew that Rome, like every other city, had men of all dispositions; and wanting a buffoon, he went into the senate-house for that which the senate-house would certainly have afforded him. He was inclined to shew an usurper and a murderer not only odious but despicable, he therefore added drunkenness to his other qualities, knowing that kings love wine like other men, and that wine exerts its natural power upon kings. These are the petty cavils of petty minds; a poet overlooks the casual distinction of country and condition, as a painter, satisfied with the figure, neglects the drapery.

The censure which he has incurred by mixing comick and tragick scenes, as it extends to all his works, deserves more consideration. Let the fact be first stated, and then examined.[9]

Shakespeare's plays are not in the rigorous and critical sense either tragedies or comedies, but compositions of a distinct kind; exhibiting the real state of sublunary nature, which partakes of good and evil, joy and sorrow, mingled with endless variety of proportion and innumerable modes of combination; and expressing the course of the world, in which the loss of one is the gain of another; in which, at the same time, the reveller is hasting to his wine, and the mourner burying his friend; in which the malignity of one is sometimes defeated by the frolick of another; and many mischiefs and many benefits are done and hindered without design.

Out of this chaos of mingled purposes and casualties the ancient poets, according to the laws which custom had prescribed, selected some the crimes of men, and some their absurdities; some the momentous vicissitudes of life, and some the lighter occurrences; some the terrours of distress, and some the gayeties of prosperity. Thus rose the two modes of imitation, known by the names of tragedy and comedy, compositions intended to promote different ends by contrary means, and considered as so little allied, that I do not recollect among the Greeks or Romans a single writer who attempted both.

Shakespeare has united the powers of exciting laughter and sorrow not only in one mind, but in one composition. Almost all his plays are divided between serious and ludicrous characters, and, in the successive evolutions of the design, sometimes produce seriousness and sorrow, and sometimes levity and laughter.

That this is a practice contrary to the rules of criticism will be readily allowed; but there is always an appeal open from criticism to nature. The end of writing is to instruct; the end of poetry is to instruct by pleasing.[10] That the mingled drama may convey all the instruction of tragedy or comedy cannot be denied, because it includes both in its alter[n]ations of exhibition, and approaches nearer than either to the appearance of life, by shewing how great machinations and slender designs may promote or obviate one another, and the high and the low co-operate in the general system by unavoidable concatenation.

It is objected, that by this change of scenes the passions are interrupted in their progression, and that the principal event, being not advanced by a due gradation of preparatory incidents, wants at last the power to move, which constitutes the perfection of dramatick poetry. This reasoning is so specious, that it is received as true even by those who in daily experience feel it to be false. The interchanges of mingled scenes seldom fail to produce the intended vicissitudes of passion. Fiction cannot move so much, but that the attention may be easily transferred; and though it must be allowed that pleasing melancholy be sometimes interrupted by unwelcome levity, yet let it be considered likewise, that melancholy is often not pleasing, and that the disturbance of one man may be the relief of another; that different auditors have different habitudes; and that, upon the whole, all pleasure consists in variety.

The players, who in their edition[11] divided our authour's works into comedies, histories, and tragedies, seem not to have distinguished the three kinds, by any very exact or definite ideas.

An action which ended happily to the principal persons, however serious or distressful through its intermediate incidents, in their opinion constituted a comedy. This idea of a comedy continued long amongst us, and plays were written, which, by changing the catastrophe, were tragedies to-day and comedies tomorrow.

Tragedy was not in those times a poem of more general dignity or elevation than comedy; it required only a calamitous conclusion, with which the common criticism of that age was satisfied, whatever lighter pleasure it afforded in its progress.

History was a series of actions, with no other than chronological succession, independent on each other, and without any tendency to introduce or regulate the conclusion. It is not always very nicely distinguished from tragedy. There is not much nearer approach to unity of action in the tragedy of *Antony and Cleopatra,* than in the history of *Richard the Second.* But a history might be continued through many plays; as it had no plan, it had no limits.

Through all these denominations of the drama, Shakespeare's mode of composition is the same; an interchange of seriousness and merriment, by which the mind is softened at one time, and exhilarated at another. But whatever be his purpose, whether to gladden or depress, or to conduct the story, without vehemence or emotion, through tracts of easy and familiar dialogue, he never fails to attain his purpose; as he commands us, we laugh or mourn, or sit silent with quiet expectation, in tranquillity without indifference.

When Shakespeare's plan is understood, most of the criticisms of Rhymer and Voltaire vanish away. The play of *Hamlet* is opened, without impropriety, by two sentinels; Iago bellows at Brabantio's window, without injury to the scheme of the play, though in terms which a modern audience would not easily endure; the character of Polonius is seasonable and useful; and the Grave-diggers themselves may be heard with applause.

Shakespeare engaged in dramatick poetry with the world open before him; the rules of the ancients were yet known to few; the publick judgment was unformed; he had no example of such fame as might force him upon imitation, nor criticks of such authority as might restrain his extravagance: He therefore indulged his natural disposition, and his disposition, as Rhymer has remarked, led him to comedy. In tragedy he often writes with great appearance of toil and study, what is written at last with little felicity; but in his comick scenes, he seems to produce without labour, what no labour can improve. In tragedy he is always struggling after some occasion to be comick, but in comedy he seems to repose, or to luxuriate, as in a mode of thinking congenial to his nature. In his tragick scenes there is always something wanting, but his comedy often surpasses expectation or desire. His comedy pleases by the thoughts and the language, and his tragedy for the greater part by incident and action. His tragedy seems to be skill, his comedy to be instinct.

The force of his comick scenes has suffered little diminution from the changes made by a century and a half, in manners or in words. As his personages act upon principles arising from genuine passion, very little modified by particular forms, their pleasures and vexations are communicable to all times and to all places; they are natural, and therefore durable; the adventitious peculiarities of personal habits, are only superficial dies, bright and pleasing for a little while, yet soon fading to a dim tinct, without any remains of former lustre; but the discriminations of true passion are the colours of nature; they pervade the whole mass, and can only perish with the body that exhibits them. The accidental compositions of heterogeneous modes are dissolved by the chance which combined them; but the uniform simplicity of primitive qualities neither admits increase, nor suffers decay. The sand heaped by one flood is scattered by another, but the rock always continues in its place. The stream of time, which is continually washing the dissoluble fabricks of other poets, passes without injury by the adamant of Shakespeare.

If there be, what I believe there is, in every nation, a stile which never becomes obsolete, a certain mode of phraseology so consonant and congenial to the analogy and principles of its respective language as to remain settled and unaltered; this stile is probably to be sought in the common intercourse of life, among those who speak only to be understood, without ambition of elegance. The polite are always catching modish innovations, and the learned depart from established forms of speech, in hope of finding or making better; those who wish for distinction forsake the vulgar, when the vulgar is right; but there is a conversation above grossness and below refinement, where propriety resides, and where this poet seems to have gathered his comick dialogue. He is therefore more agreeable to the ears of the present age than any other authour equally remote, and among his other excellencies deserves to be studied as one of the original masters of our language.

These observations are to be considered not as unexceptionably constant, but as containing general and predominant truth. Shakespeare's familiar dialogue is affirmed to be smooth and clear, yet not wholly without ruggedness or difficulty; as a country may be eminently fruitful, though it has spots unfit for cultivation: His characters are praised as natural, though their sentiments are sometimes forced, and their actions improbable; as the earth upon the whole is spherical, though its surface is varied with protuberances and cavities.

Shakespeare with his excellencies has likewise faults, and faults sufficient to obscure and overwhelm any other merit.[12] I shall shew them in the proportion in which they appear to me, without envious malignity or superstitious veneration. No question can be more innocently discussed than a dead poet's pretensions to renown; and little regard is due to that bigotry which sets candour higher than truth.

His first defect is that to which may be imputed most of the evil in books or in men. He sacrifices virtue to convenience, and is so much more careful to please than to instruct, that he seems to write without any moral purpose. From his writings indeed a system of social duty may be selected, for he that thinks reasonably must think morally; but his precepts and axioms drop casually from him; he makes no just distribution of good or evil, nor is always careful to shew in the virtuous a disapprobation of the wicked; he carries his persons indifferently through right and wrong, and at the close dismisses them without further care, and leaves their examples to operate by chance. This fault the barbarity of his age cannot extenuate; for it is always a writer's duty to make the world better, and justice is a virtue independant on time or place.

The plots are often so loosely formed, that a very slight consideration may improve them, and so carelessly pursued, that he seems not always fully to comprehend his own design. He omits opportunities of instructing or delighting which the train of his story seems to force upon him, and apparently rejects those exhibitions which would be more affecting, for the sake of those which are more easy.

It may be observed, that in many of his plays the latter part is evidently neglected. When he found himself near the end of his work, and, in view of his reward, he shortened the labour, to snatch the profit. He therefore remits his efforts where he should most vigorously exert them, and his catastrophe is improbably produced or imperfectly represented.

He had no regard to distinction of time or place, but gives to one age or nation, without scruple, the customs, institutions, and opinions of another, at the expence not only of likelihood, but of possibility. These faults Pope has endeavoured, with more zeal than judgment, to transfer to his imagined interpolators.[13] We need not wonder to find Hector quoting Aristotle, when we see the loves of Theseus and Hippolyta combined with the Gothick mythology of fairies. Shakespeare, indeed, was not the only violator of chronology, for in the same age Sidney, who wanted not the advantages of learning, has, in his Arcadia, confounded the pastoral with the feudal times, the days of innocence, quiet and security, with those of turbulence, violence and adventure.

In his comick scenes he is seldom very successful, when he engages his characters in reciprocations of smartness and contests of sarcasm; their jests are commonly gross, and their pleasantry licentious; neither his gentlemen nor his ladies have much delicacy, nor are sufficiently distinguished from his clowns by any appearance of refined manners. Whether he represented the real conversation of his time is not easy to determine; the reign of Elizabeth is commonly supposed to have been a time of stateliness, formality and reserve, yet perhaps the relaxations of that severity were not very elegant. There must, however, have been always some modes of gayety preferable to others, and a writer ought to chuse the best.

In tragedy his performance seems constantly to be worse, as his labour is more. The effusions of passion which exigence forces out are for the most part striking and energetick; but whenever he solicits his invention, or strains his faculties, the offspring of his throes is tumour, meanness, tediousness, and obscurity.

In narration he affects a disproportionate pomp of diction and a wearisome train of circumlocution, and tells the incident imperfectly in many words, which might have been more plainly delivered in few. Narration in dramatick poetry is naturally tedious, as it is unanimated and inactive, and obstructs the progress of the action; it should therefore always be rapid, and enlivened by frequent interruption. Shakespeare found it an encumbrance, and instead of lightening it by brevity, endeavoured to recommend it by dignity and splendour.

His declamations or set speeches are commonly cold and weak, for his power was the power of nature; when he endeavoured, like other tragick writers, to catch opportunities of amplification, and instead of inquiring what the occasion demanded, to show how much his stores of knowledge could supply, he seldom escapes without the pity or resentment of his reader.

It is incident to him to be now and then entangled with an unwieldy sentiment, which he cannot well express, and will not reject; he struggles with it a while, and if it continues stubborn, comprises it in words such as occur, and leaves it to be disentangled and evolved by those who have more leisure to bestow upon it.

Not that always where the language is intricate the thought is subtle, or the image always great where the line is bulky; the equality of words to things is very often neglected, and trivial sentiments and vulgar ideas disappoint the attention, to which they are recommended by sonorous epithets and swelling figures.

But the admirers of this great poet[14] have never less reason to indulge their hopes of supreme excellence, than when he seems fully resolved to sink them in dejection, and mollify them with tender emotions by the fall of greatness, the danger of innocence, or the crosses of love. He is not long soft and pathetick without some idle conceit, or contemptible equivocation. He no sooner begins to move, than he counteracts himself; and terrour and pity, as they are rising in the mind, are checked and blasted by sudden frigidity.

A quibble is to Shakespeare, what luminous vapours are to the traveller; he follows it at all adventures, it is sure to lead him out of his way, and sure to engulf him in the mire. It has some malignant power over his mind, and its fascinations are irresistible. Whatever be the dignity or profundity of his disquisition, whether he be enlarging knowledge or exalting affection, whether he be amusing attention with incidents, or enchaining it in suspense, let but a quibble spring up before him, and he leaves his work unfinished. A quibble is the golden apple for which he will always turn aside from his career, or stoop from his elevation. A quibble, poor and barren as it is, gave him such delight, that he was content to purchase it, by the sacrifice of reason, propriety and truth. A quibble was to him the fatal Cleopatra for which he lost the world, and was content to lose it.

It will be thought strange, that, in enumerating the defects of this writer, I have not yet mentioned his neglect of the unities; his violation of those laws which have been instituted and established by the joint authority of poets and of criticks.

For his other deviations from the art of writing, I resign him to critical justice, without making any other demand in his favour, than that which must be indulged to all human excellence; that his virtues be rated with his failings: But, from the censure which this irregularity may bring upon him, I shall, with due reverence to that learning which I must oppose, adventure to try how I can defend him.

His histories, being neither tragedies nor comedies, are not subject to any of their laws; nothing more is necessary to all the praise which they expect, than that the changes of action be so prepared as to be understood, that the incidents be various and affecting, and the characters consistent, natural and distinct. No other unity is intended, and therefore none is to be sought.

In his other works he has well enough preserved the unity of action. He has not, indeed, an intrigue regularly perplexed and regularly unravelled; he does not endeavour to hide his design only to discover it, for this is seldom the order of real events, and Shakespeare is the poet of nature: But his plan has commonly what Aristotle requires, a beginning, a middle, and an end,[15] one event is concatenated with another, and the conclusion follows by easy consequence. There are perhaps some incidents that might be spared, as in other poets there is much talk that only fills up time upon the stage; but the general system makes gradual advances, and the end of the play is the end of expectation.

To the unities of time and place he has shewn no regard, and perhaps a nearer view of the principles on which they stand will diminish their value, and withdraw from them the veneration which, from the time of Corneille,[16] they have very generally received, by discovering that they have given more trouble to the poet, than pleasure to the auditor.

The necessity of observing the unities of time and place arises from the supposed necessity of making the drama credible. The criticks hold it impossible, that an action of months or years can be possibly believed to pass in three hours; or that the spectator can suppose himself to sit in the theatre, while ambassadors go and return between distant kings, while armies are levied and towns besieged, while an exile wanders and returns, or till he whom they saw courting his mistress, shall lament the untimely fall of his son. The mind revolts from evident falsehood, loses its force when it departs from the resemblance of reality.

From the narrow limitation of time necessarily arises the contraction of place. The spectator, who knows that he saw the first act at Alexandria, cannot suppose that he sees the next at Rome, at a distance to which not the dragons of Medea could, in so short a time, have transported him; he knows with certainty that he has not changed his place; and he knows that place cannot change itself; that what was a house cannot become a plain; that what was Thebes can never be Persepolis.

Such is the triumphant language with which a critick exults over the misery of an irregular poet, and exults commonly without resistance or reply. It is time therefore to tell him, by the authority of Shakespeare, that he assumes, as an unquestionable principle, a position, which, while his breath is forming it into words, his understanding pronounces to be false. It is false, that any representation is mistaken for reality; that any dramatick fable in its materiality was ever credible, or, for a single moment, was ever credited.

The objection arising from the impossibility of passing the first hour at Alexandria, and the next at Rome, supposes, that when the play opens the spectator really imagines himself at Alexandria, and believes that his walk to the theatre has been a voyage to Egypt, and that he lives in the days of Antony and Cleopatra. Surely he that imagines this may imagine more. He that can take the stage at one time for the palace of the Ptolemies, may take it in half an hour for the promontory of Actium. Delusion, if delusion be admitted, has no certain limitation; if the spectator can be once persuaded, that his old acquaintances are Alexander and Caesar, that a room illuminated with candles is the plain of Pharsalia, or the bank of Granicus, he is in a state of elevation above the reach of reason, or of truth, and from the heights of empyrean poetry, may despise the circumscriptions of terrestrial nature. There is no reason why a mind thus wandering in extasy should count the clock, or why an hour should not be a century in that calenture of the brains that can make the stage a field.

The truth is, that the spectators are always in their senses, and know, from the first act to the last, that the stage is only a stage, and that the players are only players. They come to hear a certain number of lines recited with just gesture and elegant modulation. The lines relate to some action, and an action must be in some place; but the different actions that compleat a story may be in places very remote from each other; and where is the absurdity of allowing that space to represent first Athens, and then Sicily, which was always known to be neither Sicily nor Athens, but a modern theatre?

By supposition, as place is introduced, time may be extended; the time required by the fable elapses for the most part between the acts; for of so much of the action as is represented, the real and poetical duration is the same. If, in the first act, preparations for war against Mithridates are represented to be made in Rome, the event of the war may, without absurdity, be represented, in the catastrophe, as happening in Pontus; we know that there is neither war, nor preparation for war; we know that we are neither in Rome nor Pontus; that neither Mithridates nor Lucullus are before us. The drama exhibits successive imitations of successive actions, and why may not the second imitation represent an action that happened years after the first; if it be so connected with it, that nothing but time can be supposed to intervene? Time is, of all modes of existence, most obsequious to the imagination; a lapse of years is as easily conceived as a passage of hours. In contemplation we easily contract the time of real actions, and therefore willingly permit it to be contracted when we only see their imitation.

It will be asked, how the drama moves, if it is not credited. It is credited with all the credit due to a drama. It is credited, whenever it moves, as a just picture of a real original; as representing to the auditor what he would himself feel, if he were to do or suffer what is there feigned to be suffered or to be done. The reflection that strikes the heart is not, that the evils before us are real evils, but that they are evils to which we ourselves may be exposed. If there be any fallacy, it is not that we fancy the players, but that we fancy ourselves unhappy for a moment; but we rather lament the possibility than suppose the presence of misery, as a mother weeps over her babe, when she remembers that death may take it from her. The delight of tragedy proceeds from our consciousness of fiction; if we thought murders and treasons real, they would please no more.

Imitations produce pain or pleasure, not because they are mistaken for realities, but because they bring realities to mind. When the imagination is recreated by a painted landscape, the trees are not supposed capable to give us shade, or the fountains coolness; but we consider, how we should be pleased with such fountains playing beside us, and such woods waving over us. We are agitated in reading the history of *Henry the Fifth,* yet no man takes his book for the field of Agencourt. A dramatick exhibition is a book recited with concomitants that encrease or diminish its effect. Familiar comedy is often more powerful on the theatre, than in the page; imperial tragedy is always less.

The humour of Petruchio may be heightened by grimace; but what voice or what gesture can hope to add dignity or force to the soliloquy of Cato.[17]

A play read, affects the mind like a play acted. It is therefore evident, that the action is not supposed to be real, and it follows that between the acts a longer or shorter time may be allowed to pass, and that no more account of space or duration is to be taken by the auditor of a drama, than by the reader of a narrative, before whom may pass in an hour the life of a hero, or the revolutions of an empire.

Whether Shakespeare knew the unities, and rejected them by design, or deviated from them by happy ignorance, it is, I think, impossible to decide, and useless to enquire. We may reasonably suppose, that, when he rose to notice, he did not want the counsels and admonitions of scholars and criticks, and that he at last deliberately persisted in a practice, which he might have begun by chance. As nothing is essential to the fable, but unity of action, and as the unities of time and place arise evidently from false assumptions, and, by circumscribing the extent of the drama, lessen its variety, I cannot think it much to be lamented, that they were not known by him, or not observed: Nor, if such another poet could arise, should I very vehemently reproach him, that his first act passed at Venice, and his next in Cyprus. Such violations of rules merely positive, become the comprehensive genius of Shakespeare, and such censures are suitable to the minute and slender criticism of Voltaire:

> *Non usque adeo permiscuit imis*
> *Longus summa dies, ut non, si voce Metelli*
> *Serventur leges, malint a Caesare tolli.*

> [Nor time, nor chance breed such confusions yet,
> Nor are the mean so rais'd, nor sunk the great;
> But laws themselves would rather chuse to be
> Suppress'd by Caesar, than preserved by thee.][18]

Yet when I speak thus slightly of dramatick rules, I cannot but recollect how much wit and learning may be produced against me; before such authorities I am afraid to stand, not that I think the present question one of those that are to be decided by mere authority, but because it is to be suspected, that these precepts have not been so easily received but for better reasons than I have yet been able to find. The result of my enquiries, in which it would be ludicrous to boast of impartiality, is, that the unities of time and place are not essential to a just drama, that though they may sometimes conduce to pleasure, they are always to be sacrificed to the nobler beauties of variety and instruction; and that a play written with nice observation of critical rules, is to be contemplated as an elaborate curiosity, as the product of superfluous and ostentatious art, by which is shewn, rather what is possible, than what is necessary.

He that, without diminution of any other excellence, shall preserve all the unities unbroken, deserves the like applause with the architect, who shall display all the orders of architecture in a citadel, without any deduction from its strength; but the principal beauty of a citadel is to exclude the enemy; and the greatest graces of a play, are to copy nature and instruct life.

Perhaps, what I have here not dogmatically but deliberatively[19] written, may recal the principles of the drama to a new examination. I am almost frighted at my own temerity; and when I estimate the fame and the strength of those that maintain the contrary opinion, am ready to sink down in reverential silence; as Aeneas withdrew from the defence of Troy, when he saw Neptune shaking the wall, and Juno heading the besiegers.[20]

Those whom my arguments cannot persuade to give their approbation to the judgment of Shakespeare, will easily, if they consider the condition of his life, make some allowance for his ignorance.

Every man's performances, to be rightly estimated, must be compared with the state of the age in which he lived, and with his own particular opportunities; and though to the reader a book be not worse or better for the circumstances of the authour, yet as there is always a silent reference of human works to human abilities, and as the enquiry, how far man may extend his designs, or how high he may rate his native force, is of far greater dignity than in what rank we shall place any particular performance, curiosity is always busy to discover the instruments, as well as to survey the workmanship, to know how much is to be ascribed to original powers, and how much to casual and adventitious help. The palaces of Peru or Mexico were certainly mean and incommodious habitations, if compared to the houses of European monarchs; yet who could forbear to view them with astonishment, who remembered that they were built without the use of iron?

The English nation, in the time of Shakespeare, was yet struggling to emerge from barbarity. The philology of Italy had been transplanted hither in the reign of Henry the Eighth; and the learned languages had been successfully cultivated by Lilly, Linacer, and More; by Pole, Cheke, and Gardiner; and afterwards by Smith, Clerk, Haddon, and Ascham.[21] Greek was now taught to boys in the principal schools; and those who united elegance with learning, read, with great diligence, the Italian and Spanish poets. But literature was yet confined to professed scholars, or to men and women of high rank. The publick was gross and dark; and to be able to read and write, was an accomplishment still valued for its rarity.

Nations, like individuals, have their infancy. A people newly awakened to literary curiosity, being yet unacquainted with the true state of things, knows not how to judge of that which is proposed as its resemblance. Whatever is remote from common appearances is always welcome to vulgar, as to childish credulity; and of a country unenlightened by learning, the whole people is the vulgar. The study of those who then aspired to plebeian learning was laid out upon adventures, giants, dragons, and enchantments. *The Death of Arthur* was the favourite volume.[22]

The mind, which has feasted on the luxurious wonders of fiction, has no taste of the insipidity of truth. A play which imitated only the common occurrences of the world, would, upon the admirers of *Palmerin* and *Guy of Warwick*, have made little impression; he that wrote for such an audience was under the necessity of looking round for strange events and fabulous transactions, and that incredibility, by which maturer knowledge is offended, was the chief recommendation of writings, to unskilful curiosity.

Our authour's plots are generally borrowed from novels, and it is reasonable to suppose, that he chose the most popular, such as were read by many, and related by more; for his audience could not have followed him through the intricacies of the drama, had they not held the thread of the story in their hands.

The stories, which we now find only in remoter authours, were in his time accessible and familliar. The fable of *As you like it*, which is supposed to be copied from Chaucer's Gamelyn, was a little pamphlet of those times; and old Mr. Cibber remembered the tale of *Hamlet* in plain English prose, which the criticks have now to seek in *Saxo Grammaticus*.

His English histories he took from English chronicles and English ballads; and as the ancient writers were made known to his countrymen by versions, they supplied him with new subjects; he dilated some of Plutarch's lives into plays, when they had been translated by North.

His plots, whether historical or fabulous, are always crouded with incidents, by which the attention of a rude people was more easily caught than by sentiment or argumentation; and such is the power of the marvellous even over those who despise it, that every man finds his mind more strongly seized by the tragedies of Shakespeare than of any other writer; others please us by particular speeches, but he always makes us anxious for the event, and has perhaps excelled all but Homer in securing the first purpose of a writer, by exciting restless and unquenchable curiosity, and compelling him that reads his work to read it through.

The shows and bustle with which his plays abound have the same original. As knowledge advances, pleasure passes from the eye to the ear, but returns, as it declines, from the ear to the eye. Those to whom our authour's labours were exhibited had more skill in pomps or processions than in poetical language, and perhaps wanted some visible and discriminated events, as comments on the dialogue. He knew how he should most please; and whether his practice is more agreeable to nature, or whether his example has prejudiced the nation, we still find that on our stage something must be done as well as said, and inactive declamation is very coldly heard, however musical or elegant, passionate or sublime.

Voltaire expresses his wonder,[23] that our authour's extravagancies are endured by a nation, which has seen the tragedy of Cato. Let him be answered, that Addison speaks the language of poets, and Shakespeare, of men. We find in Cato innumerable beauties which enamour us of its authour, but we see nothing that acquaints us with human sentiments or human actions; we place it with the fairest and the noblest progeny which judgment propagates by conjunction with learning, but Othello is the vigorous and vivacious offspring of observation impregnated by genius. Cato affords a splendid exhibition of artificial and fictitious manners, and delivers just and noble sentiments, in diction easy, elevated and harmonious, but its hopes and fears communicate no vibration to the heart; the composition refers us only to the writer; we pronounce the name of Cato, but we think on Addison.

The work of a correct and regular writer is a garden accurately formed and diligently planted, varied with shades, and scented with flowers; the composition of Shakespeare is a forest, in which oaks extend their branches, and pines tower in the air, interspersed sometimes with weeds and brambles, and sometimes giving shelter to myrtles and to roses; filling the eye with awful pomp, and gratifying the mind with endless diversity. Other poets display cabinets of precious rarities, minutely finished, wrought into shape, and polished unto brightness. Shakespeare opens a mine which contains gold and diamonds in unexhaustible plenty, though clouded by incrustations, debased by impurities, and mingled with a mass of meaner minerals.

It has been much disputed, whether Shakespeare owed his excellence to his own native force, or whether he had the common helps of scholastick education, the precepts of critical science, and the examples of ancient authours.

There has always prevailed a tradition, that Shakespeare wanted learning, that he had no regular education, nor much skill in the dead languages. Johnson, his friend, affirms, that *he had small Latin, and no Greek*;[24] who, besides that he had no imaginable temptation to falsehood, wrote at a time when the character and acquisitions of Shakespeare were known to multitudes. His evidence ought therefore to decide the controversy, unless some testimony of equal force could be opposed.

Some have imagined, that they have discovered deep learning in many imitations of old writers; but the examples which I have known urged, were drawn from books translated in his time; or were such easy coincidences of thought, as will happen to all who consider the same subjects; or such remarks on life or axioms of morality as float in conversation, and are transmitted through the world in proverbial sentences.

I have found it remarked, that, in this important sentence, *Go before, I'll follow*, we read a translation of, *I prae, sequar*.[25] I have been told, that when Caliban, after a pleasing dream, says, *I cry'd to sleep again*, the authour imitates Anacreon, who had, like every other man, the same wish on the same occasion.

There are a few passages which may pass for imitations, but so few, that the exception only confirms the rule; he obtained them from accidental quotations, or by oral communication, and as he used what he had, would have used more if he had obtained it.

The *Comedy of Errors* is confessedly taken from the *Menaechmi* of Plautus; from the only play of Plautus which was then in English. What can be more probable, than that he who copied that, would have copied more; but that those which were not translated were inaccessible?

Whether he knew the modern languages is uncertain. That his plays have some French scenes proves but little; he might easily procure them to be written, and probably, even though he had known the language in the common degree, he could not have written it without assistance. In the story of *Romeo and Juliet* he is observed to have followed the English translation, where it deviates from the Italian; but this on the other part proves nothing against his knowledge of the original. He was to copy, not what he knew himself, but what was known to his audience.

It is most likely that he had learned Latin sufficiently to make him acquainted with construction, but that he never advanced to an easy perusal of the Roman authours. Concerning his skill in modern languages, I can find no sufficient ground of determination; but as no imitations of French or Italian authours have been discovered, though the Italian poetry was then high in esteem, I am inclined to believe, that he read little more than English, and chose for his fables only such tales as he found translated.

That much knowledge is scattered over his works is very justly observed by Pope,[26] but it is often such knowledge as books did not supply. He that will understand Shakespeare, must not be content to study him in the closet, he must look for his meaning sometimes among the sports of the field, and sometimes among the manufactures of the shop.

There is however proof enough that he was a very diligent reader, nor was our language then so indigent of books, but that he might very liberally indulge his curiosity without excursion into foreign literature. Many of the Roman authours were translated, and some of the Greek; the reformation had filled the kingdom with theological learning; most of the topicks of human disquisition had found English writers; and poetry had been cultivated, not only with diligence, but success. This was a stock of knowledge sufficient for a mind so capable of appropriating and improving it.

But the greater part of his excellence was the product of his own genius. He found the English stage in a state of the utmost rudeness; no essays either in tragedy or comedy had appeared, from which it could be discovered to what degree of delight either one or other might be carried. Neither character nor dialogue were yet understood. Shakespeare may be truly said to have introduced them both amongst us, and in some of his happier scenes to have carried them both to the utmost height.

By what gradations of improvement he proceeded, is not easily known; for the chronology of his works is yet unsettled. Rowe is of opinion, that *perhaps we are not to look for his beginning, like those of other writers, in his least perfect works; art had so little, and nature so large a share in what he did, that for ought I know*, says he, *the performances of his youth, as they were the most vigorous, were the best.*[27] But the power of nature is only the power of using to any certain purpose the materials which diligence procures, or opportunity supplies. Nature gives no man knowledge, and when images are collected by study and experience, can only assist in combining or applying them. Shakespeare, however favoured by nature, could impart only what he had learned; and as he must increase his ideas, like other mortals, by gradual acquisition, he, like them, grew wiser as he grew older, could display life better, as he knew it more, and instruct with more efficacy, as he was himself more amply instructed.

There is a vigilance of observation and accuracy of distinction which books and precepts cannot confer; from this almost all original and native excellence proceeds. Shakespeare must have looked upon mankind with perspicacity, in the highest degree curious and attentive. Other writers borrow their characters from preceding writers, and diversify them only by the accidental appendages of present manners; the dress is a little varied, but the body is the same. Our authour had both matter and form to provide; for except the characters of Chaucer, to whom I think he is not much indebted, there were no writers in English, and perhaps not many in other modern languages, which shewed life in its native colours.

The contest about the original benevolence or malignity of man had not yet commenced. Speculation had not yet attempted to analyse the mind, to trace the passions to their sources, to unfold the seminal principles of vice and virtue, or sound the depths of the heart for the motives of action. All those enquiries, which from that time that human nature became the fashionable study, have been made sometimes with nice discernment, but often with idle subtilty, were yet unattempted. The tales, with which the infancy of learning was satisifed, exhibited only the superficial appearances of action, related the events but omitted the causes, and were formed for such as delighted in wonders rather than in truth. Mankind was not then to be studied in the closet; he that would know the world, was under the necessity of gleaning his own remarks, by mingling as he could in its business and amusements.

Boyle congratulated himself upon his high birth, because it favoured his curiosity, by facilitating his access. Shakespeare had no such advantage; he came to London a needy adventurer, and lived for a time by very mean employments. Many works of genius and learning have been performed in states of life, that appear very little favourable to thought or to enquiry; so many, that he who considers them is inclined to think that he sees enterprise and perseverance predominating over all external agency, and bidding help and hindrance vanish before them. The genius of Shakespeare was not to be depressed by the weight of poverty, nor limited by the narrow conversation to which men in want are inevitably condemned; the incumbrances of his fortune were shaken from his mind, *as dewdrops from a lion's mane.*[28]

Though he had so many difficulties to encounter, and so little assistance to surmount them, he has been able to obtain an exact knowledge of many modes of life, and many casts of native dispositions; to vary them with great multiplicity; to mark them by nice distinctions; and to shew them in full view by proper combinations. In this part of his performances he had none to imitate, but has himself been imitated by all succeeding writers; and it may be doubted, whether from all his successors more maxims of theoretical knowledge, or more rules of practical prudence, can be collected, than he alone has given to his country.

Nor was his attention confined to the actions of men; he was an exact surveyor of the inanimate world; his descriptions have always some peculiarities, gathered by contemplating things as they really exist. It may be observed, that the oldest poets of many nations preserve their reputation, and that the following generations of wit, after a short celebrity, sink into oblivion. The first, whoever they be, must take their sentiments and descriptions immediately from knowledge; the resemblance is therefore just, their descriptions are verified by every eye, and their sentiments acknowledged by every breast. Those whom their fame invites to the same studies, copy partly them, and partly nature, till the books of one age gain such authority, as to stand in the place of nature to another, and imitation, always deviating a little, becomes at last capricious and casual. Shakespeare, whether life or nature be his subject, shews plainly, that he has seen with his own eyes; he gives the image which he receives, not weakened or distorted by the intervention of any other mind; the ignorant feel his representations to be just, and the learned see that they are compleat.

Perhaps it would not be easy to find any authour, except Homer, who invented so much as Shakespeare, who so much advanced the studies which he cultivated, or effused so much novelty upon his age or country. The form, the characters, the language, and the shows of the English drama are his. *He seems*, says Dennis, *to have been the very original of our English tragical harmony, that is, the harmony of blank verse, diversified often by dissyllable and trissyllable terminations. For the diversity distinguishes it from heroick harmony, and by bringing it nearer to common use makes it more proper to gain attention, and more fit for action and dialogue. Such verse we make when we are writing prose; we make such verse in common conversation.*[29]

I know not whether this praise is rigorously just. The dissyllable termination, which the critick rightly appropriates to the drama, is to be found, though, I think, not in *Gorboduc* which is confessedly before our authour; yet in *Hieronnymo*,[30] of which the date is not certain, but which there is reason to believe at least as old as his earliest plays. This however is certain, that he is the first who taught either tragedy or comedy to please, there being no theatrical piece of any older writer, of which the name is known, except to antiquaries and collectors of books, which are sought because they are scarce, and would not have been scarce, had they been much esteemed.

To him we must ascribe the praise, unless Spenser may divide it with him, of having first discovered to how much smoothness and harmony the English language could be softened. He has speeches, perhaps sometimes scenes, which have all the delicacy of Rowe, without his effeminacy. He endeavours indeed commonly to strike by the force and vigour of his dialogue, but he never executes his purpose better, than when he tries to sooth by softness.

Yet it must be at last confessed, that as we owe every thing to him, he owes something to us; that, if much of his praise is paid by perception and judgement, much is likewise given by custom and veneration. We fix our eyes upon his graces, and turn them from his deformities, and endure in him what we should in another loath or despise. If we endured without praising, respect for the father of our drama might excuse us; but I have seen, in the book of some modern critick;[31] a collection of anomalies, which shew that he has corrupted language by every mode of depravation, but which his admirer has accumulated as a monument of honour.

He has scenes of undoubted and perpetual excellence, but perhaps not one play, which, if it were now exhibited as the work of a contemporary writer, would be heard to the conclusion. I am indeed far from thinking, that his works were wrought to his own ideas of perfection; when they were such as would satisfy the audience, they satisfied the writer. It is seldom that authours, though more studious of fame than Shakespeare, rise much above the standard of their own age; to add a little of what is best will always be sufficient for present praise, and those who find themselves exalted into fame, are willing to credit their encomiasts, and to spare the labour of contending with themselves.

It does not appear, that Shakespeare thought his works worthy of posterity, that he levied any ideal tribute upon future times, or had any further prospect, than of present popularity and present profit. When his plays had been acted, his hope was at an end; he solicited no addition of honour from the reader. He therefore made no scruple to repeat the same jests in many dialogues, or to entangle different plots by the same knot of perplexity, which may be at least forgiven him, by those who recollect, that of Congreve's four comedies, two are concluded by a marriage in a mask, by a deception, which perhaps never happened, and which, whether likely or not, he did not invent.

So careless was this great poet of future fame, that, though he retired to ease and plenty, while he was yet little *declined into the vale of years*,[32] before he could be disgusted with fatigue, or disabled by infirmity, he made no collection of his works, nor desired to rescue those that had been already published from the depravations that obscured them, or secure to the rest a better destiny, by giving them to the world in their genuine state.

Of the plays which bear the name of Shakespeare in the late editions, the greater part were not published till about seven years after his death, and the few which appeared in his life are apparently thrust into the world without the care of the authour, and therefore probably without his knowledge.

Of all the publishers, clandestine or professed, their negligence and unskilfulness has by the late revisers been sufficiently shown. The faults of all are indeed numerous and gross, and have not only corrupted many passages perhaps beyond recovery, but have brought others into suspicion, which are only obscured by obsolete phraseology, or by the writer's unskilfulness and affectation. To alter is more easy than to explain, and temerity is a more common quality than diligence. Those who saw that they must employ conjecture to a certain degree, were willing to indulge it a little further. Had the authour published his own works, we should have sat quietly down to disentangle his intricacies, and clear his obscurities; but now we tear what we cannot loose, and eject what we happen not to understand.

The faults are more than could have happened without the concurrence of many causes. The stile of Shakespeare was in itself ungrammatical, perplexed and obscure; his works were transcribed for the players by those who may be supposed to have seldom understood them; they were transmitted by copiers equally unskilful, who still multiplied errours; they were perhaps sometimes mutilated by the actors, for the sake of shortening the speeches; and were at last printed without correction of the press.

In this state they remained, not as Dr. Warburton supposes, because they were unregarded,[33] but because the editor's art was not yet applied to modern languages, and our ancestors were accustomed to so much negligence of English printers, that they could very patiently endure it. At last an edition was undertaken by Rowe; not because a poet was to be published by a poet, for Rowe seems to have thought very little on correction or explanation, but that our authour's works might appear like those of his fraternity, with the appendages of a life and recommendatory preface. Rowe has been clamorously blamed for not performing what he did not undertake, and it is time that justice be done him, by confessing, that though he seems to have had no thought of corruption beyond the printer's errours, yet he has made many emendations, if they were not made before, which his successors have received without acknowledgement, and which, if they had produced them, would have filled pages and pages with censures of the stupidity by which the faults were committed, with displays of the absurdities which they involved, with ostentatious expositions of the new reading, and self congratulations on the happiness of discovering it.

Of Rowe, as of all the editors, I have preserved the preface, and have likewise retained the authour's life,[34] though not written with much elegance or spirit; it relates however what is now to be known, and therefore deserves to pass through all succeeding publications.

The nation had been for many years content enough with Mr. Rowe's performance, when Mr. Pope made them acquainted with the true state of Shakespeare's text, shewed that it was extremely corrupt, and gave reason to hope that there were means of reforming it. He collated the old copies, which none had thought to examine before, and restored many lines to their integrity; but, by a very compendious criticism, he rejected whatever he disliked, and thought more of amputation than of cure.

I know not why he is commended by Dr. Warburton for distinguishing the genuine from the spurious plays.[35] In this choice he exerted no judgement of his own; the plays which he received, were given by Hemings and Condel, the first editors; and those which he rejected, though, according to the licentiousness of the press in those times, they were printed during Shakespeare's life, with his name, had been omitted by his friends, and were never added to his works before the edition of 1664, from which they were copied by the later printers.

This was a work which Pope seems to have thought unworthy of his abilities, being not able to suppress his contempt of *the dull duty of an editor*.[36] He understood but half his undertaking. The duty of a collator is indeed dull, yet, like other tedious tasks, is very necessary; but an emendatory critick would ill discharge his duty, without qualities very different from dulness. In perusing a corrupted piece, he must have before him all possibilities of meaning, with all possibilities of expression. Such must be his comprehension of thought, and such his copiousness of language. Out of many readings possible, he must be able to select that which best suits with the state, opinions, and modes of language prevailing in every age, and with his authour's particular cast of thought, and turn of expression. Such must be his knowledge, and such his taste. Conjectural criticism demands more than humanity possesses, and he that exercises it with most praise has very frequent need of indulgence. Let us now be told no more of the dull duty of an editor.

Confidence is the common consequence of success. They whose excellence of any kind has been loudly celebrated, are ready to conclude, that their powers are universal. Pope's edition fell below his own expectations, and he was so much offended, when he was found to have left any thing for others to do, that he past the latter part of his life in a state of hostility with verbal criticism.

I have retained all his notes, that no fragment of so great a writer may be lost; his preface, valuable alike for elegance of composition and justness of remark, and containing a general criticism on his author, so extensive that little can be added, and so exact, that little can be disputed, every editor has an interest to suppress, but that every reader would demand its insertion.

Pope was succeeded by Theobald, a man of narrow comprehension and small acquisitions, with no native and intrinsick splendour of genius, with little of the artificial light of learning, but zealous for minute accuracy, and not negligent in pursuing it. He collated the ancient copies, and rectified many errors. A man so anxiously scrupulous might have been expected to do more, but what little he did was commonly right.

In his report of copies and editions he is not to be trusted, without examination. He speaks sometimes indefinitely of copies, when he has only one. In his enumeration of editions, he mentions the two first folios as of high, and the third folio as of middle authority; but the truth is, that the first is equivalent to all others, and that the rest only deviate from it by the printer's negligence. Whoever has any of the folios has all, excepting those diversities which mere reiteration of editions will produce. I collated them all at the beginning, but afterwards used only the first.

Of his notes I have generally retained those which he retained himself in his second edition, except when they were confuted by subsequent annotators, or were too minute to merit preservation. I have sometimes adopted his restoration of a comma, without inserting the panegyrick in which he celebrated himself for his achievement. The exuberant excrescence of his diction I have often lopped, his triumphant exultations over Pope and Rowe I have sometimes suppressed, and his contemptible ostentation I have frequently concealed; but I have in some places shewn him, as he would have shewn himself, for the reader's diversion, that the inflated emptiness of some notes may justify or excuse the contraction of the rest.

Theobald, thus weak and ignorant, thus mean and faithless, thus petulant and ostentatious, by the good luck of having Pope for his enemy, has escaped, and escaped alone, with reputation, from this undertaking. So willingly does the world support those who solicite favour, against those who command reverence; and so easily is he praised, whom no man can envy.

Our authour fell then into the hands of Sir Thomas Hanmer, the Oxford editor, a man, in my opinion, eminently qualified by nature of such studies. He had, what is the first requisite to emendatory criticism, that intuition by which the poet's intention is immediately discovered, and that dexterity of intellect which dispatches its work by the easiest means. He had undoubtedly read much; his acquaintance with customs, opinions, and traditions, seem to have been large; and he is often learned without shew. He seldom passes what he does not understand, without an attempt to find or to make a meaning, and sometimes hastily makes what a little more attention would have found. He is solicitous to reduce to grammar, what he could not be sure that his authour intended to be grammatical. Shakespeare regarded more the series of ideas, than of words; and his language, not being designed for the reader's desk, was all that he desired it to be, if it conveyed his meaning to the audience.

Hanmer's care of the metre has been too violently censured. He found the measures reformed in so many passages, by the silent labours of some editors, with the silent acquiescence of the rest, that he thought himself allowed to extend a little further the license, which had already been carried so far without reprehension; and of his corrections in general, it must be confessed, that they are often just, and made commonly with the least possible violation of the text.

But, by inserting his emendations, whether invented or borrowed, into the page, without any notice of varying copies, he has appropriated the labour of his predecessors, and made his own edition of little authority. His confidence indeed, both in himself and others, was too great; he supposes all to be right that was done by Pope and Theobald; he seems not to suspect a critick of fallibility, and it was but reasonable that he should claim what he so liberally granted.

As he never writes without careful enquiry and diligent consideration, I have received all his notes, and believe that every reader will wish for more.

Of the last editor it is more difficult to speak. Respect is due to high place,[37] tenderness to living reputation, and veneration to genius and learning; but he cannot be justly offended at that liberty of which he has himself so frequently given an example, nor very solicitous what is thought of notes, which he ought never to have considered as part of his serious employments, and which, I suppose, since the ardour of composition is remitted, he no longer numbers among his happy effusions.

The original and predominant errour of his commentary, is acquiescence in his first thoughts; that precipitation which is produced by consciousness of quick discernment; and that confidence which presumes to do by surveying the surface, what labour only can perform, by penetrating the bottom. His notes exhibit sometimes perverse interpretations, and sometimes improbable conjectures; he at one time gives the authour more profundity of meaning, than the sentence admits, and at another discovers absurdities, where the sense is plain to every other reader. But his emendations are likewise often happy and just; and his interpretation of obscure passages learned and sagacious.

Of his notes, I have commonly rejected those, against which the general voice of the publick has exclaimed, or which their own incongruity immediately condemns, and which, I suppose, the authour himself would desire to be forgotten. Of the rest, to part I have given the highest approbation, by inserting the offered reading in the text; part I have left to the judgment of the reader, as doubtful, though specious; and part I have censured without reserve, but I am sure without bitterness of malice, and, I hope, without wantonness of insult.

It is no pleasure to me, in revising my volumes, to observe how much paper is wasted in confutation. Whoever considers the revolutions of learning, and the various questions of greater or less importance, upon which wit and reason have exercised their powers, must lament the unsuccessfulness of enquiry, and the slow advances of truth, when he reflects, that great part of the labour of every writer is only the destruction of those that went before him. The first care of the builder of a new system, is to demolish the fabricks which are standing. The chief desire of him that comments an authour, is to shew how much other commentators have corrupted and obscured him. The opinions prevalent in one age, as truths above the reach of controversy, are confuted and rejected in another, and rise again to reception in remoter times. Thus the human mind is kept in motion without progress. Thus sometimes truth and errour, and sometimes contrarieties of errour, take each other's place by reciprocal invasion. The tide of seeming knowledge which is poured over one generation, retires and leaves another naked and barren; the sudden meteors of intelligence which for a while appear to shoot their beams into the regions of obscurity, on a sudden withdraw their lustre, and leave mortals again to grope their way.

These elevations and depressions of renown, and the contradictions to which all improvers of knowledge must for ever be exposed, since they are not escaped by the highest and brightest of mankind, may surely be endured with patience by cricks and annotators, who can rank themselves but as the satellites of their authours. How canst thou beg for life, says Achilles to his captive, when thou knowest that thou art now to suffer only what must another day be suffered by Achilles?[38]

Dr. Warburton had a name sufficient to confer celebrity on those who could exalt themselves into antagonists, and his notes have raised a clamour too loud to be distinct. His chief assailants are the authours of *the Canons of criticism* and of the *Review of Shakespeare's text;*[39] of whom one ridicules his errours with airy petulance, suitable enough to the levity of the controversy; the other attacks them with gloomy malignity, as if he were dragging to justice an assassin or incendiary. The one stings like a fly, sucks a little blood, takes a gay flutter, and returns for more; the other bites like a viper, and would be glad to leave inflammations and gangrene behind him. When I think on one, with his confederates, I remember the danger of *Coriolanus*, who was afraid that *girls with spits, and boys with stones, should slay him in puny battle;* when the other crosses my imagination, I remember the prodigy in *Macbeth*,

An eagle tow'ring in his pride of place,
Was by a mousing owl hawk'd at and kill'd.[40]

Let me however do them justice. One is a wit, and one a scholar. They have both shewn acuteness sufficient in the discovery of faults, and have both advanced some probable interpretations of obscure passages; but when they aspire to conjecture and emendation, it appears how falsely we all estimate our own abilities, and the little which they have been able to perform might have taught them more candour to the endeavours of others.

Before Dr. Warburton's edition, *Critical observations on Shakespeare* had been published by Mr. Upton, a man skilled in languages, and acquainted with books, but who seems to have had no great vigour of genius or nicety of taste. Many of his explanations are curious and useful, but he likewise, though he professed to oppose the licentious confidence of editors, and adhere to the old copies, is unable to restrain the rage of emendation, though his ardour is ill seconded by his skill. Every cold empirick, when his heart is expanded by a successful experiment, swells into a theorist, and the laborious collator at some unlucky moment frolicks in conjecture.

Critical, historical and explanatory notes have been likewise published upon Shakespeare by Dr. Grey, whose diligent perusal of the old English writers has enabled him to make some useful observations. What he undertook he has[41] well enough performed, but as he neither attempts judicial nor emendatory criticism, he employs rather his memory than his sagacity. It were to be wished that all would endeavour to imitate his modesty who have not been able to surpass his knowledge.

I can say with great sincerity of all my predecessors, what I hope will hereafter be said of me, that not one has left Shakespeare without improvement, nor is there one to whom I have not been indebted for assistance and information. Whatever I have taken from them it was my intention to refer to its original authour, and it is certain, that what I have not given to another, I believed when I wrote it to be my own. In some perhaps I have been anticipated; but if I am ever found to encroach upon the remarks of any other commentator, I am willing that the honour, be it more or less, should be transferred to the first claimant, for his right, and his alone, stands above dispute; the second can prove his pretensions only to himself, nor can himself always distinguish invention, with sufficient certainty, from recollection.

They have all been treated by me with candour, which they have not been careful of observing to one another. It is not easy to discover from what cause the acrimony of a scholiast can naturally proceed. The subjects to be discussed by him are of very small importance; they involve neither property nor liberty; nor favour the interest of sect or party. The various readings of copies, and different interpretations of a passage, seem to be questions that might exercise the wit, without engaging the passions. But, whether it be, that *small things make mean men proud,*[42] and vanity catches small occasions; or that all contrariety of opinion, even in those that can defend it no longer, makes proud men angry; there is often found in commentaries a spontaneous strain of invective and contempt, more eager and venomous than is vented by the most furious controvertist in politicks against those whom he is hired to defame.

Perhaps the lightness of the matter may conduce to the vehemence of the agency; when the truth to be investigated is so near to inexistence, as to escape attention, its bulk is to be enlarged by rage and exclamation: That to which all would be indifferent in its original state, may attract notice when the fate of a name is appended to it. A commentator has indeed great temptations to supply by turbulence what he wants of dignity, to beat his little gold to a spacious surface, to work that to foam which no art or diligence can exalt to spirit.

The notes which I have borrowed or written are either illustrative, by which difficulties are explained; or judicial, by which faults and beauties are remarked; or emendatory, by which depravations are corrected.

The explanations transcribed from others, if I do not subjoin any other interpretation, I suppose commonly to be right, at least I intend by acquiscence to confess, that I have nothing better to propose.

After the labours of all the editors, I found many passages which appeared to me likely to obstruct the greater number of readers, and thought it my duty to facilitate their passage. It is impossible for an expositor not to write too little for some, and too much for others. He can only judge what is necessary by his own experience; and how long soever he may deliberate, will at last explain many lines which the learned will think impossible to be mistaken, and omit many for which the ignorant will want his help. These are censures merely relative, and must be quietly endured. I have endeavoured to be neither superfluously copious, nor scrupulously reserved, and hope that I have made my authour's meaning accessible to many who before were frighted from perusing him, and contributed something to the publick, by diffusing innocent and rational pleasure.

The compleat explanation of an authour not systematick and consequential, but desultory and vagrant, abounding in casual allusions and light hints, is not to be expected from any single scholiast. All personal reflections, when names are suppressed, must be in a few years irrecoverably obliterated; and customs, too minute to attract the notice of law, such as modes of dress, formalities of conversation, rules of visits, disposition of furniture, and practices of ceremony, which naturally find places in familiar dialogue, are so fugitive and unsubstantial, that they are not easily retained or recovered. What can be known, will be collected by chance, from the recesses of obscure and obsolete papers, perused commonly with some other view. Of this knowledge every man has some, and none has much; but when an authour has engaged the publick attention, those who can add any thing to his illustration, communicate their discoveries, and time produces what had eluded diligence.

To time I have been obliged to resign many passages, which, though I did not understand them, will perhaps hereafter be explained, having, I hope, illustrated some, which others have neglected or mistaken, sometimes by short remarks, or marginal directions, such as every editor has added at his will, and often by comments more laborious than the matter will seem to deserve; but that which is most difficult is not always most important, and to an editor nothing is a trifle by which his authour is obscured.

The poetical beauties or defects I have not been very diligent to observe. Some plays have more, and some fewer judicial observations, not in proportion

to their difference of merit, but because I gave this part of my design to chance
and to caprice. The reader, I believe, is seldom pleased to find his opinion
anticipated; it is natural to delight more in what we find or make, than in what
we receive. Judgement, like other faculties, is improved by practice, and its
advancement is hindered by submission to dictatorial decisions, as the memory
grows torpid by the use of a table book. Some initiation is however necessary;
of all skill, part is infused by precept, and part is obtained by habit; I have
therefore shewn so much as may enable the candidate of criticism to discover
the rest.

To the end of most plays, I have added short strictures, containing a
general censure of faults, or praise of excellence; in which I know not how
much I have concurred with the current opinion; but I have not, by any
affectation of singularity, deviated from it. Nothing is minutely and particularly
examined, and therefore it is to be supposed, that in the plays which are
condemned there is much to be praised, and in these which are praised much
to be condemned.

The part of criticism in which the whole succession of editors has laboured
with the greatest diligence, which has occasioned the most arrogant ostentation, and excited the keenest acrimony, is the emendation of corrupted
passages, to which the publick attention having been first drawn by the
violence of contention between Pope and Theobald, has been continued by the
persecution which, with a kind of conspiracy, has been since raised against all
the publishers of Shakespeare.

That many passages have been passed in a state of depravation through all
the editions is indubitably certain; of these the restoration is only to be
attempted by collation of copies or sagacity of conjecture. The collator's
province is safe and easy, the conjecturer's perilous and difficult. Yet as the
greater part of the plays are extant only in one copy, the peril must not be
avoided, nor the difficulty refused.

Of the readings which this emulation of amendment has hitherto produced, some from the labours of every publisher I have advanced into the text;
those are to be considered as in my opinion sufficiently supported; some I have
rejected without mention, as evidently erroneous; some I have left in the notes
without censure or approbation, as resting in equipoise between objection and
defence; and some, which seemed specious but not right, I have inserted with
a subsequent animadversion.

Having classed the observations of others, I was at last to try what I could
substitute for their mistakes, and how I could supply their omissions. I collated
such copies as I could procure, and wished for more, but have not found the
collectors of these rarities very communicative. Of the editions which chance
or kindness put into my hands I have given an enumeration, that I may not be
blamed for neglecting what I had not the power to do.

By examining the old copies, I soon found that the later publishers, with
all their boasts of diligence, suffered many passages to stand unauthorised,
and contented themselves with Rowe's regulation of the text, even where they
knew it to be arbitrary, and with a little consideration might have found it to be

wrong. Some of these alterations are only the ejection of a word for one that appeared to him more elegant or more intelligible. These corruptions I have often silently rectified; for the history of our language, and the true force of our words, can only be preserved, by keeping the text of authours free from adulteration. Others, and those very frequent, smoothed the cadence, or regulated the measure; on these I have not exercised the same rigour; if only a word was transposed, or a particle inserted or omitted, I have sometimes suffered the line to stand; for the inconstancy of the copies is such, as that some liberties may be easily permitted. But this practice I have not suffered to proceed far, having restored the primitive diction wherever it could for any reason be preferred.

The emendations, which comparison of copies supplied, I have inserted in the text; sometimes where the improvement was slight, without notice, and sometimes with an account of the reasons of the change.

Conjecture, though it be sometimes unavoidable, I have not wantonly nor licentiously indulged. It has been my settled principle, that the reading of the ancient books is probably true, and therefore is not to be disturbed for the sake of elegance, perspicuity, or mere improvement of the sense. For though much credit is not due to the fidelity, nor any to the judgement of the first publishers, yet they who had the copy before their eyes were more likely to read it right, than we who read it only by imagination. But it is evident that they have often made strange mistakes by ignorance or negligence, and that therefore something may be properly attempted by criticism, keeping the middle way between presumption and timidity.

Such criticism I have attempted to practise, and where any passage appeared inextricably perplexed, have endeavoured to discover how it may be recalled to sense, with least violence. But my first labour is, always to turn the old text on every side, and try if there be any interstice, through which light can find its way; nor would Huetius[43] himself condemn me, as refusing the trouble of research, for the ambition of alteration. In this modest industry I have not been unsuccessful. I have rescued many lines from the violations of temerity, and secured many scenes from the inroads of correction. I have adopted the Roman sentiment, that it is more honourable to save a citizen, than to kill an enemy, and have been more careful to protect than to attack.

I have preserved the common distribution of the plays into acts, though I believe it to be in almost all the plays void of authority. Some of those which are divided in the later editions have no division in the first folio, and some that are divided in the folio have no division in the preceding copies. The settled mode of the theatre requires four intervals in the play, but few, if any, of our authour's compositions can be properly distributed in that manner. An act is so much of the drama as passes without intervention of time or change of place. A pause makes a new act. In every real, and therefore in every imitative action, the intervals may be more or fewer, the restriction of five acts being accidental and arbitrary. This Shakespeare knew, and this he practised; his plays were written, and at first printed in one unbroken continuity, and ought now to be exhibited with short pauses, interposed as often as the scene is changed, or any considerable time is required to pass. This method would at once quell a thousand absurdities.

In restoring the authour's works to their integrity, I have considered the punctuation as wholly in my power; for what could be their care of colons and commas, who corrupted words and sentences. Whatever could be done by adjusting points is therefore silently performed, in some plays with much diligence, in others with less; it is hard to keep a busy eye steadily fixed upon evanescent atoms, or a discursive mind upon evanescent truth.

The same liberty has been taken with a few particles, or other words of slight effect. I have sometimes inserted or omitted them without notice. I have done that sometimes, which the other editors have done always, and which indeed the state of the text may sufficiently justify.

The greater part of readers, instead of blaming us for passing trifles, will wonder that on mere trifles so much labour is expended, with such importance of debate, and such solemnity of diction. To these I answer with confidence, that they are judging of an art which they do not understand; yet cannot much reproach them with their ignorance, nor promise that they would become in general, by learning criticism, more useful, happier or wiser.

As I practised conjecture more, I learned to trust it less; and after I had printed a few plays resolved to insert none of my own readings in the text. Upon this caution I now congratulate myself, for every day encreases my doubt of my emendations.

Since I have confined my imagination to the margin, it must not be considered as very reprehensible, if I have suffered it to play some freaks in its own dominion. There is no danger in conjecture, if it be proposed as conjecture; and while the text remains uninjured, those changes may be safely offered, which are not considered even by him that offers them as necessary or safe.

If my readings are of little value, they have not been ostentatiously displayed or importunately obtruded. I could have written longer notes, for the art of writing notes is not of difficult attainment. The work is performed, first by railing at the stupidity, negligence, ignorance, and asinine tastelessness of the former editors, and shewing, from all that goes before and all that follows, the inelegance and absurdity of the old reading; then by proposing something, which to superficial readers would seem specious, but which the editor rejects with indignation; then by producing the true reading, with a long paraphrase, and concluding with loud acclamations on the discovery, and a sober wish for the advancement and prosperity of genuine criticism.

All this may be done, and perhaps done sometimes without impropriety. But I have always suspected that the reading is right, which requires many words to prove it wrong; and the emendation wrong, that cannot without so much labour appear to be right. The justness of a happy restoration strikes at once, and the moral precept may be well applied to criticism, *quod dubitas ne feceris* [while you doubt, do not].[44]

To dread the shore which he sees spread with wrecks, is natural to the sailor. I had before my eye, so many critical adventures ended in miscarriage, that caution was forced upon me. I encountered in every page Wit struggling with its own sophistry, and Learning confused by the multiplicity of its views. I was forced to censure those whom I admired, and could not but reflect, while I was dispossessing their emendations, how soon the same fate might happen to my own, and how many of the readings which I have corrected may be by some other editor defended and established.

> Criticks, I saw, that other's names efface,
> And fix their own, with labour, in the place;
> Their own, like others, soon their place resign'd,
> Or disappear'd, and left the first behind.
>
> Pope.[45]

That a conjectural critick should often be mistaken, cannot be wonderful, either to others or himself, if it be considered, that in his art there is no system, no principal and axiomatical truth that regulates subordinate positions. His chance of errour is renewed at every attempt; an oblique view of the passage, a slight misapprehension of a phrase, a casual inattention to the parts connected, is sufficient to make him not only fail, but fail ridiculously; and when he succeeds best, he produces perhaps but one reading of many probable, and he that suggests another will always be able to dispute his claims.

It is an unhappy state, in which danger is hid under pleasure. The allurements of emendation are scarcely resistible. Conjecture has all the joy and all the pride of invention, and he that has once started a happy change, is too much delighted to consider what objections may rise against it.

Yet conjectural criticism has been of great use in the learned world; nor is it my intention to depreciate a study, that has exercised so many mighty minds, from the revival of learning to our own age, from the Bishop of Aleria to English Bentley.[46] The criticks on ancient authours have, in the exercise of their sagacity, many assistances, which the editor of Shakespeare is condemned to want. They are employed upon grammatical and settled languages, whose construction contributes so much to perspicuity, that Homer has fewer passages unintelligible than Chaucer. The words have not only a known regimen, but invariable quantities, which direct and confine the choice. There are commonly more manuscripts than one; and they do not often conspire in the same mistakes. Yet Scaliger could confess to Salmasius how little satisfaction his emendations gave him. *Illudunt nobis conjecturae nostrae, quarum nos pudet, posteaquam in meliores codices incidimus* [Our conjectures play us for fools, and we are put to shame, when subsequently we light on better texts]. And Lipsius could complain, that criticks were making faults, by trying to remove them, *Ut olim vitiis, ita nunc remediis laboratur* [As once we labored over corruptions, so now we do the same with our corrections].[47] And indeed, where mere conjecture is to be used, the emendations of Scaliger and Lipsius, notwithstanding their wonderful sagacity and erudition, are often vague and disputable, like mine or Theobald's.

Perhaps I may not be more censured for doing wrong, than for doing little; for raising in the publick expectations, which at last I have not answered. The expectation of ignorance is indefinite, and that of knowledge is often tyrannical. It is hard to satisfy those who know not what to demand, or those who demand by design what they think impossible to be done. I have indeed disappointed no opinion more than my own; yet I have endeavoured to perform my task with no slight solicitude. Not a single passage in the whole work has appeared to me corrupt, which I have not attempted to restore; or obscure, which I have not endeavoured to illustrate. In many I have failed like others; and from many, after all my efforts, I have retreated, and confessed the repulse. I have not passed over, with affected superiority, what is equally difficult to the reader and to myself, but where I could not instruct him, have owned my ignorance. I might easily have accumulated a mass of seeming learning upon easy scenes; but it ought not to be imputed to negligence, that, where nothing was necessary, nothing has been done, or that, where others have said enough, I have said no more.

Notes are often necessary, but they are necessary evils. Let him, that is yet unacquainted with the powers of Shakespeare, and who desires to feel the highest pleasure that the drama can give, read every play from the first scene to the last, with utter negligence of all his commentators. When his fancy is once on the wing, let it not stoop at correction or explanation. When his attention is strongly engaged, let it disdain alike to turn aside to the name of Theobald and of Pope. Let him read on through brightness and obscurity, through integrity and corruption; let him preserve his comprehension of the dialogue and his interest in the fable. And when the pleasures of novelty have ceased, let him attempt exactness, and read the commentators.

Particular passages are cleared by notes, but the general effect of the work is weakened. The mind is refrigerated by interruption; the thoughts are diverted from the principal subject; the reader is weary, he suspects not why; and at last throws away the book, which he has too diligently studied.

Parts are not to be examined till the whole has been surveyed; there is a kind of intellectual remoteness necessary for the comprehension of any great work in its full design and its true proportions; a close approach shews the smaller niceties, but the beauty of the whole is discerned no longer.

It is not very grateful to consider how little the succession of editors has added to this authour's power of pleasing. He was read, admired, studied, and imitated, while he was yet deformed with all the improprieties which ignorance and neglect could accumulate upon him; while the reading was yet not rectified, nor his allusions understood; yet then did Dryden pronounce "that Shakespeare was the man, who, of all modern and perhaps ancient poets, had the largest and most comprehensive soul. All the images of nature were still present to him, and he drew them not laboriously, but luckily: When he describes any thing, you more than see it, you feel it too. Those who accuse him to have wanted learning, give him the greater commendation: he was naturally learned: he needed not the spectacles of books to read nature; he looked inwards, and found her there. I cannot say he is every where alike; were he so, I should do him injury to compare him with the greatest of mankind. He is many times flat and insipid; his comick wit degenerating into clenches, his serious swelling into bombast. But he is always great, when some great occasion is presented to him: No man can say, he ever had a fit subject for his wit, and did not then raise himself as high above the rest of poets,

> *Quantum lenta solent inter viburna cupressi.*
> [As cypresses are wont to tower amidst the supple willows]."[48]

It is to be lamented, that such a writer should want a commentary; that his language should become obsolete, or his sentiments obscure. But it is vain to carry wishes beyond the condition of human things; that which must happen to all, has happened to Shakespeare, by accident and time; and more than has been suffered by any other writer since the use of types, has been suffered by him through his own negligence of fame, or perhaps by that superiority of mind, which despised its own performances, when it compared them with its powers, and judged those works unworthy to be preserved, which the criticks of following ages were to contend for the fame of restoring and explaining.

Among these candidates of inferiour fame, I am now to stand the judgment of the publick; and wish that I could confidently produce my commentary as equal to the encouragement which I have had the honour of receiving. Every work of this kind is by its nature deficient, and I should feel little solicitude about the sentence, were it to be pronounced only by the skilful and the learned.

NOTES

1. Cf. Aristotle *Metaphysics* 1. 5.
2. Cf. Horace *Epistles* 2. 1. 39.
3. Cf. *Rasselas*, chap. 10.
4. Cf. Cicero *Ad familiares* 16. 8. 4.
5. Hierocles Alexandrinus, Greek philosopher of the fifth century A.D.
6. Cf. Johnson's *Preface to the English Dictionary*.
7. Cf. Pope's *Preface to Shakespeare* (1725), par. 4.
8. Cf. John Dennis, *An Essay on the Genius and Writings of Shakespear* (1712); Thomas Rymer, *A Short View of Tragedy* (1692); Voltaire, *Appel à toutes les nations de l'Europe* (1761) and *Dissertation sur la tragédie ancienne et moderne* (1749).
9. On tragicomedy see *Rambler* no. 156.
10. Cf. Horace *Ars poetica* 11. 333–34, 343–44.
11. John Heminge and Henry Condell, actors in Shakespeare's dramatic company, published the First Folio (1623).
12. I.e., Shakespeare has faults which would obscure any merits less estimable than those Johnson has just imputed to him. Cf. Johnson's discussion of his first defect—his lack of a moral purpose—with his remarks on *The Beggar's Opera*.
13. Cf. Pope's *Preface*, par. 18.

14. The 1778 edition reads: "have most reason to complain when he approachest nearest to his highest excellence, and seems fully resolved . . . crosses of love. What he does best, he soon ceases to do. He is. . . . "

15. Cf. Aristotle *Poetics* 7. 2–3.

16. See particularly Pierre Corneille's *Discours dramatiques* (1660). Cf. the following account of the dramatic unities and dramatic illusion with that in the *Life of Rowe*.

17. Addison's *Cato* (1713), 5. 1. 1–40.

18. Lucan *Pharsalia* 3. 138–40 (tr. Rowe).

19. Altered in later editions to "deliberately."

20. *Aeneid* 1. 610.

21. Lilly . . . Ascham: fifteenth- and sixteenth-century British educators and scholars.

22. Possibly, but not certainly, the reference is to Malory's *Morte d'Arthur* (1485).

23. In his *Appel à toutes les nations*. Cf. Johnson's discussion of *Cato* with that in the *Life of Addison*.

24. Ben Jonson, in his verses in the First Folio on Shakespeare; the quotation is corrected in the 1773 edition to "less Greek."

25. Cf. Zachary Grey, *Critical, Historical, and Explanatory Notes on Shakespeare* (1754); the references are to *Richard III*, 1. 1. 144, and Terence, *Andria*, 1. 171.

26. Cf. Pope's *Preface*, par. 15.

27. Cf. Rowe, *Some Account of the Life & c. of . . . Shakespear* (1709), par. 4.

28. *Troilus and Cressida* 3. 3. 224.

29. Cf. *Essay on the Genius and Writings of Shakespear*, par. 2. "Heroic harmony" refers to the tighter, rimed couplets characteristic of seventeenth-century heroic drama.

30. The reference is probably to Kyd's *Spanish Tragedy*.

31. John Upton, *Critical Observations on Shakespeare* (1746).

32. *Othello*, 3. 3. 269–70.

33. Cf. William Warburton's *Preface* (1747), par. 2.

34. The 1773 and later editions read: "As of the other editors, I have preserved the prefaces, I have likewise borrowed the author's life from Rowe. . . . "

35. Cf. Warburton's *Preface*, par. 4.

36. Cf. Pope's *Preface*, penultimate paragraph.

37. This is Warburton, who in 1759 had been made Bishop of Gloucester.

38. Cf. *Iliad* 21. 106–14. In the 1773 and later editions this sentence begins: "How canst thou beg for life, says Homer's hero to his captive. . . . "

39. Thomas Edwards wrote *Canons of Criticism* (1748) and Benjamin Heath *The Revisal of Shakespeare's Text* (1765). Johnson's inaccurate title for Heath is corrected in the 1778 edition.

40. *Macbeth*, 2. 4. 12–13. "An eagle" is corrected to "A falcon" in the 1773 edition.

41. The 1768 edition reads: "undertook was."

42. *2 Henry VI*, 4. 1. 106.

43. Pierre Huet, *De interpretatione libri duo* (1661).

44. Pliny *Epistles* 1. 18.

45. *Temple of Fame*, 11. 37–40 (for "efface" read "deface").

46. Joannes Andreas and Richard Bentley, both famous editors.

47. Scaliger, Salmasius, and Lipsius were all renowned classical scholars.

48. Dryden, *Essay of Dramatic Poesy* (1668); the Latin is from Virgil, *Eclogues*, 1. 25.

LIVES OF THE POETS

ABRAHAM COWLEY

Abraham Cowley was born in the year one thousand six hundred and eighteen. His father was a grocer, whose condition Dr. Sprat conceals under the general appellation of a citizen; and, what would probably not have been less carefully suppressed, the omission of his name in the register of St. Dunstan's parish, gives reason to suspect that his father was a sectary. Whoever he was, he died before the birth of his son, and consequently left him to the care of his mother; whom Wood represents as struggling earnestly to procure him a literary education, and who, as she lived to the age of eighty, had her solicitude rewarded by seeing her son eminent, and, I hope, by seeing him fortunate, and partaking his prosperity. We know at least, from Sprat's account, that he always acknowledged her care, and justly paid the dues of filial gratitude.

In the window of his mother's apartment lay Spenser's Fairy Queen; in which he very early took delight to read, till, by feeling the charms of verse, he became, as he relates, irrecoverably a Poet. Such are the accidents, which, sometimes remembered, and perhaps sometimes forgotten, produce that particular designation of mind, and propensity for some certain science or employment, which is commonly called Genius. The true Genius is a mind of large general powers, accidentally determined to some particular direction. The great Painter of the present age had the first fondness for his art excited by the perusal of Richardson's treatise.

By his mother's solicitation he was admitted into Westminster-school, where he was soon distinguished. He was wont, says Sprat, to relate, "That he had this defect in his memory at that time, that his teachers never could bring it to retain the ordinary rules of grammar."

This is an instance of the natural desire of man to propagate a wonder. It is surely very difficult to tell any thing as it was heard, when Sprat could not refrain from amplifying a commodious incident, though the book to which he prefixed his narrative contained its confutation. A memory admitting some things, and rejecting others, an intellectual digestion that concocted the pulp of learning, but refused the husks, had the appearance of an instinctive elegance, of a particular provision made by nature for literary politeness. But in the author's own honest relation, the marvel vanishes: he was, he says, such "an enemy to all constraint, that his master never could prevail on him to learn the rules without book." He does not tell that he could not learn the rules, but that being able to perform his exercises without them, and being an "enemy to constraint," he spared himself the labour. . . .

In the year 1647, his "Mistress" was published; for he imagined, as he declared in his preface to a subsequent edition, that "poets are scarce thought freemen of their company without paying some duties, or obliging themselves to be true to Love."

This obligation to amorous ditties owes, I believe, its original to the fame of Petrarch, who, in an age rude and uncultivated, by his tuneful homage to his Laura, refined the manners of the lettered world, and filled Europe with love and poetry. But the basis of all excellence is truth: he that professes love ought to feel its power. Petrarch was a real lover, and Laura doubtless deserved his tenderness. Of Cowley, we are told by Barnes, who had means enough of information, that, whatever he may talk of his own inflammability, and the variety of characters by which his heart was divided, he in reality was in love but once, and then never had resolution to tell his passion.

This consideration cannot but abate, in some measure, the reader's esteem for the work and the author. To love excellence, is natural; it is natural likewise for the lover to solicit reciprocal regard by an elaborate display of his own qualifications. The desire of pleasing has in different men produced actions of heroism, and effusions of wit; but it seems as reasonable to appear the champion as the poet of an "airy nothing," and to quarrel as to write for what Cowley might have learned from his master Pindar to call the "dream of a shadow."

It is surely not difficult, in the solitude of a college, or in the bustle of the world, to find useful studies and serious employment. No man needs to be so burthened with life as to squander it in voluntary dreams of fictitious occurrences. The man that sits down to suppose himself charged with treason or peculation, and heats his mind to an elaborate purgation of his character from crimes which he was never within the possibility of committing, differs only by the infrequency of his folly from him who praises beauty which he never saw, complains of jealousy which he never felt; supposes himself sometimes invited, and sometimes forsaken; fatigues his fancy, and ransacks his memory, for images which may exhibit the gaiety of hope, or the gloominess of despair, and dresses his imaginary Chloris or Phyllis sometimes in flowers fading as her beauty, and sometimes in gems lasting as her virtues. . . .

This year [1656] he published his poems, with a preface, in which he seems to have inserted something, suppressed in subsequent editions, which was interpreted to denote some relaxation of his loyalty. In this preface he declares, that "his desire had been for some days past, and did still very vehemently continue, to retire himself to some of the American plantations, and to forsake this world for ever."

From the obloquy which the appearance of submission to the usurpers brought upon him, his biographer has been very diligent to clear him, and indeed it does not seem to have lessened his reputation. His wish for retirement we can easily believe to be undissembled; a man harassed in one kingdom, and persecuted in another, who, after a course of business that employed all his days and half his nights in cyphering and decyphering, comes to his own country and steps into a prison, will be willing enough to retire to some place of quiet, and of safety. Yet let neither our reverence for a genius, nor our pity for a sufferer, dispose us to forget that, if his activity was virtue, his retreat was cowardice.

He then took upon himself the character of Physician, still, according to Sprat, with intention "to dissemble the main design of his coming over," and, as Mr. Wood relates, "complying with the men then in power (which was much taken notice of by the royal party) he obtained an order to be created Doctor of Physick, which being done to his mind (whereby he gained the ill-will of some of his friends), he went into France again, having made a copy of verses on Oliver's death."

This is no favourable representation, yet even in this not much wrong can be discovered. How far he complied with the men in power, is to be enquired before he can be blamed. It is not said that he told them any secrets, or assisted them by intelligence, or any other act. If he only promised to be quiet, that they in whose hands he was might free him from confinement, he did what no law of society prohibits.

The man whose miscarriage in a just cause has put him in the power of his enemy may, without any violation of his integrity, regain his liberty, or preserve his life by a promise of neutrality: for the stipulation gives the enemy nothing which he had not before; the neutrality of a captive may be always secured by his imprisonment or death. He that is at the disposal of another, may not promise to aid him in any injurious act, because no power can compel active obedience. He may engage to do nothing, but not to do ill. . . .

At the same time were produced from the same university, the two great Poets, Cowley and Milton, of dissimilar genius, of opposite principles; but concurring in the cultivation of Latin poetry, in which the English, till their works and May's poem appeared, seemed unable to contest the palm with any other of the lettered nations.

If the Latin performances of Cowley and Milton be compared, for May I hold to be superior to both, the advantage seems to lie on the side of Cowley. Milton is generally content to express the thoughts of the ancients in their language; Cowley, without much loss of purity or elegance, accommodates the diction of Rome to his own conceptions. . . .

Cutter of Coleman-street

Mr. Dryden, who went with Mr. Sprat to the first exhibition, related to Mr. Dennis, "that when they told Cowley how little favour had been shewn him, he received the news of his ill success, not with so much firmness as might have been expected from so great a man."

What firmness they expected, or what weakness Cowley discovered, cannot be known. He that misses his end will never be as much pleased as he that attains it, even when he can impute no part of his failure to himself; and when the end is to please the multitude, no man perhaps has a right, in things admitting of gradation and comparison, to throw the whole blame upon his judges, and totally to exclude diffidence and shame by a haughty consciousness of his own excellence.

For the rejection of this play, it is difficult now to find the reason: it certainly has, in a very great degree, the power of fixing attention and exciting merriment. . . .

His vehement desire of retirement now came again upon him. "Not finding," says the morose Wood, "that preferment conferred upon him which he expected, while others for their money carried away most places, he retired discontented into Surrey."

"He was now," says the courtly Sprat, "weary of the vexations and formalities of an active condition. He had been perplexed with a long compliance to foreign manners. He was satiated with the arts of a court; which sort of life, though his virtue made it innocent to him, yet nothing could make it quiet. Those were the reasons that moved him to follow the violent inclination of his own mind, which, in the greatest throng of his former business, had still called upon him, and represented to him the true delights of solitary studies, of temperate pleasures, and a moderate revenue below the malice and flatteries of fortune."

So differently are things seen, and so differently are they shown; but actions are visible, though motives are secret. Cowley certainly retired; first to Barn-elms, and afterwards to Chertsey, in Surrey. He seems, however, to have lost part of his dread of the *hum of men*. He thought himself now safe enough from intrusion, without the defence of mountains and oceans; and instead of seeking shelter in America, wisely went only so far from the bustle of life as that he might easily find his way back, when solitude should grow tedious. . . .

Cowley, like other poets who have written with narrow views, and instead of tracing intellectual pleasure to its natural sources in the mind of man, paid their court to temporary prejudices, has been at one time too much praised, and too much neglected at another.

Wit, like all other things subject by their nature to the choice of man, has its changes and fashions, and at different times takes different forms. About the beginning of the seventeenth century appeared a race of writers that may be termed the metaphysical poets; of whom, in a criticism on the works of Cowley, the last of the race, it is not improper to give some account.

The metaphysical poets were men of learning, and to shew their learning was their whole endeavour; but, unluckily resolving to shew it in rhyme, instead of writing poetry, they only wrote verses, and very often such verses as stood the trial of the finger better than of the ear; for the modulation was so imperfect, that they were only found to be verses by counting the syllables.

If the father of criticism has rightly denominated poetry τέχνη μιμητικὴ, *an imitative art*, these writers will, without great wrong, lose their right to the name of poets; for they cannot be said to have imitated any thing; they neither copied nature nor life; neither painted the forms of matter, nor represented the operations of intellect.

Those however who deny them to be poets, allow them to be wits. Dryden confesses of himself and his contemporaries, that they fall below Donne in wit, but maintains that they surpass him in poetry.

If Wit be well described by Pope, as being "that which has been often thought, but was never before so well expressed," they certainly never attained, nor ever sought it; for they endeavoured to be singular in their thoughts, and were careless of their diction. But Pope's account of wit is undoubtedly erroneous: he depresses it below its natural dignity, and reduces it from strength of thought to happiness of language.

If by a more noble and more adequate conception that be considered as Wit, which is at once natural and new, that which, though not obvious, is, upon its first production, acknowledged to be just; if it be that, which he that never found it, wonders how he missed; to wit of this kind the metaphysical poets have seldom risen. Their thoughts are often new, but seldom natural; they are not obvious, but neither are they just; and the reader, far from wondering that he missed them, wonders more frequently by what perverseness of industry they were ever found.

But Wit, abstracted from its effects upon the hearer, may be more rigorously and philosophically considered as a kind of *discordia concors;* a combination of dissimilar images, or discovery of occult resemblances in things apparently unlike. Of wit, thus defined, they have more than enough. The most heterogeneous ideas are yoked by violence together; nature and art are ransacked for illustrations, comparisons, and allusions; their learning instructs, and their subtilty surprises; but the reader commonly thinks his improvement dearly bought, and though he sometimes admires is seldom pleased.

From this account of their compositions it will be readily inferred, that they were not successful in representing or moving the affections. As they were wholly employed on something unexpected and surprising, they had no regard to that uniformity of sentiment which enables us to conceive and to excite the pains and the pleasure of other minds: they never enquired what, on any occasion, they should have said or done; but wrote rather as beholders than partakers of human nature; as Beings looking upon good and evil, impassive and at leisure; as Epicurean deities making remarks on the actions of men, and the vicissitudes of life, without interest and without emotion. Their courtship was void of fondness, and their lamentation of sorrow. Their wish was only to say what they hoped had been never said before.

Nor was the sublime more within their reach than the pathetick; for they never attempted that comprehension and expanse of thought which at once fills the whole mind, and of which the first effect is sudden astonishment, and the second rational admiration. Sublimity is produced by aggregation, and littleness by dispersion. Great thoughts are always general, and consist in positions not limited by exceptions, and in descriptions not descending to minuteness. It is with great propriety that Subtlety, which in its original import means exility of particles, is taken in its metaphorical meaning for nicety of distinction. Those writers who lay on the watch for novelty could have little hope of greatness; for great things cannot have escaped former observation. Their attempts were always analytick; they broke every image into fragments; and could not more represent, by their slender conceits and laboured particularities, the prospects of nature, or the scenes of life, than he, who dissects a sun-beam with a prism, can exhibit the wide effulgence of a summer noon.

What they wanted however of the sublime, they endeavoured to supply by hyperbole; their amplification had no limits; they left not only reason but fancy behind them; and produced combinations of confused magnificence, that not only could not be credited, but could not be imagined.

Yet great labour, directed by great abilities, is never wholly lost: if they frequently threw away their wit upon false conceits, they likewise sometimes struck out unexpected truth: if their conceits were far-fetched, they were often worth the carriage. To write on their plan, it was at least necessary to read and think. No man could be born a metaphysical poet, nor assume the dignity of a writer, by descriptions copied from descriptions, by imitations borrowed from imitations, by traditional imagery, and hereditary similies, by readiness of rhyme, and volubility of syllables.

In perusing the works of this race of authours, the mind is exercised either by recollection or inquiry; either something already learned is to be retrieved, or something new is to be examined. If their greatness seldom elevates, their acuteness often surprises; if the imagination is not always gratified, at least the powers of reflection and comparison are employed; and in the mass of materials which ingenious absurdity has thrown together, genuine wit and useful knowledge may be sometimes found, buried perhaps in grossness of expression, but useful to those who know their value; and such as, when they are expanded to perspicuity, and polished to elegance, may give lustre to works which have more propriety, though less copiousness of sentiment.

This kind of writing, which was, I believe, borrowed from Marino and his followers, had been recommended by the example of Donne, a man of very extensive and various knowledge, and by Jonson, whose manner resembled that of Donne more in the ruggedness of his lines than in the cast of his sentiments.

When their reputation was high, they had undoubtedly more imitators, than time has left behind. Their immediate successors, of whom any remembrance can be said to remain, were Suckling, Waller, Denham, Cowley, Cleveland, and Milton. Denham and Waller sought another way to fame, by improving the harmony of our numbers. Milton tried the metaphysick stile only in his lines upon Hobson the Carrier. Cowley adopted it, and excelled his predecessors, having as much sentiment, and more musick. Suckling neither improved versification, nor abounded in conceits. The fashionable stile remained chiefly with Cowley; Suckling could not reach it, and Milton disdained it.

Critical Remarks are not easily understood without examples; and I have therefore collected instances of the modes of writing by which this species of poets, for poets they were called by themselves and their admirers, was eminently distinguished.

As the authors of this race were perhaps more desirous of being admired than understood, they sometimes drew their conceits from recesses of learning not very much frequented by common readers of poetry. Thus Cowley on Knowledge:

> The sacred tree midst the fair orchard grew;
>   The phoenix Truth did on it rest,
>   And built his perfum'd nest,
> That right Porphyrian tree which did trué Logick shew.
>   Each leaf did learned notions give,
>   And th' apples were demonstrative:
> So clear their colour and divine,
> The very shade they cast did other lights outshine.

On Anacreon continuing a lover in his old age:

> Love was with thy life entwin'd,
> Close as heat with fire is join'd,
> A powerful brand prescrib'd the date
> Of thine, like Meleager's fate.
> Th' antiperistasis of age
> More enflam'd thy amorous rage.

In the following verses we have an allusion to a Rabbinical opinion concerning Manna:

> Variety I ask not: give me one
> To live perpetually upon.
> The person Love does to us fit,
> Like manna, has the taste of all in it.

Thus Donne shews his medicinal knowledge in some encomiastick verses:

> In every thing there naturally grows
> A Balsamum to keep it fresh and new,
>   If 'twere not injur'd by extrinsique blows;
> Your youth and beauty are this balm in you.
>   But, you of learning and religion,
> And virtue and such ingredients, have made
>   A mithridate, whose operation
> Keeps off, or cures what can be done or said.

Though the following lines of Donne, on the last night of the year, have something in them too scholastick, they are not inelegant:

> This twilight of two years, not past nor next,
>   Some emblem is of me, or I of this,
> Who meteor-like, of stuff and form perplext,
>   Whose what and where, in disputation is,
>   If I should call me any thing, should miss.

> I sum the years and me, and find me not
>   Debtor to th' old, nor creditor to th' new,
> That cannot say, my thanks I have forgot,
>   Nor trust I this with hopes; and yet scarce true
>   This bravery is, since these times shew'd me you.
>
> Donne

Yet more abstruse and profound is Donne's reflection upon Man as a Microcosm:

> If men be worlds, there is in every one
> Something to answer in some proportion
> All the world's riches: and in good men, this
> Virtue, our form's form, and our soul's soul is.

Of thoughts so far-fetched, as to be not only unexpected, but unnatural, all their books are full.

To a Lady, Who Wrote Poesies for Rings

> They, who above do various circles find,
> Say, like a ring th' æquator heaven does bind.
> When heaven shall be adorn'd by thee,
> (Which then more heav'n than 'tis, will be)
> 'Tis thou must write the poesy there,
> For it wanteth one as yet,
> Tho' the sun pass through 't twice a year,
> The sun, which is esteem'd the god of Wit.
>
> Cowley

The difficulties which have been raised about identity in philosophy, are by Cowley with still more perplexity applied to Love:

> Five years ago (says story) I lov'd you,
> For which you call me most inconstant now;
> Pardon me, madam, you mistake the man;
> For I am not the same that I was then;
> No flesh is now the same 'twas then in me,
> And that my mind is chang'd yourself may see.
>
> The same thoughts to retain still, and intents
> Were more inconstant far; for accidents
> Must of all things most strangely inconstant prove,
> If from one subject they t' another move:
> My members then, the father members were
> From whence these take their birth, which now are here.
> If then this body love what th' other did,
> 'Twere incest, which by nature is forbid.

The love of different women is, in geographical poetry, compared to travel
through different countries:

> Hast thou not found, each woman's breast
>   (The lands where thou hast travelled)
> Either by savages possest,
>   Or wild, and uninhabited?
>   What joy could'st take, or what repose
> In countries so uncivilis'd as those?
> Lust, the scorching dog-star, here
>   Rages with immoderate heat;
> Whilst Pride, the rugged Northern Bear,
>   In others makes the cold too great.
> And where these are temp'rate known,
> The soil's all barren sand, or rocky stone.
>
> Cowley

A lover, burnt up by his affection, is compared to Egypt:

> The fate of Egypt I sustain,
> And never feel the dew of rain,
> From clouds which in the head appear;
>   But all my too much moisture owe,
>   To overflowings of the heart below.
>
> Cowley

The lover supposes his lady acquainted with the ancient laws of augury
and rites of sacrifice:

> And yet this death of mine, I fear,
> Will ominous to her appear:
>   When sound in every other part,
>   Her sacrifice is found without an heart.
>   For the last tempest of my death
>   Shall sigh out that too, with my breath.

That the chaos was harmonised has been recited of old; but whence the
different sounds arose, remained for a modern to discover:

> Th' ungovern'd parts no correspondence knew,
> An artless war from thwarting motions grew;
> Till they to number and fixt rules were brought.
> Water and air he for the tenor chose,
> Earth made the Base, the Treble flame arose.
>
> Cowley

The tears of lovers are always of great poetical account; but Donne has
extended them into worlds. If the lines are not easily understood, they may be
read again.

> On a round ball
> A workman, that hath copies by, can lay
> An Europe, Afric, and an Asia,
> And quickly make that, which was nothing, all.
> So doth each tear,
> Which thee doth wear,
> A globe, yea world, by that impression grow,
> Till thy tears mixt with mine do overflow
> This world, by waters sent from thee my heaven dissolved so.

On reading the following lines the reader may perhaps cry out—*Confusion worse confounded.*

> Here lies a she sun, and a he moon there,
> She gives the best light to his sphere,
> Or each is both, and all, and so
> They unto one another nothing owe.
>   Donne

Who but Donne would have thought that a good man is a telescope?

> Tho' God be our true glass, thro' which we see
> All, since the being of all things is he,
> Yet are the trunks, which do to us derive
> Things, in proportion fit, by perspective
> Deeds of good men; for by their living here,
> Virtues, indeed remote, seem to be near.

Who would imagine it possible that in a very few lines so many remote ideas could be brought together:

> Since 'tis my doom, Love's undershrieve,
> Why this reprieve?
> Why doth my She Advowson fly
> Incumbency?
> To sell thyself dost thou intend
> By candle's end,
> And hold the contrast thus in doubt,
> Life's taper out?
> Think but how soon the market fails,
> Your sex lives faster than the males;
> As if to measure age's span,
> The sober Julian were th' account of man,
> Whilst you live by the fleet Gregorian.
>   Cleveland

Of enormous and disgusting hyperboles, these may be examples:

By every wind, that comes this way,
  Send me at least a sigh or two,
Such and so many I'll repay
  As shall themselves make winds to get to you.
                                        Cowley

  In tears I'll waste these eyes
    By love so vainly fed;
  So lust of old the Deluge punished.
                                        Cowley

All arm'd in brass, the richest dress of war,
(A dismal glorious sight), he shone afar.
The sun himself started with sudden fright,
To see his beams return so dismal bright.
                                        Cowley

An universal consternation:

His bloody eyes he hurls round, his sharp paws
Tear up the ground; then runs he wild about,
Lashing his angry tail and roaring out.
Beasts creep into their dens, and tremble there;
Trees, tho' no wind is stirring, shake with fear;
Silence and horrour fill the place around:
Echo itself dares scarce repeat the sound.
                                        Cowley

Their fictions were often violent and unnatural.

Of his Mistress bathing:

The fish around her crouded, as they do
To the false light that treach'rous fishers shew,
And all with as much ease might taken be,
    As she at first took me:
    For ne'er did light so clear
    Among the waves appear,
Tho' ev'ry night the sun himself set there.
                                        Cowley

The poetical effect of a Lover's name upon glass:

  My name engrav'd herein,
Doth contribute my firmness to this glass;
  Which, ever since that charm, hath been
As hard, as that which grav'd it, was.
                                        Donne

Their conceits were sometimes slight and trifling:

On an inconstant woman.

> He enjoys thy calmy sunshine now,
>   And no breath stirring hears,
> In the clear heaven of thy brow,
>   No smallest cloud appears.
> He sees thee gentle, fair and gay,
> And trusts the faithless April of thy May.
>
> Cowley

Upon a paper written with the juice of lemon, and read by the fire:

> Nothing yet in thee is seen,
> But when a genial heat warms thee within,
> A new-born wood of various lines there grows;
>   Here buds an L, and there a B,
>   Here sprouts a V, and there a T,
> And all the flourishing letters stand in rows.
>
> Cowley

As they sought only for novelty, they did not much enquire whether their allusions were to things high or low, elegant or gross; whether they compared the little to the great, or the great to the little.

Physick and Chirurgery for a Lover

> Gently, ah gently, madam, touch
>   The wound, which you yourself have made;
> That pain must needs be very much,
>   Which makes me of your hand afraid.
> Cordials of pity give me now,
> For I too weak for purgings grow.
>
> Cowley

The World and a Clock.

> Mahol, th' inferior world's fantastic face,
> Thro' all the turns of matter's maze did trace;
> Great Nature's well-set clock in pieces took;
> On all the springs and smallest wheels did look
> Of life and motion; and with equal art
> Made up again the whole of every part.
>
> Cowley

A coal-pit has not often found its poet; but that it may not want its due honour, Cleveland has paralleled it with the Sun:

> The mod'rate value of our guiltless ore,
> Makes no man atheist, nor no woman whore:
> Yet why should hallow'd vestals sacred shrine
> Deserve more honour than a flaming mine?
> These pregnant wombs of heat would fitter be

Than a few embers for a deity.
Had he our pits, the Persian would admire
No sun, but warm's devotion at our fire:
He'd leave the trotting whipster, and prefer
Our profound Vulcan 'bove that waggoner.
For wants he heat? or light? or would have store?
Or both? 'tis here: and what can suns give more?
Nay, what's the sun, but in a different name,
A coal-pit rampant, or a mine on flame!
Then let this truth reciprocally run,
The sun's heaven's coalery, and coals our sun.

Death, a Voyage:

No family
E'er rigg'd a soul for heaven's discovery,
With whom more venturers might boldly dare
Venture their stakes, with him in joy to share.
                                        Donne

Their thoughts and expressions were sometimes grossly absurd, and such as no figures or licence can reconcile to the understanding.

A Lover neither dead nor alive:

Then down I laid my head,
Down on cold earth; and for a while was dead,
And my freed soul to a strange somewhere fled:
    Ah sottish soul, said I,
    When back to its cage again I saw it fly:
    Fool to resume her broken chain!
    And row her galley here again!
    Fool, to that body to return
Where it condemn'd and destin'd is to burn!
    Once dead, how can it be,
Death should a thing so pleasant seem to thee,
That thou should'st come to live it o'er again in me?
                                        Cowley

A Lover's heart, a hand grenado.

Wo to her stubborn heart, if once mine come
    Into the self-same room,
    'Twill tear and blow up all within,
Like a grenado shot into a magazin.
Then shall love keep the ashes, and torn parts,
    Of both our broken hearts:
    Shall out of both one new one make;
From her's th' alloy; from mine, the metal take.
                                        Cowley

The poetical Propagation of Light.

> The Prince's favour is diffus'd o'er all,
> From which all fortunes, names and natures fall;
> Then from those wombs of stars, the Bride's bright eyes,
> At every glance, a constellation flies,
> And sowes the court with stars, and doth prevent
> In light and power, the all-ey'd firmament;
> First her eye kindles other ladies' eyes,
> Then from their beams their jewels lustres rise;
> And from their jewels torches do take fire,
> And all is warmth, and light, and good desire.

Donne

They were in very little care to clothe their notions with elegance of dress, and therefore miss the notice and the praise which are often gained by those, who think less, but are more diligent to adorn their thoughts.

That a mistress beloved is fairer in idea than in reality, is by Cowley thus expressed:

> Thou in my fancy dost much higher stand,
> Than women can be plac'd by Nature's hand;
> And I must needs, I'm sure, a loser be,
> To change thee, as thou'rt there, for very thee.

That prayer and labour should co-operate, are thus taught by Donne:

> In none but us, are such mixt engines found,
> As hands of double office: for the ground
> We till with them; and them to heav'n we raise;
> Who prayerless labours, or without this, prays,
> Doth but one half, that's none.

By the same author, a common topick, the danger of procrastination, is thus illustrated:

> ——That which I should have begun
> In my youth's morning, now late must be done;
> And I, as giddy travellers must do,
> Which stray or sleep all day, and having lost
> Light and strength, dark and tir'd must then ride post.

All that Man has to do is to live and die; the sum of humanity is comprehended by Donne in the following lines:

> Think in how poor a prison thou didst lie,
> After, enabled but to suck and cry.
> Think, when 'twas grown to most, 'twas a poor inn,
> A province pack'd up in two yards of skin,
> And that usurp'd, or threaten'd with a rage

> Of sicknesses, or their true mother, age.
> But think that death hath now enfranchis'd thee;
> Thou hast thy expansion now, and liberty;
> Think, that a rusty piece discharg'd is flown
> In pieces, and the bullet is his own,
> And freely flies: this to thy soul allow,
> Think thy shell broke, think thy soul hatch'd but now.

They were sometimes indelicate and disgusting. Cowley thus apostrophises beauty:

> ——Thou tyrant, which leav'st no man free!
> Thou subtle thief, from whom nought safe can be!
> Thou murth'rer, which hast kill'd, and devil, which would'st damn me.

Thus he addresses his Mistress:

> Thou, who in many a propriety,
> So truly art the sun to me,
> Add one more likeness, which I'm sure you can,
> And let me and my sun beget a man.

Thus he represents the meditations of a Lover:

> Tho' in thy thoughts scarce any tracts have been
>   So much as of original sin,
> Such charms thy beauty wears as might
> Desires in dying confest saints excite.
>   Thou with strange adultery
> Dost in each breast a brothel keep;
>   Awake, all men do lust for thee,
> And some enjoy thee when they sleep.

The true taste of Tears.

> Hither with crystal vials, lovers, come,
>   And take my tears, which are love's wine,
> And try your mistress' tears at home,
>   For all are false, that taste not just like mine.
>   Donne

This is yet more indelicate:

> As the sweet sweat of roses in a still,
> As that which from chaf'd musk-cat's pores doth trill,
> As the almighty balm of th' early East,
> Such as the sweet drops of my mistress' breast.
> And on her neck her skin such lustre sets,
> They seem no sweat drops, but pearl coronets:
> Rank sweaty froth thy mistress' brow defiles.
>   Donne

Their expressions sometimes raise horror, when they intend perhaps to be pathetic:

> As men in hell are from diseases free,
>   So from all other ills am I,
>   Free from their known formality:
> But all pains eminently lie in thee.
>   Cowley

They were not always strictly curious, whether the opinions from which they drew their illustrations were true; it was enough that they were popular. Bacon remarks, that some falsehoods are continued by tradition, because they supply commodious allusions.

> It gave a piteous groan, and so it broke;
> In vain it something would have spoke:
> The love within too strong for 't was,
> Like poison put into a Venice-glass.
>   Cowley

In forming descriptions they looked out not for images, but for conceits. Night has been a common subject, which poets have contended to adorn. Dryden's Night is well known; Donne's is as follows:

> Thou seest me here at midnight, now all rest:
> Time's dead low-water; when all minds divest
> To-morrow's business, when the labourers have
> Such rest in bed, that their last church-yard grave,
> Subject to change, will scarce be a type of this,
> Now when the client, whose last hearing is
> To-morrow, sleeps; when the condemned man,
> Who when he opes his eyes, must shut them then
> Again by death, altho' sad watch he keep,
> Doth practise dying by a little sleep,
> Thou at this midnight seest me.

It must be however confessed of these writers, that if they are upon common subjects often unnecessarily and unpoetically subtle; yet where scholastick speculation can be properly admitted, their copiousness and acuteness may justly be admired. What Cowley has written upon Hope, shews an unequalled fertility of invention:

> Hope, whose weak being ruin'd is,
>   Alike if it succeed, and if it miss;
> Whom good or ill does equally confound,
> And both the horns of Fate's dilemma wound.
>   Vain shadow, which dost vanquish quite,
>   Both at full moon and perfect night!
> The stars have not a possibility

Of blessing thee;
If things then from their end we happy call,
'Tis Hope is the most hopeless thing of all.

Hope, thou bold taster of delight,
Who, whilst thou should'st but taste, devour'st it quite!
Thou bring'st us an estate, yet leav'st us poor,
By clogging it with legacies before!
The joys which we entire should wed,
Come deflow'r'd virgins to our bed;
Good fortunes without gain imported be,
Such mighty custom's paid to thee:
For joy, like wine, kept close does better taste;
If it take air before, its spirits waste.

To the following comparison of a man that travels, and his wife that stays at home, with a pair of compasses, it may be doubted whether absurdity or ingenuity has the better claim.

Our two souls therefore, which are one,
Tho' I must go, endure not yet
A breach, but an expansion,
Like gold to airy thinness beat.

If they be two, they are two so
As stiff twin-compasses are two,
Thy soul the fixt foot, make no show
To move, but doth, if th' other do.

And tho' it in the centre sit,
Yet when the other far doth roam,
It leans, and hearkens after it,
And grows erect, as that comes home.

Such wilt thou be to me, who must
Like th' other foot, obliquely run.
Thy firmness makes my circle just,
And makes me end, where I begun.
                                                      Donne

In all these examples it is apparent, that whatever is improper or vitious, is produced by a voluntary deviation from nature in pursuit of something new and strange; and that the writers fail to give delight, by their desire of exciting admiration. . . .

In his poem on the death of Hervey, there is much praise, but little passion, a very just and ample delineation of such virtues as a studious privacy admits, and such intellectual excellence as a mind not yet called forth to action can display. He knew how to distinguish, and how to commend the qualities of his companion; but when he wishes to make us weep, he forgets to weep himself, and diverts his sorrow by imagining how his crown of bays if he had it, would *crackle* in the *fire*. It is the odd fate of this thought to be worse for being true. The bay-leaf crackles remarkably as it burns; as therefore this property was not assigned it by chance, the mind must be thought sufficiently at ease that could attend to such minuteness of physiology. But the power of Cowley is not to move the affections, but to exercise the understanding.

The *Chronicle* is a composition unrivalled and alone: such gaiety of fancy, such facility of expression, such varied similitude, such a succession of images, and such a dance of words, it is vain to expect except from Cowley. His strength always appears in his agility; his volatility is not the flutter of a light but the bound of an elastick mind. His levity never leaves his learning behind it; the moralist, the politician, and the critick, mingle their influence even in this airy frolick of genius. To such a performance Suckling could have brought the gaiety, but not the knowledge; Dryden could have supplied the knowledge, but not the gaiety. . . .

To the Miscellanies succeed the *Anacreontiques,* or paraphrastical translations of some little poems, which pass, however justly, under the name of Anacreon. Of those songs dedicated to festivity and gaiety, in which even the morality is voluptuous, and which teach nothing but the enjoyment of the present day, he has given rather a pleasing than a faithful representation, having retained their spriteliness, but lost their simplicity. The Anacreon of Cowley, like the Homer of Pope, has admitted the decoration of some modern graces, by which he is undoubtedly made more amiable to common readers, and perhaps, if they would honestly declare their own perceptions, to far the greater part of those whom courtesy and ignorance are content to stile the Learned.

These little pieces will be found more finished in their kind than any other of Cowley's works. The diction shews nothing of the mould of time, and the sentiments are at no great distance from our present habitudes of thought. Real mirth must be always natural, and nature is uniform. Men have been wise in very different modes; but they have always laughed the same way.

Levity of thought naturally produced familiarity of language, and the familiar part of language continues long the same: the dialogue of comedy, when it is transcribed from popular manners and real life, is read from age to age with equal pleasure. The artifice of inversion by which the established order of words is changed, or of innovation, by which new words or new meanings of words are introduced, is practised not by those who talk to be understood, but by those who write to be admired.

The Anacreontiques therefore of Cowley give now all the pleasure which they ever gave. If he was formed by nature for one kind of writing more than for another, his power seems to have been greatest in the familiar and the festive.

The next class of his poems is called *The Mistress,* of which it is not necessary to select any particular pieces for praise or censure. They have all the same beauties and faults, and nearly in the same proportion. They are written with exuberance of wit, and with copiousness of learning; and it is truly asserted by Sprat, that the plentitude of the writer's knowledge flows in upon his page, so that the reader is commonly surprised into some improvement. But, considered as the verses of a lover, no man that has ever loved will much commend them. They are neither courtly nor pathetick, have neither gallantry nor fondness. His praises are too far-sought, and too hyperbolical, either to express love, or to excite it: every stanza is crouded with darts and flames, with wounds and death, with mingled souls, and with broken hearts.

The principal artifice by which *The Mistress* is filled with conceits is very copiously displayed by Addison. Love is by Cowley, as by other poets, expressed metaphorically by flame and fire; and that which is true of real fire is said of love, or figurative fire, the same word in the same sentence retaining both significations. Thus, "observing the cold regard of his mistress's eyes, and at the same time their power of producing love in him, he considers them as burning-glasses made of ice. Finding himself able to live in the greatest extremities of love, he concludes the torrid zone to be habitable. Upon the dying of a tree, on which he had cut his loves, he observes, that his flames had burnt up and withered the tree."

These conceits Addison calls mixed wit; that is, wit which consists of thoughts true in one sense of the expression, and false in the other. Addison's representation is sufficiently indulgent. That confusion of images may entertain for a moment; but being unnatural, it soon grows wearisome. Cowley delighted in it, as much as if he had invented it; but, not to mention the ancients, he might have found it full-blown in modern Italy. Thus Sannazaro;

> Aspice quam variis distringar Vesbia curis,
>   Uror, & heu! nostro manat ab igne liquor;
> Sum Nilus, sumque Aetna simul; restringite flammas
>   O lacrimae, aut lacrimas ebibe flamma meas.

One of the severe theologians of that time censured him as having published *a book of profane and lascivious Verses*. From the charge of profaneness, the constant tenour of his life, which seems to have been eminently virtuous, and the general tendency of his opinions, which discover no irreverence of religion, must defend him; but that the accusation of lasciviousness is unjust, the perusal of his works will sufficiently evince.

Cowley's *Mistress* has no power of seduction; "she plays round the head, but comes not at the heart." Her beauty and absence, her kindness and cruelty, her disdain and inconstancy, produce no correspondence of emotion. His poetical account of the virtues of plants, and colours of flowers, is not perused with more sluggish frigidity. The compositions are such as might have been written for penance by a hermit, or for hire by a philosophical rhymer who had only heard of another sex; for they turn the mind only on the writer, whom, without thinking on a woman but as the subject for a task, we sometimes esteem as learned, and sometimes despise as trifling, always admire as ingenious, and always condemn as unnatural. . . .

The fault of Cowley, and perhaps of all the writers of the metaphysical race, is that of pursuing his thoughts to their last ramifications, by which he loses the grandeur of generality; for of the greatest things the parts are little;

what is little can be but pretty, and by claiming dignity becomes ridiculous. Thus all the power of description is destroyed by a scrupulous enumeration; and the force of metaphors is lost, when the mind by the mention of particulars is turned more upon the original than the secondary sense, more upon that from which the illustration is drawn than that to which it is applied.

Of this we have a very eminent example in the ode intituled *The Muse*, who goes to *take the air* in an intellectual chariot, to which he harnesses Fancy and Judgement, Wit and Eloquence, Memory and Invention: how he distinguished Wit from Fancy, or how Memory could properly contribute to Motion, he has not explained: we are however content to suppose that he could have justified his own fiction, and wish to see the Muse begin her career; but there is yet more to be done.

> Let the postilion Nature mount, and let
> The coachman Art be set;
> And let the airy footmen, running all beside,
> Make a long row of goodly pride;
> Figures, conceits, raptures, and sentences,
> In a well-worded dress,
> And innocent loves, and pleasant truths, and useful lies,
> In all their gaudy liveries.

Every mind is now disgusted with this cumber of magnificence; yet I cannot refuse myself the four next lines:

> Mount, glorious queen, thy travelling throne,
>   And bid it to put on;
>   For long though cheerful is the way,
> And life alas allows but one ill winter's day.

In the same ode, celebrating the power of the Muse, he gives her prescience, or, in poetical language, the foresight of events hatching in futurity; but having once an egg in his mind, he cannot forbear to shew us that he knows what an egg contains:

> Thou into the close nests of time do'st peep,
>   And there with piercing eye
> Through the firm shell and the thick white dost spy
>   Years to come a-forming lie,
> Close in their sacred fecundine asleep.

To the disproportion and incongruity of Cowley's sentiments must be added the uncertainty and looseness of his measures. He takes the liberty of using in any place a verse of any length, from two syllables to twelve. The verses of Pindar have, as he observes, very little harmony to a modern ear; yet by examining the syllables we perceive them to be regular, and have reason enough for supposing that the ancient audiences were delighted with the sound. The imitator ought therefore to have adopted what he found, and to have added what was wanting; to have preserved a constant return of the same numbers, and to have supplied smoothness of transition and continuity of thought.

It is urged by Dr. Sprat, that the *irregularity of numbers is the very thing* which makes *that kind of poesy fit for all manner of subjects.* But he should have remembered, that what is fit for every thing can fit nothing well. The great pleasure of verse arises from the known measure of the lines, and uniform structure of the stanzas, by which the voice is regulated, and the memory relieved.

If the Pindarick stile be, what Cowley thinks it, *the highest and noblest kind of writing in verse,* it can be adapted only to high and noble subjects; and it will not be easy to reconcile the poet with the critick, or to conceive how that can be the highest kind of writing in verse, which, according to Sprat, *is chiefly to be preferred for its near affinity to prose.*

This lax and lawless versification so much concealed the deficiencies of the barren, and flattered the laziness of the idle, that it immediately overspread our books of poetry; all the boys and girls caught the pleasing fashion, and they that could do nothing else could write like Pindar. The rights of antiquity were invaded, and disorder tried to break into the Latin: a poem on the Sheldonian Theatre, in which all kinds of verse are shaken together, is unhappily inserted in the *Musæ Anglicanæ.* Pindarism prevailed above half a century; but at last died gradually away, and other imitations supply its place.

The Pindarique Odes have so long enjoyed the highest degree of poetical reputation, that I am not willing to dismiss them with unabated censure; and surely though the mode of their composition be erroneous, yet many parts deserve at least that admiration which is due to great comprehension of knowledge, and great fertility of fancy. The thoughts are often new, and often striking; but the greatness of one part is disgraced by the littleness of another, and total negligence of language gives the noblest conceptions the appearance of a fabrick august in the plan, but mean in the materials. Yet surely those verses are not without a just claim to praise; of which it may be said with truth, that no man but Cowley could have written them. . . .

Davideis

Sacred History has been always read with submissive reverence, and an imagination over-awed and controlled. We have been accustomed to acquiesce in the nakedness and simplicity of the authentick narrative, and to repose on its veracity with such humble confidence, as suppresses curiosity. We go with the historian as he goes, and stop with him when he stops. All amplification is frivolous and vain; all addition to that which is already sufficient for the purposes of religion, seems not only useless, but in some degree profane.

Such events as were produced by the visible interposition of Divine Power are above the power of human genius to dignify. The miracle of Creation, however it may teem with images, is best described with little diffusion of language; *He spake the word, and they were made.* . . .

To the subject, thus originally indisposed to the reception of poetical embellishments, the writer brought little that could reconcile impatience, or attract curiosity. Nothing can be more disgusting than a narrative spangled with conceits, and conceits are all that the Davideis supplies.

One of the great sources of poetical delight is description, or the power of presenting pictures to the mind. Cowley gives inferences instead of images, and shews not what may be supposed to have been seen, but what thoughts the sight might have suggested. . . .

The dress of Gabriel deserves attention:

> He took for skin a cloud most soft and bright,
> That e'er the midday sun pierc'd thro' with light,
> Upon his cheeks a lively blush he spread,
> Wash'd from the morning beauties deepest red,
> An harmless flatt'ring meteor shone for hair,
> And fell adown his shoulders with loose care;
> He cuts out a silk mantle from the skies,
> Where the most spritely azure pleas'd the eyes;
> This he with starry vapours sprinkles all,
> Took in their prime ere they grow ripe and fall;
> Of a new rainbow, ere it fret or fade,
> The choicest piece cut out, a scarfc is made.

This is a just specimen of Cowley's imagery: what might in general expressions be great and forcible, he weakens and makes ridiculous by branching it into small parts. That Gabriel was invested with the softest or brightest colours of the sky, we might have been told, and dismissed to improve the idea in our different proportions of conception; but Cowley could not let us go till he had related where Gabriel got first his skin, and then his mantle, then his lace, and then his scarfe, and related it in the terms of the mercer and taylor. . . .

In the general review of Cowley's poetry it will be found, that he wrote with abundant fertility, but negligent or unskilful selection; with much thought, but with little imagery; that he is never pathetick, and rarely sublime, but always either ingenious or learned, either acute or profound.

It is said by Denham in his elegy,

> To him no author was unknown;
> Yet what he writ was all his own.

This wide position requires less limitation, when it is affirmed of Cowley, than perhaps of any other poet—He read much, and yet borrowed little.

His character of writing was indeed not his own: he unhappily adopted that which was predominant. He saw a certain way to present praise, and not sufficiently enquiring by what means the ancients have continued to delight through all the changes of human manners, he contented himself with a deciduous laurel, of which the verdure in its spring was bright and gay, but which time has been continually stealing from his brows.

He was in his own time considered as of unrivalled excellence. Clarendon represents him as having taken a flight beyond all that went before him; and Milton is said to have declared, that the three greatest English poets were Spenser, Shakespeare, and Cowley.

His manner he had in common with others; but his sentiments were his own. Upon every subject he thought for himself; and such was his copiousness of knowledge, that something at once remote and applicable rushed into his mind; yet it is not likely that he always rejected a commodious idea merely because another had used it: his known wealth was so great, that he might have borrowed without loss of credit. . . .

His diction was in his own time censured as negligent. He seems not to have known, or not to have considered, that words being arbitrary must owe their power to association, and have the influence, and that only, which custom has given them. Language is the dress of thought; and as the noblest mien, or most graceful action, would be degraded and obscured by a garb appropriated to the gross employments of rusticks or mechanicks, so the most heroick sentiments will lose their efficacy, and the most splendid ideas drop their magnificence, if they are conveyed by words used commonly upon low and trivial occasions, debased by vulgar mouths, and contaminated by inelegant applications.

Truth indeed is always truth, and reason is always reason; they have an intrinsick and unalterable value, and constitute that intellectual gold which defies destruction: but gold may be so concealed in baser matter that only a chymist can recover it, sense may be so hidden in unrefined and plebeian words that none but philosophers can distinguish it; and both may be so buried in impurities, as not to pay the cost of their extraction.

The diction being the vehicle of the thoughts, first presents itself to the intellectual eye; and if the first appearance offends, a further knowledge is not often sought. Whatever professes to benefit by pleasing, must please at once. The pleasures of reason imply something sudden and unexpected; that which elevates must always surprise. What is perceived by slow degrees may gratify us with the consciousness of improvement, but will never strike with the sense of pleasure.

Of all this, Cowley appears to have been without knowledge, or without care. He makes no selection of words, nor seeks any neatness of phrase: he has no elegancies either lucky or elaborate; as his endeavours were rather to impress sentences upon the understanding than images on the fancy, he has few epithets, and those scattered without peculiar propriety or nice adaptation. It seems to follow from the necessity of the subject, rather than the care of the writer, that the diction of his heroick poem is less familiar than that of his slightest writings. He has given not the same numbers, but the same diction to the gentle Anacreon and the tempestuous Pindar.

His versification seems to have had very little of his care; and if what he thinks be true, that his numbers are unmusical only when they are ill read, the art of reading them is at present lost; for they are commonly harsh to modern ears. He has indeed many noble lines, such as the feeble care of Waller never could produce. The bulk of his thoughts sometimes swelled his verse to unexpected and inevitable grandeur; but his excellence of this kind is merely fortuitous: he sinks willingly down to his general carelessness, and avoids with very little care either meanness or asperity. . . .

After so much criticism on his Poems, the Essays which accompany them must not be forgotten. What is said by Sprat of his conversation, that no man could draw from it any suspicion of his excellence in poetry, may be applied to these compositions. No author ever kept his verse and his prose at a greater distance from each other. His thoughts are natural, and his stile has a smooth and placid equability, which has never yet obtained its due commendation. Nothing is far-sought, or hard-laboured; but all is easy without feebleness, and familiar without grossness.

JOHN MILTON

He now hired a lodging at the house of one Russel, a taylor in St. Bride's Church-yard, and undertook the education of John and Edward Phillips, his sister's sons. Finding his rooms too little, he took a house and garden in Aldersgate-street, which was not then so much out of the world as it is now; and chose his dwelling at the upper end of a passage, that he might avoid the noise of the street. Here he received more boys, to be boarded and instructed.

Let not our veneration for Milton forbid us to look with some degree of merriment on great promises and small performance, on the man who hastens home, because his countrymen are contending for their liberty, and, when he reaches the scene of action, vapours away his patriotism in a private boarding-school. This is the period of his life from which all his biographers seem inclined to shrink. They are unwilling that Milton should be degraded to a school-master; but since it cannot be denied that he taught boys, one finds out that he taught for nothing, and another that his motive was only zeal for the propagation of learning and virtue; and all tell what they do not know to be true, only to excuse an act which no wise man will consider as in itself disgraceful. His father was alive; his allowance was not ample, and he supplied its deficiencies by an honest and useful employment.

It is told, that in the art of education he performed wonders; and a formidable list is given of the authors, Greek and Latin, that were read in Aldersgate-street, by youth between ten and fifteen or sixteen years of age. Those who tell or receive these stories, should consider that nobody can be taught faster than he can learn. The speed of the best horseman must be limited by the power of his horse. Every man, that has ever undertaken to instruct others, can tell what slow advances he has been able to make, and how much patience it requires to recall vagrant inattention, to stimulate sluggish indifference, and to rectify absurd misapprehension.

The purpose of Milton, as it seems, was to teach something more solid than the common literature of schools, by reading those authors that treat of physical subjects; such as the Georgick, and astronomical treatises of the ancients. This was a scheme of improvement which seems to have busied many literary projectors of that age. Cowley, who had more means than Milton of knowing what was wanting to the embellishments of life, formed the same plan of education in his imaginary College.

But the truth is, that the knowledge of external nature, and of the sciences which that knowledge requires or includes, is not the great or the frequent business of the human mind. Whether we provide for action or conversation, whether we wish to be useful or pleasing, the first requisite is the religious and moral knowledge of right and wrong; the next is an acquaintance with the history of mankind, and with those examples which may be said to embody truth, and prove by events the reasonableness of opinions. Prudence and justice are virtues, and excellencies, of all times, and of all places; we are perpetually moralists, but we are geometricians only by chance. Our intercourse with intellectual nature is necessary; our speculations upon matter are voluntary, and at leisure. Physical knowledge is of such rare emergence, that one man may know another half his life without being able to estimate his skill in hydrostaticks or astronomy; but his moral and prudential character immediately appears.

Those authors, therefore, are to be read at schools that supply most axioms of prudence, most principles of moral truth, and most materials for conversation; and these purposes are best served by poets, orators, and historians.

Let me not be censured for this digression as pedantick or paradoxical; for if I have Milton against me, I have Socrates on my side. It was his labour to turn philosophy from the study of nature to speculations upon life, but the innovators whom I oppose are turning off attention from life to nature. They seem to think, that we are placed here to watch the growth of plants, or the motions of the stars. Socrates was rather of opinion, that what we had to learn was, how to do good, and avoid evil.

῞Οττι τοι ἐν μεγάροισι κακόν τ᾽ ἀγαθόν τε τέτυκται.

Of institutions we may judge by their effects. From this wonder-working academy, I do not know that there ever proceeded any man very eminent for knowledge: its only genuine product, I believe, is a small History of Poetry, written in Latin by his nephew, of which perhaps none of my readers has ever heard. . . .

He that changes his party by his humour, is not more virtuous than he that changes it by his interest; he loves himself rather than truth. . . .

He published about the same time [1644] his *Areopagitica, a Speech of Mr.* John Milton *for the liberty of unlicensed Printing.* The danger of such unbounded liberty, and the danger of bounding it, have produced a problem in the science of Government, which human understanding seems hitherto unable to solve. If nothing may be published but what civil authority shall have previously approved, power must always be the standard of truth; if every dreamer of innovations may propagate his projects, there can be no settlement; if every murmurer at government may diffuse discontent, there can be no peace; and if every sceptick in theology may teach his follies, there can be no religion. The remedy against these evils is to punish the authors; for it is yet allowed that every society may punish, though not prevent, the publication of opinions, which that society shall think pernicious: but this punishment, though it may crush the author, promotes the book; and it seems not more reasonable to leave the right of printing unrestrained, because writers may be afterwards censured, than it would be to sleep with doors unbolted, because by our laws we can hang a thief. . . .

He had taken a larger house in Barbican for the reception of scholars; but the numerous relations of his wife, to whom he generously granted refuge for a while, occupied his rooms. In time, however, they went away; and the "house again," says Philips, "now looked like a house of the Muses only, though the accession of scholars was not great. Possibly his having proceeded so far in the education of youth, may have been the occasion of his adversaries calling him pedagogue and school-master; whereas it is well known he never set up for a publick school, to teach all the young fry of a parish; but only was willing to impart his learning and knowledge to relations, and the sons of gentlemen who were his intimate friends; and that neither his writings nor his way of teaching ever savoured in the least of pedantry."

Thus laboriously does his nephew extenuate what cannot be denied, and what might be confessed without disgrace. Milton was not a man who could become mean by a mean employment. This, however, his warmest friends seem not to have found; they therefore shift and palliate. He did not sell literature to all comers at an open shop; he was a chamber-milliner, and measured his commodities only to his friends.

Philips, evidently impatient of viewing him in this state of degradation, tells us that it was not long continued; and, to raise his character again, has a mind to invest him with military splendour: "He is much mistaken," he says, "if there was not about this time a design of making him an adjutant-general in Sir William Waller's army. But the new-modelling of the army proved an obstruction to the design." An event cannot be set at a much greater distance than by having been only *designed, about some time,* if a man *be not much mistaken.* Milton shall be a pedagogue no longer; for, if Philips be not much mistaken, somebody at some time designed him for a soldier. . . .

No man forgets his original trade: the rights of nations, and of kings, sink into questions of grammar, if grammarians discuss them. . . .

Cromwel had now dismissed the parliament by the authority of which he had destroyed monarchy, and commenced monarch himself, under the title of protector, but with kingly and more than kingly power. That his authority was lawful, never was pretended; he himself founded his right only in necessity; but Milton, having now tasted the honey of publick employment, would not return to hunger and philosophy, but, continuing to exercise his office under a manifest usurpation, betrayed to his power that liberty which he had defended. Nothing can be more just than that rebellion should end in slavery;

that he, who had justified the murder of his king, for some acts which to him seemed unlawful, should now sell his services, and his flatteries, to a tyrant, of whom it was evident that he could do nothing lawful. . . .

This dependance of the soul upon the seasons, those temporary and periodical ebbs and flows of intellect, may, I suppose, justly be derided as the fumes of vain imagination. *Sapiens dominabitur astris.* The author that thinks himself weather-bound will find, with a little help from hellebore, that he is only idle or exhausted. But while this notion has possession of the head, it produces the inability which it supposes. Our powers owe much of their energy to our hopes; *possunt quia posse videntur.* When success seems attainable, diligence is enforced; but when it is admitted that the faculties are suppressed by a cross wind, or a cloudy sky, the day is given up without resistance; for who can contend with the course of Nature? From such prepossessions Milton seems not to have been free. . . .

Paradise Lost

At what particular times of his life the parts of his work were written, cannot often be known. The beginning of the third book shews that he had lost his sight; and the Introduction to the seventh, that the return of the king had clouded him with discountenance; and that he was offended by the licentious festivity of the Restoration. There are no other internal notes of time. Milton, being now cleared from all effects of his disloyalty, had nothing required from him but the common duty of living in quiet, to be rewarded with the common right of protection: but this, which, when he sculked from the approach of his king, was perhaps more than he hoped, seems not to have satisfied him; for no sooner is he safe, than he finds himself in danger, *fallen on evil days and evil tongues, and with darkness and with danger compass'd round.* This darkness, had his eyes been better employed, had undoubtedly deserved compassion; but to add the mention of danger was ungrateful and unjust. He was fallen indeed on *evil days;* the time was come in which regicides could no longer boast their wickedness. But of *evil tongues* for Milton to complain, required impudence at least equal to his other powers; Milton, whose warmest advocates must allow, that he never spared any asperity of reproach or brutality of insolence.

But the charge itself seems to be false; for it would be hard to recollect any reproach cast upon him, either serious or ludicrous, through the whole remaining part of his life. He persued his studies, or his amusements, without persecution, molestation, or insult. Such is the reverence paid to great abilities, however misused: they who contemplated in Milton the scholar and the wit, were contented to forget the reviler of his king. . . .

The slow sale and tardy reputation of this poem, have been always mentioned as evidences of neglected merit, and of the uncertainty of literary fame; and enquiries have been made, and conjecture offered, about the causes of its long obscurity and late reception. But has the case been truly stated? Have not lamentation and wonder been lavished on an evil that was never felt?

That in the reigns of Charles and James the *Paradise Lost* received no publick acclamations is readily confessed. Wit and literature were on the side of the Court: and who that solicited favour or fashion would venture to praise the defender of the regicides? All that he himself could think his due, from *evil tongues* in *evil days*, was that reverential silence which was generously preserved. But it cannot be inferred that his poem was not read, or not, however unwillingly, admired.

The sale, if it be considered, will justify the publick. Those who have no power to judge of past times but by their own, should always doubt their conclusions. The sale of books was not in Milton's age what it is in the present. To read was not then a general amusement; neither traders, nor often gentlemen, thought themselves disgraced by ignorance. The women had not then aspired to literature, nor was every house supplied with a closet of books. Those indeed, who professed learning, were not less learned than at any other time; but of that middle race of students who read for pleasure or accomplishment, and who buy the numerous products of modern typography, the number was then comparatively small. To prove the paucity of readers, it may be sufficient to remark, that the nation had been satisfied, from 1623 to 1664, that is, forty-one years, with only two editions of the works of Shakespeare, which probably did not together make one thousand copies.

The sale of thirteen hundred copies in two years, in opposition to so much recent enmity, and to a style of versification new to all and disgusting to many, was an uncommon example of the prevalence of genius. The demand did not immediately encrease; for many more readers than were supplied at first the nation did not afford. Only three thousand were sold in eleven years; for it forced its way without assistance: its admirers did not dare to publish their opinion; and the opportunities now given of attracting notice by advertisements were then very few; for the means of proclaiming the publication of new books have been produced by that general literature which now pervades the nation through all its ranks.

But the reputation and price of the copy still advanced, till the Revolution put an end to the secrecy of love, and *Paradise Lost* broke into open view with sufficient security of kind reception.

Fancy can hardly forbear to conjecture with what temper Milton surveyed the silent progress of his work, and marked his reputation stealing its way in a kid of subterraneous current through fear and silence. I cannot but conceive him calm and confident, little disappointed, not at all dejected, relying on his own merit with steady consciousness, and waiting, without impatience, the vicissitudes of opinion, and the impartiality of a future generation. . . .

Milton has the reputation of having been in his youth eminently beautiful, so as to have been called the Lady of his college. His hair, which was of a light brown, parted at the foretop, and hung down upon his shoulders, according to the picture which he has given of Adam. He was, however, not of the heroick stature, but rather below the middle size, according to Mr. Richardson, who mentions him as having narrowly escaped from being *short and thick*. He was vigorous and active, and delighted in the exercise of the sword, in which he is related to have been eminently skilful. His weapon was, I believe, not the rapier, but the backsword, of which he recommends the use in his book on Education.

His eyes are said never to have been bright; but, if he was a dexterous fencer, they must have been once quick.

His domestick habits, so far as they are known, were those of a severe student. He drank little strong drink of any kind, and fed without delicacy of choice or excess in quantity. In his youth he studied late at night; but afterwards changed his hours, and rested in bed from nine to four in the Summer, and five in the Winter. The course of his day was best known after he was blind. When he first rose he heard a chapter in the Hebrew Bible, and then studied till twelve; then took some exercise for an hour; then dined; then plaid on the organ, and sung, or heard another sing; then studied to six; then entertained his visiters, till eight; then supped, and, after a pipe of tobacco and a glass of water, went to bed.

So is his life described; but this even tenour appears attainable only in Colleges. He that lives in the world will sometimes have the succession of his practice broken and confused. Visiters, of whom Milton is represented to have had great numbers, will come and stay unseasonably; business, of which every man has some, must be done when others will do it.

When he did not care to rise early, he had something read to him by his bedside; perhaps at this time his daughters were employed. He composed much in the morning, and dictated in the day, sitting obliquely in an elbow-chair, with his leg thrown over the arm. . . .

His theological opinions are said to have been first calvinistical; and afterwards, perhaps when he began to hate the Presbyterians, to have tended towards Arminianism. In the mixed questions of theology and government, he never thinks that he can recede far enough from popery, or prelacy; but what Baudius says of Erasmus seems applicable to him, *magis habuit quod fugeret, quam quod sequeretur*. He had determined rather what to condemn than what to approve. He has not associated himself with any denomination of Protestants: we know rather what he was not, than what he was. He was not of the church of Rome; he was not of the church of England.

To be of no church is dangerous. Religion, of which the rewards are distant, and which is animated only by Faith and Hope, will glide by degrees out of the mind, unless it be invigorated and reimpressed by external ordinances, by stated calls to worship, and the salutary influence of example. Milton, who appears to have had full conviction of the truth of Christianity, and to have regarded the Holy Scriptures with the profoundest veneration, to have been untainted by an heretical peculiarity of opinion, and to have lived in a confirmed belief of the immediate and occasional agency of Providence, yet grew old without any visible worship. In the distribution of his hours, there was no hour of prayer, either solitary, or with his household; omitting publick prayers, he omitted all.

Of this omission the reason has been sought, upon a supposition which ought never to be made, that men live with their own approbation, and justify their conduct to themselves. Prayer certainly was not thought superfluous by him, who represents our first parents as praying acceptably in the state of innocence, and efficaciously after their fall. That he lived without prayer can hardly be affirmed; his studies and meditations were an habitual prayer. The neglect of it in his family was probably a fault for which he condemned himself, and which he intended to correct, but that death, as too often happens, intercepted his reformation.

His political notions were those of an acrimonious and surly republican, for which it is not known that he gave any better reason than that *a popular government was the most frugal; for the trappings of a monarchy would set up an ordinary commonwealth.* It is surely very shallow policy, that supposes money to be the chief good; and even this, without considering that the support and expence of a Court is, for the most part, only a particular kind of traffick, by which money is circulated, without any national impoverishment.

Milton's republicanism was, I am afraid, founded in an envious hatred of greatness, and a sullen desire of independence; in petulance, impatient of controul, and pride disdainful of superiority. He hated monarchs in the state, and prelates in the church; for he hated all whom he was required to obey. It is to be suspected that his predominant desire was to destroy rather than establish, and that he felt not so much the love of liberty as repugnance to authority.

It has been observed, that they who most loudly clamour for liberty do not most liberally grant it. What we know of Milton's character, in domestick relations, is, that he was severe and arbitrary. His family consisted of women; and there appears in his books something like a Turkish contempt of females, as subordinate and inferiour beings. That his own daughters might not break the ranks, he suffered them to be depressed by a mean and penurious education. He thought woman made only for obedience, and man only for rebellion. . . .

In the examination of Milton's poetical works, I shall pay so much regard to time as to begin with his juvenile productions. . . . The English poems, though they make no promises of *Paradise Lost,* have this evidence of genius, that they have a cast original and unborrowed. But their peculiarity is not excellence: if they differ from verses of others, they differ for the worse; for they are too often distinguished by repulsive harshness; the combinations of words are new, but they are not pleasing; the rhymes and epithets seem to be laboriously sought, and violently applied.

That in the early part of his life he wrote with much care appears from his manuscripts, happily preserved at Cambridge, in which many of his smaller works are found as they were first written, with the subsequent corrections. Such reliques shew how excellence is acquired; what we hope ever to do with ease, we may learn first to do with diligence.

Those who admire the beauties of this great poet, sometimes force their own judgement into false approbation of his little pieces, and prevail upon themselves to think that admirable which is only singular. All that short compositions can commonly attain is neatness and elegance. Milton never learned the art of doing little things with grace; he overlooked the milder excellence of suavity and softness; he was a *Lion* that had no skill *in dandling the Kid.*

One of the poems on which much praise has been bestowed is *Lycidas;* of which the diction is harsh, the rhymes uncertain, and the numbers unpleasing. What beauty there is, we must therefore seek in the sentiments and images.

It is not to be considered as the effusion of real passion; for passion runs not after remote allusions and obscure opinions. Passion plucks no berries from the myrtle and ivy, nor calls upon Arethuse and Mincius, nor tells of rough *satyrs* and *fauns with cloven heel.* Where there is leisure for fiction there is little grief.

In this poem there is no nature, for there is no truth; there is no art, for there is nothing new. Its form is that of a pastoral, easy, vulgar, and therefore disgusting: whatever images it can supply, are long ago exhausted; and its inherent improbability always forces dissatisfaction on the mind. When Cowley tells of Hervey that they studied together, it is easy to suppose how much he must miss the companion of his labours, and the partner of his discoveries; but what image of tenderness can be excited by these lines?

> We drove a field, and both together heard
> What time the grey fly winds her sultry horn,
> Batt'ning our flocks with the fresh dews of night.

We know that they never drove a field, and that they had no flocks to batten; and though it be allowed that the representation may be allegorical, the true meaning is so uncertain and remote, that it is never sought, because it cannot be known when it is found.

Among the flocks, and copses, and flowers, appear the heathen deities; Jove and Phœbus, Neptune and Æolus, with a long train of mythological imagery, such as a College easily supplies. Nothing can less display knowledge, or less exercise invention, than to tell how a shepherd has lost his companion, and must now feed his flocks alone, without any judge of his skill in piping; and how one god asks another god what is become of Lycidas, and how neither god can tell. He who thus grieves will excite no sympathy; he who thus praises will confer no honour.

This poem has yet a grosser fault. With these trifling fictions are mingled the most awful and sacred truths, such as ought never to be polluted with such irreverend combinations. The shepherd likewise is now a feeder of sheep, and afterwards an ecclesiastical pastor, a superintendent of a Christian flock. Such equivocations are always unskilful, but here they are indecent, and at least approach to impiety, of which, however, I believe the writer not to have been conscious.

Such is the power of reputation justly acquired, that its blaze drives away the eye from nice examination. Surely no man could have fancied that he read *Lycidas* with pleasure, had he not know its author.

Of the two pieces, *L'Allegro* and *Il Penseroso,* I believe opinion is uniform;

every man that reads them, reads them with pleasure. The author's design is not, what Theobald has remarked, merely to shew how objects derive their colours from the mind, by representing the operation of the same things upon the gay and the melancholy temper, or upon the same man as he is differently disposed; but rather how, among the successive variety of appearances, every disposition of mind takes hold on those by which it may be gratified.

The *chearful* man hears the lark in the morning; the *pensive* man hears the nightingale in the evening. The *chearful* man sees the cock strut, and hears the horn and hounds echo in the wood; then walks *not unseen* to observe the glory of the rising sun, or listen to the singing milk-maid, and view the labours of the plowman and the mower; then casts his eyes about him over scenes of smiling plenty, and looks up to the distant tower, the residence of some fair inhabitant; thus he pursues rural gaiety through a day of labour or of play, and delights himself at night with the fanciful narratives of superstitious ignorance.

The *pensive* man, at one time, walks *unseen* to muse at midnight; and at another hears the sullen curfew. If the weather drives him home, he sits in a room lighted only by *glowing embers;* or by a lonely lamp outwatches the North Star, to discover the habitation of separate souls, and varies the shades of meditation, by contemplating the magnificent or pathetick scenes of tragick and epic poetry. When the morning comes, a morning gloomy with rain and wind, he walks into the dark trackless woods, falls asleep by some murmuring water, and with melancholy enthusiasm expects some dream of prognostication, or some musick plaid by aerial performers.

Both Mirth and Melancholy are solitary, silent inhabitants of the breast that neither receive nor transmit communication; no mention is therefore made of a philosophical friend, or a pleasant companion. Seriousness does not arise from any participation of calamity, nor gaiety from the pleasures of the bottle.

The man of *chearfulness,* having exhausted the country, tries what *towered cities* will afford, and mingles with scenes of splendor, gay assemblies, and nuptial festivities; but he mingles a mere spectator, as when the learned comedies of Jonson, or the wild dramas of Shakespeare, are exhibited, he attends the theatre.

The *pensive* man never loses himself in crowds, but walks the cloister, or frequents the cathedral. Milton probably had not yet forsaken the Church.

Both his characters delight in musick; but he seems to think that chearful notes would have obtained from Pluto a compleat dismission of Eurydice, of whom solemn sounds only procured a conditional release.

For the old age of Chearfulness he makes no provision; but Melancholy he conducts with great dignity to the close of life.

Through these two poems the images are properly selected, and nicely distinguished; but the colours of the diction seem not sufficiently discriminated. His Chearfulness is without levity, and his Pensiveness without asperity. I know not whether the characters are kept sufficiently apart. No mirth can, indeed, be found in his melancholy; but I am afraid that I always meet some melancholy in his mirth. They are two noble efforts of imagination.

The greatest of his juvenile performances is the *Mask of Comus;* in which may very plainly be discovered the dawn or twilight of *Paradise Lost.* Milton appears to have formed very early that system of diction, and mode of verse, which his maturer judgement approved, and from which he never endeavoured nor desired to deviate.

Nor does *Comus* afford only a specimen of his language; it exhibits likewise his power of description, and his vigour of sentiment, employed in the praise and defence of virtue. A work more truly poetical is rarely found; allusions, images, and descriptive epithets, embellish almost every period with lavish decoration. As a series of lines, therefore, it may be considered as worthy of all the admiration with which the votaries have received it.

As a drama it is deficient. The action is not probable. A Masque, in those parts where supernatural intervention is admitted, must indeed be given up to all the freaks of imagination; but, so far as the action is merely human, it ought to be reasonable, which can hardy be said of the conduct of the two brothers; who, when their sister sinks with fatigue in a pathless wilderness, wander both away together in search of berries too far to find their way back, and leave a helpless lady to all the sadness and danger of solitude. This however is a defect over-balanced by its convenience.

What deserves more reprehension is, that the prologue spoken in the wild wood by the attendant Spirit is addressed to the audience; a mode of communication so contrary to the nature of dramatick representation, that no precedents can support it.

The discourse of the Spirit is too long: an objection that may be made to almost all the following speeches: they have not the spriteliness of a dialogue animated by reciprocal contention, but seem rather declamations deliberately composed, and formally repeated, on a moral question. The auditor therefore listens as to a lecture, without passion, without anxiety.

The song of Comus has airiness and jollity; but, what may recommend Milton's morals as well as his poetry, the invitations to pleasure are so general, that they excite no distinct images of corrupt enjoyment, and take no dangerous hold on the fancy.

The following soliloquies of Comus and the Lady are elegant, but tedious. The song must owe much to the voice, if it ever can delight. At last the brothers enter, with too much tranquillity; and when they have feared lest their sister should be in danger, and hoped that she is not in danger, the Elder makes a speech in praise of chastity, and the Younger finds how fine it is to be a philosopher.

Then descends the Spirit in form of a shepherd; and the brother, instead of being in haste to ask his help, praises his singing, and enquires his business in that place. It is remarkable, that at this interview the brother is taken with a short fit of rhyming. The Spirit relates that the Lady is in the power of Comus; the brother moralises again; and the Spirit makes a long narration, of no use because it is false, and therefore unsuitable to a good Being.

In all these parts the language is poetical, and the sentiments are generous; but there is something wanting to allure attention.

The dispute between the Lady and Comus is the most animated and affecting scene of the drama, and wants nothing but a brisker reciprocaton of objections and replies to invite attention, and detain it.

The songs are vigorous, and full of imagery; but they are harsh in their diction, and not very musical in their numbers.

Throughout the whole, the figures are too bold, and the language too luxuriant for dialogue. It is a drama in the epic stile, inelegantly splendid, and tediously instructive.

The *Sonnets* were written in different parts of Milton's life, upon different occasions. They deserve not any particular criticism; for of the best it can only be said, that they are not bad; and perhaps only the eighth and the twenty-first are truly entitled to this slender commendation. The fabrick of a sonnet, however adapted to the Italian language, has never succeeded in ours, which, having greater variety of termination, requires the rhymes to be often changed.

Those little pieces may be dispatched without much anxiety; a greater work calls for greater care. I am now to examine *Paradise Lost;* a poem, which, considered with respect to design, may claim the first place, and with respect to performance the second among the productions of the human mind.

By the general consent of criticks, the first praise of genius is due to the writer of an epick poem, as it requires an assemblage of all the powers which are singly sufficient for other compositions. Poetry is the art of uniting pleasure with truth, by calling imagination to the help of reason. Epick poetry undertakes to teach the most important truths by the most pleasing precepts, and therefore relates some great event in the most affecting manner. History must supply the writer with the rudiments of narration, which he must improve and exalt by a nobler art, animate by dramatick energy, and diversify by retrospection and anticipation; morality must teach him the exact bounds, and different shades, of vice and virtue: from policy, and the practice of life, he has to learn the discriminations of character, and the tendency of the passions, either single or combined; and physiology must supply him with illustrations and images. To put these materials to poetical use, is required an imagination capable of painting nature, and realizing fiction. Nor is he yet a poet till he has attained the whole extension of his language, distinguished all the delicacies of phrase, and all the colours of words, and learned to adjust their different sounds to all the varieties of metrical modulation.

Bossu is of opinion that the poet's first work is to find a *moral,* which his fable is afterwards to illustrate and establish. This seems to have been the process only of Milton; the moral of other poems is incidental and consequent; in Milton's only it is essential and intrinsick. His purpose was the most useful and the most arduous; *to vindicate the ways of God to man;* to shew the reasonableness of religion, and the necessity of obedience to the Divine Law.

To convey this moral there must be a *fable,* a narration artfully constructed, so as to excite curiosity, and surprise expectation. In this part of his work, Milton must be confessed to have equalled every other poet. He has involved in his account of the Fall of Man the events which preceded, and those that were to follow it: he has interwoven the whole system of theology with such propriety, that every part appears to be necessary; and scarcely any recital is wished shorter for the sake of quickening the progress of the main action.

The subject of an epick poem is naturally an event of great importance. That of Milton is not the destruction of a city, the conduct of a colony, or the foundation of an empire. His subject is the fate of worlds, the revolutions of heaven and of earth; rebellion against the Supreme King, raised by the highest order of created beings; the overthrow of their host, and the punishment of their crime; the creation of a new race of reasonable creatures; their original happiness and innocence, their forfeiture of immortality, and their restoration to hope and peace.

Great events can be hastened or retarded only by persons of elevated dignity. Before the greatness displayed in Milton's poem, all other greatness shrinks away. The weakest of his agents are the highest and noblest of human beings, the original parents of mankind; with whose actions the elements consented; on whose rectitude, or deviation of will, depended the state of terrestrial nature, and the condition of all the future inhabitants of the globe.

Of the other agents in the poem, the chief are such as it is irreverence to name on slight occasions. The rest are lower powers;

> ——of which the least could wield
> Those elements, and arm him with the force
> Of all their regions;

powers, which only the controul of Omnipotence restrains from laying creation waste, and filling the vast expanse of space with ruin and confusion. To display the motives and actions of beings thus superiour, so far as human reason can examine them, or human imagination represent them, is the task which this mighty poet has undertaken and performed. . . .

To the compleatness or *integrity* of the design nothing can be objected; it has distinctly and clearly what Aristotle requires, a beginning, a middle, and an end. There is perhaps no poem, of the same length, from which so little can be taken without apparent mutilation. Here are no funeral games, nor is there any long description of a shield. The short digressions at the beginning of the third, seventh, and ninth books, might doubtless be spared; but superfluities so beautiful, who would take away? or who does not wish that the author of the *Iliad* had gratified succeeding ages with a little knowledge of himself? Perhaps no passages are more frequently or more attentively read than those extrinsick paragraphs; and, since the end of poetry is pleasure, that cannot be unpoetical with which all are pleased. . . .

The thoughts which are occasionally called forth in the progress, are such as could only be produced by an imagination in the highest degree fervid and active, to which materials were supplied by incessant study and unlimited curiosity. The heat of Milton's mind might be said to sublimate his learning, to throw off into his work the spirit of science, unmingled with its grosser parts.

He had considered creation in its whole extent, and his descriptions are therefore learned. He had accustomed his imagination to unrestrained indulgence, and his conceptions therefore were extensive. The characteristick quality of his poem is sublimity. He sometimes descends to the elegant, but his element is the great. He can occasionally invest himself with grace; but his natural port is gigantick loftiness. He can please when pleasure is required; but it is his peculiar power to astonish.

He seems to have been well acquainted with his own genius, and to know what it was that Nature had bestowed upon him more bountifully than upon others; the power of displaying the vast, illuminating the splendid, enforcing the awful, darkening the gloomy, and aggravating the dreadful: he therefore chose a subject on which too much could not be said, on which he might tire his fancy without the censure of extravagance.

The appearance of nature, and the occurrences of life, did not satiate his appetite of greatness. To paint things as they are, requires a minute attention, and employs the memory rather than the fancy. Milton's delight was to sport in the wide regions of possibility; reality was a scene too narrow for his mind. He sent his faculties out upon discovery, into worlds where only imagination can travel, and delighted to form new modes of existence, and furnish sentiment and action to superior beings, to trace the counsels of hell, or accompany the choirs of heaven.

But he could not be always in other worlds: he must sometimes revisit earth, and tell of things visible and known. When he cannot raise wonder by the sublimity of his mind, he gives delight by its fertility.

Whatever be his subject, he never fails to fill the imagination. But his images and descriptions of the scenes or operations of Nature do not seem to be always copied from original form, nor to have the freshness, raciness, and energy of immediate observation. He saw Nature, as Dryden expresses it, *through the spectacles of books;* and on most occasions calls learning to his assistance. The garden of Eden brings to his mind the vale of *Enna,* where Proserpine was gathering flowers. Satan makes his way through fighting elements, like *Argo* between the *Cyanean* rocks, or *Ulysses* between the two *Sicilian* whirlpools, when he shunned *Charybdis* on the *larboard.* The mythological allusions have been justly censured, as not being always used with notice of their vanity; but they contribute variety to the narration, and produce an alternate exercise of the memory and the fancy.

His similes are less numerous, and more various, than those of his predecessors. But he does not confine himself within the limits of rigorous comparison: his great excellence is amplitude, and he expands the adventitious image beyond the dimensions which the occasion required. Thus, comparing the shield of Satan to the orb of the Moon, he crowds the imagination with the discovery of the telescope, and all the wonders which the telescope discovers. . . .

The plan of *Paradise Lost* has this inconvenience, that it comprises neither human actions nor human manners. The man and woman who act and suffer, are in a state which no other man or woman can ever know. The reader finds no transaction in which he can be engaged; beholds no condition in which he can by any effort of imagination place himself; he has, therefore, little natural curiosity or sympathy.

We all, indeed, feel the effects of Adam's disobedience; we all sin like Adam, and like him must all bewail our offences; we have restless and insidious enemies in the fallen angels, and in the blessed spirits we have guardians and friends; in the Redemption of mankind we hope to be included; in the description of heaven and hell we are surely interested, as we are all to reside hereafter either in the regions of horror or of bliss.

But these truths are too important to be new; they have been taught to our infancy; they have mingled with our solitary thoughts and familiar conversation, and are habitually interwoven with the whole texture of life. Being therefore not new, they raise no unaccustomed emotion in the mind; what we knew before we cannot learn; what is not unexpected cannot surprise.

Of the ideas suggested by these awful scenes, from some we recede with reverence, except when stated hours require their association; and from others we shrink with horror, or admit them only as salutary inflictions, as counterpoises to our interests and passions. Such images rather obstruct the career of fancy than incite it.

Pleasure and terrour are indeed the genuine sources of poetry; but poetical pleasure must be such as human imagination can at least conceive, and poetical terror such as human strength and fortitude may combat. The good and evil of Eternity are too ponderous for the wings of wit; the mind sinks under them in passive helplessness, content with calm belief and humble adoration.

Known truths, however, may take a different appearance, and be conveyed to the mind by a new train of intermediate images. This Milton has undertaken, and performed with pregnancy and vigour of mind peculiar to himself. Whoever considers the few radical positions which the Scriptures afforded him, will wonder by what energetick operation he expanded them to such extent, and ramified them to so much variety, restrained as he was by religious reverence from licentiousness of fiction.

Here is a full display of the united force of study and genius; of a great accumulation of materials, with judgement to digest, and fancy to combine them: Milton was able to select from nature, or from story, from ancient fable, or from modern science, whatever could illustrate or adorn his thoughts. An accumulation of knowledge impregnated his mind, fermented by study, and sublimed by imagination.

It has been therefore said, without an indecent hyperbole, by one of his encomiasts, that in reading *Paradise Lost* we read a book of universal knowledge.

But original deficience cannot be supplied. The want of human interest is always felt. *Paradise Lost* is one of the books which the reader admires and lays down, and forgets to take up again. Its perusal is a duty rather than a pleasure. We read Milton for instruction, retire harrassed and overburdened, and look elsewhere for recreation; we desert our master, and seek for companions. . . .

Dryden remarks, that Milton has some flats among his elevations. This is only to say that all the parts are not equal. In every work one part must be for the sake of others; a palace must have passages; a poem must have transitions. It is no more to be required that wit should always be blazing, than that the sun should always stand at noon. In a great work there is a vicissitude of luminous and opaque parts, as there is in the world a succession of day and night. Milton, when he has expatiated in the sky, may be allowed sometimes to revisit earth; for what other author ever soared so high, or sustained his flight so long? . . .

Of *Paradise Regained*, the general judgement seems now to be right, that it is in many parts elegant, and every-where instructive. It was not to be supposed that the writer of *Paradise Lost* could ever write without great effusions of fancy, and exalted precepts of wisdom. The basis of *Paradise Regained* is narrow; a dialogue without action can never please like an union of the narrative and dramtick powers. Had this poem been written not by Milton, but by some imitator, it would have claimed and received universal praise.

If *Paradise Regained* has been too much depreciated, *Samson Agonistes* has in requital been too much admired. It could only be by long prejudice, and the bigotry of learning, that Milton could prefer the ancient tragedies, with their encumbrance of a chorus, to the exhibitions of the French and English stages; and it is only by a blind confidence in the reputation of Milton, that a drama can be praised in which the intermediate parts have neither cause nor consequence, neither hasten nor retard the catastrophe.

In this tragedy are however many particular beauties, many just sentiments and striking lines; but it wants that power of attracting the attention which a well-connected plan produces.

Milton would not have excelled in dramatick writing; he knew human nature only in the gross, and had never studied the shades of character, nor the combinations of concurring, or the perplexity of contending passions. He had read much, and knew what books could teach; but had mingled little in the world, and was deficient in the knowledge which experience must confer.

Through all his greater works there prevails an uniform peculiarity of *Diction*, a mode and cast of expression which bears little resemblance to that of any former writer, and which is so far removed from common use, that an unlearned reader, when he first opens his book, finds himself surprised by a new language.

This novelty has been, by those who can find nothing wrong in Milton, imputed to his laborious endeavors after words suitable to the grandeur of his ideas. *Our language*, says Addison, *sunk under him*. But the truth is, that, both in prose and verse, he had formed his stile by a perverse and pedantick principle. He was desirous to use English words with a foreign idiom. This in all his prose is discovered and condemned; for there judgement operates freely, neither softened by the beauty nor awed by the dignity of his thoughts; but such is the power of his poetry, that his call is obeyed without resistance, the reader feels himself in captivity to a higher and a nobler mind, and criticism sinks in admiration.

Milton's stile was not modified by his subject: what is shown with greater extent in *Paradise Lost*, may be found in *Comus*. One source of his peculiarity was his familiarity with the Tuscan poets: the disposition of his words is, I think, frequently Italian; perhaps sometimes combined with other tongues. Of him, at last, may be said what Jonson says of Spenser, that *he wrote no language,* but has formed what *Butler* calls a *Babylonish Dialect,* in itself harsh and barbarous, but made by exalted genius, and extensive learning, the vehicle of so much instruction and so much pleasure, that, like other lovers, we find grace in its deformity.

Whatever be the faults of his diction, he cannot want the praise of copiousness and variety: he was master of his language in its full extent; and has selected the melodious words with such diligence, that from his book alone the Art of English Poetry might be learned. . . .

Rhyme, he says, and says truly, *is no necessary adjunct of true poetry.* But perhaps, of poetry as a mental operation, metre or musick is no necessary adjunct: it is however by the musick of metre that poetry has been discriminated in all languages; and in languages melodiously constructed, by a due proportion of long and short syllables, metre is sufficient. But one language cannot communicate its rules to another: where metre is scanty and imperfect, some help is necessary. The musick of the English heroick line strikes the ear so faintly that it is easily lost, unless all the syllables of every line co-operate together: this co-operation can be only obtained by the preservation of every verse unmingled with another, as a distinct system of sounds; and this distinctness is obtained and preserved by the artifice of rhyme. The variety of pauses, so much boasted by the lovers of blank verse, changes the measures of an English poet to the periods of a declaimer; and there are only a few skilful and happy readers of Milton, who enable their audience to perceive where the lines end or begin. *Blank verse,* said an ingenious critick, *seems to be verse only to the eye.*

Poetry may subsist without rhyme, but English poetry will not often please; nor can rhyme ever be safely spared but where the subject is able to support itself. Blank verse makes some approach to that which is called the *lapidary stile;* has neither the easiness of prose, nor the melody of numbers, and therefore tires by long continuance. Of the Italian writers without rhyme, whom Milton alleges as precedents, not one is popular; what reason could urge in its defence, has been confuted by the ear.

But, whatever by the advantage of rhyme, I cannot prevail on myself to wish that Milton had been a rhymer; for I cannot wish his work to be other than it is; yet, like other heroes, he is to be admired rather than imitated. He that thinks himself capable of astonishing, may write blank verse; but those that hope only to please, must condescend to rhyme.

The highest praise of genius is original invention. Milton cannot be said to have contrived the structure of an epick poem, and therefore must yield to that vigour and amplitude of mind to which all generations must be indebted for the art of poetical narration, for the texture of the fable, the variation of incidents, the interposition of dialogue, and all the stratagems that surprise and enchain attention. But, of all the borrowers from Homer, Milton is perhaps the least indebted. He was naturally a thinker for himself, confident of his own abilities, and disdainful of help or hindrance: he did not refuse admission to the thoughts or images of his predecessors, but he did not seek them. From his contemporaries he neither courted nor received support; there is in his writings nothing by which the pride of other authors might be gratified, or favour gained; no exchange of praise, nor solicitation of support. His great works were performed under discountenance, and in blindness, but difficulties vanished at his touch; he was born for whatever is arduous, and his work is not the greatest of heroick poems, only because it is not the first.

EDMUND WALLER

When he had lost all hopes of Sacharissa, he looked round him for an easier conquest, and gained a lady of the family of Bresse, or Breaux. The time of his marriage is not exactly known. It has not been discovered that his wife was won by his poetry; nor is any thing told of her, but that she brought him many children. He doubtless praised many whom he would have been afraid to marry; and perhaps married one whom he would have been ashamed to praise. Many qualities contribute to domestick happiness, upon which poetry has no colours to bestow; and many airs and sallies may delight imagination, which he who flatters them never can approve. There are charms made only for distant admiration. No spectacle is nobler than a blaze. . . .

Cromwell, now protector, received Waller, as his kinsman, to familiar conversation. Waller, as he used to relate, found him sufficiently versed in ancient history; and when any of his enthusiastick friends came to advise or consult him, could sometimes over-hear him discoursing in the cant of the times: but, when he returned, he would say, "Cousin Waller, I must talk to these men in their own way"; and resumed the common stile of conversation.

He repaid the Protector for his favours (1654), by the famous panegyrick, which has been always considered as the first of his poetical productions. His choice of encomiastick topicks is very judicious; for he considers Cromwel in his exaltation, without enquiring how he attained it; there is consequently no mention of the rebel or the regicide. All the former part of his hero's life is veiled with shades, and nothing is brought to view but the chief, the governor, the defender of England's honour, and the enlarger of her dominion. The act of violence by which he obtained the supreme power is lightly treated, and decently justified. It was certainly to be desired that the detestable band should be dissolved, which had destroyed the church, murdered the king, and filled the nation with tumult and oppression; yet Cromwel had not the right of dissolving them, for all that he had before done, could be justified only by supposing them invested with lawful authority. But combinations of wickedness would overwhelm the world by the advantage which licentious principles afford, did not those who have long practised perfidy, grow faithless to each other. . . .

Shorter Poems

Of these petty compositions, neither the beauties nor the faults deserve much attention. The amorous verses have this to recommend them, that they are less hyperbolical than those of some other poets. Waller is not always at the last gasp; he does not die of a frown, nor live upon a smile. There is however too much love, and too many trifles. Little things are made too important; and the Empire of Beauty is represented as exerting its influence further than can be allowed by the multiplicity of human passions, and the variety of human wants. Such books therefore may be considered as shewing the world under a false appearance, and so far as they obtain credit from the young and unexperienced, as misleading expectation, and misguiding practice. . . .

It has been the frequent lamentation of good men, that verse has been too little applied to the purposes of worship, and many attempts have been made to animate devotion by pious poetry; that they have very seldom attained their end is sufficiently known, and it may not be improper to enquire why they have miscarried.

Let no pious ear be offended if I advance, in opposition to many authorities, that poetical devotion cannot often please. The doctrines of religion may indeed be defended in a didactick poem; and he who has the happy power of arguing in verse, will not lose it because his subject is sacred. A poet may describe the beauty and the grandeur of Nature, the flowers of the Spring, and the harvests of Autumn, the vicissitudes of the Tide, and the revolutions of the Sky, and praise the Maker for his works in lines which no reader shall lay aside. The subject of the disputation is not piety, but the motives to piety; that of the description is not God, but the works of God.

Contemplative piety, or the intercourse between God and the human soul, cannot be poetical. Man admitted to implore the mercy of his Creator, and plead the merits of his Redeemer, is already in a higher state than poetry can confer.

The essence of poetry is invention; such invention as, by producing something unexpected, surprises and delights. The topicks of devotion are few, and being few are universally known; but few as they are, they can be made no more; they can receive no grace from novelty of sentiment, and very little from novelty of expression.

Poetry pleases by exhibiting an idea more grateful to the mind than things themselves afford. This effect proceeds from the display of those parts of nature which attract; and the concealment of those which repel the imagination: but religion must be shewn as it is; suppression and addition equally corrupt it; and such as it is, it is known already.

From poetry the reader justly expects, and from good poetry always obtains, the enlargement of his comprehension and elevation of his fancy; but this is rarely to be hoped by Christians from metrical devotion. Whatever is great, desireable, or tremendous, is comprised in the name of the Supreme Being. Omnipotence cannot be exalted; Infinity cannot be amplified; Perfection cannot be improved.

The employments of pious meditation are Faith, Thanksgiving, Repentance, and Supplication. Faith, invariably uniform, cannot be invested by fancy with decorations. Thanksgiving, the most joyful of all holy effusions, yet addressed to a Being without passions, is confined to a few modes, and is to be felt rather than expressed. Repentance, trembling in the presence of the Judge, is not at leisure for cadences and epithets. Supplication of man to man may diffuse itself through many topicks of persuasion; but supplication to God can only cry for mercy.

Of sentiments purely religious, it will be found that the most simple expression is the most sublime. Poetry loses its lustre and its power, because it is applied to the decoration of something more excellent than itself. All that verse can do is to help the memory, and delight the ear, and for these purposes it may be very useful; but it supplies nothing to the mind. The ideas of Christian Theology are too simple for eloquence, too sacred for fiction, and too majestick for ornament; to recommend them by tropes and figures, is to magnify by a concave mirror the sidereal hemisphere.

JOHN DRYDEN

Secret Love, or the Maiden Queen, is a tragi-comedy. In the preface he discusses a curious question, whether a poet can judge well of his own productions: and determines very justly, that, of the plan and disposition, and all that can be reduced to principles of science the author may depend upon his own opinion; but that, in those parts where fancy predominates, self-love may easily deceive. He might have observed, that what is good only because it pleases, cannot be pronounced good till it has been found to please. . . .

The Tempest is an alteration of Shakespeare's play, made by Dryden in conjunction with Davenant. . . . The effect produced by the conjunction of these two powerful minds was, that to Shakespeare's monster Caliban is added a sister-monster Sicorax; and a woman, who, in the original play, had never seen a man, is in this brought acquainted with a man that had never seen a woman. . . .

The two parts of the *Conquest of Granada* are written with a seeming determination to glut the publick with dramatick wonders; to exhibit in its highest elevation a theatrical meteor of incredible love and impossible valour, and to leave no room for a wilder flight to the extravagance of posterity. All the rays of romatick heat, whether amorous or warlike, glow in Almanzor by a kind of concentration. He is above all laws; he is exempt from all restraints; he ranges the world at will, and governs wherever he appears. He fights without enquiring the cause, and loves in spite of the obligations of justice, of rejection by his mistress, and of prohibition from the dead. Yet the scenes are, for the most part, delightful; they exhibit a kind of illustrious depravity, and majestick madness: such as, if it is sometimes despised, is often reverenced, and in which the ridiculous is mingled with the astonishing. . . .

All for Love, or the World well lost, a tragedy founded upon the story of

Antony and Cleopatra, he tells us, *is the only play which he wrote for himself;* the rest were given to the people. It is by universal consent accounted the work in which he has admitted the fewest improprieties of style or character; but it has one fault equal to many, though rather moral than critical, that, by admitting the romantick omnipotence of Love, he has recommended as laudable and worthy of imitation that conduct which, through all ages, the good have censured as vitious, and the bad despised as foolish. . . .

In 1681, Dryden became yet more conspicuous by uniting politicks with poetry, in the memorable satire called *Absalom and Achitophel,* written against the faction which, by lord Shaftesbury's incitement, set the duke of Monmouth at its head.

Of this poem, in which personal satire was applied to the support of publick principles, and in which therefore every mind was interested, the reception was eager, and the sale so large, that my father, an old bookseller, told me, he had not known it equalled but by Sacheverel's trial.

The reason of this general perusal Addison has attempted to derive from the delight which the mind feels in the investigation of secrets; and thinks that curiosity to decypher the names procured readers to the poem. There is no need to enquire why those verses were read, which, to all the attractions of wit, elegance, and harmony, added the co-operation of all the factious passions, and filled every mind with triumph or resentment.

It could not be supposed that all the provocation given by Dryden would be endured without resistance or reply. Both his person and his party were exposed in their turns to the shafts of satire, which, though neither so well pointed nor perhaps so well aimed, undoubtedly drew blood.

One of these poems is called *Dryden's Satire on his Muse;* ascribed, though, as Pope says, falsely, to *Somers,* who was afterwards Chancellor. The poem, whose soever it was, has much virulence, and some spriteliness. The writer tells all the ill that he can collect, both of Dryden and his friends.

The poem of *Absalom and Achitophel* had two answers, now both forgotten; one called *Azaria and Hushai;* the other, *Absalom senior.* Of these hostile compositions, Dryden apparently imputes *Absalom senior* to Settle, by quoting in his verses against him the second line. *Azaria and Hushai* was, as Wood says, imputed to him, though it is somewhat unlikely that he should write twice on the same occasion. This is a difficulty which I cannot remove, for want of a minuter knowledge of poetical transactions.

The same year he published the *Medal,* of which the subject is a medal struck on lord Shaftesbury's escape from a prosecution, by the *ignoramus* of a grand jury of Londoners.

In both poems he maintains the same principles, and saw them both attacked by the same antagonist. Elkanah Settle, who had answered *Absalom,* appeared with equal courage in opposition to the *Medal,* and published an answer called *The Medal reversed,* with so much success in both encounters, that he left the palm doubtful, and divided the suffrages of the nation. Such are the revolutions of fame, or such is the prevalence of fashion, that the man whose works have not yet been thought to deserve the care of collecting them;

who died forgotten in an hospital; and whose latter years were spent in contriving shows for fairs, and carrying an elegy or epithalamium, of which the beginning and end were occasionally varied, but the intermediate parts were always the same, to every house where there was a funeral or a wedding; might, with truth, have had inscribed upon his stone,

Here lies the Rival and Antagonist of Dryden.

Settle was, for this rebellion, severely chastised by Dryden under the name of *Doeg,* in the second part of *Absalom and Achitophel,* and was perhaps for his factious audacity made the city poet, whose annual office was to describe the glories of the Mayor's day. Of these bards he was the last, and seems not much to have deserved even this degree of regard, if it was paid to his political opinions; for he afterwards wrote a panegyrick on the virtues of judge Jefferies, and what more could have been done by the meanest zealot for prerogative? . . .

Soon after the accession of king James, when the design of reconciling the nation to the church of Rome became apparent, and the religion of the court gave the only efficacious title to its favours, Dryden declared himself a convert to popery. This at any other time might have passed with little censure. Sir Kenelm Digby embraced popery; the two Rainholds reciprocally converted one another; and Chillingworth himself was a while so entangled in the wilds of controversy, as to retire for quiet to an infallible church. If men of argument and study can find such difficulties, or such motives, as may either unite them to the church of Rome, or detain them in uncertainty, there can be no wonder that a man, who perhaps never enquired why he was a protestant, should by an artful and experienced disputant be made a papist, overborne by the sudden violence of new and unexpected arguments, or deceived by a representation which shews only the doubts on one part, and only the evidence on the other.

That conversion will always be suspected that apparently concurs with interest. He that never finds his error till it hinders his progress towards wealth or honour, will not be thought to love Truth only for herself. Yet it may easily happen that information may come at a commodious time; and as truth and interest are not by any fatal necessity at variance, that one may by accident introduce the other. When opinions are struggling into popularity, the arguments by which they are opposed or defended become more known; and he that changes his profession would perhaps have changed it before, with the like opportunities of instruction. This was then the state of popery; every artifice was used to shew it in its fairest form; and it must be owned to be a religion of external appearance sufficiently attractive.

It is natural to hope that a comprehensive is likewise an elevated soul, and that whoever is wise is also honest. I am willing to believe that Dryden, having employed his mind, active as it was, upon different studies, and filled it, capacious as it was, with other materials, came unprovided to the controversy, and wanted rather skill to discover the right than virtue to maintain it. But enquiries into the heart are not for man; we must now leave him to his Judge. . . .

There are men whose powers operate only at leisure and in retirement, and whose intellectual vigour deserts them in conversation; whom merriment confuses, and objection disconcerts; whose bashfulness restrains their exertion, and suffers them not to speak till the time of speaking is past; or whose attention to their own character makes them unwilling to utter at hazard what has not been considered, and cannot be recalled.

Of Dryden's sluggishness in conversation it is vain to search or to guess the cause. He certainly wanted neither sentiments nor language; his intellectual treasures were great, though they were locked up from his own use. *His thoughts*, when he wrote, *flowed in upon him so fast, that his only care was which to chuse, and which to reject.* Such rapidity of composition naturally promises a flow of talk, yet we must be content to believe what an enemy says of him, when he likewise says it of himself. . . .

Of the mind that can trade in corruption, and can deliberately pollute itself with ideal wickedness for the sake of spreading the contagion in society, I wish not to conceal or excuse the depravity.—Such degradation of the dignity of genius, such abuse of superlative abilities, cannot be contemplated but with grief and indignation. What consolation can be had, Dryden has afforded, by living to repent, and to testify his repentance.

Of dramatick immorality he did not want examples among his predecessors, or companions among his contemporaries; but in the meanness and servility of hyperbolical adulation, I know not whether, since the days in which the Roman emperors were deified, he has been ever equalled, except by Afra Behn in an address to Eleanor Gwyn. When once he has undertaken the task of praise, he no longer retains shame in himself, nor supposes it in his patron. As many odoriferous bodies are observed to diffuse perfumes from year to year, without sensible diminution of bulk or weight, he appears never to have impoverished his mint of flattery by his expences, however lavish. He had all the forms of excellence, intellectual and moral, combined in his mind, with endless variation; and when he had scattered on the hero of the day the golden shower of wit and virtue, he had ready for him, whom he wished to court on the morrow, new wit and virtue with another stamp. Of this kind of meanness he never seems to decline the practice, or lament the necessity: he considers the great as entitled to encomiastick homage, and brings praise rather as a tribute than a gift, more delighted with the fertility of his invention than mortified by the prostitution of his judgement. It is indeed not certain, that on these occasions his judgement much rebelled against his interest. There are minds which easily sink into submission, that look on grandeur with undistinguishing reverence, and discover no defect where there is elevation of rank and affluence of riches. . . .

Dryden may be properly considered as the father of English criticism, as the writer who first taught us to determine upon principles the merit of composition. Of our former poets, the greatest dramatist wrote without rules, conducted through life and nature by a genius that rarely misled, and rarely deserted him. Of the rest, those who knew the laws of propriety had neglected to teach them.

Two *Arts of English Poetry* were written in the days of Elizabeth by Webb and Puttenham, from which something might be learned, and a few hints had been given by Jonson and Cowley; but Dryden's *Essay on Dramatick Poetry* was the first regular treatise on the art of writing.

He who, having formed his opinions in the present age of English literature, turns back to peruse this dialogue, will not perhaps find much increase of knowledge, or much novelty of instruction; but he is to remember that critical principles were then in the hands of a few, who had gathered them partly from the Ancients, and partly from the Italians and French. The structure of dramatick poems was not then generally understood. Audiences applauded by instinct, and poets perhaps often pleased by chance.

A writer who obtains his full purpose loses himself in his own lustre. Of an opinion which is no longer doubted, the evidence ceases to be examined. Of an art universally practised, the first teacher is forgotten. Learning once made popular is no longer learning; it has the appearance of something which we have bestowed upon ourselves, as the dew appears to rise from the field which it refreshes.

To judge rightly of an author, we must transport ourselves to his time, and examine what were the wants of his contemporaries, and what were his means of supplying them. That which is easy at one time was difficult at another. Dryden at least imported his science, and gave his country what it wanted before; or rather, he imported only the materials, and manufactured them by his own skill.

The dialogue on the Drama was one of his first essays of criticism, written when he was yet a timorous candidate for reputation, and therefore laboured with that diligence which he might allow himself somewhat to remit, when his name gave sanction to his positions, and his awe of the public was abated, partly by custom, and partly by success. It will not be easy to find, in all the opulence of our language, a treatise so artfully variegated with successive representations of opposite probabilities, so enlivened with imagery, so brightened with illustrations. His portraits of the English dramatists are wrought with great spirit and diligence. The account of Shakespeare may stand as a perpetual model of encomiastick criticism; exact without minuteness, and lofty without exaggeration. The praise lavished by Longinus, on the attestation of the heroes of Marathon, by Demosthenes, fades away before it. In a few lines is exhibited a character, so extensive in its comprehension, and so curious in its limitations, that nothing can be added, diminished, or reformed; nor can the editors and admirers of Shakespeare, in all their emulation of reverence, boast of much more than of having diffused and paraphrased this epitome of excellence, of having changed Dryden's gold for baser metal, of lower value though of greater bulk.

In this, and in all his other essays on the same subject, the criticism of Dryden is the criticism of a poet; not a dull collection of theorems, nor a rude detection of faults, which perhaps the censor was not able to have committed; but a gay and vigorous dissertation, where delight is mingled with instruction, and where the author proves his right of judgement, by his power of performance.

The different manner and effect with which critical knowledge may be conveyed, was perhaps never more clearly exemplified than in the performances of Rymer and Dryden. It was said of a dispute between two mathematicians, 'malim cum Scaligero errare, quam cum Clavio recte sapere'; that *it was more eligible to go wrong with one than right with the other*. A tendency of the same kind every mind must feel at the perusal of Dryden's prefaces and Rymer's discourses. With Dryden we are wandering in quest of Truth; whom we find, if we find her at all, drest in the graces of elegance; and if we miss her, the labour of the pursuit rewards itself; we are led only through fragrance and flowers: Rymer, without taking a nearer, takes a rougher way; every step is to be made through thorns and brambles; and Truth, if we meet her, appears repulsive by her mien, and ungraceful by her habit. Dryden's criticism has the majesty of a queen; Rymer's has the ferocity of a tyrant.

As he had studied with great diligence the art of poetry, and enlarged or rectified his notions, by experience perpetually increasing, he had his mind stored with principles and observations; he poured out his knowledge with great liberality, and seldom published any work without a critical dissertation, by which he encreased the book and the price, with little labour to himself; for of labour, notwithstanding the multiplicity of his productions, there is sufficient reason to suspect that he was not a lover. Two write *con amore*, with fondness for the employment, with perpetual touches and retouches, with unwillingness to take leave of his own idea, and an unwearied pursuit of unattainable perfection, was, I think, no part of his character. . . .

Criticism, either didactick or defensive, occupies almost all his prose, except those pages which he has devoted to his patrons; but none of his prefaces were ever thought tedious. They have not the formality of a settled style, in which the first half of the sentence betrays the other. The clauses are never balanced, nor the periods modelled; every word seems to drop by chance, though it falls into its proper place. Nothing is cold or languid; the whole is airy, animated, and vigorous; what is little, is gay; what is great, is splendid. He may be thought to mention himself too frequently; but while he forces himself upon our esteem, we cannot refuse him to stand high in his own. Every thing is excused by the play of images and the spriteliness of expression. Though all is easy, nothing is feeble; though all seems careless, there is nothing harsh; and though, since his earlier works, more than a century has passed, they have nothing yet uncouth or obsolete.

He who writes much, will not easily escape a manner, such a recurrence of particular modes as may be easily noted. Dryden is always *another and the same*, he does not exhibit a second time the same elegancies in the same form, nor appears to have any art other than that of expressing with clearness what he thinks with vigour. His stile could not easily be imitated, either seriously or ludicrously, for being always equable and always varied, it has no prominent or discriminative characters. The beauty who is totally free from disporportion of parts and features cannot be ridiculed by an overcharged resemblance.

From his prose however, Dryden derives only his accidental and secondary praise; the veneration with which his name is pronounced by every cultivator of English Literature, is paid to him as he refined the language, improved the sentiments, and tuned the numbers of English Poetry.

After about half a century of forced thoughts, and rugged metre, some advances towards nature and harmony had been already made by Waller and Denham; they had shewn that long discourses in rhyme grew more pleasing when they were broken into couplets, and that verse consisted not only in the number but the arrangement of syllables.

But though they did much, who can deny that they left much to do? Their works were not many, nor were their minds of very ample comprehension. More examples of more modes of composition were necessary for the establishment of regularity, and the introduction of propriety in word and thought.

Every language of a learned nation necessarily divides itself into diction scholastick and popular, grave and familiar, elegant and gross; and from a nice distinction of these different parts, arises a great part of the beauty of stile. But if we except a few minds, the favourites of nature, to whom their own original rectitude was in the place of rules, this delicacy of selection was little known to our authors; our speech lay before them in a heap of confusion, and every man took for every purpose what chance might offer him.

There was therefore before the time of Dryden no poetical diction, no system of words at once refined from the grossness of domestick use, and free from the harshness of terms appropriated to particular arts. Words too familiar, or too remote, defeat the purpose of a poet. From those sounds which we hear on small or on coarse occasions, we do not easily receive strong impressions, or delightful images, and words to which we are nearly strangers, whenever they occur, draw that attention on themselves which they should convey to things.

Those happy combinations of words which distinguish poetry from prose, had been rarely attempted; we had few elegancies or flowers of speech, the roses had not yet been plucked from the bramble, or different colours had not been joined to enliven one another.

It may be doubted whether Waller and Denham could have over-born the prejudices which had long prevailed, and which even then were sheltered by the protection of Cowley. The new versification, as it was called, may be considered as owing its establishment to Dryden; from whose time it is apparent that English poetry has had no tendency to relapse to its former savageness. . . .

In an occasional performance no height of excellence can be expected from any mind, however fertile in itself, and however stored with acquisitions. He whose work is general and arbitrary, has the choice of his matter, and takes that which his inclination and his studies have best qualified him to display and decorate. He is at liberty to delay his publication, till he has satisfied his friends and himself; till he has reformed his first thoughts by subsequent examination; and polished away those faults which the precipitance of ardent composition is likely to leave behind it. Virgil is related to have poured out a great number of lines in the morning, and to have passed the day in reducing them to fewer.

The occasional poet is circumscribed by the narrowness of his subject.

Whatever can happen to man has happened so often, that little remains for fancy or invention. We have been all born; we have most of us been married; and so many have died before us, that our deaths can supply but few materials for a poet. In the fate of princes the publick has an interest; and what happens to them of good or evil, the poets have always considered as business for the Muse. But after so many inauguratory gratulations, nuptial hymns, and funeral dirges, he must be highly favoured by nature, or by fortune, who says any thing not said before. Even war and conquest, however splendid, suggest no new images; the triumphal chariot of a victorious monarch can be decked only with those ornaments that have graced his predecessors.

Not only matter but time is wanting. The poem must not be delayed till the occasion is forgotten. The lucky moments of animated imagination cannot be attended; elegancies and illustrations cannot be multiplied by gradual accumulation; the composition must be dispatched while conversation is yet busy, and admiration fresh; and haste is to be made, lest some other event should lay hold upon mankind. . . .

Annus Mirabilis

His description of the Fire is painted by resolute meditation, out of a mind better formed to reason than to feel. The conflagration of a city, with all its tumults of concomitant distress, is one of the most dreadful spectacles which this world can offer to human eyes; yet it seems to raise little emotion in the breast of the poet; he watches the flame coolly from street to street, with now a reflection, and now a simile, till at last he meets the king, for whom he makes a speech, rather tedious in a time so busy; and then follows again the progress of the fire. . . .

Absalom and Achitophel is a work so well known, that particular criticism is superfluous. If it be considered as a poem political and controversial, it will be found to comprise all the excellencies of which the subject is susceptible; acrimony of censure, elegance of praise, artful delineation of characters, variety and vigour of sentiment, happy turns of language and pleasing harmony of numbers; and all these raised to such a height as can scarcely be found in any other English composition.

It is not, however, without faults; some lines are inelegant or improper, and too many are irreligiously licentious. The original structure of the poem was defective; allegories drawn to great length will always break; Charles could not run continually parallel with David.

The subject had likewise another inconvenience: it admitted little imagery or description, and a long poem of mere sentiments easily becomes tedious; though all the parts are forcible, and every line kindles new rapture, the reader, if not relieved by the interposition of something that sooths the fancy, grows weary of admiration, and defers the rest.

As an approach to historical truth was necessary, the action and catastrophe were not in the poet's power; there is therefore an unpleasing disproportion between the beginning and the end. We are alarmed by a faction formed out of many sects various in their principles, but agreeing in their purpose of mischief, formidable for their numbers and strong by their supports, while the king's friends are few and weak. The chiefs on either part are set forth to view; but when expectation is at the height, the king makes a speech, and

Henceforth a series of new times began.

Who can forbear to think of an enchanted castle, with a wide moat and lofty battlements, walls of marble, and gates of brass, which vanishes at once into air, when the destined knight blows his horn before it? . . .

Not long afterwards he undertook, perhaps the most arduous work of its kind, a translation of Virgil, for which he had shewn how well he was qualified by his version of the Pollio, and two episodes, one of Nisus and Euryalus, the other of Mezentius and Lausus.

In the comparison of Homer and Virgil, the discriminative excellence of Homer is elevation and comprehension of thought, and that of Virgil is grace and splendor of diction. The beauties of Homer are therefore difficult to be lost, and those of Virgil difficult to be retained. The massy trunk of sentiment is safe by its solidity, but the blossoms of elocution easily drop away. The author, having the choice of his own images, selects those which he can best adorn: the translator must, at all hazards, follow his original, and express thoughts which perhaps he would not have chosen. When to this primary difficulty is added the inconvenience of a language so much inferior in harmony to the Latin, it cannot be expected that they who read the Georgick and the Eneid should be much delighted with any version.

All these obstacles Dryden saw, and all these he determined to encounter. The expectation of his work was undoubtedly great; the nation considered its honour as interested in the event. One gave him the different editions of his author, and another helped him in the subordinate parts. The arguments of the several books were given him by Addison.

The hopes of the publick were not disappointed. He produced, says Pope, *the most noble and spirited translation that I know in any language.* It certainly excelled whatever had appeared in English, and appears to have satisfied his friends, and, for the most part, to have silenced his enemies. Milbourne, indeed, a clergyman, attacked it; but his outrages seem to be the ebullitions of a mind agitated by stronger resentment than bad poetry can excite, and previously resolved not to be pleased. . . .

When admiration had subsided, the translation was more coolly examined, and found, like all others, to be sometimes erroneous, and sometimes licentious. Those who could find faults, thought they could avoid them; and Dr. Brady attempted in blank verse a translation of the Eneid, which, when dragged into the world, did not live long enough to cry. I have never seen it; but that such a version there is, or has been, perhaps some old catalogue informed me.

With not much better success, Trapp, when his Tragedy and his Prelections had given him reputation, attempted another blank version of the Eneid;

to which, notwithstanding the slight regard with which it was treated, he had afterwards perseverance enough to add the Eclogues and Georgicks. His book may continue its existence as long as it is the clandestine refuge of schoolboys.

Since the English ear has been accustomed to the mellifluence of Pope's numbers, and the diction of poetry has become more splendid, new attempts have been made to translate Virgil; and all his works have been attempted by men better qualified to contend with Dryden. I will not engage myself in an invidious comparison, by opposing one passage to another; a work of which there would be no end, and which might be often offensive without use.

It is not by comparing line with line that the merit of great works is to be estimated, but by their general effects and ultimate result. It is easy to note a weak line, and write one more vigorous in its place; to find a happiness of expression in the original, and transplant it by force into the version: but what is given to the parts, may be subducted from the whole, and the reader may be weary, though the critick may commend. Works of imagination excel by their allurement and delight; by their power of attracting and detaining the attention. That book is good in vain, which the reader throws away. He only is the master, who keeps the mind in pleasing captivity; whose pages are perused with eagerness, and in hope of new pleasure are perused again; and whose conclusion is perceived with an eye of sorrow, such as the traveller casts upon departing day.

By his proportion of this predomination I will consent that Dryden should be tried; of this, which, in opposition to reason, makes Ariosto the darling and the pride of Italy; of this, which, in defiance of criticism, continues Shakespeare the sovereign of the drama. . . .

One composition must, however, be distinguished. The ode for *St. Cecilia's Day*, perhaps the last effort of his poetry, has been always considered as exhibiting the highest flight of fancy, and the exactest nicety of art. This is allowed to stand without a rival. If indeed there is any excellence beyond it, in some other of Dryden's works that excellence must be found. Compared with the Ode on Killigrew, it may be pronounced perhaps superiour in the whole; but without any single part, equal to the first stanza of the other.

It is said to have cost Dryden a fortnight's labour; but it does not want its negligences: some of the lines are without correspondent rhymes; a defect, which I never detected but after an acquaintance of many years, and which the enthusiasm of the writer might hinder him from perceiving.

His last stanza has less emotion than the former; but it is not less elegant in the diction. The conclusion is vitious; the musick of Timotheus, which *raised a monarch to the skies*, had only a metaphorical power; that of Cecilia, which *drew an angel down*, had a real effect: the crown therefore could not reasonably be divided.

In a general survey of Dryden's labours, he appears to have had a mind very comprehensive by nature, and much enriched with acquired knowledge. His compositions are the effects of a vigorous genius operating upon large materials.

The power that predominated in his intellectual operations was rather strong reason than quick sensibility. Upon all occasions that were presented, he studied rather than felt, and produced sentiments not such as Nature enforces, but meditation supplies. With the simple and elemental passions, as they spring separate in the mind, he seems not much acquainted; and seldom describes them but as they are complicated by the various relations of society, and confused in the tumults and agitations of life.

What he says of Love may contribute to the explanation of his character:

> Love various minds does variously inspire;
> It stirs in gentle bosoms gentle fire,
> Like that of incense on the altar laid;
> But raging flames tempestuous souls invade;
> A fire which every windy passion blows,
> With pride it mounts, or with revenge it glows.

Dryden's was not one of the *gentle bosoms:* Love, as it subsists in itself, with no tendency but to the person loved, and wishing only for correspondent kindness; such love as shuts out all other interest; the love of the Golden Age, was too soft and subtle to put his faculties in motion. He hardly conceived it but in its turbulent effervescence with some other desires; when it was inflamed by rivalry, or obstructed by difficulties; when it invigorated ambition, or exasperated revenge.

He is therefore, with all his variety of excellence, not often pathetick; and had so little sensibility of the power of effusions purely natural, that he did not esteem them in others. Simplicity gave him no pleasure; and for the first part of his life he looked on Otway with contempt, though at last, indeed very late, he confessed that in his play *there was Nature, which is the chief beauty.*

We do not always know our own motives. I am not certain whether it was not rather the difficulty which he found in exhibiting the genuine operations of the heart, than a servile submission to an injudicious audience, that filled his plays with false magnificence. It was necessary to fix attention; and the mind can be captivated only by recollection, or by curiosity; by reviving former thoughts, or impressing new: sentences were readier at his call than images; he could more easily fill the ear with some splendid novelty, than awaken those ideas that slumber in the heart.

The favourite exercise of his mind was ratiocination; and, that argument might not be too soon at an end, he delighted to talk of liberty and necessity, destiny and contingence; these he discusses in the language of the school with so much profundity, that the terms which he uses are seldom understood. It is indeed learning, but learning out of place.

When once he had engaged himself in disputation, thoughts flowed in on either side: he was now no longer at a loss; he had always argument at command: *verbaque provisam rem*—give him matter for his verse, and he finds without difficulty verse for his matter.

In Comedy, for which he professes himself not naturally qualified, the mirth which he excites will perhaps not be found so much to arise from any original humour, or peculiarity of character nicely distinguished and diligently pursued, as from incidents and circumstances, artifices and surprizes; from jests of action rather than of sentiment. What he had of humorous or passionate, he seems to have had not from nature, but from other poets; if not always as a plagiary, at least as an imitator.

Next to argument, his delight was in wild and daring sallies of sentiment, in the irregular and excentrick violence of wit. He delighted to tread upon the brink of meaning, where light and darkness begin to mingle; to approach the precipice of absurdity, and hover over the abyss of unideal vacancy. This inclination sometimes produced nonsense, which he knew; as,

> Move swiftly, sun, and fly a lover's pace,
> Leave weeks and months behind thee in thy race.
>   Amariel flies
> To guard thee from the demons of the air;
> My flaming sword above them to display,
> All keen, and ground upon the edge of day.

And sometimes it issued in absurdities, of which perhaps he was not conscious:

> Then we upon our orb's last verge shall go,
>   And see the ocean leaning on the sky;
> From thence our rolling neighbours we shall know,
>   And on the lunar would securely pry.

These lines have no meaning; but may we not say, in imitation of Cowley on another book,

> 'Tis so like *sense* 'twill serve the turn as well?

He had a vanity unworthy of his abilities; to shew, as may be suspected, the rank of the company with whom he lived, by the use of French words, which had then crept into conversation; such as *fraicheur* for *coolness*, *fougue* for *turbulence*, and a few more, none of which the language has incorporated or retained. They continue only where they stood first, perpetual warnings to future innovators.

These are his faults of affectation; his faults of negligence are beyond recital. Such is the unevenness of his compositions, that ten lines are seldom found together without something of which the reader is ashamed. Dryden was no rigid judge of his own pages; he seldom struggled after supreme excellence, but snatched in haste what was within his reach, and when he could content others was himself contented. He did not keep present to his mind an idea of pure perfection; nor compare his works, such as they were, with what they might be made. He knew to whom he should be opposed. He had more musick than Waller, more vigour than Denham, and more nature than Cowley; and from his contemporaries he was in no danger. Standing therefore in the highest place, he had no care to rise by contending with himself; but while there was no name above his own, was willing to enjoy fame on the easiest terms.

He was no lover of labour. What he thought sufficient, he did not stop to make better; and allowed himself to leave many parts unfinished, in confidence that the good lines would overbalance the bad. What he had once written, he dismissed from this thoughts; and, I believe, there is no example to be found of any correction or improvement made by him after publication. The hastiness of his productions might be the effect of necessity; but his subsequent neglect could hardly have any other cause than impatience of study.

What can be said of his versification, will be little more than a dilatation of the praise given it by Pope.

> Waller was smooth; but Dryden taught to join
> The varying verse, the full-resounding line,
> The long majestick march, and energy divine.

Some improvements had been already made in English numbers; but the full force of our language was not yet felt; the verse that was smooth was commonly feeble. If Cowley had sometimes a finished line, he had it by chance. Dryden knew how to chuse the flowing and the sonorous words; to vary the pauses, and adjust the accents; to diversify the cadence, and yet preserve the smoothness of his metre. . . .

Of Dryden's works it was said by Pope, that *he could select from them better specimens of every mode of poetry than any other English writer could supply.* Perhaps no nation ever produced a writer that enriched his language with such variety of models. To him we owe the improvement, perhaps the completion of our metre, the refinement of our language, and much of the correctness of our sentiments. By him we were taught *sapere & fari,* to think naturally and express forcibly. He taught us that it was possible to reason in rhyme. He shewed us the true bounds of a translator's liberty. What was said of Rome, adorned by Augustus, may be applied by an easy metaphor to English poetry embellished by Dryden, *lateritiam invenit, marmoream reliquit,* he found it brick, and he left it marble.

JONATHAN SWIFT

He wrote the same year [1711] a *Letter to the October Club,* a number of Tory Gentlemen sent from the country to Parliament, who formed themselves into a club, to the number of about a hundred, and met to animate the zeal and raise the expectations of each other. They thought, with great reason, that the Ministers were losing opportunities; that sufficient use was not made of the general ardour of the nation; they called loudly for more changes, and stronger efforts; and demanded the punishment of part, and the dismission of the rest, of those whom they considered as publick robbers.

Their eagerness was not gratified by the Queen, or by Harley. The Queen was probably slow because she was afraid, and Harley was slow because he was doubtful; he was a Tory only by necessity, or for convenience; and when he had power in his hands, had no settled purpose for which he should employ it; forced to gratify to a certain degree the Tories who supported him, but unwilling to make his reconcilement to the Whigs utterly desperate, he corresponded at once with the two expectants of the Crown, and kept, as has been observed, the succession undetermined. Not knowing what to do, he did nothing; and with the fate of a double-dealer, at last he lost his power, but kept his enemies.

Swift seems to have concurred in opinion with the *October Club;* but it was not in his power to quicken the tardiness of Harley, whom he stimulated as much as he could, but with little effect. He that knows not whither to go, is in no haste to move. Harley, who was perhaps not quick by nature, became yet more slow by irresolution; and was content to hear that dilatoriness lamented as natural, which he applauded in himself as politick.

Without the Tories, however, nothing could be done; and as they were not to be gratified, they must be appeased; and the conduct of the minister, if it could not be vindicated, was to be plausibly excused.

Swift now attained the zenith of his political importance: he published (1712) the *Conduct of the Allies,* ten days before the Parliament assembled. The purpose was to persuade the nation to a peace, and never had any writer more success. The people, who had been amused with bonfires and triumphal processions, and looked with idolatry on the General and his friends, who, as they thought, had made England the arbitress of nations, were confounded between shame and rage, when they found that *mines had been exhausted, and millions destroyed,* to secure the Dutch or aggrandise the Emperor, without any advantage to ourselves; that we had been bribing our neighbours to fight their own quarrel; and that amongst our enemies we might number our allies.

That is now no longer doubted, of which the nation was then first informed, that the war was unnecessarily protracted to fill the pockets of Marlborough; and that it would have been continued without end, if he could have continued his annual plunder. But Swift, I suppose, did not yet know what he has since written, that a commission was drawn which would have appointed him General for life, had it not become ineffectual by the resolution of Lord Cowper, who refused the seal.

Whatever is received, say the schools, *is received in proportion to the recipient.* The power of a political treatise depends much upon the disposition of the people; the nation was then combustible, and a spark set it on fire. It is boasted, that between November and January eleven thousand were sold; a great number at that time, when we were not yet a nation of readers. To its propagation certainly no agency of power or influence was wanting. It furnished arguments for conversation, speeches for debate, and materials for parliamentary resolutions.

Yet, surely, whoever surveys this wonder-working pamphlet with cool perusal, will confess that its efficacy was supplied by the passions of its readers; that it operates by the mere weight of facts, with very little assistance from the hand that produced them. . . .

Swift, being now the declared favourite and supposed confidant of the Tory Ministry, was treated by all that depended on the Court with the respect which dependents know how to pay. He soon began to feel part of the misery of greatness; he that could say he knew him, considered himself as having fortune in his power. Commissions, solicitations, remonstrances, crouded about him; he was expected to do every man's business, to procure employment for one, and to retain it for another. In assisting those who addressed him, he represents himself as sufficiently diligent; and desires to have others believe, what he probably believed himself, that by his interposition many Whigs of merit, and among them Addison and Congreve, were continued in their places. But every man of known influence has so many petitions which he cannot grant, that he must necessarily offend more than he gratifies, as the preference given to one affords all the rest a reason for complaint. *When I give away a place,* said Lewis XIV., *I make a hundred discontented, and one ungrateful.*

Much has been said of the equality and independence which he preserved in his conversation with the Ministers, of the frankness of his remonstrances, and the familiarity of his friendship. In accounts of this kind a few single incidents are set against the general tenour of behaviour. No man, however, can pay a more servile tribute to the Great, than by suffering his liberty in their presence to aggrandize him in his own esteem. Between different ranks of the community there is necessarily some distance: he who is called by his superior to pass the interval, may very properly accept the invitation; but petulance and obtrusion are rarely produced by magnanimity; nor have often any nobler cause than the pride of importance, and the malice of inferiority. He who knows himself necessary may set, while that necessity lasts, a high value upon himself; as, in a lower condition, a servant eminently skilful may be saucy; but he is saucy only because he is servile. Swift appears to have preserved the kindness of those that wanted him no longer; and therefore it must be allowed, that the childish freedom, to which he seems enough inclined, was overpowered by his better qualities. . . .

In 1723 died Mrs. Van Homrigh, a woman made unhappy by her admiration of wit, and ignominiously distinguished by the name of Vanessa, whose conduct has been already sufficiently discussed, and whose history is too well known to be minutely repeated. She was a young woman fond of literature, whom Decanus the Dean, called Cadenus by transposition of the letters, took pleasure in directing and instructing; till, from being proud of his praise, she grew fond of his person. Swift was then about forty-seven, at an age when vanity is strongly excited by the amorous attention of a young woman. If it be said that Swift should have checked a passion which he never meant to gratify, recourse must be had to that extenuation which he so much despised, *men are but men:* perhaps however he did not at first know his own mind, and, as he represents himself, was undetermined. For his admission of her courtship, and his indulgence of her hopes after his marriage to Stella no other honest plea can be found, than that he delayed a disagreeable discovery from time to time, dreading the immediate burst of distress, and watching for a favourable moment. She thought herself neglected, and died of disappointment; having ordered by her will the poem to be published, in which *Cadenus* had proclaimed her excellence, and confessed his love. . . .

The great acquisition of esteem and influence was made by the *Drapier's Letters* in 1724. One Wood of Wolverhampton in Staffordshire, a man enterprising and rapacious, had, as is said, by a present to the Dutchess of Munster, obtained a patent empowering him to coin one hundred and eighty thousand pounds of half-pence and farthings for the kingdom of Ireland, in which there was a very inconvenient and embarrassing scarcity of copper coin; so that it was possible to run in debt upon the credit of a piece of money. The cook or keeper of an alehouse could not refuse to supply a man that had silver in his hand, and the buyer would not leave his money without change.

The project was therefore plausible. The scarcity, which was already great, Wood took care to make greater, by agents who gathered up the old half-pence; and was about to turn his brass into gold, by pouring his treasures of his new mint upon Ireland, when Swift, finding that the metal was debased to an enormous degree, wrote Letters, under the name of *M. B. Drapier,* to shew the folly of receiving, and the mischief that must ensue, by giving gold and silver for coin worth perhaps not a third part of its nominal value.

The nation was alarmed; the new coin was universally refused: but the governors of Ireland considered resistance to the King's patent as highly criminal; and one Whitshed, then Chief Justice, who had tried the printer of the former pamphlet, and sent out the Jury nine times, till by clamour and menaces they were frighted into a special verdict, now presented the *Drapier,* but could not prevail on the Grand Jury to find the bill.

Lord Carteret and the Privy Council published a proclamation, offering three hundred pounds for discovering the author of the Fourth Letter. Swift had concealed himself from his printers, and trusted only his butler, who transcribed the paper. The man, immediately after the appearance of the proclamation, strolled from the house, and staid out all night and part of the next day. There was reason enough to fear that he had betrayed his master for the reward; but he came home, and the Dean ordered him to put off his livery, and leave the house; "for," says he, "I know that my life is in your power, and I will not bear, out of fear, either your insolence or negligence." The man excused his fault with great submission, and begged that he might be confined in the house while it was in his power to endanger his master; but the Dean resolutely turned him out, without taking further notice of him, till the term of information had expired, and then received him again. Soon afterwards he ordered him and the rest of the servants into his presence, without telling his intentions, and bade them take notice that their fellow-servant was no longer Robert the butler; but that his integrity had made him Mr. Blakeney, verger of St. Patrick's; an officer whose income was between thirty and forty pounds a year, but he still continued for some years to serve his old master as his butler.

Swift was known from this time by the appellation of *The Dean.* He was honoured by the populace as the champion, patron, and instructer of Ireland;

and gained such power as, considered both in its extent and duration, scarcely any man has ever enjoyed without greater wealth or higher station.

He was from this important year the oracle of the traders, and the idol of the rabble, and by consequence was feared and courted by all to whom the kindness of the traders or the populace was necessary. The *Drapier* was a sign; the *Drapier* was a health; and which way soever the eye or the ear was turned, some tokens were found of the nation's gratitude to the *Drapier*.

The benefit was indeed great; he had rescued Ireland from a very oppressive and predatory invasion; and the popularity which he had gained he was diligent to keep, by appearing forward and zealous on every occasion where the publick interest was supposed to be involved. Nor did he much scruple to boast his influence; for when, upon some attempts to regulate the coin, Archbishop Boulter, then one of the Justices, accused him of exasperating the people, he exculpated himself by saying, "If I had lifted up my finger, they would have torn you to pieces." . . .

He returned to a home of sorrow: poor Stella was sinking into the grave, and, after a languishing decay of about two months, died in her forty-fourth year, on January 28, 1728. How much he wished her life, his papers tell us; nor can it be doubted that he dreaded the death of her whom he loved most, aggravated by the consciousness that himself had hastened it.

Beauty and the power of pleasing, the greatest external advantages that woman can desire or possess, were fatal to the unfortunate Stella. The man whom she had the misfortune to love was, as Delany observes, fond of singularity, and desirous to make a mode of happiness for himself, out of the general course of things and order of Providence. From the time of her arrival in Ireland he seems resolved to keep her in his power, and therefore hindered a match sufficiently advantageous, by accumulating unreasonable demands, and prescribing conditions that could not be performed. While she was at her own disposal he did not consider his possession as secure; resentment, ambition, or caprice, might separate them; he was therefore resolved to make *assurance double sure,* and to appropriate her by a private marriage, to which he had annexed the expectation of all the pleasures of perfect friendship, without the uneasiness of conjugal restraint. But with this state poor Stella was not satisfied; she never was treated as a wife, and to the world she had the appearance of a mistress. She lived sullenly on, in hope that in time he would own and receive her; but the time did not come till the change of his manners and depravation of his mind made her tell him, when he offered to acknowledge her, that *it was too late.* She then gave up herself to sorrowful resentment, and died under the tyranny of him by whom she was in the highest degree loved and honoured.

What were her claims to this excentrick tenderness, by which the laws of Nature were violated to retain her, curiosity will enquire; but how shall it be gratified? Swift was a lover; his testimony may be suspected. Delany and the Irish saw with Swift's eyes, and therefore add little confirmation. That she was virtuous, beautiful, and elegant, in a very high degree, such admiration from such a lover makes it very probable; but she had not much literature, for she could not spell her own language; and of her wit, so loudly vaunted, the smart sayings which Swift himself has collected afford no splendid specimen.

The reader of Swift's *Letter to a Lady on her Marriage,* may be allowed to doubt whether his opinion of female excellence ought implicitly to be admitted; for if his general thoughts on women were such as he exhibits, a very little sense in a Lady would enrapture, and a very little virtue would astonish him. Stella's supremacy, therefore, was perhaps only local; she was great, because her associates were little.

In some Remarks lately published on the Life of Swift, this marriage is mentioned as fabulous, or doubtful; but, alas! poor Stella, as Dr. Madden told me, related her melancholy story to Dr. Sheridan, when he attended her as a clergyman to prepare her for death; and Delany tells it not with doubt, but only with regret. Swift never mentioned her without a sigh. . . .

His asperity continually increasing, condemned him to solitude; and his resentment of solitude sharpened his asperity. He was not, however, totally deserted: some men of learning, and some women of elegance, often visited him; and he wrote from time to time either verse or prose; of his verses he willingly gave copies, and is supposed to have felt no discontent when he saw them printed. His favourite maxim was *vive la bagatelle;* he thought trifles a necessary part of life, and perhaps found them necessary to himself. It seems impossible to him to be idle, and his disorders made it difficult or dangerous to be long seriously studious, or laboriously diligent. The love of ease is always gaining upon age, and he had one temptation to petty amusements peculiar to himself; whatever he did, he was sure to hear applauded; and such was his predominance over all that approached, that all their applauses were probably sincere. He that is much flattered, soon learns to flatter himself: we are commonly taught our duty by fear or shame, and how can they act upon the man who hears nothing but his own praises? . . .

When Swift is considered as an author, it is just to estimate his powers by their effects. In the reign of Queen Anne he turned the stream of popularity against the Whigs, and must be confessed to have dictated for a time the political opinions of the English nation. In the succeeding reign he delivered Ireland from plunder and oppression; and shewed that wit, confederated with truth, had such force as authority was unable to resist. He said truly of himself, that Ireland was his debtor. It was from the time when he first began to patronize the Irish, that they may date their riches and prosperity. He taught them first to know their own interest, their weight, and their strength, and gave them spirit to assert that equality with their fellow-subjects to which they have ever since been making vigorous advances, and to claim those rights which they have at last established. Nor can they be charged with ingratitude to their benefactor; for they reverenced him as a guardian, and obeyed him as a dictator.

In his works, he has given very different specimens both of sentiment and expression. His *Tale of a Tub* has little resemblance to his other pieces. It exhibits a vehemence and rapidity of mind, a copiousness of images, and vivacity of diction, such as he afterwards never possessed, or never exerted. It is of a mode so distinct and peculiar, that it must be considered by itself; what is true of that, is not true of any thing else which he has written.

In his other works is found an equable tenour of easy language, which rather trickles than flows. His delight was in simplicity. That he has in his works no metaphor, as has been said, is not true; but his few metaphors seem to be received rather by necessity than choice. He studied purity; and though perhaps all his structures are not exact, yet it is not often that solecisms can be found; and whoever depends on his authority may generally conclude himself safe. His sentences are never too much dilated or contracted; and it will not be easy to find any embarrassment in the complication of his clauses, any inconsequence in his connections, or abruptness in his transitions.

His stile was well suited to his thoughts, which are never subtilised by nice disquisitions, decorated by sparkling conceits, elevated by ambitious sentences, or variegated by far-sought learning. He pays no court to the passions; he excites neither surprize nor admiration; he always understands himself, and his reader always understands him: the peruser of Swift wants little previous knowledge: it will be sufficient that he is acquainted with common words and common things; he is neither required to mount elevations, nor to explore profundities; his passage is always on a level, along solid ground, without asperities, without obstruction.

This easy and safe conveyance of meaning it was Swift's desire to attain, and for having attained he certainly deserves praise, though perhaps not the highest praise. For purposes merely didactick, when something is to be told that was not known before, it is in the highest degree proper, but against that inattention by which known truths are suffered to lie neglected, it makes no provision; it instructs, but does not persuade.

By his political education he was associated with the Whigs; but he deserted them when they deserted their principles, yet without running into the contrary extreme; he continued throughout his life to retain the disposition which he assigns to the Church-of-England Man, of thinking commonly with the Whigs of the State, and with the Tories of the Church.

He was a churchman rationally zealous; he desired the prosperity and maintained the honour of the Clergy; of the Dissenters he did not wish to infringe the toleration, but he opposed their encroachments.

To his duty as Dean he was very observant. He managed the revenues of his church with exact œconomy; and it is said by Delany, that more money was, under his direction, laid out in repairs than had ever been in the same time since its first erection. Of his choir he was eminently careful; and, though he neither loved nor understood musick, took care that all the singers were well qualified, admitting none without the testimony of skilful judges.

In his church he restored the practice of weekly communion, and distributed the sacramental elements in the most solemn and devout manner with his own hand. He came to church every morning, preached commonly in his turn, and attended the evening anthem, that it might not be negligently performed.

He read the service rather with a strong nervous voice than in a graceful manner; his voice was sharp and high-toned, rather than harmonious.

He entered upon the clerical state with hope to excel in preaching; but complained, that, from the time of his political controversies, he could only preach pamphlets. This censure of himself, if judgement be made from those sermons which have been published, was unreasonably severe.

The suspicions of his irreligion proceeded in a great measure from his dread of hypocrisy; instead of wishing to seem better, he delighted in seeming worse than he was. He went in London to early prayers, lest he should be seen at church; he read prayers to his servants every morning with such dexterous secrecy, that Dr. Delany was six months in his house before he knew it. He was not only careful to hide the good which he did, but willingly incurred the suspicion of evil which he did not. He forgot what himself had formerly asserted, that hypocrisy is less mischievous than open impiety. Dr. Delany, with all his zeal for his honour, has justly condemned this part of his character.

The person of Swift had not many recommendations. He had a kind of muddy complexion, which, though he washed himself with oriental scrupulosity, did not look clear. He had a countenance sour and severe, which he seldom softened by any appearance of gaiety. He stubbornly resisted any tendency to laughter.

To his domesticks he was naturally rough; and a man of a rigorous temper, with that vigilance of minute attention which his works discover, must have been a master that few could bear. That he was disposed to do his servants good, on important occasions, is no great mitigation; benefaction can be but rare, and tyrannick peevishness is perpetual. He did not spare the servants of others. Once, when he dined alone with the Earl of Orrery, he said, of one that waited in the room, *That man has, since we sat to the table, committed fifteen faults.* What the faults were, Lord Orrery, from whom I heard the story, had not been attentive enough to discover. My number may perhaps not be exact.

In his œconomy he practised a peculiar and offensive parsimony, without disguise or apology. The practice of saving being once necessary, became habitual, and grew first ridiculous, and at last detestable. But his avarice, though it might exclude pleasure, was never suffered to encroach upon his virtue. He was frugal by inclination, but liberal by principle; and if the purpose to which he destined his little accumulations be remembered, with his distribution of occasional charity, it will perhaps appear that he only liked one mode of expence better than another, and saved only that he might have something to give. He did not grow rich by injuring his successors, but left both Laracor and the Deanery more valuable than he found them.—With all this talk of his covetousness and generosity, it should be remembered that he was never rich. The revenue of his Deanery was not much more than seven hundred a year.

His beneficence was not graced with tenderness or civility; he relieved without pity, and assisted without kindness, so that those who were fed by him could hardly love him.

He made a rule to himself to give but one piece at a time, and therefore always stored his pocket with coins of different value.

Whatever he did, he seemed willing to do in a manner peculiar to himself, without sufficiently considering that singularity, as it implies a contempt of the general practice, is a kind of defiance which justly provokes the hostility of ridicule; he therefore who indulges peculiar habits is worse than others, if he be not better.

In the intercourse of familiar life, he indulged his disposition to petulance and sarcasm, and thought himself injured if the licentiousness of his raillery, the freedom of his censures, or the petulance of his frolicks, was resented or repressed. He predominated over his companions with very high ascendency, and probably would bear none over whom he could not predominate. To give him advice was, in the stile of his friend Delany, to venture to speak to him. This customary superiority soon grew too delicate for truth; and Swift, with all his penetration, allowed himself to be delighted with low flattery.

On all common occasions, he habitually affects a stile of arrogance, and dictates rather than persuades. This authoritative and magisterial language he expected to be received as his peculiar mode of jocularity; but he apparently flattered his own arrogance by an assumed predomination, in which he was ironical only to the resentful, and to the submissive sufficiently serious.

He told stories with great felicity, and delighted in doing what he knew himself to do well. He was therefore captivated by the respectful silence of a steady listener, and told the same tales too often.

He did not, however, claim the right of talking alone; for it was his rule, when he had spoken a minute, to give room by a pause for any other speaker. Of time, on all occasions, he was an exact computer, and knew the minutes required to every common operation.

It may be justly supposed that there was in his conversation, what appears so frequently in his Letters, an affectation of familiarity with the Great, an ambition of momentary equality sought and enjoyed by the neglect of those ceremonies which custom has established as the barriers between one order of society and another. This transgression of regularity was by himself and his admirers termed greatness of soul. But a great mind disdains to hold any thing by courtesy, and therefore never usurps what a lawful claimant may take away. He that encroaches on another's dignity, puts himself in his power; he is either repelled with helpless indignity, or endured by clemency and condescension.

Of Swift's general habits of thinking if his Letters can be supposed to afford any evidence, he was not a man to be either loved or envied. He seems to have wasted life in discontent, by the rage of neglected pride, and the languishment of unsatisfied desire. He is querulous and fastidious, arrogant and malignant; he scarcely speaks of himself but with indignant lamentations, or of others but with insolent superiority when he is gay, and with angry contempt when he is gloomy. From the Letters that pass between him and Pope it might be inferred that they, with Arbuthnot and Gay, had engrossed all the understanding and virtue of mankind, that their merits filled the world; or that there was no hope of more. They shew the age involved in darkness, and shade the picture with sullen emulation.

When the Queen's death drove him into Ireland, he might be allowed to regret for a time the interception of his views, the extinction of his hopes, and his ejection from gay scenes, important employment, and splendid friendships; but when time had enabled reason to prevail over vexation, the complaints, which at first were natural, became ridiculous because they were useless. But querulousness was now grown habitual, and he cried out when he probably had ceased to feel. His reiterated wailings persuaded Bolingbroke that he was really willing to quit his deanery for an English parish; and Bolingbroke procured an exchange, which was rejected, and Swift still retained the pleasure of complaining.

The greatest difficulty that occurs, in analysing his character, is to discover by what depravity of intellect he took delight in revolving ideas, from which almost every other mind shrinks with disgust. The ideas of pleasure, even when criminal, may solicite the imagination; but what has disease, deformity, and filth, upon which the thoughts can be allured to dwell? Delany is willing to think that Swift's mind was not much tainted with this gross corruption before his long visit to Pope. He does not consider how he degrades his hero, by making him at fifty-nine the pupil of turpitude, and liable to the malignant influence of an ascendant mind. But the truth is, that Gulliver had described his *Yahoos* before the visit, and he that had formed those images had nothing filthy to learn.

ALEXANDER POPE

Almost every poem, consisting of precepts, is so far arbitrary and immethodical, that many of the paragraphs may change places with no apparent inconvenience; for of two or more positions, depending upon some remote and general principle, there is seldom any cogent reason why one should precede the other. But for the order in which they stand, whatever it be, a little ingenuity may easily give a reason. *It is possible,* says Hooker, *that by long circumduction, from any one truth all truth may be inferred.* Of all homogeneous truths at least, of all truths respecting the same general end, in whatever series they may be produced, a concatenation by intermediate ideas may be formed, such as, when it is once shewn, shall appear natural; but if this order be reversed, another mode of connection equally specious may be found or made. Aristotle is praised for naming Fortitude first of the cardinal virtues, as that without which no other virtue can steadily be practised; but he might, with equal propriety, have placed Prudence and Justice before it, since without Prudence Fortitude is mad; without Justice, it is mischievous.

As the end of method is perspicuity, that series is sufficiently regular that avoids obscurity; and where there is no obscurity it will not be difficult to discover method. . . .

It is reasonable to infer, from his Letters, that the verses on the

Unfortunate Lady were written about the time when his *Essay* was published. The Lady's name and adventures I have sought with fruitless enquiry.

I can therefore tell no more than I have learned from Mr. Ruffhead, who writes with the confidence of one who could trust his information. She was a woman of eminent rank and large fortune, the ward of an unkle, who, having given her a proper education, expected like other guardians that she should make at least an equal match, and such he proposed to her, but found it rejected in favour of a young gentleman of inferior condition.

Having discovered the correspondence between the two lovers, and finding the young lady determined to abide by her own choice, he supposed that separation might do what can rarely be done by arguments, and sent her into a foreign country, where she was obliged to converse only with those from whom her unkle had nothing to fear.

Her lover took care to repeat his vows; but his letters were intercepted and carried to her guardian, who directed her to be watched with still greater vigilance; till of this restraint she grew so impatient, that she bribed a woman-servant to procure her a sword, which she directed to her heart.

From this account, given with evident intention to raise the Lady's character, it does not appear that she had any claim to praise, nor much to compassion. She seems to have been impatient, violent, and ungovernable. Her unkle's power could not have lasted long; the hour of liberty and choice would have come in time. But her desires were too hot for delay, and she liked self-murder better than suspense.

Nor is it discovered that the unkle, whoever he was, is with much justice delivered to posterity as a false Guardian; he seems to have done only that for which a guardian is appointed; he endeavoured to direct his niece till she should be able to direct herself. Poetry has not often been worse employed than in dignifying the amorous fury of a raving girl. . . .

The *Rape of the Lock* stands forward, in the classes of literature, as the most exquisite example of ludicrous poetry. Berkley congratulated him upon the display of powers more truly poetrical than he had shewn before; with elegance of description and justness of precepts, he had now exhibited boundless fertility of invention.

He always considered the intertexture of the machinery with the action as his most successful exertion of poetical art. He indeed could never afterwards produce any thing of such unexampled excellence. Those performances, which strike with wonder, are combinations of skilful genius with happy casualty; and it is not likely that any felicity, like the discovery of a new race of preternatural agents, should happen twice to the same man. . . .

When we find him translating fifty lines a day, it is natural to suppose that he would have brought his work to a more speedy conclusion. The *Iliad*, containing less than sixteen thousand verses, might have been despatched in less than three hundred and twenty days by fifty verses in a day. The notes, compiled with the assistance of his mercenaries, could not be supposed to require more time than the text. According to this calculation, the progress of

Pope may seem to have been slow; but the distance is commonly very great between actual performances and speculative possibility. It is natural to suppose, that as much as has been done today may be done to-morrow; but on the morrow some difficulty emerges, or some external impediment obstructs. Indolence, interruption, business, and pleasure, all take their turns of retardation; and every long work is lengthened by a thousand causes that can, and ten thousand that cannot, be recounted. Perhaps no extensive and multifarious performance was ever effected within the term originally fixed in the undertaker's mind. He that runs against Time, has an antagonist not subject to casualties. . . .

A grotto is not often the wish or pleasure of an Englishman, who has more frequent need to solicit than exclude the sun; but Pope's excavation was requisite as an entrance to his garden, and, as some men try to be proud of their defects, he extracted an ornament from an inconvenience, and vanity produced a grotto where necessity enforced a passage. It may be frequently remarked of the studious and speculative, that they are proud of trifles, and that their amusements seem frivolous and childish; whether it be that men conscious of great reputation think themselves above the reach of censure, and safe in the admission of negligent indulgences, or that mankind expect from elevated genius an uniformity of greatness, and watch its degradation with malicious wonder; like him who having followed with his eye an eagle into the clouds, should lament that she ever descended to a perch. . . .

The filial piety of Pope was in the highest degree amiable and exemplary; his parents had the happiness of living till he was at the summit of poetical reputation, till he was at ease in his fortune, and without a rival in his fame, and found no diminution of his respect or tenderness. Whatever was his pride, to them he was obedient; and whatever was his irritability, to them he was gentle. Life has, among its soothing and quiet comforts, few things better to give than such a son. . . .

Pope's epistolary excellence had an open field; he had no English rival, living or dead. . . . It is indeed not easy to distinguish affectation from habit; he that has once studiously formed a style, rarely writes afterwards with complete ease. Pope may be said to write always with his reputation in his head; Swift perhaps like a man who remembered that he was writing to Pope; but Arbuthnot like one who lets thoughts drop from his pen as they rise into his mind. . . .

About this time Warburton began to make his appearance in the first ranks of learning. He was a man of vigorous faculties, a mind fervid and vehement, supplied by incessant and unlimited enquiry, with wonderful extent and variety of knowledge, which yet had not oppressed his imagination, nor clouded his perspicacity. To every work he brought a memory full fraught with a fancy fertile of original combinations, and at once exerted the powers of the scholar, the reasoner, and the wit. But his knowledge was too multifarious to be always exact, and his pursuits were too eager to be always cautious. His abilities gave him an haughty confidence, which he disdained to conceal or mollify; and his impatience of opposition disposed him to treat his adversaries with such contemptuous superiority as made his readers commonly his enemies, and excited against him the wishes of some who favoured his cause. He seems to have adopted the Roman Emperor's determination, *oderint dum metuant;* he used no allurements of gentle language, but wished to compel rather than persuade.

His style is copious without selection, and forcible without neatness; he took the words that presented themselves: his diction is coarse and impure, and his sentences are unmeasured.

The Use of Riches

Into this poem some incidents are historically thrown, and some known characters are introduced, with others of which it is difficult to say how far they are real or fictitious; but the praise of Kyrl, the Man of Ross, deserves particular examination, who, after a long and pompous enumeration of his publick works and private charities, is said to have diffused all those blessings from five hundred a year. Wonders are willingly told, and willingly heard. The truth is, that Kyrl was a man of known integrity, and active benevolence, by whose solicitation the wealthy were persuaded to pay contributions to his charitable schemes; this influence he obtained by an example of liberality exerted to the utmost extent of his power, and was thus enabled to give more than he had. This account Mr. Victor received from the minister of the place, and I have preserved it, that the praise of a good man being made more credible, may be more solid. Narrations of romantick and impracticable virtue will be read with wonder, but that which is unattainable is recommended in vain; that good may be endeavored, it must be shewn to be possible. . . .

He afterwards (1734) inscribed to Lord Cobham his *Characters of Men*, written with close attention to the operations of the mind and modifications of life. In this poem he has endeavoured to establish and exemplify his favourite theory of the *Ruling Passion*, by which he means an original direction of desire to some particular object, an innate affection which gives all action a determinate and invariable tendency, and operates upon the whole system of life, either openly, or more secretly by the intervention of some accidental or subordinate propension.

Of any passion, thus innate and irresistible, the existence may reasonably be doubted. Human characters are by no means constant; men change by change of place, of fortune, of acquaintance; he who is at one time a lover of pleasure, is at another a lover of money. Those indeed who attain any excellence, commonly spend life in one pursuit; for excellence is not often gained upon easier terms. But to the particular species of excellence men are directed, not by an ascendant planet or predominating humour, but by the first book which they read, some early conversation which they heard, or some accident which excited ardour and emulation.

It must be at least allowed that this ruling passion, antecedent to reason and observation, must have an object independent of human contrivance; for there can be no natural desire of artifical good. No man therefore can be born, in the strict acceptation, a lover of money; for he may be born where money does not exist; nor can he be born, in a moral sense, a lover of his country; for society, politically regulated, is a state contradistinguished from a state of nature; and any attention to that coalition of interests which makes the happiness of a country, is possible only to those whom enquiry and reflection have enabled to comprehend it.

This doctrine is in itself pernicious as well as false: its tendency is to produce the belief of a kind of moral predestination, or overruling principle which cannot be resisted; he that admits it, is prepared to comply with every desire that caprice or opportunity shall excite, and to flatter himself that he submits only to the lawful dominion of Nature, in obeying the resistless authority of his ruling passion. . . .

Arbuthnot was a man of great comprehension, skilful in his profession, versed in the sciences, acquainted with ancient literature, and able to animate his mass of knowledge by a bright and active imagination; a scholar with great brilliancy of wit; a wit, who, in the crowd of life, retained and discovered a noble ardour of religious zeal. . . .

Letter from Cibber to Pope

The pamphlet was written with little power to thought or language, and, if suffered to remain without notice, would have been very soon forgotten. Pope had now been enough acquainted with human life to know, if his passion had not been too powerful for his understanding, that, from a contention like his with Cibber, the world seeks nothing but diversion, which is given at the expence of the higher character. When Cibber lampooned Pope, curiosity was excited; what Pope would say of Cibber nobody enquired, but in hope that Pope's asperity might betray his pain and lessen his dignity.

He should therefore have suffered the pamphlet to flutter and die, without confessing that it stung him. The dishonour of being shewn as Cibber's antagonist could never be compensated by the victory. Cibber had nothing to lose; when Pope had exhausted all his malignity upon him, he would rise in the esteem both of his friends and his enemies. Silence only could have made him despicable; the blow which did not appear to be felt, would have been struck in vain.

But Pope's irascibility prevailed, and he resolved to tell the whole English world that he was at war with Cibber; and to shew that he thought him no common adversary, he prepared no common vengeance; he published a new edition of the *Dunciad*, in which he degraded Theobald from his painful pre-eminence, and enthroned Cibber in his stead. Unhappily the two heroes were of opposite characters, and Pope was unwilling to lose what he had already written; he has therefore depraved his poem by giving to Cibber the old books, the cold pedantry and sluggish pertinacity of Theobald.

Pope was ignorant enough of his own interest to make another change, and introduced Osborne contending for the prize among the booksellers.

Osborne was a man intirely destitute of shame, without sense of any disgrace but that of poverty. He told me, when he was doing that which raised Pope's resentment, that he should be put into the *Dunciad;* but he had the fate of Cassandra; I gave no credit to his prediction, till in time I saw it accomplished. The shafts of satire were directed equally in vain against Cibber and Osborne; being repelled by the impenetrable impudence of one, and deadened by the impassive dulness of the other. Pope confessed his own pain by his anger; but he gave no pain to those who had provoked him. He was able to hurt none but himself; by transferring the same ridicule from one to another, he destroyed its efficacy; for by shewing that what he had said of one he was ready to say of another, he reduced himself to the insignificance of his own magpye, who from his cage calls cuckold at a venture.

Cibber, according to his engagement, repaid the *Dunciad* with another pamphlet, which, Pope said, *would be as good as a dose of hartshorn to him;* but his tongue and his heart were at variance. I have heard Mr. Richardson relate, that he attended his father the painter on a visit, when one of Cibber's pamphlets came into the hands of Pope, who said, *These things are my diversion.* They sat by him while he perused it, and saw his features writhen with anguish; and young Richardson said to his father, when they returned, that he hoped to be preserved from such diversion as had been that day the lot of Pope. . . .

While he was yet capable of amusement and conversation, as he was one day sitting in the air with Lord Bolingbroke and Lord Marchmont, he saw his favourite Martha Blount at the bottom of the terrace, and asked Lord Bolingbroke to go and hand her up. Bolingbroke, not liking his errand, crossed his legs, and sat still; but Lord Marchmont, who was younger and less captious, waited on the Lady; who, when he came to her, asked, *What, is he not dead yet?* She is said to have neglected him, with shameful unkindness, in the latter time of his decay; yet, of the little which he had to leave, she had a very great part. Their acquaintance begun early; the life of each was pictured on the other's mind; their conversation therefore was endearing, for when they met, there was an immediate coalition of congenial notions. Perhaps he considered her unwillingness to approach the chamber of sickness as female weakness, or human frailty; perhaps he was conscious to himself of peevishness and impatience, or, though he was offended by her inattention, might yet consider her merit as overbalancing her fault; and, if he had suffered his heart to be alienated from her, he could have found nothing that might fill her place; he could have only shrunk within himself; it was too late to transfer his confidence or fondness.

In May 1744, his death was approaching; on the sixth, he was all day delirious, which he mentioned four days afterwards as a sufficient humiliation of the vanity of man; he afterwards complained of seeing things as through a curtain, and in false colours; and one day, in the presence of Dodsley, asked what arm it was that came out from the wall. He said, that his greatest inconvenience was inability to think.

Bolingbroke sometimes wept over him in this state of helpless decay; and being told by Spence, that Pope, at the intermission of his deliriousness, was always saying something kind either of his present or absent friends, and that his humanity seemed to have survived his understanding, answered, *It has so.* And added, *I never in my life knew a man that had so tender a heart for his particular friends, or a more general friendship for mankind.* At another time he said, *I have known Pope these thirty years, and value myself more in his friendship than*—his grief then suppressed his voice.

Pope expressed undoubting confidence of a future state. Being asked by his friend Mr. Hooke, a papist, whether he would not die like his father and mother, and whether a priest should not be called, he answered, *I do not think it essential, but it will be very right; and I thank you for putting me in mind of it.*

In the morning, after the priest had given him the last sacraments, he said, "There is nothing that is meritorious but virtue and friendship, and indeed friendship itself is only a part of virtue." . . .

The person of Pope is well known not to have been formed by the nicest model. He has, in his account of the *Little Club,* compared himself to a spider, and is described as protuberant behind and before. He is said to have been beautiful in his infancy; but he was of a constitution originally feeble and weak; and as bodies of a tender frame are easily distorted, his deformity was probably in part the effect of his application. His stature was so low, that, to bring him to a level with common tables, it was necessary to raise his seat. But his face was not displeasing, and his eyes were animated and vivid.

By natural deformity, or accidental distortion, his vital functions were so much disordered, that his life was a long disease. His most frequent assailant was the headach, which he used to relieve by inhaling the steam of coffee, which he very frequently required.

Most of what can be told concerning his petty peculiarities was communicated by a female domestick of the Earl of Oxford, who knew him perhaps after the middle of life. He was then so weak as to stand in perpetual need of female attendance; extremely sensible of cold, so that he wore a kind of fur doublet, under a shirt of a very coarse warm linen with fine sleeves. When he rose, he was invested in boddice made of stiff canvas, being scarce able to hold himself erect till they were laced, and he then put on a flannel waistcoat. One side was contracted. His legs were so slender, that he enlarged their bulk with three pair of stockings, which were drawn on and off by the maid; for he was not able to dress or undress himself, and neither went to bed nor rose without help. His weakness made it very difficult for him to be clean.

His hair had fallen almost all away; and he used to dine sometimes with Lord Oxford, privately, in a velvet cap. His dress of ceremony was black, with a tye-wig, and a little sword.

The indulgence and accommodation which his sickness required, had taught him all the unpleasing and unsocial qualities of a valetudinary man. He expected that every thing should give way to his ease or humour, as a child, whose parents will not hear her cry, has an unresisted dominion in the nursery.

C'est que l'enfant toujours est homme,
C'est que l'homme est toujours enfant.

When he wanted to sleep, he nodded in company; and once slumbered at his own table, while the Prince of Wales was talking of poetry.

The reputation which his friendship gave, procured him many invitations; but he was a very troublesome inmate. He brought no servant, and had so many wants, that a numerous attendance was scarcely able to supply them. Wherever he was, he left no room for another, because he exacted the attention and employed the activity of the whole family. His errands were so frequent and frivolous, that the footmen in time avoided and neglected him; and the Earl of Oxford discharged some of the servants for their resolute refusal of his messages. The maids, when they had neglected their business, alleged that they had been employed by Mr. Pope. One of his constant demands was of coffee in the night, and to the woman that waited on him in his chamber he was very burthensome; but he was careful to recompense her want of sleep; and Lord Oxford's servant declared, that in a house where her business was to answer his call, she would not ask for wages.

He had another fault, easily incident to those who, suffering much pain, think themselves entitled to whatever pleasures they can snatch. He was too indulgent to his appetite; he loved meat highly seasoned and of strong taste; and, at the intervals of the table, amused himself with biscuits and dry conserves. If he sat down to a variety of dishes, he would oppress his stomach with repletion, and though he seemed angry when a dram was offered him, did not forbear to drink it. His friends, who knew the avenues to his heart, pampered him with presents of luxury, which he did not suffer to stand neglected. The death of great men is not always proportioned to the lustre of their lives. Hannibal, says Juvenal, did not perish by a javelin or a sword; the slaughters of Cannæ were revenged by a ring. The death of Pope was imputed by some of his friends to a silver saucepan, in which it was his delight to heat potted lampreys.

That he loved too well to eat, is certain; but that his sensuality shortened his life will not be hastily concluded, when it is remembered that a conformation so irregular lasted six and fifty years, notwithstanding such pertinacious diligence of study and meditation.

In all his intercourse with mankind, he had great delight in artifice, and endeavoured to attain all his purposes by indirect and unsuspected methods. He hardly drank tea without a stratagem. If, at the house of his friends, he wanted any accommodation, he was not willing to ask for it in plain terms, but would mention it remotely as something convenient; though, when it was procured, he soon made it appear for whose sake it had been recommended. Thus he teized Lord Orrery till he obtained a screen. He practised his arts on such small occasions, that Lady Bolingbroke used to say, in a French phrase, that *he plaid the politician about cabbages and turnips.* His unjustifiable impression of the Patriot King, as it can be imputed to no particular motive, must have proceeded from his general habit of secrecy and cunning; he caught an opportunity of a sly trick, and pleased himself with the thought of outwitting Bolingbroke.

In familiar or convivial conversation, it does not appear that he excelled. He may be said to have resembled Dryden, as being not one that was distinguished by vivacity in company. It is remarkable, that, so near his time, so much should be known of what he has written, and so little of what he has said: traditional memory retains no sallies of raillery, nor sentences of observation; nothing either pointed or solid, either wise or merry. One apophthegm only stands upon record. When an objection raised against his inscription for Shakspeare was defended by the authority of *Patrick,* he replied—*horresco referens*—that *he would allow the publisher of a Dictionary to know the meaning of a single word, but not of two words put together. . . .*

Of this fortune, which as it arose from publick approbation was very honourably obtained, his imagination seems to have been too full: it would be hard to find a man, so well entitled to notice by his wit, that ever delighted so much in talking of his money. In his Letters, and in his Poems, his garden and his grotto, his quincunx and his vines, or some hints of his opulence, are always to be found. The great topick of his ridicule is poverty; the crimes with which he reproaches his antagonists are their debts, their habitation in the Mint, and their want of a dinner. He seems to be of an opinion not very uncommon in the world, that to want money is to want every thing.

Next to the pleasure of contemplating his possessions, seems to be that of enumerating the men of high rank with whom he was acquainted, and whose notice he loudly proclaims not to have been obtained by any practices of meanness or servility; a boast which was never denied to be true, and to which very few poets have ever aspired. Pope never set his genius to sale; he never flattered those whom he did not love, or praised those whom he did not esteem. Savage however remarked, that he began a little to relax his dignity when he wrote a distich for *his Highness's dog.*

His admiration of the Great seems to have increased in the advance of life. He passed over peers and statesmen to inscribe his *Iliad* to Congreve, with a magnanimity of which the praise had been compleat, had his friend's virtue been equal to his wit. Why he was chosen for so great an honour, it is not now possible to know; there is no trace in literary history of any particular intimacy between them. The name of Congreve appears in the Letters among those of his other friends, but without any observable distinction or consequence. To his latter works, however, he took care to annex names dignified with titles, but was not very happy in his choice; for, except Lord Bathurst, none of his noble friends were such as that a good man would wish to have his intimacy with them known to posterity: he can derive little honour from the notice of Cobham, Burlington, or Bolingbroke.

Of his social qualities, if an estimate be made from his Letters, an opinion too favourable cannot easily be formed; they exhibit a perpetual and unclouded effulgence of general benevolence, and particular fondness. There is nothing but liberality, gratitude, constancy, and tenderness. It has been so long said as to be commonly believed, that the true characters of men may be found in their

Letters, and that he who writes to his friend lays his heart open before him. But the truth is, that such were simple friendships of the Golden Age, and are now the friendships only of children. Very few can boast of hearts which they dare lay open to themselves, and of which, by whatever accident exposed, they do not shun a distinct and continued view; and, certainly, what we hide from ourselves we do not shew to our friends. There is, indeed, no transaction which offers stronger temptations to fallacy and sophistication than epistolary inter-course. In the eagerness of conversation the first emotions of the mind often burst out, before they are considered; in the tumult of business, interest and passion have their genuine effect; but a friendly Letter is a calm and deliberate performance, in the cool of leisure, in the stillness of solitude, and surely no man sits down to depreciate by design his own character.

Friendship has no tendency to secure veracity; for by whom can a man so much wish to be thought better than he is, as by him whose kindness he desires to gain or keep? Even in writing to the world there is less constraint; the author is not confronted with his reader, and takes his chance of approbation among the different dispositions of mankind; but a Letter is addressed to a single mind, of which the prejudices and partialities are known; and must therefore please, if not by favouring them, by forbearing to oppose them.

To charge those favourable representations, which every man gives of himself, with the guilt of hypocritical falshood, would shew more severity than knowledge. The writer commonly believes himself. Almost every man's thoughts, while they are general, are right; and most hearts are pure, while temptation is away. It is easy to awaken generous sentiments in privacy; to despise death when there is no danger; to glow with benevolence when there is nothing to be given. While such ideas are formed they are felt, and self-love does not suspect the gleam of virtue to be the meteor of fancy.

If the Letters of Pope are considered merely as compositions, they seem to be premeditated and artificial. It is one thing to write because there is something which the mind wishes to discharge, and another, to solicit the imagination because ceremony or vanity requires something to be written. Pope confesses his early letters to be vitiated with affectation and ambition: to know whether he disentangled himself from these perverters of epistolary integrity, his book and his life must be set in comparison.

One of his favourite topicks is contempt of his own poetry. For this, if it had been real, he would deserve no commendation, and in this he was certainly not sincere; for his high value of himself was sufficiently observed, and of what could he be proud but of his poetry? He writes, he says, when he has just nothing else to do; yet Swift complains that he was never at leisure for conversation, because he had always some poetical scheme in his head. It was punctually required that his writing-box should be set upon his bed before he rose; and Lord Oxford's domestick related, that, in the dreadful winter of Forty, she was called from her bed by him four times in one night, to supply him with paper, lest he should lose a thought.

He pretends insensibility to censure and criticism, though it was observed by all who knew him that every pamphlet disturbed his quiet, and that his extreme irritability laid him open to perpetual vexation; but he wished to despise his criticks, and therefore hoped that he did despise them.

As he happened to live in two reigns when the Court paid little attention to poetry, he nursed in his mind a foolish disesteem of Kings, and proclaims that he never sees Courts. Yet a little regard shewn him by the Prince of Wales melted his obduracy; and he had not much to say when he was asked by his Royal Highness, *how he could love a Prince while he disliked Kings?*

He very frequently professes contempt of the world, and represents himself as looking on mankind, sometimes with gay indifference, as on emmets of a hillock, below his serious attention; and sometimes with gloomy indignation, as on monsters more worthy of hatred than of pity. These were dispositions apparently counterfeited. How could he despise those whom he lived by pleasing, and on whose approbation his esteem of himself was superstructed? Why should he hate those to whose favour he owed his honour and his ease? Of things that terminate in human life, the world is the proper judge; to despise its sentence, if it were possible, is not just; and if it were just, is not possible. Pope was far enough from this unreasonable temper; he was sufficiently a fool to Fame, and his fault was that he pretended to neglect it. His levity and his sullenness were only in his Letters; he passed through common life, sometimes vexed, and sometimes pleased, with the natural emotions of common men.

His scorn of the Great is repeated too often to be real; no man thinks much of that which he despises; and as falsehood is always in danger of inconsistency, he makes it his boast at another time that he lives among them.

It is evident that his own importance swells often in his mind. He is afraid of writing, lest the clerks of the Post-office should know his secrets; he has many enemies; he considers himself as surrounded by universal jealousy; *after many deaths, and many dispersions, two or three of us,* says he, *may still be brought together, not to plot, but to divert ourselves, and the world too, if it pleases;* and they can live together, and *shew what friends wits may be, in spite of all the fools in the world.* All this while it was likely that the clerks did not know his hand; he certainly had no more enemies than a publick character like his inevitably excites, and with what degree of friendship the wits might live very few were so much fools as ever to enquire.

Some part of this pretended discontent he learned from Swift, and expresses it, I think, most frequently in his correspondence with him. Swift's resentment was unreasonable, but it was sincere; Pope's was the mere mimickry of his friend, a fictitious part which he began to play before it became him. When he was only twenty-five years old, he related that a glut of study and retirement had thrown him on the world, and that there was danger lest a glut of the world should throw him back upon study and retirement. To this Swift answered with great propriety, that Pope had not yet either acted or suffered enough in the world to have become weary of it. And, indeed, it must be some very powerful reason that can drive back to solitude him who has once enjoyed the pleasures of society.

In the Letters of both Swift and Pope there appears such narrowness of mind, as makes them insensible of any excellence that has not some affinity with their own, and confines their esteem and approbation to so small a number, that whoever should form his opinion of the age from their representation, would suppose them to have lived amidst ignorance and barbarity, unable to find among their contemporaries either virtue or intelligence, and persecuted by those that could not understand them.

When Pope murmurs at the world, when he professes contempt of fame, when he speaks of riches and poverty, of success and disappointment, with negligent indifference, he certainly does not express his habitual and settled sentiments, but either wilfully disguises his own character, or, what is more likely, invests himself with temporary qualities, and sallies out in the colours of the present moment. His hopes and fears, his joys and sorrows, acted strongly upon his mind; and if he differed from others, it was not by carelessness; he was irritable and resentful; his malignity to Philips, whom he had first made ridiculous, and then hated for being angry, continued too long. Of his vain desire to make Bentley contemptible, I never heard any adequate reason. He was sometimes wanton in his attacks; and, before Chandos, Lady Wortley, and Hill, was mean in his retreat.

The virtues which seem to have had most of his affection were liberality and fidelity of friendship, in which it does not appear that he was other than he describes himself. His fortune did not suffer his charity to be splendid and conspicuous; but he assisted Dodsley with a hundred pounds, that he might open a shop; and of the subscription of forty pounds a year that he raised for Savage, twenty were paid by himself. He was accused of loving money, but his love was eagerness to gain, not solicitude to keep it.

In the duties of friendship he was zealous and constant: his early maturity of mind commonly united him with men older than himself, and therefore, without attaining any considerable length of life, he saw many companions of his youth sink into the grave; but it does not appear that he lost a single friend by coldness or by injury; those who loved him once, continued their kindness. His ungrateful mention of Allen in his will, was the effect of his adherence to one whom he had known much longer, and whom he naturally loved with greater fondness. His violation of the trust reposed in him by Bolingbroke could have no motive inconsistent with the warmest affection; he either thought the action so near to indifferent that he forgot it, or so laudable that he expected his friend to approve it.

It was reported, with such confidence as almost to enforce belief, that in the papers intrusted to his executors was found a defamatory Life of Swift, which he had prepared as an instrument of vegeance to be used, if any provocation should be ever given. About this I enquired of the Earl of Marchmont, who assured me that no such piece was among his remains.

The religion in which he lived and died was that of the Church of Rome, to which in his correspondence with Racine he professes himself a sincere adherent. That he was not scrupulously pious in some part of his life, is known by many idle and indecent applications of sentences taken from the Scriptures;

a mode of merriment which a good man dreads for its profaneness, and a witty man disdains for its easiness and vulgarity. But to whatever levities he has been betrayed, it does not appear that his principles were ever corrupted, or that he ever lost his belief of Revelation. The positions which he transmitted from Bolingbroke he seems not to have understood, and was pleased with an interpretation that made them orthodox.

A man of such exalted superiority, and so little moderation, would naturally have all his delinquences observed and aggravated: those who could not deny that he was excellent, would rejoice to find that he was not perfect.

Perhaps it may be imputed to the unwillingness with which the same man is allowed to possess many advantages, that his learning has been depreciated. He certainly was in his early life a man of great literary curiosity; and when he wrote his *Essay on Criticism* had, for his age, a very wide acquaintance with books. When he entered into the living world, it seems to have happened to him as to many others, that he was less attentive to dead masters; he studied in the academy of Paracelsus, and made the universe his favourite volume. He gathered his notions fresh from reality, not from the copies of authors, but the originals of Nature. Yet there is no reason to believe that literature ever lost his esteem; he always professed to love reading; and Dobson, who spent some time at his house translating his *Essay on Man*, when I asked him what learning he found him to possess, answered, *More than I expected*. His frequent references to history, his allusions to various kinds of knowledge, and his images selected from art and nature, with his observations on the operations of the mind and the modes of life, shew an intelligence perpetually on the wing, excursive, vigorous, and diligent, eager to pursue knowledge, and attentive to retain it.

From this curiosity arose the desire of travelling, to which he alludes in his verses to Jervas, and which, though he never found an opportunity to gratify it, did not leave him till his life declined.

Of his intellectual character, the constituent and fundamental principle was Good Sense, a prompt and intuitive perception of consonance and propriety. He saw immediately, of his own conceptions, what was to be chosen, and what to be rejected; and, in the works of others, what was to be shunned, and what was to be copied.

But good sense alone is a sedate and quiescent quality, which manages its possession well, but does not increase them; it collects few materials for its own operations, and preserves safety, but never gains supremacy. Pope had likewise genius; a mind active, ambitious, and adventurous, always investigating, always aspiring; in its widest searches still longing to go forward, in its highest flights still wishing to be higher; always imagining something greater than it knows, always endeavouring more than it can do.

To assist these powers, he is said to have had great strength and exactness of memory. That which he had heard or read was not easily lost; and he had before him not only what his own meditation suggested, but what he had found in other writers that might be accommodated to his present purpose.

These benefits of nature he improved by incessant and unwearied diligence; he had recourse to every source of intelligence, and lost no opportunity of information; he consulted the living as well as the dead; he read his compositions to his friends, and was never content with mediocrity when excellence could be attained. He considered poetry as the business of his life, and however he might seem to lament his occupation, he followed it with constancy; to make verses was his first labour, and to mend them was his last.

From his attention to poetry he was never diverted. If conversation offered any thing that could be improved, he committed it to paper; if a thought, or perhaps an expression more happy than was common, rose to his mind, he was careful to write it; an independent distich was preserved for an opportunity of insertion, and some little fragments have been found containing lines, or parts of lines, to be wrought upon at some other time.

He was one of those few whose labour is their pleasure: he was never elevated to negligence, nor wearied to impatience; he never passed a fault unamended by indifference, nor quitted it by despair. He laboured his works first to gain reputation, and afterwards to keep it.

Of composition there are different methods. Some employ at once memory and invention, and, with little intermediate use of the pen, form and polish large masses by continued meditation, and write their productions only when, in their own opinion, they have completed them. It is related of Virgil, that his custom was to pour out a great number of verses in the morning, and pass the day in retrenching exuberances and correcting inaccuracies. The method of Pope, as may be collected from his translation, was to write his first thoughts in his first words, and gradually to amplify, decorate, rectify, and refine them.

With such faculties, and such dispositions, he excelled every other writer in poetical prudence; he wrote in such a manner as might expose him to few hazards. He used almost always the same fabrick of verse; and, indeed, by those few essays which he made of any other, he did not enlarge his reputation. Of this uniformity the certain consequence was readiness and dexterity. By perpetual practice, language had in his mind a systematical arrangement; having always the same use for words, he had words so selected and combined as to be ready at his call. This increase of facility he confessed himself to have perceived in the progress of his translation.

But what was yet of more importance, his effusions were always voluntary, and his subjects chosen by himself. His independence secured him from drudging at a task, and labouring upon a barren topick: he never exchanged praise for money, nor opened a shop of condolence or congratulation. His poems, therefore, were scarce ever temporary. He suffered coronations and royal marriages to pass without a song, and derived no opportunities from recent events, or popularity from the accidental disposition of his readers. He was never reduced to the necessity of soliciting the sun to shine upon a birth-day, of calling the Graces and Virtues to a wedding, or of saying what multitudes have said before him. When he could produce nothing new, he was at liberty to be silent.

His publications were for the same reason never hasty. He is said to have sent nothing to the press till it had lain two years under his inspection: it is at least certain, that he ventured nothing without nice examination. He suffered the tumult of imagination to subside, and the novelties of invention to grow familiar. He knew that the mind is always enamoured of its own productions, and did not trust his first fondness. He consulted his friends, and listened with great willingness to criticism; and, what was of more importance, he consulted himself, and let nothing pass against his own judgement.

He professed to have learned his poetry from Dryden, whom, whenever an opportunity was presented, he praised through his whole life with unvaried liberality; and perhaps his character may receive some illustration, if he be compared with his master.

Integrity of understanding and nicety of discernment were not allotted in a less proportion to Dryden than to Pope. The rectitude of Dryden's mind was sufficiently shewn by the dismission of his poetical prejudices, and the rejection of unnatural thoughts and rugged numbers. But Dryden never desired to apply all the judgement that he had. He wrote, and professed to write, merely for the people; and when he pleased others, he contented himself. He spent no time in struggles to rouse latent powers; he never attempted to make that better which was already good, nor often to mend what he must have known to be faulty. He wrote, as he tells us, with very little consideration; when occasion or necessity called upon him, he poured out what the present moment happened to supply, and, when once it had passed the press, ejected it from his mind; for when he had no pecuniary interest, he had no further solicitude.

Pope was not content to satisfy; he desired to excel, and therefore always endeavoured to do his best: he did not court the candour, but dared the judgement of his reader, and expecting no indulgence from others, he shewed none to himself. He examined lines and words with minute and punctilious observation, and retouched every part with indefatigable diligence, till he had left nothing to be forgiven.

For this reason he kept his pieces very long in his hands, while he considered and reconsidered them. The only poems which can be supposed to have been written with such regard to the times as might hasten their publication, were the two satires of Thirty-eight; of which Dodsley told me, that they were brought to him by the author, that they might be fairly copied. "Every line," said he, "was then written twice over; I gave him a clean transcript, which he sent some time afterwards to me for the press, with every line written twice over a second time."

His declaration, that his care for his works ceased at their publication, was not strictly true. His parental attention never abandoned them; what he found amiss in the first edition, he silently corrected in those that followed. He appears to have revised the *Iliad*, and freed it from some of its imperfections; and the *Essay on Criticism* received many improvements after its first appearance. It will seldom be found that he altered without adding clearness, elegance, or vigour. Pope had perhaps the judgement of Dryden; but Dryden certainly wanted the diligence of Pope.

In acquired knowledge, the superiority must be allowed to Dryden, whose education was more scholastick, and who before he became an author had

been allowed more time for study, with better means of information. His mind
has a larger range, and he collects his images and illustrations from a more
extensive circumference of science. Dryden knew more of man in his general
nature, and Pope in his local manners. The notions of Dryden were formed by
comprehensive speculation, and those of Pope by minute attention. There is
more dignity in the knowledge of Dryden, and more certainty in that of Pope.

Poetry was not the sole praise of either; for both excelled likewise in prose;
but Pope did not borrow his prose from his predecessor. The style of Dryden is
capricious and varied, that of Pope is cautious and uniform; Dryden obeys the
motions of his own mind, Pope constrains his mind to his own rules of
composition. Dryden is sometimes vehement and rapid; Pope is always
smooth, uniform, and gentle. Dryden's page is a natural field, rising into
inequalities, and diversified by the varied exuberance of abundant vegetation;
Pope's is a velvet lawn, shaven by the scythe, and levelled by the roller.

Of genius, that power which constitutes a poet; that quality without
which judgement is cold and knowledge is inert; that energy which collects,
combines, amplifies, and animates; the superiority must, with some
hesitation, be allowed to Dryden. It is not to be inferred that of this poetical
vigour Pope had only a little, because Dryden had more; for every other writer
since Milton must give place to Pope; and even of Dryden it must be said, that
if he has brighter paragraphs, he has not better poems. Dryden's performances were always hasty, either excited by some external occasion, or
extorted by domestick necessity; he composed without consideration, and
published without correction. What his mind could supply at call, or gather in
one excursion, was all that he sought, and all that he gave. The dilatory
caution of Pope enabled him to condense his sentiments, to multiply his
images, and to accumulate all that study might produce, or chance might
supply. If the flights of Dryden therefore are higher, Pope continues longer on
the wing. If of Dryden's fire the blaze is brighter, of Pope's the heat is more
regular and constant. Dryden often surpasses expectation, and Pope never
falls below it. Dryden is read with frequent astonishment, and Pope with
perpetual delight.

This parallel will, I hope, when it is well considered, be found just; and if
the reader should suspect me, as I suspect myself, of some partial fondness for
the memory of Dryden, let him not too hastily condemn me; for meditation and
enquiry may, perhaps, shew him the reasonableness of my determination. . . .

One of his greatest though of his earliest works is the *Essay on Criticism*,
which, if he had written nothing else, would have placed him among the first
criticks and the first poets, as it exhibits every mode of excellence that can
embellish or dignify didactick composition, selection of matter, novelty of
arrangement, justness of precept, splendour of illustration, and propriety of
digression. I know not whether it be pleasing to consider that he produced this
piece at twenty, and never afterwards excelled it; he that delights himself with
observing that such powers may be so soon attained, cannot but grieve to think
that life was ever after at a stand.

To mention the particular beauties of the Essay would be unprofitably tedious; but I cannot forbear to observe, that the comparison of a student's progress in the sciences with the journey of a traveller in the Alps, is perhaps the best that English poetry can shew. A simile, to be perfect, must both illustrate and ennoble the subject; must shew it to the understanding in a clearer view, and display it to the fancy with greater dignity; but either of these qualities may be sufficient to recommend it. In didactick poetry, of which the great purpose is instruction, a simile may be praised which illustrates, though it does not ennoble; in heroicks, that may be admitted which ennobles, though it does not illustrate. That it may be complete, it is required to exhibit, independently of its references, a pleasing image; for a simile is said to be a short episode. To this antiquity was so attentive, that circumstances were sometimes added, which, having no parallels, served only to fill the imagination, and produced what Perrault ludicrously called *comparisons with a long tail*. In their similies the greatest writers have sometimes failed; the ship-race, compared with the chariot-race, is neither illustrated nor aggrandised; land and water make all the difference: when Apollo, running after Daphne, is likened to a greyhound chasing a hare, there is nothing gained; the ideas of pursuit and flight are too plain to be made plainer, and a god and the daughter of a god are not represented much to their advantage by a hare and dog. The simile of the Alps has no useless parts, yet affords a striking picture by itself; it makes the foregoing position better understood, and enables it to take faster hold on the attention; it assists the apprehension, and elevates the fancy.

Let me likewise dwell a little on the celebrated paragraph, in which it is directed that *the sound should seem an echo to the sense;* a precept which Pope is allowed to have observed beyond any other English poet.

This notion of representative metre, and the desire of discovering frequent adaptations of the sound to the sense, have produced, in my opinion, many wild conceits and imaginary beauties. All that can furnish this representation are the sounds of the words considered singly, and the time in which they are pronounced. Every language has some words framed to exhibit the noises which they express, *as thump, rattle, growl, hiss*. These however are but few, and the poet cannot make them more, nor can they be of any use but when sound is to be mentioned. The time of pronunciation was in the dactylick measures of the learned languages capable of considerable variety; but that variety could be accommodated only to motion or duration, and different degrees of motion were perhaps expressed by verses rapid or slow, with very little attention of the writer, when the image had full possession of his fancy; but our language having little flexibility, our verses can differ very little in their cadence. The fancied resemblances, I fear, arise sometimes merely from the ambiguity of words; there is supposed to be some relation between a *soft* line and *soft* couch, or between *hard* syllables and *hard* fortune.

Motion, however, may be in some sort exemplified; and yet it may be suspected that even in such resemblances the mind often governs the ear, and the sounds are estimated by their meaning. One of the most successful attempts has been to describe the labour of Sisyphus:

> With many a weary step, and many a groan,
> Up a high hill he heaves a huge round stone;
> The huge round stone, resulting with a bound,
> Thunders impetuous down, and smoaks along the ground.

Who does not perceive the stone to move slowly upward, and roll violently back? But set the same numbers to another sense;

> While many a merry tale, and many a song,
> Chear'd the rough road, we wish'd the rough road long.
> The rough road then, returning in a round,
> Mock'd our impatient steps, for all was fairy ground.

We have now surely lost much of the delay, and much of the rapidity.

But to shew how little the greatest master of numbers can fix the principles of representative harmony, it will be sufficient to remark that the poet, who tells us, that

> When Ajax strives—the words move slow.
> Not so when swift Camilla scours the plain,
> Flies o'er th' unbending corn, and skims along the main;

when he had enjoyed for about thirty years the praise of Camilla's lightness of foot, tried another experiment upon sound and time, and produced this memorable triplet:

> Waller was smooth; but Dryden taught to join
> The varying verse, the full resounding line,
> The long majestick march, and energy divine.

Here are the swiftness of the rapid race, and the march of slowpaced majesty, exhibited by the same poet in the same sequence of syllables, except that the exact prosodist will find the line of swiftness by one time longer than that of tardiness.

Beauties of this kind are commonly fancied; and when real, are technical and nugatory, not to be rejected, and not to be solicited.

To the praises which have been accumulated on *The Rape of the Lock* by readers of every class, from the critick to the waiting-maid, it is difficult to make any addition. Of that which is universally allowed to be the most attractive of all ludicrous compositions, let it rather be now enquired from what sources the power of pleasing is derived.

Dr. Warburton, who excelled in critical perspicacity, has remarked that the preternatural agents are very happily adapted to the purposes of the poem. The heathen deities can no longer gain attention: we should have turned away from a contest between Venus and Diana; the employment of allegorical persons always excites conviction of its own absurdity; they may produce effects, but cannot conduct actions; when the phantom is put in motion it dissolves; thus Discord may raise a mutiny, but Discord cannot conduct a march, nor besiege a town. Pope brought into view a new race of Beings, with powers and passions proportionate to their operation. The sylphs and gnomes act at the toilet and the teatable; what more terrifick and more powerful phantoms perform on the stormy ocean, or the field of battle, they give their proper help, and do their proper mischief.

Pope is said, by an objector, not to have been the inventor of this petty nation; a charge which might with more justice have been brought against the author of the *Iliad*, who doubtless adopted the religious system of his country; for what is there but the names of his agents which Pope has not invented? Has he not assigned them characters and operations never heard of before? Has he not, at least, given them their first poetical existence? If this is not sufficient to denominate his work original, nothing original ever can be written.

In this work are exhibited, in a very high degree, the two most engaging powers of an author. New things are made familiar, and familiar things are made new. A race of aerial people, never heard of before, is presented to us in a manner so clear and easy, that the reader seeks for no further information, but immediately mingles with his new acquaintance, adopts their interests, and attends their pursuits, loves a sylph, and detests a gnome.

That familiar things are made new, every paragraph will prove. The subject of the poem is an event below the common incidents of common life; nothing real is introduced that is not seen so often as to be no longer regarded, yet the whole detail of a female-day is here brought before us invested with so much art of decoration, that, though nothing is disguised, every thing is striking, and we feel all the appetite of curiosity for that from which we have a thousand times turned fastidiously away.

The purpose of the Poet is, as he tells us, to laugh at *the little unguarded follies of the female sex*. It is therefore without justice that Dennis charges the *Rape of the Lock* with the want of a moral, and for that reason sets it below the *Lutrin*, which exposes the pride and discord of the clergy. Perhaps neither Pope nor Boileau has made the world much better than he found it; but if they had both succeeded, it were easy to tell who would have deserved most from publick gratitude. The freaks, and humours, and spleen, and vanity of women, as they embroil families in discord, and fill houses with disquiet, do more to obstruct the happiness of life in a year than the ambition of the clergy in many centuries. It has been well observed, that the misery of man proceeds not from any single crush of overwhelming evil, but from small vexations continually repeated. . . .

The Epistle of *Eloise to Abelard* is one of the most happy productions of human wit: the subject is so judiciously chosen, that it would be difficult, in turning over the annals of the world, to find another which so many circumstances concur to recommend. We regularly interest ourselves most in the fortune of those who most deserve our notice. Abelard and Eloise were conspicuous in their days for eminence of merit. The heart naturally loves truth. The adventures and misfortunes of this illustrious pair are known from undisputed history. Their fate does not leave the mind in hopeless dejection; for they both found quiet and consolation in retirement and piety. So new and so affecting is their story, that it supersedes invention, and imagination ranges at full liberty without straggling into scenes of fable.

The story, thus skilfully adopted, has been diligently improved. Pope has left nothing behind him, which seems more the effect of studious perseverance and laborious revisal. Here is particularly observable the *curiosa felicitas*, a fruitful soil, and careful cultivation. Here is no crudeness of sense, nor asperity of language. . . .

Translation of "The Iliad"

The chief help of Pope in this arduous undertaking was drawn from the versions of Dryden. Virgil had borrowed much of his imagery from Homer, and part of the debt was now paid by his translator. Pope searched the pages of Dryden for happy combinations of heroick diction; but it will not be denied that he added much to what he found. He cultivated our language with so much diligence and art, that he has left in his *Homer* a treasure of poetical elegances to posterity. His version may be said to have tuned the English tongue; for since its appearance no writer, however deficient in other powers, has wanted melody. Such a series of lines so elaborately corrected, and so sweetly modulated, took possession of the publick ear, the vulgar was enamoured of the poem, and the learned wondered at the translation.

But in the most general applause discordant voices will always be heard. It has been objected by some, who wish to be numbered among the sons of learning, that Pope's version of Homer is not Homerical; that it exhibits no resemblance of the original characteristick manner of the Father of Poetry, as it wants his awful simplicity, his artless grandeur, his unaffected majesty. This cannot be totally denied; but it must be remembered that *necessitas quod cogit defendit;* that may be lawfully done which cannot be forborn. Time and place will always enforce regard. In estimating this translation, consideration must be had of the nature of our language, the form of our metre, and, above all, of the change which two thousand years have made in the modes of life and the habits of thought. Virgil wrote in a language of the same general fabrick with that of Homer, in verses of the same measure, and in an age nearer to Homer's time by eighteen hundred years; yet he found, even then, the state of the world so much altered, and the demand for elegance so much increased, that mere nature would be endured no longer; and perhaps, in the multitude of borrowed passages, very few can be shewn which he has not embellished.

There is a time when nations emerging from barbarity, and falling into regular subordination, gain leisure to grow wise, and feel the shame of ignorance and the craving pain of unsatisifed curiosity. To this hunger of the mind plain sense is grateful; that which fills the void removes uneasiness, and to be free from pain for a while is pleasure; but repletion generates fastidiousness; a saturated intellect soon becomes luxurious, and knowledge finds no willing reception till it is recommended by artificial diction. Thus it will be found, as learning advances, that in all nations the first writers are simple, and that every age improves in elegance. One refinement always makes way for another, and what was expedient to Virgil was necessary to Pope.

I suppose many readers of the English *Iliad,* when they have been touched with some unexpected beauty of the lighter kind, have tried to enjoy it in the original, where, alas! it was not to be found. Homer doubtless owes to his translator many Ovidian graces not exactly suitable to his character; but to have added can be no great crime, if nothing be taken away. Elegance is surely to be desired, if it be not gained at the expence of dignity. A hero would wish to be loved, as well as to be reverenced.

To a thousand cavils one answer is sufficient; the purpose of a writer is to be read, and the criticism which would destroy the power of pleasing must be blown aside. Pope wrote for his own age and his own nation: he knew that it was necessary to colour the images and point the sentiments of his author; he therefore made him graceful, but lost him some of his sublimity.

The copious notes with which the version is accompanied, and by which it is recommended to many readers, though they were undoubtedly written to swell the volumes, ought not to pass without praise: commentaries which attract the reader by the pleasure of perusal have not often appeared; the notes of others are read to clear difficulties, those of Pope to vary entertainment.

It has however been objected, with sufficient reason, that there is in the commentary too much of unseasonable levity and affected gaiety; that too many appeals are made to the Ladies, and the ease which is so carefully preserved is sometimes the ease of a trifler. Every art has its terms, and every kind of instruction its proper style; the gravity of common criticks may be tedious, but is less despicable than childish merriment. . . .

The *Essay on Man* was a work of great labour and long consideration, but certainly not the happiest of Pope's performances. The subject is perhaps not very proper for poetry, and the poet was not sufficiently master of his subject; metaphysical morality was to him a new study, he was proud of his acquisitions, and, supposing himself master of great secrets, was in haste to teach what he had not learned. Thus he tells us, in the first Epistle, that from the nature of the Supreme Being may be deduced an order of beings such as mankind, because Infinite Excellence can do only what is best. He finds out that *all the question is whether man be in a wrong place.* Surely if, according to the poet's Leibnitian reasoning, we may infer that man ought to be, only because he is, we may allow that his place is the right place, because he has it. Supreme Wisdom is not less infallible in disposing than in creating. But what is meant by *somewhere* and *place,* and *wrong place,* it had been vain to ask Pope, who probably had never asked himself.

Having exalted himself into the chair of wisdom, he tells us much that every man knows, and much that he does not know himself; that we see but little, and that the order of the universe is beyond our comprehension; an opinion not very uncommon; and that there is a chain of subordinate beings from infinite to nothing, of which himself and his readers are equally ignorant. But he gives us one comfort, which, without his help, he supposes unattainable, in the position *that though we are fools, yet God is wise.*

This Essay affords an egregious instance of the predominance of genius, the dazzling splendour of imagery, and the seductive powers of eloquence.

Never was penury of knowledge and vulgarity of sentiment so happily disguised. The reader feels his mind full, though he learns nothing; and when he meets it in its new array, no longer knows the talk of his mother and his nurse. When these wonder-working sounds sink into sense, and the doctrine of the Essay disrobed of its ornaments, is left to the powers of its naked excellence, what shall we discover? That we are, in comparison with our Creator, very weak and ignorant; that we do not uphold the chain of existence, and that we could not make one another with more skill than we are made. We may learn yet more; that the arts of human life were copied from the instinctive operations of other animals; that if the world be made for man, it may be said that man was made for geese. To these profound principles of natural knowledge are added some moral instructions equally new; that self-interest, well understood, will produce social concord; that men are mutual gainers by mutual benefits; that evil is sometimes balanced by good; that human advantages are unstable and fallacious, of uncertain duration, and doubtful effects; that our true honour is not to have a great part, but to act it well; that virtue only is our own; and that happiness is always in our power.

Surely a man of no very comprehensive search may venture to say that he has heard all this before; but it was never till now recommended by such a blaze of embellishment, or such sweetness of melody. The vigorous contraction of some thoughts, the luxuriant amplification of others, the incidental illustrations, and sometimes the dignity, sometimes the softness of the verses, enchain philosophy, suspend criticism, and oppress judgement by overpowering pleasure.

This is true of many paragraphs; yet if I had undertaken to exemplify Pope's felicity of composition before a rigid critick, I should not select the *Essay on Man;* for it contains more lines unsuccessfully laboured, more harshness of diction, more thoughts imperfectly expressed, more levity without elegance, and more heaviness without strength, than will easily be found in all his other works. . . .

Pope had, in proportions very nicely adjusted to each other, all the qualities that constitute genius. He had *Invention,* by which new trains of events are formed, and new scenes of imagery displayed, as in the *Rape of the Lock;* or extrinsick and adventitious embellishments and illustrations are connected with a known subject, as in the *Essay on Criticism.* He had *Imagination,* which strongly impresses on the writer's mind, and enables him to convey to the reader the various forms of nature, incidents of life, and energies of passion, as in his *Eloisa, Windsor Forest,* and the *Ethick Epistles.* He had *Judgement,* which selects from life or nature what the present purpose requires, and by separating the essence of things from its concomitants often makes the representation more powerful than the reality: and he had colours of language always before him, ready to decorate his matter with every grace of elegant expression, as when he accommodates his diction to the wonderful multiplicity of Homer's sentiments and descriptions.

Poetical expression includes sound as well as meaning; *Musick,* says Dryden, *is inarticulate poetry;* among the excellencies of Pope, therefore, must be mentioned the melody of his metre. By perusing the works of Dryden, he discovered the most perfect fabrick of English verse, and habituated himself to that only which he found the best; in consequence of which restraint his poetry has been censured as too uniformly musical, and as glutting the ear with unvaried sweetness. I suspect this objection to be the cant of those who judge by principles rather than perception; and who would even themselves have less pleasure in his works, if he had tried to relieve attention by studied discords, or affected to break his lines and vary his pauses. . . .

It is remarked by Watts, that there is scarcely a happy combination of words, or a phrase poetically elegant in the English language, which Pope has not inserted into his version of Homer. How he obtained possession of so many beauties of speech, it were desirable to know. That he gleaned from authors, obscure as well as eminent, what he thought brilliant or useful, and preserved it all in a regular collection, is not unlikely. When, in his last years, Hall's *Satires* were shewn him, he wished that he had seen them sooner.

New sentiments and new images others may produce; but to attempt any further improvement of versification will be dangerous. Art and diligence have now done their best, and what shall be added will be the effort of tedious toil and needless curiosity.

After all this, it is surely superfluous to answer the question that has once been asked, Whether Pope was a poet? otherwise than by asking in return, If Pope be not a poet, where is poetry to be found? To circumscribe poetry by a definition will only shew the narrowness of the definer, though a definition which shall exclude Pope will not easily be made. Let us look round upon the present time, and back upon the past; let us enquire to whom the voice of mankind has decreed the wreath of poetry; let their productions be examined, and their claims stated, and the pretensions of Pope will be no more disputed. Had he given the world only his version, the name of poet must have been allowed him: if the writer of the *Iliad* were to class his successors, he would assign a very high place to his translator, without requiring any other evidence of Genius. . . .

On Mrs. Corbet, who died of a Cancer in her Breast

> Here rests a woman, good without pretence,
> Blest with plain reason, and with sober sense:
> No conquests she, but o'er herself desir'd;
> No arts essay'd, but not to be admir'd.
> Passion and pride were to her soul unknown,
> Convinc'd that Virtue only is our own.
> So unaffected, so compos'd a mind,
> So firm, yet soft, so strong, yet so refin'd,
> Heaven, as its purest gold, by tortures try'd,
> The saint sustain'd it, but the woman dy'd.

I have always considered this as the most valuable of all Pope's epitaphs;

the subject of it is a character not discriminated by any shining or eminent peculiarities; yet that which really makes, though not the splendor, the felicity of life, and that which every wise man will choose for his final and lasting companion in the languor of age, in the quiet of privacy, when he departs weary and disgusted from the ostentatious, the volatile, and the vain. Of such a character, which the dull overlook, and the gay despise, it was fit that the value should be made known, and the dignity established. Domestic virtue, as it is exerted without great occasions, or conspicuous consequences, in an even unnoted tenor, required the genius of Pope to display it in such a manner as might attract regard, and enforce reverence. Who can forbear to lament that this amiable woman has no name in the verses?

If the particular lines of this inscription be examined, it will appear less faulty than the rest. There is scarce one line taken from common places, unless it be that in which *only Virtue* is said to be *our own*. I once heard a Lady of great beauty and elegance object to the fourth line, that it contained an unnatural and incredible panegyrick. Of this let the Ladies judge.

WILLIAM COLLINS

About this time I fell into his company. His appearance was decent and manly; his knowledge considerable, his views extensive, his conversation elegant, and his disposition chearful. By degrees I gained his confidence; and one day was admitted to him when he was immured by a bailiff, that was prowling in the street. On this occasion recourse was had to the booksellers, who, on the credit of a translation of Aristotle's Poeticks, which he engaged to write with a large commentary, advanced as much money as enabled him to escape into the country. He shewed me the guineas safe in his hand. Soon afterwards his uncle, Mr. Martin, a lieutenant-colonel, left him about two thousand pounds; a sum which Collins could scarcely think exhaustible, and which he did not live to exhaust. The guineas were then repaid, and the translation neglected.

But man is not born for happiness. Collins, who, while he *studied to live,* felt no evil but poverty, no sooner *lived to study* than his life was assailed by more dreadful calamities, disease and insanity.

Having formerly written his character, while perhaps it was yet more distinctly impressed upon my memory, I shall insert it here.

"Mr. Collins was a man of extensive literature, and of vigorous faculties. He was acquainted not only with the learned tongues, but with the Italian, French, and Spanish languages. He had employed his mind chiefly upon works of fiction, and subjects of fancy; and by indulging some peculiar habits of thought, was eminently delighted with those flights of imagination which pass the bounds of nature, and to which the mind is reconciled only by a passive acquiescence in popular traditions. He loved fairies, genii, giants, and monsters; he delighted to rove through the meanders of inchantment, to gaze on the magnificence of golden palaces, to repose by the water-falls of Elysian gardens.

"This was however the character rather of his inclination than his genius;

the grandeur of wildness, and the novelty of extravagance, were always desired by him, but were not always attained. Yet as diligence is never wholly lost; if his efforts sometimes caused harshness and obscurity, they likewise produced in happier moments sublimity and splendour. This idea which he had formed of excellence, led him to oriental fictions and allegorical imagery; and perhaps, while he was intent upon description, he did not sufficiently cultivate sentiment. His poems are the productions of a mind not deficient in fire, nor unfurnished with knowledge either of books or life, but somewhat obstructed in its progress by deviation in quest of mistaken beauties.

"His morals were pure, and his opinions pious: in a long continuance of poverty, and long habits of dissipation, it cannot be expected that any character should be exactly uniform. There is a degree of want by which the freedom of agency is almost destroyed; and long association with fortuitous companions will at last relax the strictness of truth, and abate the fervour of sincerity. That this man, wise and virtuous as he was, passed always unentangled through the snares of life, it would be prejudice and temerity to affirm; but it may be said that at least he preserved the source of action unpolluted, that his principles were never shaken, that his distinctions of right and wrong were never confounded, and that his faults had nothing of malignity or design, but proceeded from some unexpected pressure, or casual temptation.

"The latter part of his life cannot be remembered but with pity and sadness. He languished some years under that depression of mind which enchains the faculties without destroying them, and leaves reason the knowledge of right without the power of pursuing it. These clouds which he perceived gathering on his intellects, he endeavoured to disperse by travel, and passed into France; but found himself constrained to yield to his malady, and returned. He was for some time confined in a house of lunaticks, and afterwards retired to the care of his sister in Chichester, where death in 1756 came to his relief.

"After his return from France, the writer of this character paid him a visit at Islington, where he was waiting for his sister, whom he had directed to meet him: there was then nothing of disorder discernible in his mind by any but himself; but he had withdrawn from study, and travelled with no other book than an English Testament, such as children carry to the school: when his friend took it into his hand, out of curiosity to see what companion a Man of Letters had chosen, *I have but one book,* said Collins, *but that is the best.*"

Such was the fate of Collins, with whom I once delighted to converse, and whom I yet remember with tenderness. . . .

To what I have formerly said of his writings may be added, that his diction was often harsh, unskilfully laboured, and injudiciously selected. He affected the obsolete when it was not worthy of revival; and he puts his words out of the common order, seeming to think, with some later candidates for fame, that not to write prose is certainly to write poetry. His lines commonly are of slow motion, clogged and impeded with clusters of consonants. As men are often esteemed who cannot be loved, so the poetry of Collins may sometimes extort praise when it gives little pleasure.

THOMAS GRAY

Gray's Poetry is now to be considered; and I hope not to be looked on as an enemy to his name, if I confess that I contemplate it with less pleasure than his life.

His ode on *Spring* has something poetical, both in the language and the thought; but the language is too luxuriant, and the thoughts have nothing new. There has of late arisen a practice of giving to adjectives, derived from substantives, the termination of participles; such as the *cultured* plain, the *daisied* bank; but I was sorry to see, in the lines of a scholar like Gray, the *honied* Spring. The morality is natural, but too stale; the conclusion is pretty.

The poem on the *Cat* was doubtless by its author considered as a trifle, but it is not a happy trifle. In the first stanza *the azure flowers* that *blow*, shew resolutely a rhyme is sometimes made when it cannot easily be found. *Selima,* the *Cat,* is called a nymph, with some violence both to language and sense; but there is good use made of it when it is done; for of the two lines,

> What female heart can gold despise?
> What cat's averse to fish?

the first relates merely to the nymph, and the second only to the cat. The sixth stanza contains a melancholy truth, that *a favourite has no friend;* but the last ends in a pointed sentence of no relation to the purpose; if *what glistered* had been *gold,* the cat would not have gone into the water; and, if she had, would not less have been drowned.

The *Prospect of Eaton College* suggests nothing to Gray, which every beholder does not equally think and feel. His supplication to father Thames, to tell him who drives the hoop or tosses the ball, is useless and puerile. Father Thames has no better means of knowing than himself. His epithet *buxom health* is not elegant; he seems not to understand the word. Gray thought his language more poetical as it was more remote from common use: finding in Dryden *honey redolent of Spring,* an expression that reaches the utmost limits of our language, Gray drove it a little more beyond common apprehension, by making *gales* to be *redolent of joy and youth.*

Of the *Ode on Adversity*, the hint was at first taken from *O Diva, gratum quæ regis Antium;* but Gray has excelled his original by the variety of his sentiments, and by their moral application. Of this piece, at once poetical and rational, I will not by slight objections violate the dignity.

My process has now brought me to the wonderful *Wonder of Wonders*, the two Sister Odes; by which, though either vulgar ignorance or common sense at first universally rejected them, many have been since persuaded to think themselves delighted. I am one of those that are willing to be pleased, and therefore would gladly find the meaning of the first stanza of *The Progress of Poetry*.

Gray seems in his rapture to confound the images of *spreading sound* and *running water. A stream of musick* may be allowed; but where does *Musick,* however *smooth and strong,* after having visited the *verdant vales, rowl down the steep amain,* so as that *rocks and nodding groves rebellow to the roar?* If this be said of *Musick,* it is nonsense; if it be said of *Water,* it is nothing to the purpose.

The second stanza, exhibiting Mars's car and Jove's eagle, is unworthy of further notice. Criticism disdains to chase a school-boy to his common places.

To the third it may likewise be objected, that it is drawn from Mythology, though such as may be more easily assimilated to real life. Idalia's *velvet-green* has something of cant. An epithet or metaphor drawn from Nature ennobles Art; an epithet or metaphor drawn from Art degrades Nature. Gray is too fond of words arbitrarily compounded. *Many-twinkling* was formerly censured as not analogical; we may say *many-spotted,* but scarcely *many-spotting.* This stanza, however, has something pleasing.

Of the second ternary of stanzas, the first endeavours to tell something, and would have told it, had it not been crossed by Hyperion; the second describes well enough the universal prevalence of Poetry; but I am afraid that the conclusion will not rise from the premises. The caverns of the North and the plains of Chili are not the residences of *Glory* and *generous Shame.* But that Poetry and Virtue go always together is an opinion so pleasing, that I can forgive him who resolves to think it true.

The third stanza sounds big with *Delphi,* and *Egean,* and *Ilissus,* and *Meander,* and *hallowed fountain* and *solemn sound;* but in all Gray's odes there is a kind of cumbrous splendor which we wish away. His position is at last false: in the time of Dante and Petrarch, from whom he derives our first school of Poetry, Italy was over-run by *tyrant power* and *coward vice;* nor was our state much better when we first borrowed the Italian arts.

Of the third ternary, the first gives a mythological birth of Shakespeare. What is said of that mighty genius is true; but it is not said happily: the real effects of his poetical power are put out of sight by the pomp of machinery. Where truth is sufficient to fill the mind, fiction is worse than useless; the counterfeit debases the genuine.

His account of Milton's blindness, if we suppose it caused by study in the formation of his poem, a supposition surely allowable, is poetically true, and happily imagined. But the *car* of Dryden, with his *two coursers,* has nothing in it peculiar; it is a car in which any other rider may be placed.

The Bard appears, at the first view, to be, as Algarotti and others have remarked, an imitation of the prophecy of Nereus. Algarotti thinks it superior to its original; and, if preference depends only on the imagery and animation of the two poems, his judgement is right. There is in *The Bard* more force, more thought, and more variety. But to copy is less than to invent, and the copy has been unhappily produced at a wrong time. The fiction of Horace was to the Romans credible; but its revival disgusts us with apparent and unconquerable falsehood. *Incredulus odi.*

To select a singular event, and swell it to a giant's bulk by fabulous appendages of spectres and predictions, has little difficulty, for he that forsakes the probable may always find the marvellous; and it has little use, we are affected only as we believe; we are improved only as we find something to be imitated or declined. I do not see that *The Bard* promotes any truth, moral or political.

His stanzas are too long, especially his epodes; the ode is finished before the car has learned its measures, and consequently before it can receive pleasure from their consonance and recurrence.

Of the first stanza the abrupt beginning has been celebrated; but technical beauties can give praise only to the inventor. It is in the power of any man to rush abruptly upon his subject, that has read the ballad of *Johnny Armstrong*.

> Is there ever a man in all Scotland—

The initial resemblances, or alliterations, *ruin, ruthless, helm nor hauberk,* are below the grandeur of a poem that endeavours at sublimity.

In the second stanza the *Bard* is well described; but in the third we have the puerilities of obsolete mythology. When we are told that *Cadwallo hush'd the stormy main,* and that *Modred* made *huge Plinlimmon bow his cloud-top'd head,* attention recoils from the repetition of a tale that, even when it was first heard, was heard with scorn.

The *weaving* of the *winding sheet* he borrowed, as he owns, from the northern Bards; but their texture, however, was very properly the work of female powers, as the art of spinning the thread of life in another mythology. Theft is always dangerous; Gray has made weavers of his slaughtered bards, by a fiction outrageous and incongruous. They are then called upon to *Weave the warp, and weave the woof,* perhaps with no great propriety; for it is by crossing the *woof* with the *warp* that men *weave* the *web* or piece; and the first line was dearly bought by the admission of its wretched correspondent, *Give ample room and verge enough.* He has, however, no other line as bad.

The third stanza of the second ternary is commended, I think, beyond its merit. The personification is indistinct. *Thirst* and *Hunger* are not alike; and their features, to make the imagery perfect, should have been discriminated. We are told, in the same stanza, how *towers* are *fed.* But I will no longer look for particular faults; yet let it be observed that the ode might have been concluded with an action of better example; but suicide is always to be had, without expence of thought.

These odes are marked by glittering accumulations of ungraceful ornaments; they strike, rather than please; the images are magnified by affectation; the language is laboured into harshness. The mind of the writer seems to work with unnatural violence. *Double, double, toil and trouble.* He has a kind of strutting dignity, and is tall by walking on tiptoe. His art and his struggle are too visible, and there is too little appearance of ease and nature.

To say that he has no beauties, would be unjust: a man like him, of great learning and great industry, could not but produce something valuable. When he pleases least, it can only be said that a good design was ill directed.

His translations of Northern and Welsh Poetry deserve praise; the imagery is preserved, perhaps often improved; but the language is unlike the language of other poets.

In the character of his Elegy I rejoice to concur with the common reader; for by the common sense of readers uncorrupted with literary prejudices, after all the refinements of subtilty and the dogmatism of learning, must be finally decided all claim to poetical honours. The *Church-yard* abounds with images which find a mirrour in every mind, and with sentiments to which every bosom returns an echo. The four stanzas beginning *Yet even these bones,* are to me original: I have never seen the notions in any other place; yet he that reads them here, persuades himself that he has always felt them. Had Gray written often thus, it had been vain to blame, and useless to praise him.

BIBLIOGRAPHY

GENERAL

Abrams, M. H. *The Mirror and the Lamp: Romantic Theory and the Critical Tradition.* New York: Norton, 1958.

Anderson, Howard, and Shea, John S., eds. *Studies in Criticism and Aesthetics, 1600–1800: Essays in Honor of Samuel Holt Monk.* Minneapolis: University of Minnesota Press, 1967.

Bate, W. J. *From Classic to Romantic: Premises of Taste in the Eighteenth Century.* Cambridge: Harvard University Press, 1946.

Bateson, Frederick Wilse. *English Comic Drama, 1700–1750.* New York: Russell and Russell, 1963.

———. *English Poetry; a Critical Introduction.* London: Longmans, 1966.

———. *English Poetry and the English Language.* Oxford: Clarendon Press, 1973.

Beljame, Alexandre. *Men of Letters and the English Public in the Eighteenth Century.* Translated by E. O. Lorimer. London: Kegan, Paul, Trench, Trubner & Co., 1948.

Bentley, Eric. *The Life of the Drama.* New York: Atheneum, 1964.

Berlin, Isaiah. *Vico and Herder: Two Studies in the History of Ideas.* New York: Viking Press, 1976.

Bond, D. F., ed. *The Eighteenth Century.* Northbrook, Ill.: AHM, 1975.

Bond, R. P. *Studies in the Early English Periodical.* Chapel Hill: University of North Carolina Press, 1957.

Bosker, A. *Literary Criticism in the Age of Johnson.* New York: Hafner Publishing, 1953.

Boswell, James. *The Life of Johnson*, edited by George Birbeck Hill. 6 vols. Oxford: Clarendon Press, 1934–50.

Brook, Stella. *The Language of the Book of Common Prayer.* London: Oxford University Press, 1965.

Brooks, Cleanth. *The Well-Wrought Urn.* New York: Harcourt, Brace & World, 1947.

Butt, John. *The Augustan Age.* London: Hutchinson University Press, 1965.

———. *The Mid-Eighteenth Century.* Oxford: Clarendon Press, 1979.

Camden, Charles Carroll, ed. *Restoration and Eighteenth Century English Literature: Essays in Honor of Allan Dugald Mckillop.* Chicago: University of Chicago Press, 1963.

Cassirer, Ernst. *The Platonic Renaissance in England.* Translated by J. Pettegrove. Austin: University of Texas Press, 1953.

———. *The Philosophy of the Enlightenment.* Translated by Fritz Koella and James Pettigrove. Boston: Beacon Press, 1955.

Clifford, James, ed. *Eighteenth Century English Literature: Modern Essays in Criticism.* New York: Oxford University Press, 1959.

Congleton, J. E. *Theories of Pastoral Poetry in England, 1684–1798.* Gainesville, Fla.: University of Florida Press, 1963.

Craig, David. *Scottish Literature & The Scottish People, 1680–1830.* London: Chatto and Windus, 1961.

Dobree, Bonamy. *Restoration Tragedy, 1670–1720.* Oxford: Clarendon Press, 1929.

———. *Men of Letters and the English Public in the Eighteenth Century, 1660–1744.* Translated by E. O. Lorimer. London: Kegan, Paul, Trench, Tubner, 1948.

———. *English Literature in the Early Eighteenth Century, 1700–1740.* Oxford: Clarendon Press, 1959.

——. *Three Eighteenth Century Figures: Sarah Churchill, John Wesley, & Giacomo Casanova*. New York: Oxford University Press, 1962.

Empson, William. *Some Versions of Pastoral*. London: Chatto and Windus, 1935.

——. *The Structure of Complex Words*. Norfolk, Conn.: New Directions, 1951.

Ford, Boris, ed. *From Dryden to Johnson*. Baltimore: Johns Hopkins University Press, 1963.

Goldberg, Rita. *Sex and Enlightenment: Women in Richardson and Diderot*. New York: Cambridge University Press, 1984.

Goldman, Lucien. *The Philosophy of the Enlightenment*. London: Routledge and Kegan Paul, 1973.

Grave, S. A. *The Scottish Philosophy of Common Sense*. Oxford: Clarendon Press, 1960.

Greene, Donald. *The Age of Exuberance*. New York: Random House, 1970.

Hazlitt, William. *Lectures on the English Comic Writers*. In *The Collected Works*, vol. 8. Edited by A. B. Waller and Arnold Glover. London: J. M. Dent, 1902–04.

Humphreys, Arthur. *The Augustan World: Life and Letters in Eighteenth Century England*. New York: Harper and Row, 1974.

Johnson, Howard and Shea, John, eds. *Studies in Criticism and Aesthetics, 1600–1800*. Minneapolis: University of Minnesota Press, 1967.

Johnson, Samuel. *The Lives of the Poets*, edited by G. B. Hill. 3 vols. Oxford: Clarendon Press, 1905.

Lansdale, Roger, ed. *The History of Literature in the English Language*. London: Barrie and Jenkins, 1971.

Lipking, Lawrence. *The Ordering of the Arts in Eighteenth Century England*. Princeton: Princeton University Press, 1970.

Loftis, John. *Comedy and Society from Congreve to Fielding*. Stanford: Stanford University Press, 1957.

Lucas, Frank Lawrence. *The Search for Good Sense: Four Eighteenth Century Characters; Johnson, Chesterfield, Boswell and Goldsmith*. London: Cassell, 1958.

Maclean, Kenneth. *John Locke and English Literature of the Eighteenth Century*. New Haven: Yale University Press, 1936.

Mcfarland, Thomas. "The Originality Paradox." *New Literary History* 5 (1974): 447–76.

Monk, Samuel H. *The Sublime: a Study of Critical Theories in Eighteenth Century England*. Ann Arbor, University of Michigan Press, 1960.

Paulson, Ronald. *English Satire*. Los Angeles: University of California Press, 1972.

——. *The Fictions of Satire*. Baltimore: Johns Hopkins Press, 1967.

Pottle, Frederick A. *The Idiom of Poetry*. Bloomington: Indiana University Press, 1963.

——. *James Boswell: The Earlier Years*. New York: McGraw Hill, 1966.

Pound, Ezra. *ABC of Reading*. New York: New Directions, 1960.

Singleton, Charles, ed. *Interpretation: Theory and Practice*. Baltimore: Johns Hopkins University Press, 1969.

Sparrow, John. *Visible Words: A Study of Inscriptions in and as Books and Works of Art*. Cambridge: Harvard University Press, 1969.

Stephen, Leslie. *English Literature and Society in the Eighteenth Century*. New York: Barnes and Noble, 1962.

——. *History of English Thought in the Eighteenth Century*. 2 vols. New York: Harcourt, Brace, 1962.

Taylor, Duncan Burnett. *Fielding's England*. New York: Ray Publishers, 1967.

Tillotson, Geoffrey. *The Continuity of English Poetry from Dryden to Wordsworth*. England: Nottingham, 1967.

————. *Augustan Poetic Diction*. London: University of London, Athlone Press, 1964.

————. *Augustan Studies*. London: University of London, Athlone Press, 1961.

Trickett, Rachel. *The Honest Muse: A Study in Augustan Verse*. Oxford: Clarendon Press, 1967.

Wasserman, Earl. "Nature Moralized: The Divine Analogy in the Eighteenth Century." *English Literary History* 20 (1957): 39–76.

Watson, George. *The Literary Critics*. Baltimore: Johns Hopkins University Press, 1962.

Watt, Ian P. *The Rise of the Novel*. London: Chatto and Windus, 1957.

Weinbrot, Howard D. *The Formal Strain: Studies in Augustan Imitation and Satire*. Chicago: University of Chicago Press, 1969.

Weinsheimer, Joel. *Imitation*. Boston: Routledge and Kegan Paul, 1984.

Wellek, Rene. *A History of Modern Criticism: 1750–1950, vol. 1: The Later Eighteenth Century*. New Haven: Yale University Press, 1955.

EARL OF SHAFTESBURY

Bernstein, J. A. *Shaftesbury, Rousseau, & Kant: An Introduction to the Conflict between Aesthetic and Moral Values in Modern Thought*. Rutherford, N.J.: Fairleigh Dickinson University Press, 1980.

————. "Shaftesbury's Identification of the Good with the Beautiful." *Eighteenth Century Studies* 10 (Spring 1977): 3.

Brett, R. L. *The Third Earl of Shaftesbury; a Study in Eighteenth Century Literary Theory*. New York: Hutchinson's University Library, 1951.

Fessenden, Anne Lathrop. *Shaftesbury & Diderot; a Study in Inter-Connectedness*. New York: Columbia University Press, 1971.

Grean, Stanley. *Shaftesbury's Philosophy of Religion and Morals; a Study in Enthusiasm*. Athens: Ohio University Press, 1967.

Marsh, Robert. "Shaftesbury's Theory of Poetry: The Importance of the Inward Colloquy." *English Literary History* 28 (1959): 67–58.

Rogers, Pat. "Shaftesbury and the Aesthetics of Rhapsody." *British Journal of Aesthetics* 12 (1972): 244–57.

Schlegel, Dorothy B. *Shaftesbury and the French Deists*. Chapel Hill: University of North Carolina Press, 1956.

Sotlnitz, Jerome. "On the Significance of Lord Shaftesbury in Modern Aesthetic Theory." *Philosophical Quarterly* 11 (1961): 97–113.

Tuveson, Ernest. "Shaftesbury and the Age of Sensibility." In *Studies in Criticism and Aesthetics, 1600–1800*, edited by Howard Johnson and John Shea. Minneapolis: University of Minnesota Press, 1967.

Uphaus, R. W. "Shaftesbury on Art: The Rhapsodic Aesthetic." *Journal of Aesthetic and Art Criticism* 27 (1959): 341–48.

ADDISON & STEELE

Bateson, F. W. "Addison, Steele and the Periodical Essay." In *History of Literature in the English Language*, edited by Roger Lonsdale. London: Barrie & Jenkins, 1971.

Beljame, Alexandre. "Joseph Addison." In *Men of Letters and the English Public in the Eighteenth Century*. Translated by E. O. Lorimer. London: Kegan, Paul, Trench, Trubner and Co., 1948.

————, eds. *Addison & Steele, The Critical Heritage*. Boston: Routledge and Kegan Paul, 1980.

Bloom, Edward A. and Lillian D. *Joseph Addison's Sociable Animal: In the Market Place, On the Hustings, In the Pulpit*. Providence, R.I.: Brown University Press, 1971.

Bond, Richard P. *The Tatler: The Making of a Journal*. Cambridge: Harvard University Press, 1971.

Courthope, W. J. *Addison*. New York: AMS Press, 1968.

Dammers, R. H. *Richard Steele*. Boston: Twayne Publishers, 1982.

Elioseff, Lee Andrew. *The Cultural Milieu of Addison's Literary Criticism*. Austin: University of Texas Press, 1963.

Gay, Peter. "The Spectator as Actor: Addison in Perspective." *Encounter* 29 (1967): 27–32.

Goldgar, Bertrand A. *The Curse of Party; Swift's Relations with Addison and Steele*. Lincoln: University of Nebraska Press, 1961.

Hansen, David A. "Addison on Ornament and Style." *Studies in Criticism and Aesthetics, 1600–1800: Essays in Honor of Samuel Holt Monk*. Minneapolis: University of Minnesota Press, 1967.

Humphreys, A. R. "Steele, Addison and Their Periodical Essays." London: British Council Pamphlet, 1959.

Johnson, Samuel. "Life of Addison." In *Lives of the English Poets*. London: J. M. Dent, 1925.

Lannering, Jan. "Studies in the Prose Style of Joseph Addison." In *Essays and Studies on English Language and Literature*, vol. 9. Cambridge: Harvard University Press, 1951.

Lewis, C. S. "Addison." In *Eighteenth Century English Literature: Modern Essays in Criticism*. Ed. James Clifford. New York: Oxford University Press, 1959.

Loftis, John. *Steele at Drury Lane*. Berkeley: University of California Press, 1952.

Otten, Robert M. *Joseph Addison*. Boston: Twayne Publishers, 1982.

Smithers, Peter. *The Life of Joseph Addison*. Oxford: Clarendon Press, 1968.

Thorpe, Clarence DeWitt. "Addison's Contribution to Criticism." In *The Seventeenth Century: Studies by R.F. Jones and Others*. Stanford: Stanford University Press, 1951.

————. "Addison's Theory of Imagination as Perceptive Response." *Papers of the Michigan Academy of Arts and Sciences* 21(1936): 509–30.

Winton, Calhoun. *Captain Steele; the Early Career of R. Steele*. Baltimore: Johns Hopkins Press, 1964

————. *Sir Richard Steele, M.P., the Later Career*. Baltimore: Johns Hopkins Press, 1970.

JOHN GAY

Armens, Sven. *John Gay, Social Critic*. New York: Octagon Books, 1966.

Bronson, Bertrand H. "The Beggar's Opera." *Studies in the Comic: University of California Publications in English* 2 (1941): 197–231.

Brown, Wallace Cable. "Gay: Pope's Alter Ego." In *The Triumph of Form*. Chapel Hill: University of North Carolina Press, 1948.

Empson, William. "The Beggar's Opera: Mock-Pastoral as the Cult of Independence." In *Some Versions of Pastoral*. Norfolk, Conn.: New Directions, 1960.

Irving, William Henry. *John Gay, Favorite of the Wits*. Durham, N.C.: Duke University Press, 1940.

Johnson, Samuel. "Gay." In *Lives of the English Poets*, edited by George Hill. 3 vols. Oxford: Clarendon Press, 1905.

Noble, Yvonne, ed. *Twentieth Century Interpretations of the Beggar's Opera; a Collection of Critical Essays*. Englewood Cliffs, N.J.: Prentice Hall, 1975.

Schultz, William Eben. *Gay's Beggar's Opera; its Content, History, and Influence*. New York: Russell and Russell, 1967.

Spacks, Patricia Ann. *John Gay*. New York: Twayne Publishers, 1965.

Sutherland, James. "John Gay." In *Eighteenth Century English Literature: Modern Essays in Criticism*, edited by James L. Clifford. New York: Oxford University Press, 1959.

JONATHAN SWIFT

Brown, N. O. "Swift's Apocalypse: The Excremental Vision." *Life Against Death; the Psychoanalytic Meaning of History*. New York: Random House, 1959.

Crane, R. S. "The Houyhnhnms, the Yahoos, and the History of Ideas." In *Reason and Imagination*, edited by J. A. Mazzeo. New York: Oxford University Press, 1962.

Downie, J. A. *Jonathan Swift, Political Writer*. Boston: Routledge and Kegan Paul, 1984.

Ehrenpreis, Irvin. *The Personality of Jonathan Swift*. London: 1958.

———. *Swift: The Man, His Works, and the Age*. London: 1962.

Elliott, R. C. *The Literary Persona*. Chicago: University of Chicago Press, 1982.

Ewald, William B. *The Masks of Jonathan Swift*. Cambridge: Harvard University Press, 1954.

Fabricant, Carole. *Swift's Landscape*. Baltimore: Johns Hopkins University Press, 1982.

Fussell, Paul. "The Frailty of Lemuel Gulliver." In *Essays in Literary History*, edited by Rudolf Kirk and C. F. Main. New Brunswick, N.J.: Rutgers University Press, 1960.

Knight, G. Wilson. "Swift and the Symbolism of Irony." In *Poets in Action*, edited by G. Wilson Knight. London: Methuen, 1967.

Lock, F. P. *The Politics of Gulliver's Travels*. Oxford: Clarendon Press, 1980.

———. *Swift's Tory Politics*. London: Duckworth, 1983.

Louis, Frances D. *Swift's Anatomy of Misunderstanding: A Study of Swift's Epistemological Imagination in* A Tale of a Tub *and* Gulliver's Travels. London: G. Prior, 1981.

Murry, John Middleton. *Jonathan Swift, a Critical Biography*. New York: Noonday Press, 1955.

Price, Martin. *Swift's Rhetorical Art*. New Haven: Yale University Press, 1953.

Probyn, Clive T., ed. *The Art of Jonathan Swift*. London: Vision Press, 1978.

Rawson, Claude Julien. *Gulliver and the Gentle Reader; Studies in Swift and Our Time*. Boston: Routledge and Kegan Paul, 1973.

Reilly, Patrick. *Jonathan Swift: The Brave Desponder*. Carbondale: Southern Illinois University Press, 1982.

Steele, Peter. *Jonathan Swift, Preacher and Jester*. Oxford: Clarendon Press, 1978.

Tuveson, Ernest, ed. *Swift; a Collection of Critical Essays*. Englewood Cliffs, N.J.: Prentice Hall, 1964.

Zimmerman, Everett. *Swift's Narrative Satire: Author and Authority*. Ithaca: Cornell University Press, 1983.

ALEXANDER POPE

Barnard, John, ed. *Pope: the Critical Heritage*. Boston: Routledge and Kegan Paul, 1973.

Edwards, Thomas B., Jr. *The Dark Estate: A Reading of Pope*. Berkeley: University of California Press, 1963.

Empson, William. "Wit in the Essay on Criticism." In *The Structure of Complex Words*. Norfolk, Conn.: New Directions, 1951.

Erskine-Hill, H. *The Social Milieu of Alexander Pope: Lives, Example, and the Poetic Response*. New Haven: Yale University Press, 1975.

Fraser, G. S. *Alexander Pope*. Boston: Routledge and Kegan Paul, 1978.

Gooneratne, Yasmine. *Alexander Pope*. New York: Cambridge University Press, 1976.

Guerinot, J. V. *Pope; a Collection of Critical Essays*. Englewood Cliffs, N.J.: Prentice Hall, 1973.

Jackson, Wallace. *Vision and Revision in Alexander Pope*. Detroit: Wayne State University Press, 1983.

Kenner, Hugh. "Pope's Reasonable Rhymes." *English Literary History* 41 (1974) 74–88.

Knight, G. W. *Laureate of Peace; on the Genius of Alexander Pope*. New York: Oxford University Press, 1955.

Mack, Maynard, ed. *Essential Articles for the Study of Alexander Pope*. Hamden, Conn.: Archon Books, 1968.

———. *The Garden and the City; Retirement and Politics in the Later Poetry of Pope, 1731–1743*. Toronto: University of Toronto Press, 1969.

Morris, David B. *Alexander Pope: The Genius of Sense*. Cambridge: Harvard University Press, 1984.

Nicolson, Marjorie, and G. S. Rousseau. *"This Long Disease, My Life": Alexander Pope and the Senses*. Princeton: Princeton University Press, 1968.

Russo, J. Paul. *Alexander Pope; Tradition and Identity*. Cambridge: Harvard University Press, 1972.

Sitwell, Dame Edith. *Alexander Pope*. New York: Norton, 1962.

Spacks, Patricia Ann. *An Argument of Images; the Poetry of Alexander Pope*. Cambridge: Harvard University Press, 1971.

Tillotson, Geoffrey. *On the Poetry of Pope*. Oxford: Clarendon Press, 1950.

———. *Pope and Human Nature*. Oxford: Clarendon Press, 1963.

Warren, Austin. *Alexander Pope as Critic and Humanist*. Gloucester, Mass: Peter Smith, 1963.

Weinbrot, Howard D. *Alexander Pope and the Traditions of Formal Verse Satire*. Princeton: Princeton University Press, 1982.

Wimsatt, W. K. "One Relation of Rhyme to Reason: Alexander Pope." *Modern Language Quarterly* 5 (1949): 323–38.

———. "Rhetoric and Poems: The Example of Pope." *English Institute Essays* (1949): 179–207.

GIAMBATTISTA VICO

Berlin, Isaiah. *Vico and Herder: Two Studies in the History of Ideas*. New York: Viking Press, 1976.

Componigri, Aloysius Robert. *Time and Idea: the Theory of History in Giambattista Vico*. Notre Dame, Ind.: University of Notre Dame Press, 1968.

Croce, Benedetto. *The Philosophy of Giambattista Vico*. Translated by R. G. Collingwood. New York: Russell and Russell, 1964.

Flint, Robert. *Vico*. New York: Arno Press, 1979.

Grimaldi, Alfonsia. *The Universal Humanity of Giambattista Vico*. New York: S. F. Vanni, 1958.

Manson, Richard. *The Theory of Knowledge of Giambattista Vico*. Hamden, Conn.: Archon Books, 1969.

Mooney, Michael. *Vico in the Tradition of Rhetoric*. Princeton: Princeton University Press, 1984.

Pompa, Leon. *Vico: A Study of the New Science*. New York: Columbia University Press, 1975.

Tagliacozzo, Giorgio, ed. *Vico, Past and Present*. Atlantic Highlands, N.J.: Humanities Press, 1981.

Verene, Donald Phillip. *Vico's Science of Imagination*. Ithaca: Cornell University Press, 1981.

HENRY FIELDING

Alter, Robert. *Fielding and the Nature of the Novel*. Cambridge: Harvard University Press, 1968.

Blanchard, F. T. *Fielding, the Novelist; a Study in Historical Criticism*. New York: Russell and Russell, 1966.

Digeon, Aureliaen. *The Novels of Fielding*. New York: Russell and Russell, 1962.

Empson, William. "Tom Jones." *Kenyon Review* 20 (1958) 217–49.

Goldberg, H. "Comic Prose Epic or Comic Romance: The Argument of the Preface to Joseph Andrews." *Philological Quarterly* 43 (1964): 193–215.

Golden, Morris. *Fielding's Moral Psychology*. Amhearst: University of Massachussetts Press, 1966.

Greene, Graham. "Fielding and Sterne." In *The Lost Childhood and Other Essays*. London: Eyre and Spottiswoode, 1951.

Hatfield, Glenn W. *Henry Fielding and the Language of Irony*. Chicago: University of Chicago Press, 1968.

Hunter, J. *Occasional Form: Henry Fielding and the Chains of Circumstance*. Baltimore: Johns Hopkins University Press, 1975.

Iser, Wolfgang. *Die Weltanschaunng Henry Fielding*. Tubingen: M. Niemeyer, 1952.

Johnson, Maurice O. *Fielding's Art of Fiction; Eleven Essays*. Philadelphia: University of Pennsylvania Press, 1961.

Kalpakgian, Mitchell. *The Marvellous in Fielding's Novels*. Lanham, Md.: University Press of America, 1981.

Levine, George Richard. *The Techniques of Irony in the Major Early Works of Henry Fielding*. New York, 1961.

Murry, J. Middleton. "In Defense of Fielding." In *Unprofessional Essays*. London: Cape, 1956.

Paulson, Ronald, ed. *Henry Fielding; the Critical Heritage*. London: Routledge and
     Kegan Paul, 1969.
Rawson, Claude Julien. *Henry Fielding and The Augustan Ideal Under Stress*. Boston:
     Routledge and Kegan Paul, 1972.
Sacks, Sheldon. *Fiction and the Shape of Belief; a Study of Henry Fielding*. Berkeley:
     University of California Press, 1964.
Wright, Andrew H. *Henry Fielding, Mask and Feast*. Berkeley: University of California
     Press, 1965.

OLIVER GOLDSMITH

Black, William. *Goldsmith*. New York: AMS Press, 1968.
Forster, John. *The Life of Oliver Goldsmith*. Westport, Conn.: Greenwood Press, 1971.
Hopkins, R. H. *The True Genius of Oliver Goldsmith*. Baltimore: Johns Hopkins Press,
     1969.
Jackson, R. Wyse. *Oliver Goldsmith; Essays Toward an Interpretation*. Plainview,
     N.Y.: Books for Libraries Press, 1974.
Kirk, Clara. *Oliver Goldsmith*. New York: Twayne, 1967.
Quintana, Ricardo. *Oliver Goldsmith; a Georgian Study*. New York: Macmillan, 1967.
Sells, Arthur Lytton. *Oliver Goldsmith: His Life and Works*. New York: Barnes and
     Noble, 1974.
Sherburn, George. "The Periodicals and Oliver Goldsmith." In *A Literary History of
     England*, edited by A. C. Baugh. New York: Appleton, 1950.
Swarbrook, Andrew, ed. *The Art of Oliver Goldsmith*. London: Vision, 1984.

EDMUND BURKE

Cameron, David R. *The Social Thought of Rousseau and Burke: a Comparative Study*.
     Toronto: University of Toronto Press, 1973.
Canavan, Francis P. *The Political Reason of Edmund Burke*. Durham, North Carolina:
     Duke University Press, 1960.
Chapman, Gerald Wester. *Edmund Burke, the Practical Imagination*. Cambridge:
     Harvard University Press, 1967.
Cobban, Alfred. *Edmund Burke and the Revolt Against the Eighteenth Century; a
     Study of the Political and Social Thinking of Burke, Wordsworth, Coleridge and
     Southey*. New York: Barnes and Noble, 1961.
Freeman, Michael. *Edmund Burke and the Critique of Political Rationalism*. Oxford:
     Blackwell, 1980.
Kramnick, Isaac. *The Rage of Edmund Burke: a Portrait of an Ambivalent Conserva-
     tive*. New York: Basic Books, 1977.

DENIS DIDEROT

Barzun, Jacques. "Diderot as Philosopher." *Diderot Studies* 22 (1986): 17–26.
Blum, Carol. *Diderot: the Virtue of a Philosopher*. New York: Viking Press, 1974.
Bremner, Geoffrey. *Order and Chance: the Pattern of Diderot's Thought*. New York:
     Cambridge University Press, 1983.

Caplan, Jay. *Framed Narratives: Diderot's Genealogy of the Beholder*. Minneapolis: University of Minnesota Press, 1985.

Crocker, Lester G. *Diderot's Chaotic Order; Approach to Synthesis*. Princeton: Princeton University Press, 1974.

———. *Two Diderot Studies: Ethics and Esthetics*. Baltimore: Johns Hopkins Press, 1952.

France, Peter. *Diderot*. Oxford: Oxford University Press, 1983.

Goldberg, Rita. *Sex and Enlightenment: Women in Richardson and Diderot*. New York: Cambridge University Press, 1984.

Josephs, Herbert. *Diderot's Dialogue of Language and Gesture: Le Neveau de Rameau*. Columbus: Ohio State University Press, 1969.

Mehlman, Jeffrey. *Cataract, a Study in Diderot*. Middleton, Conn.: Wesleyan University Press, 1979.

Sherwin, Carol. *Diderot and the Art of Dialogue*. Geneve: Librarie Droz, 1976.

THOMAS GRAY

Blake, William. *Water Colours Illustrating the Poems of Thomas Gray*. Chicago: J. P. O'Hara, 1972.

Brooks, Cleanth. "Gray's Storied Urn." In *The Well Wrought Urn*. New York: Harcourt, Brace and World, 1947.

Cecil, Lord David. *The Poetry of Thomas Gray*. London: G. Cumberlege, 1946.

———. *Two Quiet Lives: Dorothy Osborne, Thomas Gray*. Indianapolis: Bobbs-Merrill Co., 1948.

Dyson, A. E. "The Ambivalence of Gray's Elegy." In *Essays in Criticism*, edited by F. W. Bateson. Oxford, 1957.

Empson, William. "Proletarian Literature." In *Some Versions of Pastoral*. London: Chatto and Windus, 1935.

Golden, Morris. *Thomas Gray*. New York: Twayne, 1964.

Jack, Ian. "Gray's Elegy Reconsidered." In *From Sensibility to Romanticism: Essays Presented to F. A. Pottle*, edited by F. W. Hilles and Harold Bloom. New York: Oxford University Press, 1965.

Jones, William Powell. *Thomas Gray, Scholar*. Cambridge: Harvard University Press, 1937.

Reed, Amy Louise. *The Background of Gray's Elegy; a Study in the Taste for Melancholy Poetry, 1700–1751*. New York: Russell and Russell, 1962.

Starr, Herbert Willmarth, ed. *Twentieth Century Interpretations of Gray's Elegy; a Collection of Critical Essays*. Englewood Cliffs, N.J.: Prentice Hall, 1968.

———. *Gray as a Literary Critic*. Folcroft, Pa.: Folcroft Press, 1969.

EDWARD YOUNG

Bailey, Margery. "Edward Young." In *The Age of Johnson: Essays Presented to Chauncey Brewster Tinker*. New Haven: Yale University Press, 1949.

Clark, H. H. "A Study of Melancholy in Edward Young." *Modern Language Notes* 39 (1924).

Kind, J. L. *Edward Young in Germany*. New York: AMS Press, 1966.

Mutschmann, Heinrich. *The Origin and Meaning of Young's "Night Thoughts."* Folcroft, Pa.: Folcroft Press, 1969.

Pettit, Henry. *A Bibliography of Young's "Night Thoughts."* Boulder: University of Colorado Press, 1954.

Shelley, Henry Charles. *The Life and Letters of Edward Young.* New York: Pitman, 1914.

Weinsheimer, Joel. *Imitation.* Boston: Routledge and Kegan Paul, 1984.

SAMUEL JOHNSON

Bate, W. J. *The Achievement of Samuel Johnson.* New York: Oxford University Press, 1961.

———. *Samuel Johnson.* New York: Harcourt, Brace and Jovanovich, 1977.

Bloom, E. A. *Samuel Johnson in Grub Street.* Providence: Brown University Press, 1957.

Boswell, James. *The Life of Samuel Johnson, L.L.D.* edited by G. B. Hill. 6 vols. Oxford: Oxford University Press, 1934–50.

Bronson, B. H.—*Johnson Agonistes and Other Essays.* Berkeley: University of California Press, 1965.

Chapin, C. F. *The Religious Thought of Samuel Johnson.* Ann Arbor: University of Michigan Press, 1968.

Damrosch, Leopold. *Samuel Johnson and the Tragic Sense.* Princeton: Princeton University Press, 1972.

———. *The Uses of Johnson's Criticism.* Charlottesville: University Press of Virginia, 1976.

Edinger, William. *Samuel Johnson and Poetic Style.* Chicago: University of Chicago Press, 1977.

Fussell, Paul. *Samuel Johnson and the Life of Writing.* New York: Harcourt, Brace and Jovanovich, 1971.

Greene, Donald. *The Politics of Samuel Johnson.* New Haven: Yale University Press, 1960.

———. *Samuel Johnson, 1709–84.* New York: Oxford University Press, 1984.

———, ed. *Samuel Johnson: A Collection of Critical Essays.* Englewood Cliffs, N.J.: 1965.

Hagstrum, Jean. *Samuel Johnson's Literary Criticism.* Minneapolis: University of Minnesota Press, 1952.

Hardy, J. P. *Samuel Johnson: A Critical Study.* Boston: Routledge and Kegan Paul, 1979.

Lascelles, M. M.; Clifford, J. L.; Fleeman, J. D.; and Hardy, J. P, eds. *Johnson, Boswell and their Circle: Essays Presented to Lawrence Fitzroy Powell.* Oxford: Oxford University Press, 1965.

McIntosh, Carey. *The Choice of Life: Samuel Johnson and the World of Fiction.* New Haven: Yale University Press, 1973.

Sachs, Arieh. *Passionate Intelligence: Imagination and Reason in the Work of Samuel Johnson.* Baltimore: Johns Hopkins Press, 1967.

Voitle, Robert. *Samuel Johnson the Moralist.* Cambridge: Harvard University Press, 1961.

Wimsatt, W. K., Jr. *The Prose Style of Samuel Johnson.* New Haven: Yale University Press, 1941.

———. *Philosophic Words: A Study of Style and Meaning in the 'Rambler' and 'Dictionary' of Samuel Johnson.* New Haven: Yale University Press, 1948.

Acknowledgements

SHAFTESBURY

"A Letter Concerning Enthusiasm" is from *The Complete Works, Selected Letters, and Posthumous Writings of Anthony Ashley Cooper, Third Earl of Shaftesbury*, edited by Gerd Hemmerich and Wolfram Benda, copyright © 1981 by Fromann-Holzboog GmbH. Reprinted by permission.

ADDISON & STEELE

The selections from *The Spectator* are taken from *The Spectator: A New Edition with Biographical Notices*, published by Applegate & Co. (Cincinnati), 1860.

The selections from *The Tatler* are taken from *The British Essayists*, Volume I, edited by Alexander Chalmers, published by Sargeant & Ward (New York), 1809.

The selections from *The Guardian* are taken from *The Guardian*, Volume I, published by Jacob and Richard Tonson (London), 1756.

JOHN GAY

"On the Present State of Wit" is taken from *John Gay: Poetry & Prose*, Volume I, edited by Vinton A. Dearing, copyright © 1974 by Oxford University Press. Reprinted by permission.

JONATHAN SWIFT

"A Tritical Essay" is taken from *The Prose Works of Jonathan Swift*, Volume I, edited by Temple Scott, published by George Bell & Sons (London), 1900.

"A Proposal for Correcting the English Tongue" is taken from *A Proposal for Correcting the English Tongue, Polite Conversation, Etc.*, edited by Herbert Davis with Louis Landa, copyright © 1957 by Basil Blackwell & Mott, Ltd. Reprinted by permission.

"A Letter to a Young Poet" and *The Tatler* (#230) are taken from *Satires and Personal Writings by Jonathan Swift*, edited by William Alfred Eddy, copyright © 1932 by Oxford University Press. Reprinted by permission.

ALEXANDER POPE

"An Essay on Criticism" is taken from *Pastoral Poetry and An Essay on Criticism*, edited by E. Audra, copyright © 1961 by E. Audra and Aubrey Williams. Reprinted by permission.

. The "Preface to the Iliad" is taken from *The Prose Works of Alexander Pope*, Volume I, edited by Norman Ault, copyright © 1936 by The Shakespeare Head Press (Basil Blackwell & Mott, Ltd.). Reprinted by permission.

"The Epistle to Dr. Arbuthnot" and the "Epilogue to the Satires" are taken from *Imitations of Horace,* edited by John Butt, copyright © 1939 by Yale University Press. Reprinted by permission.

GIAMBATTISTA VICO

The selections from "The New Science" are taken from *Principles of the New Science of Giambattista Vico Concerning the Common Nature of the Nations,* translated and edited by Thomas G. Bergin and Max Fisch, copyright © 1984 by Cornell University Press. Reprinted by permission.

HENRY FIELDING

The "Preface to Joseph Andrews" is taken from *Joseph Andrews,* edited by Martin C. Battestin, copyright © 1967 by Martin C. Battestin. Reprinted by permission.

OLIVER GOLDSMITH

The selections from the *Essays* are taken from *The Miscellaneous Works of Oliver Goldsmith,* Volume I, edited by James Prior, published by Derby & Jackson (New York), 1857.

EDMUND BURKE

The selections from the "Essay on the Sublime and Beautiful" are taken from *The Works of the Right Honorable Edmund Burke,* Volume I, published by Little, Brown & Co. (Boston), 1865.

DENIS DIDEROT

"The Paradox of Acting" is taken from *The Paradox of Acting, and Masks or Faces?,* copyright © 1957 by Hill & Wang, Inc. Reprinted by permission.

THOMAS GRAY

"Observations on English Meter" is taken from *The Works of Thomas Gray in Prose and Verse,* Volume I, edited by Edmund Gosse, published by H. Gregory (Providence, R.I.), 1884.

EDWARD YOUNG

"Conjectures on Original Composition" is taken from *The Complete Works, Poetry and Prose of the Rev. Edward Young,* Volume II, edited by James Nichols, published by William Tegg & Co. (London), 1854.

SAMUEL JOHNSON

"An Essay on Epitaphs" is taken from *Samuel Johnson,* edited by Donald Greene, copyright © 1984 by Oxford University Press. Reprinted by permission.

The selections from *The Rambler* (excluding #176) are taken from *The Works of Samuel Johnson,* Volume II, edited by W. J. Bate, copyright © 1963 by Yale University Press. Reprinted by permission.

The selections from *The Idler* and *The Adventurer* are taken from *The Idler and The Adventurer,* edited by W. J. Bate, J. M. Bullitt, and J. F. Powell, copyright © 1963 by Yale University Press. Reprinted by permission.

The "Preface to the Dictionary," the "Preface to Shakespeare," and *The Rambler* (#176) are taken from *Samuel Johnson's Literary Criticism,* edited by R. D. Stock, copyright © 1974 by the University of Nebraska Press. Reprinted by permission.

The selections from "The Lives of the Poets" are taken from *Johnson: Prose and Poetry,* edited by Mona Wilson, copyright © 1951 by Harvard University Press. Reprinted by permission.